PR.

Counterc

"A painfully honest memoir of a girl who grew up in one of the largest and long-lived of the 1960s-era communes. The good, the bad, and the ugly are all here—but mainly just memories of growing up in the idealistic, if imperfect, world of the hippie spiritual seekers."

Timothy Miller, Professor of Religious Studies at the University of Kansas at Lawrence and author of:
The 60s Communes: hippies and beyond (1999); *America's Alternative Religions* (1995); and *The Hippies and American Values* (1991)

"Rachel takes us on an amazingly colorful journey through her childhood. It is a captivating story of what life was like growing up in the early years of the hippie counter culture. Rachel encompasses her own personal experiences with relevant historical facts, giving readers insight into the early hippie days of alternative lifestyles, communal living, and living off the grid. Even though she faced many "hardships" like hitchhiking with her single mom and living without running water and electricity, Rachel portrays her experiences with positivity and grace.

Having personally grown up in the hippie counter culture, I am astounded by the similarities and recollections that Rachel and I share. Our journeys briefly crossed as I too stayed with the Love Family; a unique Christian commune, where everyone is "eternal." I can relate so well with the various events Rachel describes in her book with such fascinating detail.

Rachel's writing style is easy to follow and her book is hard to put down. A wonderful authentic narrative, that is very informative and appropriate for all ages."

Anastasia G. Ewing (Machacek), Author of *Growing Up Hippie*

"This is an intriguing first-hand recollection by Rachel Israel. As a child she lived in the Love Israel Family, a countercultural commune of the late 20th century located in western Washington State. Based on reminiscences the author wrote shortly after she left the Family in her early teens, her recollections have been amplified by research and other studies during her adult years. Thus, her book has the credibility of first hand observations by a child at critical moments of her life but enriched by a later perspective based on studies of psychology and cultural issues.

The account begins with the reminiscences of this very young girl experiencing a hippie life with her mother whose wanderings eventually led them into a commune rigidly controlled by a dominant leader who had assumed the name Love Israel. What follows is a frank account of the experiences, views, and often bewildering challenges faced by a child who is buffeted by adults and situations she is not equipped to understand. She recounts living conditions, social practices, daily life, schooling, rituals, and adult behavior as seen through her young eyes. After several years in the commune a new set of challenging circumstances forced her sudden departure and entry into the traditional "World"; suddenly she was a teen-ager in a city with neighborhoods, with a school and classmates that were foreign to her. Rachel's struggles both during and after her communal life are explored with convictions and an effort to comprehend it all. Hers is a compelling and even unique life story."

Charles P. LeWarne, author of
The Love Israel Family: Urban Commune, Rural Commune

"Among the thousands of communal experiments of the late 1960s and early '70s, the Love Family was one of the biggest and most successful, as well one of the most controversial. Opponents accused it of brainwashing and child abuse, whereas supporters saw it as an admirable social experiment and a welcome addition to Seattle's diverse cultural scene. Yet, surprisingly little has been written about the Love Family, and, until now, nothing at all from the perspective of a second-generation member.

Rachel Israel's account is really two stories woven into a single narrative. The first is her personal story. She describes joining the Love Family with her mother when she was just six years old; learning to navigate daily life in a world where everyone was expected to be perfect; and ultimately leaving the community and struggling to readjust to life in "the World." The second story is the story of the Love Family itself--from its origins in an LSD trip during the "Summer of Love" in 1967 to its calamitous breakup and near demise in 1984. Based on both her personal observations and interviews with other members, Ms Israel provides rich descriptions of virtually every aspect of community life, including all the topics commonly covered in professional ethnographies. Given recent academic interest in second-generation members of new religious movements, her descriptions of childhood and adolescence are especially important.

In addition to general readers, this book should be of special interest to sociologists, historians, and students of communal societies, as well as counselors and psychologists who work with former members of high-control religious communities."

Rob Balch, Professor Emeritus, Dept. of Sociology, University of Montana, retired 2013 but still teaching Sociology of Alternative Religions

COUNTERCULTURE CROSSOVER

GROWING UP *in the* LOVE FAMILY

A MEMOIR

By Rachel Israel

Life Story PRESS

Web Address: RachelIsrael.net

Publisher's Address:
Life Story Press
P.O. Box 472
Maple Valley, WA 98038-9998

ISBN-13: 978-1-7322400-1-8

Disclaimer:

This is a work of creative nonfiction. The events are portrayed to the best of Rachel Israel's memory. While all the stories in this book are true, some names and identifying details have been changed or omitted to protect the privacy of the people involved. Furthermore, there are events from the author's life that were omitted that were not significant to this memoir.

The chapters of this book are organized by subject but are chronological within each subject. The chapters do not stand alone; they must be read in the order they were presented for the story to make sense as each chapter is built on the knowledge of the previous chapter.

ACKNOWLEDGMENTS

First, I'd like to thank my mother, Karen, for her courage to live the life she believed in, without which, I wouldn't have had such an interesting and eventful early life. I will be eternally grateful that she was open to talking about a difficult subject and help give me an understanding of her point of view. The greatest gifts she taught me was to honor my instinct, to be willing to accept discomfort if it means doing what's right, and to have pride in my history.

To my special friends, Laurie McConnachie and Rebecca Stewart for all their advice, support and encouragement along my journey; for believing in me and giving me valuable and honest feedback when I needed it.

My gratitude for their early and constant support goes to Larry Israel, Understanding Israel, Eve and Definition, Helpful, Bliss, Ethan, Lydia, Atarah, Zarah, Ravah and Bright, my brave interviewees who helped me deepen my understanding and expand my views of some key events that took place during my childhood. Thank you all for your faith and encouragement.

Thank you to George R. Harker, Paul Wood, Ron Reeder, Tom Collins, and Robert and Matthew Gilman for sharing their history and thoughts about a chapter of their life story, which helped me understand my own history.

For their kindness, encouragement, and thoughtful advice, I thank Chuck LeWarne, Rob Balch, Timothy Miller, and Paul Andrews. What a burst of luck that they were set in my path. I appreciate the extra support and encouragement I received from them, as I traveled forward with my book project.

I also want to express gratitude to Summit admin and teachers for giving me and my peers from the commune the opportunity to have a relaxed and supportive academic environment during our transition to the outside and for years later, sharing their memories of that critical juncture in my life.

I can never adequately thank my husband, Ken, who persuaded me that it was time to tell my story and encouraged me during the process, providing me with feedback as well as technical help with some of the more challenging obstacles on my path. I am also thankful to have my two wonderful daughters in my life who have given me great joy and inspiration to finish writing my story.

If it wasn't for all the encouragement and support that I received from those I've mentioned, but also from many others along the way, this story would've never been told.

INTRODUCTION

When I was almost seven years old, my mother joined the Love Family, a controversial religious commune with several hundred members, founded in Seattle in 1968. A dangerous cult to some but a happy community to others, the Love Family was highly successful compared to a lot of similar groups, having a life span of almost 50 years.

I was a child member of the Love Family for eight years, from the summer of 1975 when I arrived with my mother, to the summer of 1983 when I left at nearly 15 years old. I was a baptized member, but I did not join the Love Family; I was only there was because my mother brought me, so because of this, I don't have the guilt or shame that many ex-members have about their involvement or the defensiveness that current members or loyalists have, both of which has contributed to an environment of secrecy surrounding the Love Family. But growing up there was a major part of my early history and has had a very significant impact on my life, positive and negative.

There are a few things that are unique about my memoir: I include excerpts from my childhood diary. I do this for a couple of reasons: They are another way of showing the reliability of my memories, and they also remind my reader of my youth and the fact that my story primarily takes place during my childhood.

My narrative style is to switch back and forth between my perspective as a child and my perspective as an adult. This was easy to do, because, I didn't wait 35 years and then write my memoirs. A lot of my writing was done in my early adulthood, not long after I left the community; I was writing at a critical time when my memories were fresh. Then I added to those writings as an adult, looking back, which was enhanced by my studies of sociology, psychology, and cultural issues.

Another way that my memoir stands out was I chose to bring in other voices besides my own. I interviewed adult ex-members, particularly those who were involved with the children. I also interviewed adult ex-members who were former child members of the community, who had been in my peer group. Bringing in other voices provides evidence that my story is a true story and builds credibility with my readers; I also include other voices to add rich detail and expand the awareness of the complexities of my story; And finally, I believe in the power of story and feel honored to hear the stories of others who are willing to share and contribute to my understanding.

There's one final reason why my memoir is not typical: I include an unusual amount of historical detail in my descriptions and discuss openly subjects that have been untouched by other authors that have written about the Love Family. I shed light on the dark, conflicted, and more controversial aspects of the Love Family's history.

For those who are willing to accompany me on this journey, I am confident that I accomplish what I set out to do, which is to tell a captivating and informative story of what it was like being raised in the Love Family.

TABLE OF CONTENTS

CHAPTER I

Makena Beach:
A Hippie Heaven in Paradise

For the first six and a half years of my childhood, I didn't live in the Love Family; I lived with my mom in the hippie counterculture, where my mom lived various alternative lifestyles. There are 18 chapters in this book; The first two I don't even mention the Love Family. There's a reason for this: Before I even got to the Love Family, there were a few events that took place before I came that are important to know because of what happened later, once I became a member of the Love Family.

My very first memories were of life camping on a hippie beach in Hawaii. I didn't have a stable home early on, so it started out as an adventure, going from one place to another as my mom's side kick. I called my mom by her first name, who I will call 'Karen.' It was common, during those days, for hippie kids to call their parents by their first names.

When I was not even two years old, Karen left my dad and flew to Maui. We ended up living there for almost a year on a popular hippie beach, Makena Beach.

It was 1970. The Vietnam war was still raging, and anti-war protests continued. Movements for change were growing, and my mom was looking for the hippie good life.

"I wasn't ready to settle down," Karen says. "Your dad was doing a lot of speed, and I was sick of society. He was devastated and begged me to come back. You cried a lot."

My mom believed that straight culture and the whole system was going to come down, and that it was time to buy land and become self-sufficient. The word had been out about Makena Beach since early 1969—the police are gentle, the locals are generous, and there's plenty of free tropical fruit, sunshine, and good surf.

When Karen heard the news from her friend Sherry, she took her savings from a job where she had been working as a maid, cleaning motel rooms and bought us a ticket to Maui. Sherry was already there, staying at a place known as the Banana Patch in Haiku, which was near Makena Beach. She had two kids named Cuzan and Oona. I also played with two other kids—Guava Doo Da and Hasha Banana.

The first thing to know is that Makena Beach is one of the largest and most beautiful beaches in Maui. Located on the South side of East Maui and surrounded by green kiawe or mesquite trees, it is shielded from regular trade winds. There are wide sandy beaches, clear blue-turquoise ocean, and an abundance of coral strewn between the black lava beds. The 360-ft. cinder cone, Pu'u Olai or Red Hill dominates the middle ground between two connected Beach areas—Big Beach and Little Beach. One can get to Little Beach by going up a path that winds through lava rocks and takes you over a bluff. Mt. Haleakala dominates the background for the entire beach area.

I talked to Robert Gillman, a photographer, who also lived on Makena Beach during the same time we were there. He was there for 18 months, living with his wife and his son. Raised in an Irish neighborhood of Boston, a self-described "beatnik in the 1950s" and "hippie in the 1970s," Robert ended up settling on the Island and making it their permanent home. He talked about his memories of how the Island has changed since he first arrived so many years ago:

> It's hard for People to realize it but it's still the United States. Hawaii is the farthest point on the planet from any other place. It is the most isolated land mass on the planet… Maui in 1970 was kind of like Guam. I mean there just wasn't much here. The very first time we drove down North Kihei road, which is the road that hugs Ma'alaea Harbor, heading towards Kihei, and it was past sunset—there were no lights at all—nowhere. Nowadays the whole hillside is lit up and Kihei is lit up, but it was like going into a National Forest. There was hardly anything in Kihei. There was a dirt road all the way down to Makena from the end of Kihei. And the people who lived in Kihei weren't too thrilled with the hippies being down

on Makena, and they were heavily discriminatory. There were two general stores in the area. One was called Azeka which was a combination of a gas station and general store in the middle of Kihei, and then, at the beginning of Kihei, was a similar establishment called Suda that was a gas station and a general store as well. Now Suda is an ABC store—40 years later—and Azeka is now a shopping center.

Despite its isolated location, hippies from far and near were drawn there, trying to get away from civilization. 'Makena's a far-out place,' said David Gunner in the *Honolulu Advertiser* on March 16, 1970. 'There's a very high energy level out there. You know, they used to bury old kahunas up there on Red Hill (pg. A4). In the late 1960s and early 1970s, Makena was the place to be. Jane and Peter Fonda, singer Steve Miller, members of Big Brother and the Holding Company, and the Grateful Dead—all had visited Makena.

It was a small adventure to even get to there. After the long flight, you had to hitchhike, which was against the law. That is, hitching with your thumb pointed down the road. Just standing by the side of the road was tolerated.

According to my mom, we did not have any trouble when we hitchhiked from the airport:

"We did end up having to walk a lot of the way," she says. For an almost three-year-old kid, it was a lot of walking, but I was mature for my age and am told I was an, "early talker." Instead of peak-a-boo, I would say, poo-po-boo," my mom recalled. I also apparently liked to hold hands with my mom and would offer her my hand and say, "Mama han, Mama han."

It was hot, and we were from Seattle, but we kept walking.

"A lot of the hippies there were from Tahiti or California, so it was obvious from how overdressed we were that we were from the Northwest," Karen says. "All that clothing that we brought—it turned out we didn't need any of it." We went "naked mostly," and at other times, we wore the "traditional, Hawaiian dress called a Muumuu."

I don't remember a lot about Makena Beach because I was so young, but I do remember some things. As we walked along the road, my mom told me we were passing sugar cane. So as any child who hears the word sugar, I thought to myself, Oh Candy! even though my mom called it, "Shit food." There was no candy. I looked out and saw a huge field of golden sugar cane stalks.

We finally got to Kihei. My mom arranged to get her driver's license and bought a used station wagon for $75. To get to the beach, it was five miles down what Makena hippies referred to as 'Desolation Road,' a narrow, six-mile, extremely bumpy, two-lane dirt road. It would take 45 minutes for a car to navigate it, although, Karen says that "cars usually didn't make it down this road more than once." A 4-wheel drive was essential.

We made it, somehow, but we still had half a mile of strenuous hike through a thicket of Kiawe trees, which are a spreading bush or moderately sized tree, bearing small leaves and spikes or thorns. The path was barely visible through the thick over-grown, vegetation. Of course, back then, there were no Public restrooms or parking lots. Even now, there is still only a Porta-Potty.

We finally arrived. It was august, 1970— Everyone was still talking about the Jimmy Hendrix concert, even though it had already been a month since the event which took place at Haleakala Crater.

The beauty of Makena beach was breathtaking. The first thing we saw when we got there was nearly a mile of perfect orange and white sand, cliffy dramatic landscape, and water that was brilliant blue and green. There was little reef, which made the sand bottom shine up through the water to give it that tropical inviting brightness. To top it off, there were close to 200 people camped out in a variety of ways: tree houses, a cave, abandoned vehicles, make-shift tents of old tarp, card board, scrap metal or whatever they could find. Somebody even had revamped an old artillery bunker. My mom's friend Sherry, who was the one who had originally invited us to Makena, had moved from the Banana Patch and set up a little living room back in the Kiawe trees with a rug, a couch, and a table.

Just a year before we got there, in 1969, there were only around 30 campers. A year later, when we got there, there were almost 150 people just at Little Beach, not including Big Beach. A year after we left, there were approximately 300–400 people. The actual number of people there was impossible to count, though, because the crowd at Makena was constantly changing and shifting. There were evictions and arrests at different points and different reasons why people came and went. As time went on though, there were more people arriving than there were leaving.

At first, we stayed in the station wagon that didn't run anymore, but then someone gave us a little pup tent, which we set up on the rocks between Big and Little Beach. Sometime later, we moved from the tent into what Karen called the "House of Doors," which was a shack made up entirely of old, wooden doors.

When my mom and I first arrived, we stayed on Big Beach but as time went on, we began to camp at Little Beach where the people lived more communally and ate meals together.

Years and years later, as an adult, I went to Maui to do some research on Makena Beach and was put in touch with several people who lived on the beach during the same time that we did: Robert Gillman, who I already mentioned earlier as well as his son Matthew, who was just a couple years older than I was. I also talked to Ron Reeder, Tom Collins, Jeanice Barcelo, George R. Harker, PhD, Paul Wood and Gill Engledow. Some of them I quote and others I didn't quote but all were influential in my thinking about Maui history, including the events, over the years, at Makena Beach.

Ron had just graduated from art school, then went to Maui, looking for a friend and ended up staying at Little Beach. He talked about mealtimes and how people ate:

"It was more communal at Little Beach," Ron says. "There were teams of people who would go to this place where they could get 50-pound bags of rice for a couple of dollars," Ron explained. "When the rats had chewed a hole in the bag, it was cheaper for the company to just get rid of the bag for a loss than it was to cut it open, clean it, dry it, and re-bag it." He says that people would go around and "collect opihi to eat," which were small, cone-shaped mollusks that had to be detached from the surfaces of rocks near the ocean.

"The moon was the only light source at night," Ron says, "so when the moon was full, people would stay up later." He saw people eating out of coconut bowls. "When the fire went out, dinner was done. People took turns collecting firewood or washing dishes."

I talked to a couple of local Mauians who I met at a bar on the Island. This was on that same visit years later as an adult. One of the ladies had lived on the Island her whole life. She said that several women from Makena had miscarried, and it was thought that it was because of their diets; They were eating nothing but fruit!

I ate a lot of fruit in those days! One memory that I have is of visiting Sherry, back at her campsite in the Kiawe trees. She always had a lot of bananas, which were the kind that had to be cooked. I was stuffing myself with the bananas and noticed her watching me. I stopped and offered her a bite.

"Oh God! No!" Sherry cried. "I have eaten so many of those—they make me sick!"

Sick? I thought. It puzzled me. *How could anyone be sick of something that tasted so good?*

My mom explained the various ways people ate: First, there were some very "generous locals." Secondly, a lot of people had money or food stamps," which she says that "back then were easier to get." Finally, a lot of people would "just eat fruit or whatever they could find." There were "organized fruit runs to certain parts of the Island," and then "trucks would arrive stuffed with fruit."

On that same trip to Maui, which I took years later as an adult, I met a Gill at the Maui Historical Society and got to talking to her about Makena. She told me that she had adopted a little girl from Makena beach. The little girl had been found on the beach without any parents.

"Papayas were being picked from fruit trees in a nearby park," Gill says, "and one old guy was so upset about it that during the night, he went and cut the trees down."

"A lot of people would just go look for mango trees, avocado trees," says Robert, "and if you were considerate, you would knock on the person's door and say, 'May I have a couple mangos, or may I have some avocados?' And if not, then you would just steal them and that was one of the things people were upset about. People were stealing fruit off their fruit trees."

Water was more of a problem than food though, according to Robert:

"There were four or five houses on the South side of Makena. And if you knocked on the door and asked them for some water, they'd let you fill up a water jug or five-gallon cans, so I am sure they passed out 100 gallons a day. The bottom line was that the water line from the beginning of Kihei all the way to La Perouse Bay was just a thin half inch line so there wasn't much water pressure in either Kihei or Makena in those days. But we always had enough fresh water. And we would get it either by getting it just how I described or when we went in town, taking a five-gallon plastic thing and filling it up at Kalama Park. To get to a public spigot, you had to hike a couple miles, but to get to a private one, like I said there were private homes at the South end of the beach. Water was a never-ending problem but because I had an automobile, I had more access."

Tom, a Vietnam veteran wanted to preserve his anonymity after the war, since when he returned, he had been attacked and harassed by antiwar protesters. He had gone to Maui to buy land, then ended up staying at Makena for various periods of time over a seven-year period. Tom discussed with me his memories of the challenges of getting water to the beach:

We took turns going and getting water. I was one of the few that was clean cut. I didn't have long hair. I didn't have a long beard. I walk straight up. I just carry an aura about me that is carried over from being in the marine core. I would be the leader and walk up to the house and very politely say, 'We have 30 people over there that need water. Can we have some of your water?' 'How much do you want?' 'We each have two gallons.' And by the way, I didn't just walk up to the house and knock on the door. I would call out well before we got to the house because everyone had weapons. And yes, I hate to say it, but they pissed the neighbors off by taking water without asking first. Otherwise you had to go all the way to the shops at Wailea to get water cause there was only one little rinky-dink line coming down there. And it was for the horse ranch and the two other houses that were down there in that area. When I was getting water with those four-other people. I would always ask. They were pretty stingy, so if they said no, then fine, we would just hitchhike to Wailea. We had to have the water. And back then, the shops in Wailea were just these plywood shacks.

Some people feel that life is difficult because of imposed forces beyond one's control, but I was learning early on: Life was not easy, but we liked it that way. It was self-chosen survival: We do it our way, and we accept the challenges that come along with that choice.

Robert's son, Matthew was six years old when he lived on Makena for 18 months with his parents in 1971. Now, all grown up, he paints houses and is well known on Maui as an actor in several local films, one of which was called Lima Post and another film called Aloha Daze among others. Matthew described what he remembered about his early years at Makena Beach:

"There were so many different types of people there," he says. "Every night, everyone would get together for a big bon fire and hang out." Matthew's worst memory was seeing people "freak out," and not understand why.

"A lot of times at night, people would get too high or too drunk and make a big commotion," Matthew says. "There was just a lot of flipping out. There were a lot of sex and drugs and people were having sex with somebody's person, so there was a lot of stuff going on."

According to Matthew, there were quite a few children that lived on the beach with their parents. There were "at least twenty or twenty-five" children, he remembered.

Matthew told me his best memories were of running around and playing with the other children there. "The adults," he says, "were in their own little world, so it was a free for all for the kids in a lot of ways." He talked about what it was like visiting peoples' camps:

"Somebody would give us some jelly rolls," Mathew explained, "and then somebody else would say 'Hey do you want to sit down and listen to us play some music?' The beach was so big," he says, "that it took "an average adult 15 minutes to walk across," but for Matthew, who was only six, it took a lot longer. "As a kid, it was just so big," he says. "We'd spend three quarters of the day, walking around talking to people, and then making it back to our own camps."

I was only three years old and too young to run around with the older kids who were trying to score donuts. Instead, I was busy trying to keep up with my mom. One of my earliest and most vivid memories took place right at the edge of the Pacific Ocean. My mother held a large, black inner-tube.

She wades out into the waves. I watch in horror as more and more of her disappears under the water line. Farther out, two heads were bobbing on the surface. She doesn't seem to be coming back for me. Scared, I run out into the water, and it slows me down. Her head is getting smaller each second, her hair floating, streaming out behind her on the surface of the ocean. I scream out for her. She turns her head, exasperated.

"Go back!" she says.

I refuse. I make my way back and quickly locate a small, clear plastic inner-tube, decorated with surfing teddy bears. The inner-tube sits near a woman. I grab it. "Mine!" I said and claimed the inner-tube.

I hear a child scream from behind me. I turn and notice a chubby girl around my age running after me. I run faster.

Her mother is watching me. "You can use it," she says with a smile.

Saved! I throw the inner-tube over my head and paddle like mad out to my mom. As soon as I reach her, I grab a clump of her hair to hold onto.

"Ow!" She winces, trying to pry lose my fingers.

I hold on tighter.

I guess that's how I felt for a lot of my early childhood—that no matter what, I was determined to keep up. Only a few of my memories during this time are vivid like this one.

Five months before we even arrived on Little Beach, Maui police had served over 100 evictions to Makena area dwellers. (Honolulu Advertizer, Mar 14, 1970). Despite the evictions, we were able to move right in without any harassment or trouble and live there with everyone else, like we did, for almost a year. Every so often, there were beach raids after the eviction notices were ignored. The evictions didn't work: The beach population continued to grow over about a five-year period.

A Clash of Cultures

In 1969, when people, from the counterculture, began arriving at Makena beach and other hippie enclaves on the Island, they (the hippies) were seen, by locals, as a threat. Not only did they look and act different, they were also seen as a problem to the budding tourism industry.

The business community was the most directly impacted by the newcomers. One storekeeper raved, "They steal things, they panhandle in front of the store, and sometimes eat things and don't pay for them. I have to track after them when they come in…they smell and a lot of them come in with no underpants on." (*Honolulu Advertiser*, Mar 16, 1970 A4)

In a strongly worded address to the West Maui Business Association, President elect David Williams said the groups' single, most important task is "to make Lahaina less attractive to the hippies and to discuss what legal steps could be taken to solve the hippie problem." (*Maui News*, June 20th, 1970).

One of the first things the State did was to make hitchhiking illegal, and this of course, made it more difficult to get around the island. (*Maui News*: May 7, 1969).

It wasn't a new law; it was a reinterpretation of an old, vague law, which applied only to hippies. It didn't apply to college students trying to get to and from their classes, and it didn't apply to motorists who might break down and need a ride to and from their vehicle.

Regarding the law, Maui County Attorney Kase Higa was reported by the local newspaper to object to the term 'hippie' because it was "undefined." (*Maui News*, May 7, 1969). As a result of the objection, the law was amended using the term 'strange people.'

Meanwhile, the papers continued to print a slew of articles which had a negative slant towards the hippies. The *Maui News* editorialized, "These [hippies] are parasites who deride our society, contribute nothing to it, but use the services provided by our 'grubby' tax dollars to further their indolent, squalid existence." (*Maui News*, Aug 1, 1970, B2).

Predictably, the negative press contributed to an attitude, among some local Mauians, of intolerance towards the hippies.

Discrimination, something most of these hippie refugees were not used to dealing with, ran rampant.

"I remember getting the evil eye wherever I went, says my mom. "I felt like a [Ni**er]. "When we got back to Seattle," she says, "I couldn't believe how friendly people were."

Anti-hippie sentiment festered, and city officials lost restraint when the director of the Maui Chamber of Commerce asked for community vigilante action to rid the Island of hippies. "Harassment or anything, I don't care," he said to Robert Johnson…Even goon squads…" (*Honolulu Advertiser*, Jan 15, 1969 A5)

In response, there was an increase in violence towards hippies. There were beatings and several rapes reported over one summer as locals attacked hippies (*Honolulu Advertiser* March 16, 1970, A4). As part of a panel discussion to address the communications gap between the "establishment and the transients," Attorney Sanford Langa gave his view on the change in assault and battery statistics, "[It] has to be blamed on the mayor and the *Maui News*, because to some extent there has been a tendency to cultivate the idea that it's alright to commit assault and battery on some people" (*Maui News*: Dec 12, 1970).

I asked Ron about the violence toward Makena hippies. He talked about two incidents:

> There was a time when some people came and knocked a lot of people unconscious in the middle of the night and stole a bunch of things from people on the big beach. They didn't even know I was there. They didn't see me. They could have killed them. They hit em in the head with 2 X 4s. The wounds were like the size of a 2 X 4 on the side of their heads. They stole a couple of surf boards and some snorkeling gear and stuff like that. I was fine but my friends, no one knew what was going to happen with them. We had no ice to put on it. Damp clothes, that's all we had. The ocean was the coldest thing we had around. And you know how cold that is. It's like 80 degrees!

"Some [locals] were wonderful and others were lousy," Ron says. "I can remember going and having Hukilau at the park with some people and them just being wonderful and then walking across the street to a bar where the cars were parked and having people try to kill us, he says. "One night, one guy told me, 'we got rifles in the car, we kill all you haoles.' While I talked, my friends went and got the car. I had to run and jump in the back window as we were driving, just to get away."

I asked Tom if he faced harassment while he was at Makena. Tom was very open about his experiences on Makena. He described that he was his family's 'rebel child,' having come from a large Catholic family. When he injured his back in Vietnam, he returned home. He was then regularly harassed as people were angry about the war. That's one of the reasons he moved to Maqui, to get away from it. Once Tom got to Makena, no one bothered him:

"Everyone could tell I was a marine, because of my short hair," he says, "but no one cared."

He didn't face harassment from the Makena crowd or local Mauians about being a vet, but he did face it because he was hippie:

"The first three years, I was a "Fucking Haole," he says then continued, "The first time I went to Hana, I went out on the pier, and the next thing I know, there were five, big Hawaiian dudes standing there. 'Don't even get out of your car, fucking Haole,' they told him. Tom argued with them: 'I live in Kihei.' The Hawaiians said, 'No, go back to your real home!'

There was a point when Matthew's parents put him in public school on the Island. Matthew remembered the harassment he got for being "a hippie kid:"

"Kindergarten was kinda tough," Matthew says. "I was a hippie kid coming into a full-on, local, very conservative school on the Island. "I fought every single day. They didn't like hippies. Eventually they became my friends, but back then they called me Fuckin' Haole. "They still had 'Kill Haole Day' on Fridays when I went to school," Matthew remembered.

'Haole' is a Hawaiian derogatory term that is used to refer to a white person. Wikipedia explains the etymology of the term. 'Ha' means inner breath of our being, where truth resides. 'A'ole' means no or none. Haole is a contraction of the two words meaning "no inner breath" or "not coming from truth."

A lot of the discrimination against the hippies stemmed from the nudity. It was very offensive to a lot of the locals who came from very conservative, religious backgrounds.

Although, Ron, whose heritage was First Nations, explained that it wasn't always that way: Originally, before the missionaries came in 1820 and converted most of the Island's indigenous peoples from Polynesian based religions, to Christianity, they might not have been so offended by nudity. Hippies and locals Mauians, back then, might've been more similar, in a spiritual sense, than a lot of them were during the counterculture era of the late 1960s and 1970s. Author and researcher Pali Jae Lee writes: "During these ancient times, the only 'religion' was one of family and oneness with all things. The people were in tune with nature, plants, trees, animals, and each other. They respected all things and took care of all things.

In ancient Hawai'ian society, sex was without guilt, shame, or sin. Nudity was not sexualized or considered indecent or a perversion. It was ritualized and seen as a sign of respect. When missionaries came, one of the first things they did was ban surfing, because the surfers stood unashamedly naked on their boards. These findings were derived from anthropological records and by personal interviews conducted with Hawaiian elders, called Kupuna (Diamond, 2004).

Hippies went naked, but it was because no one cared, not because being nude was the end to some means or the means to some end.

Like Matthew, I became accustomed to nudity early on. It seemed like it was no big deal. I didn't hear people comment on it or make an issue of it, but to many locals who weren't used to it, the nudity was quite offensive. It didn't help that a lot of the local Hawaiians made up the police force and Island government.

The police were known to fly in with helicopters and arrest nude people. Makena beach was an isolated location, so it might have been a lot easier to go by way of helicopter, than to try to drive up Desolation Road. Photos of nude beach goers ended up on the front pages of local newspapers. I guess they had nothing better to write about than naked people on the beach way out in the middle of nowhere. Eventually, a committee formed to study the problem of transients on Maui. They requested to have made available all-terrain vehicles in order so that they could conduct 'surveillance of the transients' which could make it easier to make arrests.

I don't remember the raids, but Matthew did:

"The main detective for the vice squad, Solomon Lee, would come down and tell everybody to put their clothes on or they were going to jail," Matthew explained. "I mean everybody had drugs, so if they searched people, they could have found it, but all in all, everybody was living down there, it's a public beach and everybody is naked."

"What did you think of the arrests?" I asked him.

"I thought it was lame," Matthew answered, "because after a while, you just get used to it—and here we were out in the middle of nowhere!"

The *Maui News* was littered with articles about different people who were arrested for indecent exposure. Typically, at the sentencing, Magistrate Shimoda would indicate that any of those sentenced would not have to serve their jail terms, if they just left the State, and then those charged were offered a one-way ticket to the mainland. (*Maui News*: Wed. Aug 20, & Jul. 9, 1969). Apparently, over the years, even to recently, this practice is still used to encourage transients leave the Island.

Karen remembered the arrests, although, she says that people didn't take them too seriously:

"The running joke at Makena was that "the [police] were looking for the hippie with the biggest shlong," she says. "It was just a big joke."

From time to time people were randomly arrested during beach raids that took place every so often. Beachgoers were booked and had to post $50 bail. Some people would just swim out in the ocean and not comeback till the police were gone.

Tom explained that it got so bad that certain beach residents took watch at certain check-points to alert their fellow beach mates that the police were coming:

"A variety of people got arrested," Tom says. "They let them put their swim suits on and they took them into Wailuku. Booked them, had to post $50 bail. It was utterly ridiculous," he explained. "I was exceedingly a good swimmer and still am, and when [the police] would come over, I'd hit the water and didn't come back till they left."

"The religious right ran this Island for a long time," Tom explained.

Former Maui officer Charles Kauluwehi Maxwell Sr. recalled that he would go with a team of officers before sunup to surprise the nude beachgoers, only to watch them scamper into the ocean, waiting sometimes for hours for them to come back in (*Honolulu Advertiser* Nov 26, 2001 pg. 2).

I was nude too, just a little chubby hippie kid. My almost white, blond hair wasn't that long yet, just below my ears. I still had my baby fat. I have a couple pictures of me on the beach without clothes on, holding what looked like a soiled diaper in one hand as I stood on the wide sandy beach. At three years old, I was too young to get arrested.

I don't think I had any idea at that point of the significance of the events taking place around me. I still feel that way sometimes.

I have these faded snap-shots in my head of images or situations. One image I have is of huddling under this palm tree with my mom, trying to take advantage of every piece of its not very generous shadow.

Another memory is of getting all these itchy bumps all over my body from a staph infection. They were not little bumps either; they were mini infected volcanoes scattered about on my skin. Some people had bumps the size of a small tangerine.

Staph was spread person-to-person but was also spread from contact with the sand. The mosquitoes made it worse because if you scratched the bites, they became open sores and vulnerable to infection. "Don't scratch!" Karen told me, over and over. It was no use.

Anytime there are too many people in one spot and especially with a constant flow of newcomers, you're going to have bacterial problems unless there are sanitation procedures in place that everyone is expected to follow. Some people there had more experience than others about how to stay healthy without modern plumbing and toilets. It was a learning curve, so it was trial and error to some degree. The Makena community learned how to keep the water bottles clean with bleach to avoid spreading illness.

No one knows exactly why there were problems with dysentery too. Some speculated that it was brought by a batch of bad poi. Poi is the Hawaiian word for the starchy, potato-like root that is a Polynesian staple. Tom described it as tasting like, "Elmer's Glue." Others thought that the water source may have been the problem.

"There's always a problem with dysentery," Tom says. "And I'm also speaking as a Vietnam Veteran. If you drink water that is not actually purified or boiled, then yes. And I am sure that those three people, except the one who had the horse ranch, that they had a way to purify or filter their water. But I honestly feel that [the water] made people sick."

In response to the dysentery, the state set up clinics and offered free gamma globulin shots at Makena. A group of social workers arrived at the beach and were giving out shots. They demonstrated how to wipe the mosquito bites with cotton and peroxide. Peroxide killed the existing staph, but calamine worked better to get rid of the itch. Unfortunately, when new bites would occur, then new bouts with staph would follow.

I ended up getting sick with dysentery, so my mom took me into town to see Dr. Fleming. Dr. Fleming was known as the doctor that took care of Makena people. It was pay what you could. He was even known to do trades such as medical treatment for a box of fruit. (*Honolulu Advertiser*, March 16, 1970, A5) Dr. Fleming gave me a shot of penicillin.

It was three days before Christmas. We had been living on Makena Beach for almost six months, when there was a terrible storm. They say it was the worst storm in 30 years, putting snow on Mt Haleakala. Many of the plastic campsites blew over, so we had to move back into the station wagon, but because I was so sick, social workers arranged to have us stay in a hotel for a couple nights. After that, we stayed for a short time with Astrid Watanabe, an artist painter who lived in Kihei. Then Karen decided to leave me with Sherry for a month in the kiawe trees while she looked for a place.

While she was gone, she arranged that we would stay with these nice Christian ladies in their home, and that is where we stayed for the remainder of our time in Maui, which was a couple months, although we still went back periodically and stayed for shorter periods of time on Makena beach.

During this time, I apparently potty trained myself.

"One day, you hopped up on the toilet and went," bragged my mom.

"Look what I did!' I announced proudly."

"I was into the natural thing, hippie that I was," says my moom, "so you just peed on the ground. If you took a crap on the ground, I would just pick it up and throw it in the toilet, but from that day on, you were potty trained."

I don't remember that, but I do remember that when I got that shot of penicillin, it left a small, round scar on my shoulder. I liked the scar because I found it useful as a topic for conversation. "See, look!" I showed it to everyone. I lifted my sleeve and pointed to the scar. Every time I showed someone, they would come close and look carefully with a concerned expression. I followed their eyes and studied their expression as they looked.

"What happened?" they would ask, giving me, each time, a chance to explain.

As I got older, my vocabulary increased, and there were more words to describe it. It was a great way to get attention. It did eventually fade, which ended up being disappointing.

I think I wanted something to hold on to, something permanent. I was attracted to the scar's durability. It was there day after day when other aspects of my life were not. Most children seem to be inclined to show off their injuries but for me, the scar represented a symbol of permanence in a time when our life was shifting from environment to environment. Here was this little scar that told a story—my story. My mom had her story, and I was a part of hers, but I had my own story too.

In my story, it was 1971. It had been a year since we had first arrived in Maui. We were just beginning to get settled with the Christian ladies, when my mom decided it was time to leave. She had talked to my dad and was under the impression that they were to reunite. That never ended up happening though, so Karen always talked about how happy we were with the Christian ladies and how she wished she had never left Maui.

Over the years, Karen bragged about her time in Maui; she was proud of it, but I was there too, so I took on her pride as if it were my own, without really understanding why. After doing my research, I learned that the alternative culture that was there when we were there continued to thrive on that beach. There have been continuing struggles though, between people who go there and the State police. A lot of the conflict is still over the nudity issue, but there have also been a lot of battles that center around people who want to protect the area from development and preserve the animal and plant diversity that exists there.

A couple years after we left, the Makena crowd was largely evicted. But the culture that had evolved there, over the years, continued. Today, Little Beach is one of the most popular, unofficial, nude beaches in the world! Despite the assaults, harassment, arrests, beach raids, and court battles, the counterculture there has persisted. Once the beach was shut down for camping, many of the hippies left back to the mainland, but many also stayed on and became part of the fabric of the local society.

Jeanice lived for years on Makena beach. She explained that starting in 2000, there have been "ongoing battles" around Little Beach in particular because of the drum circle happening there on Sunday evenings.

"People used to be able to be out there all night," Jeanice says, "then they suddenly changed it to 9:00pm. Then they changed it to 6:00pm, so people couldn't even stay till sunset." Beach goers "made such a stink about it," that the time was then changed to 8:00pm. "All of this was to get the drum circle to come to a close," says Jeanice.

I was only three, but Makena Beach just the beginning of my childhood in the counterculture. From Makena on, it was one adventure after the other.

BIBLIOGRAPHY (CHAPTER 1)

Barcelo, Jeanice. Personal Interview. October 3, 2011.

Bronson, Cliff. *Maui News*. Hitchhiking Law Change Opposed and Supported, May 7, 1969.
Collins, Tom. Personal Interview. November 7, 2010.

Diamond, Milton. Ph.D. (2004). Sexual Behavior in Pre Contact Hawai'i: A Sexological
Ethnography. University of Hawaii, Pacific Center for Sex and Society. Published in Revista
Espanola del Pacifico, 16: 37-58.

[Karen], Personal Interviews. June 13 and 21, September 27, all 2001.

Gilman, Matthew. Personal Interview. February 16, 2011.

Gilman, Robert. Personal Interview. October 19, 2010.

Hurley, Timothy. *Honolulu Advertiser*, Maui County Bureau. At Little Beach, Hippies Naked
Legacy Endures. Monday, November 26, 2001 pg. 2.

Honolulu Advertiser. 100 Maui Beach-Dwelling Hippies Get Eviction Notices. Mar 14, 1970.

Johnson, Robert. *Honolulu Advertiser*. Maui Vigilante Action Against Hippies Urged. Wednesday,
Jan 15, 1969, A5.

Lee, Pali Jae. (2007). Ho'opono. *Lightning Source Inc.* p. 28.

Lueras, Leonard. *Honolulu Advertiser*. Makena: A Unique Place Under the Sun. Mar 16, 1970,
A4–A5.

Maui News. Distorted View August 1, 1970 B2.

Maui News. 'Hippies our biggest problem'—Williams. June 20, 1970.

Maui News. 8 Arrested for Nudism at Makena. Wednesday, August 20.

Maui News. Five of 14 Still in Jail. July 9, 1969.

Maui News. Politics Part Of 'Problem,' Attorney Says. August 5, 1970.

Reeder, Ron. Personal Interview. December 2, 2010.

CHAPTER 2

On the Road: Hitchhiking and Other Adventures

I was three when we left Maui. Karen thought she and my dad were getting back together, but that never happened. For six months or so, we were between things, staying at communal houses, hitchhiking from place to place, hanging out at various hippie hot spots in the University District of Seattle.

Mostly, I was with her as her little side kick, but there were times when she left me with Gramma or Grampa.

Between the age of three and four, my Gramma Phyllis says that I was "friendly and talkative," and that I would frequently strike up a conversation with anyone who seemed receptive.

"You were not shy," my gramma says. "You would love to talk to anyone who would talk to you. It was so cute. You would say, 'Hi. How ya doin?'"

When I was little, there weren't a lot of other kids in the hippie counterculture yet, so I got quite a bit of attention everywhere we went from adults. The hippies hadn't yet started procreating in large numbers.

My mom would take me to the Open-Door Clinic which was a free medical clinic that operated in the University District. Its focus was serving the counterculture. They provided medical service and did triage with police and hospitals but also were supportive, offering referrals and counseling. The downstairs was a free medical clinic and upstairs was a referral agency and area where you could sit and hang out.

We were at the Open-Door Clinic onetime, and we were in the back where there was this hot-plate. Karen opened a can of food and put it on the burner.

"Some crazy guy kept coming up and stirring the can, just trying to be a pain," my mom says. "I got sick of it and went up to him and said, 'Fuck off, Asshole!'

The guy kept stirring it.

Karen went up to him again and said, 'Fuck off,' again, and "slugged" him. "Security came right away."

During this time, we had no regular meal times. I stood there with her while she panhandled for "Spare Change." If we didn't have money, she would pull "perfectly good" donuts or bagels out of the dumpster behind the grocery store for us to eat. When we hitchhiked, often the people who gave us rides would offer us food or a place to crash; sometimes they offered to take us to a restaurant. There was a song I heard a lot during this period. It was a Rolling Stones song, "You can't always get what you want." The song irritated me. I thought, *Why not? Why can't I get what I want?* I guess that's life, I learned. People had to even sing about it, like it was this thing to sing about.

Karen was a self-proclaimed "Dylan Freak." Freak was a term used in the hippie counterculture which means a person who is really into something, like wildly and almost obsessively. Music was a big part of the countercultural scene. It seemed like everywhere we went, people were playing music. I heard Dylan and a lot of other music of that period, such as Carol King's, "You've Got a Friend." I heard other songs like Paul Simon's "Skarborough Fair." Then there was "50 ways to Leave Your Lover," which I liked because of how it rhymed, "Get on the bus, Gus." The music of those times is like a backdrop for my childhood.

Every time we were near the UW Campus, I would ask to go to the used bookstore where the lady had free cookies. I was too young to be ashamed. It wasn't like we were the only ones; It seemed a lot of people in our circles at that time were creative types as well.

There were certain restaurants that would let you eat in exchange for washing a few dishes. Yeah, things have changed, and one can't even imagine things like that now. We once went into this diner. My mom asked to wash some dishes in exchange for food. They didn't need any help this time. They said somebody had already been there, just before we got there. Disappointing!

Sometimes my mom and I ate free meals with the Hari-Krishna people. Eating with them was called Pasha dim. They were very holy and clean. We would sit on tapestries on the floor. Before we ate, we would dance with finger symbols and pray. We ate the same thing every time. These brown, golfball sized balls of this bland mixture that had a slightly nutty flavor. I don't know exactly what was in those balls, but I was told they were made from a 5000-year-old recipe.

There always seemed to be a group of Hare Krishna wherever hippies hung out. They seemed to have this symbiotic relationship. The Hare Krishna managed to convert a lot of hippies, and the hippies were always welcomed by them and could eat with them for free.

Bald and in groups, they danced in a circle, each one draped in a brightly colored robe. They carried identical brown books held tightly to their abdomens.

They would chant:

"Hare Krishna, Hare Krishna, Krishna-Krishna, Hare Hare, Hare Rama."

It was an easy song for me to learn. Karen and I also frequented the Last Exit, a well-known restaurant/hippie hang out in the University District. Many of the regulars knew us by name and would invite me to eat and chat. I specifically remember that there were always a lot of alfalfa sprouts on the sandwiches, which I quickly learned to love. Musicians of various skill levels took turns on an old rickety piano in the corner. Karen would often play the flute with the piano player.

There was this perpetual feeling of movement and noise at the Last Exit. There were high ceilings, so the noises of the restaurant echoed on top of each other. Smoke curled upwards. I was hearing the faint clicks of the Go-players, the low rumble of voices, and laughter, someone clunking on the piano there, and plates being loaded into the dishwasher from the kitchen. There were huge, spacious windows which overlooked a collage of bicycles parked out front. Some played chess; others read from textbooks or drew on pads of paper. Margie, the waitress pitter-pattered from table to table wearing her pink, ballet slippers and an apron over her bell bottoms. With her tip money, she often bought me hot cocoas with a swirl of whip cream on top. Margie was my mom's friend.

In the back of the restaurant, there were these wooden steps and there was this small outdoor area where people could eat or hang out. I saw people buy marijuana, LSD or mushrooms. Nobody was trying to hide anything from me.

My mother and I lived in two different communal hippie houses. I specifically remember one of these hippie houses. For one thing, the refrigerator had food, but you couldn't just eat it. There were refrigerator rules. Everyone who lived there had their own food.

I didn't like that rule, plus there were strange noises from behind closed doors. I was walking by and from behind one of the closed bedroom doors, I heard people yelling and loud crashes and bangs. I went and told my mom and she said to just ignore it. A young guy walked by and said they were "balling," which meant having sex in hippie talk, and that they always did that. It sounded to me like there was someone in trouble, so it did not make sense to just ignore it, but I did as I was told.

The house was Andy Worhol-style with rugs on the walls. It had several floors with rooms on each landing. At night, everyone would get together for the rap session, which were long discussions about the war and straight society and how screwed up it all was.

My most vivid memory of the communal house was laying there in bed and being unable to move because my back hurt. The Easter bunny had come and brought a basket, but it was downstairs. My mom brought me a chocolate Easter egg from the basket up to my bed on the top floor. I wish I had more memories like this one.

Years and years later, during college, I was a volunteer phone worker on a crisis line. While I was there, I met this man named Eric who was also working the phones next to me. When I told him my name, he said, "Is your mom's name Karen?" He was the same Eric that had been my mom's boyfriend during that time when we lived at the communal house. I didn't remember him at all. He gave me Margie's phone number. I remembered her. Margie was the waitress at the Last Exit that used to give me those hot cocoas with the whip cream. I called Margie and we went out for lunch. I asked her what she remembered about me. Margie said that one day, she and Eric took me to this rock concert at a local park. They babysat me sometimes for my mom. Margie said they had lost track of me and sometime later, when they found me, my eyes were very dilated. Margie suspected that someone had fed me LSD. She said that I was pretty upset for hours and hours. She said that neither she nor Eric could console me. I sort of wished she hadn't told me that.

During this time, there was a movement that was brewing which was called the Back-to-the-Land movement. A lot of hippies, including my mom began to see that as the next step. Communes began sprouting up in the thousands all over the United States, many of which were rural. The idea was to buy land, on your own or with other similar-minded people, and live off the grid, grow your own food and live more healthful, simply and close to nature. Karen was ultimately looking for a commune but was biding her time to find the right one. Until then, she was looking for that ultimate back to the land experience where she could be self-sufficient and grow her own food. That was what drew her to Makena Beach, originally.

Then Karen met these two guys that changed her life. They also were interested in the idea of going 'back-to-the-land.' They took Karen under their wing and set about to helping her learn how to manage herself 'on-the-road.'

"Frankie and Leo were violent, jail-house, street-trip guys—they had hard lives," explained my mom. "Frankie was a blond Mexican who, as a child, had been given up for adoption because of the color of his hair after his mother had had an affair. Leo was black and had dreadlocks."

"When Caucasian hippie chicks started approaching Leo, telling him how cool his hair was, he shaved his dreadlocks them off," she says.

Frankie and Leo thought Karen was a 'crappy' mom. They offered to take care of me to demonstrate to her and help her learn how to have a more functional relationship with me. I would throw tantrums when I didn't get what I wanted. I was demanding and spoiled, to the point where people at the Last Exit "got sick of it" and would give us "the look," when we came in. "'Oh, here comes the lady with the kid,' people would say."

"You would fuss and tantrum a lot," my mom remembered. "You would demand a glass of water, saying, 'I'm thirsty,' then when the glass was brought, you would scream, 'No! I want a different one!' My mom never thought much about it and just patiently gave me what I wanted until Frankie and Leo came along.

Frankie and Leo taught my mom about discipline, positive reinforcement, and how to set boundaries in a loving way. When I was crying or not being nice, they would just ignore me, and when I was nice, they would give me heapings of attention or sometimes an ice cream cone. They also taught Karen all about the importance of a respectful, equal friend relationship with me, but 'equal' in the sense that Karen was still the decision maker. They explained to her that 'spoiling a child is one of the most unloving things a parent can do.' Within two weeks, I was transformed. My mom took me into the Last Exit, and people were saying, "Woh, Lois sure is happy!"

Frankie and Leo taught Karen how to survive on-the-road and how to protect me. Frankie, Leo and my mom were at the Open-Door Clinic one day, and while we were there, this creepy guy came up to me.

"Hi, little girl," the 'creepy guy' says, his voice syrupy and too friendly.

My mom says that Frankie looked at her with a knowing look in his eye, then went up to the guy and said, 'Back off man!' and "kicked the guy across the room."

Karen learned a lot from Frankie and Leo in those days, especially how to survive on-the-road. They taught her to 'never smoke pot' when she was on-the-road, and that it was 'important to be clear headed' and 'aware' of what was going on around her at all times. They taught her how to have her 'act together' and how to fight. She learned blindfolded how to pitch a tent in the dark and how to repair it. She learned what to carry in her pack. When we were on the road, she always carried medical supplies, food, a shovel, hatchet, air-mattress, toiletries, a pan, utensils, tent, full rain-suits and an extra outfit—just the bare minimum. I had a little school pack and carried my own coat and lunch. I wore my hiking boots and jeans.

"Everyone thought you were so cute," says Karen, "but that wasn't why; it was not to be cute, but just because we needed to."

My mom thought that Frankie and Leo were not really hippies: They were against what they called 'hippie-dippie, peace and love folks.' They told her that Hippie-dippie peace and love people 'were distinct and identifiable on the road;' they were 'usually in groups' and 'never knew what they were doing.' They taught Karen how to hitchhike the 'right' way: 'the fewer people there are,' they explained to her, 'the higher chances of getting a ride.' Karen learned that if she was with a small group of friends, they would all hitchhike separately and meet somewhere; they wouldn't go together. Frankie and Leo told her, 'always look nice and clean on the road; wear a nice pair of jeans and a turtleneck; always be polite; never flip a car off. If they don't give you a ride, they don't owe you any favors, and you don't owe them any favors.' Frankie and Leo taught my mom which ride to take, which ride not to take, and how to trust her instincts.

Karen's new friends, Leo and Frankie, also taught her about the 'social female' and the 'big bad man,' way of acting, which were stereotyped roles that were to be avoided. It was more important to be 'more real.' A social female 'was helpless and weak and allowed people to make her weaker.'

When we were on the road, guys would always offer to carry my mom's pack, and she would say, 'No, forget it, I will do it myself.' That's how independent she was. She was always amazed at how many men would get offended because she wouldn't let them help her with her pack. Leo and Frankie taught Karen that 'the system wanted to weaken her.' They told her that she 'was smart for carrying her own pack because it kept her strong.'

They also taught my mom that the social female 'was manipulative' and did not just come out and say, 'Let's ball,' (have sex) but instead 'had all these little courting games.'

Big bad man was a macho way of acting: it was men who acted in stereotypical and superficial ways as opposed to approaching people as just friends. I heard them talking about it a lot, because my mom even remembered that I would say it too, but in my own way—"Sho sho meo," and "Big big man," I would say. My mom had this "rap" down about everybody. It helped her to be strong on the road to know these principles. She was very idealistic and "into it, almost religiously."

"Even today they are a part of who I am," she says.

Frankie and Leo were planning on staking out land in Alaska and my mother was going to meet them there. She ended up hitchhiking to Alaska twice before we actually went there to live there.

Karen, with me in tow, hitchhiked through Canada to Fairbanks twice, up the Alaskan Canadian Highway, (AlCan) through the Yukon and NW Territories. The ALCan Highway was built during WWII for the purpose of connecting the United States to Alaska through Canada.

"It was 1400 miles of dirt road back then," Karen says. "We would travel 200–300 miles a day." That was her rule so that we didn't get too "burned out." Then we would have time to make dinner and set up camp. We went fishing and traveled with these different people. "It was easy to get rides and plenty of people were giving us food."

The hardest part was crossing the border. Just before we got to the border, my mom dressed me up in a pink pant-suit, and she wore a pink dress just for the occasion. These were outfits that she kept in the bottom of her backpack, just for border crossing.

"Borders were a big hassle," she says. Each time we prepared to cross, she had to "dump out" all her vitamins, so they wouldn't think they were drugs.

On one of our trips, hitchhiking the AlCan to Alaska, something happened: We had gone to Fairbanks to a college town, to the University of Alaska. Frankie and Leo taught "They told me to, 'go straight to the student union' where there is often free food, lots of other hippies to meet up with, and resources," they taught her.

We met Frankie and Leo there as well as my mom's best friend Debbie. Everyone had hitchhiked separately so it wouldn't take as long. We stayed in our tent in these woods behind the student union at night. During the day, in the union, there was a piano there that my mom liked to play.

"I had to wait long periods of time for it," says my mom, "because there was this crazy guy there, who also liked to play it." This time though, there was no one there, so Karen sat down to play. Suddenly she was "grabbed" from behind by her wrists and "yanked backward off the bench." Karen "jumped him" and was "punching" him—adrenaline just took over," she says. Of course, security broke it up right away.

Then something else happened. Debbie, my mom's best friend was very "uptight" because apparently there was some guy "bad vibing" her and "staring at her." Debbie kept saying, over and over 'I wish he would fucking stop!' Finally, "Debbie got up and went over to him, picked up this trash can that was full of trash, lifted it over her head and hit him with it," my mom says. "My jaw dropped," my mom continued. "I was sitting there watching the whole thing, just shocked. Security came right away." Karen and Debbie were kicked out.

"I wasn't very in touch with my feelings back then," my mom says. "We were hardened at that point and were attracting that sort of energy. I was really muscular and in shape."

So once again, back on the road hitchhiking. It was sometimes a long time to wait for a four-year-old. This time, we had been standing on the side of the road for almost an hour. There was a light rain, and it was totally silent except the sound of our steps as we walked. Evergreens lined the wet pavement as the road wound off into what seemed like nowhere. It was early evening and getting cooler. I was beginning to feel hungry and tired. Walking became a way of life because even if we didn't get the rides, eventually we would get there, if we just keep walking.

We walked and walked, and when we heard the engine, everything stopped and became still, her thumb went out and we waited until the vehicle approached. If it passed without stopping, then there would be disappointment. One time, we had been waiting for a ride. It had been a while, and finally there was a truck coming. But it passed us without stopping.

That was it! Karen kicked her pack, which was very heavy, it only moved a grudging couple of inches. I hoped she hadn't crushed my animal crackers, which she had put in that pocket.

"Come on," she said, "we'll start walking again."

I thought *no way*. I knew better than to start complaining though. I got up and walked boldly up to the road and flung out my arm and thumb; I would help, even though I knew she would not let me.

The crease in her brow disappeared, and she rolled her eyes and laughed. I think she was tired of the waiting and it was cold.

I bravely faced the edge of the road, my arm parallel, my thumb tilted the wrong way.

Amused, she walked up behind me, put her arms around me and rearranged my thumb.

I was probably around 4 but I remember it so vividly as it was a special moment between us. I often felt like I couldn't keep up with her, and now she would show me how. I could do this too! Her long braid tickled my face as she raised my arm about two inches and swung it out to the opposite side of the road, turning my body slightly toward on-coming traffic. She stood in place behind me, shifted the padded shoulder strap of her pack, and confidently walked backwards. I took a step back, gravel shifting under my feet. Before I knew it, she was several yards up the road. As she walked, I could see the handle of the Bowie survival knife hidden in her boot, as I ran towards her. It was big enough that she used it to chop kindling sometimes.

Years later, I said to my mom, "I remember hitchhiking."

"No, I never let you hitchhike, and if I did it was a onetime thing," she says, "but I can see how that might have happened if there were no cars coming for a long time.

"Frankie and Leo taught me, 'Never use your kid as a meal ticket to survive'—They'd beat me up if they knew," she explained.

But usually, there was no problem getting rides along the AlCan, In the winter time, at least back then, "it was illegal to pass up a hitchhiker, because they could die if they are left out there too long."

Each night, on our way up the AlCan, towards Alaska, we would set up the tent, make a fire, and cook potatoes. Karen would dig a little pit around the tent with her pick so that the water would run off if it rained.

Leo and Frankie had taught her that potatoes were good food for the road, and she always carried them in her pack.

"Potatoes are a good source of starch, very filling, with lots of vitamins and could easily be wrapped in tinfoil and thrown on a fire," Karen explained. She also carried things like tubes of mayonnaise and canned milk and other things that mountain climbers used.

"You were so content," my mom says. "I gave you a can of milk, and you would chug the whole thing down. It sounds so gross to me now, but it was so filling and so full of nutrition."

One of the cutest things that I did, she says, was when people offered me candy or cookies, I would say, 'No, but I'll have a glass of milk.' I didn't like candy because I never had it. I knew I needed nourishment. My mom says that I was 'very verbal and so smart.' I 'talked a mile a minute.'

Karen and I were closer during these years than at any other time in my life. So far, it was just her and me on this adventure. She told me about one of the times that we were hitchhiking up the AlCan. We were on our way to meet Frankie and Leo, Debbie, and another friend named Suzie.

"Everyone was meeting in Kodiak," says my mom. "We had gotten a good ride," and were in the back camper of a pick-up truck. Both of us "had to pee really bad," so we ended up "banging on the window of the cab for hours."

The people driving couldn't hear us. Finally, "we decided to pee our pants" as "there was no other option."

But just then, the driver stopped.

"We raced into this restaurant to see who could get there first," says my mom.

I won. I sat up on the toilet.

Karen had to go so bad, that she sat up on the sink, and it broke off the wall.

"We laughed so hard, she says. "We were like equals then that I'm kind of ashamed of now."

At the time, Karen says that she was "hard core into this honesty approach." She went in and just told the restaurant staff what had happened. But she also knew that if she didn't tell them, that we might be standing there for hours, waiting for a ride. She didn't want them "bad vibing" us.

Because these hitchhikes down the AlCan to Alaska were so huge, my mom stopped off in Canada to check out this commune that she had heard about where she "could crash, relax and get ready" for her journey to Alaska. It was muddy and a difficult trek down the trail. We had to carefully step on the boards that had been placed on the path, so we would avoid sinking in the mud. When we got there, they didn't have much food and were rationing sugar. I only got one teaspoon of sugar on my oatmeal each morning. While we were there, we were told about another commune, that was not rationing sugar, but that was a very long hike. A nice man drew her a map.

"He was a great big guy with a big beard, and he had just walked 30 miles down this dirt road to get there," my mom explained. He left his pack 15 miles back. The man offered to take us to the commune, but my mom refused. She was determined to do it on her own.

We left and followed the man's map through the woods to the road, found the gate, and followed the path. We walked and walked. Karen had her great big pack on and I had my little pack. After a while, she did not see the path anymore.

"It was a freaky feeling," my mom says. "Nothing like that had ever happened to me. Our canteen of water was running low." Even though she was scared, she did not show it, so I would not panic. We walked all day. It was starting to get dark when we finally found a stream to fill our canteen.

Then we set up our tent for the night. I helped my mom clear a space, and she put potatoes on the fire for dinner. After we ate, we snuggled up in the sleeping bag that we shared.

In the morning, we could see that there was a farm in the distance, but there was some risk in approaching the house since we were out in the middle of nowhere. They could shoot at us or they might have a dog. Suddenly, we heard horses' hooves clomping up, approaching our tent. Karen threw on her pants and got out her knife:

"Stay in the tent and don't come out!" she growled at me.

There were "two Indian guys" and they sounded friendly.

"I am here with my daughter and we are lost," Karen said. "Can you tell us where we are?"

"Surely," the men said and told us to walk about a mile that way and we would hit the road.

We packed up, hiked out of there and got to the road in no time.

We still had 50 miles to hitchhike down the dirt road to get to this ferry that would take us across the Fraser River. Then we would have to hike in eight miles. There were no cars out there. We had been hiking for a long time when along came the nice man from the commune. He had worried that we would get lost, so he followed us, then he lost our tracks and knew we had gotten lost. Even though my mom had refused his help getting to the commune, he now insisted.

It was a long truck drive to the ferry. When we got there, it was just a great big raft that we went across with this rope, just like a hundred years ago. I got to ride on the nice man's shoulders the whole way.

"It was treacherous and scary," my mom says. "If I had done that alone, we would have been dead." We were at the top of a desert mountain, cactus all around. It was beautiful country, but it was hot. We were exhausted.

"I can't go on," Karen told the nice man.

"Yes, you can," he answered, firmly.

We made it to the top, and we looked down this huge ravine that went way, way, down, and at the bottom of it was the Liberal River and this little house that looked like a dot it was so far away. To get there, we had to go down these switchbacks.

My mom was interested in living in a commune, so whenever she heard about one, she wanted to visit. When we finally arrived, all the people there were "very muscular—like Amazons. They had to pack everything in and were in really good shape."

"You can work in the kitchen with the women," said the man who owned the place to Karen.

"I ain't staying in the kitchen with the women," Karen told him, "I will get out and help clear rocks." So, every day, my mom was out with the men, with a wheel barrow, helping to clear rocks. The owner didn't seem to mind. He was "a little Greek guy," who had three wives, one of whom herded goats all day.

"I'll never forget," says my mom, "He came in from the field that night, and he asked his wives, 'Who is going to fuck me tonight?' It was not really hippie but more just old-fashioned."

We didn't stay long at this commune. Karen was back on the mission. She was going to find Frankie and Leo in Alaska.

For me, being on-the-road, wasn't a stable home, and I didn't have kid friends, but I learned to love being close to nature, and I enjoyed the adventure and being close to my mom. She taught me how to hug trees and told me how important trees were to our planet and to all life. Trees have feelings too, I learned. We were sitting in the park eating a sandwich, when this work crew pulled up in a truck. They took out their chainsaws, and right in front of us, were cutting the trees down. I was overwhelmed with sadness and started crying. My mom says that I became "transfixed."

"As the tree fell," she says, "I'll never forget. Your mouth was really wide and went 'Waaaaa!' It looked just like this famous comedian, Joey Brown, who had this big mouth."

We were stuck in Prince George, which is one of the last main towns before you get up into the Yukon. She took a job babysitting, but it paid so little that she was unable to save any money for our trip to Alaska. Then she lost her purse, which had the little bit of money she had saved from babysitting.

Things hadn't worked out too well in Prince George, so the only option at that point was to go back to the commune where they were rationing sugar. Karen told me we needed to "eat and crash." This commune was on the last leg before you reach the border to Alaska. Karen said the hippies there "were losers," but it was a place that at least we could stay.

On our way and before we arrived, this older man picked us up in a pickup truck and offered my mom a job.

"Can you cook?" he asked.

"Hell, yeah!" she answered enthusiastically. But really, she didn't know how to cook anything. "I had never made a made a pot of coffee in my life. I had never cooked a steak in my life," she admitted to me. The owner, an outfitter with teams of cowboy-like guides, took actors from the States out hunting for weeks at a time. "He was kind of like a John Wayne," she remembered.

Before our trip up into the mountains for this job, the man let us stay in Lillooet where his wife and children had a house. Lillooet is a community on the Fraser River in British Columbia, Canada, about 240 km up the British Columbia Railway from Vancouver and 518 km from Prince George. Lillooet was an important location in Aboriginal history and culture and remains one of the main population centers of the St'at'imc (Lillooet Nation) where the population of indigenous people form the majority of people living there.

We stayed with John Wayne's family for a couple of weeks, waiting for the hunting season to start, then we were taken into the mountains for the job.

"I had to make big steaks for the cowboys and big pots of coffee," My mom remembered. The job was way up at timberline in these beautiful mountains. Her boss called my mom 'Cookie,' and he called me 'Charlie Brown,' because I always wore these overalls. They were my Osh Kosh B'Gosh overalls, which I remember to this day because I thought it was so great to say that name "Osh Kosh B'Gosh," which I would say whenever I had an opportunity.

Karen loved the job, and I ended up enjoying it too. The nice hunters gave me rides on the horses. My mom learned how to butcher animals with an ax, breaking the bones up if they brought deer back. She learned how to make stews with the meat. She was taught how to make pie and washed their long johns too. We made friends with this old man there named Uncle Kenny who taught my mom how to chop wood.

"He was really nice to us," my mom says, "and was always there to help when the people would go out hunting.

When they went hunting, it was for weeks at a time and we were left to our own devices, except for Uncle Kenny. There were these shelves near the stove, lined with cans of corned beef hash. Whenever I was hungry, I could ask Karen for corned beef hash and there I had it. Instant gratification.

I was now almost four years old. My life had really changed. I was no longer palling around in the University District in Seattle; now we lived in the mountains and ate corned beef hash. I got to ride horses. No more hitchhiking around from place to place, panhandling, or hanging around the Last Exit.

In the end, after all that hitchhiking back and forth, we ended up just flying to Alaska. She bought our tickets out of the $800 that she had earned from her job cooking in the mountains.

"Eight hundred was a lot more back then," she says.

BIBLIOGRAPHY (CHAPTER 2)

[Karen], Personal Interviews. June 13 and 21, September 27, all 2001.

CHAPTER 3

Back to the Land: Living in the Alaskan Wilderness

Winter, 1972. We moved to Alaska when I was four where we lived for almost three years. Karen had met this guy on the road who was from Homer who said we could stay with him.

Her original plan, with some friends of hers from Seattle, including Debbie, Susie, Frankie and Leo, was to go work in Alaska in the canneries. They would each save $2000, then they were going to Canada to buy land.

That plan fell through, but she had the money that she had earned in Canada, so she bought us a plane ticket, and we flew to Anchorage. From there, we took a small plane to Homer. As soon as we got off the plane, it was so cold that we went right away with the remaining money and bought warm boots and coats, the snowpack kind.

Karen could not remember the name of the guy who invited us. She says we stood in front of the post office, and she asked everyone that walked by, "Hey, do you know two brothers that live together?"

They looked at her like she was crazy. Eventually, two people came walking towards us.

"That's them!" Karen cried. Then when they got closer, she said, "Hi, remember me?"

He did remember. His name was Marty and he lived with his brother Bill near Lake Beluga. Marty had gentle features. He had freckles and shoulder length, wavy medium-brown hair; crooked teeth. Nineteen years old, he was just a year or so younger than my mom. Bill, his brother, was taller than Marty and had freckles, a mustache and super short hair that he wore in a warm, black ski hat.

We went back to their cabin in the woods. Bill had built it himself; It was rustic with no electricity or running water. The cabin was on a little lake that froze every winter. In the middle of the night, we would walk out onto the middle of it just for fun. Unfortunately, Bill turned out to be an alcoholic, so we moved into his friend's trailer nearby.

"All we had to do was open the little door of this trailer," my mom explained, "and instantly, the whole trailer was freezing." We had arrived in Alaska during the coldest part of the winter, and we lived in that trailer for a few months.

At that time, Homer was a town of about 4000. It was like a cross between a little Western town and a fishing village, right on the sea. I could smell saltwater no matter where we were in Homer, and there were beaches everywhere. Right across Kachemak Bay from Homer were the Kenai mountains, which raise about 10,000 feet, straight up from sea level. Then pouring into the bay from the Kenai mountains were three glaciers that opened right up into the ocean itself. Most people don't ever see a glacier in their whole lives, but here, there were three of them.

I felt right at home and was glad to not be hitchhiking around anymore. The trailer was cozy and my mom seemed happy. This place that was now my home. I was amazed as it was so different than anything I had ever seen, and I had seen quite a bit for my age by now. Suddenly, the pace, which had been going rather fast thus far, slowed down, dramatically to almost a standstill.

Homer wasn't as cold as a lot of places in Alaska because of the Japanese current. The main thing that was so beautiful was the air was so clean, and it was so quiet. I didn't hear trucks going by at all on a freeway anywhere. I didn't hear planes going by like we did in Seattle or when we were hitchhiking around from place to place. It was just silent and beautiful, pristine, and white.

Soon after we got settled into the trailer, Karen started working at the cannery. I got to go see where she worked once or twice. The cannery was on the Homer Spit, a skinny piece of land that went out five miles into the ocean. There was a cannery and a restaurant at the end of it. The Spit was only as wide as the road going out there. There was a beach on either side. I found it entertaining that it was called "The Spit." Karen and I used to spit off the Spit, just for fun. Once when we were there, I found a piece of petrified wood on the beach that I kept for years after that. I think I still have it.

Alaskan author Charles Wohlforth who has written *Frommer's Alaska* as well as several other travel guides, described Homer his way: "Homer is full of outspoken, unusual, and even odd individualists," he writes. "It has gathered certain people here the way currents gather driftwood on the town's pebble beaches..." and "believers of one kind or another have washed up here for decades." (Wohlforth, pg 305)

I never saw anyone "washed up," when I was spitting off the Spit. No one seems to know exactly why the Spit is even there, but some speculate that it is a moraine left behind by glaciers retreating into the Kenai Mountains on the far side of the bay. (Pascall, 1998)

To get to work at the cannery on the Spit, Karen would hitchhike every day. We didn't have a car until almost a year later; we mostly walked everywhere or hitchhiked. Marty took care of me a lot and would pull me in the sled. My mom made sure I wore as much clothing as there was to wear, but even then, it was still cold. Then there was the wind chill factor—it was well below zero.

Marty loved me a lot and became like a dad to me. I didn't even remember my biological dad by now. My mom was always very careful about who she let talk to me.

"When we were on the road," Karen remembered, "it was rare to actually find someone who could relate to children. Most people go 'Oh, the chick with the kid.' But "Marty was different."

"He thought you were just wonderful, and he was super nice to you," My mom remembered. "He didn't goo goo talk at you."

Marty just talked to me like a friend. Then he and Karen fell in love.

In the spring, Marty found us a little house for $50 a month in town. It had electricity and running water. It didn't have any furniture or anything, but it didn't matter, it was heaven. Karen used the gas stove to cook meals, and we had company over all the time. This is where we lived for our first summer in Alaska.

Around that time, Marty began working at the cannery too, so then they worked different shifts, and Marty could take care of me while Karen worked.

Karen was against getting welfare or food stamps.

"You absolutely did not get help from the government! That was a Frankie and Leo thing," she explained emphatically. And we didn't even need government help.

"That first winter we had two hundred pounds of steak, a whole quarter of a moose," my mom says and explained that quite often, people would end up with a quarter of a moose because "It takes about four people to pack it out." We ate moose all the time. We ate seal meat too. We even had a friend that let us try some of his bear jerky, and we ate a lot of halibut. The average halibut was about a hundred pounds. Marty would work on the docks from time to time, and he had lots of friends who he would go fishing with.

We had plenty of homemade bread too. Karen found a grinder at the dump and began grinding her own flour to make bread. We found all kinds of things at the dump. The dump was this gigantic, football field sized pile of stuff that was fenced off. We could walk right in and climb on top of it. Everything was hard and frozen, quiet. I could hear the seagulls.

"A lot of people would move to Alaska, and after their first winter, they would say 'Forget it,' My mom explained. "They didn't want to bring all their stuff back down the AlCan or ship it back, so they would just take it to the dump." We found furniture there. We got all our pots and pans there. Karen found a down coat that she wore the whole time we were in Alaska. There was lots of frozen meat, because people would empty their freezers out.

"The packages usually had dates on them, so we would know how old they were," Karen says.

By one way or another, we got what we needed, and even though we were settled in this little house that had electricity and a gas stove, Karen hadn't given up on buying land, just like she had originally planned with Frankie and Leo.

To buy land, Karen and Marty decided they could make some quick cash if they worked on the fishing boats. They would be gone for a month, so they left me with a friend, Sherry, who lived on East End Road. This was a different Sherry from the one who lived with us on Makena beach. This Sherry had three daughters who I could play with while Karen and Marty were gone. I heard about the fishing trip after they returned. They actually told it many times since there had been a terrible accident at sea, and they had almost died.

While they were out there working on the boat, there was an accident and the ship hit a rock.

It was a 300-foot barge. Karen and Marty wore aprons and helped process the herring at large tables. At night, they slept on the tug boat that pulled the barge. At one point, the boat was going through this narrow passage, and it hit a rock. Suddenly, they heard a crash, then the boat started tipping. This was around nine at night when they were all going to bed.

"The guy above us really had his act together," Karen says. "I saw him jump from the bunk and land directly with both feet into his boots." They were scrambling to get their pants and boots on. "We all met up on the deck, and we looked up and saw the stars, the Northern Lights going across the sky. We are all freaked, and we are all looking at each other."

The boat was on the rock on some deserted island out in the middle of nowhere. Karen looked up at the boat and saw that it was solid ice.

'Pump the bilge!' the captain yelled.

"As the water was being pumped, the boat started to jack knife really slowly," remembered Karen. Luckily, the pilot radioed the pilot boats who came right away, and they tied up and pulled the barge out, so it stopped jack knifing. They then put the anchor down to stabilize the boat.

"You could hear the wench creaking and pulling us off the rocks," my mom says.

Karen could have died, really. Apparently, the captain had fallen asleep after "getting drunk and stoned with these two hippie chicks."

"It was an illegal operation and was devastating the herring population," my mom explained. One week later, we heard that the captain died; "He was hit by a one-ton crate of herring,"

I don't remember staying with Sherry and her daughters. All I remember is hearing about the wreck afterward and having nightmares about it for a long time.

Right after this disaster happened was when Karen heard, through a friend, about the Open Entry project.

Open Entry was an opportunity to buy land in Denali National Park, a mountainous region adjacent to Talkeetna near Mt McKinley. Mt McKinley is a mountain now known as Mt Denali. It has been renamed to what the Native Alaskans originally called it before white settlers came along.

Denali National Park and Preserve notes that "Mt Denali is the highest peak in North America, at 20,320-ft. It has numerous active glaciers, which continue to shape a landscape of broad U-shaped valleys and small kettle lakes (Microsoft Encarta Online Encyclopedia 2001).

Back when the Open Entry parcels of land became available, the State of Alaska was encouraging settlement in this remote location to encourage growth. For $32 dollars a year, you could take out two, five-year leases with the option to buy at $100 an acre. The project included periodic surveys of residents who had settled in the area, complete with ecological recommendations. A majority of the people who settled were "young, countercultural hippie types." (Durr 1974)

This was just the opportunity my mom was looking for. She wanted to buy land, and land was available, but she had to go and stake it out herself.

She says that Marty took care of me while she was gone, so I wasn't there, but she told me what happened:

First, she hitchhiked 225 miles to the land office in Anchorage. Once she got there, there were hippies who helped her study the photographic aerial maps to pick out her parcel. Then she had to go and stake it out herself, so she hitchhiked 100 miles to Talkeetna, then took a train another 50-miles to Curry, which was on the East bank of the Susitna River.

Curry was just wilderness; there were no signs of human habitation anywhere. There was just this one guy working the train station, which was this little shack out in the middle of nowhere. But early on, when they were building the Alaskan Railroad, Curry was a railroad construction camp and roadhouse.

It was originally called 'Dead Horse Hill' because it was a notorious place where horses would lose their footing and fall. It was renamed Curry in 1922 when it became the railroad construction camp and roadhouse.

The roadhouse and railroad camp were run by a very well-known and well-loved early Alaskan Pioneer—Nellie Neal Lawing—commonly known as "Alaska Nellie." She ran the roadhouse where she provided food and lodging to government employees and other tourists and important heads of government. She was, in fact, the first woman to ever be awarded a lucrative government contract for the Alaskan Engineering Commission. In addition to her duties at the roadhouse, Alaska Nellie was also a fisherman, a hunter, a trapper, a guide for big game hunters, and had an impressive collection of trophies of her own. She ran a dog team in the winter and was known to keep a pet bear cub. A movie short was made about her called, "Land of Alaska Nellie" (1940) produced by Metro-Goldwyn-Mayer Studios. She died almost 15 years before Karen took her journey to stake out property in the wilderness in Curry.

Because of a cliff between her and her parcel, Karen had to go up the riverbed all the way until she hit Dead Horse Creek. The riverbed was shallow, but the current was strong. At one point, her pack was so heavy, that she fell backwards into the creek and got all wet. It was hot out though, so she dried off as she hiked. Once she followed the creek all the way up, it led her to this little lake, right where land was available. She walked around all day until she found this beautiful spot on the creek. Then she paced out five acres on really overgrown wilderness.

Karen used a compass to find the corners of the parcel, and on each one of her stakes, she put a lidded jar with a note in it, claiming the land, just as she was instructed. She then put little red flags on the trees where she was required to. She had carried a tent, a hatchet, and a shovel as well as food for the trip. The whole thing took her two days. On the way down, she took a shortcut down through these alder trees towards the tracks, instead of going back down the riverbed. My mom described her trip down:

"I was seeing so much bear shit," she says. The whole time, she was singing really loud, going 'La la la la!' and was clapping her hands really loud and laughing and saying, 'Ha! Ha! here I come!' Karen was smart for doing that. It's not a good idea to surprise a mother bear in the spring, which is when she was there. That is when the bears come out of hibernation and eat tons of berries which were everywhere, and then the berries ferment in their stomach, and they get drunk. My mom explained that a lot of people who get attacked by bears, it usually happens in the spring when the bears are drunk.

"I was scared shitless," she says.

It took Karen four hours to get back to the railroad tracks. On the way down, suddenly, she began to feel feverish and nauseous. She had drunk bad water. Her foot was bothering her, but she made it to the train stop.

Then she hitchhiked back to the land office and filled out the paper-work. She learned she would be required to name the little lake that was on her parcel, so she named it Lake Ptarmigan, named after the wild birds that she saw there that were like, "wild chickens." She got her lease.

After considerable thought, Karen decided the land was unlivable. "It was above timberline and 60 degrees below in the winter." Just to live there, there would have to be a dug-out that would climb 10 feet through the snow. There wouldn't be enough firewood. Water could be a problem too; The stream dried up in the summer and in the winter, snow would have to be melted. Another problem was that the trail would have been too difficult for me to get to the school bus. She had considered homeschooling me, which was common among hippie families, but if we lived there, there wouldn't be an option. Plus, just to move there, all our supplies would have to be helicoptered in.

"There were hippies that did that," Karen explained solemnly, "but in the end, it just seemed like too much trouble."

While Karen was up north claiming her open entry land, Marty found a beautiful abandoned cabin in Homer that was a hundred-year old squared-log cabin. The original white settlers of Alaska built squared-log cabins because of their heat efficiency. Squared log cabins are warmer than round-log cabins because they retain heat better. The squared logs fit perfectly together and don't require chinking, or stuffing. Log cabins were the typical dwellings of early American Pioneers during the Westward expansion after 1765.

We found out that the cabin wasn't abandoned; Someone owned the cabin, so we got permission from the owner to live there for a year. In exchange, Marty would do some remodeling. It didn't have any windows, but apparently none of the abandoned cabins up there did. Marty put double layered Visqueen, a plastic sheeting in them. Everyone we knew used Visqueen. The cabin was about a mile from town near the hospital, off this trail. We could sled on the trail and take it all the way to town, which we often did for supplies. One of my favorite memories was when I was allowed to go sled by myself down the hill to a store that was at the bottom of the hill. One time, Marty gave me 50 cents, so I could buy an ice cream cone. At almost six years old, I was beginning to get a little more independent now. Karen and Marty used the sled to bring wood to the cabin. They cut it by hand with a bow saw, then chopped it with an ax. I helped stack it.

My mom seemed happy there, even though she says, "the rednecks hated us." Homer had a strong artist community though, and there were a lot of hippies and alternative types there too.

"The hippies we knew were constantly cross-country skiing. Marty did a lot of cross-country skiing too," Karen remembered.

I was happy too. Karen was no longer a vagabond, traveling from one place to another without a home, she was settling down and in more of a domestic role.

In the evenings, there was the warmth of the wood stove in the cabin as I slept, sometimes listening half asleep to people talking or playing guitar. My bathtub was a metal washtub that hung outside the front door.

Every couple of days or so, I looked forward to going to the laundromat with Karen. I loved it because it was a chance for us to just hang out while we waited for the wash. She would often get a treat from the vending machine, and we would sit and share it. One day, we were there, and I had these itchy, uncomfortable bumps all over my skin. She put calamine lotion on them, and told me they were scabies, little bugs that lived under your skin. I was horrified as I tried to imagine their little lives under my skin. I imagined them sitting around a little firepit, since the bumps were uncomfortably hot and itchy.

When we were at the laundromat, there were Russian women there doing laundry too.

"They were friendly and would talk to us, even though they were very private and usually did not socialize outside their group," My mom explained. "They were very discriminated against by the local rednecks who hated them because they worked so hard and made such good money." They built their own boats; They made their own wine and raisins; They dried noodles.

A lot of them worked at the cannery with my mom and Marty. They had lots of houses and lived in a large community that they started in Anchor Point, which was right near where we ended up living the following year.

When they needed someone to marry their child, someone would come up from Oregon so that they wouldn't intermarry. Some of their fishermen stopped by and visited us a couple of times and brought us some food.

"They hated hippies in a way because they were really conservative in a Christian way, but they liked us," Karen says, "because we were kind of different. We were not quite your average hippies. Here we were living in a very rustic situation, and they knew I had my baby at home."

The Russians had settled in Alaska just a few years before we got there, around 1965. They were peasant-costumed and wore long colorful homemade skirts or dresses and scarves; their bearded men wore rubashki, the hand-embroidered blouses of old 17th century Russia.

Their story was that 300 years ago, their ancestors refused to accept the reforms of the rites of the Russian Orthodox Church. Because of that, they were excommunicated. These dissenters became known as the "Old Believers" and were persecuted. Many paid with their lives. In the next several decades, thousands committed suicide rather than follow the new order. Elders of the Alaska group had fled from the Soviet Union to China in the 1920's and 1930's. They migrated through Hong Kong, to Brazil, then ended up in Oregon. When their numbers grew too large, there was a crew that moved to Alaska, and started a village in Anchor Point, about 30 minutes from Homer. (Rearden, National Geographic, 1972, pg. 401-405).

We didn't just go to the laundromat to do laundry though. We also went there to bathe. Karen would pay a couple dollars and we could take a shower. It was common for showers to be available to anyone who might need one. Even the hotels offered them to the public. People got really dirty in Homer, especially once the snow started melting and the streets turned to mud. Karen remembered that one day, we were showering, and the hotel owners found out there were hippies in the shower. It upset them.

"It was really mean of them the way they kicked us out. I felt really sad about it," my mom told me.

At least I could still take a bath in my metal tub back at the cabin, but now Karen and Marty were back to sponge baths since we didn't have running water at home.

Around the time that I started Kindergarten, which would've been the Fall of 1973, Marty brought a puppy home, and named him Yusef, "after the famous jazz musician named Yusef Latif." Yusef was a beautiful dog. "His mother was a full-blooded wolf. His father was a Husky German Shepherd." He was large, the size of an Alaskan wolf, and he was wild. We didn't even have to feed him. He caught animals and fed himself. He was very protective, loving and super smart. He always greeted me when I got off the school bus. When people saw him, they got scared, and if strangers came anywhere near our cabin, he would bark and scare them away very easily.

When Yusef first came home, he would "shit all over the cabin." Every time he did it, Marty would stick his nose in it, and Yusef would cry out. This upset me very badly, so I told Marty he was being mean. Marty explained to me that this was how you train a dog to live in the house with people. I still didn't like it.

One night we came home and it was freezing. Yusef had ripped out the visqueen covering in the windows.

"He did that a couple times," my mom explained. Eventually though, he learned.

I loved Yusef. One day I got home from school, and Marty was using his pliers to remove porcupine quills from Yusef's mouth and face. He apparently had gotten into some trouble in the woods. Each time that Marty would yank a quill out with the pliers, Yusef would yelp. Each quill was the size of a large sewing needle, but it was striped white and brown and black. I tried to help but it was horrible torture to watch. Those were the quills Karen used to make beads. Each quill is hollow so when it is cut it into slices, it would make beautiful beads, which she used to make jewelry.

Karen was very resourceful. She used to take me mushroom picking. We ate puffballs and wild edible mushrooms that grew everywhere. Karen knew a lot about wild herbs and plants that had medicinal or edible qualities. She had taken a class at the University of Alaska on plants and animals of the Kenai Peninsula, and she brought home a lot of the specimens that she collected in the field during the class.

Then Karen discovered nettle. We ate it like spinach almost every night. We drank a lot of nettle tea too. Then, she learned to make nettle bread from Yule Kilcher. Yule Kilcher had a homestead in Homer that we visited from time to time, and he had visited our cabin a couple times.

"He was famous for his nettle bread. He would put one cup of nettle flour into each loaf; the loaves were huge," Karen bragged.

Yule Kilcher lived out East End Road. He was a famous Alaskan homesteader and former state Senator who helped sign Alaska's constitution. When we would visit them, I would play with the children there. He had eight children, one of whom was named Jewel, who was just a baby when we knew them. This was the same Jewel that later became the famous singer-songwriter. Yule had a huge garden and grew lots of potatoes. He was well known for his hash browns too. Yule's original goal when he moved from Switzerland to Alaska in 1940 was to start a colony of self-sufficient craftsmen, independent of modern technology. I think Karen and Yule Kilcher were similar in some ways. (The Bush Blade, issue #11 Nov. 1999)

I knew all about nettle and how to harvest it. I was taught exactly how to pick it so that I didn't get stung by its leaves. After it is cooked like spinach, it doesn't sting, but there is a certain way to eat it raw by folding the stinging part of the leaves a certain way. One day, when we were picking nettle, Karen told me about Milarepa, the Buddhist saint and yogi who went on a fast and ate nothing but nettle for a year. She said "it ended up turning him green." I got a kick out of trying to imagine that.

I celebrated my first Halloween that fall. Mom dressed me up like a Hobo; she put soot on my nose and gave me a walking stick with a red bandana tied to the end of it. Inside the bandana was a half of a sandwich, an apple, and a small blanket. I wore a flannel, which was stuffed to make it look like I had a big, round belly.

What's a hobo? One definition that I found: "A hobo is someone who lives on the road, has lived on the road for a while, likes living on the road, and intends to keep living on the road." (Niman, 1997) Karen dressed me up as a hobo, but in real life, we had not too long ago, been living a nomadic life style on the road, just like real Hobos.

Life in the cabin felt like home. Karen was pregnant and thought Marty "would be a wonderful dad." And even though our life was more stable, she was still very free-spirited in her thinking.

"We didn't have a ceremony," she says resolutely. "I was against the institution of marriage and was pretty hard core into my thinking then."

Karen was five months pregnant, but now our one-year lease was up. It was spring, and the landlord came by for a visit. It was just after the snow had melted and uncovered piles of toilet paper and shit that the snow had covered up. The landlord was not happy. There was an outhouse out back, a short distance from the cabin, but the roof was caving in. Plus, if it was snowing real hard, you couldn't even see it. "Once the snow melted, it looked pretty bad." Suddenly, we were apparently living in squalor. We got evicted.

It was taking longer than she thought to find us a new home. We were about ready to go into our second Winter in Alaska. My mom said that we were getting desperate, and that she was "going to have the baby any minute." We ended up "crashing at this funky cabin" in Anchor Point that had a floor that was "caving in."

We set up camp there. I was disappointed to leave our cozy cabin that had been in Homer, and now I would have to go to a new school. Karen was resourceful, though, as I had seen many times. She would find us a new place.

While we were squatting in this cabin, An Italian family we knew agreed to let us live on their property for a year. They lived just down the road from where we were squatting. Karen wanted to set us up in a tepee. She paid a few hundred for the roof and a few hundred for the liner, but for Marty to get the poles for the tepee, we would need a car.

Karen and Marty bought a car for $50. Up to that point, we had been just hitchhiking or walking. Marty took some of his buddies and drove 150 miles to go get the tepee poles. There was a forest up in Kenai that had trees that were tall and skinny enough to make the poles. He and his friends used a tool to skin the trees to make them beautiful. Then, the poles were tied to the roof of the car and driven back to where our new home would be.

It was 1974, and we had now been living in Alaska for two years. Marty prepared the new home site for the tepee. They wanted to have it ready for when the baby was born. In the tepee, Marty built a platform where we kept our beds and clothes. There was a loft with a ladder where I would sleep. There was a fence where we would step down to the area that had a dirt floor.

"Dirt floors are actually one of the warmer kinds of floors," Karen explained. Then Marty built shelves between each pole all the way around the teepee. He put in two wood stoves, right in the middle of the tepee floor and right next to each other. One stove was a big barrel stove that had to be stoked constantly to keep us warm. The other stove was a little cook stove with a small oven that did not work very well.

The property was beautiful, wooded and next to an alpine lake and a blueberry bog; It was right off this little road that had 50 lakes on it. So wherever one lived on this road, they were right by a lake that they could go swimming in, and that they could get drinking water from.

We did not have time to move into the tepee before the birth, so Karen and Marty set up Marty's brother Bill's cabin for the birth. His cabin would be best anyway, since it was closer to the hospital which was in Homer, just in case.

To prepare for the birth, Karen studied "Swedish and midwife manuals" and took "a Lamaz course." She was "exercising and doing yoga every day for months just to be ready." She didn't drink or smoke and was eating health food.

"I was nervous about a home birth," she says, "so I wanted to be in tiptop shape."

Her mother, my grandmother Phyllis had been a forerunner in the Natural Birth Movement and had a midwife attend when Karen was born, which back then was considered radical. Unfortunately, Karen could not find a midwife, and it was impossible to get a doctor to attend at a home birth, especially in the rustic conditions we were living in, way out in the boondocks. She was just going to have to figure it out on her own.

Karen went into labor at 5am. She and Marty loaded up the truck. "The birthing instruments were in alcohol." There was a special bed built at Bill's, waiting for her arrival. I overheard them arguing about how fast to drive. They had a stop watch and were timing the contractions as we went. I believe it was about a 30-minute drive or so to Homer. Once we got there, we had to hike on this trail to get to Bill's cabin. As we were hiking the trail, every 300 yards or so, Karen would stop, get down on her knees and have major contractions. It was slow going with all the supplies we also had to carry.

We finally got there. Karen says she laid out the sterilized sheets on the bed, but when she laid on them, sawdust got all over them. Bill had a sawdust floor. She felt "silly," after all the work she had done to boil them and hang them in the sun to dry.

It was a three-hour labor. I stood next to Karen's bed and played with the stethoscope. At the last-minute, right before the baby came out, I was told to go outside with Bill. I went outside, but I could still see everything. The bed was built right by the window frame of the cabin, which was empty, so I could see in just as easily as if I were inside.

"I didn't think I wanted you to see me like that," my mom explained, "but then I realized—Oh yeah, what difference does it make?" Karen gave out instructions as the birth went along, so that everything went smoothly. As the baby came out, Karen held up a mirror, so she could see what was happening and watched the birth. Marty wore rubber gloves. Bill was upset with all the intensity and went for a walk in the woods to play his flute. Our friend Mark was there and held Karen's hand and said prayers while she labored. Finally, she said I could go back in.

"I see the head!" I heard Marty cry. Marty used two pieces of dental floss to tie the cord as was the plan.

The baby popped out perfectly. They suctioned off the fluids out of his nose.

Once the placenta came out, which everyone was calling the 'afterbirth,' it was cooked up and everyone ate it with biscuits and gravy.

"I loved it," my mom says. She told me that God made the placenta to taste good to the mother. "It does not taste like liver like you might think. It tasted more like veal." Eating the placenta was natural, she told me, plus, eating placenta has been in practice around the world throughout history by many cultures, she explained.

She was right. In Western Medicine, the placenta is thought of as human waste, but in other cultures and places around the world, it is seen differently. There are cultures that promote cooking and eating it as a celebration of life and as a rich source of nutrients. In fact, most placental mammals do it.

In Chinese medicine, for example, eating placenta is considered a powerful and sacred medicine to help support and help heal a mother after childbirth. It contains oxytocin which has been shown to dramatically increase the pain threshold in rats, plus improves energy, mood and lactation. (Kristal, 1991; 2012).

I don't specifically remember what the afterbirth tasted like or anything about the meal, but my mom and Marty believed it was natural and that eating it wasn't weird or gross but part of a long history of cultural tradition that went way back.

Karen named the baby, Forest, because that is where he was born—in the forest. My brother and I had modest names, really, considering we were hippy kids. But between the two of us, I had the more 'normal' sounding name since when I was born, my mom hadn't yet become a hippie. Other hippie kids weren't so lucky. We knew this family who lived in a cabin in the woods. It was a very long hike to get there. She had a home birth too and named her baby 'Eva By the River Valley.'

Once Forest was born, we moved right into the tepee that was all set up. Karen had decorated it with furs and put up tapestries that she had brought from Seattle, just to make the tepee more like home. I now had my own room in the loft that Marty built. Except for a slight smoky odor and a few spiders, the attic was cozy warm. The chimneys from the stoves came right up through the floor to my loft, so it was like I had my own heater.

One day, I climbed up the ladder to my loft and when I got there, I looked and there was our cat after having just given birth at the end of my bed. It was a messy scene I will never forget, but low and behold, there were five kittens—three gray ones, a black one and a white one. Birth seemed like a very natural, everyday experience in our family. I fell instantly in love with all of them and was so excited that I ran to a neighbor's house to tell her what had happened. I got to play with them for a couple of months before Karen took them to the post office in a cardboard box. We stood outside the entrance and gave them away to whoever would take them. I cried terribly, begging Karen to let us keep them. Her mind was set. I was so mad. How could she just give them away? They needed their mother just like I needed her.

That night, I had a terrible nightmare. In my dream, the kittens were crying and trying desperately to climb the ladder to my loft in the tepee. They kept falling off and climbing back up, trying to reach me.

Karen didn't seem to care about the kittens losing their mother. She was now very absorbed with the new baby, so I began to feel closer to Marty. He and I were good friends anyway, but now we spent more time together. I would watch him work, keep him company, and help when I could. I also helped with the new baby and helped collect kindling for the fire in the woods outside our tepee. I liked to feel helpful and do my part. One day, I was watching Forest. A couple minutes went by and I realized that he was gone. I looked around and didn't see him. Karen joined the hunt and soon enough, we found him. He had crawled out of the tepee and down the dirt driveway towards the main road. He had gotten almost to the road when we found him. Karen freaked out.

I started First grade that fall at the school in Anchor Point. When my teacher saw the cradleboard that Karen was carrying my brother in, she asked her about it. It was a Sioux Indian cradle board made of raw caribou and bear hide. Our friend Mark built it for her. The cradleboard had these two big wooden poles, carved wood in the Sioux tradition with feathers and beads. Then between the poles was a huge moccasin made of moose, which was raw and hard, made by stretching it wet, then drying it. The interior of the back-pack was lined with moose fur. It had round beaded rosettes, and it had a piece of bear hide in it, which came up over Forest's head and buried him, so he was encompassed by the hide.

When we went into town, people would stop and stare at us and ask where the cradleboard came from. Forest was carried everywhere in it. It was like a shoe that if the strings were pulled, he would be cinched up tight as if in a portable fur womb. It was so sturdy that if there was a fall, he wouldn't even feel it, and if he pooped in it, Karen would just rinse it out.

Karen never did bring it in for that show and tell like my teacher re-quested. Here we were in school learning the history of the Alaskan Natives, and when I went home each day, we lived similarly to how the Natives did. One day at school, every child was asked to draw a picture of their home. I took some crayons, and I drew this simple drawing of our tepee with the poles sticking out the top. I drew Marty and Karen, myself and little baby Forest, probably not much more than a few stick figures all standing in front of the tepee.

My teacher seemed very interested in my picture, so much so, that she called over another teacher to take a look. The two women looked at my picture, then looked at each other, then me, then back at the picture. Finally, they gave it back to me. I enjoyed the extra attention, but I also felt puzzled why they would make such a deal of it. When the teacher put all the draw-ings up on the classroom wall, I saw that my home looked very different than all of the other drawings. I will never forget that moment when they saw my drawing, because it was one of the first times when I began to realize that we lived very differently than other families.

I loved our life when we lived in the tepee. I played outside quite a bit and picked blueberries from the bog that was right next to the little lake on the property. The blueberries were gigantic. In fact, I have never seen blueberries that big or tasted blueberries that plump and juicy since. Sometimes I played in this old, rusted out van that sat there across from the tepee. It might have belonged to the Italian family that let us stay on their property. Across the lake was a rotting, stump of a tree. When it was dark, the stump looked spooky and I imagined that it looked like a bear. It looked a lot like the black bear that I had seen at our old cabin. I had seen a lot of wild animals since we lived in Alaska. Moose had come right up to the cabin, especially at night. They would just stand there, trying to keep warm. When we would go into town, I would see the moose standing by the theater. They just stood there, chewing their cud, like cows, just part of the scenery.

It was very cold during the winters, even considering it was a bit warmer than other areas because of the Japanese current. To stay warm, we burned a lot of wood and we got coal for free from the beach.

It was bituminous coal. On the bottom of cook Inlet was a coal deposit. Once a year, before everything froze over, there would be rip tides that would come through and tear coal up from the floor of Cook Inlet and wash it ashore. It was called float coal. It would bounce on the surface and then float in. The tide would come in and leave tons of coal right on the beach. I helped to collect it with Marty and Karen. A lot of people did that.

Karen seemed happy that year and almost like a traditional stay-at-home mom. She baked cornbread and custard pie in the little oven that Marty put in the tepee for her. She also sewed me some hippie-style clothes for school. Sewing was one of her childhood loves, so she bought a truck for $100 and drove all the way to Anchorage, 225 miles so she could buy an antique treadle sewing machine. I got a green corduroy skirt and matching shirt that I wore to school all the time. She made Marty black caribou pants and a patchwork shirt. Karen began to wear dresses that she had sewn for herself too, which was different, since the only time I had ever seen her wear a dress was when we had crossed the border.

One of my favorite things to do was make ice cream. It was easy. Just go outside, collect snow. Then mix it with milk and sugar. Then I served it in bowls to Karen, Marty, and people who were visiting. It was a hit! Everyone commented on how good it was.

I was starting to feel secure, and it was nice having a stable home. My worst memory during this time was when I stuck my tongue on the front entrance to the tepee, which was just a flap of canvass, and my tongue got frozen to it. I ended up having to just rip it off which took a few taste buds with it. At school the next day, I stuck my tongue out to show my teacher where I had lost the taste buds. She didn't seem impressed. I had hoped to earn her sympathy after she had complained to my mom that I wasn't learning three letter words.

After we moved into the tepee, Marty built a sauna by the lake, so we could bathe. After he took a sauna, Marty would jump through the ice, into the lake. He had to keep a hole in the ice all winter, so we had drinking water. Each morning, Marty would go and chop the hole to keep it from freezing over.

After the sauna was built, I would play at the sauna with Brenda like it was our playhouse. She was my first good friend. She lived with her family not too far down the road. Brenda was just a year or so older than I was. She was skinny and had shoulder length, wavy brown hair.

One day we swam in the lake, then went into the sauna to dry off. It was still warm from earlier that day when Karen and Marty had bathed there. I looked down, and on my ankle, was a black, slimy leech. It was about an inch long and a centimeter wide. We couldn't seem to pry it loose from my skin, so we ran to the tepee and Brenda asked Karen for some salt. Brenda then sprinkled the salt on the leech. Once we got back to the sauna, the leech slid off my ankle onto the floor. Brenda used a butter knife to cut it up into pieces and stuffed the pieces into a crack between the boards. To our utter dismay, each piece began to slither out of the crack. I carried a leech-shaped scar on my ankle for a long time after that. I have always wondered what sort of leech that was.

Brenda taught me a lot about safety and playing in the woods. Once we saw a porcupine.

"Don't be afraid. I see those all the time," she said nonchalantly. She knew about plants such as Devil's Club, also known as Alaskan Ginseng and other plants like Poison Hemlock, one of the most poisonous plants there is. It was nice to have a friend. I didn't have other children to play with very often when we were on the road or when we were in Maui or Canada, before we got to Alaska.

For being such an isolated life living in the wilderness, we had plenty of friends. Suzanne was my mom's best friend. She had long, shiny, golden blond hair and blue eyes. She helped my mom put in a garden and taught her how to do beadwork on a loom.

Suzanne was an artist. One way she made money was to do simple little paintings of trees and cabins and other scenery on small screens. She then sold them to stores who would resell them to people who wanted to do needlepoint. My mom took me to visit her at a bead shop in Homer where she sold some of the paintings. Suzanne was super nice to me and would take me skiing behind the cabin. Once Suzanne made a delicious fruit salad with Karen, and they came to a potluck at my school.

Another time, Karen and Suzanne went skiing and discovered seal-skins that were preserved in oil, in an old abandoned log cabin. In the same cabin, they also found these old photographs of an Eskimo woman who must have lived there, a long time ago. In the photos, her teeth were all worn down at an angle from chewing the skins.

Karen and Suzanne also found a bunch of unfinished skins. They tried to soak them in chemicals, but it didn't work to soften them. I saw them chewing on the skins as they tried to make them beautiful. They said it didn't taste bad, but I didn't want to try it.

Marty would go out with our dog Yusef, and the dog would catch squirrels and rabbits. We ate squirrel meat—it was delicious! The squirrel hides were soaked for a couple of weeks and then my mom worked the hides in her teeth for a few hours, so they could be ready to use. Squirrel skin is thin and not very durable, so she would cut it into strips that could be woven together into a quilt.

Suzanne made Karen a beautiful purse out of the baby seal hides. Karen made a vest for herself out of bear hide, then she made Forest a hat out of red fox.

It had been over a year since we lived in the tepee, and the Italian family wanted their land back. They were nice about it, but it was time for us to go. We packed up and went just down the road, to the cabin where we had lived before. This time, it was all fixed up and more livable. Suzanne had been living there, and she and her boyfriend had put in a new floor. But they didn't live there anymore, and we didn't know where they had gone.

Karen was worried about what had happened to Suzanne. I missed her too. She had spent a lot of time with me and was a good friend to me too. We found out where she was, because some men from a commune called the Love Family visited our tepee one day and used our sauna. While they were visiting, they told us Suzanne had gone to the Love Family. The men told us exactly where the commune was. It was in Homer off East End Road at the head of the bay.

Just a couple weeks earlier, we had already met the leader of the Love Family. He just happened to be at the bar in Homer. He had said his name was 'Love.'

"I like your outfit man!" my mom had said to him.

"Yes, my sisters made it for me," he had answered. Love dressed very differently than anyone we had seen in Homer. He wore purple velvet, and no one in Homer wore purple velvet. Whether you were straight, redneck or hippie—everyone wore dirty jeans and down coats.

My mom decided to go out to the Love Family homestead and visit Suzanne. The homestead was at the end of East End Road in Homer. With Forest on her back in the cradleboard, Karen and I hitchhiked a total of about 50 miles to where their homestead was. First, it was about 25 miles from Anchor Point to Homer, along the Sterling highway. Then once we got to Homer, it was another 25 miles down East End road to where we were told the Love Family's homestead was located.

East End road was famous because it was so bad during break up. 'Break-up' happens in the spring when all the ice melts everywhere, and all the roads turn into great big muddy messes. Every now and then, we would hear about some car getting sucked into this almost quicksand like mud. There would be these sensational stories of cars that were unable to get out. Things will freeze right on the road itself, and there would be great big potholes and mud that would freeze and become road. It never dried out really, so when it would thaw in the spring, there would be mud all over everything in the town—all over the people—everywhere.

Once we got to the end of East End Road, it was a five-mile hike to the homestead. Karen was following directions she had received from one of the men who had visited our tepee. The guy had said his name was 'Innocence.' The name was unusual but not to us, considering we were hippies and we used to all kinds of names.

I was six and a half now—a five-mile hike was nothing to me. My mom said I could hike well by the age of two. I had hiked all over the place by now.

Once we got to the end of East End Road, the journey began with a half-mile hike across a horse ranch that was private property. There wasn't an actual road that led to the homestead, which wasn't that weird in the mostly undeveloped area of Alaska where we were living. It was common for people to have to hike across each other's properties since there weren't a lot of roads yet. Once we got across the horse ranch, it was about a mile down these steep switchbacks toward the beach. We heard later stories of horses that had lost their footing on these switchbacks and had fallen off. That had happened during the coldest part of the winter.

Once we got to the beach, we had to hike four miles to the head of the bay. As we hiked, there were millions of tiny light-pink shells that had washed up along the shoreline, which I filled my pockets with on the way.

Even though there wasn't a road that got you there, everyone wanted a homestead at the head of the bay, including Karen and Marty. It was considered the choicest, most valuable land.

We were walking down the beach, and I began to wonder if we were ever going to get there. Just then, we saw two figures coming toward us in the distance. As we walked closer and closer, we saw that it was two kids. They were older than I was, maybe 11 or 12. They were boys and they had long hair, which was unusual for their age. They were playing on the driftwood as we approached.

"Hi," they said cheerfully.

We told them we were looking for Suzanne and the Love Family.

"You're going the right way," the boys said helpfully. "We will take you up there," they offered. They said their names were Hope and Elimelech.

When we got up to where the property was, there was a big, maybe 25-acre pasture that bordered the bay. Then, as we walked into their land, we followed a trail up into a canyon that came to a gate. On the gate in very ornate carved lettering it said Israel. Then, we saw a naked lady with long red hair, running across the meadow. We found out later her name was Nerai. Then we saw the house, which was a sturdy, nice big beautiful house on a slightly elevated hillside. It was made from rough-cut lumber and was about 30 feet wide by about 50 feet long. It had two stories and was a large house with a lot of bedrooms.

Hope, one of the boys who we had met on the beach, was now helping with the younger children in the house. While my mom was visiting Suzanne, I was with some other children there under Hope's care. He was really nice to me and got crayons and paper for me. There was a baby there who was Forest's age. Her name was 'Better.'

We saw Dan there. He was a guy who we had known from our early days in Homer. He was slender, tall and had long brown hair, a mustache, and bushy eye-brows. He was one of three hippie guys that lived on some property at the head of the bay who called themselves the 'Unimoggers.' They were well known in town after they invented this vehicle that they called a 'Unimog.' The vehicle could easily travel along the beach, over rocks and even driftwood. It had one big wheel and two small wheels on the front, two wheels in the back, and a long thing with poles in the middle.

My mom played her flute with some members of the Love Family who were playing music. After a little while, a man with a long beard and long hair named Meekness asked Karen to stop playing her flute. When he told her to stop, it hurt my mom's feelings. I could tell she was mad after that. She complained about it a lot to Suzanne. Years later, she told me,

"That was kind of that whole male dominated, sexist trip that the Family was into," Karen remembered, "and I wasn't used to that. I was my own woman at that point, so it really offended me."

The ladies that were there at the Love Family homestead helped prepare Karen for meeting Love—even though we had already met him at the bar earlier that spring. All the ladies were slender and wore long, flowing, ethnic looking dresses. The ethnic look reminded me of the Russian women at the laundromat, except that the Love Family women were all skinny, whereas the Russian women were all mostly very large.

The women pushed Karen into the sauna. Forest was screaming, as he wasn't used to being without her, but he was attended to by a couple of the women there. They seemed to be in a hurry since Love, their leader, would be there shortly. As I said, we had already met him though; he was the guy who was at the bar in Homer, wearing the purple robe. Right, this was long enough ago, that children could go into the bar with their parents. Then they changed the rule and I had to wait outside.

After her sauna, they dressed Karen in a long skirt and blouse and combed her hair. They were preparing a banquet, and everyone seemed to be in a bustle to make it ready for Love's arrival. While everyone was getting ready, I played nearby with Hope and the other children.

We stayed overnight. My main memory of our visit to the Love Family homestead was of running across the floor to show Karen my picture. As I was running, I fell into this hole in the floor. It was quite deep, maybe 10 or 15 feet. At the bottom, I fell on a metal tub and hurt myself. The hole was so deep that the cellar had a wooden ladder that was used to climb in and out of it safely. Usually the cellar was covered and under a rug, but for some reason, it had been left open.

We left the homestead later that day. It was all uphill on the way back. I was still in pain from my fall and cried the whole way out.

My mom remembered hearing my "Really far away scream," when I fell down the cellar.

"It was just one more awful thing to happen there," Karen says. She didn't like the Love Family, at first. She had just gone to see Susanne.

Soon after our visit, my mom's friend, Suzanne left Alaska to go live in Seattle where the Love Family had a home base. She had decided to join.

Later that summer, Karen decided to go visit Suzanne in Seattle at the Love Family headquarters. Susanne had sounded very enthusiastic about the group and had encouraged my mom to come and see for herself. My mom was curious, despite how she felt about her unpleasant Love Family visit in

Homer. Karen planned a trip to go visit my grandpa, who lived in Bellevue, which was not too far from where the community was located. That way, she could visit her dad and her friend Suzanne during the visit. My grampa, Truman paid for the plane tickets.

It was August 1975. I was almost seven years old now. On the flight out of there, this old man gave me a little bag of peanuts to eat and a deck of cards.

"I have jet lag," he told me.

"What's that?" I asked him.

He told me his legs were so stiff, he couldn't move them anymore. If it happens to a horse, they "have to shoot it," he explained.

I guess he was joking? It upset me a little bit.

When we arrived, mom left me with Grampa. She borrowed his car and visited her friend from high school, three-time Washington State Chess Champion John Braley. Then afterward went and saw Suzanne at the Love Family.

"I was just going to check it out," my mom says. "I wasn't planning on staying."

When Grampa found out that she borrowed his car to visit the commune, he was mad at her. She was supposed to be visiting him, he thought.

When we got to the Love Family, I didn't know we wouldn't be going back to Marty and our life in Alaska. I'm not sure if she knew either.

Why didn't you go back?" I asked her years later.

"We were out of time where the tepee had been set up," she says. "Marty wasn't coming through. He drank a lot and had seizures. I didn't really have anything to go back to," she figured.

I was there one day when Marty had a seizure. He was on the bed, and my mom put something in his mouth, so he wouldn't choke. I don't remember him having them regularly though. It was rare. I don't remember him drinking that much either. They both went to the bar occasionally. I know because I went with them until the rule changed.

If Karen was so unhappy there, in Alaska, unhappy enough to leave Marty and our life there, then why has she always talked over the years about how happy she was in Alaska? Why would she just pick up and leave? And she left all of our stuff too. It was always somewhat of a mystery to me.

"Life was hard [in Alaska]," she once told me. "I just got sick of it."

I know that was part of it, but from my memories, and from all the stories I have heard of our life there, it wasn't Marty's fault. He did everything he could to make her happy. He did end up with a serious drinking problem that progressed over the years, but that was after Karen left him. He lost Karen, he lost me, and he lost his one-year old son, Forest.

For many years after that, Marty was angry and resentful. He could never let it go. Why would she do that to him or to me? Marty was like a dad to me. I never stopped missing him and the life that we all had together in Alaska for the rest of my life.

BIBLIOGRAPHY (CHAPTER 3)

Shrief, Lynnea. (2016). Placenta History. *Independent Placenta Encapsulation Network* (IPEN). 2016.

The Bush Blade. issue #11. November, (1999). Kachemak Bay, AK. The Bush Blade is a monthly statewide publication that focuses on ecological investigative reporting.

[Karen] Personal Interviews. June 13 and 21, September 27, all 2001.

Kristal, Mark B. (May 2012). Placentophagia in Humans and Nonhuman Mammals: Causes and Consequences. (PDF) *Ecology of Food and Nutrition*.

Kristal, Mark B. (1991). Enhancement of Opiod-Mediated Analgesia: A Solution to the Enigma of Placentophagia. *Neuroscience and Biobehavioral Reviews*.

Denali National Park and Preserve. (2001). *Microsoft Encarta Online Encyclopedia*. The MSN Encarta site was closed on October 31, 2009.

Dictionary of Alaskan Place Names. (1967). *Alaskan Engineering Commission Annual Report*. (USGS Professional Paper 567). pg. 260.

Durr, Robert R. (1974). Land: Bridge to Community Report. *Talkeetna Historical Society*.

Hegener, Helen. (August 24, 2014). *Alaska Dispatch News*. Alaska Nellie Lived a Life to Remember, Deserves an Epitaph to Match.

Niman, Michael. (1997). *People of the Rainbow*. University of Tennessee Press, Knoxville.

Noyes, Pierrepont B. (1937). *My Father's House; An Oneida Boyhood* Published by Farrar & Rinehart Incorporated.

Pascall, Jane M. (1998). *The Homer Tribune*. Alaskan Homer Visitor's Guide.

Rearden, Jim. (1972). Nikolaevsk: A bit of old Russia takes root in Alaska. *National Geographic*. September 1972, pg. 401–424.

Shrief, Lynnea. (2016). Placenta History. *Independent Placenta Encapsulation Network* (IPEN). 2016.

Wohlforth, Charles. (2008). *Frommer's Alaska*. Wiley Publishing, Inc Hoboken, NJ.

CHAPTER 4

My First Year in the Love Family

"I was born and brought up in a strange world—a world bounded on all four sides by walls of isolation; a world wherein the customs, laws, religions, and social formulas accumulated by civilization came to us only as the faint cries of philistine hordes outside our walls. Within that protected area, a prophet and his followers, having separated themselves from the rest of mankind, were trying to live as lived those members of the Primitive Christian Church of whom it is written, "No man called aught his own." That little world was called the Oneida Community, and that prophet was my father."
—Pierreponte Noyes, 1937, pg. 3

1975. I was almost seven when we left Alaska. We flew to Seattle, visited grandpa, then went right up to Queen Anne Hill to visit the Love Family. We hadn't been back to Seattle since after Maui, in the days when we were hitchhiking and hanging around the University District. Little did I know that I would spend the next almost eight years of my childhood living in the Love Family and would be there until I was almost 15 years old.

From grandpa's house, we went to visit Suzanne at the Love Family's Front Door Inn, a hosting station for new members or visitors. The Front Door Inn was like the main door to the Love Family. One could not just walk up to any of the houses that they owned. You would be redirected right away to the Inn.

Back in Alaska, at the Love Family homestead, there were probably 10 to 15 members who had been there that day when we had visited. But in Seattle, there were probably more than 160 people who were all living communally in the eight to ten houses that they owned. All their houses were located within a several block area, on the top of Queen Anne Hill. The house where we initially stayed was a house that was behind the Front Door Inn, but it was attached to the Inn. There was a passageway from the upstairs of the house that entered the upper loft of the Inn.

Karen, Forest, and I slept in an unfinished, small, closet-sized cubby, and for the next three weeks, my mom attended classes and meetings for prospective members. I hung out with a boy around my age named Seth. His parents were the elders of the Inn, which meant they oversaw those who lived at the Inn and made sure the Inn ran smoothly. Their names were Certain and Goodness. They were both very tall and slender people who were loving and kind. Their little boy Seth was skinny with shoulder length, stringy hair and freckles. There were no other kids our age who lived at the Front Door Inn at this time, so I got the sense Seth appreciated having me there to play with.

When we got to the Love Family, it was like walking into another land. It was so different than anything I had ever seen that it was like being dropped into an ancient tribe in some remote place in the world, where people spoke another language and where one has no familiarity with the customs or traditions. If I hadn't been on other adventures with my mom in the counterculture before we got there, it might've been more frightening. But I was young and had visited different alternative groups and environments in the past, so I knew how to blend and imitate like a well-mannered guest would. It wasn't too hard to figure out what the customs were. All I had to do was look around and do what I saw others doing.

One of the main topics of conversation were spiritual concepts. It was different than hippie 'rap' sessions where everyone talked about how screwed up society was. As soon as we arrived, I began learning the Love Family philosophies too, just like all new members were taught. It was like a crash course in Love Family. The only option was to just start participating in the life, which was certainly an adjustment.

But back to the names, which pretty much made a huge impression on most people who were trying to understand what it was all about, including myself.

A lot of the people I met, like Certain and Goodness, had virtue names. My understanding about these names came to be that the virtue names that people were given, represented the thoughts in the mind of Jesus Christ.

Members believed that when the thoughts (virtues) of Jesus had been gathered together, then the second coming or 'Armageddon' would be complete. They didn't believe that Jesus was going to return as a person; they believed that the members themselves, as a group, were Jesus's second coming. Jesus had returned, and he was alive in all of us. On one of the walls, I saw a gigantic, wall-sized painting of Jesus, and in his face were the faces of the membership.

Not everyone had a virtue name though. A lot of people had a Hebrew name that had been picked out of the Bible, as they had not yet earned or been given a virtue name. At certain times, Love, who was the head and founder of the Love Family, would give someone a virtue name, and it would be a significant and sacred moment for that person and for the Love Family.

When I came, there was an adult member that already had my name, Lois, which I learned was a Bible name. In a small community that was like family, it became a source of confusion, that there were two 'Lois's, so for a short time, I was called "Little Lois." A little boy named Shivaya who was around five or six started the trend. He had come from India with his sister Parvati and their parents Deepesh and Lakshi. They did not have dark skin and were not of East Indian descent; the family had just lived In India and had been there on a spiritual quest before they met the Love Family. Shivaya called the other Lois, "Big Lois," although, she wasn't big at all but slender like most of the women there. Big Lois was warm and kind with long brown hair, bright blue eyes, and a great sense of humor.

One day, Big Lois took me aside, and we looked through the Bible at names together. Eventually after leafing through several pages, she said,

"Do you like the name Rebekah?" she asked after she leafed through several pages.

"No," I said matter-of-factly.

She looked a little disappointed but kept leafing through the pages. "How about Rachel?" she asked.

I liked that one, so from then on, that was what they called me. It wasn't too long after that when I discovered more about my new name—it bothered me. 'Rachel' means lamb of God in the Bible. In John 1:29 and John 1:36 Jesus was called the 'lamb of God,' because he was considered the perfect and ultimate sacrifice for sin. So, I didn't like the idea that the meaning of my name meant sacrifice or basically the killing of an innocent lamb. Furthermore, the sacrifice of lambs played a very important role in the ancient Jewish religious life and sacrificial system. This was important, because I heard that the Love Family celebrated Passover, and that there would be a lamb that would give his life. I knew that a 'sacrificial lamb' meant a lamb that had given his life like Jesus had given his life, because that's what I was being taught. The kids in the Love Family were learning the same things the adults were learning, but just instead of being taught directly by Love, we were taught by caretakers and members who acted as spiritual teachers for the young.

I learned right away that names, in the Love Family, had great meaning and were a common topic of conversation. But I always tried to avoid sharing the meaning of my name. It wasn't just the meaning, though, it was also the biblical story. Rachel, the second wife of Jacob, died in childbirth. I knew that someday, I wanted to give birth—I just tried not to think about it.

The meaning of virtue names was important too. Virtue names were not just pulled out of a hat; they were given by Love to a person who he felt was spiritually "ready" for the name. Most of the time, the name would be inspired by a dream, a vision, or a revelation of one of the members. At other times, there would just be a clear recognition by Love himself of someone's virtue. For example, I heard that was how Cheerful got his name. When I came to the Family, I had met this boy named, Cheerful, who was around my age. Love just recognized the boy's personality as being cheerful, and so he was named. Cheerful was, in fact, very cheerful and had a very contagious laugh, that most people who were there remember. It was very distinct, and it was impossible to hold a straight face when anyone heard it.

Once someone received their virtue name, it could be taken from them. I was told that a man named Israel had gotten the name Reality until he was caught chasing his "wants." He was going to Queen Anne neighbors and drinking coffee and eating bacon, which was totally not what people did in the Love Family. Pork was not allowed, which was considered biblically unclean, and there were times when the Love Family did not drink coffee either, and his indiscretion took place during one of those times, so he lost his name and went back to his Bible name, Israel. By the way, everyone in the Love Family had the last name of Israel, so in the case of Reality, he went back to his Bible name, which would've made his full Love Family name, 'Israel Israel.'

Another example was Hope, the boy who was walking on the beach in Homer and helped give us directions to the Love Family homestead. He was unruly and was refusing to do his school work, so he lost his virtue name and was called by his Bible name, Carmi. Eventually, he got it back. Since Carmi continued to misbehave even after he had lost his name, it was many years before eventually people started calling him Hope again. It was an unusual case because Love never officially gave him his name back as was the custom; everyone just started calling him Hope again, and Love—surprisingly—never made an issue of it. My brother Forest, who was only one-year old, kept his name. Apparently, Love liked it so much that he let him keep it.

Originally, Hebrew names were given by Love, but then it was changed: Love said that when people came, they could pick out their own name, until they were baptized. Actually, very early on, before we came, I understand that adult members were originally referred to as 'Man' and 'Woman.' As more and more people joined, though, it became too confusing because there were too many mans and womans, so it changed. That's when Love began giving out Bible names. Kids, who were born into the Family, usually got a virtue name automatically; it was like a birthright.

Kids who were not born into the Family, who came with their parents, like myself, got a Bible name, just like their parents. Usually everyone who joined got a Bible name, then at some point, certain people received their virtue name. Some adult members got their virtue names right away when they joined, but others had to wait for years.

In some ways, being a child was an advantage, spiritually. I heard the Bible quoted, "Verily I say unto you, accept ye be converted, and become as little children, ye shall not enter into the kingdom of heaven. (Matthew 18:3, *King James version*) Children were seen as pure, because we were untainted by the World. I always heard people call the children "beautiful." That was coming from the spiritual side of things. Children were respected in the sense that they were seen as spiritually innocent, starting out fresh with a virtue, angelic.

Children in the Love Family were being protected from the World. Compared to the other children there, I knew more about the outside world than they did. I went to Kindergarten in Homer, Alaska, so I suppose I was a bit tainted from that. Plus, I had a close relationship with my mom, and that prior relationship, since it was an outside bond and not communal, was considered 'Worldly' conditioning. Many of the children in the Love Family who were born there, did not have an exclusive bond with their mom or dad; they were being taken care of communally by members designated to care for the children. I heard the big people talk about 'baggage.' It was not literal baggage; it was figuratively the Worldly influences that one brought with them to the Love Family. Baggage had negative connotations. The children's innocence was spiritually idealized, so we could be angelic, virtuous without even trying. Adult members had so much more conditioning from the outside world to fight against. Lucky me, I guess.

To me though, in one's "baggage" are items that are used for survival in a foreign place, not something to throw away all together. There might be something valuable in that suitcase, like a sock or one's toothbrush. A little baggage could've been just what was needed.

There was a little boy there who was around my age. His name was Bright. When Bright first came, his name had been Sunhawk. There was already a little boy there named Sun, so to lessen the confusion, he got a virtue name right away—Bright.

There were many people who never received their virtue names. They were said to "be on their own trip." These were people who had an agenda and tried to make things happen on their own, and because of that, they didn't earn much status. To receive a virtue name, one had to give over their individuality completely and become a totally humble servant to Love's vision.

It seemed to me that the kids didn't take names as seriously as the adults did. There were times when I heard kids making fun of the names. There was, it seemed, a name for everything, even private parts. "Mena" was the name used for vagina, and "pison" was the name used for penis. There was a woman who came who wore a burka. Her skin tone and facial features indicated she might've been from a Middle East country. Her name was Femina, and the last syllable of her name was pronounced like "mena" with a long 'e,' just like the name for a woman's private part. Many a laugh was had behind her back about her name. We were just kids being kids, I guess.

Then there was Eliab who was Elimelech's brother, Elimelech being one of the boys we met along the beach in Homer on our way to the Love Family homestead. The brothers were about four or five years older than me and were very close in age; they were almost like twins. They looked so very similar, that people often got them mixed up. Both were slender boys with long blond hair and blue eyes. They didn't have parents in the Love Family. All I knew was that their dad was a police officer and lived far away. Their mother, Cheryl, was said to have schizophrenia and was not welcome in the Family. Someone said that their dad had once hit their mom over the head with a frying pan. I wasn't sure if that was the reason she wasn't welcome. The older boy, Eliab, tended to be negativistic and down on people. He would call anyone he thought wasn't cool, "Jerkaniah," a generic but descriptive term that only people from the Love Family would understand, since so many of the Bible names ended with "iah."

Maybe for the kids, it was about trying to see the humor in a culture that was so very serious so much of the time. Who had a virtue name? Who had a Bible name? What did the name mean? The meaning of someone's name was seen as saying something about the person who carried it. Names were an indication of status and a big deal. But, at least for some of the kids, making fun of names was a natural reaction to try to lighten things up and just be our silly selves instead of being so serious all the time.

The adults were mostly very serious. I hardly ever just saw people casually hanging out, laughing. As a young child entering the community, my impression was that in the Love Family, the culture was serious, quiet, and strict, where everyone was focused on spiritual concepts and the Bible.

I knew my mom was spiritual, because she had talked about God often when she had explained things, but until this point, I hadn't been exposed to the Bible at all. So, for me, it was very noticeable when I didn't see books around, except the Bible, *King James Version*, and of course, the Love Family Charter, which was shown to me at the Front Door Inn. One or the other could be found in almost every room, opened on the tables or dressers, waiting to be read at any time.

My only memory, at this point, of learning about the Bible was early on, during the period when my mom and I lived with the Christian ladies after I got sick on Makena beach. I still remember going to Sunday school in

Maui and singing, *"Jesus loves me this I know, for the Bible tells me so..."*

Little did I know that the Bible would now be playing a huge role in my upbringing from here out. The books of Genesis and Exodus had to be read in their entirety before prospective members could be considered for membership. Of course, the kids were too young to do that, but I learned Bible stories from the caretakers who were in charge of the kids.

Not just anyone could become a member; it was a lot of self-discipline. After the adults read Genesis and Exodus, they were expected to take Charter classes and go on a seven day fast, (three of those days without water). That requirement wasn't popular, but it thinned out the ranks. If they were still interested after all that, they were sent to an elder's counsel to see if they were ready for baptism. The prospective member would be asked: "Do you believe in Jesus Christ? Do you believe in Love as our head and as the final, absolute authority in all matters? Are you willing to give your life for your Family? Are you willing to leave behind your past?" Once baptized, they had to give up sex and become celibate for at least six months. During the baptism, the new member would recite, "Jesus Christ is Lord." Since the expectations were the same for everybody, it was well known what was required to become a member. Plus, later on in this chapter, I talk about an adult baptism that I witnessed, then discuss my own baptism.

When we lived at the Front Door Inn, not a lot was expected of me, since I was still very young and not even seven. But even at this age, being very impressionable, it was clear that this group of people lived very differently from anything I had ever experienced. Even considering that for a child, I had seen quite a bit from living in the counterculture before we got there, including living and visiting communes along the way.

One of my earliest memories took place on a holiday the Love Family called 'Flower Day.' It was what most people in America know as May Day. I sat with Family women and other children learning to make baskets out of paper. Then we put flowers in the baskets and walked around the neighborhood, putting them on people's doorsteps. Afterward, everyone met at Parsons Gardens where they set up a May pole.

Parsons Gardens was a small city park, a short distance from the Front Door Inn that was taken care of by the Love Family for the city of Seattle.

I loved Parson's Gardens. It was a magic garden as far as I was concerned. There were cherry trees that would blossom and flower beds that were carefully maintained. Every spring, it was full of gorgeous flowers—hyacinths, daffodils, tulips and other beautiful plants. There were little walkways and paths that went through the garden.

That day, everyone gathered around the maypole. I got to dance around it with some other girls and women. Men and women stood around us in a circle and watched as we would weave in and out, going around the pole. I heard someone playing a tune on the fiddle and someone else played the flute. Everyone—men and women—had long, flowing hair. The men all had beards and wore long robes or cotton drawstring pants. The women all wore long, ankle length, ethnic dresses. I held one of the long ribbons and carefully went over one person, then under another until the streamers formed a colorful, woven glove around the pole. As I danced round and round the pole, the ribbon I was holding got shorter and shorter as it braided down the pole to the base where it became increasingly difficult to maneuver over and under the other dancers.

Everyone seemed so happy and joyful as we danced round and round. Lots of people were clapping and cheering as they watched us go. It could easily have been 100 people or more at that gathering from the pictures of it that I saw. It was a time I will always remember because I was so new in the Family, and it was my first glimpse of communal life. I felt like I was in another world with all these people who loved me, and in some ways, it was so much more love than I had ever felt before.

As a child, I was trying to find my footing. Here I was now living in a huge community where I had a new family and lots of children to play with. It was so different than the quiet life we had had living in the tepee in Alaska.

On the main floor of the Front Door Inn, way in the back, there was a small kitchen that was always bustling with activity and serving meals to visitors who were sat with and explained things.

At the Front Door Inn, upstairs, there were a lot of musical instruments in an area designated for playing music. Seth and I would play the instruments to pass time. He showed me this closet space way in the back behind this curtain. There on the shelf was this box of large glossy postcards.

The painting on the cards in large lettering read, "We Are One." The simple sentence filled up the entire card. Each letter was filled in with drawings of the faces of all the members of the Love Family, at least members who were there prior to 1975 which was when we came. I recognized people and children I had already met such as Hope and some of the other children.

The three central beliefs that shaped my life in the Love Family:

We are one.
Now is the time.
Love is the answer.

I include an excerpt from my childhood diary here to illustrate how even as young as I was, I was trying to internalize everything that I was learning about how the Love Family thought. I was trying, in a hurry, to mold myself to what was expected.

Dear Diary,

What we believe:

We are one
Love is the answer
Jesus Christ is real
God is our father
God is love
God sent us down to help the earth
Now is the time.

Rachel Israel

Another entry read:

Dear Diary,

My prayer for tonight.

Dear Father,
Bless my sleep with good dreams and bless everyone in the whole world
for coming home. There are 300 people in my new family and millions
are coming home.
I know you're real.
For Jesus Christ

Amen
Rachel Israel

My mom later explained to me that one of the main things that attracted her to the Love Family, that she found amazing, was that the Family's ideas were the same spiritual realizations that she had come to on her own.

"To me, 'we are one,' wasn't just this thing in the sky," she says. "I had really realized that everyone is really a part of one big consciousness." Karen continued. "We didn't use the term "philosophy" in the Family, but whatever it was, it was amazingly what I believed."

While Karen was going to new members' classes, Seth, who had befriended me, was trying to help me understand certain things too. One day we were trying to find something to do, and we found a copy of the Love Family Charter. The Charter was a parchment booklet with hand-lettered calligraphy that described the basis of what the Love Family believed. It was what people had to agree to when they joined. There were a lot of biblical passages quoted in it. From what I understand, each chapter in the Charter was written by a different elder, so it was a compilation that had been put together into a document. It was titled, 'Church of Armageddon Charter,' which throughout was decorated with symbols, some of which were the symbols of Love Family elders. The lettering was calligraphic, and it described Love Family beliefs in black; other lettering was red, indicating rubric quotes from the Bible or when Jesus's name was mentioned. On the first couple of pages before the table of contents, it was decorated with a symbol that a member named Hananiah created. It was a star of David. Inside the star was a cross, then the star, with its imbedded cross, were surrounded by a perfect circle border. From what I was later told, when he came, Hananiah was into numerology and symbology and was very good at creating mathematical designs. Love put his skills to use, creating symbols that had great meaning to the Love Family.

Seth and I leafed through the Charter that day. He turned the pages until he came to the chapter on children. Then he found certain passages within that chapter to show me. As I read it, he watched me quizzically, looking for my reaction. Since I could already read chapter books by the time I came to the Family, I was able to read what it said: It read:

"Chasten thy son while there is hope, and let not thy soul spare for his crying. (Prov. 19:18). Foolishness is bound in the heart of a child; but the rod of correction shall drive it far from him. (Prov. 22:15) Withhold not correction from the child: For if thou beatest him with the rod, he shall not die. (Prov. 23:13) He that spareth his rod, hateth his son; but he that loveth him, chasteneth him be-times." (Prov. 13:24). "Thou shalt beat him with the rod, and shalt deliver his soul from hell." (Prov. 23:14)

I finished reading it and felt a sense of dread.

"This is how it is here," Seth informed me with a serious expression.

I didn't know what to say. I had never been 'beat' with a stick, let alone even a hand. It was an unusually serious moment between two young children, Seth and myself. Within that same year, a kind woman named Probity was assigned to teach me and some other children Charter classes. Luckily, I was too young to do any of the other requirements to become a member, such as the 'seven-day fast' or 'address the council.'

My mom continued taking the new members' classes, but she was not doing well. In Homer, she had been "really confident" and like the "queen" of her home, but in the Family, she was the low man on the totem pole. She said she felt "unusually shy, self-conscious." We had been living a very quiet life, in the woods, but now we lived in close quarters with a lot of unrelated people.

Karen remembered that when she felt uncomfortable, she blamed herself but has since changed her views:

"Now, looking back," she says, "it was my real instincts trying to tell me something. It was my good intuition talking. I wish I had followed it."

It was in the third week of those classes when Karen had a run in with the elder, Certain. Apparently, from what she explained, Certain told her to go take a shower, and she told him to "Fuck off!" He didn't like that very well and kicked her out of the Family. She told him she didn't have anywhere to go, and he told her she could leave the kids while she went and figured out what she was going to do. She was gone for a month.

"I felt uncomfortable [in the Love Family]" she says, "but I also thought it was neat too, and a place where I was free from what I saw as weirdness in the world."

When Karen was kicked out, Forest and I were sent to Encouragement's household. This was in one of the houses that was in what they called 'Serious's Area' where there were four houses, one of which was Encouragement's. Encouragement and his then elder lady, Lois were the elders of the household where I was sent to live with a small group of members. Encouragement had dark, almost black, long bushy hair and a long beard. He had a medium build and had slightly, darker skin than most. I found out years later that he came from a Native American heritage. He was a Family musician who often played the guitar and sang songs with the group of children who I now spent most of my time with. He was very loving and fatherly to me and to Forest. He seemed overly concerned with some acne on my nose and helped teach me how to wash my face properly. Another time, when I had a cold, he taught me to eat a spoonful of hot sauce, to "clean my system out." My cold did seem to go away within no time after I ate it. After that, I went to the refrigerator with another girl my age from the household, and we dared each other to take the spoonful of hot sauce. It got to the point where it didn't taste hot anymore, so I just did it to show off. I could now impress people with my bravery.

Encouragement was strict though and was rule-bound in terms of Love Family custom and culture. Lois, his elder lady seemed overwhelmed by my brother Forest's constant crying, since Karen was gone now. At this point, Big Lois had no children of her own, but was now in charge of an angry baby,

Forest, as well as the other children who lived there. Besides myself and Forest, there were two other boys named Sun and Benjamin who were always getting in trouble.

One morning, I was in the shower with Sun. It was not uncommon for kids and adults to share in the bathing experience. At least to me, it was not ever sexual or weird but more just convenient and part of communal life. Before we came to this commune, nudity in the counterculture was treated similarly, especially at Makena Beach in Maui where everyone went naked all the time anyway.

When I was in the shower with Sun, it was that day when I began to realize what was really meant by the Family's "Spare the rod and spoil the child" mentality. We were soaping up, and I saw these bruises all over his body. They were blue and purple centimeter wide lines on his legs and back.

"What are those?" I asked him innocently, having never seen anything like it.

"I got the rod," he answered soberly.

When Sun showed me his bruises, it concerned me. I always tried to be nice to Sun anyway, but especially after that shower, because I felt bad for him always getting in trouble. Mostly he left me alone because I was nice to him, but it was hard because he would sometimes do things like come up and pull my hair or poke me and then sit back and wait for my reaction, which he seemed thoroughly amused by. Rumor had it that he had 'a leather butt,' but I didn't understand what was meant by that until I got older: The physical punishment obviously wasn't working. My friendship with him at times was a liability too, because if I wasn't careful, I could get in trouble right along with him, so I was always aware of that factor whenever I played with him.

We both lived at Encouragement's at that time, even though Serious, an elder who lived in the next house over was his dad. His mom's name was Miriam who I had met a couple times. She was not a member of the Love Family but only came for occasional visits. She was full figured and wore long skirts with boots and blouses with scarves. Her brown hair was long but because it was frizzy, it puffed out into a ball and only stretched to her shoulders.

Sun's story is part of my story. His experience had a huge impact on my own experience. I was living in an environment where beatings like this could happen, so I was afraid to do anything but obey and submit. From seeing what happened to Sun and others, it was clear to me that there was no room to protest. He was like a brother to me now, and it hurt to see him hurt. Since we lived in the same household, we spent a lot of time together. One of the things we used to do was sing together. He had a gift to where he could harmonize his voice to my singing. People who heard us would often comment and say our singing was beautiful.

One evening, someone heard us singing in the basement of one of the households.

"What tape is that?" they called down the stairs, asking.

"It's Rachel and Sun," we answered them.

"Wow!" I heard a couple of women exclaim, sounding amazed.

Sun's mom, Miriam, would only come for visits to the Family. I heard that she was not welcome because she had not been as submissive to the authority as was expected. She was considered too independent minded to be accepted. It was determined that she would be a bad influence on her son, Sun. My mom was still kicked out, so neither one of us had a mom there, so right away, I felt I could relate to him.

Sun's name was Moon when he came, but then he got the virtue name Son of Righteousness. Everyone just called him, Son though. Then, when he had some behavior problems, which may have been exacerbated by his separation from his mother, he lost his original virtue name and became known as, Sun. It was a different spelling but a very significant change symbolically. He didn't seem to mind. I heard him correct people a lot if they spelled his name wrong.

"It is spelled, S.U.N.!" he would emphatically spell it out.

For adults who lost their name, it was more how it was in the military if you were stripped of your honors and demoted. It would be a total embarrassment where you could be shunned and shamed. It did not seem to me like the kids really cared one way or the other if they lost their name.

It didn't work as a punishment when Hope lost his name who I talked about earlier, and it didn't work at all when Son of Righteousness lost his name.

Instead, other consequences would be used. If there was crying, the child would sometimes be put in a closet until they decided to stop, or they might just be put into some distant room by themselves. As a child, my reaction to the restrictive and controlling environment was just to comply as best as possible and not risk getting in trouble. It wasn't worth it. I learned that my body was a temple and to keep Satan out. Satan, which I understood to be an evil spirit, could apparently make kids cry or misbehave.

I had heard that little Benjamin had gone 3 days without food because they didn't want to feed a "negative spirit." Other children were put in closets if they cried where they would stay until they would get Satan out of their temples. My body was a holy place of God now.

I had the opportunity to read a former member's account of his experiences in the Love Family in the early 1970s (Israel, 1978). He goes by the name Larry now, but during the four years Larry spent in the Love Family, he was known as Consideration. My mom and I came and joined six months after he was already gone, so I never actually met him until many years later, after I read his manuscript.

Consideration had shoulder-length dark, almost black curly hair, dark eyes. He was a gentle, soft-spoken man, a very considerate person as it happened to be. His parents were Jewish, so his skin tone was a bit darker than a lot of the other members.

Larry wrote about his memories of the discipline of children in his manuscript. He wrote that children were "not allowed to cry, and if they persisted, they would be spanked and sometimes put into a closet, until they stopped." When he was a member, he wrote, the Love Family children were the most beautiful children that he had ever seen and the "best behaved." At the time, he thought that the way we were disciplined "worked," and "made sense." His observation was that, "Love's wisdom in handling children plus following what the Bible said could not be denied," then continued, "Love always seemed to know what to do with each child in each particular situation and the elders were learning fast (pg. 262)."

My first Christmas there, Sun had been so naughty that Santa Claus put rotten oranges in his stocking. He had the last laugh though because he got up earlier than the other children and went to open his stocking before anyone had gotten up. When he found the rotten oranges in his stocking, he went and took the candy out of another child's stocking—it was Bright's stocking—and left the rotten oranges for Bright to find. Bright was a boy around my age who was probably one of the most well-behaved boys there. Bright opened his stocking that morning to find rotten oranges, and Sun had eaten all his candy.

Bright's all grown up now, but I had a chance to interview him about what he thought of the discipline of children in the Love Family. He recalled an incident in which Sun stole something and had to sit on his hands for an entire day. I remembered it too. In fact, it seemed that one child's punishment sometimes became legendary. It would be a reminder to all the kids for years to come of what could happen if someone stepped out of line.

"My personal response there was just to be as good as I could," Bright says. "I remember begging Integrity not to spank me one time. Literally, I was down on my hands and knees, because I hadn't bowed. I was also punished severely for wetting the bed."

Zarah spent a lot of her growing up years in the Love Family. She was a few years younger than me. She recalled that she and one of her close friends, Purity, had been fighting over a quarter on Christmas Eve. The next morning, she woke up to this "horrible smell." They went to open their stockings:

"Purity didn't have anything in her stocking," Zarah recalled, "and instead found a small pile of compost near her bed." The only present Purity got that year was a toddler-sized rocking horse that she was too old to play with. On it, it said, 'To Persnickety.' Zarah remembered that Purity was always getting in trouble for being mean to the other kids and says, "I had been fighting with her just the night before over that quarter, but I didn't get compost."

In the early years, physical punishment was more systematic and pervasive, but in later years, that extreme, spare the rod, spoil the child mentality relaxed a bit, although there was still some of that going on, especially with certain individuals, in certain households.

In the end, though, what I took from it was just to never, ever misbehave. Mostly I did not much get in trouble. It was rare. The fear of the rod or banishment, separation, or exclusion was frightening. I didn't really see there as being any option other than to just become the model kid and stay out of trouble. I modeled myself after those in authority out of survival like any kid would. There really wasn't much room for anybody to relax. If adults stepped out of line, they could lose their name, they could get kicked out, or they could be ostracized and shamed. If any adult complained about something or expressed opposition, they would be criticized for it and confronted by the group, usually at meetings. When that happened, the person getting criticized could not get defensive. Instead they had to "Take it up," or "Shine it on," as it was referred to.

Physical punishment was usually reserved for the kids; however, on rare occasions, even the adults could be physically punished. One adult man who stepped out and had sex with a woman who was not in the Love Family got 40 swats as his punishment. Unfortunately, for certain kids like Sun or like Benjamin, physical punishment was not occasional, it was the standard when I got there, and that was definitely true during the early years of the Love Family. There was a time in my life when I denied that the physical punishment was as bad as it was. I wanted to only look at the positive aspects of my childhood. It has taken me time to come to terms with the full picture.

During the time period when Karen was gone and when Forest and I were placed at Encouragement's, Sun and I were down in the basement playing. We heard these noises coming from the garage. There was scraping and growling. Sun opened the garage door and there was Elimelech, Eliab, and Hope wielding their pocket knives as if to attack us. They contorted their faces like beasts. Sun and I were so freaked out that we ran for our lives up the stairs to tell Big Lois. Out of breath and probably unintelligible, we told her what happened. Lois did not like the noise and did not seem concerned at all. In fact, she was highly irritated and refused to let us come upstairs. She locked the door to the basement, trapping us down there with the weapons welding older boys. We started screaming and crying and went and hid in the basement bedroom. The boys came after us, so we ran and hid in Gideon's bed. Then we heard uncontrolled laughing. Sun and I went out, and there they were laughing their heads off. One of them was on the floor holding their belly. They thought it was hilarious! I did not think so at all. That was the day I learned how important it was to be one of the kids they liked. Years later, I asked Eliab what he remembered about me.

"I remember that you were one of the ones we liked," he says with a devious expression.

Hope would do stuff like that when he was with Elimelech and Eliab, but when it was just him, he was really nice. I went to Coe School with all the kids, just to play, and Hope would play dodge ball with us. We would all line up against the wall and he would throw the ball at us, trying to take us out one by one.

Hope and Elimelech, as I said, were the boys that were on the beach at the homestead in Alaska when my mom and I came hiking up the beach looking for the Love Family. They had been there in the first place, because they had been banished as punishment, for being out of control and for refusing to participate in Family life.

I liked it when Hope was around. He was like a big brother. He taught us how to play 'kick-the-can,' and we would play it in Love's Area by the sandbox between the Caretaker's House and the Kids' House.

Hope's mom was Truthfulness, and she was Love's elder lady, so Hope was somewhat privileged. He couldn't be kicked out like an adult could, and he was on his own in a way, because his mom was busy helping Love run the Family. With his mom unavailable, he was relegated to being guardianed by different members, none of whom he respected and none of whom could control him. His dad, Faith, had lived in the Family initially, but had done something wrong and lost his name and took on the Bible name, Joah. Joah ended up leaving the Family. I heard it had something to do with a decision that involved his wife, Kemuel having a baby outside of the Family, which was not how things were done. Love Family women were expected to have their babies at home, in the Love Family. As a result of that decision, she lost her name too, which had been Benevolence until that point.

I also heard that Hope had, at one point, went and tried to live with his dad, Faith/Joah, but apparently, he came back after his dad hit him with a shovel. Most people thought that Hope was unruly and uncooperative, and because of that, there were many who tried to beat him into submission. It didn't help one bit. He wasn't going to go with the Love Family program.

I didn't see him as a problem. I admired Hope. He was one of us, (a kid) but he was a rule breaker and had his own mind. He never gave up on himself. He was always bucking authority, because he made it clear, with his attitude and behavior, that he thought most things going on in the Love Family were BS, so he would never just fall in line. There were few people I saw who got away with that, not even Sun who was bucking the system the whole time. Sun never got away with it. Instead, he suffered mercilessly. Hope on the other hand, maybe because people gave up trying to control him and because he was Truthfulness's son, he just managed to not give a care in the world what people thought of him. There was nothing that I didn't admire about that, considering the culture around me was very strict with what seemed like arbitrary rules about everything, none of which made any sense.

One night, I was at a sleep over with one of Love's daughters, Gentle, who was around my age. I was sitting there talking with some other children from Love's household and Hope was there too. After dinner dishes, the kids were clustered around Hope, who had these sunglasses. No one in the Love Family wore sunglasses, but somehow, Hope had a pair, and he was letting us try them on.

One by one, we each put them on our face and he would chuckle like he was super amused. When it was my turn to try them on, I was a little apprehensive at what I would see, since I had never worn shades before. Nothing happened. Hope laughed the hardest when I put them on. I was the only one who just sat there with a dead-pan expression on my face, totally nonchalant and unamused. The other kids were posing and pouting and making all these attempts to get his attention. I just put them on and looked like—so what. He got such a kick out of it, that he let me wear them all afternoon. Every time he saw me walk by, he would chuckle in amusement. There were not many like Hope who could get away with wearing a pair of sunglasses.

For the adults, it seemed they were trying hard to keep themselves in line with the accepted customs and practices of the community. Having contrary points of view meant they were being "separate." If someone was separate, there might be a loss of vertical mobility and a loss of status. My view as a child was that the adults around me—their focus was on self-discipline. Total conformity. Nobody wanted to get kicked out which was almost like being banished from utopia. Members were passionately committed to the vision that was divinely inspired by Love. When people left or were kicked out, they were said to have, 'lost their vision.'

All of the adults around me were trying hard to control their every impulse to live out Love's vision. They were working hard to repress their every baser impulse in order to avoid expulsion. This impressed upon me the message that the world outside must really be a terrible place for all these people to be afraid to leave. It was a giant PR machine made out of people. To my own naïveté, it was convincing. If they believed this strongly in what they were doing, it seemed likely that what they were doing was that important. It was circular, but I think it fed itself in terms of the impression that was created on others coming in and even staying the course. I came to truly believe that this Family was everything that it was created to be. Everyone there believed it, then there were all the dreams and visions that were attestations of peoples' faith, which was evidence even more of the importance of the Love Family. The dreams and visions were spiritual and were testimonials of how people had been led to Love.

Meanwhile, Life at Encouragement's house was very controlled and strict. I was on my own to figure out the best way to deal with it, since Karen was still gone. Everything I did was with the group. We ate together twice a day; there was no lunch, only popcorn for a snack. There might have been 12 members, including children that lived there at the house with me. Everyone was totally silent during meals, except the elder. We would always chant for several minutes before the meal, then there was a prayer, led by the elder. "Thank you, Abba for our food." Every time I ate with them, they told me I was eating "the blood and the body of Christ." It sounded disgusting to me. Little Benjamin was being fed in the high chair, and the one feeding him would take the spoonful of food and before each bite say, "body of Christ," so he would know and appreciate what he was eating. If he cried, the food would not be served until the crying stopped. It scared me to think that maybe I would not be fed, so I made sure that with every bite I took, I would say to myself, 'This is the body of Christ.' The prayer would close with "in Jesus name."

The food was very different than how I had been fed in Alaska. There was no meat or fish at all. We ate mostly the same thing each night. It was brown rice. There was no butter. It was served with soy sauce and olive oil. There might be a small salad served with the rice and sometimes home-made bread.

I always knew exactly what was for breakfast and what was for dinner. I did not have to ask. On a typical day, I ate hot oatmeal or hot farina in the morning, sometimes fruit. When I first got there, I got to drink this delicious drink they called Pua. It was made from wheat berries that a crew of men would collect from the base of Queen Anne hill at a grain factory.

The exception to the simple diet was Holy Day, which was Sunday or what was then called Laodicea. On that day, there would be a feast of cheeses, homemade bread, homemade mayonnaise and mustard. There would be fruit on the table from the harvests in Eastern Washington, fruits and other treats. On Holy Day, the Family would all eat together and not just with our individual households. They would set up tables in the yard, and everyone would dress in their finest clothes.

On Holy Day, I would get homemade yogurt and homemade granola for breakfast. Then that afternoon, when everyone spent time together in the yard, I would pick whatever I wanted off the tables. One Holy Day, peaches were put on my granola, and they tasted like hot sauce. None of the kids would eat it, including myself. The peaches had come from a cannery that the Family owned in Eastern Washington where just the year before, the buckets had been used for hot sauce.

There was a girl there that day with her mother. They were visitors. Her mother was standing by the tables nibbling cheese and talking to Serious. The girl was around my age. She and I played the whole day together. I wanted to know all about her. This was still my first year in the community, so I was very curious to understand what this place was all about. I don't remember the little girl's name who I befriended that day, but she told me that she and her mother had come from a community in Canada that believed in Satan. I was incredulous!

"Satan?" I asked. I thought to myself, how could that be? Here I was living in a community that believed in love, oneness and Christ. It was hard to imagine anything on the opposite spectrum.

She told me they hung pentagrams on the walls and in the closets. I did not know what a pentagram was so she drew me a picture. It was a five-pointed star inside of a circle.

It reminded me of a similar decorative symbol that was used in the

Love Family. It was a star of David inside a circle, and inside the star was a cross. The star of David had great symbolic meaning for our community. It was used a lot in decorating books for children, on official documents, in artwork that one might see on the walls, even embroidered onto the clothing that people wore. It seemed to be a symbol that was representative of our identity as a family.

Everything that I heard from newcomers taught me something about the culture outside. People out there believed all sorts of things. We believed in God; there was a commune in Canada that believed in Satan. I guess to each his own. I had questions though: What is this Love Family? Why do they think that out there is bad? Everyone always said don't do this or that, because it is 'Worldly.' 'The world' or outside culture had negative connotations. It was confusing, because I had lived on the outside and it hadn't been all that bad, at least that I knew of, and if they were trying to keep it from me, what was it that they didn't want me to know?

It was impossible to understand the larger context because I was too young. Adult members had all been raised in the "world" so they already knew what only seemed like a mystery to me. As the months went by, I became more familiar with customs and expectations.

When it was time to eat, I sat cross-legged on the floor, around a low table as I saw others do. Everyone in the Love Family lived in different households that were like clusters of people who lived together, communally. Each cluster was headed by a Family elder. I was told to chew my bite 30 times, and as I chewed, I was to think of Jesus Christ with each bite. The food was absolutely pulverized by the time I was swallowing it. As I chewed, I wondered if the girl who had come from the Satan group in Canada, if she had been told to think of Satan with each bite.

A Love Family elder, Serious Israel, was quoted in the newspaper discussing the eating ritual when he said, "We really feel that all meals should be approached as a holy experience with time to stop and focus and remember that we really are eating the body and blood of Jesus Christ." (*Seattle Times* Jan 23rd, 1982 Sat. A10)

The Bible was instructive for the Love Family regarding this:

For my flesh is meat indeed and my blood is drink indeed (John 6:55, *KJV*).

He that eateth my flesh and drinketh my blood dwelleth in me and I in him (John 6:56 *KJV*, See also John 6:33, 48–58 *KJV*)

Whosoever eateth my flesh and drinketh my blood hath eternal life (John 6:54 *KJV*)

At mealtimes, everyone was totally silent as they focused on Jesus Christ. Even something as simple as a shared meal was a highly structured spiritual exercise. As people chewed their food, I was learning to become conscious of something that I had done over and over again each day without even thinking about it. I learned that everything that we all did together—singing, meditating, chanting, working—we were raising our state of consciousness, even being aware of my breathing—breath in Jesus Christ—breath out—negativity, doubt, separation, etc.

I couldn't just slouch. I had to always sit up straight. When I went to the bathroom, I was told to only use three squares. My poop was now called, "Leat Da," and my pee was called, "Leat Ain." Love had developed a lot of language for things, including written symbols that we used.

The bathroom had a wooden rack with a line of hooks on it that hung by the toilet. On each hook was what was called, a 'bottom towel,' and next to the shelf was a squirt bottle that was to be used beforehand. Each bottom towel had a name embroidered on it that labeled it as belonging to someone in the household. This is what we were to use to wipe with after we went leat da. That was a short-lived custom though because it became the source of many jokes, including the rumor that Eliab had been switching them around to confuse things, which he probably found quite humorous.

Most of the virtue names also had a written symbol that was attached to them, but there were a lot of symbols for written words too. I never forgot a lot of those symbols and even today, I use them for a sort of shorthand for taking notes. In college, it saved me quite a bit time, during lectures. One day, someone from my class saw my lecture notes and they couldn't quit asking about them. None of the symbols can be found on any word processor around.

The rules were strict around meals and eating. I wasn't allowed to eat unless it was a meal time. No one could just go get food out of the refrigerator. Apparently, before Karen and I got there, someone had taken bread and was punished for it after no one confessed.

Larry/Consideration, who has since raised a family and works as a caregiver, remembered much about his Love Family days. He remembered the stolen bread incident.

When the bread was taken, he described the event as the "heaviest" he had encountered. He said that everyone was "extremely nervous," and that it seemed as if "hell awaited." He described that one morning, everyone was called together for a family meeting. The atmosphere was "silent, quiet, and serious." About 40 people sat cross legged waiting to hear what was going on. During this time, in the early 1970s, the only way that food could be distributed was through the elders. When the bread was taken, no one confessed, so each person had to file into Love's room and be asked individually whether they had stolen the bread or not. A man named Reverence was to be the oracle to determine if the person was lying. Reverence was lying down, and his arms would raise-up, indicating innocence or guilt. After everyone had come in and left, no one was determined guilty. It was then decided to draw straws in order for justice to prevail. The shortest straw would give indication of the offender, and they would have to leave the Love Family forever. A man named Healing was picked. That night, Healing was made to leave. (pp 198–200).

Years and years later, the real thief admitted their deed, which made everyone realize that Healing had been innocent all along and had been banished from the Kingdom of Heaven forever for something he didn't do.

Larry wrote that he was not allowed to go into the refrigerator whenever he wanted. He said, "We were taught not to want or expect anything. We no longer had any rights. There was no more I, me, or my own."

The relevant biblical quote that applied to this was from Psalm 23 and says, "The Lord is my Shephard, I shall not want." Therefore, it was taught that "to want anything was wrong and simply not trusting God to take care of us."

Everything that took place in the Love Family had an underlying spiritual purpose. It permeated the culture on every level. There was a poster that I always would read when I saw it, and I saw it all the time because it was on the wall in a room in one of the houses, a room that was used for children's Bible classes. It was a standard sized poster that listed all the different names of God. There was God, Allah, Yahowah, Father, Yahweh, Abba, Lord, Jehovah, Elohim, King of Kings, Lord of Lords, Lord of Hosts, Adonai–The list went on and on, filling up the whole poster. It seemed like every part of my life became a discipline, a spiritual exercise. There was always something to meditate on. Each bathroom would be like a little sanctuary, with a Bible and a candle. There would be a thought jar there, so I could pick a thought. A thought jar was a bowl or dish with tiny little cards and each card was printed a virtue, like confidence or grace. Consequently, many of the virtues on the cards were the names of people who I now lived with. Each time I went to the bathroom, I would pick one and meditate on it, just as I was instructed to do.

I was smart enough that I knew, even at age seven, that my survival in this group depended on my ability to get along, so I tried hard to do as I was told and to understand what I was being taught. I wondered when Karen would come back for me, but I didn't have time to feel sorry for myself. I was absorbed with the adjustment, and there were so many people and other children who were now my family.

One of the things that I had to get used to was a whole new way of thinking. It wasn't optional. To get along there, I was suddenly being expected to become aware of my thoughts. I often heard the mantra, "Thoughts create." I was learning that every time I spoke, I was putting thoughts in other people's minds. If I voiced things that I wished for, I would be lectured and told that my thoughts were "wants." I was learning to ignore my wants and wishes, and ultimately, my needs, because it wasn't clear to me who was going to determine which of my wants was a want and not an actual need.

I heard a lot of talk about being "positive." One day, I was in one of the household sanctuaries, and a nice man who helped take care of the kids a lot, especially in the early days, was there. His name was Ezra. He made the kids laugh and would sometimes put on a red rubber nose. Every time I or one of the kids would squeeze it, he would make the nose squeak, which one kid after the other would do, resulting in laughter each time. Anyway, in the sanctuary, Ezra heard me say something negative, a complaint of some sort. I don't remember what it was exactly, but he immediately went and got a half a glass of water and brought it to me.

"Is it half full or half empty" he asked, studying my face.

I didn't answer him and thought it was a bit of a trick question.

"It is important to look at things like the glass is half full," he answered himself. "We have a choice in how we look at things."

I think that was the first time that I began to more deeply understand all the talk about 'be positive' and 'thoughts create.' As a child, I was learning the power of my thoughts, which is good to learn no matter what age, but it also, to some extent, took the levity out of play and it became more of a spiritual shtick. Everything became part of this spiritual drama which while it was good mental training, it was also a bit much at times.

Not only was I supposed to try and control my inner thoughts, I was also supposed to express my positive thoughts externally. If I didn't, someone might comment on it. It seemed a lot of people walked around like they were in perpetual bliss. Maybe they were. Members would constantly remind one another to smile. When I was told to smile, it thoroughly irritated me. I liked to just be myself. There was so much focus on being positive and "Thoughts create," and "Take it up," that it got to me. It felt repressive; I came to my own conclusion, that my thoughts and feelings are mine, and I don't have to share them if I don't want!

Rob Balch, a sociologist who visited and wrote about the Love Family talked about some of his observations in an article he wrote for a book titled, "Sects, Cults, & Spiritual Communities: A Sociological Analysis. He wrote that people in the Family behaved differently than he had ever seen before, the most noticeable being eye contact, which he wrote, "There was more of it," more than he was used to. He said that as he got to know the members, he could see differences in their personalities, but "still there was a remarkable uniformity in their expressions, inflections, tone of voice, and way of relating to each other. Members spoke softly, went through their routines quietly and efficiently, and always seemed cheerful about whatever they were doing." (pg. 74)

One of the reasons I liked to befriend new members was because they had not taken on that uniformity. They were more interesting. They didn't know the rules yet, so they would be more open about their past. I liked to hear about where they came from and what their life had been like on the outside. Because in the Love Family, I was told that the present was all the mattered; the past was nothing more than the past and wasn't important anymore. People did not generally discuss their past, which included anything that took place before they joined the Love Family. They also did not talk about their past in the Family; in other words, I did not hear people sitting around talking about what happened last year, last month, last week, or even yesterday. Everyone was trying to live in the present moment. As I said earlier, 'Now is the time,' was one of the main beliefs that underlay all of life in the Love Family, with exception to 'Love is the answer,' and 'We are one.'

As a child, I was always very curious about people and culture. I enjoyed talking to new people because it seemed like they were still individuals, and they had not yet changed or become "one" with everyone else. When they did, they quit answering questions about their past. In the Family, we were told to "Stay present," that the past didn't matter anymore. Once they took on that uniformity, they would change and become uninteresting to me, boring frankly, and just like everybody else. For such a non-conformist group, there sure was a lot of conforming going on!

The adults would often look at one another for minutes at a time. Sometimes they would look when they were seated across from each other or next to each other, and sometimes it was just in the casual moving about during the day. The purpose of this, I was told, was to "give love to one another." They were radiating love through their eyes. Larry wrote about the extended eye contact between people. He explained how when people stared at each other, it was a way for people to get to know one another, to "really see" the other person and break down the walls that consisted of the fears of relating to and loving each other (Israel, 1978).

I heard people ask each other, "What kind of thoughts are you getting?" After anything was said, it seemed there was a sort of scrutiny that would occur that would determine whether the thought was from God. If someone answered, "I was thinking that we were one person," then it was a thought from God, but if someone said, "I'm thinking about having something to eat," then I imagine that would've been considered 'separate' or from Satan.

Before I came to the Love Family, I had been talkative, friendly, and outgoing. But once I began adjusting to life inside the Love Family, I became shy and quiet, in part because to say anything meant that my thoughts were held up to a light to determine whether they met certain spiritual criteria that was occurring underneath the surface. Being quiet was a way of protecting my inner privacy and right to have my own thoughts without judgment.

Years later when I went into the outside culture, I would stare at people without realizing it was offensive. Guys thought I was interested when in truth, I was just looking around and sending out love as I had been taught for so many years. I still catch myself sometimes and think, *Oh, right—not that.* It is like a language that I learned as a child, my first language that is hard to extinguish, as an accent might be for someone from South America.

If I wasn't cheerful, I would be told to "Brighten up," and that I was being, "dark." If I had a contrary point of view or was questioning the way things were, I was told that I was thinking with a small "I," and having "separate" thoughts rather than thinking with the big "I" and submitting to the will of the group. I tried to be positive, because I didn't want someone calling me on my behavior all the time. I was irritated though at the constant pressure to be positive and bright. It did not feel genuine to have a big grin on my face all the time.

Despite the mental training, I still had fun with the other children and didn't feel sad or down most of the time. I just learned how to deal with it. The uniformity of thought and behavior drove me to have a rich inner life as a way of coping. Inside my head I could be alone. Inside my head, no one could tell me what to do or what to think. This was when I began to learn how to keep my feelings hidden. Literally, I would hide them. When I wrote in my diary, I would use a secret code, just in case someone read it. I made the code up myself and hid it inside the back cover, which had a not very noticeable rip between the vinyl cover and the cardboard.

I didn't get my diary, though, until a few years later. Earlier on, during my first year living at Encouragement's, I was only seven years old and was still getting familiar with my new home in the community and how things were laid out.

I now lived in a yellow house that was in an area called Serious's Area, just a few blocks from the Front Door Inn. Serious's Area was composed of four houses that were connected; their yards were landscaped together, communally. There were also well-maintained lawns and flower beds that defined the shared boundaries. There were nine bee hives located near a tree house in the center of the shared yard, and along the paths were perfectly trimmed box bushes.

The area, which included these four houses was called Serious's Area, because Serious, a high-status elder oversaw the entire area for Love. Serious lived with his household in the light blue house next to Encouragement's household where I lived.

Serious was a tall, pale skinned, slender man with long, straight, dark-brown hair, that was—like all Love Family members—parted in a perfect line going down the middle of his scalp. He had the brightest of blue eyes, and had a long beard and mustache, just like most the men there. Serious functioned as Love's business manager and second in command, but then he also had a role with the kids as well. There was a time when I went over to his house with other children every morning to do meditations with him.

One day, after the meditation, Serious talked about what an aura was. There were around seven or eight kids at that time that he would teach. We all sat in a version of the lotus (cross-legged) on the floor in a half circle around him.

"Does anyone know what an aura is?" Serious asked. Then he told us that an aura was an energy field that emanates from one's body and reflects their spiritual state of consciousness. "Do you see it?" He insisted, expectantly. Then he told us to look carefully at the person across from us to see if we could see the white light radiating from their head. All the kids began staring at one another with concentrated expressions.

I looked at Serious. I stared for a minute or more at him while he talked.

"Who can see it?" he asked again?

I kept looking at him. *I saw it! No wait, yes, it was there!* I saw a very light, white energy field emanating from around his head. It was about 2 inches wide; I could see very faintly the boundary of this light. It was translucent, almost invisible. The only way I could tell that it was there was that I could see the slight movement, as it vibrated ever so slightly.

I didn't raise my hand when he asked who saw it because I didn't want to bring attention to myself. Maybe I imagined it. I saw it but then the light was so subtle that I wasn't totally sure, because when I looked again, after doubting myself, it wasn't there. The other kids who were there, some of them raised their hands and said they saw it; others were still trying, with puzzled expressions on their faces. He had said, "It takes practice." I saw it—again, I think. It really wasn't important to me whether it was there or not though; what was important was avoiding getting in trouble and doing everything I could to understand the concepts I was being taught and gain the approval of my elders.

Serious's household where we would meditate was on one side of Encouragement's household. On the other side of Encouragement's household was Meekness's household. A couple lived there named Salmon and Duel who had a little boy named Worth, who looked blue. He had a slight blue hue to his skin. Worth did not play with the other children. I wasn't told why initially.

All three houses, Encouragement's, Serious's and Meekness's, were on eighth Avenue. Across the yard on Ninth, there was another house where an elder named Integrity lived with his elder lady named, Together.

All three houses on 8th and the one on 9th all comprised what was called, Serious's Area. A couple of blocks over from Serious's Area, on Sixth Avenue, there were several more houses that were connected communally— that was called Love's Area.

Rob Balch described the Family compound as a "tranquil village-like atmosphere in the middle of a densely populated urban neighborhood." (pg. 75). The two Areas of houses were connected by a designated circuit. The 'Circuit' was certain streets that members walked that kept everyone connected socially and defined our boundaries as a group from outsiders. The Front Door Inn was on that Circuit as well as other Family houses that were acquired over time in that same several-block area. The Circuit went anywhere that members commonly went, including Parson's Gardens, the neighborhood park a short distance from the Front Door Inn where everyone had celebrated Flower Day.

The Circuit was a designated, commonly shared way to travel to and from Love Family houses. I knew about the Circuit. But when I walked it, I was with other children there, and we were guided by our guardian who would keep us on the right streets. The Circuit was one of those unwritten rules the Love Family kept. It helped make living in a big city feel like a small town, because everywhere I went on the circuit, there would be other Love Family members also on the Circuit that would pass, on their way to wherever, on their different missions. Life in the community had a close-knit feel. The circuit delineated and defined the Love Family world. I didn't think about it much; it was just the way things were. It gave me the feeling when we walked it that we weren't just walking in the outside society, but we were walking on streets defined by us as being ours.

The circuit passed by a lot of neighbors, people who lived along the circuit who were considered our friends. The Love Family considered anyone on that circuit to be our neighbors, even if they were several blocks away. It was on the top of Love's list to have good relationships with the neighbors. Crews of men from the Family would go and help the neighbors in their yards. Other members would visit the elderly folks, help clean their houses, bring them food or read the Bible to them. At the Front Door Inn, there were bins of fresh produce that were free for the taking. I saw little old ladies stop by and put items into their bags. Especially early on, there was a lot of altruism, just helping people out.

At Christmas-time I went with the kids and our guardians to neighbors' houses, and when they opened the door, we would sing the standard Christmas carols. We also sang them a Love Family Christmas carol, that was written and put to music by one of the musicians in the community. It went:

> God shown down upon a great light,
> The angels were there and filled the air,
> With hope and gladness and singing.
> La la la la—la la la la,
> With hope and gladness and singing...

The relationships that were formed were such that from time to time I went with Probity and other women and we could pick flowers from their yards. Then the flowers were used to decorate Love Family homes or for special events such as Flower Day or Holy Day.

My clearest memories though are of the many times that we were taken to different neighbors who were especially fond of the children. I looked forward to going to Loretta's house who lived on the Circuit, going from Love's Area to the Front Door Inn. Loretta lived across from Coe School. She was a very large, nice older lady who was always talking about her latest diet and called us "the Loves." She loved to sew, and she made several of the girls dresses. She made me a dress that I wore all the time. It was a white, ankle length dress with little light-green flowers. She made the dresses in the style of Love Family custom-wear, just to be helpful but probably knowing we would not wear them if she didn't. Every time we went to visit her, she gave us cookies too. We never got cookies in the Love Family except for on a day the Family called 'Cookie Day' (Halloween) so it was a real treat to go to Loretta's.

A lot of those neighbors really seemed to appreciate the friendship with the Family and my guess is they probably looked the other way when weird stuff happened. There was a period of time when we marched, military style formation right under the watchful gaze of many of our neighbors. I know they thought that was weird, because I heard there were complaints. Even the kids marched. I wondered later what the neighbors' must have thought to see us marching. We marched down Sixth Avenue and over at Coe school in the open field where we would've been very visible to the neighbors on both sides of the school.

Strength was like the commander, and as we marched, he would yell out, *"Aman, aman, aman, samal, aman,"* which means—right, right, right left right in Hebrew. The children would be lined up by size which caused some complaint by some of the children who had to be in the back of the line each time because they weren't as tall. The guardian tried to make it a learning moment by quoting the Bible, saying, "So the last shall be first, and the first last: for many be called, but few chosen." In the moments after he said it, all the kids stopped talking and just stood there in silence thinking about it, not sure what to make of it. It stopped the complaining though as suddenly it no longer mattered who was in front or who was last in the line. We only did that marching for a short period of time though because it made some of the neighbors nervous.

Even if we weren't marching, the Love Family was still a very visible presence on the Hill. We would all go on family walks sometimes on Holy Day. Can you imagine 150 people on a walk? It was just a casual stroll in the densely populated Queen Ann neighborhood where we lived. Everyone would be decked out in their Holy Day gear, with handmade robes and fine dresses, our regular, hippie–ancient Israeli look. When we were walking by, sometimes I would see the neighbors peeking out their windows at us passing by.

I went and visited the Queen Anne News to do some research on what they had printed about the Love Family in those days and surprisingly, they did not publish hardly anything. I asked the editor why. She told me that they did not like to write about it since the *Seattle Times* was regularly covering it. I didn't buy it. I speculated that the real reason was that they didn't want to publish negative stories about the Family; they were trying to preserve the peace on the Hill since we had so many friends.

It was a high priority to Love that the neighbors be happy. One day, the kids were making too much noise at the Kids' House, and there was a neighbor who complained. Right away, Love's response was to send all the kids out to live at the Ranch with our guardians. There had already been complaints about the bleating of a little lamb that had been put in Love's Area for Passover the previous spring. There had also already been complaints about the rooster, so because we were making too much noise, we were sent to the Ranch.

'The Ranch' was what everyone called a 350-acre farm that the Love Family owned in Arlington, Washington. For the kids who stayed in town, they were no longer allowed to have recess in Love's Area. They had to go to Roger's Park for recess each day, which was a substantial walk for a lot of the kids who were still quite young.

I was one of the kids who was banished to the Ranch. It was all over a game of tug-o-war. Part of the problem was that it wasn't just a few kids anymore; the group of us was getting larger in number as more and more people joined the Love Family. Of course you're going to have more noise—more kids? More noise.

The noisy game was Logic's idea. As it happened to be, Logic was the famous Steve Allen's son, but in the Love Family, he was a high-status elder named 'Logic.' Logic, besides fulfilling his regular duties of running a household and helping Love run the Family, he would often go way out of his way to help solve practical problems for the caretakers and guardians in charge of the kids. That day he was just having fun with us. It was the girls against the boys. We had this big rope and we started tugging. We were laughing and screaming. Logic got carried away because he was winning, and he was pulling us out of the Kids' House. He was laughing with total glee, like a big kid, and not even aware that we were making noise because we were having so much fun. That evening, Co-op (Cooperation) showed up at the Kid's House with serious news. With a stern expression on his face he reminded us that we had been warned and that we were all to go live at the Ranch where it wouldn't matter if we made noise.

So, I and a group of about 15 other children of various ages and sizes, with our guardians and helpers, all went out and lived in what everyone called the 'Barn.' It was a big barn, just like what most people think of a barn—a large structure on a farm for animals. But this was no typical barn. It was transformed over the years into a major central gathering point, including being made into a school for the children, and eventually was made into Love's home. When we were sent to live in it though, this was early on, just after the property had been acquired, so the Barn was rustic and unheated. It was more like a two-week long camping trip—but that is just one example of the lengths that Love went to make the neighbors happy. One of the designated guardians on that trip remembered seeing the station wagon all loaded up with kids, and on the roof of the vehicle were strapped "five pottys."

It seemed that the efforts made a difference because we did not have too many problems with the neighbors for the most part. In the papers, there were neighbors quoted, making comments about what they thought of us:

One neighbor was quoted as saying, "They are our neighbors, and very good neighbors, at that. They are all out, early in the morning, picking up the street. They place those baskets of free food on their porches with those signs: "Please share in our abundance." (*Seattle Times* Jan 31, 1976 A1) Another neighbor was quoted as saying,

"They paid their rent on-time. And, although they trooped in and out of their houses in droves, they didn't disturb the neighborhood with noisy parties." (*Seattle Post-Intelligencer*, Sunday May 14, 1978 A13 BM).

There was one neighbor on Queen Anne who liked us so much, she ended up joining and donating her house to Love. That was a member who became known as Wisdom.

Most of the neighbors did not have a problem with us or fear the hippie image. For the most part, they liked having the Family on the hill and felt secure because we were always around.

There were members on 'Watch,' every day and every night. They were stationed at the Front Door Inn was the front door to the Love Family. The household that lived there in the house that was attached to it would help people who came in off the street, feed them if needed. Someone would be there, playing guitar or they would read the Bible with people who came in. They hosted visitors and would deliver messages to Love and tell him what was going on. I figured all this out right away when we stayed there as new members.

During the night, there would be people on watch as well; they called it the Nux Watch. Nux in Greek, according to Strong's Greek dictionary, means 'night' or 'by night.' Twice a night, at around 1am and again at 4am in the morning, two people would go on the circuit to the different houses and check on people. I heard they would collect peoples' dreams and communicate love to each person, although thankfully, they did not wake up the kids.

Finally, there were relationships that the Love Family fostered that gave us standing in the community. For example, the Love Family was also known as the Church of Armageddon in the church community. We had applied for status as a church and became observers on the Church Council of Greater Seattle. (*Seattle Times*, November 11, 1976 B3) That was a big deal, because it was an organization that was city wide and had a lot of notoriety. Observer status was important because it put us in line for actual membership. It was not without controversy though, because when the Love Family and the Church Council jointly sponsored an event, there were those who protested our involvement. They stood outside with picket signs. (*Seattle Times* January 25th, 1982 C2)

In the Northwest section of the *Seattle Times*, the Council was quoted saying they had received "numerous letters and telephone calls objecting to the liaison" but stated, "We have found, in our four-year association with the Church of Armageddon, that many of the accusations against the church have no basis in fact…" (*Seattle Times* Dec 15, 1981 B1 Northwest). Another article reported that the Church Council of Greater Seattle and the Love Israel Family had an "open and friendly" relationship without conflicts or problems. The Church Council had found us to be a "gentle people seeking to have a meaningful life in a communal society of [our] own creation."

The kids were taught to be respectful of the neighbors. Anytime I saw trash, I learned to pick up the litter and create a more beautiful place. On a walk one day, I had seen a notice on one of the candy wrappers that said that if I sent the company 50 candy-bar wrappers, that they would send me five dollars rebate. It did not take me long since we picked up trash everywhere we went. I put them all in a manila envelope and sent them off to the address. I never heard back from them, even though it was a fun exercise. Each time I was out and about, I looked forward to getting more wrappers off the street and spent a lot of time thinking about what I might do with the five dollars.

Looking back, maybe they did send me the five dollars, but maybe I just didn't get it; it probably went to the "Center." The Center was where everything went that was turned in to Love by members when they joined. It wasn't an actual place; it was a person or persons, working under the guidance of Love, who would decide whether an item would be gotten rid of, sold, returned to the person who turned it in, or redistributed to another member or members. When members joined, they turned everything they owned into Love, to the Center. If they received anything from outsiders while they were a member, they would also turn that in.

There was something that happened that gave me my first lesson on how that worked. I was somewhere between seven and eight; it was during my first year there. Serious took the kids to Parsons Gardens to play. I went to play behind the building where they kept all the garden tools. When I was back there, I found a large pile of pennies. There were probably 100 or more, just piled up in the dirt behind the lattice. It was treasure! I stuffed my pockets with as many as I could, then came out from behind the building with dirt all over my hands. I was so proud of my discovery that I went and showed Serious. I wore the dress that Loretta had made me with big pockets. I had bluish green eyes and wore my blond hair in two braids, one going down each side of my head past my shoulders. I no longer looked like the ragged Alaskan hippie kid; I looked more like Laura, from Little House on the Prairie who might've lived on a farm in biblical times. When Serious saw my pennies, he told me they were from God, and I needed to turn them in to the Center. He took all my pennies and I never saw them again. He didn't do it to be mean; he did it because that's how it was, and he had to teach me the way of the Love Family. I silently let the reality sink in, but since I didn't grasp the full meaning of it, I felt disappointed and confused.

It was a small example of what was happening on a much wider scale in the community. If members received gifts from outside relatives or friends, those gifts were to be turned in to the Center as well.

The Love Family had a lot of property. Incoming members would donate houses and other properties when they joined, but other houses that we owned had been deteriorated Hill properties that had been scrubbed, repaired, and brought up to code.

There were properties such as: a horse ranch near Goldendale; an old minesweeper re-christened the Abundance used as a fishing boat; a seven-seated aircraft piloted by Noble Israel; 140-acre homestead on the Kenai Peninsula in Alaska, where we had met the Family; a hydroelectric project in Northport; a 350-acre ranch near Arlington, Washington, with a ranch house and a barn; a remote one-acre outpost in Hilo, Hawaii with a large house; and a total of 306 acres in the Skagit, Yakima, and Columbia Valleys.

The Love Family also owned a wide assortment of vans, trucks, buses, and other vehicles, including at least 2 Hanomags. Love's bus was called the 'Blue Bus,' and was a 1947 Mack, which contained two stoves and a bath tub.

The Love Family also had quite a few businesses that were developed by the members once they had joined: There was a construction and home-repair company, a roofing company, a cabinet shop; a natural foods grocery; an art gallery and a crafts store; a traveling espresso bar that catered affairs at the Westin Hotel and Paramount Theater, a wine-making operation called Israel Brothers and a cannery in Eastern Washington that had been donated by an in-coming member.

These properties were not all owned when we got there, although a lot of them were; Many of them were acquired or developed over time.

Just on Queen Anne Hill in Seattle, the Family owned many houses.

It was common for ten to fifteen people to share a house. In the basement of Love's house, there was a windowless room called Cube City where at one-time, 16 people, many of whom were children, lived in eight tiny cubicles.

All the Family houses had tailored architecture. The houses were re-modeled in Shaker-like quirky ways that could accommodate larger numbers of people. Basements, attics and closets were remodeled into living quarters; everything was remodeled to make room for more people to sleep. On certain holidays, there were many more people that would fill the homes than just the regular number who lived there all year round.

Whenever there was a gathering in the city, there might be 20 or 30 people who slept in a house for a weekend. For certain holidays, like Christ-mas, everyone would come to the city from the different outposts, so every-body was sleeping everywhere. In the morning, everyone would roll up their sleeping and carry bags and put them out of the way to accommodate the sanctuaries for day use.

At Encouragement's house where I stayed while Karen was gone. In the basement, there were a lot of small rooms and spaces with bunk beds, including a bed-sized cupboard or storage cabinet that had been made into a sleeping space. At the time, there was a heavyset man that slept in there, a new member named Gideon. We would go in there sometimes and visit him.

He had put a clock on the wall and obviously didn't realize that it wasn't appropriate to do that in the Love Family. It was not common to see clocks, and people did not carry watches on their wrists. Even the Bible had references that bolstered our beliefs:

> "Now is the accepted time, behold now is the day of salvation." (2 Cor. 6:2)

> "Now is our salvation nearer than when we believed." (Rom. 13:11, See also 1 Cor. 15:23; Eph. 2:13, 14, 19; 1 Cor. 12:18–20, 24, 25, 27)

Everyone believed in living the present moment and being in 'the now.' I heard people tell each other all the time to "Stay present." Everything would happen when it was supposed to happen. We did not live by clocks. 'Now' was the only time. If a member planned an event in the future with another member, even then, the plan was only tentative, and I heard them say they would be there, but only "God willing..."

One day, Sun and I went into Gideon's cubicle to play when he wasn't there. The clock was still on his wall, but it would not be long before he was talked to about it; he was a new guy and didn't understand the way things were there.

Sun stood up on Gideon's bed and started playing with the clock. Sun had shoulder length, curly, blond hair and blue eyes. He stood on Gideon's pillow, so he could reach the clock.

"I know how to tell time," he bragged.

"I don't know how to tell time," I answered him proudly.

"Oh, it's easy, I'll teach you," He insisted.

"No, that's OK, I don't want to learn," I told him. I was trying to be a good girl. "Now" was always what time it was.

He moved the clock hands around and told me what time it was each time he moved them. He didn't care.

It made me nervous. I decided it was best to leave Gideon's room before anyone saw us. "Come on, let's get out of here," I said as I stepped down out of the cubby.

I was being taught that the Worldly conceptions of "past" and "future" were merely illusions. One day, I was thinking about all this, trying to understand it, philosophically. I had gone to the park with the kids and our guardians. It was dusk. I wandered off by myself and followed this little trail, across the grass and through a patch of trees. I began thinking about the concept of time. *Stay present.* I walked slowly down the woodsy path, contemplating the idea. I came to a place on the path where this branch had fallen, right over the path. I had to cross, step over the branch to continue on. I thought, *I can stand here and not step over that branch and remain on this side of the branch. If I do that, then remaining on this side of the branch will be my destiny. But, if I cross over the log and continue, then continuing will be my destiny.* I stood there thinking for a few long moments. The future seemed like a contradiction. Whatever I ultimately chose to do was what the future held. Was there such thing as destiny? It seemed strange to me. I stood there in the woods, thinking about the concept of past, present, and future. I stepped over the branch, then stepped back across a couple times just to process my thoughts. Where I stood on the path—that was the present; the steps I had just taken— that was the past; the steps I now planned to take—that was the future. And once time passed, I could not go back and change it. To me, the past was very real, and the future would be set upon a foundation of what had happened before. So how could that not matter?

I could see that 'now is the time' was a belief, a social construction. Outsiders who chose to live by a clock were choosing to divide up their day by these arbitrary time slots. In the Love Family, we were choosing to put our focus on the present. I wanted it to make sense. If I was going to accept the beliefs, I wanted to at least understand them.

It seemed to me that time was a relative concept. What time it was depended on who I asked. I guess it didn't really matter too much to me, because in the end, it was the big people who made all the decisions, including when we were to leave the park that day.

The Family also did not have televisions, radios or phones in any of the houses, at least that I was aware of. To communicate what was happening, Love would send out messages through messengers. Although apparently, I heard that there was a phone in the Family's business office used for business purposes only, not general use. Years later, Cube City got a TV, but it was only used on certain rare times for movies that were screened and arranged in advanced for the children. I was often in the care of a woman named Understanding who would mute the commercials and act them out. She would make up funny scripts for the people selling the products in the commercials. I looked forward to the commercials when it was comic relief time. Coming from Alaska, though, it was nothing new to me to not have TV, since we never had modern conveniences such as phones or television there either.

The Love Family lifestyle was clean and simple, with very little furniture. People sat on the floor, basically. There were no couches, chairs or tables. I saw that when people ate, they often sat cross legged in a circle on a drop cloth, or in some cases, they sat cross legged on the floor around a table that was very low to the ground, like no higher off the ground than for an adult to just barely get their legs under.

Members generally did not sleep in typical beds either. It was only the elder of the household that had an actual bed and his own room. Because there were so many people, every bedroom wall had a double bunk, like a submarine. In the men's rooms, they often just used a sleeping bag in their bunk, but in the women's rooms, I noticed they had blankets and sheets that they used. There were others that used a foam pad on the floor for their bed scene, which would be rolled up during the day.

Also, there were no washers and dryers in the homes, so I saw people, men and women, helping with the laundry. Many times, I walked into the bathroom and saw members washing their laundry in the bathtub. Then it was wrung out and hung on the lines in the yards. No more trips to the laundromat as I had done so many times with my mom in Alaska.

Chores like laundry and yardwork were shared; members worked together in a teamwork like way in groups to get things done. Each Saturday, the day before Holy Day would be a day of work. Everyone would gather from the different houses in the common yards to work. I was too young to do very much at this point, so I ran around with some of the girls, collecting flower petals for fairy potions. I would squeeze the juice from the petals into a small bottle, then add other ingredients from the kitchen such as iodine, soy sauce and whatever I could find to give the potions special powers.

I loved playing with the other children who lived in Serious's Area. I had never had so many friends in my life. Until this point, I had only one friend, Brenda, and she had lived next door to us when we lived in Alaska in the tepee. But now I played with all sorts of kids.

We liked to play in this wonderful tree-house. It was the coolest treehouse I had ever seen. Right in the middle of the joining yards in Serious's Area was this gigantic Maple tree. Wooden stepping sticks were nailed into the trunk that went way up where there was a little house. I lugged pillows and blankets up the steps for a slumber party. Then, if you kept climbing past the treehouse, there was an even larger fenced platform or balcony that overlooked the entire yarded area between the houses. It was scary climbing up. One time, one of the stepping sticks gave way, and Cheerful fell and hurt himself—hit his head pretty hard. I don't remember if he ended up getting stitches or how badly he was hurt. He got hurt all the time because he played so rough, but he never seemed to mind. Cheerful was there mostly without his parents. I don't know what happened to his dad; His mom, Grace, was an artist, but was only there part of the time. Cheerful was very external about his emotions. He was true to his name which was cheerful quite a bit and had that contagious giggle, but when he was mad, he would fight.

One day we were playing near the tree-house.

"Punch me as hard as you can!" he challenged.

I wouldn't do it, at first, but he begged me.

"Oh, come on!" he whined.

Eventually, I punched him in the stomach, like he asked, and he didn't flinch.

"OK, now you try it," he challenged me. He made it look so easy.

"Why not?" I agreed.

He punched me, and I literally couldn't breathe for a few moments. I doubled over and almost passed out. Everything seemed a little woozy and I sat down. It was not taking long to get to know my new family.

The tree house was a center point of play during those years. There was a sandbox in this area too. We ran around freely in the yard and between the houses quite a bit. Gardens and lawns were immaculately maintained, lovingly cared for, and much commented on by adults. I loved to walk around and enjoy the flowers. There were a lot of daffodils and tulips that were a part of the landscaping, and coming from Alaska, I had never seen such flowers. Compared to the wild, untamed wilderness of Alaska, they seemed so domesticated and tame, yet simple and beautiful.

One day, I was playing with other children in the yard. We were by the clothes lines, just outside of Serious's house. Suddenly, a whole cacophony of male and female voices began to chant together. The chanting was coming out of the open window of Serious's house, just a few feet from where we were playing.

I heard a lot of chanting in the Love Family, especially before meals, and at meetings and gatherings. Whether there were four or thirty people present or whether there were one hundred or more, people regularly chanted together. It was a regular part of the culture. People would stand or sit in a circle, often holding hands while they chanted. When we first got there, I wondered about it and had questions. I asked one of the kids, "How do they chant that long?" The chanting would go on and on for minutes and minutes, but it seemed that when I chanted, I would quickly run out of breath. It was explained to me that when there is a group of people chanting, they all start and stop at different times, so it just sounds like it's a long time. Made sense.

As the chanting continued, a boy named Ravah sat down in the grass as if to meditate. He was one of the kids around my age. When I got there, he had shoulder length brown hair that he kept braided, and he wore a woven rainbow headband that held his hair out of his blue eyes. The chanting was particularly loud. When Ravah heard the chanting coming out of the window, he chose the moment to make fun of the chanting. He sat cross legged in the grass and sat up so straight that it looked like he was going to fall over, drunk. He got this very serious expression on his face and closed his eyes as we all sat there and watched. He opened his mouth way wider than one might need to chant. His chant sounded deep and throaty, like a cow. I couldn't help but laugh with the other children. It was good to feel like there were those there who I could relate to.

We weren't the big people, we were just us, the kids. At times, I saw the big people passing what they called the "tau" (pipe) or the bong around the circle. They were smoking marijuana which they called "mashish." If I was sitting in the meeting too, they passed it around me, since I was a kid and it was assumed I didn't do that. Marijuana was considered a sacrament. Hallucinogens such as LSD, mushrooms and peyote were less common but also considered sacraments. Sacraments were a controlled substance and handled by the elder or Love's priests and were considered holy, part of a spiritual, ritualistic activity that reinforced the Family's feeling of being one.

The kids did not do sacraments for the most part, especially in the early years when we were so young. If they did, I didn't know about it. Sacrament was something the big people did, at meetings or other holy events. I had no idea that there was a world on the outside that felt very differently about our "sacrament." Even before I got to the Love Family, I lived with my mother in the counterculture where marijuana was normal. But what was different for me was now seeing it in the context of a spiritual community where it was controlled and considered holy.

After I had been in the Love Family for several years, I was told by a member that if I smoked the flowers of Scotch Broom, that it would make me high. Scotch Broom was a shrub that grew, and it had the brightest of yellow flowers. The member said that if the leaves were smoked, it would be like the high of mashish but just "milder." Just for fun, I went with another girl out in the yard where we knew it grew and collected it. I helped to pack it into the bong, then we took turns inhaling it. It was a terrible tasting smoke. Maybe I didn't inhale it properly, or maybe we didn't smoke enough of it, but I never felt any different, just a sore throat for a while. It just confirmed my overall total disinterest in such a thing as sacrament.

My brother Forest had a memory that he shared with me about sacrament. He says he was probably around 7 when it happened, which means it was years after we joined.

"I wasn't really interested [in smoking mashish]," Forest recalled, "but one-time, Brotherhood and I took some [mashish] from someone's stash box and we took it out in the woods and wrapped it in newspaper and tried to smoke it, which didn't work at all. I think it just fell out onto the ground."

Bright also discussed with me his memories of sacrament:

"Unlike other kids, I wasn't exposed to drugs really," he says. "Way back when, somebody had given me a pipe to take a toke and I blew out. It all went flying! (laughing) That was about as close as I got, but I wasn't really drawn to it; I wasn't one of the one's asking for it."

Zarah remembered that mashish was "something that the adults did." She remembered seeing a secret area where it was kept, but said, "I didn't think of it as illegal; I just thought of it as normal."

Mashish was just one of those things that the big people did. It was as normal as a lot of the chanting that we did. I loved the chanting and thought it was beautiful. At meetings or special get togethers, Love would use his hand to act as a sort of conductor for everyone. He would indicate with his hand the notes, as if on a scale, that the men were to sing. At first, the men and women would chant together. Then, a woman named Simplicity would use her hand and direct the women's chanting. The notes the women would sing would often be higher on the scale to compliment the lower notes that the men were reaching. Once Simplicity directed the women's chanting for a period, Love, would direct the men's chanting. The chanting was a back and forth sort of relay between the genders, then Love and Simplicity both would bring the men's and the women's voices together in harmony. It was amazing to me to hear so many voices at the same time, all creating the same rich sound. That was one of the more beautiful sides of the oneness that we all shared and the oneness that I began to appreciate and feel a part of.

The chanting was one of the unique things that members of the Love Family would do together to express their oneness. Chanting happened every day, maybe twice a day or more. Another thing that was unique about the Love Family was the music. People usually did not play the radio or listen to music from the outside society. Instead, most of the music was written and put to music by members of the community who were musicians. Everyone would then sing songs together, daily. Music was an integral aspect of Love Family life. It unified us as a group and as a culture.

The lyrics for the songs we all sang together talked about our life in the Family, what we believed, and who we were as a group. Some lyrics were taken straight out of the Bible and put to music. Other lyrics came from the spiritual dreams or visions of individual members. The music was ethnic and folksy and had a distinct Love Family flavor.

Most of the music was created within our culture, but there were some songs that were incorporated from the outside culture into our music scene. There were a couple of Dylan songs that we sang, one of which was "Forever Young." Karen sang that one with the ladies in the choir, which she loved because she had always been a Dylan Freak before she came to the Family. Integrity's band did "Desolation Row." We also did that one by the Youngbloods, "Get together." At Christmas, we sang a lot of the standard Christmas carols too. We also sang the Beatles, "Let It Be." I'm sure there were others, but mostly the music was homegrown.

The kids sang right along with the adults, although, there were songs that were especially easy and fun, that the kids would sing more often. One of the songs I sang was, *"Glad to be a happy one, in the kingdom of heaven..."*

Dear Diary,

A Family song is going through my head:
"Here Oh Israel,
the Lord our God,
the Lord our God is one."

Rachel Israel

In addition to all the singing that everyone did, the Love Family had their own rock bands, that were composed of members who were musicians. The bands would play at Love Family parties or they would sometimes perform outside of the Family. The Family's 'National Band' appeared on rock concert bills at the Eagles Auditorium with established groups like Junior Cadillac and others. Resolve and Solidity, two brothers who were members, had a jazz band called the Solid Resolve. The Love Family bands would play at the Seattle Peace Concerts at Gasworks or Volunteer Park. I got to go too, at times, because Understanding took a group of children with her, and she would put on puppet shows for the children at the concert to entertain them. I helped her set up and take down a gigantic puppet theater that had been made for her that she would use. I ran around freely during the concert or climbed the monkey trees to peak out the branches at the band and everyone while they danced.

The crowd at the Peace concert was diverse and more of a counterculture type scene, mostly young, hippie types. I watched the dancers and took note of how differently they danced from Love Family people. They would wiggle around and do all these moves that I didn't see in the Family. Love Family people would dance in this distinct way. They would twirl around, lift-up their arms, sway back and forth. It was these generic, conservative moves, again and again. Whereas the people who were not from the Love Family were boogying down in all sorts of suggestive ways. I loved to dance, so I got out there and started wiggling around. No one in the Love Family would wiggle when they danced. Understanding saw me dancing, and later I overheard her telling another member about how funny it was to see me wiggling around.

Understanding was very theatrical. She wiggled around, imitating the way I had danced. She was making fun of me, but she made it funny, so I laughed too and enjoyed the extra attention.

The Love Family was a conservative community in a lot of ways. Even at the peace concert, Love Family people all dressed similarly in a style of dress that was unique to the Family. All the children that I played with were dressed similarly in handmade, ethnic cotton clothing. The Women and girls wore hand-made long dresses or long skirts; Everyone had long hair, even the men and boys. Everyone usually wore their hair in braids to keep their hair out of their faces. The men and boys also often wore a headband. All the adult men had full mustaches and long beards.

The Bible was very specific in its instruction to not cut hair:

Ye shall not round the corners of your heads, neither shalt thou mar the corner of thy beard. (Leviticus 19:27, *KJV*)

The Bible didn't say anything about women shaving legs and armpits, but in the Love Family, women didn't do that either. Men and women just letting their hair grow wasn't just a biblical thing, though, it was also just because it was natural, which was in line with countercultural thinking of the times.

When I came to the Love Family, I noticed that the women would brush the hair of the men and helped keep everyone's hair braided. There might have been a hundred people or more, on any given morning, that all needed their hair braided, because everyone had long hair. I learned right away how to braid my own hair and always kept it out of my face that way. I sometimes would help brush and braid some of the women's hair, just to help out. There was a woman named Jezreal who had long, thick, black curly hair, and she would seek me out to help her brush her hair. She said I did it the best, so I was glad to help her out whenever I could. In the Love Family, there were no mirrors of any kind in any of the rooms, which was to encourage people to see themselves in others and to avoid the pitfalls of vanity.

The dress codes were strict in the early days. Over time, it became somewhat more relaxed but not a whole lot. On special occasions and at morning meetings, the men wore robes, and women wore their finest dress and a shawl around their shoulders. I didn't have summer clothes that I would wear in the summer and winter clothes that I wore in the winter. It was the same dress code all year round. In the summer, almost no one wore shorts, but on hot days, the men and boys would often wear a kiltlike loincloth around.

The kids pretty dressed like the adults for the most part. We clearly looked like little hippie kids dressed in ethnic fashions. I heard the boys complain that when they went on a trip to the World, they had been mistaken for girls; I could tell they were bothered by that and a bit embarrassed.

The way we dressed was more noticeable when we went to places like the circus, which we sometimes did, or to a public park. I got used to people staring at us. The way they stared did not seem hostile, it just seemed like they were curious. There was this whole mentality, that I was now a part of, which was an 'us and them' mentality, and the way that people dressed in the Family differentiated us from them. But I never made judgments about people in that way, at least not consciously. My mind went to just trying to understand the deeper meanings. People remember me as a quiet child, but my mind was not quiet; I was often deep in the many layers of my thoughts. There were times when I would walk by Coe school with other Family children on our way to and from the Front Door Inn to Love's or Serious's Areas. We would watch the kids playing at recess as we walked by. Clearly, we were different. One day, I was walking with other Family children. We were passing Coe School during their recess. A couple of the children at recess came up to the fence as we walked by:

"Why aren't you in school?" one of them asked us, in a snotty manner.

"Why are you dressed that way?" another child asked us.

"I don't know, why are you in there?" one of the Family kids I was with answered rhetorically, and "Why are you dressed that way?"

They just stared back at us from behind the chain-link fence, silently. We kept walking.

As I walked, I thought about their question. Why were we dressed this way? I wasn't sure why. We just were. All my clothes up to this point had been hand-made, so the outfits that Karen had made for me in Alaska fit right in with the Love Family look. The way that we dressed in the Love Family was not hippie-dippy with tie-dyes and trippy peace symbols and such; it was hippie in some ways, but it was more a cross between that and an ancient biblical, Old Testament look.

A diary entry I had made talked specifically about clothes:

Dear Diary,

My favorite clothes:
My long, blue velvet and satin skirt,
Green, blue, and white silk, hand woven skirt and blouse,
Long white dress that used to be a wedding dress.
My blue and brown Afghani dress
My pink and purple Afghani dress

Rachel Israel

When I came to the Love Family, as I said, I got to keep some of my clothes that I had brought from Alaska. They fit into the Love Family's style, but many people did not get to keep things they brought with them when they joined. Everything was turned into the center as a donation. Upon joining the Love Family, members gave up Worldly belongings, including jewelry, money, property, or anything else that would then be donated to the Center, and then, as I discussed earlier, Love would redistribute it as he saw fit.

A Bible passage in the book of Acts addressed it:

"And the multitude of them that believed were of one heart and of one soul: neither said any of them that ought of the things which he possessed was his own; but they had all things common." Acts 4:32 (*King James Version*)

I imagine though that our system of distribution was more communistic, than it was Biblical or similar to the hippie communes of the times. Communism would be a society in which all property is publicly owned, and each person works and is paid according to their abilities and needs. Right, this would fit the Love Family, as long as it was clear that Love was the absolute overarching authority who was in charge of the entire operation. And 'publicly owned' would mean, essentially, Love owned. And of course, no one got paid, but Love did make an attempt to utilize some members abilities and meet certain basic needs, more so earlier on.

It had been a few years after losing my pennies that day at Parsons Gardens. My grandmother, Phyllis bought me these gold post earrings. I had desperately wanted to get my ears pierced and was so happy to get them, but after she gave them to me, an elder took me aside and told me I had to turn them in to Love. I was very disappointed and sad. I turned them in as I was instructed, and Love gave them to Wisdom. I would see her wearing them and I would have to hold back my tears. I was hoping Love would've given them back to me. He sometimes would do that.

My mom was still gone after she'd been kicked out. She was trying to decide if she wanted to join or where we would go or live instead. While she was gone, I tried to do the best I could to get along and get used to how things worked. But without her, I was pretty much on my own to figure it out. Forest cried a lot. Neither one of us was used to being without her, but I could handle it better since I was quite a bit older. Forest was now talking and had started calling me, "La-la."

I felt like I had walked into another world. No one sat me down and gave me the handouts. One day, I was over at Serious's house and I walked across the room and opened this glass door to the sanctuary. Usually I went in there to play with the piano over by the fireplace, but this time, I unknowingly walked in on a bunch of people having a meeting. There were at least 40 to 50 people, maybe more, all silent and sitting cross-legged on the floor in a huge circle. Before I realized I was interrupting a meeting, I had already walked several paces into the room. Everyone stared at me, jarred. I was frightened, like a deer caught in the headlights. Serious addressed me in an authoritarian tone:

"Please leave and come back in and bow."

Confused and frightened, I walked out of the room and came back in and stood there, ashamed and embarrassed. I wasn't sure what he wanted of me.

The people in the room were all still silent and watchful. Serious sat at the head of the circle and looked up at me expectantly as he put his hands together and tilted his head forward in a bow. Everyone watched him bow.

When he was done with his demonstration, he looked directly at me and waited. The people in the room all silently watched me bow.

"When you enter into the presence of Jesus Christ, we bow," Serious instructed.

I had no idea what he was talking about, but I did as I was told. It was that moment when I realized how serious this life was, how one little thing like walking into a room could be the end of me.

There was a lot of bowing that was expected. I was to bow when I enter a room, when I see an elder, and certainly when I see Love.

Ravah would imitate bowing to make us laugh. With an extremely serious expression on his face, he held his palms together and tilted his head forward in a pretend, exaggerated bow. As his head came forward, his whole body became stiff, and he fell forward, so his face gently hit the ground and flattened out his nose. He bulged out his eyes to look like a zombie as he bowed to no one in particular. The seriousness of the moment didn't last a second before we were all busting up laughing. We each took our turns bowing to each other in mock seriousness. It became a mini competition to see who could get the most laughs. It was good we had each other so as not to take it all too seriously.

I knew eventually Karen would be back. She always came back for me, but I also missed Marty and our life in Alaska. I was just going to have to be careful and learn how to live here and adapt. I didn't have much of a choice. Karen taught me survival from early on. She taught me how to be resilient and creative. I had seen, as a young child, how people lived on the beach in Maui; I had seen very young, how to live on the road with just a backpack and some potatoes; and I had lived with my family in a tepee in the woods without tap water or electric heat. It was pretty clear to me here in this environment that survival, in this case, meant get with the program.

After about a month, Karen did end up coming back. I walked in on her, crying on Encouragement's shoulder. She had decided to stay for good and had to tell Marty. The ladies at Encouragement's household were so happy that she was back, because baby Forest had been a handful. She wrote Marty and told him we weren't coming back. He didn't know and just thought we were visiting grandpa.

My mom never talked to me about her decision, but over time, it just became self-evident. Our home was now with these people. We weren't going back to our life in Alaska.

Marty was hurt. Karen invited him to come and join the Love Family too, but he said no. That's why he had moved from LA in the first place; it was to get away from all the people. He was happy in Alaska. Even if Marty had joined, our family unit would have been finished. The whole nature of relationships was changed in the Love Family.

How it worked was that people didn't get "married," in the Love Family. Love, the leader, would decide that two people could be together, and he would 'sanction' them. So, if a couple was sanctioned, then that would be like saying they were married. Only with Love's blessing could individuals be sanctioned. If a couple came to the Family already married, they would usually not be together once they joined. The past and any relationship associated with it was no longer an important part of one's identity. "The past is the past" I heard people say, which meant that who they were before they joined wasn't important anymore. They had given up their former lives to be a part of the group.

Not only that, but when they came, each adult member would be expected to be celibate for at least six months. Sex was not called "sex." It was called "getting together." Either way, you couldn't do that for at least six months. A lot of people assume that because the Love Family was so alternative and communal, that sex was freely shared around. It was not that way. Sexual relations were very controlled. Men and women slept separately in different quarters. Members also could not get together with someone who lived on the outside. I had heard of a member who had been kicked out for having relations with someone who wasn't a member. Especially in the earlier years, it was very strict. Some people were celibate for a lot longer than just six months, sometimes several years or more. One man who I talked to said he was celibate the entire time he was there–eight years! Karen was celibate for many years as well. Celibacy weeded out the less committed and provided an environment where men and women could relate to each other on non-sexual terms, like brothers and sisters. I talk more about this subject in a later chapter.

Of course, kids didn't get sanctioned, but there were teenagers that came to the Love Family who ended up in adult roles and sanctioned, with some controversy in certain cases. A man named Israel told me he was 17 when he joined. A woman named Serenity was 16. I know of others who were 15 and 16 years old when they came, even younger than that. There was one girl who came who was only eight years old! She came on her own without her parents, claiming to have had visions that drew her, just like a lot of the other, older people who joined. Children weren't generally sanctioned into sexual relationships, but how do you define "child?" In the Love Family, no one had ages; everyone was considered, 'eternal.'

"Why did you join the Love Family?" I asked my mom, years later.

She told me that she had been looking for a commune, but that the Love Family wasn't really a commune.

"It was a kingdom," she explained. "Typically, a commune is where a bunch of hippies live in a house and share each other's clothes," she explained, and "everybody is equal in everything. We had visited communes like that, where there was no continuity, where everyone was always arguing and interrupting each other." The Love Family wasn't like that at all. It had a clear hierarchy where some people had more than others. It was more of an alternative community, very organized. It "had its act together" my mom had thought. She liked also that it had a school with real teachers. She had been considering homeschooling me but thought that the Family school "was a nice middle ground."

Another thing that she said she liked:

"Nobody smoked or drank [cigarettes or alcohol], and there wasn't any heavy drug taking. "It was a chore to get accepted though," she says. "You had to do things the way the head lady said to do them."

My mom had always been her own head lady but now she had to learn how to live with a whole bunch of people, where there were proscribed roles and clear patterns of authority.

"[In the Love Family,]" my mom continued, "we were super into cleanliness in a way that I wasn't used to. In Alaska, you just got used to dirtiness. It was clean dirt, you were out in the woods."

When my mom came to the Love Family, she was ambivalent:

"I had mixed feelings," she says, "but not enough to head out on my own. I figured that what I didn't like about the Family was a lot less than what

I didn't like about the World." She says that she was "disgusted with society and with the values that were common, like materialism."

One day, I was watching my mom. She had recently returned and was in the kitchen, and there was a woman teaching her how to make rice. I couldn't believe it. She knew how to cook rice! She had been a survivalist in Alaska. In the Love Family though, members had their own unique way of doing things. It was the Family way, and if someone couldn't accept it, then they had to leave.

"It was hard to accept the hierarchy, but you had to" she says.

Even though Karen was back, she wasn't back in terms of taking care of me. It seemed she no longer made the decisions. Love did. Love was the anointed King. I realized over time the significance of this and how that would play out in my life, but early on, I learned right away that this man was a very big deal—and don't ever forget to bow when you see him!

One day, I was with some of the children who lived there, and we walked casually pass Love, chatting and laughing, as children do, without paying him any attention. He stopped us with an air of indignant, parental authority and sternly asked, "Why didn't you bow to me?" He sounded perturbed and hurt.

Love continued to look at us expectantly, waiting for us to bow to him. I stood there with maybe three or four other children of varying ages. We all bowed to him in unison. It was a serious moment. I obviously had screwed up, again.

Not bowing to Love was one small example of how I learned how to get along there. I learned mostly through imitation, trial and error. There was quite a bit of natural incentive to just do what you see others doing. If a child got in trouble, they would either be called on the floor for it and that could be humiliating, possibly very embarrassing, or downright upsetting. If children were naughty, they would also sometimes get the 'rod,' as I had found out early on when I went over the Charter with Seth. The other thing that could happen, if they didn't get the rod, would be separation, and separation could be worse than a verbal or physical lashing. I saw the pain it caused, when children were separated out, put in a closet or in some isolated room. I learned pretty fast how to avoid getting into trouble. I went above and beyond avoiding to where I would try to be a helpful and a positive spirit to those around me, insuring their affection and admiration so I never had to worry about punishment.

It was especially important to be good around Love, and everyone seemed to be under more pressure, when he was around, to make sure he was happy. From day one, Love had more privileges than anyone else. He ate better for one. When I would have a sleepover at his house with one of his daughters, for example, I noticed that they had better food, special cheeses, eggs and meats. It was quite different than in my own household where we would eat a lot of brown rice and salad. That discrepancy in privilege was not as noticeable in the early years, but over time, it became more pronounced and problematic and will be discussed as my story unfolds.

"What did you think of Love?" I ask my mom one day after we had left the community. I wanted to know what her initial impressions of him had been.

"He wasn't that great," she says, "but he was a draw in that he started this thing and held it together for that long. It was kind of like if you lived in a little country and there was a king. It wasn't a big deal if I was compatible with the king. What was a big deal was that he held the kingdom together so that I could live there."

As a child, I had a constant opportunity to observe this king and his relationships with people who joined. He was served and waited on like a real king. When he came in the room, he instantly became the center of attention. At all times, at every moment, he was in command, orchestrating the social and physical landscape. He was adored by all and feared by most, described by adults as handsome and charismatic. When he looked at me, it felt like he could see right through me and read my innermost feelings and thoughts.

On the outside, he seemed to care how the children were getting along, but I grew to fear him, because of the great power that he had over everyone's lives. He had blue eyes and long, medium brown hair and a long beard, just like all the adult men, but he carried himself with authority and with an attitude of self-importance. He also dressed more like a king. He wore his robe more often. I noticed at times he wore a gold and lapis necklace. I heard that lapis was his favorite. When he wore his robe, he wore it with a wide sash that made him look more like royalty. Without his leadership, it was assumed, the entire Love Family machinery would grind to a halt. His authority was absolute in almost every imaginable way.

It seemed out-of-the-blue, when Love decided that Encouragement and Lois, the elders at our household, were going to Hawaii. Suddenly, we didn't have a household anymore.

I was sent to go live next store, at Serious's household where I was taken care of by the teachers—Eve and Caleb. Eve had long, brown hair, and freckles. She was in the process of taking classes at the University, so she could help keep the Love Family school certified and legal. While she was gone, Caleb, who later became known as Definition, oversaw the kids. I liked him right away. He was a very easy-going guy and seemed to know how to relate to the kids. He was tall and skinny. His light brown hair was long, just past his shoulders and held back in a ponytail or braid. He wore a shorter, almost goatee like beard, not on purpose but just because that is the way it grew. We would all chant the times tables together aloud to memorize them.

I would see my mom sometimes, but mostly I did not see her much. I am not sure where she was living. She wasn't involved with the kids as a caretaker. It seemed that the kids were somewhat segregated from adults and from their parents. We would all be together, but the kids would be separate. For example, if everyone went out in the yard to work, all the kids would be working together with caretakers on a certain area of the yard. The adults would be working amongst themselves on other areas nearby. It wasn't always like that, but it was a lot.

The Love Family was communal, so biological family units were not recognized or emphasized. So even though my own mother was not involved in my care now, it seemed that it was like that for a lot of children. Designated members took care of the kids. Some kids were in the same households with their parents, but they still were taken care of by teachers, guardians, caretakers and members who were like nannies.

If there was a parent who was involved with the kids, it was in a lesser role as a helper or guardian, or they just happened to be assigned to what was called, 'Kid Watch.' People would ask, "Who's on 'Kid Watch' today?"

Understanding was in charge of the kids most the time. She was like the head kid lady. She made all the major decisions under the guidance of Love. But she had helpers who were assigned to her on a regular basis.

Parent-child relationships weren't a focus, so the attachment to my own mother was not fostered. It had been replaced. I had new attachments to the other children who I was close to and to my new caretakers, who became like family to me. I attached myself to those who were more involved in my care on a day to day basis, out of survival. I didn't see much choice. I saw what happened to kids who protested the loss of their parents; they didn't get love and attention from anybody when they were getting in trouble all the time.

If a child was misbehaving, they would be assigned a personal guardian and would often be separated out from the main group of children. I was paying attention to who was getting in trouble and why, since I was trying hard to get along. At some point, I was sent from Serious's house to go live with Understanding. She resided with the largest group of the community's children, in Love's Area in a house everyone called, the 'Kids' House.' This was all still during the first year that I was in the Love Family, so 1975. Understanding was warm and focused entirely on caring for the needs of the children in her care. Instead of oatmeal, I ate granola with milk and honey at her table with maybe 10–15 other children. At the Kids' House, most of the children shared a room. I shared the bottom bunk of a Queen-sized bed with three other girls around my age, Neriah, Heaven, and Gentle.

Living at the Kids' House was much more relaxed than living in a household full of adult members, like I did when I lived at Encouragement's or Serious's. Understanding would let us have contests to see who could stay up the latest. There were times, the kids played Monopoly all night. There would be kids crashed out on the floor in the morning. Fake money would be everywhere.

On one occasion, Understanding let Heaven and I stay up really late. For some reason, she and I had Understanding to ourselves one night. I am not sure where the other children were that evening. We asked Understanding to tell us the story of the apple tree. It was our favorite at that time. The tree had a magical world underneath it. Understanding made Heaven and I characters in the story just to make it more fun. There was a magical opening in the trunk to get to the world under the tree. Later that night and after the story, Understanding let us cut up goat cheese (Gjetost) into little squares, and we pretended that the cheese squares were medicine. We ate them slowly, so the squares would last all night long. We ended up eating the whole brick that night. The cheese was a special treat, because at that time, it was only served on Holy Day. I enjoyed living at the Kids' House with Understanding, who seemed like she just wanted us to have fun.

At the Kids' House, I didn't know how old any of the other kids were. I was taught that I was 'eternal,' which meant that people in the Love Family did not celebrate their birthdays and believed we would live forever.

The Bible is littered with references that were used to bolster the basis of our beliefs:

> Verily, verily, I say unto you, He that believeth on me hath everlasting life. (John 6:47; See also John 5:24, 11:25–26; Romans 6:6–7, all *KJV*)

I internalized that belief to the point where it became seamless. For example, Understanding took a group of children to the circus one year. We each got a bag of home popped popcorn and we sat down to eat it, filling up three rows. Since we all dressed ethnically and looked distinct as a group, there were people who sat near our rows who looked at us curiously. There was a couple of women in a nearby row that I saw talking to Understanding. They asked her questions about us.

"How old are they?" They wanted to know.

"Why don't you ask the children?" Understanding answered one of the women, then stepped over to where I was sitting and asked me to come with her. She also asked Cheerful to come too. We followed her over to where the women were sitting. We stood in front of them with Understanding behind us. They smiled at us. We stared back at them, silent, awkward.

"How old are you?" one of the women asked.

"Eternal."

"What?" she says, looking confused.

"Eternal," I tell her again.

She looked at Understanding confused.

Understanding told the women that in our family, we did not celebrate birthdates. We believed "we were spiritual beings and would live forever."

While she continued talking to the lady, Cheerful and I were directed to return to our seats. It was a curious interaction to me where the boundary became evident between where the Love Family ended and where the world outside began. It was a rare moment of clarity for me to see people from outside of our culture looking at us like we were different. I did not often get that perspective when I lived in the Love Family, because we were living in our own little world that had little contact with outsiders who, to me themselves, seemed like the ones' who were different and who I was curious about.

"What was it like being eternal?" I asked Bright, many years later.

"I felt self-conscious about being eternal," he answered. "I usually told people I was a turtle as a joke which confused them," he says. "Or sometimes, I would make up an age. I said I was six for a few years. Then, I thought, well by now I must be about nine, so then I said nine." Bright continued, "I was self-conscious about some of the clothes I wore too and my long hair."

I did not feel embarrassed or self-conscious about being eternal. I was more curious about what it meant. I wanted to understand. *Who were we? Who were they? Why do we believe this? What does it mean?*

I knew that the Seattle Police had a problem with us being eternal, because the Love Family resisted Worldly laws and regulations when it came to age. Everyone was 'eternal,' so it made it impossible for people to get driver's licenses. I knew there had been arrests. Members of the Love Family were sent to jail for refusing to provide their age. My caretaker, Understanding was one of those that this happened to. She was pulled over for running a stop sign while riding a bicycle. When she was questioned by the police, she told them her name, 'Understanding,' and that she had no identification or date-of-birth, because she was eternal. She was arrested and taken to jail.

It took several hours to book her, because when they entered her name into the computer, the machine did not recognize 'Understanding' as a name. The machine started printing out hundreds of pages of random numbers. A *Seattle Times* reporter named Diane Alters wrote a comical article about it the next day, titled, "Jail? It's a misUnderstanding." (*Seattle Times*, Aug 16, 1977 pg. C19)

The Seattle Police eventually became more tolerant of the Love Family's beliefs and practices, but in other parts of the country, in places where they were not familiar with the Love Family, they often were not as sympathetic. There were members who spent weeks in jail, others who were interrogated, beat up and assaulted, which I talk about shortly.

It is hard for me to imagine Understanding being arrested after coming to know her like I did, but her story was unusual to begin with. From time to time, she would tell us about how she came to the Love Family. She had been married to Phil Rockefeller, a politician, and he had taken her daughters from her when she joined. She told us in detail about how her ex-husband had her locked up in a psychiatric ward, and how she had been put in a straightjacket to keep her from leaving him, to force her into marital counseling. People did not talk about the past in the Family, but this part of her past was important because it was part of her testament of faith that brought her to Love. In other words, nothing could keep her from Love and from taking care of us here in the Kingdom of Heaven, not Phil Rockefeller, not a strait Jacket. She told that story many times. I always felt sad that she had been unable to bring her daughters to the Love Family, and it angered me when she explained how her ex-husband knew the judges and treated her so unfairly. Phil Rockefeller was a person of much power and influence. Understanding explained how he had used it to influence the system in his favor. Her daughters would have been like sisters to me.

Her ex-husband was from a place everyone called, "The World." I got the impression, at least according to how it was talked about, that the world was a pretty bad place. If something was "Worldly," that had negative connotations. I heard that a lot. The world was a place where people were lost and someday, they would all realize and "come home." They would come home to us, to their real family, the family of God.

The way things were done in the World was not how we did them in the Love Family, down to every last detail. For example, women in the Family did not wear make-up because that was considered Worldly. It was superficial, fake, not natural.

When my gramma Phyllis came for a visit once, she was wearing make-up, and her make-up, style of dressing, and even her mannerisms were considered very Worldly. She was from "The World."

I now lived on a spiritual plane and didn't live anymore in that ungodly place. The message I got was, this is who we are; and that is who they are, and that doesn't belong here. There was a lot of distinguishing going on and a lot of defining of boundaries. Logic told a *Weekly* reporter, "We're trying to do our darndest to keep the church free, clean, and innocent of The World." (*Weekly*, Dec 1–7, 1982 pg. 33) Logic was a head elder. He was higher up in the hierarchy of elders, close to Love. He was just one step down from Love himself, along with Serious. If the church was 'free, clean, and innocent," what did that make the World? The message to me was that the World was not-free, unclean, and not-innocent, and I was receiving messages like this constantly. I heard a lot that 'we were in the world but not of the World.' There were several passages that I heard read and quoted often.

> If ye were of the world, the world would love his own: but because ye are not of the world, but I have chosen you out of the world, therefore the world hateth you. John 15:19 *KJV*

> They are not of the world, even as I am not of the world. (John 17:19 *KJV*)

> Do not love the world or the things in the world. If anyone loves the world the love of the father is not in him. (John 2:15 *KJV*)

The World must be a bad place, if the Bible said there was no God in the World. Not only that but the Bible was saying that if I were to love the World, then God would not be in me. The message was pretty clear to my child-like mind. *The World was bad. The Love Family is good.*

The Love Family's view of the outside culture was influenced by the Bible, but it was also consistent with the thinking of the times. Before I was brought to the community when my mom and I were on the road: The main attitude among countercultural hippie types was that society was "screwed up," and the larger culture's predominant mainstream institutions were "bad." The messages about mainstream society that I was receiving in the Love Family were similar to what I received before we joined: My new family was holier than, better than those on the outside. Everyone in the Love Family saw the 'truth' and had 'come home' to Heaven on Earth. People in the outside culture were lost, confused, and living mundane, superficial lives that weren't real. This was what I was taught, year after year, growing up in the Love Family.

All the adults around me were enthusiastic, very idealistic and passionate about what they believed. And I wanted to believe with them that my family, the Love Family was this important place. I felt the excitement too, without understanding the full picture.

In my day-to-day life at the Kids' House I was taught the skills needed to connect, to be a fully spiritual being, such as meditation. I sat on the floor cross legged in a circle with the other children. If I wasn't sitting up straight enough, Understanding would walk around with a long, skinny stick and tap lightly on my back. For those children who refused to sit still, they would have to go sit by themselves in the back bedroom or would be placed in the care of a personal guardian. If I peeked my eyes open, I would be told to shut them. I was taught to sit in the half lotus which was to sit cross legged but with one calf and foot on top of the other. Some kids seemed double jointed and could sit in the full lotus, which was cross legged, but looked like one's legs were tied in a knot. One kid would get up, while he sat in the full lotus, and he would walk around on his knees, just to show off.

When I meditated, I was told to 'give light,' and to 'love the entire universe.' Then I was taught to focus on what was called the Golden Triangle.' It was an exercise that helped rid my mind of those distracting thoughts. I tried to imagine a golden triangle in my mind, but try as I might, I never could see it.

One of my clearest memories of meditating was a meditation led by one of my teachers, a woman named Dedication. I sat with several other children on a Persian carpet in the sanctuary by the window. There was a sanctuary in every house. It was an unfurnished room with just a carpet. There were usually small square decorative pillows for seating, placed in a circle on the carpet. Then, along one wall, sat a small table covered with a table runner or embroidered doily, upon which sat a Bible, a Charter, a candle, or sometimes incense in a brass incense holder.

All the children sat with Dedication in a circle near the window where the light poured in on us. We needed the window light since in the Love Family, we did not use electricity for heating or lighting. For this meditation, I was told to imagine leaving my body. I floated up with the other children as I was told, in my imagination. We looked down at the house and at all of us, sitting there in a circle meditating. Then I was told to keep going higher, so now I could see the rooftops of several houses, then higher to where I could see the whole neighborhood. I could see the sandbox and the treehouse, and the street. Then slowly, we floated back down into our bodies, opened our eyes and saw one another once again. I preferred to go on trips like this, above our house than just sitting there and unsuccessfully trying to see a golden triangle.

There was a lot of meditation in the Love Family. Every morning, before school, there was a meditation for the kids. I preferred not to meditate, but it ended up being helpful to me as it taught me self-control, will power and ways to manage stress. But back then, meditation was a daily spiritual practice that was mostly very boring as it required long periods of time just sitting.

The meditations with the children were facilitated by different members at different times. But during my first year in the Love Family, it was Understanding that did them each morning. Understanding was strict, but she was also very loving. During times when we weren't in school, she served hot cocoa for us and would let us have little tea parties with a tea set of small, doll-sized dishes. She was a gifted storyteller and told us stories about the Grabbits and the Snatchems. If I lost my coat or other items, it was the Grabbits and Snatchems that took it. Understanding said that they were little people that lived underground in a place that reminded me of Willy Wonka's chocolate factory. As we traveled through their land, they could grab children if they were fighting. Each child who was listening to the story got to be a character in the story, and our characters in the story were identical to our characters in real life. It was fiction, but because each child was in the story, it seemed to be so much more. The characters in the story would say things that sounded like something the child would say in their real life outside the story, which made it more believable. Understanding was also gifted with theater skills, so she would act out the parts to make it more like a movie, which made it more interesting and funny.

Understanding told us about the 'La's and the Va's' which were two opposing families of people that lived on separate hills, but hills that were right next to one another. The two family's fought, but eventually the La's and the Va's stopped being 'separate' and against each other and came together to form the word 'Love.' I actually thought that it was a Bible story, because the story had such a strong moral component, but eventually I realized it was just made up. There were other stories she told as well. Some were based on the Old Testament like Noah's ark and Adam and Eve. Others were stories based on the New Testament and the parables of Jesus. One of my favorites was about the man who built his house on the rock and the man who built his house on the sand. It came from a parable that Jesus told as part of the Sermon on the Mount as told in Matthew, 7:24-27). Understanding dramatized this story and personally acted out each part of each family member in these two families, so it became this elaborate story with complex characters and a layered storyline. Understanding was fantastically entertaining and talented, and she was a gifted comedian as well.

Bright also remembered Understanding and her stories.

"The Bible stories that we read [with Understanding] embodied moral lessons," he says. "I came away with who I approved of and who I didn't in those characters and stories."

Bright was smart and clear-eyed, a natural leader, and very well liked among the kids.

"It was like [Understanding] had a natural gift for stage production and script writing," Bright says. "But she used that gift to tell us stories. It was very entertaining and especially since there were no televisions in the Love Family."

Understanding was an amazing puppeteer as well and would put on full scale shows using a puppet theater. She had a large-scale toothbrush, and the puppets would talk about the importance of brushing one's teeth.

Understanding was not a teacher. She was more our main caretaker or guardian who took care of us outside of school. She was a natural teacher, though, and even though she did not teach academics, I learned other things from her. She taught meditation. She taught about the Bible. She also taught Native and African American culture and history. Understanding had Native

American heritage, and she felt strongly that we needed to learn about diversity, because while the Love Family was somewhat diverse, she was concerned that it was also predominantly Caucasian. So one of the things she did was she would take us on fieldtrips to local Indian reservations where we sang Love Family songs for the Native children.

One year, Understanding had us pick out one of our favorite toys. We were to give it to one of the Native children for Christmas. All I had to give was this stuffed snowman. It was called a 'Snowboy.' He was given to me by a man everyone called, Chuck the Cheese Man. I wrapped up my Snowboy, and I got to give him to one of the Native children on the reservation. It was an exercise in giving and sharing with those in need, but here I was with nothing myself. Luckily, I wasn't super attached to it. Kids in the Love Family did not have commercial toys like children did in the World. If there were any toys, they were handmade, and so far, I didn't have any of those.

There were other things that Understanding did to build us a multi-cultural awareness. There were at least two or three years in a row when she took us to the Indian Pow Wow. We would sing our Love Family songs for them, then we participated in their cultural dances. In front of the tribe, we all danced the Native way, round and round to the drumming. We couldn't just dance any dance; there was only one we were allowed to dance. It was called the 'Honkey' dance. Honkey was a derogatory name for white people, I learned. I was fascinated by their dress and celebration. I was learning that there were others, Native Americans, who saw us differently than how we saw ourselves, and that they had different lives and histories.

When I was under Understanding's care, she made sure I was fed and clothed and that I had a nap each day. I never had to take naps before. This was when I lived at the Kid's House, very early on. One day she had a difficult time getting all the kids to nap. There was crying and tantrums. As she walked towards the door after we had all finally laid down to nap, she said to no one in particular, "You don't want a nap now, but someday you are going to really look forward to having one!" then she walked out and firmly shut the door, and I thought, *how could that ever be?*

Understanding was considered like an elder for the kids. She worked closely with Love to make sure we were learning the spiritual beliefs of the

Love Family and passing on to us what Love wanted us to learn.

Love wanted us to learn the arts, so he was encouraging when she arranged for me and a group of other children to take ballet lessons from a man named John George. There were already a group of Family women who were taking ballet over at Coe school down the street, so it seemed to make sense that the children would get to do it too.

Dear Diary,

I got to take ballet lessons at Coe school with a man named John George. Hope and Bright were the only two boys in the class, but then Bright ended up the only boy because Hope dropped out complaining that he was getting unwanted sexual attention.

Rachel Israel

Bright was one of the children that lived at the Kids' House with me. He had long brown hair that he mostly wore in a long braid down his back.

"What do you remember about Understanding?" I asked him, in recent years.

"I have only good memories of Understanding," he says. "She was looking out for the kids' interests and did an outstanding job with the resources. She was one of the few people that went out of their way to be with the kids and seemed to really genuinely love what she was doing."

The first time Bright went to buy shoes, it was with Understanding:

"Before she got me those shoes," Bright remembered, "I had walked around and stubbed my toes constantly, and had bloody toes, from walking around on the cement of Seattle on Queen Anne, barefoot…"

When I lived at the Kids House with Understanding, I met a lot of interesting new friends. Neriah, one of the girls I shared a bed with, seemed to think she knew how old she was and told me she was nine. She had a little brother who was quite younger than her named Zoar. Zoar was very fair skinned. He had such blond hair that his hair truly looked white. Then, he had blue eyes and round, rosy cheeks. Neriah looked nothing like her brother.

She had long, brown hair, brown eyes and bucky looking teeth. She seemed very serious all the time and was mature enough that Understanding would assign her to help with younger kids. When Neriah was taking care of the younger kids, she did this thing where she would bite the kids, if they didn't behave themselves.

There was one day when I was helping Neriah with the younger children. One of the kids was not listening to her and she bit him. She warned me though:

"Make sure you don't bite them if they are old enough to talk," she told me. Maybe she was too young herself to be babysitting.

One of the most amazing things that I learned from Neriah was about fairies. She would take me, and other girls our age, out in the garden, and she would tell us stories of the fairies lives. In vivid detail, I learned how they lived and how to make fairy potions. We made them houses to live in. We would leave the fairies gifts of marbles, which they seemed to take in the night, because in the morning, when we went out to check, the marbles were gone. It was wonderful fun to know the fairies had been there and had taken the marbles.

Neriah and Zoar came with their mother, Salem and their step-father Nathaniel. They all had lived in a commune in Canada before they came. I heard that she and Zoar had been given hallucinogenic mushrooms before they came to the Love Family. A few years later, their parents died in a car accident and Neriah was taken out of the Love Family by her grandmother, so I never saw her again. I always missed her after that and I was sad to lose her as a sister.

There was another girl who I lived with at the Kids' House, who I knew by a couple different names, but who eventually became known as Heaven. She was a couple years younger than I and still had her baby fat, so if I was seven when I came, she must've been five or six. She had long, brown hair. Her skin was a little darker than mine and she had a few freckles sprinkled on her nose.

Heaven and I hit it off right away and after that, always considered ourselves best friends. We would tell one another our 'secrets' and offer one another 'surprises' in exchange for favors, such as company to the bathroom or company on an errand. Over time, it became a joke, because neither one of us had any surprises to offer to offer. But we still said it anyway, just to laugh at ourselves.

"I'll give you 20 surprises, if you go with me," I offered her, sweetly.

"OK," she'd easily agree, then we'd break down in laughter as we knew there was no such thing as 20 surprises, let alone one surprise. It was nice to have someone to be silly with, with all the seriousness going on that made up our life during these early childhood years.

One day at Roger's Park, which was a park on Queen Anne Hill, not too far from the neighborhoods where the Love Family lived. Heaven and I had wandered off and sat down in the grass together by this maple tree. I told her I missed Yusef and Marty. She told me she missed her mom, that her mom had left her there with the Love Family and was following Maharaj Ji around. Maharaj Ji was a spiritual leader of a Hindu sect called the Divine Light Mission, which had thousands of devoted followers in the early and mid-1970s. She told me that her mom was jealous of Maharaj Ji's wife Durga Ji, and that she brought him offerings of watermelon.

When I told Heaven about Marty and Yusef, I started crying. She cried too and said she missed her mom.

Dear Diary,

Heaven, my best friend is very pretty, has brown long hair, and is very funny and silly. We have fun together.

*Rachel Is*rael

I felt sad for Heaven who didn't have a mom in the Love Family, but I could totally understand. I felt I didn't have a mom either. My mom had just left me there too. Even though she was there–she wasn't there. I heard she had gone out on the ship that the Family owned, the Abundance.

I didn't see Karen more than occasionally anyway, and when I did, she would give me a big hug. We each had different roles now. I was in the kids' group, and she was serving Love. In other words, she was back, but she wasn't involved in the Kid Scene, and we didn't live together. Our relationship now was more that we belonged to the same community.

While she was gone, working on the ship, I missed my mom, and just knowing that she was on the Abundance worried me. After what had happened in Alaska when she and Marty went out on the fishing boat that crashed when they almost died—it worried me. While she was out at sea on the Love Family's boat, I had a nightmare that the boat crashed, and she fell overboard and was struggling to swim.

I guess it was my body's way of trying to process our separation. We were in this large group of people now, and she wasn't in charge of me anymore. Love was in charge, and he designated who would take care of the kids. If Understanding needed granola or honey or milk for the kids, she would ask Love. My own mom wasn't in the loop.

I missed my mom, and I was angry with her for allowing this group to separate us, but I was also absorbed with adapting to all the change. Plus, the social environment was almost designed to supplant those biological ties. I had other people taking care of all my basic needs, and I had a lot of new friends and family now. Plus, my mom was still there—it's just that her status in my life had changed—drastically. I would see her at meetings and helping in the ways that she was assigned. Forest was still so young that he was still in her care a lot. I did not see her very often though, and there was no visitation or special time for parents to spend time with their kids.

When I went to live at the Kids' House with Understanding, a group of girls about my age—there were at least 5 or 6 of us—would be sent twice a week to go take a shower at Imagination's household where there was a group shower. The Kids' House was in Love's Area, so we would just walk across the yard to Imagination's house. There were at least three showerheads in there and it was definitely large enough for a small group of kids.

I was impressed with the shower room. It was inlaid with glass and semiprecious stones into a sort of clay plaster. I had never been in such a beautiful shower. I had been used to just taking a sponge bath or taking a quiet bath in my small, round metal tub in the cabin or later, in the tepee sauna. This group shower experience though, was something else with all these other girls. Lined along the wall were several different fancy shampoos. There was this deep red, strawberry shampoo, that smelled like real strawberries, that became the favorite. We made it foam up; putting it on our chins like we had beards. Then, we put it on our heads like cone-head hats. Everyone broke out in giggles after one of the girls made herself some breasts out of soap bubbles. It was all very hilarious. We were shrieking and giggling, and it was making a ton of noise, echoing off the walls. Then we all took our towels and went into the little sauna at the end of the hallway from the shower. It was the most fun shower that I had ever had at that point.

After our group shower, I had gone upstairs with another girl, for some reason to get towels. At the top of the stairs, there was this little window. I stopped to peek out the window, and there below, on the deck was a hot tub. There were a group of people standing around the hot tub wearing holy-day clothes. There were men in robes and women dressed in their finest white dresses. I saw Love there presiding over Nerai's baptism. She had been the naked redhead, who had been running across the meadow at the Love Family homestead in Homer when my mom and I had hiked in to visit for the first time. Now she stood naked again, but this time in a hot tub with two priests on each side of her. I saw the men hold her under the water for a few moments, then she came up out of the water smiling.

I always loved Nerai, although for most of the years that I knew her, her name was Listening. Nerai/Listening always remembered me from Alaska. When she saw me, she would give me a huge smile. She'd hug me and tell me how she remembered when I fell down that cellar at the homestead in Homer. She still seemed genuinely concerned for me even after our lives had changed so drastically. Plus, her even mentioning our shared past was against Love Family thinking. No one usually talked about or referred to the past.

All that mattered now was the present. "Stay present," I always heard. My life in Alaska was just the past now. It apparently didn't matter anymore. No one ever asked me about my past, so it was very nice that Nerai would mention it when she saw me.

When I first went to live at the Kids' House, there were maybe 10–15 kids of various ages who were old enough to live with Understanding. Over the years that I was there, though, there ended up being a total of 269 children in the Love Family, 134 of whom were born there. It's interesting that in the newspapers and in other things written about the Love Family, they always underestimated the number of members in the community. They always wrote that there were about 300 members in the Love Family. But those reported numbers don't include the children, so including the children, the membership was actually more like almost 600 at its height. I have documentation of the list of children for those who do not have their own numbers, and that figure only covers the eight years that I was there. Many more children were born into the group after I left.

Some of the kids I was with early on had come with their parents like I did. But there were some who were dropped off, like Heaven, and there were others still who didn't have parents there, and I wasn't sure why.

In the Family, adults were not called adults. At least I never heard them called that. I always just heard them referred to collectively as, the "big people." I guess there was no real sense to be made of age; since we were all eternal anyway. It depended somewhat on the child or person's maturity what grouping they fell into.

Over the years, as an adult, I kept track of how many kids I had grown up with. I eventually came back into contact with an ex-member, Wisdom. I told her that I was making a list of children who were raised in the Love Family. She gave me a list of babies that had been born in the Family. It was a birth record that she had kept in secret, since in the Love Family birth records were not officially kept, and since we didn't keep track of ages.

Once I had Wisdom's list of all the babies that had been born there, I used it to create a more encompassing list of every child who had ever lived in the Love Family, while I was there. Just to make sure I was accurate, I cross checked my lists. I talked to those who had been teachers, caretakers and guardians for the children. I talked to those who had been raised there as a child and asked them to list anyone who was not on my list, just to make sure I didn't miss anyone.

There are lots of things that make this writing challenging, but one thing that helps it along is that I can easily verify information by talking to those who were also there. The Love Family was a small, tight knit community, so it has been easy to cross check stories by just making a few phone calls, visiting a few old friends.

Getting the numbers right is important to me. This was my family, this was my history. It bothers me that the children weren't included in the estimates. Didn't we count too? I was a baptized member!

I was baptized almost a year after we had arrived. It was the spring of 1976. Everyone had gone out to a farm that the Love Family owned to celebrate Passover. The event would be held on a 350-acre parcel of property that the Love Family had recently acquired in Arlington, Washington, which everyone started calling, the 'Ranch.' The previous year, Passover had been celebrated in Love's Area on Queen Anne, but there had been complaints from the neighbors about the noise of the lamb and the rooster, which I discussed earlier. So, because of the complaints, that spring it was decided that everyone would go to the Ranch for the festivities.

During the week before Passover, there was to be a large baptism. It would be held at the shore of a small lake that was situated on the Ranch. Before the baptism, it was custom for those who were to be baptized, such as myself, to fast. It was a seven day fast; the first three days were no food or water; the last four days were water only. I was told I could fast if I wanted to, but because I was still growing, I was allowed to only do three days, not the full seven.

Everyone had set up tents in the pasture in preparation for Passover and was going to camp out for two weeks, then we would all go back to the City when it was over. Just to be clear, this was the year before everyone moved to go live permanently at the Ranch (1976). I decided to fast to see if I could do it. Just for fun, I asked Heaven to do it with me, so I wouldn't be the only kid fasting.

The first day was easy. The second day, I was beginning to feel weak and sick. By that afternoon, it wasn't very much fun to play softball with the boys in the pasture. The next morning on the third day of our fast, I was so weak that I was having difficulty trying to make my bed. Our fast ended when the adults made us eat breakfast that day, so we didn't make it all the way through to that evening when it would've been officially three days. Even so, fasting for two days was a lot, considering I was just a kid, and now I had done my best to prepare for my baptism. The fast wasn't fun, but Heaven and I were proud of our accomplishment. It became more of a bonding experience with my best friend than anything else.

Until this point, I was not a baptized member. I had gotten my Bible name, 'Rachel' early on, but only because there was already a 'Lois' there and people had gotten us mixed up. At that time, most people had to wait until they were baptized before they received their Bible names. My mom was still going by the name Karen; she hadn't yet been baptized, which may have had to do with the fact that she had been kicked out, early on. I guess they still had her on a watch list to make sure she was going to work out. But apparently, I was working out just fine. This was an important point, because my own mom wasn't allowed to see my baptism. She wasn't yet baptized herself, and only baptized members could witness a baptism.

Resolve, the piano player was there guarding the gate and told her she couldn't come in as was the rule. As a result, she had to go hike up on the knoll to watch it from afar. Marty, from our Alaska days, just happened to be visiting during that time and watched it with her. Unfortunately, the knoll wasn't close to the lake, so they couldn't see my baptism very well. My mom talked about what she remembered from that day.

"It made me really sad, because at that time, baptism seemed so important to me," she says. "I was still trying to be accepted, and the last thing you'd do is complain. Karen continued. "A lot of the philosophy of the family was that you kind of deny yourself. You take a humble spot, but I was so proud though that you were being baptized."

The day I was baptized, there were thirteen people there, including myself. We all stood in the water at the same time. The following Passover, there was another baptism, and I have heard from their memories that there was also a large group that was baptized, but that only two at a time went.

It wasn't like that for my baptism. We all stood naked in the water at the same time, all lined up along the shore. Each person was standing next to a priest, so all together, there were some 26 people in the water, preparing to be baptized. A red carpet had been rolled out on the dock and Love sat in a chair on the end of it, directing the event.

Love prayed to begin the ceremony. I was nervous and a bit frightened, so I don't think I was paying much attention to what he said. But I heard Love say something about giving up our former selves and receiving our new names to symbolize our commitment to the Family. It was the Love Family style version of a baptism ceremony through immersion.

Baptisms were very holy, ceremonial events, like weddings. They were symbolic of identity transformation and rebirth. By that afternoon, I would be a baptized member. Even though there were no other children at the baptism that morning, I had seen baptisms in Love's hot tub earlier on and knew what would happen. Although at my baptism, as I will discuss shortly, there had to be a little unplanned snafu.

A man named Israel was the guy that baptized me. He was sanctioned to Radiance who we had known in Alaska as Suzanne. Israel was a slender man and had straight, long, dark brown hair. He was the one who, earlier on, had lost his virtue name, Reality because he had fallen to his 'wants.' He got caught eating bacon and drinking coffee at one of the Queen Ann neighbors' houses. At least that is what was said about him. I assume that was why he lost his name, but maybe it was something else. Wanting was a big no-no in the Love Family. That was what everyone was trying to get away from when they left the World. I heard that the World was a place where greed had taken over and where people had forgotten about the simple things in life, like loving each other.

I took all my clothes off my eight-year-old body with the others who were to be baptized that day. Each of us waded into the water along the shore of the lake and stood waiting for Love to direct the ceremony. I stood nervously next to Israel. He smiled down at me paternally to try and put me at ease, flashing a perfect set of straight, white teeth. I managed to return the smile, but I was starting to feel scared. Everyone was silent as Love talked, but I wasn't really listening. When he was done talking, Israel and the other priests, all at the same time, held the person assigned to them under the water. So, I was dunked by Israel in the lake at the exact same time that the other 13 people were being dunked by their priests. The water enveloped me and I thought I was dying. I gasped for air but drew in water. I struggled to the surface, against his grip, splashing desperately. When I breached, I looked around and saw that the others were still under. Israel glared at me. He looked at Love, fearfully, and asked Love a question. I couldn't hear, because my ears were full of water. Love answered Israel, his mouth moving in round vowels. He looked irritated. *Had I done something wrong?* Israel bent down and told me to hold my breath longer this time. Then he put his arms around me and dunked me under, again. This time I held my breath and let the still water hold me for a moment, and this time Israel brought me up sooner and just after the others had come up.

Lois no longer existed. My old eight-year old self was dead. I was a new person, a baptized member of the Love Family. I would now be 'Rachel Israel,' officially. In the Bible, Rachel, meaning 'Lamb of God,' was the second wife of Jacob who bore Benjamin and Joseph, two of the twelve sons who were the fathers of the 12 tribes of ancient Israel. The story of Rachel was not just some Bible story, it was a legacy that now belonged to me as a member of the Love Family since everyone believed we were the descendants of the ancient Israelites from the tribe of Judah.

Once the baptism was complete, we stepped out of the water and onto the shore of the lake. A group of women descended on us, bringing us something to wear. Each of the men were given a new robe. I was given a long, white dress of fine linen. Someone said it used to be a wedding dress. There were other women there who were also given white dresses.

We were all ushered toward a huge tent with cedar double doors. I stood for a moment, deciding whether I wanted to join the others inside. After the baptism, I wasn't sure I was up for much more. The Family woman who had dressed me stood several feet ahead, waiting for me to catch up. From the looks on their faces, it was clear I didn't have a choice.

There was total silence inside the tent as the newly baptized members filed in one by one. I hesitated just inside the door for a moment then moved forward and took a seat. Nothing exciting happened in the tent. It was just a long, boring ceremonial gathering. Love gave a talk and directed the meditation and prayer.

Afterward, I didn't really feel any different than I did before, but maybe some of the others did as they were much older than I and had more knowledge about the event and the context. As for myself, I was just glad it was over.

It wasn't until the following year that Karen was baptized, and her Bible name became 'Elkanah.' I didn't see her baptism, because it took place in town, in Love's hot tub, just like Nerai's baptism. From then on, I called my mom by her Love Family name, Elkanah. In the Love Family, children addressed their parents by their first names, so calling her Elkanah did not seem strange or unusual, just a part of how it was there. Even before I came to the Family, as I've said, I never called her mom; I called her by her first name, as was common for hippie kids in the counterculture.

When Elkanah was baptized, she had to sign a hand-lettered document called a 'Last Will and Testament.' It was a document which bequeathed all Worldly possessions to the 'Church of Armageddon,' the Commonwealth of Israel, which was a name that reflected our status in the World as an official and recognized church. The document further decreed that the Church had full power of attorney concerning Elkanah's former name. It stated:

> As far as I am concerned, I am dead to the past and baptized into a new life through Jesus Christ with a new name and purpose... I hereafter have no longer any responsibilities connected to my past name. The Church elders and authorities have permission to sign my old name in all matters of my past life.

The witnesses and the notary on the document were the former names of four elders of the Church. I didn't have to sign it because I was a kid, and because I wasn't old enough to have responsibilities or possessions connected to my old name.

In the Journal of Cooperative Living, Serious Israel had written: "We each discarded our old names and assumed the new name "Israel...we claimed the right to essentially start over fresh severing ourselves from our previous identities with all their trappings of birth records, driver's licenses, and other legal identifiers." (1994, pg. 55).

I did not have ID or other records of my previous identity, although my birth certificate was probably filed in some office somewhere in California, since I was born years before Karen joined.

Talking about baptism, Serious had been quoted in the paper: "We don't rush into that. It may take a year or longer for someone actually to be baptized...baptism announces a person's commitment to the Family and represents almost a marriage to the Family...We really realize that we are married to God through Jesus Christ." (*Seattle Times* Jan 23rd, 1982 Sat. A10)

Serious often acted as a spokesperson for reporters or others asking questions in our dealings with the outside society. He explained: "We feel that everyone has a second chance. That old part of us is dead, that we have been reborn. This name I now have, I will have forever." (*Seattle Times* January 25, 1972 Tue A20).

What was the biblical basis for Love's ideas about names?

In the Love Family Church of Armageddon Charter, it stated that "God has blessed each of us with a holy name." (29-30):

> One shall say I am the Lords…and surname himself by the name of Israel." (Isaiah 44:5 *KJV*).

The Charter then stated our duty: "to show mankind that Love is Real, by bringing the love of Christ out from within each of us."

My last name was now Israel and carried with it an importance and biblical history all its own. The name 'Israel, means 'Prince of God.' Love's claim was that we were Jesus Christ returned. But there was also another layer of meaning in the name for us; Israel meant "Is Real," even though we didn't spell it like that. Jesus Christ is real. Love is real. Our official name was the Love Israel Family, but for us, it also meant, the Love IS REAL Family. Love considered that we were descendants of the tribe of Judah, because Jesus was from the tribe of Judah. Jacob's descendants came to be known as the Israelites, eventually forming the tribes of Israel. According to Love and everyone who joined the Love Family, this was now my heritage.

Carrying the name Israel was not taken lightly. Members of my new Family had been arrested, harassed and jailed, even beaten and assaulted because of our name, because over time, there were a bunch of people who had run ins with the law about the name Israel.

One example was when Love sent Larry, who was then known as Consideration, to Ohio. He was to hitchhike to his parents' house to get the rest of his money, which was $2000. A man named Happiness also went. On the way back, they were stopped and asked for their I.D.'s, which of course they didn't have, because when people joined the Family, they gave up their previous identities and all the evidence that went along with it.

The police asked them what their real names were. Consideration and Happiness stuck to what they believed, telling the police their Love Family names, and it angered the police. The police were laughing at them and called them 'freaks.' The more they refused to give them their real names, the angrier the police got. For Consideration and Happiness, it was a harrowing and traumatic experience. Consideration was punched in the face. Then the officer held a gun to his head with the notch pulled back to get him to give his old name. Happiness was "slapped around and handed off to a few wild men" in a cell where he was assaulted. They spent six days in jail. I got these details about their situation from Larry's manuscript and from subsequent discussions with him about what happened (Israel, pp. 214-218, 1978). Even after everything they endured, neither of the men gave up their old names, which shows just how firm members could be in their beliefs. I talked earlier about Understanding's arrest—the Love Family was very stubborn about this issue. (*Seattle Times* February 22, 1979 D5)

As I said earlier, the Love Family was granted observer status on the Church Council of Greater Seattle. A state senator from Queen Anne named Ray Moore introduced a bill on the Love Family's behalf that would have made it possible to get a driver's license without a birth date. (*Weekly*, December 1-7th 1982) The bill failed, but the Seattle Police Department solved the problem another way. They began issuing Love Family members special identification cards bearing their Israel Family names and the word "legal" in the space reserved for their ages. (Balch, pgs. 75–76)

I wasn't old enough to have to worry about getting arrested and having to produce an ID. I was fine with my new name, Rachel Israel, but knew that someday I would receive a virtue name. The idea of having a virtue name, though, did not appeal to me. I knew it would mean more responsibility, because having a virtue name would mean I would represent that virtue in Christ for the whole community. I would be held to a higher spiritual standard when it was already hard enough. No thanks!

It was a concern. One morning, I woke up and I'd had a nightmare about my virtue name. I dreamed that the elders surrounded me on the sanctuary floor at Encouragement's house. They bent over and put their hands on my back and head. They were "laying hands" on me in prayer, which was a spiritual ritual facilitating healing. In the dream, I knelt on the floor while a special holy oil was poured over my head. While the anointing took place, Love spoke with authority, proclaiming, "Your name shall be Experience!" In the dream, I was overcome by fear. It was fear of the unknown. What experiences? I felt the pain of what I had been through so far. "No!!" I screamed in the dream, "I'm not strong enough to face the pain; I don't want to go through it!"

It was a relief to wake up from that dream with just the lowly Bible name Rachel. Shortly after my baptism, Love sent for me. I don't remember who took me to him, but when I got there, he gave me a ring. It was a simple gold band with a large ruby. It probably had been turned in by a new member. I took the ring and put it on my finger and stared down at it, mesmerized. I had never had a ring before. I held my hand out and smiled up at Love, genuinely touched by the gift. He smiled at me and said, "You are a princess of God." It seemed after that, that everyone stopped to look at my ring and comment on its beauty. People knew that Love had given it to me, and that he had honored me in this way.

And that was the end of my first year in the Love Family.

BIBLIOGRAPHY (CHAPTER 4)

Alters, Diane. *Seattle Times*. Love Israel: Jail? It's a MisUnderstanding. August 16, 1977. pg. C19.

Balch, Rob. (1998). The Love Family: Its formative years. *Religion in the Age of Transformation: Sects, Cults and Spiritual Communities: A Sociological Analysis*. Ed. Marc Petrowsky, William W. Zellner. Praeger Publishers, Westport, CT.

Bryant, Hilda. *Seattle Post-Intelligencer*. Love Family is Gaining Ground. Sunday. May 14, 1978. A13–14 BM.

Church of Armageddon Charter of the Love Israel Family.

Downey, Roger. *Seattle Weekly*. All in the Love Family. December 1982. pgs. 30–35.

[Karen]. Personal Interview. September 27, November 10, December 20, June 21, all 2001.

Hinterberger, John. *Seattle Times*. Love Family: Sect Wants to Rule Magnolia and Queen Anne. Tuesday, January 25, 1972. A20.

Hinterberger, John. *Seattle Times*. A Minesweeper for the Love Family: Owners for Kathy Jo. January 31, 1976 A1.

Israel, Larry. (Consideration) 1978. Unpublished Manuscript.

Israel, Serious. Community as Crucible: The Love Israel Family. *Communities: Journal of Cooperative Living*, no. 85 (Winter, 1994) pp. 52–55.

Ruppert, Ray. *Seattle Times*. Church Council Hit for Love Israel Liaison. December 15, 1981. NWB1.

Ruppert, Ray. *Seattle Times*. A New look at Seattle's Church of Armageddon. Saturday. January 23, 1982. Sat. A10.

Ruppert, Ray. *Seattle Times*. Love Israel Family Wants to Join Area Church Council November 11, 1976. B3.

Seattle Times. Sign-Carrying Pickets Hold Peaceful Protest. January 25, 1982 C2.

Seattle Times. Church Refuses to Yield on Driver's License Issue. February 22, 1979. D5.

CHAPTER 5

Why Love? The Jesus People and Armageddon

This chapter is dedicated to my husband. After he read the previous chapter, which talks about my first year living in the Love Family, he looked at me with a confused expression on his face:

"Why would anyone want to join this group? He asked.

"That's a very good question," I answered him. "I'll get right on that." I decided right then—that question would be my next chapter. So here it is:

Why would anyone want to join the Love Family? It might have been easier to understand 30 or more years ago when the 1960s and 1970s were fresh in peoples' minds. Now the counterculture, at least in the popular media, are prepackaged stereotypes, bundled into advertising or upcycled into the latest fashion trends.

I was there. I was just a kid, but I was being raised in an alternate society where the adults around me were trying to build a better world. Better than what, I wasn't sure, but with the power of their mind and sheer will, they were going to drop out and reject the conventional mainstream institutions that they didn't believe in anymore.

Being raised the way I was, I also had a question: Why was my childhood so damn different than everybody else's. Plus, there are obvious questions: Why was there such thing as the Love Family? Why would anyone want to join such a group? I have to ask these questions, because I wasn't an adult member: I wasn't attracted to Love or the Love Family. I was only there because my mom was there. The questions aren't easy either, because everyone who came to the Love Family, has a different story about why they joined. But, even so, it's important to me to try and understand as much of the larger picture as possible. Since the more I understand, I have found, the less it seems like just bad fortune.

I have to start by explaining the fundamentals: Why would anyone want to join a community that required that they give up everything they owned? This is one of the first questions that people have, and it is one of the hardest to understand. I touched on this subject earlier. As I said, some people didn't have to give up much, because they didn't have anything when they came. My mom left most of what she owned with Marty in Alaska, which wasn't much. The tepee. She let Marty have the money from the sale of the property on Mt Denali. She felt bad for leaving him, so she sent it to him thinking that he would need it more than her.

"Love never knew about that one," she says.

I got to keep a lot of the clothes I brought. I had beautifully, hand-sewn hippie-ethnic, styled outfits my mom had made for me when we lived in the tepee in Alaska, but we didn't need much now. Our new life was simple. No one seemed to have anything more than a sleeping bag and one bag of clothing. Once we joined, my mom made me a patchwork quilt style duffle bag with a nice shoulder strap. It was what I used for the next few years of my childhood to store my belongings.

Everything that I had to give up, was immaterial. It had sentimental value, such as my close relationship with my mom, Marty, and the familiarity of life as I had known it.

Adult members gave up everything to be a member. There were those who gave up degrees and status, houses, cars, property and fine personal belongings. Dan, the Unimogger from Homer, who was now called, 'Richness,' was a DuPont heir when he joined; I heard everything he owned was 2 or 3 million dollars, most of which was said to be in the form of property. The Alaska Homestead was one such property.

People gave up everything they owned, including their former identities and personalities.

People would no longer be independent thinkers with needs and wants of their own. They would now embrace a collective consciousness or Christ mind, represented by Love Israel. One of the main tenants there was 'We are one.' What this meant was that instead of having a group of people who all had their own minds, the idea was that everyone in the group shared a single mind.

When people who came to the Love Family and decided to give up everything, including their minds, this was way before they'd had time to be a member; It was conditional for membership. Thus, it was impossible to explain their decision to undergo this transformation by brainwashing. It hadn't been long enough to use that explanation. They weren't even allowed in unless they'd done it.

When I talk about what it was like growing up there, it is a little awkward to say, "I did this," or I did that," because when I was there, "I" didn't do anything. We did this, and we did that. My mind was part of a collective consciousness, where my mind was, in theory anyway, part of this—oneness, part of this—everyone else. It wasn't just theory, because most everything that happened took place within a group context. As a result, all my memories in the Love Family were formed when I shared the group consciousness. It's one of those things that makes writing about the Love Family technically challenging. When I say, "we," it sounds like I'm speaking for everybody else. When I say, "I," it can portray me as this solo character who was acting alone, when actually, my identity was enmeshed with all these other people and our shared mind.

As a child, it was an amazing feeling to be a part of 'one' mind. I felt a sense of belonging and purpose, and there was a closeness there, an almost spiritual, otherworldly warmth and belonging. I felt a sense of awe in that everything that happened was an outgrowth of Love's vision. There was a sense of importance about what we were doing and why. We were creating a new world, a new society that would be significant to people all over the planet. What we believed placed the Love Family at the center of everything. Of course, I believed it. All of the hundreds of adults that were now my family believed it. I was too young to question whether it was right or not. And since my family did not interact with outsiders much, there wasn't much reason to question it, since I wasn't exposed to those who might've questioned it.

The downside of living in such a close space with others, physically, psychologically, and emotionally is that it felt oppressive. I wasn't really allowed to dwell in my own mind. 'We are one,' is what we believed. Being "negative" wasn't allowed. Complaining was out. We kept 'our mind' clear, focused on love and beauty and other virtues, but I felt very controlled in terms of what I could think. I understood it, but I also craved my own mind. There were times when I would sneak off by myself, just to be alone. I took a little blanket and I would find somewhere to hide and read my book. When everyone went to the farm, I would hike off away from the group encampments where there was this little patch of clearing in the trees that I had found. No one knew I was there. I would sit out in the woods where the sunshine would hit me just right as I read or wrote in my diary. Here is a story I wrote on one such excursion, taken from my then diary.

Dear Diary,

Once upon a time there was a frog, and he liked to croak, but all the other frogs liked to squeak, so they thought he was weird. He didn't think he was weird and kept on croaking. One day he went and told the other frogs to croak like him. They threw him out. He was sad and didn't know what to do. He decided to trust in God. The next day, he found a pool with lots of frogs just like him; they all croaked and not one squeaked. He was very happy. The End.

Rachel Israel

The first time that story is read, it might sound like a child-like fairytale. On the second reading, though, one might see that the story is about preserving one's individuality and not succumbing to group pressures.

As an adult, Karen had the choice to give up everything; I didn't have that choice, I had to. The frog in my story didn't give up his croak. Well, to join the Love Family, one had to give up their croak.

I wrote that story into my diary without thinking much about it, but now I can see that it was a story about my family, the Love Family, and it also was about conformity and social control, which is what I was seeing in the group dynamics that were playing out before me.

When I snuck off by myself, I felt free. I could usually be gone for short periods of time, and no one seemed to even notice that I was gone. I loved that feeling of being by myself—so rare. When I was with the children and we wanted to do something or go anywhere, we always had to have a guardian. We were never usually just left to our own devices. I never was given my own space unless it was punishment, and I never had my own room, where I could just be by myself or daydream. This was in line with the thinking: We are one. We are not separate individuals with personal needs and attachments to our own stuff. No one, except maybe Love, the elders, and maybe a few exceptions, had their own space in the Love Family. When I lived at the Kids' House, I slept in a room with a ton of other kids. We shared the bunks, and Understanding slept in the same room, in the hide-a-bed.

The adults didn't do things by themselves. I often heard a passage from the Bible that was used to justify our custom:

"For where two or three are gathered together in my name, there am I in the midst of them." (Matthew 18:20; *KJV*).

There wasn't an overt rule that one could not do things alone, but everyone there was trying hard to be one-minded and do everything together, communally. I heard one former elder say, "There were no rules, there were only "agreements," but of course the agreements were determined by Love and everyone followed them. And if someone didn't follow the "agreements," then they would have to leave; What is that called if it's not a rule?

A lot of the agreements were written out in the Love Family's Charter. The Church of Armageddon Charter, (1971) stated:

Love Israel represents Christ and God as the final word in all matters concerning the church, by the total consent of all members. He is a parent in all spiritual things, a minister and guide worthy of all respect and obedience (pg. 6).

Love's power was consistent over time too. Ten years after the Charter was written, a statement was issued by the council of elders that described Love's power: [Love] is the point of agreement between us, the central thought in our mind, the mind of Christ, the point of final resolve in all matters that concern us."

To become a member, one had to give over their property, money, any statuses and anything associated with who they used to be before they joined, including relationships. In addition to giving up all this, a person who joined the Love Family had to give up their autonomy and agree to let Love Israel make all the decisions in their life.

My former teacher, Eve, talked about how that "agreement" to have someone with her, had an impact on her. She and Serious had to go talk to the Department of Education regarding the requirements to keep the Love Family school legal.

Eve had to take some classes at the University, which meant she needed to take someone with her to class every day.

"Because we were eternal, we had no birthdates; I had no I.D., no record of myself as the person who had gotten the certificate in the first place," Eve explained. She had to convince the president of the university to allow her to use her old I.D number to access her old school records. On the first day of class, she brought another member with her, and she had to explain to the instructor that in the Family, there was a philosophy. She had to have someone with her in class every day. One of her instructors refused, and when Eve went to that class, the fellow member assigned to accompany her, had to sit outside the door and wait for her.

Larry wrote his then understanding of why people did not go places alone.

"The reason for this was for our protection from getting into our own thoughts if we went by ourselves," he explained, "plus it was good to express our oneness by doing things together..." (184)

My understanding of this 'agreement' was that Armageddon could happen at any time, so members needed to have a brother or a sister there to back them up and support them. This was especially important when going into the World. If one were confronted or challenged by an outsider or an authority, it would be easier to stand together in opposition to back one another up, if needed. It was kind of like a buddy system, except there was more. It was also a way to help people stay bright and not "doubt." When one is alone with their individual thoughts, one could be susceptible to having dark thoughts that were from Satan. People were trying to keep their thoughts on a spiritual plane. Everyone was trying to do this together, because it was 'our mind.' It was a lot easier to avoid being alone with one's thoughts when there were others who were trying to do the same thing, to hold them in line.

I saw people struggle. If someone did something out of step with the thinking, they would risk expulsion. They could get kicked out. They might be considered to be 'separate.' They would be confronted about it from the group or shunned. It was conformity to the extreme. Observing this as a child made me wonder if I would get kicked out. It scared me. I overheard people talking about it. I would overhear that someone had been "raked over the coals." It meant they were confronted about their behavior, by the group. Once judgment was passed, there was no court of appeals. Everyone would ostracize them, and the challenge for them would be to change and just "give light." "If they could do it," Eve says, "then they could survive there."

If they responded negatively to that criticism, it was said that they were, 'dark,' or 'going through changes.' It wasn't just the adults that went through that self-inculcation. I was a kid, but I also had to learn. Sometimes if I showed that I was unhappy, I was called 'dark,' and expected to 'change.' No one said, 'What's bothering you?' or 'Tell me all about it.'

There were adults who couldn't handle it and left the Family. When people asked what happened to them, it was said that they had, 'lost their vision,' or that they 'gave in to a negative spirit.'

Anytime anyone got wrapped up in their own ideas or ways of doing things, they would be told to 'get out of their head.' When I heard this, I always wondered: *If they were supposed to get out of their head, then who is supposed to be there?* I guess Love was supposed to be there now.

I could tell that people were afraid that they would slip as they fought to repress their urges and natural protests that came from their individual selves. It was a conscious and intentional process. In some ways, I think it was easier for me, since I was young and more malleable, but even for me, it was irritating to constantly monitor my thoughts and behaviors. I heard people years later complain that the self-monitoring was "exhausting."

They were captive, in a way, captive in the oneness. If they didn't like it, they could leave, but for a lot of years, most people stayed. They placed their total loyalty and trust in Love and had complete faith in him and in his teachings.

I talked about it with a man who was known as Ethan. He was one of my main teachers and a caretaker for children, along with Eve and Definition. Ethan was tall and slender and had long, bushy, blond hair and a goatee beard. He was a very dedicated person who spent all of his time helping take care of children and teaching.

"Everyone was in awe of Love, because he had so much power," Ethan says. "Love was like Jesus and promised eternal life for those who could be one-minded. People were at different places in terms of how much they gave up their own mind," he explained. "If he [Love] had asked me to go kill some of the children or jump off a cliff, I wouldn't have done it. But there were those who would have," he says soberly.

There was a dark side, and there was a light side. The light side was a sense of community, a brotherhood and a sisterhood and lots and lots of family. After meals, everyone would all help with dishes, taking turns with the different stations. Someone would be playing guitar as everyone worked together to clean up. They all sang together as they washed, rinsed, or dried, *"We're going to build ourselves—a brand new country yeah…"* Other memories I have is walking into the kitchens and seeing groups of women all making bread together, or I went out into the gardens and ran around with the kids while the big people all worked in the gardens, trying to make the gardens beautiful. One ex-member, who was there early on, said,

"It was like walking into heaven," one ex-member says.

There is a really good film out there that captures the external beauty that the Love Family offered. It is a film called, "It Takes a Cult," by Eric Johannsen. It includes amazing footage of communal life that is difficult to really convey without seeing.

With so many people all living together, one would think that it would be a noisy, busy environment, but in his manuscript, (1978) Larry described just the opposite: "There was an air of real quiet, unity and attentiveness at all times…There could only be one conversation going on at a time in the room since we were only one person with one mind." (169–170) As a child, I tried to be quiet too. I didn't dare make a bunch of noise, which would've been a sure-fire way of getting in trouble real fast.

Larry had an unusual story. Six months before we arrived at the Front Door Inn, his parents hired Ted Patrick, who was a notorious anti-cult deprogrammer, to kidnap their son, then Consideration, lock him up, and force him to undergo deprogramming sessions. They believed that he was in the Love Family against his will and that he had been brainwashed. For anyone wishing to learn more about Ted Patrick and who he was, there is a 78-minute docufilm called, "Deprogrammed," which chronicles Ted Patrick's anti-cult crusade. The film looks at the deprogramming era (1971–1990) and asks questions about whether the practice was a result of moral panic or a matter of cultic mind control.

When I came to the Love Family in 1975, it was in the 'Year of Consideration.' Every year, it was custom for Love to name the previous year. He would make the announcement at Passover. But when we joined, Passover had already happened, and it had been months after he was taken. No one talked about it, so I never knew about it. I only found out years later, after I left the community and read his manuscript. I then contacted him, and we met. In his manuscript, he discusses his kidnapping, then I also talked to him about how he had survived it.

What happened was that Consideration had gotten permission from Love to visit his parents in Ohio with another member, Cooperation. Once he got there, he was lured over to a relative's house. Suddenly three strange figures walked in the room, whom he'd never seen before. He wrote, "fear shot through my whole being, as I realized what was happening." His Uncle Ralph followed the figures into the room behind him and shut the door. When Consideration asked if he could leave, they told him no, emphatically. When they refused to let him leave, he "curled up in a little ball" and knew he wasn't going anywhere (321–22).

The men refused to call him Consideration and said that they weren't going to hurt him, but that he had been deceived. 'Larry, Love is a thief, a con man, and a liar," they told him and tried to convince him that he had been brainwashed. It was a very frightening and traumatic experience for him. He felt alone and trapped.

For months, he was kept a prisoner. The doors and windows were locked so he could not escape. They cut his hair and beard. His captors were his parents and former members of another group called the Children of God, a group who were also considered dangerous. They took turns talking to him. They argued with him about how the Love Family was misinterpreting the Bible. They kept repeating that 'Consideration is dead' and 'Larry is alive.' He was told over and over that everything he had believed in was 'a lie' and that 'Love was Satan, a snake…You can't do anything without them telling you what to do,' they repeated.

Larry's deprogramming experience was so traumatic and stressful that he had a mental breakdown which led to several psychiatric hospitalizations. During the first hospitalization, he called the Love Family and asked them to help rescue him. It was then that the court gave his parents legal guardianship; they became his "conservator."

The kidnapping was being viewed as a domestic matter. Serious had been quoted in the papers and had said, "We are really concerned about this guardian thing. It might become a pattern for other parents who are anxious to get their children, who are legally adults, away from the sect." (*Seattle Times* April 23, 1975 B1). For more details about Consideration's kidnapping, see also *Seattle Times* April 25, 1975 B3.

Larry eventually was able to heal and overcome the difficulties. He has attributed his recovery to his relationship to Jesus. He studied the Bible and has tried to understand how the Love Family strayed. He explained that Love put himself between members and Jesus by being the final authority in all matters. This took away a person's personal relationship with Christ. Love had ultimate authority, but he was human and fallible and vulnerable to sin. This, Larry said, was what led to the eventual downfall of the Love Family.

Larry's parents, Abe and Betty Israel (just a coincidence that their last name was also 'Israel.') had been in contact with Steve Allen, since Allen had a son in the Love Family, "Logic." Steve Allen befriended a lot of other parents who also had adult children in the Love Family. Allen published some of their letters in his book, "Beloved Son." Despite their complaints, Steve Allen always carried an open, nonjudgmental mind about the Love Family, even expressing his support for the Family publicly, which outraged a lot of the parents who had major concerns about the group. Steve Allen had told a reporter:

"It seems to me the parents who are most critical are basing their opposition on assumptions that are not factual. They don't understand the phenomenon of religious conversion. Then Allen made a comment about the 'children.' He says: "The one important question about social experiments is the fate of the children," he said. "The happiness of the children is ultimately one of societies measuring mechanisms," (*Seattle Times* May 2, 1975 A4).

As a child who was raised in the Love Family, I happen to agree with Steve Allen that children raised in the Love Family are a measure of the group's success or failure, that what we think, is an important indicator.

Steve Allen though was in an interesting position. I don't know exactly what it was like for him, but my guess is that he expressed support for us and defended us to the press as a way of keeping his relationship with his son Logic and his grandchildren positive. If he had expressed concern about the Family, it might have spurned massive negative press. Can you imagine the headline, Steve Allen's Son Joins Dangerous Cult! It would have been the basis for a media vulture feeding. He must have struggled with the question of how to deal with the truth in a way that minimized harm to his career, his public image, and his family.

In the end, Larry chose to never return to the Love Family. Whether one believes that Larry or any of the members were brainwashed or not, the fact remains that his kidnapping was traumatic and led to his mental breakdown. There have been a lot of conversations about it over the years, but I want to point something out. Let's look at the word, "kidnapping." The first three letters of this word are K.I.D. KIDnapping. But Larry wasn't a kid—I was.

I was a kid. Larry was an adult whose parents had decided they did not like their adult child's decisions. They chose to put their adult son under a psychologically highly stressful situation, which had severe consequences to him.

Over time, it became clear that many adult members, the ones who weren't kidnapped, came to rethink their choices—on their own—without intervention.

Usually when brainwashing techniques are discussed, they can be handily appropriated by anyone to support their claims of their opponent. When using the term brainwashing, it also assumes that someone's opponent is applying with forethought and force, a tool by which to accomplish some end result.

Love had a vision and a set of ideas about how to live a vision. Everybody there wanted what he wanted. Love was not Jesus, he was a human, and peoples' expectations of him were not realistic. I never forgot that quote, by Sir John Dalberg-Acton "Power tends to corrupt, and absolute power corrupts absolutely. Love was given absolute power by everybody there, and no human can handle absolute power.

Serious told a *Seattle Times* reporter, "We believe that Love is the representation of God. He is our authority figure." (*Seattle Times* January 25, 1972 Tuesday A20)

When my mom and I had still been living on Makena Beach in Maui, Love had been anointed King in a ceremony in 1971. He was seen as having the divine right of a king's authority.

It is funny that even in conventional relationships between two people, that which draws you to them, sometimes becomes this curse later. From day one, Love had more privileges than anyone else. He always had his own room. He ate better. He had personal servants and had complete and total authority over every aspect of the group's development and expression.

Sociologist Rob Balch wrote, "Love's followers believed that his special privileges were justified because he was their king. They gave him authority because they believed he embodied their highest ideals. From their perspective, Love deserved the privileges he enjoyed." (Balch, pg. 77)

In the end, that was held against *him*, not them for having faith in something that wasn't real. Larry was right. Love was a human and susceptible to sin. He wasn't the embodiment of Christ, like he had convinced people. But I am getting ahead of myself, again.

What I have been discussing in the last few pages is what people were giving up when they joined. It was everything, including their minds—willingly. If they owned houses, property, degrees, titles, jewelry, books, they gave it up to join. If they were married or had committed relationships, they gave it up. If they had parents or relatives on the outside, they gave them up. If they had children, they gave them up. In a sense, I was given up. I was given over to the care of others. One could say, that I was turned-in to 'the center,' since from the time I came, I was parented communally.

Not only did people give up all this, as I've discussed, they also gave up the right to make their own decisions and the right to their individual thoughts and feelings. "They" were being replaced—by Love.

Why would anyone want to do this? I am almost sure there will be no way to explain this. However, I am going to try:

People were attracted to the Love Family, because it was an alternative society, a society that was organized around one man's vision, a vision that was easy for a lot of people, during that time in history, to relate to, because it encompassed important ideals of the hippie counterculture. Ethan once told me that when he first met Love, he was like the "king of the hippies." A lot of Love's ideas that became a part of his vision for the Love Family came from ideas that were already popular in the hippie counterculture. And one of the main ideas that Love offered was the idea of 'Oneness.' It wasn't just some cool spiritual idea to talk about; it would now be actualized in a real-life situation with a whole community of people. It wasn't a new concept. In the 1960s and 1970s, the idea of "oneness" with the universe was a popular concept that grew with the spread of hallucinogens such as LSD. Plus, the idea of oneness, in general, was consistent with other ideals in the counterculture which were oriental in nature such as the rejection of individualism and such as the openness towards communal living.

It was oneness, but it was also a chance to live communally. In the larger counterculture, during that time, most hippies had rejected capitalism, competition and private property. Communes were very popular. The idea of giving up everything one owned and living simply and with nothing was exactly the sort of idea that inspired people back then.

One way I try to understand why people joined the Love Family is to look at the zeitgeist, the popular ideas that were sprouting from the tray, the tray being the societal and cultural landscape. No matter how out-of-the-box it was, there was no shortage of membership. There was no need to proselytize or make much effort to recruit new members. Instead, there were droves of people joining, so many that there ended up a need to screen out people who did not fit in. Those who were disruptive or who could not submit to the practices, were sent out on their own. Those who suffered from mental illness or who were not mentally stable enough were rejected. I saw people who never made it past the Front Door Inn. There was a lady who used to come by often asking to join. Her name was Debbie. I felt sorry for her, because she seemed desperate to get in, and no one wanted her around. Every time she showed up, she would tell people her new virtue name, and each time, it was a different name. She didn't understand how it worked. I heard people say that she was "crazy."

Looking back from today's world, it would seem to be absolutely insane for anyone to want to join the Love Family, but to really understand it, one has to look at it from back then. Let's start with maturity. The average age of a Love Family member was probably 22 or 23. Young adults. People who were deemed old enough to make their own decisions, but people who still had a lot to learn.

Most people were in their early 20s, living in the 1960s time-period. The year I was born, 1968, was the year that Love started the Love Family. People were looking for alternatives, and there were those who were offering them up. I talked in an earlier chapter about the Back-to-the-Land movement. There were so many countercultural types looking to drop out of the predominant society, to live in a commune or to live off the land and get back to nature. The Love Family was one avenue by which to do just that. It was an alternative society made up of people who had already dropped out and had built a life, a society on its own accord.

For many years, the Love Family's secluded, 350-acre ranch in Arlington, WA was an attractive feature. It was mostly wooded, but there was a pretty lake on the property and lots of space to garden and tend animals. Eventually, members lived and camped out on this property for many years. That was an ideal for some people, to find an alternative but one that included community and society, instead of doing it on their own.

It wasn't just the idea of an alternative for the sake of living differently. The Back-to-the-Land movement was also an expression of protest of what was often negatively referred to the "establishment."

"The way to change things, is just to drop out," my mom always said, and "if enough people did it," she explained, "it could gradually change the world." A lot of the communes that formed back then were anarchistic for a reason. No one wanted to trust authority anymore. The Vietnam war was the truest and most present example of abuse by those in control during that time.

People were against a lot of the institutions that had held the fabric of society together—military, government, education, family, church, marriage, and a lot of the social norms that many were now willing to throw out the window. The norms of society and the institutions upon which the culture sat were being challenged on a wide scale.

The Love Family was one communal experiment among many. A lot of the communes that formed were dirty and disorganized, and because there was a resistance to authority, everyone was seen as equal. There would be a lot of arguing and interrupting, and no one could agree on who was going to do what. There was no order or authority structure in these communes, which could act to coordinate peoples' efforts and lives. There were those, though, who would rather tolerate a dirty, disorganized, anarchistic commune than tolerate living in what was then traditional American culture.

The Love Family offered something different, an alternative society with the hippie ideals of the times, a place close to nature, a commune but one that had order. It was highly organized. There was a hierarchy and a leadership structure that was well defined.

The sort of hippie that was attracted to the Love Family was one who was not drawn to the communes that were available at that time. They wanted out, but they were discouraged by the typical communes available. They were commune-less people in a sense.

One cannot talk about hippie counterculture without talking about drugs. The Love Family was attractive as well because marijuana and hallucinogens were an integral part of the culture.

Marijuana was a real draw. In the Love Family though, we didn't call it pot or marijuana. We had our own name for it; It was called 'mashish.' In fact, mashish and LSD were not considered drugs at all, instead they were called, 'sacraments.'

When people took sacraments, they weren't just sitting around doing it whenever they felt like it. In the Love Family, it was a controlled substance. It was given out by priests in a ceremonial, spiritual way. I have heard people say that it was more like how the Native Americans were about, say, peyote. The visions induced during the taking of sacrament were considered holy and spiritually significant. Members often had deep spiritual experiences, on many occasions, ranging from intuitive revelations to dramatic visions that became part of the community's cultural practice. Books could be written just about the subject of the dreams and visions of members and how they were significant in terms of their spiritual guidance for the community.

One of the things that members talked about all the time were the visions and dreams that they claimed were influential in guiding them to the Love Family. A lot of adults would say that they had been looking for something, and that they had finally found it when they discovered the Love Family. They would say, "It was like coming home." I heard that over and over. People said they had seen Love and the Kingdom of Israel in their dreams and visions before they had even met Love or knew about the Love Family. The way it was talked about led me to believe that my family was so important that people had been led home by a real God, by unseen magical forces.

Marijuana, spirituality—what more could anyone want? I grew up in a community where everyone was always meditating, chanting and reading the Bible; there wasn't a separation between the spiritual life of the community and the personal and social lives of members. It was one and the same. It was like being in church all the time, not just on Sundays for an hour. When we were eating dinner that night or when we went to the bathroom, it was a spiritual practice, that included reading the Bible and meditating, focusing on God. The culture existed on a spiritual plane. As a child, I was swimming in it, soaking it in through osmosis if nothing else.

I had a vision too. During the time when I was living at the kids' house, I became very ill. I had a hoarse voice and felt terrible. Despite my predicament, I was able to momentarily manage a smile when someone said I sounded like Janis Joplin. When it didn't clear up, I was sent to Love's house to be cared for by one of his wives, although they weren't called 'wives.' Her name was Bliss. Bliss was a very loving presence to be around. She waited on me hand and foot, taught me little breathing techniques to bring my fever down and help minimize coughing. She brought me a couple of Babar books about the little elephant, which until that point, I had never seen any children's books in the Love Family. Since I was staying in Love's house, I assumed that the books were there for Love's kids and not for the general population of community kids.

I was there under Bliss's care for a couple weeks. While I was there in my bed one day, I looked, and I saw an angel sitting by my bed. I could distinctly see her but only if I didn't look directly at her, so I watched her from my side-glance. She was very beautiful as she kneeled in prayer. I could see her hands together as she prayed, palm-to-palm against her chest. I was so amazed that I spent the next couple hours or so watching her to see if she would disappear, which she did eventually. Next time Bliss came to check on me, I told her.

"Oh, there is an angel watching over you," she said matter-of-factly, as she smiled warmly.

Maybe I was delirious or maybe I really saw a vision, an angel. I don't know but I never forgot it. The power of belief. Some people have said that, 'you have to see it to believe it,' but it is also true that, 'you have to believe it to see it.'

Cheerful had a dream. Everyone had heard about this dream and the knowledge of it was discussed widely in the community. Cheerful was around my age. It was that camping trip where we were all rolled out our sleeping bags in the Barn. The kids had been sent to the farm after the neighbors had complained about our noise. In the middle of the night, I awoke to the sounds of a child screaming. It was Cheerful. He told us there was a lion in his dream. Abishai calmed him down, told him not to be afraid, that it was the lion of Judah. The Love Family saw itself as the tribe of Judah, and the tribe of Judah's symbol was the lion.

For some time after that, it was talked about like gossip, but good gossip, because everyone was so impressed that such a young kid would have this very significant spiritual dream. Cheerful got all this attention for it, and I noticed that after that, some of the other kids were also having dreams. The attention was enough to encourage them to just make it up. It worked, because I saw Understanding take each child aside and with a notebook, she wrote down what they told her, showing them the utmost interest.

Zarah was around seven years old when she decided to "make up" her brother Reconciliation's symbol. I already explained that a written symbol could be attached to someone's virtue name as an additional status sign. Her brother had not been given one yet, and she knew, like we all did, that the way that someone got his/her symbol was usually through a member's dream or a vision. Zarah wanted her brother to have one too. Who wouldn't, her little brother was the cutest little thing. The next morning, she got up and told everyone her dream.

Years later, she told me what happened. 'I had a dream!' she said excitedly. "God came and there was a big rainbow and God said," 'this is Reconciliation's symbol!' she told people. Her mom and some other householders had her draw it and she was taken to Love. The drawing was a circle with a dot in the center. It had points coming out from the center to create an eight-pointed star. Dignity, a Family artist was there on the bus with Love, and Love asked him to simplify the design, which then became her brother's symbol. Zarah explained, "I was being consistent with my lie, but I will always know that I didn't really have that dream."

Zarah later learned that the symbol that she drew as a child actually does mean harmony in Tibetan culture, and harmony is a synonym for Reconciliation.

I found an entry in my then diary about a conversation between Zarah and myself when we lived together in the same household:

Dear Diary,

I asked Zarah last night, what are you going to dream about? She said goats and horse leeto I said, "I am going to dream about God's angels."

Rachel Israel

I don't know what that was about. Maybe it was just us, goofing off. I really had dreams about Angels though. Whenever I had a dream, I would be asked to share it and to write it down, so sometimes I just kept it private, since I didn't feel like sharing it. Understanding kept a file with a lot of the kids' visions and dreams in it. She would share them with Love when she determined the dream might have a message for the Family.

I had a dream once about fairies and I know she wrote that one down, and I assume she shared it with Love.

Years later, I had another dream. It was after reading a book that was assigned to me in school, *The Diary of Anne Frank*. I was deeply moved by her story. I had received a diary sometime after that and began to write in.

In the dream, I came upon a huge, intricately carved wooden, bookshelf. I pulled out a book from that shelf that read, *The Book of Life*. I was aware, by then, that in the book of Revelations, it talked about a list of those who will live with God forever in heaven, and that it had said that "whoever was not found written in the book of life would be cast into the lake of fire," (20:15) But in my dream, when I opened the 'Book of Life,' I did not see a list of names. Instead, I saw that it was my life story. It hit me. I knew there was something important about the dream. Here I had read Anne Frank's diary and had received my own diary, and now this dream, of my own story sitting there on this bookshelf?

I began to see my life in the Love Family was part of my story, a story that I would someday read. It gave me a whole new perspective on my life. I thought to myself, *so I am here now, but someday, this is just going to be a part of my story.*

I was brought up within a spiritual environment where symbolism and deeper meanings were a fundamental part of life. I was being taught that dreams were meaningful and had messages.

It seemed I heard a lot of members talk about dreams they had had, dreams that had messages that led them to the Love Family. I heard a lot of people say that before they joined, they had "been asleep," and when they came to the Love Family, they had been "awakened." I wanted to know what that meant, and how it might apply to me.

And that's the one weakness in my perceptions and memories of life growing up in the Love Family. I was a child, and I missed out on a whole realm of spirituality that only the adults would understand and be able to talk about. I did have spiritual experiences that helped me understand what I was being taught, but I also had an interest there that drew me towards the spirit world. But it was limited compared to what the adults experienced. It's impossible for me to explain the adult perspective about their spiritual experiences and what it was like for them to be drawn to the Love Family.

I can still ask the questions though and try to come up with answers. Why were people joining the Love Family? They had told me. They had been 'awakened.' They were joining because the Love Family 'awakened' something in them spiritually.

In his book, *Religion, Culture and Society: A Global Approach*, Andrew Singleton wrote that in the 1960s and 1970s, there was a period of "awakening," fueled by the massive mood of counterculture where teens and young adults "shunned the strictures of organized religion." Singleton talked about the "spiritual marketplace," where there was a "plethora of spiritual alternatives." It was during this time that many alternative, spiritual groups arose such as the Krishna Consciousness Society, the Unification Church and many others (116).

At the same time that this 'Awakening' was happening, communes were sprouting up everywhere.

Before 1960, there were hardly any communes. Miller, (1990) documented only 225 during the 100-year period between 1860 and 1960. Then, in the late 1960s, there was a huge resurgence of hippie communes.

By 1971, the National Institute of Health estimated over three thousand communal groups in the U.S., and over 800 were deemed to be part of the Jesus People Movement (DiSabatino, 1994: Chapter III). That estimate is consistent with another estimate done by David Benjamin Zablocki, a professor of sociology at Rutgers University. Zablocki is widely published on subjects such as charismatic religious movements. He wrote: "I estimate that there are currently about a thousand rural hippie communes in North America, and at least twice that many urban communes. I have personally visited close to a hundred of these in the last five years." (Zablocki, 1971, pg. 300)

After 1960, many communes were formed in connection with the hippie movement, but the Encyclopedia of American Religions explains that numerous Christian communes also sprang up. Among the hippies, there emerged a Christian evangelical movement; it was joined by occult, Eastern, and New Age communities which combined hippie values with their own ideas of communes as transforming agents in society (1999).

As stated above, almost a third of the communes that sprung up were rooted in the Jesus People Movement. June 21st, 1971, on *Time Magazine* was a full-page, graphic image of Jesus Christ. Above his head was a halo-like label that read, "The Jesus Revolution." The feature article inside of that issue was called, "The New Rebel Cry: Jesus is Coming!" The article is hopeful sounding as Church leaders and others discuss a resurgence of followers to the Christian faith, where massive numbers of hippie youth were passionately joining and returning to churches across the country. "Communal Christian houses are multiplying like loaves and fishes," it read. "It has been a startling development for a generation that has been constantly accused of tripping out or copping out with sex, drugs and violence." The photos included with the article are amazing shots of large groups of young hippies praying together, expressions of ecstasy on their faces as they look upward in prayer.

I heard them called 'Jesus Freaks.' The word "Freak" wasn't a bad word in the counterculture. It was used to describe anyone who was into something so much that they "freaked out." A freak is someone who has gone to an extreme on anything, so there were "acid freaks," or "speed freaks" or some other kind of "freak," depending on what they were "freaked out" on.

Before my mom joined the Love Family, she was a self-proclaimed, 'Dylan Freak,' but the Love Family did not describe ourselves as 'Jesus Freaks.'

I sometimes wonder if the Love Family was a result of a marriage between the Back-to-the-Land, counter-cultural Movement and the Jesus Movement. Then throw in some Eastern spiritual influences, some ancient Judaism and voila!

It was as simple as a bunch of people looking for an alternative to the alternatives. Societal institutions that held people together no longer were meeting their needs, and a lot of people were free spirited seekers, feeling lost after having given up on the more traditional answers that were available. Others were rebelling against the religions of their birth families which left a vacuum. Some communes had five or six people, others had thousands of members such as the Hare Krishna and East Indian groups like the one led by Maharaj Ji.

I came up with the perfect prototype of someone attracted to the Love Family: They were:

Sick of the current values and norms of society,
Angry about Vietnam or other injustices of the times,
Naturally rebellious,

A creative personality,

Turned off to traditional religion but still believed in God,

Believed in the hippie idealism of that era,

Negative experiences with the typical communes of the time,

Actively looking for alternatives with a desire to drop out.

Another thing that may have attracted some people to the Love Family, was the fact that nobody worked traditional jobs. Things that were needed were obtained through trade or barter or bought in large quantities such as bulk foods. Then there were some efforts to create self-sufficiency such as through gardening or harvesting produce in Eastern Washington.

One year it seemed so many of the ladies were crocheting hats made out of human hair, so every time I brushed my hair, I would clean out my brush and put the hair into some bag to be used by someone to make a hat with. It sounds gross to me now, but back then, it was just this fad for a short time.

In terms of whether we were doing enough gardening to be self-sufficient, it would depend on which year. There were some years when we were living on the farm when I had to trek up to the gardens each evening to gather food for dinner. We ate every night from the garden. I would pick carrots and kale and other veggies that were in season or ready for harvest. But we were never totally self-sufficient. There was always 'the store,' where foods for the households were kept in bulk bins such as rice, beans, oats, olive oil, soy sauce and other necessities.

Just because people didn't work conventional jobs, doesn't mean everyone was sitting around all day either. People worked very hard within the community. The idea was that everyone worked together to make sure everything got done. Every day, the men and women went to an early morning meeting to determine what the tasks were for the day. I saw the men working together on different projects such as irrigation digging or other construction or landscaping projects. The women would coordinate cleaning, caring for children and making sure everyone was fed and clothed. Plus, there were some family businesses that had to be tended such as the cannery, the vineyards and wine making operation. There was also the work that we did in the orchards each year in Eastern, Washington. Then the Family would all get together for other tasks that were not relegated to one gender or another such as landscaping or gardening tasks.

For someone considering joining the Love Family, it might have been an appealing idea to join a community where people didn't work. Instead of getting paid, they would get to work in a nontraditional sense in a communal setting. One could do what was needed in order to build what they might've thought was a new society, a utopian dream world, a worthy purpose with meaning.

A lot of people were sick and tired of society at that point. They had had enough. The idea of coming together with other like-minded people and living off the grid was a popular concept. The Love Family was totally off the map. It was unique, and it was able to maintain that uniqueness because there was little interaction with outsiders.

William Partridge was an anthropological researcher who was interested in the hippie movement. While he was an instructor of Social Sciences at the University of Florida, he prepared a case study and published a book called, *The Hippie Ghetto*. The book is based on his experiences when he moved into a hippie neighborhood (ghetto) and took notes on the social organization, beliefs, and activities of his fellow residents. It was Height Ashbury. In order to do that effectively, he had to become a participant in the hippie subculture. After his experience, he refused to define what a hippie was and wrote: "…as any resident of San Francisco will testify, there are many different hippie cults and many different kinds of hippies…so there are drug groups, nudist groups, vegetarians, communes, Jesus Freaks, Krishna devotees, and virtually hundreds of other subdivisions of the larger group called hippies." (Partridge, p.10)

My point in bringing this up is to shed some light on the term 'hippie,' which is used very loosely and indiscriminately in our society today, and as a consequence, a lot of the diversity that existed within the counterculture was eliminated by the use of certain terminology. As a result, trying to explain how a place or thing, such as the Love family could exist, will pretty much take up this whole chapter.

There were a lot of "hippies" who joined the Love Family from the counterculture, but not everyone. There were people who joined who were living "straight" lives, and they came and just fell in love with what was happening. Some came from dysfunctional backgrounds, but then there were others who came from good homes and families. Despite the stereotypes of 'hippies coming from upper-middleclass homes, in my view of the many I met, they came from a wide diversity of economic backgrounds too. I knew a guy who had been severely abused and had been passed from foster home to foster home as a child, before he joined. There were others who came from poverty stricken families. Then I knew members like Understanding, who had been an airline stewardess and a politician's wife. She had never smoked pot in her life when she joined. Some people were very independent types who had been traveling all over, were educated or had some accomplishments under their belts, others didn't and had been just kicking around after high school. At least to me, it seems from everyone I have talked to, I have never been able to make much sense of the "type" of person who would join the Love Family.

The Love Family itself did not fit neatly into any predefined set of boxes. Religion is something that is used to identify differences among peoples and groups, but Love was able to assimilate eclectically a lot of different spiritual ideas and practices from different religions. This has made it difficult to explain to anyone what the Love Family was.

The Love Family had Eastern influences, such as meditation, which helps teach mental control and concentration. I had years of meditation, starting on day one of my life there as I have already described.

One of our core beliefs was Buddhist in nature; it was our focus on living in the present moment. "Now is the time." That was a big one. That's why when people joined, they did not talk about their past or who they were. It almost became like a past life all together that they couldn't remember. A lot of members' biological parents were heart broken and felt they had lost their children, because once people joined, their parents were now considered "earthly parents," and just part of the past, no longer considered important. Of course, parents of adult members were invited to come and join, one older couple did. Others would come and visit from time to time, but most did not.

The Love Family also had Judeo Christian roots. Ancient Israel was a model for social organization. The Love Family was considered a Christian community, a patriarchal kingdom based on Love's image of the tribe of Judah. According to the Love Family Charter, our purpose was to fulfill the prophecies of the New Testament by following the example of Jesus Christ.

The Love Family even celebrated Lent, a Catholic holiday; it was just a one-day event where members fasted. I didn't pay much attention to Lent though, because it was an adult holiday and not one the kids celebrated.

Love was drawn to Jewish beliefs as well. We celebrated Passover for example, but we did not celebrate it as modern-day Jews do; we celebrated it like the ancient Israelites did with a focus on the Old Testament. There were quite a few members in the Love Family who came from Jewish backgrounds, probably 20 or more from the list I developed with the help of other ex-members.

I would go up to the Front Door Inn and there were times when I saw the Hassid there visiting. Hassidic Judaism is a branch of Orthodox Judaism that promotes spirituality through the popularization and internalization of Jewish Mysticism as the fundamental aspect of the faith. (Wikipedia)

One time, I walked into the Front Door Inn, and there were all these men, doing this rousing singing, "Shema Yisrael Hashem Elokeinu Hashem Echad" which means, Hear O Israel, the Lord our God is one, and they were dancing in circles. The men would never look at any of the Family women when they came. It was amazing that they became friends with us since they were so fundamentalist in their religion, but my mom once speculated about that:

"Maybe they were trying to pull the Jewish boys that were in the Family back into the Jewish fold," she says.

It has never been easy to explain to people what my religious upbringing was. "It was very eclectic," I say. "VERY eclectic!"

The Love Family had all sorts of influences, such as Jewish, Buddhist, Christian, and a lot of New Age spiritual ideas derived from the hippie counterculture, and Love had woven them all together, so they fit neatly together with the ideals of oneness.

There is a place in the Bible where it talks about that oneness, and it's an important verse because it helps make the transition from seeing Jesus as a separate and elevated personality, which is how traditional Christianity understands Jesus, to more how the Love Family saw Jesus, which was more of a phenomenon that was allowing mankind to re-access their inherent oneness.

In Christ's prayer that he prayed at the last supper—a prayer found only in the Gospel of John, Chapter 17, verses 21–23, it says:

> Father…I pray…that they may be one; as thou Father, art in me, and I in thee, that they may be one, even as we are one…(*KJV*)

Sociologist Rob Balch, as I've said, came and lived for a time with the Love Family in order to study our group and write about his findings. He wrote that we were based on a *Monistic* conception of God. "Monism," he wrote, "means we are all part of God" or, put another way, that "there is a spark of divinity in each of us." Monism, Balch explained, is basic to Buddhism and Hinduism, whereas orthodox Christianity teaches that God is a separate entity and that humanity is fundamentally sinful."

I was taught that God was in me, and that we were all essentially one being, separated only by our egos and selfish desires. This understanding of God was what I learned was the true revelation of Jesus Christ. Here is Balch's explanation of how the Love Family thinking diverged from Christian orthodox teachings:

> Through his example of perfect love, Christ represented the spirit of God in man, but when Jesus died on the cross, the essence of his vision was lost and mankind succumbed to the forces of darkness and separation…Love claimed that during the 1960s, the spiritual consciousness of mankind had reawakened, and once again people had begun to recognize their oneness with God and each other. By dropping their worldly egos, loving each other, and living in agreement instead of conflict and competition, people could manifest the reality of Jesus Christ. For members of the Love Family, this was the real meaning of the resurrection. They were the body of Christ, forgiven for their sins, and they expected to live forever in a state of perpetual harmony and bliss without experiencing disease and death." (Balch, 1998, pg. 70).

Love Israel was once quoted saying, "I am merely the voice of

Christ. The body of Christ has many parts…there are the eyes, the heart, the feet, the hands. No one part has any more importance than the others, and the body needs all of its parts to function properly," he explained. "Our family, unified through love, is the living body of Jesus Christ… I speak the message of Christ, and I would be unable to do that if it were not for the other parts of my body" (*The Rocket* pg. 23 1984).

One of the central ideas underlaying the Love Family's belief system was 'We are one,' and the way that was interpreted was biblical:

> For as the body is one, and hath many members, and all the members of that one body, being many, are one body: so also is Christ (1 Cor, 12:12 *KJV*).

> For by one Spirit are we all baptized into one body, whether we be Jews or Gentiles, whether we be bond or free; and have been all made to drink into one Spirit (1 Cor, 12:13 *KJV*).

> So we, being many, are one body in Christ, and every one members one of another (Rom, 12:5 *KJV*).

Christ had returned, through us, and we all were the body of Christ. I talked in the previous chapter about how each virtue named person represented that virtue in the mind of Christ. For example, one elder there was named Humility, so he was seen to represent the humility of Christ. Then there was a man named Integrity; He was the integrity of Christ. They represented that virtue—in the mind of Christ.

It seems difficult to place the Love Family's version of spirituality into any one box. One thing is for certain, there was a complete and total focus on the Bible, especially the Old Testament. It was a guidepost for our lives.

When I first got there, I started school with the other children around my age, and the only book we had was the Bible. We had paper. We had crayons, and we had the Bible. It was a major change for me, because before I came, I had been reading all sorts of children's books. Now, except the Bible, there were no books whatsoever. This was especially true in the early days, which was at least the first five years I was there.

The Bible was central to community life, so much so, that I even remember it in my sleep. One morning, the big people were having a morning meeting. It was very early, so the kids were allowed to keep sleeping through the meeting, as we did every morning during that time. Since spaces were so often multipurpose and shared, it sometimes meant, I was sleeping in the same space while a meeting was taking place. As I was sleeping, I could hear the people talking, praying, and reading the Bible together. It was quite a lot of activity for me to try to sleep through, but eventually I got used to it and could mostly sleep through it. On this particular morning, I would float in and out of consciousness as the meeting droned on. A man named Frankness would read the Bible. There was probably 10 people at the meeting. They all sat on the floor in a circle. I lay half-awake behind a tapestry on the top bunk, just a few feet away. I listened to the biblical passage as it was read. I found out later it was from the book of John, 6:17-21, which was a passage about one of the miracles Jesus performed. As I listened to Frankness read, I began to dream about the verses as he talked. I thought it was very strange when I awoke and recalled the entire dream. I was literally dreaming the Bible. It's like I was there. Jesus's disciples got in a boat and set off for Capernaum. They hit rough waters, then were totally amazed to see Jesus walking on water towards them. The whole thing ended up in my dream in amazing detail. It was very strange to wake up and realize I had dreamed a story right out of the Bible as it was being told.

It was a lot of Bible for a kid—a lot of Bible, but overall, it wasn't so bad; there were a lot of things about growing up in the Love Family that were not so great, but for me, the Bible made more sense to me than some of the other things going on around me.

The Bible was a centerpiece in the spiritual landscape of my childhood. It was a strong value system that was being transmitted and ingrained into my brain. Kids on the outside might've been going to church on Sunday, and then throughout the week, going home to who-knows-what. But for me, there was a consistency there that was grounding and meaningful. The Bible was a way of life. I saw the adults open the Bible without looking, then place their finger down on a passage and just start to read. It was just for fun, as if it were their horoscope for the day. I would do it too and try to figure out what it meant, which wasn't easy because it was *King James Version*, which was not like some of the newer translated versions of today. I found it interesting, especially since there was nothing else to read, and I was naturally a reader and enjoyed ideas.

From growing up there, it seemed that was why a lot of people came and joined—for the spirituality and for the community, especially the community—I think that's what was seen as missing in the world they left behind, a world with big freeways and billboards and houses packed tight into big urban mega-cities; it was a world where no one knows anybody, and life is working 9 to 5 with no sense of meaning—no community.

The Love Family was seen as a viable way of life. They could live communally and work towards a common good. They had friends. They could earn status or position within the group. There was the camaraderie. Relationships were built. Children were born. People were bonded. There was a culture there that included its own language. Leaving meant losing all of that.

A lot of people joined because of Love himself. I have heard a lot of people who knew Love say that he was "handsome" and "charismatic." I saw his charisma, but handsome—no. As a child, I didn't see that at all. Love's face, to me, looked a lot like what you imagine Christ would look like in the pictures that you commonly see, except that Love's face was fuller and not so gaunt. He had people sew him beautiful clothes. He stood out in a crowd, like a star. He walked like royalty, like a king. He was extremely confident and would look people straight in the eye and say:

"Welcome home where we are building the kingdom of God."

I had very few personal interactions with Love myself. Mostly he addressed me as part of the group of children. I saw him all the time, walking about with his entourage of personal servants and priests. There were days when the Family all worked together, landscaping or doing yard work. He would be there helping out, but he always maintained his kingly status to where it was obvious that he was the king and not just some lowly member, working in the yard. He would have his robe on and he would walk about as people worked. He was kind of like a CEO of a major corporation. He would oversee and coordinate, make sure that the musicians were there and playing as we worked. He was bright and friendly as he oversaw the operation. He would go up to people as they worked and connect with them with his eyes and say something inspiring about oneness or something else that was spiritually significant. He seemed to be constantly concerned with how people were feeling and with the group mood. He worked to make everyone feel connected to each other.

He would at times call everyone to a Family meeting or gathering and lead the prayer and meditation. Wherever he went, he was always the center of attention at all times. He was micromanaging and orchestrating the entire group every minute, every day.

It was impossible not to see him or to see what a huge influence he was over everyone. Things were a little bit more relaxed when he wasn't around, but not a whole lot, because then there were the elders who took on his duties when he wasn't there. The elders idolized Love and always were trying to be like him. In this kingdom, I wasn't close to the king; I was close to the children and to the members who took care of the children.

As a child, it was very boring to me to hear Love talk. He seemed to say the same things over and over again. I would much have preferred to go play or do just about anything, really, than just sit there and listen to him talk. But that is the difference I think at least for a lot of the kids there as opposed to the adults there. There wasn't anything he ever said to me that struck me as relevant to my life. There was a time when Love had this meeting with the kids. It was the older kids, which by now, there were about 30 of us in this meeting. It was my peers and the kids who were a couple years younger. We all sat in our finest linens, sitting in the half lotus in a circle. Love paced around the outside of the circle, talking animatedly to us. Usually he talked about spiritual concepts and expected us to respond to him like the big people would; If we didn't, he seemed irritated, befuddled. But this time, He gave us instruction on how to breath if we were all stranded in the ocean without a boat. I learned from him that day, that there was a specific way to breath and hold my arms in just such a way that I would not expend much energy. If I could do it, I could wait in the ocean for a longer period of time until I was rescued. At that point, I hadn't been to the ocean since Maui, and I never had swimming lessons, although I taught myself the dog paddle. As he talked, I wondered why he was he telling us this. I guess it was somewhat interesting, at least compared to some of the talks he usually gave.

I got the sense that the big people responded to him very differently. It seemed that everything he said was golden. People would take him very literally, and everything he said was taken very seriously. That is why I always heard everyone saying, "Love said this..." or "Love said that..." When Love made a decision, I often heard that "It had come down." In other words, as if from heaven, because Love represented God, so it was assumed that whatever Love decided had such importance attached to it as if God himself had decided. Everything Love said was what people lived their lives by. Even the papers reported on what Love said:

> I had a revelation or just a remembrance that I am one with every-one...I felt the whole earth was actually a family and connected. We don't want to hide anything. We just want to be able to be eternal subjects of God and claim the inheritance of Jesus Christ. I was not a totally religious man, and I saw Jesus Christ. I saw that we were all one. At that moment, we really came together and saw Jesus Christ...It was obvious we were being called together...There is go-ing to be a day when everybody is going to see Jesus Christ. We did. And we didn't think we would." (*Seattle Times* Jan 23, 1982 A10)

Love often talked about the vision that he and Logic had when they were living in the Height Ashbury district just before he started the Love Family. He and Logic had looked into each other's face and each saw the face of Jesus Christ in the other. I want to touch on that for a moment, because I heard people talk a lot about seeing Jesus Christ in each other's faces. The Charter of the Love Family stated, that we were founded on the revelation of Jesus Christ, and that without this revelation we would never understand our purpose on this earth or our relationship to one another. One of the aspects of that revelation that seemed unique to our Family's shared experience was the phenomenon of seeing the fully recognizable face of Jesus Christ superim-posed on someone else's face.

I also saw what I was being told was the face of "Jesus Christ" in someone else's face. It happened during a meditation. Serious was overseeing the meditation. All the kids were sitting as usual on the floor cross-legged in a circle, which was the standard way to sit there, especially during meetings or meditations. Serious talked to the kids about Jesus Christ and how Jesus was in all of us and that if I looked, I could see Jesus Christ in peoples' faces. So, he instructed us all to look across the circle and into the face of the child across from us.

I kept staring and staring into the face of the child across from me. I don't remember who it was, but it was a long time to stare into someone's face, probably minutes. Kids who couldn't handle it were taken out of the circle and away as to not distract the rest of us. As I stared into the child's face across from me, her face began to change. Her face became unfamiliar to me. It was frightening to see someone's face distort into a face I didn't recognize. Serious said I was seeing Jesus Christ in her face. Maybe it was, or maybe it was some sort of natural distortion. Faces aren't designed to be stared at for endless periods of time.

Another time, I was watching Serenity. She was a dainty and petite, small brunette. She reminded me of some of the Disney pictures I had seen of Snow White. I stared at her beautiful jewelry. She wore pretty rings and several bracelets on each wrist. She was working over a wood stove and I became mesmerized by her. I was staring and staring at her for a long time. I was suddenly jolted into thought when I noticed her face change into a strange face that I did not recognize. I thought, *Am I seeing the face of Jesus Christ? Is this what everyone is talking about?*

Years later, I went to a public high school, and I told my best friend Kate to stare at me until my face changed. She looked at me like I was strange, but she did it anyway. I was just going to do it as an experiment to see if I could make it happen again, and because I was bored. We stared and stared for minutes, trying to contain our laughter.

"Weird! She suddenly stopped and exclaimed. "Your face changed! How did that happen?" Her face had changed too just like Serenity's had changed years earlier.

Did I see Jesus in my friend? Did she see Jesus in mine? Or was there some scientific explanation?

Apparently, there may be a scientific basis for it. A recent discovery made by vision researcher Giovanni Caputo from the University of Urbino in Italy and reported in Scientific America magazine, found that staring for a prolonged period of time into someone's eyes has the ability to affect our consciousness and cause hallucinations. Many of the subjects in Caputo's study began to experience altered states of consciousness in less than 1 minute. "According to the feedback received, 90% of the participants saw the faces of other participants change shape and warp, 75% saw the appearance of monsters or animals, and in some cases, 15% saw deceased family members." This phenomenon was named the "strange-face illusion."

Illusion or not, Love said he saw the face of Jesus Christ in Logic and that he had a deep realization of the oneness of humanity, which inspired him to such a degree that he started a community based on that vision and idea. Why did people join the Love Family? They joined because they could relate to Love's vision of oneness. I had the childhood that I had because of the power of an idea.

There was another part of the story that Love told, It was a story about how Love's name came to be "Love."

Apparently, Love was riding a bus in Texas when he had a vision. His name was Paul, although members did not talk about the names they had before they joined. The vision was of a white stone and inscribed on this white stone was the name, "Love." In correlation with this was the verse in Revelation 2:17, "He that hath an ear, let him hear what the Spirit saith unto the churches; To him that overcometh will I give to eat of the hidden manna, and will give him a white stone, and in the stone a new name written, which no man knoweth saving he that receiveth it." (*King James Version*).

Love's original vision of oneness changed his life and led him to start the Love Family. His entire mission for everyone was to build a family where he could make his vision a reality, and that's what he did for the rest of his life.

Love was always asking people to share their visions of Jesus, of oneness. He was totally convinced that it was important. When it was quiet during the meeting, Love would ask everyone questions. There were certain things that he said all the time. Love would always ask, "Who here has seen Jesus Christ?" or "Who here has seen we are all one?" or "Who here has seen Love is the answer?" or "Has anybody had any revelations?" Everyone was real quite once he asked the question. Then someone might speak up and share a vision or revelation. Once they were done sharing, Love would comment on it and show how the revelation fit in with his vision. In this way, it was like everyone had an opportunity to contribute to the vision that guided the community.

"What have you seen?" he would say as he looked directly at someone. Then, I would hear people reply:

"I just see my family," or "I see the beauty of the present moment," or "I just see myself," or "I just see the importance of staying in the now and loving."

"Who has seen totally beyond a shadow of a doubt that this is it?" Love would always ask. Everyone would raise their hand.

"God showed me love was the answer and it was time to get together," he would say. Love was in total command, and there was total silence and attentiveness to him at all times.

Oftentimes a scripture was shared, such John 15 where Jesus declared that he is the vine and we are the branches. It was easy to see our oneness in these verses from the Bible. Love was always pointing out that the Bible was "just us." He said, "We just have to bring the Kingdom down." These things Love said, he said them all the time, not just at meetings, then the elders all had their own versions of similar comments. Then everybody was just repeating a lot of the ideas that came from Love. There were times when the kids were absent from whatever the big people were doing, especially the younger children. But each year, I was a little older and more and more included in the spiritual life.

Love seemed to care deeply about people's revelations. He made them important. That is how many people would receive their name, but also, people's visions and dreams were affirmations of his vision. For example, and this is just an example, so I am making it up, but if Love told us that there was a castle in the sky. If someone had a dream about that castle, then that dream became proof of the castle's existence. Dreams and visions were unifying, and their symbolism was significant. They were influential in creating the world that I lived in as a child.

Love would say:

"I went up and became one with everything and came down and saw all my parts and knew we had to get together. I knew someone had to do it. The only way out was to love my way out and give my life."

Love would say that God showed him that Jesus Christ was in everyone. Jesus Christ was in me too. Jesus had risen from the dead, and he had come back through all of us. I was part of the body of Christ now.

When I was younger, it would be hard for me to sit for long periods. I sometimes couldn't wait for the meetings to be over. If one can imagine how this sort of conversation might have sounded to a young child. One memory that I have is a day when Love was having a meeting with the kids. After the meditation, he looked directly at me.

"What have you seen?" He asked me.

The children were raising their hands and telling him of certain dreams they had had or in some cases visions, making it up as they went from what I have heard years later.

I hadn't "seen" anything. I just wanted him to look away.

Another child, was raising his hand, waving it all around, seemingly desperate to be called on.

I wished that he would call on that child, but he didn't. I didn't know what to say. I was scared. I didn't want to displease him, but it seemed that he was expecting something, because he kept staring into my eyes in front of everybody. I could feel myself blushing. I was embarrassed, but I was also angry that he would single me out in this way. Several long moments went by while he continued to stare.

"Why is your face so red?" Love finally asked, sounding curious.

What was I supposed to say? I thought.

Finally, he moved on, but again, one of those horrible moments when I had failed to live up to Love's expectations, when he wanted me to say something of value and I had nothing to share.

Love was considered like our dad, a dad to the children but also even, as I heard later, a lot of the adults felt that way about him. He made all the decisions about everything, even about the children. At Christmastime, all the presents were from Love. To me though, I had known Marty, who had been like a real dad to me, so Love was fatherly, but he seemed more like a distant stepdad, but not like a dad at all, really; he was more like a powerful King, a powerful ruler of which I was a subject, someone who I would never want to cross.

My impression of Love was that he was a perfectionist. He was very critical and noticed everything, so around him, I felt self-conscious. He wasn't just another person, he was Love. The most important person there, and he was very particular and could easily be displeased.

Certainly nothing like the gentle, humble Marty who lovingly took care of me when I was sick in Alaska. Marty would hang out and talk to me like a friend in what now seemed like an increasingly, distant and fading past life.

People had different impressions of Love. Sociologist Rob Balch who is a sociologist at the University of Montana teaches courses on unconventional religious groups. He is best known for his studies of Heaven's Gate (with David Taylor), the Aryan Nations, and the Love Family. He met Love at a meeting that took place at the Rainbow Gathering one year. He wrote about what it was like meeting Love for the first time:

> "On the floor of Love's spacious, octagonal tent was a huge Persian rug. The white tent flaps had been rolled up to let in the sunlight, and crystals dangling from the wooden frame sent rainbows dancing around the space. Seated on a pillow that elevated him above everyone else, Love Israel resembled an Old Testament patriarch. He was tall and slender, with clear blue eyes, long brown hair, and a full beard. He wore a spotlessly clean, sleeveless robe tied at the waste with a red sash. His neatly combed hair reached down to the middle of his back. As the meeting got under way, beautiful women in long handmade dresses poured mugs of freshly ground coffee with honey and cream, taking care to serve the most influential guest first. It was, I thought, a magical scene out of a Hollywood version of *The Arabian Nights*." (64)

Understanding once explained it to me this way:

"Love's charisma was beyond what we'll ever know," she explained. "People who were well known for their charisma, people like Richard Nixon,

Dr. King, or Robert Kennedy, at the end of the day, many of those people who served them, if they weren't paid, they would be gone the next day. But Love's charisma was such that people served him for many years without pay. People would have given their lives for him."

People in a group called the People's Temple died for Jim Jones, the leader who claimed to be the reincarnation of Jesus, as well as other charismatic leaders who had great power such as Ikhnaton, Buddha, Lenin, and Father Divine. I always have wondered what sort of charisma Mr. Jones might have had to make them drink poison.

When the mass suicide took place in 1978, I didn't know about it. As far as I know, most people in the Love Family didn't know about it, since members did not keep themselves informed about what was happening in the outside culture.

Unbeknownst to most members, on November 18th, 1978, over 909 people were found dead in what was considered a 'mass suicide' in northern Guyana. At the bidding of Jim Jones, all his people drank poison in what Temple members considered a "revolutionary suicide" protesting capitalism in favor of socialism.

I sometimes have pondered whether Love would've ever done something like that to us. He didn't, but I can easily see that he could have. Love had the kind of power that Jim Jones had.

Love offered people a vision. I heard all the time that "Heaven was coming down." Love was bringing heaven down to earth. We were creating heaven on earth. Heaven wasn't this place somewhere up in the sky. Heaven was right here, right now. And it was up to each one of us to help create heaven on earth. I learned that I can make life hell by being negative and unloving, or I can create heaven by my kindness and love towards others. I always heard people say that the Love Family was the kingdom of heaven. I was aware of what I was being taught, because it was being taught year after year.

When visitors came, I noticed they had this look of wonder on their faces. It didn't seem to take them long to decide to join.

Understanding lived in Love's household for many years since she helped take care of his kids. Her impression of Love:

"He was like a movie director," she explained. "He knew how people fit into the larger picture and how everyone had a place," she says. Then Understanding gave me an example of how that was true. She told me about Red. She says that there was this guy who came named Red who was extremely good at sorting garbage, and his name became Essential. His name seemed so perfect for him. Love had seen Red's gift. He came as a total nobody, and now he was an 'Essential' part of Christ. "Love was really good about seeing people's gifts." He was very "demanding" though, Understanding explained. He had "an absolute clear prescription." It was "very strict." To get along there, one had to "bow to the system." If they could do that, "they had a feeling of being part of the chosen people. They got a name. They were given an identity and status." For example, "Love loved the artists, so he set them up. They often had their own house. He made sure they had paint. Then, if someone showed exceptional leadership skills, they often would be made an elder. Others," Love thought, "were better serving."

There was a man who came. He was a dentist. He was also a gifted hiker, backpacker and outdoorsman. Love honored those gifts in him. In other words, Love allowed him to fix people's teeth and to help train people for outdoor sports. Then Love honored him with a virtue name—Presence. Presence was a really fun guy, like a big kid himself.

He once let me and Esther sit in his dental chair and clean each other's teeth. It was fun to use the electric toothbrush and pretend to be her dentist. Another time, Presence took some of the kids' whitewater river rafting. He did that a few times. What a blast it was getting sprayed with water as we screamed our way through the rapids down the river. Once we got to still waters, Understanding brought out her famous banana and peanut butter sandwiches made with homemade wheat bread, a hippie staple for a lot of hippie kids during those times. I also remember a trip with Presence to Mt. Adams. I was amazed by the beauty on that trip. As I hiked up to base camp with another girl, Gentle, who was also on the trip, I saw little animals peek out from the rocks. The climate and wildlife were so different at that elevation. Gentle and I collected pinecones and woodsy treasures like fungus and mosses to bring back home. There was another trip that was very memorable. Presence took a group of kids and other guardians to Lake 22 in the middle of winter. When we got there, the lake was frozen, so we got to do a little impromptu ice skating in our everyday shoes.

I loved going on adventures with Presence. He was someone whose gifts were recognized and made a part of our life, but not everyone's gifts were recognized.

There were those who felt that they were not able to contribute in the ways that they were gifted. My mom had gifts that were not recognized or honored by Love. She was a talented seamstress and had been sewing since the age of six. That was one reason she sewed so much so she could prove that she was good at something.

There were times when her skills were put to use. She tells me proudly that, at one point, she was assigned to work for eight months with Vortex. Vortex was working on a project to make the sanctuary tent, which was a huge, beautiful, white, eight-sided, tent with mosquito netting. Plus, my mom could play the piano and flute as well, but instead of being able to contribute her gifts, sadly, she felt that she was placed in more serving roles, household labor such as cooking and cleaning mostly.

My teacher Ethan said he felt that his gifts as a musician were not honored either. Ethan ended up being more assigned to help with the kids, gardening and with the animals. Why did Love honor some but not others?

There were so many members, it might not have been practical to honor everyone's talents. One ex-member said that the musicians that were chosen to be honored had an exclusive mentality, a sort of in-group-out-group click that had the effect of keeping some people out. I heard that if a woman wasn't skinny or pretty enough, her gifts might not be honored. Maybe they weren't submitted enough to Love or maybe they didn't have enough to offer. I am not sure what Love was thinking, but I am sure there were many people who wanted to be honored by Love in any way that they could, so it must've been disappointing when it didn't happen for them.

Even if there were members whose gifts were not utilized, they still came, made it their home, and were convinced in Love's vision enough to live their lives there. Relative to the number of members, very few were elders, most were at the bottom of the hierarchy. Thus, status in and of itself must not have been a motivator for people who joined. It must've been something much greater, a simple life, serving God, being a part of a community.

It didn't cost anything, but it wasn't free. It was almost like the opposite—people paid by giving up everything, including their former lives and anything they owned.

As I have described throughout this chapter, there were many societal and cultural factors that made the Love Family an attractive place. But none of it would've happened if it hadn't been for Love. To even be a part of the Love Family, they had to have been convinced that what Love was offering far outweighed any costs or people wouldn't have joined, and many wouldn't have stayed for as long as they did.

People joined or stayed because they believed in Love. Love once said something that struct me as interesting. He was interviewed by historian Chuck LeWarne for his book called, *The Love Israel Family: urban commune, rural commune.* Love was asked about the period of time before he started the Love Family when he was a television salesman, and his name had been Paul Erdmann. Love told Chuck LeWarne, 'When I was selling, I realized that people believed me.' And it made him feel 'guilty.' Love continued, 'People actually believed me when I told them something! I realized I should be telling them the truth…[I was] making things sound better than they really were as all salesman do.' That was when he decided 'to get into something more real.' (LeWarne, 2009, pg. 18)

It wasn't that long after that when Paul, after having life changing visions, became known as 'Love' and founded the Love Israel Family where he lived as the founder and leader of said community for the remainder of his days, which was the next 45 or more years of his life.

What was Love's background? Were there clues from his childhood that would explain who he became? Love, of course, rarely talked about his childhood. As a hippie turned guru, he taught about the importance of 'staying present' and not focusing on the past. So, everything I have gathered about his childhood, that I am about ready to share, is based on my conversations with Understanding who talked to Love's mom, Omi. Love had sent Understanding to visit Omi who lived in Astoria, Oregon. Omi needed help with smelt season, so there was a crew of kids that went to help her for a few days.

Their job was to stand in the river and help catch the smelt in buckets, then clean and prepare them, so that Omi could put the cleaned fish in the smokehouse. During the day, Love would leave while Understanding and the kids stayed behind to help his mom. When Love was gone, that's when Omi began to talk about Love's upbringing to Understanding.

Omi said that Love was born in Germany as Paul Erdman in 1939. This was towards the end of WWII. Paul's family were wealthy; his grandpa, (Omi's dad) had been German nobility and a Baron.

When Paul was four years old, the Allies started bombing the area where Paul and his family lived, and the Germans took over the family's mansion. That is when the family went and lived in an apartment in Berlin. When the Dutch Underground began circulating pictures of what Hitler was doing to the Jews, Paul's dad, Hubert began to think that Hitler was mad and might get everybody killed. He began listening to Radio Free Europe.

A neighbor overheard it and turned Hubert in, and he was sent to prison. The prison was a holding place for political prisoners, some of whom were known to end up in concentration camps. Omi had to sell a few valuables she had hidden away, and with the help of a wealthy relative was able to use a bribe to get Hubert released. The bribe was risky, so once he was released, the family went into hiding in Holland. Omi's mom (Paul's grandmother) had the neighbor, who originally turned Hubert in, killed, because he was supposed to testify against Hubert at an upcoming hearing. Omi said they buried the neighbor in the back yard in the vegetable garden behind the mansion.

There is one report I saw that said that the neighbor suicided. Since I am assuming that report came from Love, it is my guess, since his report conflicts with his mother's, who said the neighbor was murdered to keep him quiet, it makes sense to me that suicide is what the children (Love and his siblings) were told. Love was under seven when all this happened.

Anyway, when the family was living in Holland, it was safer, but not much. To lower the risk that they would be detected, Paul was taught to be a deaf mute each time he went to fetch the mail. There was concern that if he talked, someone would hear his accent and reveal that they were German. One day, when Paul went out to get the mail, he didn't return, and the family were terrified that something had happened to him. Hubert went out looking for Paul and found him. He had joined a funeral Cortez, thinking that it was a parade.

Omi talked about the day they had all gone to Church when a regi-men of Hitler's soldiers marched into the church and removed the minister, who was reading an anti-Hitler document. The family watched as another minister got up and continued reading the document; he also was removed, then another and another. Every one of the ministers who were taken that day, were never heard from again.

The family was forced to leave the apartment in Berlin and they found a field in the country where they camped for a period of time. In the same field, there was another family with young children who also lived there. All the kids would play together. Paul had two brothers and a sister. His two brothers were Peter and Bob. Peter was the oldest. Bob was around Paul's age and had been adopted when the child's family was killed in a bombing. Paul's sister Mary was the youngest. One day, they were playing with the neighbor's kids when the field was bombed. Paul and his siblings narrowly escaped death, but all the neighbor's kids were killed in the bombing.

Then after the field was bombed, the family went and lived in a bomb shelter. They stayed there until one day, it was quiet; they thought it was safe to come out. As everyone was leaving the shelter, suddenly bombs started raining again and there was a mad dash to return to the shelter. It became a stampede where several people got trampled to death. 'Paul saw the whole thing, perched on his dad's shoulders.'

The family were unable to get back into the shelter, because of the stampede, so the they hid in a nearby grocery store. They had just barely gotten safely into the grocery store when the bomb shelter was hit by a bomb and everyone in it died, but because Paul and his family had hidden in the grocery store, they all lived.

Paul came close to death again when there was an accident. It hap-pened once the family was able to return to their mansion. The Allies had taken back possession of their home from the Germans and had turned it into a makeshift hospital. The home was full of soldiers and artillery, but at least they were safe—until Paul was seriously injured. He was playing on a tank when he accidentally drove it through a brick wall.

With so many accidents and near misses in Paul's early life, Omi said she always thought her son, Paul was 'special,' and claimed that when he was an infant, she had seen an angel over his cradle.

Omi had dual citizenship as a German and American, so after the war, the family came to America. Paul was just seven years old, but still remembered that it was a 'rough' adjustment.

Once they were living in America, there was a divorce. Omi said that 'Hubert had a problem molesting little girls in the family.' She then married a man named Charlie and they raised the kids together. As he was growing up, Paul traveled freely to visit relatives in Switzerland and was sent to a private high school while he was there.

After high school, Paul went into business and ended up bankrupt by the time he was 21. He gave up business, moved to the Height Ashbury District in San Francisco, a hippie ghetto and began exploring Eastern religion. During this period, he had a back injury and ended up in the hospital where' he saw a vision of Jesus Christ,' then in that same time frame, he had the vision that I discussed earlier when he was riding on a bus in Texas.

Not many in the Love Family knew much about Love's past, other than his visions and revelations, which he shared freely. And even though Love didn't talk about his early childhood, somehow it must've been important in terms of who he became and some of the choices that he made. One thing that seems clear to me, was that Love wasn't just some average American Joe; he had an unusual family background. He suffered trauma in his early childhood, then had a difficult adjustment in school when his family moved to America. Once he moved, he had to adjust to Catholic school as a 'German kid,' where he got into frequent fights (LeWarne, 2009, 16-17).

After Understanding talked to Omi about Love's childhood and upbringing, she also had the opportunity to talk to Hubert who confirmed what Omi had told her. Understanding and a group of Love's kids had stopped off to see Hubert and his wife, Bell in Utah, on their way to the Arizona Rainbow Gathering.

Then Understanding also talked to Peter, Love's older brother who also confirmed the story and had more to add. Peter showed Understanding a photo of their old mansion, where the neighbor, the witness who was to testify against Hubert, was buried.

......

I am sure there is a lot more that I could learn about why people joined the Love Family. It's like a painting that never gets finished. But I have laid out some of the major things that were going on, culturally, during that time in history to help explain it. I guess, for me, I have had to struggle with trying to make sense of my past.

My mom just happened to be in Homer Alaska and heard about this commune that also lived there. My mom just happened to have a friend, Suzanne, who joined and encouraged her to also join. If we hadn't gone to Alaska, would my mom have eventually gone back to Seattle anyway? Would she have ended up finding out about the Love Family and then joining at that point? Maybe. Word gets around in the counterculture, and the Love Family was one of the largest and most well-known groups to come out of the Seattle area. She was looking for a commune, so there's a good chance I would've ended up being raised in the Love Family.

This was how I was raised. It's different, for sure, but the more I have tried to understand why, the easier it has been to accept. Not everyone needs to understand everything, but for me, I was born curious and with a natural drive to understand things. It has been easier to accept once I put the thought into understanding how the Love Family even happened in the first place? Who was Love? Why did people join? I have tried to turn what has been a negative in my life in certain ways, into something positive, something that interests me, something to figure out and understand.

The scope of this chapter was not to come to any definitive conclusions. It was written for my husband and for anyone wanting some explanation as to why anyone would want to join this group; For them, I suspect that I have only made things more of a riddle. Funny thing is, that I have found that the more I tell someone about the Love Family, the more curious and confused they become. It has been so frustrating that its ends up being one of the reasons why I don't talk about it.

In the next chapter, I provide a lot more detail about the Love Family hierarchy and how it transformed all social life. I include my memories of what it was like as a child growing up in a community that was governed very differently than how things are governed in America.

BIBLIOGRAPHY (CHAPTER 5)

Balch, Rob. (1998). The Love Family: Its Formative Years. *Religion in the Age of Transformation: Sects, Cults and Spiritual Communities: A Sociological Analysis* Ed. Marc Petrowsky, William W. Zellner. Praeger Publishers, Westport, CT.

DiSabatino, Dave. (1994). *History of the Jesus Movement*. Chapter III. McMaster University

Donovan, Mia. *Deprogrammed*. 78-minute docufilm EyeSteelFilm, Montreal, Quebec, Canada.

Galanter, Marc. (1989). *Cults: Faith, Healing and Coercion*. New York: Oxford University Press

[Ethan]. Personal Interview. November 16, 2015.

[Eve], Personal Interview. September 30, 2001.

Eichhorn, Dennis P. *Rocket*. Love Israel: On the Road Again. August 1984 pg. 23.

Hinterberger, John. *Seattle Times*. Love Family: Sect Wants to Rule Magnolia and Queen Anne. Tuesday. January 25, 1972. A20.

Holy Bible (*King James Version*) World Bible Publishers.

Israel, Larry. (1978). Unpublished Manuscript, pp. 170–281.

Israel, Betty. (2008). *Fighting the Storm*. Unpublished Manuscript.

Johannsen, Eric. (movie). *It Takes a Cult*. Produced by Santiago Films.

Martinez-Conde, Susana. & Macknik, Stephen L. (July 1, 2013). Illusory Scenes Fade into and Out of View. *Scientific American*, a division of *Nature America Inc.* (2017).

Melton, Gordon J. (1999). *Encyclopedia of American Religions*. First published in 1978; Consortium Books. McGrath Publishing Company.

Miller, Timothy. (1990). *American Communes, 1860–1960: A Bibliography*. Garland Publishing, Inc. New York and London.

Partridge, William L. (1973). *The Hippie Ghetto; A Natural History of a Subculture*. Georgia State University. Waveland Press Inc. Prospect Heights, Illinois.

Ruppert, Ray. *Seattle Times*. A New Look at Seattle's Church of Armaggedon January 23, 1982. A10.

Seattle Times. Ohio Court to Weigh Seattle Sect Member's Guardianship. April 23, 1975 B1.

Seattle Times. Steve Allen Carries an Open Mind to Son in Love Family. May 2, 1975. A4.

Seattle Times. Religious Sect Seeks Man's Return Despite Court Decision. April 25, 1975 B3.

Singleton, Andrew. (1999). *Religion, Culture and Society: A Global Approach*. Sage Publishers.

Time Magazine. The New Rebel Cry: Jesus is Coming! June 21, 1971. Pg. 56–63.

Understanding Israel, Personal Interview. December 13, 2015.

Understanding Israel, Personal Interview. December 29, 2001.

Zablocki, Benjamin David. (1971). *The Joyful Community: An Account of the Bruderhof: A Communal Movement Now in its Third Generation*. Baltimore: Penguin Books.

[Zarah]. Personal Interview. December 13, 2001. Maple Valley, WA.

CHAPTER 6

The Hierarchy: An Imbalance of Power

Before I begin with any discussion of the hierarchy, I must start by describing a certain document called 'Common Sense.' It was an especially important document to the Love Family's leadership.

Common Sense was written on parchment paper and composed with blue and gold calligraphic lettering. Each time the word 'Love' is mentioned, and it is mentioned quite frequently, it was in gold lettering. It was a one-page document, and it basically was the Love Family's version of the United States Constitution.

Common Sense established a government that existed as a separate, and superior entity from the U.S. Government. Its explained "purpose" was to tie its people together in "spiritual unity…leading to the conscious realization of the oneness of mankind." It's stated goal was the "complete liberation of all mankind from the tyranny of hate and greed, and the bondage of fear, loneliness, pain and death," for all people.

The Document proclaimed that "NOW is the time" for all people to affirm their "allegiance" to the "government of Love," and it proclaimed the right to "be free of all existing man-made laws…" It freed "any man from the demands and limitations of all lesser systems of government." Furthermore, Common Sense declared "independence from all existing financial systems," and stated that it was "sustained and supported, not by taxation, but by faith and unselfish devotion to the service of mankind."

Basically, it was screw the United States Government. Now that that has been made clear, I will now go on to describe the Love Family hierarchy. It was a very clear hierarchy from top to bottom.

At the top of the hierarchy, there was Love, who had total, unchecked authority. The next tier down were the elders. Elders were appointed by Love and were part of an inner circle, a governing body or council. Love ruled directly, but he also ruled through the elders. At the bottom of the hierarchy was everybody else.

On a regular basis, Love would hold Family meetings. There were meetings where everyone would attend, then at times, he would hold meetings for the men and the women separately. Then, he would hold meetings just for the elders. I attended the all-Family meetings and the meetings he would hold for the kids. I also went to a few Morning Meetings, which were all-family daily meetings held in the early mornings and included discussions of what work projects had to be completed that day. Meetings were a regular part of the life there. They were important times when Love would impart information about decisions he had made, and for people to meditate, read the Bible, smoke mashish, and share their revelations, dreams and visions. Meetings also functioned to emphasize and constantly remind everyone of the hierarchy.

Morning meetings were typically daily meetings that took place wherever members lived. There was one at the ranch for people that lived at the ranch. There was one in town, for people who lived in town. There was one at the cannery for people who lived in the house at the cannery, and so on. Love would sometimes meet with the elders who lived in the city separately. Then he would meet with those elders who lived on the Ranch. Those elders who lived in the city, tended to be higher up in the hierarchy but not always. Love was always switching things around and moving different elders to different outposts or houses.

There were about 20 elder men and about the same number of elder ladies. Each elder lady was paired with, sanctioned to an elder man. Each elder man was considered the head of a household and would run the household with the help of his elder lady. The household, though, was considered to belong to the elder man, not the elder woman.

A household was made up of the elder and his elder lady and all the non-elder members—men, women and children, sometimes referred to as "younger" members. Each household had various numbers of people in them but probably anywhere from as few in number as eight to as many as 20 people, not including children. Over time, the number of people in each household grew as more people joined the Love Family and as more children were born.

Relationships between biological family members were less valued in the Family, and communal ties were strongly valued and more emphasized, so households were composed mostly of unrelated individuals.

Everyone living in the household was under the authority of the elder of that household, so anything that anyone wanted had to be approved by the elder, although Love could supersede on any level.

Each elder lady was like a co-leader of her household, however; the elder man was considered the symbolic head of that household. The Love Family hierarchy was, at its core, patriarchal.

The relationship between Love and the elders was like the relationship between an elder and his household. Each household, in some ways, was like a mini Love Family.

There was even a hierarchy within the elder circle, with some elders having more status since they were closer to Love. Each elder had their own personality too, where some were more strict or lax than others. I lived in Helpful's household for certain periods of time. He was way less strict as an elder. It was still the same culture, the same way of life; but it was more relaxed, with more laughing and less work.

When I was in Helpful's household, instead of using baking soda to brush my teeth, I got to use real toothpaste powder, at least for a time. There was this old can of powdered Pepsodent that was just sitting in the bathroom, and no one seemed to care. Maybe a new member brought it and it never got turned in. I wasn't sure, but I looked forward to going to brush my teeth so I could use it. Although, eventually Dedication caught me and asked me sternly why I had used it. It was the one and only time I ever remember Dedication being uptight with me, and even though she wasn't that mad, it still scared me. Then the Pepsodent disappeared after that, and I never got to use it again.

Another thing that happened in Helpful's household was I would go visit a new member named Eliada. She and I would sit, chat, and drink a powdered coffee alternative called Postum. I enjoyed that no one from the household seemed to notice or mind our visits.

Even though some households were more lax than others, it was still a strict culture that Love designed and that was followed by the elders. It was kind of like the way Taco Bell is run. Each Taco Bell serves the same menu, but each Taco Bell is slightly different in how fresh the food is and how quickly one can get through the drive thru. Each Taco Bell has a store manager, but the store manager follows the rules set by the franchise owner, who essentially follows the rules of the regional owner. There was no complaint process either. If one didn't feel like wearing the silly outfit, then oh well, time to move on.

The Love Family was the opposite of a democracy. It was more like an autocracy. An autocracy is a system of government by one person with absolute power. Love had absolute power. His elders were like the arms of a dictator. An elder or anybody, could come to Love with a problem or a need, and Love might or might not accommodate them, which was very similar to how ancient kings ruled their kingdoms.

This hierarchy had a huge impact on my life. It wasn't just this theoretical concept of authority. My own mother was not considered an authority over me. My direct elders were the teachers and the caretakers who were designated by Love to take care of me, but my teachers and caretakers were submitted to the elders of their households, and the elders of their households were submitted to Love. But everyone, no matter who you were, was first submitted to Love. There was a definite order that everyone followed.

As a child, even though it was set up this way, I learned how to work the system so that I could sometimes get what I wanted. One situation took place long after I had lived in the Kids' House. I was staying in one of the households.

One day, Gentle invited me to spend the night at her house. Gentle was Love's biological daughter and because of that was like a royal princess. For me to get permission to have a sleepover at her household, which was Love's household, I had to ask my elder. I didn't even have to ask my own mom. It was the elder lady who made all the decisions about the kids in my household, so I asked her permission. If I had asked the elder man, who was her elder, he would've said 'Yes, but first ask the elder lady.' So to save time, I just went right to the elder lady.

"No, sorry. I need your help here to help watch the babies," my elder lady said.

Then, Gentle and I talked privately.

"Come on, let's just go ask Love," Gentle suggested. She and I walked over to ask Love.

"Of course!" Love said, enthusiastically. We went back to my household and began packing up my duffle bag.

"What are you doing? My elder lady asked angrily. "I thought I told you no."

"Love said," Gentle told her matter-of-factly. There was an awkward pause.

"Okay, see you tomorrow," My elder lady said tightly and softened her expression.

Oh okay, so this is how it's done! I thought as we walked down the path.

Many times, I went with other children to Love for permission for different things that we wanted. It especially worked if it was with one of his own kids. He seemed to enjoy listening to what we wanted and would often grant the requests. I became aware of that fact and realized I had a backup plan if all else failed. Once we had Love's permission, everyone else fell in line—every time.

As I have discussed so far, there was the hierarchy with Love as the head and under him were the elders, but within that hierarchy, there was another hierarchy, which was men over women. There was a double hierarchy.

From before to well after the time period when the women's liberation movement was in full swing, hundreds of men and women became members of the Love Family, a community where men were defined as the head.

The power differential in the Love Family was enshrined in our doctrine, 'the Charter.' On page 22, it stated, "As one body we are married to Christ, *for the husband is the head of the wife, even as Christ is the head of the Church.*" (Eph. 5:23) This was the charter we lived our lives by and the Bible, as Love interpreted it, was our daily guide.

Love's main philosophy was, the man was 'the head' and the woman was 'the heart,' and that the best way that men and women could work together is for man to represent the direction and for women to be the supporting element, the heart. He was quoted in the PI as saying, "We're building sex stereotypes, making sure ladies are ladies and men are men. I think we have eliminated the need for women's liberation by being righteous with each other." (*Seattle Post-Intelligencer*, Sunday May 14, 1978 A13-14BM)

As a girl child, when I heard the philosophies, I didn't like it. I didn't dwell on it, but it bothered me to hear it. I thought to myself, *That's not fair.* But all the women around me seemed to accept it, so I just accepted it too, as just the way things were.

I talked to a former member known as Lydia and asked her to explain how she thought about it when she was a member. She left the Family during the mid-eighties, but had spent years of her life working as a teacher in the community school. She eventually was sanctioned to my teacher Ethan and they had a little baby named, Discretion.

"There were different interpretations of men's and women's roles," Lydia says. "Men were most definitely in positions of authority, that was a big reason it was called 'the head and the heart.' She continued. "At the time, I saw that it was clearly sexist, but there were some beneficial aspects to being in an intentional community of people."

So, the benefits of living in a communal experiment outweighed the costs of joining, such as everything they had to give up to be there in the first place, as I have explained earlier, and now on top of that, a rigid and arbitrary hierarchy that diminished their autonomy as feminine beings.

Only women who accepted the dogma and submitted to the hierarchy, to the brotherhood, to Love, were even accepted into the Family. Verbal or outspoken (challenging, confrontational) women need not apply. All the women who joined the Family had to accept the hierarchy as Love defined it before they could even join.

The power differential between men and women was significant, especially in the early years. One example was written about in Larry/Consideration's manuscript (1978).

Consideration had hitchhiked hundreds of miles with two other members, a man named Reuel and a woman named Adiel. Love had sent them to visit Billy Graham and deliver him a copy of the Love Family's Charter. They had all finally gotten a ride and were sitting in the back seat of a car. As they rode, the three of them got into an argument about something. The two men determined that the woman, Adiel, would not submit to their authority and was giving them "bad vibrations." Adiel didn't back down and continued to stand her ground. Since Adiel "didn't change," the men, believed they had no other recourse than to let her out on the side of the road. Consideration wrote, "It was too bad it had to happen, but I had to do what was right in the situation." (265)

Consideration and Reuel were not elders, they were just regular members, but yet, they were considered Adiel's elders in that situation, because they were men and she was expected to submit to them, because she was a woman.

When the driver, who had picked up the hitchhikers saw the men let Adiel out of the car, way out in the middle of nowhere, he got upset about it and asked the men to get out of the car. Then he turned around and went back and got Adiel, leaving Consideration and Reuel on the side of the road by themselves.

Okay so it was the Family way or the freeway. It was not up for discussion. It was a given. I was taught that women were not decision makers. We were the heart, the daughters of God, and the man is our head.

Understanding talked to me in an interview about the Love Family hierarchy. This was years later, after she had left the community and had gotten her own apartment with her then two young sons:

"The man was to make the logical decisions, and the woman was to keep pumping him with energy," she explained. Then with a hint of sarcasm, "We definitely knew the "heart" meant stir the granola, raise the kids, don't give him any trouble if he brings another woman home."

I asked my mom what she thought of the head and the heart philosophy in the Love Family. It had been many years since she left, and she now could look back and reflect.

"A lot of people from the hippie standard community figured we were repressed," she explained, "but really it was refreshing in a way that didn't seem oppressive most of the time. I actually appreciated it when I was carrying something heavy up the trail—a brother wouldn't even have thought twice—of course they would help me carry it," she says.

I was amazed to hear her say that. Just a few years earlier when she was hitchhiking on the road to Alaska, she would never have let a man carry her backpack for her—and now she appreciated it?

My mom says she didn't see the Family as sexist but saw it more as a step up because to her, the Family "didn't compare to the big, sexist society" that she had come from.

"In the world, there was and is so much wanting of sexuality and being sucked up into unrealistic body images and the commodity that sex has become," she says. "People try to play these subtle manipulative games and roles," In the Family, "it wasn't like that." She said that one year, the women got into wearing leotards under their dresses because they looked beautiful. Some members from another commune had joined, and they wore leotards, so the Family women started wearing them too. But then a rule came down that the women were to stop wearing them because they were too revealing in terms of the nipples.

"It was considered a little too naked," my mom explained.

Women in the Love Family didn't wear bras, just like most of the women in the hippie counterculture at that time. There was less pressure on women as far as their physical appearance because natural beauty was the standard, but it is hard for me to see how the Love Family was a step up for women as they were in defined roles and had to defer to men to make the major decisions. It might've been fine for a while, but how would that work out in practice when there was conflict?

It reminded me of comments I had read from Middle Eastern women when they had said, 'Yes, I have to wear a cloth over my face and yes, I am not allowed to ride a bike or participate in politics or the Olympics, but at least I don't live in America where women are treated like sex objects and molested in the street.'

I asked my former teacher, Eve to talk about how she felt about the power differentials in the Family between men and women.

"Especially in the early days, it didn't feel sexist," Eve says, "because it was a whole community of brothers and sisters, being real, just hanging out together. We tried to be positive, be light, be bright, and we helped each other do that so that drama didn't dominate our lives." If somebody felt doubt or negativity, the whole idea was that they would "squelch" it. "It was an incredible freedom and felt ideal most of the time," she says, then admitted, "but there were underlying issues."

Even though Love Family women were not seen as holders of power, officially. Unofficially, there were some pretty powerful women in the

Love Family.

Understanding, for example, was not an elder, but she was in a powerful position because Love depended on her to take care of the community's children. She had direct contact with him constantly about the children's needs and activities. Love also chose her to be on the council, which was a small council of elders that Love chose to consult regarding important issues.

Eve was another exception. She had a unique role as head teacher, so her position was a position of power. She was involved in a political way with the State Department to get the school certified. Plus, she was building a whole school structure, so she had a lot of power and influence in the Family, because she was directing the school and telling people what needed to be done. She would talk directly to Serious and Love all the time about her needs for the school.

Then there was another woman who was particularly powerful, and her name was Wisdom. Wisdom was older than most and had beautiful long white hair. She had donated a house to Love when she joined and always lived with Love in his household. She was very involved with taking care of his children and the children in his household, but she also acted as Love's personal advisor. Some said that Love "sought her approval" like he would his own mother, and that she was "like a mother figure to him." He listened to her when she voiced concern, which she did a lot, especially about the children. Wisdom made sure there was money set aside for things the kids needed, like socks or coats. She made sure that there were funds for the kids to have their teeth fixed too. It wasn't just the kids that she focused on either. I heard a former member say that he didn't have a robe, and Wisdom made sure that he got one, as well as, a warm sweater that he wore all the time.

Wisdom was also not sanctioned to an elder, and she, like Understanding, was also on the Council and attended elders' meetings. Understanding and Wisdom both lived in Love's household, and they both worked closely together since they were both primarily concerned with the children.

"When [Wisdom] wanted something, she went in and talked to Love—and she got it!" says Understanding. "Onetime, Wisdom found out that Love was telling people to 'use a belt on the kids if they needed a whack.' Wisdom 'became irate' and went and told Love, 'I don't want one of these kids hit with a belt. This could leave marks. What are you doing here?' she ranted. "The next thing I knew," Understanding says, "Love sent Cooperation over with a message that belts were never to be used again—That was the sort of influence that Wisdom had."

Wisdom was a unique case, other than exceptions, such as Eve and Understanding. The only other women who were considered women of power were the elder ladies. In terms of actual power though, that is debatable; what they really had was status and indirect power because they were sanctioned to elders.

I asked Eve, my former teacher, to talk about the role of women in the Love Family:

"An elder lady had power?" I asked her at one point during the discussion.

"An elder lady," Eve says, "had certain power within her household, but outside the household, she didn't have the authority. To be successful there," Eve continued, "you had to be sensitive to the form or everybody got on you about it. That was the cause of many household meetings. People that just couldn't do that." This was especially true in the earlier days, says Eve. "If there was a man who was telling a woman what to do, and the woman had a problem with it, she had to do what he asked, respectfully, and not answer him back. If she still had a problem with it, she privately could go and talk to her elder about it, then the elder could choose to go talk to the man about it or not, depending on the situation."

Elder ladies, though, had power within their households over the members who resided there. Then, they could influence their elder man who then had influence with other elder men or with Love, so indirectly, an elder lady could be quite powerful in certain ways.

Then, certain elder ladies were more powerful than other elder ladies, because of who they were sanctioned to. For example, there was Truthfulness who was Love's elder lady; She had to have been one of the more powerful elder ladies there were.

The most power an elder lady had was, as Eve says, within her household, over the members in that household and over how the household was run. Then they also went to elder ladies' meetings where they made decisions.

Although, from what I have heard their power was limited in scope as many of their decisions might have involved what to eat at Passover, how to get people in their households' clothes and food, or who was going to do laundry or kid watch that day. Certainly important!

They also had influence in that Love would, at times, consult with them before he made decisions.

For example, my former teacher, Definition told me that Love once asked him which woman he was interested in and Definition told him, 'Eve.' If Definition had been an elder, Love might've said yes right away, but he wasn't. So, Love's answer was, 'wait,' until he consults with the elder ladies at the next meeting. "There were politics to consider," says Definition thoughtfully. "Eve was seen more as an elder lady, even though, she wasn't officially an elder lady."

"Love didn't like to make decisions like that on his own," Definition says. "He wanted to know if that was a good idea. He wanted to know what the women thought about things like that." Definition speculated that Serious had planned to make Eve his second lady eventually. "But it wasn't Serious that drove Love's decision, it was [Probity.] She didn't want to deal with a second lady, so she really discouraged it."

Love had absolute power, but he wasn't stupid. Understanding explained to me that Love would pay attention to what people were seeing in their visions and dreams. She remembered that onetime, Love had a large number of members write down their visions and dreams, then he read them out loud in private with just a few members from his household who were present, including Understanding. One by one, the papers were read from the stack. A lot of people had had dreams and visions about one of the elders named Strength.

"Love wasn't threatened by it at all," says Understanding. "He was trying to figure out how people saw the power. He wanted to know if people were having visions about anyone besides him," she says. "Strength's pile was totally fat." He was an elder who was "well-loved and fatherly." After that, Love put more power into Strength because he decided that Strength was a 'man of the people.' That's when Love made Strength the head elder at the Ranch, the rural property outside of Arlington that the Family came to own.

It's hard to pigeon hole Love's thinking about how he distributed power. Men were the official holders of power, but that didn't mean that women were totally powerless.

Strong women did make it into the Love Family. They weren't all screened out. They were there, even if they had to repress parts of themselves to be accepted. Others seem to exert influence behind the scenes, like Wisdom, Love's personal advisor, like Understanding, head kid lady, like Eve who found a niche in the school as a teacher, and like some of the elder ladies who were in powered relationships with high status elder men.

My own mother was at the bottom of the Love Family hierarchy. Before we came, she had been a very strong, independent, adventurous woman, her own boss. It was devastating, to see her join and lose all that and have no status at all, nothing that defined her as somebody important and someone to respect. It was difficult for me to see that downfall. It was one reason I was drawn to strong women in the Family, women like Understanding and Eve and others who had status and decision-making power. It was women like them that carried on my mom's earlier legacy and gave me a sense of self-importance as a feminine being.

The main problem with the hierarchy was that there wasn't a clear and fair way to resolve conflicts between people. It was all about submission and total, unquestioning loyalty to one's elder. No one was voting on anything, and nothing was reached by consensus. It was one person at the top, Love, making all the decisions. The hierarchy was set in stone pretty much, but People were willing to accept this arrangement and enjoy the benefits of living in an alternative society and community, rather than accept the democratic society they had come from.

The Love Family hierarchy wasn't something that people could get away from and just be themselves; it was a fundamental aspect of our lives, a set of powered relationships that dominated Family life.

I couldn't go anywhere without seeing the symbolism, which was the external expression of the hierarchy. The boundaries of Love's authority were defined on every level, in every facet of organized life. For example, on Queen Anne, I could not just run around in Love's Area without being questioned as to what I was doing. This was Love's Area, and that boundary defined Love's importance; This was *his* backyard; this wasn't *our* backyard.

When I had lived in Serious's Area, it had been more relaxed; the yard felt more shared, so when I went to go live in Love's Area at the Kids' House, the difference was noticeable. Love's house was not somewhere that I could just go walk in and see who is around to play with. It was a holy sanctuary. One had to be there for a reason and with specific permission. Although on occasion, I did go in there to use the bathroom downstairs; no one seemed to care about that, but sometimes I was there to play with one of Love's kids. If I was stopped and asked what I was doing, that was my answer. At times, depending on who it was that asked, I noticed that they might listen to my explanation, pause and think about it. There were a lot of folks that were more rule bound than others. I usually got a pass each time, especially if I was with one of Love's kids. Love's kids had a certain level of authority. Everyone knew they usually had Love's permission, and at least from what I observed, most people didn't dare challenge it. Maybe they figured the risk of Love's condemnation was too high if they did.

The shared yard in Love's Area had fruit trees, and even though fruit would be hanging low and inviting, I couldn't just run up and start picking the fruit. It was "Love's yard," even though all the houses shared the yard. It was a combined, communal yard, but it was considered an honor to even go there.

In the individual households, Love's authority was represented by the elder. In a household, for example, the elder would have his own room. Everyone else would use shared spaces. There were rooms that the men shared, and there were rooms that the women shared, and then there were kids' rooms. The kids' rooms were full of bunk beds, but in some of the households, the men had bunk beds in their rooms too.

Here is another example of how the power structure was displayed externally: At mealtimes, the elder of each household sat at the head of the table, and the members who lived in his household would sit according to rank. Children sat separately usually on a drop cloth or low table, nearby or in another room.

The seating arrangements also displayed the power structure. In a Family meeting, for example, Love would be at the head of a circle or half circle. He would always sit on a pillow. Sometimes the elders would sit on a floor pillow as well. Then everyone would sit according to their status. The elders, who were the next highest status under Love, would sit next to Love. Then next to them, the elders with the next highest status and so on. Once the elders were in their strategic places, usually, but not always, everyone else was arranged by gender. The men would sit on one side, the women on the other side. The children were often placed in the middle or would sit in front or close to Love which meant all eyes were on us. I would have preferred to sit a little bit more inconspicuously, but I was used to it. Sometimes Love would place me and some of the other girls next to him. I would be on one side of him and Gentle or Heaven would be placed on his other side. I don't know why he did that.

At other times and especially when we were younger, Love would place all the children in the middle of the circle. If one were to look down upon the meeting from above with a bird's eye view, it would look like a circle with a dot in the middle. We were the dot. A circle with a dot in the middle was Love's symbol, coincidentally. It seemed that there wasn't a facet of life there that wasn't touched by the physical representation of power.

As I've said, the arrangement of seating at meal times displayed the hierarchy, even the serving of plates—who was served first, next. Men were served first. It was made sure they had the largest portions too. I thought this was stupid. I clearly remember that when the kids were served, the boys too were served first. It bothered me every time. I felt it was unfair and sent the message that the boys were more important, which I knew wasn't true. Maybe they were thinking that someday, these boys would be elders with their own households, so they needed to eat first and learn, early on, their role of authority and self-importance.

Women would do things that showed their subservience to the men. For example, the women would brush and braid the men's hair each day. They were mostly quiet, unless spoken too, and never showed any signs that they were unwilling or resistant to the power structure that placed them in lesser roles. Predominantly, men and women were in socially defined roles, and although everyone was subservient to Love or their direct elders who were under Love, it was mostly the women who were in domestic or subservient roles such as cooking, serving and caretaking. Although, there were always exceptions to everything.

If one were to look at the Love Family from the perspective of a church, Love made all the church elders men. Every member of the Love Family was considered to 'serve' Love. But in Love's own personal household, which he stocked with those he considered the most good-looking and the most talented, these servants had a slightly elevated status, due to the fact that they were in Love's household. He had a lot of servants in his household, but it was the male servants in his household who were called 'priests.' Love gave them additional status through their title. But there was a downside to additional status: they had given up their egos and had submitted to the group mind with their souls to a far greater extent than the masses of those with far less status. I hope one of them ends up writing a book someday about what that was like. I heard years later that a lot of people were glad they had stayed at the bottom of the ladder where they could just relax and be a humble servant.

Consideration/Larry made a note of his observations of women in his manuscript, (1978) when he noted that women only spoke when spoken to. "Surely, the only place a woman could ever be happy was in submission, just loving, and being the heart," he wrote. "In fact, this is truly what made the women of Israel beautiful and they were a very important part of our life." (261)

It wasn't just symbolic either. Everything that happened took place within the boundaries of Love's vision of heaven on earth. People would say, "Have you checked with Love?" People were reluctant to do anything that hadn't been cleared with Love.

The Love Family hierarchy was not influenced by money, although I am sure there were exceptions to this as, again, there were exceptions to just about everything. Usually though, how much money you gave Love when you joined made no difference in terms of whether you became an elder or not. For example, Dan, who had now become known as Richness, brought millions of dollars to the Family, yet he never was an elder. A man named Joab brought the cannery to the Family, but he did not become an elder until many years after that. Love wanted to make it clear that money was not a reason someone would be honored with a leadership role.

Ethan explained that status was something that Love was able to "bestow" on people readily at any time. "Love could give someone a virtue name or status if they did something good, or he could take it away. And "some people got status quicker than others. "Sometimes someone new would join and within a year have their virtue name and be an elder," Ethan says, "but there were others who were there for at least ten years who would still be 'a nobody.' Submission was everything."

"The hierarchy was very rigid, but it changed all the time," Ethan says. "People could be demoted." He talked about a man named Respect: Respect, "was high up in the echelons" of the Love Family, but he made the "mistake of questioning Love" about his total authority. He questioned him about the fact that Love thought he was Jesus Christ, and "because he doubted Love, he was kicked out of the Family." When he came back, he didn't get his name back, and he never got his stature back; He became just a "regular" person. "If you did something stupid or something Love didn't like, you were excluded," Ethan says. "You wouldn't be invited to meetings anymore."

Despite the fact that Respect never got his respect back, there was another elder who left, but he did get his name and elder status back. It was Logic. This was sometime before I came. Understanding told me that after Logic had joined the Love Family, there was a point when he had "runaway." He had joined the Source Family, another spiritual commune in Los Angeles.

Now typically, if you left the Love Family, you would lose all your status, including your virtue name, if you had one, and any standing that you had. Logic was one exception to this. Logic and Love were very close; Logic was the highest status elder in the Love Family, next to Serious, both second only to Love himself.

When Logic left, Love was devastated. Understanding remembered that Love would sit in his bathtub for very long periods of time, brooding about it, visibly upset that Logic would leave him. Eventually, Logic asked to come back, but he would not do so unless Love let him have his elder status, his name and his household back. Love agreed. He did not want to lose Logic. Understanding called the situation, "Love's black eye."

Over time, things changed, people got status, others lost it, people were kicked out, others joined, but for the most part, there was a core group of elders who were there the whole time, and the way the hierarchy was structured and the politics surrounding it, pretty much stayed the same.

Women's lack of voice was still a problem until the end though. Understanding expressed frustration about it, since she felt that their lack of voice had a direct impact the children, who were her total focus.

"The men made all the real decisions," Understanding says. "The women we're the ones who took care of the kids, and other than a few exceptions, no one stood up for the kids who was a man," she says. "It was always the women. The women were concerned about the kids, the women were the ones to ask for food for their kids, it was the women who were bonded to the kids."

Why did women put up with this? Why didn't all the women stand up together and demand change? I posed this question to a former member known as Atarah. Atarah was a talented artist and seamstress, tall and graceful, with long, light brown hair. She shared a memory of a ladies' meeting with Love. At that meeting, Simplicity spoke up for all the women and complained about how the women were being treated.

"Love came down on her hard and told her in front of everyone at the meeting, that she was 'speaking for Satan, being negative,' and 'questioning our oneness,' says Atarah. "But Simplicity went toe-to-toe with Love and argued with him in front of everyone at the meeting. She spoke for all of us," Atarah continued. "To this day, I regret that I didn't speak up and agree with her—everybody backed him of course. If I had, maybe someone else would have too, and then someone else. It might have changed the course of history."

Atarah explained that even amongst the women in private, women held themselves in line and didn't complain much. "You couldn't just talk about it if you were having a hard time; You had to keep up the role. It was very exhausting."

I was being raised in a patriarchal society, and since I didn't see women protest or standup for themselves, it appeared as if they had accepted it. Here I was a young girl getting closer and closer each year to becoming a woman, and I didn't look forward to being in that powerless role.

Women's lack of voice and lack of prominence in the leadership of the community bothered me. It wasn't something I thought much about, but I felt it intuitively. I knew it wasn't fair. I usually didn't make comments when I noticed something that didn't sit well with me, but apparently, Understanding remembered a comment I had once made to her. I had said to her, "It's not fair, the boys get to wear pants, and the girls have to wear dresses, so we have to be cold all the time!" I don't remember saying that, but that winter; it was freezing. Eventually I figured out how to wear two pairs of tights underneath my dress, one right on top of the other; that helped some.

Women's lack of authority in the Family wasn't just a problem for them. It was also a big problem for the children who were under their care. In my case, it had a huge impact on me, which I discuss in a later chapter, but my own mother was not considered my elder. 'Elder' could mean a church elder, but it was also used as a term to indicate authority, and who had authority over who. As I explained earlier, my elders were, for many years, the members who were directly taking care of me, such as the caretakers or the teachers. They in turn were under the direct authority of their elders such as Serious or Logic, who were under the authority of Love. Everyone had a place in the hierarchy. So, in every situation, there was no gray area. It was clear who was in charge.

Eventually though, as I got older, I no longer lived with Understanding in the Kids' House. There was a time when I ended up living in the same household with my mom. Even living with her in the same household, the hierarchy was still the same. My mom lived there as a householder, but it was the elder lady of the household that was my direct elder, not my mom, and the elder lady was submitted to the elder of the household, who she was sanctioned to, both of whom were submitted to Love, of course.

What this meant for many children is that their own mother didn't have a say in their care. Let me give an example of how the Love Family's hierarchy was a disservice to children.

I had heard that us girls, the older girls like myself had been given permission by Love to take sacrament at King Lake. It was not just marijuana or mushrooms, which were also referred to as sacrament. It was LSD 'sacrament.' The Love Family, like most Amazonian and Native American tribes saw hallucinogenic intoxication as a collective journey into the subconscious and as such, it was essentially a social event. It had been determined that we seemed mature enough to partake in the community sacrament ritual.

I couldn't have been older than 12, maybe 13, but no one knew how old we really were since we were considered eternal. I was immature for my age, considering I was being raised in the shelter of an isolated commune, not precocious at all, and very naïve. I was always considered one of the 'big' kids though. I was in the first generation, other than a few teenagers who were older, but who there were so few of that they never formed their own generation.

It was a very timeless experience being in the Love Family. Living in the present and letting go of the past wasn't just this theoretical concept, it was a belief that was put into practice. People weren't keeping track of how old they were or even when things happened. There were no clocks and no one was keeping calendars. When people avoided talking about the past, their memories faded a lot quicker too.

If I want to know when something happened, the most reliable way to figure it out is to ask a bunch of different people what they remember. If they don't know, I go to the rainbow gathering website where they list out every gathering, which state it was in, and what year it was held. Every year, the Love Family sent a crew to the gathering, so whole sets and subsets of memories can be placed in time by which gathering took place that year. Plus, a lot can be determined by just observing when we lived in different places or who joined and when. This was because as soon as one crossed the line from or into the outside society where calendars and clocks rule the day, the crossing itself becomes a marker in time, as one travels from a time zone into or out of a Love Family nether zone.

Unfortunately, no matter what, it has still been somewhat of a guessing game. Human experience is formed by markers, labels and tags, within predetermined time frames, so without all that, memories are formed without boundaries in our brains, and the years go by, one year flowing into the next year without distinction.

Big or small, ready or not, the leader of my family had determined that I would go and do sacrament, a clear example of how the hierarchy worked; Love made all the decisions about the children's care. Our biological parents were not in the loop.

The sacrament aspect of it was over my head. I just looked forward to the campout with my friends. There were around five or six of us on that trip, all around the same age, give or take a year or two. It was going to be a one-night campout at one of the lakes on the Love Family's ranch, the property that was owned in Arlington, Washington. This was about a 45-minute drive from the residential properties on Queen Anne Hill in Seattle. The actual hike to King Lake was another 45-minute hike through the woods.

Love had given his permission for us to take sacrament, but there were certain guidelines we had to follow. For one, we had to have an adult guardian. Second, the girls and the boys would go up to the lake separately, on separate trips. Lastly, before we left, we had to meet with someone who would educate us about the meaning of sacrament within our culture.

It wasn't like they just let us go do it, it was more like they sat us down and had this serious talk with us, like a rite of passage. At the meeting, it was explained that sacrament was supposed to allow us to have a spiritual "revelation" that would "wake us up to the oneness of mankind." They said that our "thoughts and vision will change," and it will be a part of God.

Love appointed an elder who volunteered to be our guardian, Nobility. I was packing up my sleeping bag and a few other items, when Elkanah happened to come by to see what I was doing.

"Where are you going?" she asked.

"We are going to King Lake to take sacrament," I told her matter-of-factly.

"I don't think that is a good idea!" She said in an alarmed, raised voice.

"We have a guardian—Love said," I responded, indignantly.

She shut her mouth, with tight lips. Her eyes bulged out. Her face grew red, then she stomped off.

Off I went too, in the opposite direction. I felt self-righteous because the leader of our community, Love, had given his permission, and he thought we were mature enough to go and have a spiritual trip. What was her problem? She was no authority over me! Why the hell not anyway? Taking sacrament was a part of our culture. Her concern made no sense.

An hour later, we were hiking up to King Lake. On the way, there was a conversation. Two of the girls were laughing sarcastically:

"Love wants us to see visions, so that when we turn 18, we will want to stay in the Love Family."

"Sorry Love, we are leaving you anyway!" The other girl chimed in.

I looked back at them as they hiked along the path. There was laughter.

One of the girls rolled her eyes as if exasperated.

The other girl looked smug.

I hiked along in silence and wondered what sort of vision I might have that would make me want to stay in the Love Family forever. I just enjoyed being on the adventure as we all hiked through the woods to the lake, carrying our sleeping bags and other things that we would need. Usually when I went to King Lake, it was just for a few hours to swim or just to go on a short hike to get away for a while. I don't remember any other time when I hiked to King Lake to camp out. It was a bit further than I was used to for carrying all my stuff.

When we got to the lake, Nobility helped us set up our campsite, just a large tarp that we all laid our sleeping bags out on, under some large cedar trees. Afterward, we all sat on the large rocks together, and I put the sacrament under my tongue, just as I was instructed. It was three 'hits.' The hits were tiny, little square pieces of white paper, a couple millimeters long by another couple millimeters wide.

Thirty minutes later, I began to feel very different. All the colors from the lake and surrounding wilderness began to appear more vibrant, more intense. The trees and large rocks that surrounded the lake began to feel alive, more beautiful than I could've ever imagined.

It was dusk and the sun was getting ready to set. We decided to go swimming. From the tarp, where all of our sleeping bags and things were, it was maybe 25 or 30 feet through some trees and brush to get to the lake's edge. All my senses were magnified to such a degree that I found I could not walk. I got down and crawled, bound and determined to get to the water. It did not seem strange to crawl, it just seemed natural, which then in itself seemed strange that it didn't seem strange. I felt my hands in the dirt and it was dirt that I was a part of and that was a part of me. I was so distracted by the feeling, that I had to tell myself to keep going over and over or I would get lost in the experience of my perceptions. We crawled to the lake's edge, which seemed to take an eternity. It was a beautiful and timeless eternity though.

Nobility, our guardian was keeping an eye out for us. I could see him standing off behind a bush, watching us carefully. The other girls were all getting in the water, a couple of them were already swimming. I walked carefully out on this humongous log that sat at the lake's edge from which I planned to get into the water. The beauty of the lake and all the wildlife around me was overwhelming, so as I was walking out on the log, I slipped and fell off into the water. I felt my feet hit sharp objects, which turned out to be rocks, just under the surface of the lake. I didn't feel anything, but the girls were asking me if I was ok.

As I swam out into the water, I drank in the beauty of the sun, casting reflections off the lake's surface. The water was clear and cool. As I swam, I was astounded by how the water felt on my skin; it was almost like a deep sense of love from the earth, filling me up and inviting me and warming my soul. I didn't fight it or second guess what was happening. I allowed myself to be drawn in to the experience of connection to the earth, to the sky, to the universe.

For some inexplicable reason, I was drawn, almost like a magnet towards the far side of the lake where I saw the sun setting behind the trees. I swam in a sort of invisible channel where the rays were creating sparkles as the shimmering light hit the water.

I felt this intense desire to reach the sun, to touch it, to be with it, become one with it. It was a breathtaking beauty that drew me, invited me to be a part of it. Nothing else seemed to matter.

I got to the other side. I wasn't alone. Heaven had been swimming with me. It seemed it had taken hours to get across but really it was probably ten minutes if that. We climbed out of the water and began climbing through the woods, up the cliffs. I wanted to get to the top, so I could see the sun, because it was slipping behind the hillside as it was setting, but when I looked down at my legs, there were scratches all over them and they were bleeding. I felt nothing, which struck me as odd. Heaven had scratches on her legs too. I wanted to keep going. We were naked, which was normal. Most people went nude to swim, especially on our own property, and certainly way out in the middle of nowhere at King Lake. We were all family anyway. I was barefoot, and the terrain was rough, but my love for the universe, for this oneness that I felt, took away all my concerns that I usually had. I knew intuitively that what I was feeling was God. It was so powerful that my awareness for the minor discomfort of wearing no shoes or clothes and hiking through rocky terrain covered with thorn covered sticker bushes was absent. I was the water. I was the sky. I was the blackberry bushes. I was the earth, and it was me.

I was connected to the earth, all life, the universe; it wasn't this separate thing. There I was my heart pouring out love and knowing with my inner most being what a miracle it all was and how grateful I was to be alive, to be a part of it.

Meanwhile, Nobility, our guardian had been watching Heaven and I the whole time as she and I attempted to climb the overgrown, steep backside of the lake, which was becoming more cliff-like as we tried to get closer and closer to the sunset. I heard him yell from the other side of the lake from where we were. His voice echoed across the water:

"OK, You girls get back down here now!" Nobility called loudly.

"We're fine!" I yelled back.

"You girls come back down here, or I will come after you!" he insisted loudly.

I could tell he meant it, so I turned around and started heading back. Heaven and I swam back to the others. I was disappointed but only momentarily. The experience of the oneness and of enlightenment continued. It was one timeless moment after the next of being just totally absorbed into this alternate awareness, although it was less like an alternate awareness and more like an awareness that I already had, that was exaggerated or amplified for my benefit. The closest thing I have ever felt to that feeling is the feeling of being in love with someone, except that it wasn't someone, it was all life and the planet, and it was much more intense than just being in love with another human.

Later that night, no one could sleep. Suddenly, Gentle, who was laying in her sleeping bag next to me, screamed. It scared me.

"There's spider webs falling on me!" she cried. A couple minutes later, "Look! There's another one!"

"It's just the needles from the tree," I told her calmly.

"You don't believe me," she whined.

There was no way I could sleep. Every so often, she would let out another scream.

It was beginning to get light. I don't think any of us slept that night. I was trying to arrange my sleeping space and kept losing my hairbrush, then

I would find it, then I would lose it again. I began to get distressed, so that the other girls were trying to help me find it—again. As we all looked for the brush, items were being moved about on the tarp such as sleeping bags, flashlights, clothing, and other things we had brought, which made it even more difficult to find them.

With Gentle screaming every so often and with my inability to locate my hairbrush, this is how I spent the rest of the early morning until it was time to get up.

Once it was light out, Nobility made a fire and cooked us steaks, which I knew was against the rules since, in general, we did not eat meat as a culture. Nobody seemed to notice or care after the night we had all had, and everyone was famished. There was also a box of butterscotch pudding in the bag, which I prepared in the pan and set it on the fire. I stirred the pudding with a stick since there was no utensil.

After we ate, we packed up all our stuff and started back home. There wasn't much talking along the way. I was too tired after the long night, so I took the time to think about things. *'Your thoughts and vision will change,'* and *'It will be a part of God,'* I had been told. *'It will be the same revelation that the Love Family was built on.'* It was all starting to come together in terms of my understanding of what Love was teaching everyone. *'We are one,'* was suddenly taking on a new meaning for me. It no longer was just something I was being told; it was something I had experienced, something I had felt, that was very real, a way of thinking that was now part of my awareness.

There was something else that I learned, that was part of my revelation. It was that, no matter how connected I felt, to life, to the earth, to the universe, to God—my humanity had held me back. I couldn't be totally 'one' because I was human, and I could bleed. As I was climbing the cliff to reach the sun, if Nobility hadn't called me back, maybe I could've been seriously hurt. My humanity held me back and it grounded me. God was a part of me and I was a part of God, but I was still only human. It was a humbling realization.

When we all got back, it was over. That was that. No one talked about the King Lake trip, and I never told anyone what had happened to me. The kids usually did not talk about spirituality to one another; That was something the adults did.

We ran into the boys. They had gone up the day before, and when they had seen us come off the trail into the open field with our stuff, they approached us. There was an awkward silence, then one of the boys said the trip was "ridiculous," and that they had lost the radio and their sleeping bags in the lake. They didn't even need to explain. I understood.

I am not sure exactly what happened up there for each of the kids that went besides me, but all in all, from the Love Family's point of view, sacrament was the apple of knowledge, and I had been given the right to take a bite. What I have been chewing on ever since is a mixture of thoughts. On the one hand, I learned a valuable lesson on that trip. The lesson has become foundational in terms of my spiritual understanding of my connection to something bigger than myself, which has been a source of strength to me throughout my life.

On the other hand, I feel that it was wrong. It was wrong that my own mother was out of the loop about it, that she couldn't protect me or say no. I ended up alright, but what if I hadn't? It scares me to think how vulnerable children were in the Love Family that something like this could happen.

Something like this can happen in any place where women aren't allowed to help run things. That was the problem with one man being the leader and creating a hierarchy dominated by men, who live by the mantra that men are the head and women are the heart—it doesn't work. In any society, women must be leaders too, so they can represent their own needs, which include protecting and nurturing their young. A balance of powers with checks and balances is essential in any society in order to avoid people getting hurt. We are a part of God, and God is a part of us—but we are still only human.

As a child, one of the things that affected me the most in a negative way was the Love Family hierarchy. There was a pecking order and people could get hurt. It was just like chickens that cruelly peck on one another, sometimes to the death. Certain members would get ostracized, pecked on if they weren't submissive enough to the order. If they were considered different, if they complained too much, if they were judged to be dark or too negative, whatever it was—everyone would band together and pick on them, be critical of them until they changed or left. It was peer group pressure, suppressing doubt and resistance to Love's programming, by exploiting peoples' need to belong and their desire to be a part of the community.

It was chicken coop politics. There was a time when the Love Family had farm animals at the Ranch. I used to go out to the chicken coop and watch the chickens as they went about their business. When I saw one of the chickens being pecked on, I would open the gate and run in there and chase the bullies away. I would stand there and wait, ready to pounce on any chicken that came along to try and pick on the weaker chicken. It drove me nuts, because they were going to do it anyway as soon as I left.

Chickens were like humans in this way, I thought. Why did it have to be that way? In my own way, I tried to right the wrongs. I tried to help those who I saw as vulnerable in some way. If there was another child who was being picked on and it seemed unfair to me, I always tried to intervene as best I could.

There was this girl who was around my age who came. Her Bible name was Sarai. Sarai was picked on for no reason, other than she was considered "fat." I wasn't going to go along with making fun of the fat girl. It wasn't right! It wasn't fair!

I became good friends with Sarai. She knew how to have a good laugh. She was easy going and had a gentle spirit. She and I would have sleepovers. She was tall and somewhat heavier than the other children for her height and body structure, but I didn't think it was by that much. She was a pretty girl, with blond, shoulder length hair, blue eyes, and big round, rosy red cheeks.

Unfortunately, the kids would make fun of her and try to exclude her. There was nothing wrong with her that I could tell. I didn't see her overeat; there wasn't much opportunity to overeat anyway in the Love Family since we all pretty much ate the same things, and portions were mostly controlled. I think the problem was also that she didn't stand up for herself very well.

One day, I came upon a situation where she was being made fun of. There were two boys who were sneering at her, calling her names as she attempted to steer herself clear of a mud puddle. I could see that it was difficult for her as the puddle was wedged between two trees on a narrow path. They called her, "Stupid," and were pointing at her as she struggled around it, trying not to get wet. I came upon the scene and grew angry at the boys. "You leave her alone!" I said sternly. The boys ran quickly off, with guilty expressions. These were boys who were more popular than some of the others, leaders of the pack type. I didn't care who they were. I was going to challenge the status quo if it meant protecting my friend from being unfairly picked on.

Sarai trusted me and told me in private how she was picked on by the adults too. It was about her weight. There was a lot of pressure on women in the Love Family to be skinny. I don't remember which adults she identified or what they said to her, but I could tell that the comments had upset her.

One day we were walking along, chatting as we went.

"My virtue name is going to be Firm," she said matter-of-factly.

Hardly likely, I thought to myself. It seemed she had internalized some of the negative attention she got about her weight, and she fantasized about the day when she would be "skinny," and would be recognized by Love and accepted by the other kids.

I was taught to swim against the current. Everyone who had thus far helped to take care of me from my birth mother to these people in the Love Family were all rebels in a sense, strictly following a rebel leader, Love. They were all swimming against the current in terms of their life choices. As the fish were going upstream, I was naturally diverging off from the main group of up-streamers.

I was willing to confront my peers and risk condemnation. There were kids in my peer group who didn't like it that I tried to include kids, who had been determined uncool or who were excluded for one reason or another. It was a source of frustration for the other kids because they wanted to be more selective about who was included. To me, the unspoken rules of exclusion sickened me. It was that same old in-group out-group mentality that the Love Family was all about, and I fought it.

One day, I saw Ravah and Cheerful, walking across the pasture carrying a white five-gallon bucket. This was about a year or so after we had come to the Family, and people were beginning to set up campsites at the Family Ranch. The boys walked up to me and let me look in the bucket. It was full of grass and sticks. I looked and saw a couple of garter snakes not looking very happy. The boys were so proud though and watched for my reaction as I looked in the bucket. I kept a straight face and managed a smile, but I felt sad for the snakes. They were curled up because they had nowhere to slither.

Suddenly, for some unknown reason, Ravah and Cheerful dashed off behind one of the tents nearby and left their bucket sitting alone next to me.

I saw my chance. Once they were out of sight, I lightly kicked the bucket over with my foot "by accident." The snakes slithered freely into the tall grass and disappeared. A few seconds later, the boys returned, and they saw me standing there with the bucket tipped over. I must've looked guilty as they looked from the bucket to me, then back to the bucket. "Whadga do that for? they snarled, stomping off resolutely into the tall grasses yonder.

I didn't care; I had saved the snake's life. Every life was worth saving to me.

One winter, at the Ranch, I was at the lake's edge jabbing a stick through ice shards and stirring them around like stew, when I spotted a frog. It was motionless in the icy water. I stared at it for several moments after I thought I saw it move. Maybe it was dead, but I couldn't tell. It was frozen and certainly needed my help. I picked up his stiff body and brought it into the sanctuary tent to see if I could help him.

To my amazement, once the frog thawed out, it came back to life. Ethan just happened by and came and took a look at him. He said it had been sleeping for the winter, and that it would wake up in the spring. I took it back to the lake, so the frog could finish his winter nap and live happily ever after. When I got there, I realized that all its friends were still asleep. He was awake and all by himself. I watched him for the longest time, waiting for him to get sleepy, but he never did. *What have I done?* I thought. The lonely frog opened its wide eyes and peered out as if in utter disbelief, staring out across the empty plain of ice that covered the lake.

I learned an important lesson that day: Make sure if you are helping someone, that you really are helping them and not just making things worse.

I couldn't help it, in a way, because I was trying to equalize the playing field for those who were at a disadvantage. It was the only way that I could help. I wanted to see the world as a fair place where people had a chance. The snake got a chance. That frog got a chance. Sarai got a chance. Situations where animals or people were being hurt impacted me the most. I remember them as clear as day. In the case of people, it didn't make sense. Here I was being taught to love and that we were Jesus Christ, but it seemed that in the Love Family, arbitrary authority took precedence over people's individual needs and feelings.

Another child who was on my radar, was Sun. I was closer to him in some ways because I was often in the same households as he was. I felt sorry for him. None of the kids wanted to play with him, so he was ostracized, excluded from the games. Despite being excluded, he never gave up, and he always tried to include himself anyway. It didn't matter to him what people thought of him. I admired that. When the group would try to ditch him, I felt bad for him. I found, though, that if I stood up for him, I sometimes would be excluded as well, so there was a limit in what I could do to help him. I was nice to him though, and as I said earlier, he did not pick on me as much as he did the other kids.

At times, when I played with the big kids, I was able to smuggle one of the younger kids into the game. I did not like it that there was this unspoken rule regarding age. Even though we didn't know how old anyone was, there was still 'the big kids' and then there was 'the little kids.' It was taboo to include the little kids who were of various ages and sizes and were not as sophisticated. But I could never understand why there was this arbitrary separation. I preferred for the kids to play together in a more inclusive way.

"Why do you want to hang out with them?" I was asked.

Why not? To me, there was richness in our diversity where there were a multitude of perspectives and experiences. Maybe I was just born that way, or maybe it was a direct result of seeing the adults around me live according to a completely arbitrary and undemocratic system of governance. I was trying to even things out; I only wanted to see a just world and was trying to make that happen on my small scale.

For a lot of years, because we were so young, it seemed our futures had already been determined. Someday I would be a grownup. Whose household would I be in? Would I be sanctioned to an elder and be an elder lady? Understanding said that the boys, especially those who had shown leadership qualities, were being primed to one day be elders, and that Love had made comments about certain boys who he thought showed promise.

I asked Ravah to talk about the hierarchy.

"That's what young boys were striving to be—elders and householders," he says. "I knew that I was going to be an elder, and I wondered who would be in my household."

The hierarchy wasn't something I thought much about; it was just how things were. But whether I thought about it or not, it had an impact on my life. For example, I sometimes went for a sleepover at Love's household. I was invited by his daughter Gentle or sometimes by Heaven when she lived in his household later on.

When I went to Love's household, there were perks. There was much better food—eggs for breakfast, cheese, and lots of good snacks, that I never saw in my own household. Plus, we could pretty much do whatever we wanted because all we had to do was ask Love for permission. Since when we asked him for things, he usually said yes, no one could do anything about it. In my own household and in other households I was in, things were strict. If I brought a girl to my house to spend the night or for dinner, we would eat beans and rice, then I still would be expected to do my chores and help out. In Love's big house in town, we would be allowed to sleep on the deck by ourselves and we were pretty much left to our own devices, whereas at my household, we would sleep in the same space with everyone else and be expected to help out with things. Also, in my household, everyone was submitted to someone above them, so getting permission to do anything was a task; It was a lot of trouble to go up the chain of command, whereas at Love's house, it was easy, because the top decision maker was right there in the same house, and if we asked him, it would eliminate all the middlemen.

The Love Family hierarchy was a big deal, and almost everything that happened in the Love Family took place within its framework. In the next chapter, I discuss examples of how the Love Family was not just an autocracy, it was a *totalitarian* autocracy, and I will show exactly why that was true.

BIBLIOGRAPHY (CHAPTER 6)

Atarah. Personal Interview. August 7, 2002. Seattle, WA 6–7pm.

Bryant, Hilda. *Seattle Post-Intelligencer*. Love Family is Gaining Ground. Sunday. May 14, 1978. A13–14 BM.

Church of Armageddon Charter of the Love Israel Family.

[Karen]. Personal Interview. October 21, 2001.

[Ethan]. Personal Interview, November 16, 2015.

[Eve and Definition]. Joint Personal Interview. September 30, 2001. Magnolia Hill, Seattle, WA.

Holy Bible, *King James Version*. Eph. 5:23.

Israel, Larry. (Consideration) Unpublished Manuscript, 1978, pp. 261–265

Israel, Understanding. Personal Interview. September 15, 2002.

[Lydia]. Personal Interview. February 20, 2002. Seattle, WA.

[Ravah]. Personal Interview, March 19, 2002. Tuesday. 7:45pm.

CHAPTER 7

Marriage, Sex, and Relationships

In the last chapter, I discussed the framework of the Love Family's hierarchy. In this next chapter, I am going to explain some of the finer details of how relationships between people were governed. As I have already explained, the Love Family was an autocracy, which is a system of government by one person with total authority. The Love Family was more than just an autocracy, though. It was a *totalitarian* autocracy. Totalitarianism is a political system in which the state recognizes no limits to its authority and strives to regulate every aspect of public AND private life wherever feasible. Not only did Love have absolute authority in the public sphere, he also had absolute power in the private sphere. He made all the decisions about relationships and sex, which is usually considered, by most modern societies, to be in the private domain, not state regulated.

In order to describe the reach of Love's power, I will need to provide all the details about marriage, sex, and relationships in the community, a community in which everyone was married to everyone in a sort of group marriage. Say what?

The Charter was very clear:

> Worldly marriage is null and void; all Worldly relationships dissolve upon joining the Church." (pg. 21) All other customs of matrimony in the Church will be spiritually determined by the word of God and will be established by the Church." (24).

Since Love was the head of the church, what that really meant was that Love would determine all customs of matrimony.

Once a person joined the Love Family, any marriage contract or other committed love relationship, that was formed before someone joined, was no longer recognized. The Charter referenced the Bible in authoritative terms:

> "There will be no marriage in the resurrected state. For in the resurrection they neither marry, nor are given in marriage but are as the angels of God in heaven." (Matt 22:30, see also Mark 12:25, both *KJV*).

Of course, Love was the one who decided how we would interpret the Bible, and his interpretation was that we were the resurrected state.

We were considered Jesus Christ returned, He was alive in us, so in the Love Family, there was no one-on-one monogamous marriage in the classic sense where the relationship was characterized by ideas of ownership and exclusivity. The Love Family Charter stated:

> Thus we, being each married to the body of Christ, are married one to another in Christ Jesus Our Lord." (23) Wherefore, my brethren, ye also are become dead to the law by the body of Christ; that we should be married to another, even to him who is raised from the dead. (Rom 7:4, *KJV*).

Once someone was baptized into the membership, they were now considered part of the marriage to Christ. In theory and practice, everyone was married to everyone through Jesus Christ, with Love as the head of the Church.

The idea of group marriage is not common, but it occurred occasionally in communal societies founded in the 19th and 20th centuries. The Oneida community (1848–1879) was a tight knit, thriving communal society of Christian communists living in upper New York State. Their leader was a man named John Humphrey Noyes. They believed that God's kingdom on earth would soon be established led by the armies of Christ. Everyone, which was just over 300 people at its height, was married to everyone in what they called "Complex marriage." Complex Marriage was an attempt to liberate men and women from what they saw as the "narrowing confines" of monogamy and conventional family life.

John Humphrey Noyes's idea of "perfectionism" stressed the possibility of achieving an ideal society on earth under divine leadership. After restoring "right religious principles," the second step in achieving the kingdom of heaven on earth was to restore right relations between the sexes. Existing marriage practices and relations between the sexes "were unnatural and harmful." Following Jesus's statement reported in Matthew, Mark, and Luke that there would be no marriage in the resurrected state, Noyes argued that in the heavenly society, there would be no monogamous marriage, no exclusive sexual and emotional ties between the sexes, and no ownership of women by men" (as cited in Foster, 1997, 262). "Women would have sexual relations only with whom they pleased, and no woman had to bear more children than suited her." (Kephart, 1963 pg. 7) Instead there would be a complex marriage in which all loved each other and placed the concerns of the community above their private selfish interests."

I bring up Oneida because that community might have been the most comparable to the Love Family of any of the groups that I have looked at. Oneida did not practice celibacy though like the Love Family did.

In the Love Family, just because everybody was married to everybody, didn't mean that anyone could just go sleep with anyone. It was not a free love, anything goes hippie commune; it was an almost puritanical, highly structured, complex community where the nature of family and marital relationships was completely transformed, and where Love decided who would sleep with who and when. At any time, he could disrupt a relationship. It was not an organic process at all; it was orchestrated.

After baptism, everyone had to go through a period of celibacy. This was about giving up the physical for the spiritual. I asked my mom years later what is was like between men and women.

"The family had such a plutonic feel with the men and women," she says. "You knew you were not going to bed with anyone, so you could kind of relax a little more."

Consideration wrote in his manuscript about his then perception of the marriage in the Love Family. This was the early 1970's time period, before he was kidnapped out by his parents, vis a vie Ted Patrick. He wrote about relationships between men and women:

> To know that we belonged to one another, that we had passed from death unto life…The women to me were wonderful sisters, down to earth people that didn't put on airs and who would accept me. I really enjoyed their company and being a brother to them. As far as sexual desires toward the women, I didn't feel them at all. I didn't try to figure out why, I only knew I had given that up. It was no longer a concern of mine or something I had to try and satisfy. I really saw women as persons to be loved and to be known." (172–173)

My former teacher known as Definition discussed some of the ideas behind the practice of celibacy:

"The priority was to build the Love Family first, not one's own personal relationship with a man or a woman," Definition explained. "The purpose of celibacy" was to change one's thinking in order to be a part of God's family, a family where "men and women were like brothers and sisters," he says. "If you take the sex out, you can then have women that are friends."

There were also "spiritual underpinnings," Definition explained. "Roman Catholic priests are celibate—they are marrying the church." In the Love Family as well, when someone joined, they were marrying the church. "Celibacy works in that if you are married to the church your spiritual concerns are much higher than carnal concerns," Definition continued. "It was very much a spiritual thing. The influence of sex can corrupt and eventually ruin people's lives because they can never get a handle on that," he says. "If you just drop it completely, it changes everything."

Atarah's perspective was that when she began to check out the Love Family, she thought it might be "a really great thing to be a part of." She had worked in nightclubs in the mid-1970s and had been exposed to what she called the "meat market" a lot:

"It was rock 'n' roll, party till you drop, smoke pot, drink, sleep with someone different every night. It was a screwed-up world at that point," she explained. "Sexual freedom didn't benefit women. It just meant your having sex with a bunch of guys. Who does that benefit? The bunches of guys that are getting sex now because before good girls wouldn't do that." Once Atarah came to the Love Family, she found that everyone was celibate. "I had been this rampant sexual being, and now I became this non-sexual being for months if not more, even then it had to be approved," she says.

"This was during the sexual revolution when everybody was on birth control," Eve says, then continued, "but one of the things that attracted me to the Family was the men. Everyone was celibate. There were just a few elders who were together," she recalled. "There was a real beauty in that because you didn't have to play a lot of sex games—All that was eliminated. You could just be with your brother and hang out with them and be close to them. Over time, that changed, Eve explained, but "in the early years, that's what it was like. It was beautiful. It was wonderful."

"Everyone was married to everyone in a sort of group marriage," Ethan says. "If a man and a woman really liked each other or fell in love, they could not just have sex, which was called, 'getting together.' They had to have Love's approval." Ethan continued. "If a man wanted to get together with a woman, he had to go ask Love. Love might say no, she is mine, or he might say go ask all other people involved with that person."

Not only did Love decide who would be with who, he also decided how many would be with who. He allowed "certain elders" to be in what was called, 'multiple relationships,' which were essentially polygamous relationships. Ethan explained that this was so that "people wouldn't get hung up on each other," because "Love was trying to build a community where men and women didn't own each other" in exclusive, one-on-one relationships. "If a couple joined the family, he would break them up, Ethan explained. "Once they finished the required celibate period of six months, sometimes Love would tell a couple they could get back together—but he did not usually do that. There were a few exceptions but Love almost always split couples up when they joined."

In the Love Family, sexual relationships (getting together) could only take place if one was sanctioned, which meant that the relationship was approved by Love. Once someone became sanctioned, they could no longer get together with someone who was not sanctioned.

"With Love's approval, elders could have more than one woman, called a 'multiple relationship,' says Eve, "but it was usually within house-holds; Elder ladies did not have the same freedoms." The elder man could add partners without his elder lady's approval. Although, as the years went by, "it changed somewhat" in that "the elder lady also had to agree."

Other than the rare affair or exception, I don't know of any woman, elder lady or not, who was able to add another man to her relationship. That was a choice that it seemed only elder men had.

Thankfully, I never had to deal with some of the things that the adult members had to deal with, like who I was sanctioned to—of course I was celibate, I was just a kid. I was a long way from having to worry about getting sanctioned or getting together. I was being raised in a culture where an elder could have more than one woman. Would I, someday, be sanctioned to an elder? Which of the boys would be an elder? I had a crush on a certain boy. Would I, someday, have to share him with one of my friends? I couldn't even imagine that.

When we got there in 1975, Love had two wives, Truthfulness and Bliss. None of the other elders had two. For most of the years that I was there, it stayed that way. In time, Love allowed Integrity to have two. He felt that Integrity could handle it. Integrity had Together and Submission, and on the surface, at least, it seemed to work as far as most people could tell.

My mom discussed her perspectives about how the Family saw mul-tiple relationships.

"Love liked to try new things a little bit at a time to see how it worked out, but for many years, that was how it remained, just an idea in its initial stages of experimentation." My mom continued, "Any elder could ask Love if they wanted to, but for many years, none of them did. A lot of communities that we knew were trying different things, and we were watching it all," she says. "Love thought that in general, nobody was mature enough to handle any relationships. In his thinking, as we all matured together as a family—the ideal that he presented, and it might take us 20 years—was that eventually we would all be with each other." Love explained how marriage was to be seen in the community. "[He] always said that we were all married with each other," my mom remembered. "We heard that over and over."

Multiple relationships were part of Love's vision; he just wanted to make sure that people were "ready," that they could handle it. Love's vision was, of course, influenced by his own fantasies of how he felt the world should be. And of course, in the Bible, polygamy was never condemned; in fact, the Bible is littered with references of men who had multiple wives, including David, Soloman, Abraham, Jacob, and many others. Women who joined the Love Family and saw what was happening, either went along with it or overlooked it, to be a part of the community.

Love was the apex or center. He was the visionary for the entire Love Family, down to every aspect of peoples' relationships with one another. Therefore, it was totalitarian and not just an autocracy.

Sex outside of the marriage was not allowed. If someone had sex outside of a sanctioned relationship or if they had sex with someone who was not in the Love Family, they could be asked to leave. It was very serious. The Love Family was endogamous, which means allowing marriage within, but not outside the group.

As the big people persevered in their quest to live out Love's vision, my childhood continued to unfold. Years were going by; I was growing up. Even though I was 'eternal' and my birthday was not celebrated, my body continued to get taller and it began to occur to me on concrete terms that someday I would be an adult.

That same year, Hope decided he was too old to find eggs on Easter. Instead, he would help hide the eggs with the adults. When I heard it, I had a hard time imagining any kid not wanting to find eggs on Easter. From the expressions on the kids' faces when they heard that Hope would hide eggs, I knew that nobody could believe it. I liked the idea of Hope hiding the eggs for us, but it was, at least for me, an ominous reminder that adulthood was somewhere around the bend.

Even Love had made a comment once when he saw me walk by with another girl. He said that we were "becoming young women." It irritated me to hear him say it. I didn't feel like a young woman, I still felt like a young girl.

Then something happened that sticks out in my mind. It was a warm afternoon, and everyone had gathered at the edge of one of the fields. It must've been Passover time, which after a certain point, was spent at the Love Family' Ranch.

Humility, who was Bright's dad was playing the sitar. The sitar is a type of guitar, a plucked instrument used mainly in Hindustani music and Indian classical music. Everyone, maybe one or two hundred people were gathered in a half circle around Love, sitting in the grass, meditation style. I sat with some of the other children near Love where he had indicated he wanted us to sit. Everyone was silent, listening to the sounds of the sitar being played, waiting for Love to talk. The reverberating buzzing sounds of the strings created a sort of hypnotic, mesmerizing ambiance for the gathering.

At times like these, Love chose Endurance to dance, or sometimes other women who he considered beautiful. Endurance was dancing this time. She danced on the outside of the circle of people. Her dancing was not in front of everybody, but more off to the side where it was just part of the background and was more part of the ambiance as opposed to it being a performance. If you look at the photo section of this book, there is a group shot of people meeting in the barn. The photo belongs to photographer, Rich Frishman. In the photo, you can see that off to the side, there are two women dancing. That was not uncommon. Love often did that.

I liked to watch the women dance. As a kid, it was more interesting than listening to Love talk. I watched Endurance. She would twirl her skirt around and throw up her arms in a variety of ways. She had long, very dark, almost black hair. Her ethnic, long skirt twirled out, so I could see her legs carrying her about. Her dancing was discrete but vibrant and active. It had a very non-western, ethnic quality that was complimentary to the sounds of the sitar. Everyone was quiet and in the moment of the experience. Nothing needed to be said. I looked at the trees up behind the group which swayed with the warm, light breeze then across the field towards the lake. Nature was the back drop for this scene, this moment in time. I watched the trees sway in motion together on the hillside. Not only was I slowly, ever so slowly becoming an adult, but there was something else that was new, and that was a spiritual awareness within me about the idea of oneness. Maybe it started with my experience at King Lake, but when I saw the trees swaying back and forth on the hillside behind the gathering, I felt that there was a consciousness that connected me, that permeated everything, the trees, me, the people around me. It seemed that my whole body filled up with light. The sitar droned on in the back of my awareness as I just sort of let myself enjoy the beauty of the gathering.

One of the reasons why I think I remember those moments so well was because of what happened next.

Suddenly, I heard Love's voice say that he wanted some of the girls to dance. Usually he only asked adult women to dance. He would ask one or more of the women that he considered the most beautiful to dance, such as Endurance or Empathy. I did not see myself as fitting into that category, I was a child, so it made me uncomfortable.

All the light drained out of me in one instant as I realized what he wanted to have happen. Even though I didn't want to dance, I felt like I had no choice. Love was the creator, a sort of supreme being, orchestrating our life like a dance. Everyone there expected of me what Love expected of me. Those were the expectations of the community that I was a part of. No one that I knew of had ever challenged Love. When I got up to dance, my body felt heavy and stiff. I tried to move with the music, but it was like slow motion. I was painfully self-conscious, and because of it, I was unable to even coordinate my movements. I saw four or five other girls, around my age, dancing, evenly spread around the perimeter of the group. Love had placed us strategically around the half circle of adults. We stood and danced; everyone else was sitting on the grass in the lotus.

My legs were stiff. If I refused, it would disappoint the King. It would disappoint everyone. From then on, I might be the source of consternation. I might be singled out as being a problem. I might get lectures on being dark or negative. *Just dance,* I told myself. *Dance, Dance. We are one. We are one,* reverberated in my thoughts. I began to feel light headed. Each moment went on forever. Love was beginning to see us like "young women." *Just dance.* In my view when Love asked adult women to dance at a gathering, it seemed that he was trying to create a subtle, sexual vibe to the ambiance. I was perceptive enough to realize what he was doing. He didn't ask the boys to dance; it was just the big girls, so it seemed to me that he was wanting to show off the beauty of the community's young women, but I wasn't ready to see myself that way. To me, it just felt gross. I did not want to see myself as beautiful.

It wasn't just the dancing, Love also began to ask the big girls to sit by him at meetings where he knew everyone would be looking at him and us.

I was disgusted by the attention. It was offensive to me that he would use us to try and create an impression, a subtle sexual vibe. It felt violating. As we danced, the sitar music continued to vibrate in its hypnotic way throughout the whole thing. The oneness, the beautiful moment of shared consciousness that I witnessed earlier, was gone. *We are one, but we are still human.* It was a lesson that had hit me at King Lake when I took sacrament, and there was a resonance within me in this situation here in the pasture when Love asked us to dance. Love was only human. He wasn't Jesus Christ, although he probably saw himself that way. I don't think Jesus would've asked me to dance.

Things were changing; I wasn't sure I liked it. One day, I walked into one of the classrooms, and there were some of the older boys. They were all standing by the chalkboard where there was a drawing of a naked lady. When they saw me, they all jumped in front of the chalkboard in a line and froze. They all looked at me with intense expressions on their faces, trying to figure out what to do next. I had a journal entry in my then diary about the incident:

Dear Diary,

Today I walked into the Barn classroom. The boys were looking at a naked drawing of a woman on the chalkboard. Bright held me off and told me not to come in. Woopde doo! so that's the latest fad?!

Rachel Israel

It seemed that sex had become a topic for conversation among the kids, because I overheard the boys talking about masturbation. I didn't know what that was but wasn't sure I wanted to. Then some of the older kids had played spin the bottle out in the pasture one evening, and I had heard there had been kissing. I wasn't there for that one, but I heard about it for a couple of weeks after that as they had to keep talking about it. Something new was happening. Our relationships were changing. It seemed almost everyone knew who everyone else "liked."

Not too long after that, there was a slumber party up in the Barn for the kids. Seth and I rolled our sleeping bags in the upper loft of the Barn where the school library was. Seth had been one of the ones who had played spin the bottle, so he got it in his head that he wanted to kiss me. He said he wanted to French kiss.

"No way! I said adamantly.

"Please! Please!" Seth kept begging me.

"No! Yuck!" I kept saying. The thought of it was disgusting. I saw Seth and the boys who were around my age more as brothers, the result of years of living in a commune where we all had just been considered family.

As kids, I guess we were dealing with a lot of the same things that kids on the outside deal with, but the culture that we were embedded in was anything but conventional. I was raised in a polygamous community. I was raised in a world where the government (Love) made all the decisions about who will and won't be married.

I was raised in a community where I was taught that someday, when I was ready for love, I may not have a say in who I end up with, or I could end up having to share the person I love with someone else. This was just how it was. Way back when I had lived in Alaska, my mom and Marty had a somewhat normal relationship, although they weren't ever married and that was their choice, but those memories were fading. This new normal was what it was like for me, growing up in the Love Family.

BIBLIOGRAPHY (CHAPTER 7)

[Atarah]. Personal Interview. August 7, 2002. 6–7pm. Seattle.

Church of Armageddon Charter of the Love Israel Family. (1971).

Conquest, Robert. (1999). *Reflections on a Ravaged Century.* p. 74. ISBN 0-393-04818-7.

[Definition]. Personal Interview. September 30, 2001. Magnolia Hill, Seattle.

[Karen]. Personal Interviews. July 11, November 10, both 2001. West Seattle.

[Ethan]. Interview with Chuck LeWarne. February 18, 1998.

[Eve]. Personal Interview. September 30, 2001.

Foster, Lawrence. (1997). *Americas Communal Utopias.* Ed. Donald E. Pitzer. The University of North Carolina Press, 1st New Edition.

Government and Law. (2009). Volume Library 1. The Southwestern Company. p. 11.

Israel, Larry. (Consideration) (1978) Unpublished Manuscript. pp. 172–173.

Israel, Understanding, Personal Interview. September 15, 2002. Lake Forest Park, WA.

Klaw, Spencer. (1993). *Without Sin: The Life and Death of the Oneida Community.* New York: Allen Lane, Penguin Press.

Kephart, William M. (1963). Experimental Family Organization: An Historico-Cultural report on the Oneida Community. *Marriage and Family Living.* Vol. 25 (3), pp. 261–271.

LeWarne, Charles P. (2009). *The Love Israel Family: Urban Commune, Rural Commune.* University of Washington Press, Seattle and London.

[Zarah] Personal Interview. December 13, 2001. Maple, Valley, WA.

Zablocki, Benjamin. (1971). The Joyful Community. Penguin Press

CHAPTER 8

Chicken Pox, Fat Camp and Life on the Funny Farm

am now going back in time to 1976. I had been in the Love Family for over a year. The Love Family acquired a 350-acre parcel of property in Arlington, donated to Love by Richness, who we had known as 'Dan' before we joined. Everyone called the new property 'the Ranch.' Since there was a lot of driving back and forth between Queen Anne and the Arlington Ranch, the time it took was well known—it was about a 45-minute drive. The only other property that we owned at this point was the big house in Hawaii. I heard that the property in Homer, Alaska was sold. This was sometime after the house that was there burned down. I paid attention to that piece of information because that is where we had first met the Family. It was hard to imagine that large house not being there. That was the house where I had fallen down that cellar and hurt myself pretty bad.

Apparently, once Richness decided to join, the homestead was sold and a down payment was made on the Arlington ranch. Even though the Love Family was a small community, I never knew Richness that well, but from what I could tell, he was a kind man. When I saw him walk by or when I saw him in a gathering, I noticed that he had these deep-set eyes, bushy eye brows and mustache. I always thought that even if he wasn't smiling, it looked as if he was. It was just his natural expression.

The property near Arlington was beautiful. There was a house and a barn and pastures, and a lot of open spaces for gardens as well as lots of woods for hiking and camping. There were also three small lakes on the property, several creeks and a small waterfall.

Sometime after the Ranch was bought, Love sent one household out there to live in the house and help take care of the animals. At first, there were at least two cows, horses, a large coop of chickens, and a pig. I also remember a peacock, some ducks and a goose as well.

I got to see these different animals, because about a year after I had come to the Love Family, I caught the chicken pox and it was decided that I would be quarantined at the Ranch. This was when there were hardly any other people that lived there yet. They decided it would be an ideal place to keep me isolated from the other kids, who were all still living in town and could catch it.

I had been living in Love's Annex, which was the house right next to Love's house in Love's Area. Eventually there was a construction project where Love's Annex was attached to Love's house, so that it became one house, Love's 'big house.' But before that, it was Encouragement's house after he got back from Hawaii. Deepesh and Lakshi were there with their two kids Parvati and Shivaya. The family had lived in several Ashrams in India, including Swami Omkar's Ashram on the east coast of India. Swami Omkar was a Hindu yogi and saint under the rubric of the Divine Life Society, founded by Sri Swami Sivananda. The Society dealt with all aspects of yoga and Vedanta, ancient medicine, ancient traditions and cultural practices, and ran conferences and training centers. Parvati and Shivaya had lived at this Ashram on the Ganga. Parvati was closer to my age; Shivaya, Parvati's brother, was a year or two younger than Parvati and had the longest hair I had ever seen on a kid, that he kept in a long braid that hung down his back. Parvati had very long hair too and wore her hair in pigtails.

When all the kids would meditate, Shivaya and Parvati could meditate for very long periods of time, much longer than any of us, which was impressive. A lot of the kids in the Love Family were just learning to meditate when they came.

In India, they had suffered from a staph infection, like I did in Makena, but instead of taking antibiotics, they had been taught to drink their own urine as a cure. When I heard about that, I saw that some kids laughed; others were sort of horrified. Their family came and stayed for various periods of time as visitors. They never joined or stayed on permanently. Deepesh and Lakshi, Shivaya and Parvati's parents wore beautiful, fine cotton clothes from India when they came. Joya, their mother, had pale ivory skin, long red hair, and wore silk scarves around her head, black eyeliner, and at times had a third eye painted on her forehead just above and between her eyebrows.

Parvati and Shivaya and their parents were staying in the Annex during this time, so I often played with them. Then one day, I was taking a bath with them when I noticed they had all these red, itchy bumps. Soon after that bath, I had the bumps too. Deepesh and Lakshi and their kids left after that for a while, but I was sent to the Ranch on a quarantine for two weeks or more. During the quarantine, I lived in the house that was there. Innocence was the elder of the household. This was early on, when hardly anyone lived at the Ranch; the property was still pretty new to us.

I knew Innocence fairly well. Before he became an elder, I had lived with him when he was a member of Encouragement's household. He was tall, slender and had straight, long, blond hair and a strawberry blond beard. He had a slender face and a long, slender nose. Blue eyes. He also was one of the men, along with a guy named Enthusiasm, who had visited our tepee in Alaska before we came. They had spent the night, then had used our sauna, and then they all went and helped our friend Suzanne get her stuff on her way to join the Love Family.

But now, just over a year later, he did not seem to recognize me, and now eldered the Ranch house. His elder lady Piety took care of me. Piety was pretty, with full, rosy cheeks and long, light-brown hair. She drew me hot baths when my blistering bumps itched miserably, and dabbed calamine lotion on them to relieve my discomfort. I would watch her knit tiny booties and baby hats. She said she was going to send the hats and booties to town for the ladies whose babies were due soon.

Then, there were a group of about 12 women who were sent to the Ranch. While I stayed in the Ranch house, they were working and living in the Barn. They would take care of the animals and clean their pens. I heard they were there to lose weight. None of them were actually fat, they were just full-figured women who were no more than 5–20 pounds heavier than Love considered ideal. Love had definite ideas about femininity and acceptable shapes for women.

The Ranch was being used as a 'fat camp' for Family women who were deemed 'fat.' I was told that Love had said the women were 'to become the true image of their spirits,' and that they were 'poor examples of Jesus Christ.'

The women had to live in the Barn, which wasn't heated, although at that time, there was a wood stove in the tack room. I would see them huddled around the stove, eating fried rice and raw veggies or reading the Bible. When they weren't working, they were crocheting hats and booties for the Family's new babies. I made myself useful, learning how to milk the cows and helping them take care of the animals, but then I was told not to talk to them.

I was only there because I had chicken pox. Eve was there, but this was before she started teaching classes at the Family school. Eve was not fat, she was shapely and beautiful. I have learned since that women come in all shapes and sizes and are not chattel to be compared and judged to fit one man's ideal.

Luckily, a lot of the pressures on the adult women to be underweight were over my head because of my age. It was more this subtle background noise. Love was the patriarch, and it was his vision that women should be skinny. The degrading and insensitive expectations for women regarding their weight must've been a lot of pressure for women. For myself, to not hear any public discussion or protest about it had a negative impact on me in that it was, once again, women's silence with its concurrent message of acceptance.

The fat camp ordeal did not happen again, although there were still the pressures on women to keep their weight low. Some women were more impacted by it than others. I did hear that a few years after fat camp, there was a woman who had confronted Love about the issue. Apparently, she was very mad and went and railed on Love about why such a big deal was made about women's weight. He wasn't very receptive from what I've heard. It wasn't long after that when she left the Family.

When I felt a little better, I would go collect the eggs from the chicken coop for Piety. I had a craving for maternal energy and she was very loving to me. I appreciated having this one-on-one time with her when there were no other children there to play with.

I was lonely and miserable as my chicken pox were very hot and itchy. The only relief were the warm baths. Piety could tell that I need a playmate, so she talked to Innocence who talked to Love in town and soon after, they sent a girl out there for me to play with, someone to be my play-mate until my chicken pox were gone and I could return to town.

The girl they sent to me was Hadassah. They said she already had the pox and couldn't catch them again. I really didn't know her that well. She was new and a couple of years older than I. We looked very different. I was not as tall as she was and had very light, golden blond hair. She had pale skin and long, dark brown hair, brown eyes and very delicate facial features. Before her mother had dropped her off in the Love Family, she had been a member of the Source Family, the spiritual commune that Logic had joined and then returned from.

The Source Family's full name was actually called, Brotherhood of the Source. It was led by a man called Yahowah, whose prior or Worldly name had been Jim Baker. They also were known to have called him, "Yod," which was a planet in some planetary constellation.

Yahowah/Jim Baker had been an American Marine, having earned a silver star during WWII and was an expert karate fighter of Jujitsu. He was said to be one of the first non-Japanese Karate experts. He also was known to have been a Vedantic monk for a while and had followed yogi Bhajan, a Sikh spiritual teacher and leader of Kundalini yoga. After following the yogi, he had come to Hollywood to work as a stuntman when he founded the Source community in Hollywood Hills.

The Source community was wealthy, they drove Rolls Royces, lived communally in a mansion they called the 'Mother House,' where they slept in cubes stacks four high. Yahowah, who had twelve wives, decided who slept with who each night.

There were 140 original Source members, less than half of the Love Family membership. Their men all had long hair and long beards and wore short, white robes with a belt. Their women all had long hair and wore tightly fitted, opalescent, Grecian type dresses made of synthetic, shiny fabric. Members wore large, Egyptian symbols around their necks.

They also had a band that played experimental, psychedelic rock that was gaining in popularity in the Hollywood Hills where they lived.

The Love Family had lost one of our members to the Source, Joah, and almost lost Logic, of course, as I already explained. Despite that, the Love Family and the Source Family were friends. It was somewhat of a competitive relationship to some degree though, due to our competition for members.

The Source were like the Love Family in thinking to the extent that it was an eclectic mix of all sorts of spiritual influences: They were influenced by the Bible too, but they also were influenced by astrology and numerology, Hindu-yoga, Persian and Middle Eastern religions, Christian Science, power of positive thinking, as well as hippie counterculture idealism.

It wasn't just Hadassah that had come from the Source; eventually a lot of their members came and joined the Love Family. That happened because of an accident that took place in Hawaii.

Yod had moved his followers from Sunset Boulevard to Hawaii, because he had become convinced that the end of civilization was fast approaching, and that the American mainland was going to be destroyed.

The Source lived in Kauai and spent time hand gliding and training in Karate. Yahowah was hand gliding in Oahu at Kilpani cliffs when he broke his back and refused to get medical attention. He launched from a point too high for his level of experience and crashed into a group of campers in a nearby parking lot. Yahowah didn't believe in the value of medical science and was dead nine painful hours later on August 25th, 1974. This was not too long before we showed up at the Front Door Inn. When we came, there were members I was meeting who had come from the Source.

Yahowah had been friends with Love and had told his followers that if anything ever happened to him, they were to go to the Love Family. I played with a girl named Sacred who was around my age who had come from the Source. She taught me some of the Source Family songs. I loved the music. It was ethereal, hypnotic compared to the Love Family's more folksy sound. She sang, *"If you want to keep something sacred, keep it in the silence of your heart…"* And instead of chanting, *"Aaaaah,"* like we did, they sang Yahowah's name repeatedly. It followed a melody, it wasn't just monotone: *"Yahowah, Yahowah, Yahowah, Yahowah."* For more information on the Source Family, see a 98-minute documentary called, "The Source Family" 2012, directed by Jodie Wille and Maria Demopoulos.

Hadassah, the girl sent to keep me company while I suffered with chicken pox, had come with about 20 other Source members, some I got to know better than others. One of the things that was really great about when the Source joined us was they brought us alfalfa sprouts, wheat grass, whole grains and nutritional yeast. They did not cook and had owned a health foods restaurant on Sunset Strip and believed in eating raw foods only. That was one way that they influenced our culture. From that point on, I put nutritional yeast on everything—rice, popcorn, sprouts, even oatmeal. It was delicious!

Hadassah told me that the Source would jump off cliffs. There would be a group of people at the bottom of the cliff, holding their arms out waiting to catch the people who jumped. It was an exercise in belief. The whole idea was to jump and totally believe that you would fly. If you didn't fully believe it, you would fall into the safe arms of those waiting at the bottom. Hearing what these people would do, the idea of it frightened me. Just the thought of people jumping off a cliff, thinking that they might fly. From that point on after I heard that, I would have this recurring dream.

In the dream, I can fly but only if I truly believe it. If there was any doubt, then I am grounded and go nowhere. In the dream, I am only as powerful as my mind will allow, so it is this mental exercise where I must let go of one belief system and embrace another. In the dream, I focus my mind and as I do, I begin to fly. Throughout the dream though, I am dealing with periodic bouts of doubt that bring me crashing to the ground. In the dream, I continually mentally fight to overcome the doubt, so that I can return to flight.

I was so happy when Hadassah showed up to keep me company while I had chicken pox. We became like best friends for a couple weeks or so.

Hadassah and I played together in the Barn a lot. At the time, the Barn's upper floor was full of bales of hay, stacked all the way up to the rafters. There was also a basketball hoop in the Barn, where the men from Innocence's household would play. When the men played, Hadassah and I would be cheerleaders and would kick our legs in the air and chant, *"2-4-6-8, who do we appreciate..."* We also would visit the Barn animals and play in the tack room where they kept the saddles.

One evening, Hadassah and I were in the Barn. We climbed up the stacks of hay and brought blankets and some snacks. The hay was stacked up almost to the top, so we were near the rafters. We had set our blankets just right and knew that soon the men would be in to play basketball.

We were eating our snacks, when suddenly several black bird-like things swooped past our heads.

"Oh birds?! I asked.

"Bats!" Hadassah screamed, in a blood curdling voice.

I didn't know what she was afraid of, but I screamed too. It must be pretty serious for her to scream like that. We fell from bale to bale as we scrambled out of there. We screamed all the way down and out the Barn. The men were just coming up the stairs on their way to play basketball as we stumbled past them, waving our arms around.

"We were attacked by bats!" Hadassah told them, frantically.

They did not seem concerned at all and just started laughing as we almost fell down the stairs past them. It took a while for us to calm down, but Hadassah and I had bonded for life.

That was my experience with chicken pox. I was miserable and lonely, only really able to talk to Piety because the fat ladies were working, until Hadassah came out to keep me company, which even though we were attacked by bats, ended up being fun anyway.

For years afterward, whenever I saw Hadassah, we'd say, "Remember when we were attacked by bats?" We would laugh about it. I had so much fun at the Ranch that winter with her that I almost forgot I'd been banished because of the pox.

......

It wasn't until the following year (1977) that people began trickling out to the Ranch in larger numbers to set up what became permanent encampments. Before that, the only people living at the Ranch were the people who were living in the Ranch house who were taking care of the animals. The migration was gradual, but over time, the largest contingency of the Love Family lived at the Ranch. This is where I spent a majority of the next few years of my childhood.

Our life at the Ranch was an evolution of sorts. Each elder and their respective household was set up with a surplus Army tent that was placed in a circle in one of the large fields by the lake. The Army tents were large, 16' by 32' dark Army green tents that could accommodate households of 12 or more people.

In the center of the circle of tents was a fire pit with benches. Near the lake a wooden sauna was built which was a center for bathing and laundry. If one looked at the encampment of tents from above, it looked like a circle with the firepit being the dot in the middle, a Love symbol, just like how people were arranged for meetings and gatherings. Things often had a staged feel to them where every arrangement seemed to place Love at the center of all life in every context.

To me, the arrangement of tents in the circle seemed more communal in some ways, than when we all lived in the City, because now all the households shared a front yard, whereas in the City, a lot of the houses were located on different streets in clusters.

By the following year, 1978, the Army tents were built upon and remodeled to accommodate a more permanent way of life. I heard people refer to them as 'shack-tents.' Wood Platforms were built for some of the tents to sit on to get them up off the ground. They had full kitchens, covered entranceways, usually made from wood, although, some used clear plastic sheeting. The kitchen was sometimes built as an attachment to the tent, and at other times, it was built inside the tent at the far end. Inside the main tent area was a multipurpose, carpeted space where people could have meetings during the day or for eating and sleeping at night.

Eventually, after living in the Army tents in the pasture for two years, there was a change. People spread out and began living in 24' diameter canvas and vinyl Mongolian yurts that were moved out of the pasture and were set up around the lake. The yurts sat on wooden platforms, that were high enough off the ground that it created a lower living area underneath the yurts. The lower stories were enclosed and used as kitchens and dining areas, while the upstairs yurts served as bedrooms.

The Ranch was a big place. There was a large Barn, that was set up with electricity and plumbing. There was also a shed attached to the Barn and another outbuilding nearby that was used as another shed. There was a fully functioning and livable house and fenced pastures with farm animals. It was 350 acres when it was initially acquired. Much of it was wooded, but there were large areas of just open pastures and areas for agriculture. There were three small lakes on the property as well, one that was centrally located near where the tents were set up. The other two lakes were within a short hike's distance.

Eventually most people lived at the Ranch, but not everyone. Some of the houses on Queen Anne were sold, but there were certain elders who stayed in town and lived with their households in the remaining houses, and Love kept his area of houses.

Life at the Ranch was more similar in some ways to my life in Alaska than living on Queen Ann, so going from living in town to living in tents on a farm was not that difficult for me. I had already learned to live rustically when my mom and I were on the road and when we lived in the tepee and log cabins in Alaska.

The Ranch was way more isolated than living in town. It was outside of Arlington in a rural area at the end of Mattson road, which was a country, gravel road with tons of potholes. We had one neighbor, across the road, Jerry Firnstahl who also had a farm, but because of the long driveway, he couldn't see much, if anything from his standpoint.

Anyone visiting would come up directly to a dead end where there was a gate and a small wooden shed, which everyone called the 'Gatehouse.' Members took turns keeping a 24-hour watch over who came and went. There was always two people on watch, keeping in line with the Family's custom of oneness and readiness for Armageddon. The Gatehouse was so small, that it only had room for a bed and a small wood stove. It was a cozy place though where the gatekeepers could rest, eat, read the Bible and stand guard. Just to the side of the main gate, was a hand-carved wooden plaque that read:

> Sanctuary
> Please enter
> silently, prayerfully
> with peace under your feet.
> God Bless
> Family Council

I was too young to take my turn at the gate, but to pass time, I would take a walk down the driveway from the Barn area to visit whoever was on watch that day. It was just something to do. Sometimes we would stop by there and chat on our way to or from the sheep pasture or to take a bike ride. The sheep pasture was a triangular shaped pasture with a sheep shed that was less than a quarter mile down the road from the Ranch. It was detached from the main property but was part of the owned property.

During the whole time I lived at the Ranch, I generally wore flip flops or rubber boots. I didn't have tennis or other fancy shoes. It was communal farm living. I went barefoot all the time. The members on Watch always seemed to enjoy visits from the kids, at least every time I stopped by. I imagined how boring it must be to sit there all day and night, as they waited to see who would be coming or going and why. One day, I was passing through on my way to the sheep pasture to play, and the person on watch commented on my calloused feet. The way they said it made me feel proud, so I and a couple of girls I was with had a contest to see who could walk the farthest on the gravel with our bare feet, just to impress the gatekeeper. The gravel of Mattson was sharp but I did pretty well.

From the Gatehouse, there was a long dirt driveway that led directly to the Ranch house. Just past the house was the gigantic Barn next to a shed that ended up being called the 'pottery shed.' It had two potting wheels, a kiln and other supplies for making pottery. It was a large enough shed, that one side of it was used for a candle making operation as well.

At first, the 2nd floor of the Barn just had stacks of bales of hay, but then overtime, it was remodeled and turned into a community sanctuary and meeting room used for meals, meetings, and parties. Once it was remodeled, for many years, the sanctuary had a red and gold, large print paisley carpet. Hung along each wall were 12 hand-sewn and embroidered large, maybe four feet wide by five feet in height, banners, each displaying pictography representing one of the Twelve Tribes of Israel. Above the sanctuary was a loft that eventually was turned into school rooms. The Barn was constantly changing and being remodeled as our life evolved, and different rooms changed functions as our needs changed.

At some point, there was an addition built upon the Barn that had a big, restaurant-style kitchen with stainless steel ovens and countertops. I learned how to make bread and pies there. I made a pecan pie once. It was during a slumber party in the Barn, and each kid there got to make their own pie. An elder lady named Appreciation sent someone to the store in Arlington to get the ingredients. Afterward, we all shared the pies, so I got to taste lemon meringue and chocolate and others. Since there were around 10 of us there, there were a lot of different kinds of pie to sample. I had never even had pie at that point in my life, so it was a super fun time.

Early on, the main floor of the Barn, was just cement, with stalls for milking cows. It had a small room for processing the milk, a tack room, and another storage room that became what everyone called 'the store,' where bins of bulk foods were kept for the households. There was also a laundry room where there was a washer and dryer, and another room became a community shower.

Once the upstairs of the Barn was turned into a sanctuary and the kitchen was added, there was a community boot room built at the base of the stairway leading from the main floor of the Barn to the upper floor. I was taught to remove my shoes before I entered the carpeted areas upstairs. Neat rows of muddy black or Army green boots, shoes and flip flops filled the shelves that lined the walls of the boot room. I would straighten the boots and shoes each time I went through there, as I was taught. We were creating the kingdom of God by helping to beautify our life. Understanding taught the kids, 'Always leave it better than you found it.' When I reminded her about that, years later, she answered quickly, "Yes, but I was teaching you what Love taught me."

Above the sanctuary, on the wall that faced the lake and the circle of tents, there was a large window that was put in that was in the shape of a star of David. The window cast light across the sanctuary floor and lightened the entire space. Although there were electric hook ups for the band equipment that was used during parties, the light from the new window was needed since electricity was not used for lighting. The window could be seen from the outside for quite a distance due to its size. It was distinct and gave the Barn its unique Love Family personality. If I was out in the gardens on the backside of the Barn, I could see the light reflect off the glass from all angles. I could even see it from the pasture down by the lake where all the tents were set up, which could've been about at least a ten-minute walk from the Barn, depending on one's size.

In the Barn, right in the center of the sanctuary, was a knotted, rope ladder. Each knot reached higher and higher until it finally came into a tiny look-out room with excellent views. I was told that this room was designed to circulate the air in the Barn. As I looked out, I could see a lot of the developed areas. Towards the front, I could see the dirt round-a-bout and driveway that went out past the Ranch house to the gate. If I looked out another angle, I could see the pottery/candle shed. If I looked another angle, I could see the gardens and greenhouses, the swing set and the fruit trees. I could also see the huge pasture where the horses grazed and another pasture where cows swished their tails. I could see a small part of the lake and part of the pasture where the tents were set up next to it, but it was hard to see the tents themselves from the look-out room because of the knoll. The knoll was a wooded hill that to me almost seemed more like a small mountain. It was big enough that there was a hiking trail that went up and over it.

Love had designated the knoll for meditation and prayer, so we were not allowed to talk on the knoll; it was for total silence. I loved to go there, and I would say a little prayer as I got to the top where there was this little natural rock formation with moss on it, surrounded by sword ferns and trees. It was my magic spot. One day, I was up on the knoll with Heaven, and we were picking huckleberries. The huckleberry bushes were on the side of the knoll that had fewer trees and rose above the woodchip walking path that went right by on its way towards the lake and tent pasture. While we were picking, Love walked by with his elder lady, Truthfulness and a couple other people. He often had a little entourage of servants or priests with him who would assist him as he needed. He looked up at us and smiled as he walked by, then his expression turned to concern. The entire entourage also stopped and waited for him. He called up to us, loud enough for us to hear him.

"You girls aren't talking up there, now are you?" he asked.

I felt like it was a trick question. I had to answer Love, because to not answer him wouldn't be right, but if I answered him, I would be breaking the 'no talking' rule. We just smiled back sweetly from behind the berry bushes, trying to decide if we should answer him. "No Love!" we yelled down to him. It seemed too rude to just not say anything.

He seemed happy enough with that answer, thankfully, and kept walking by. Love was headed away from the barn area and down the wood chip path that went past the knoll. He would come to the main grassy field by the lake with the circle of tents that sat right next to Butterfly Lake.

Butterfly lake was awesome because it was centrally located near the tents where we lived. I played at the lake with the other children all the time. There was a beach area, a dock, and a zip-line that went across a portion of the lake. If I climbed the tree by the edge of the lake, I could hang onto the zip-line, and it would carry me across to where I could jump off into the water.

Another great place to swim was at a place everyone just called 'Jordan River.' It was located near Jordan Store, which was off Jordan Road. In the summer, I went with groups of Family children with our guardians to swim. It would take too long to get there if we had to walk down Mattson road, then down Jordan road, so usually, unless we road our bikes, which we sometimes did, we usually would all hike through the woods off the property, across a neighbor's property, past a small nickel mine and onto a back road that led right to the small store and river. I think it took almost an hour to get there, which wasn't bad since we were used to hiking around the Ranch all the time.

We had to wear clothes at Jordan River though when we went to swim, not go naked as we did back home at the Ranch. Our guardians told us there had been complaints by the neighbors who lived on the opposite side of the river in houses overlooking the river when they had seen a few of the Love Family kids swimming naked. Love Family kids weren't used to having to worry about that. We all just swam at lakes on our property where nudity was no big deal.

There were several swimming options. If we were willing to take a short hike through the woods, there was another lake we could swim at, King Lake. At King Lake, the water was deeper, more clear and cooler than Butterfly Lake. There was also nobody there, except those who were willing to do the hike, whereas back home, at Butterfly lake where everyone lived right next to the it, it was more populated. I swam out, and if I got into just the right place, I could feel the colder, spring water flowing up through my legs. Right next to the edge of King Lake were these gigantic rocks that were man sized with big, flat surfaces, so I could find just the right rock to sunbathe on. We would each get our own rock—that was the deal. Then we would jump from our claimed rocks into the water— which was what was necessary—since there was nowhere else to enter the water from the shore; there was no beach access.

I don't know how many people knew about it, but there was a small waterfall up there as well. It wasn't at King Lake; it was on another hike that eventually went above King Lake; It was very steep to try and climb it though. Understanding once took all the kids on a hike above the waterfall. I had to yank myself up by the tree branches and roots just to get to the top. It was quite a struggle and ended up not being that worth it.

The Ranch was a beautiful place! Another thing that I didn't mention was that on the hike to King Lake, there was, what we called, 'the Rock Gardens.' It was this area deep in the woods where there were these gigantic rocks. They were huge, some the size of small rooms in a house. The rocks were bare; they were not covered in moss, although they were quite slippery when they were wet. They were so big that I was nervous to try and climb them. Many of the rocks were piled up on each other, creating cave-like dwellings underneath them.

Just the lake that we all lived next to, Butterfly Lake, was gorgeous. It was very peaceful, serene and surrounded on most sides of it by forest. There were hillsides that gradually rose behind it. There were trails that led to what everyone called, the 'Lookout.' It was a hefty climb that led up steeply enough that when I got there, there were outstanding views of a lot of the property, way, way, way down below, including neighboring farms. The Ranch was situated on the outskirts of Arlington, Washington, which was in the western foothills of the Cascade Range. The Lookout was a steeper hike than some of the other hikes, but once we got to the top, if I looked straight down, I could see all the little Army tents in a circle in the pasture by the lake. I could see Butterfly Lake, the Barn, the knoll, and dot-like teeny, tiny miniature people walking about.

How lucky I was, as a kid, to live in such beautiful places, starting out in my early childhood living in Maui and then Homer Alaska, two of the most beautiful places on earth. Then to also live on this ranch for several years was amazing, just from an environmental perspective.

As I said earlier, we didn't stay in the circle of tents. There was a turning point when households began moving into yurts that were set up around the perimeter of the lake, instead of right next to it. The migration, which started in 1978, was gradual and took maybe two or three years. It didn't happen all at once. Eventually, most elders, who lived at the Ranch, had a permanent spot on the Lake. If I walked a short distance from my household site to the edge of the lake, I could look and see other yurt sites on the opposite side of the lake. In the winter, I could see the little trails of smoke coming out their chimneys and spreading out into the sky above the encampments. There was a hiking trail that went around the lake from household campsite to household campsite, so in looking across, I saw little mini people walking on the trail, going in and out of little yurts. I found it entertaining to watch. Since the lake carried sound, I could sometimes hear people singing or Ezra yodeling.

If I was really quiet, I could hear faint voices of people talking, laughing, and chanting. Other typical sounds coming from a household's campsite would be a baby fussing, someone chopping wood or playing guitar. If I came closer, the sounds of cedar wood crackling in the wood stove, peoples' conversations that could easily be heard through the thin walls of the canvas tents.

There are certain memories about what it was like to live there that will always stay with me: like the sounds of frogs chanting each night during certain times of the year; like the faraway calls of coyotes on certain nights; like dragonflies darting around in the cattails at the edges of the lake; like swimming at the dock and chasing tiny, black pollywogs, who would wiggle in swarms of thousands where it was warmer, in the shallow beach areas. Occasionally, a fish would jump, causing circular ripples that spread out over the surface of the water. There were water mosquitoes who would scoot with their little jet-ski like legs from one place to another.

The lake was this ceaseless center of curiosity and exploration. Tobiah taught biology for a time in the Family school and would take the kids in his class on nature walks around the lake to gather pond scum and pieces of plant that we took back to look at under the microscope. I was amazed to see all different sort of creatures that were invisible to our human eyes.

Then there was the Frog Club. Since there were a ton of frogs that lived in the lake, including bull frogs, the frog club was formed. Each of the girls in the club had a different frog name, such as 'Big Frog' or 'Slimy Frog.' I was 'Little Frog.' We each had to kiss a frog to be in the club. We could not get many other girls to be in the club because of that requirement, so there were just a few of us. Plus, you also had to drink a small glass of wheatgrass juice, that was made for us special by a woman who had come from the Source family. We did not drink wheat grass juice in the Love Family, but she didn't care what anybody thought and continued to make it, drink it and talk about how beneficial it was to whoever would listen. The juice was gross; it was dark green and very strong, the perfect thing to require of our members—because it was so disgusting. I was only able to drink it because I drank it quickly with my nose plugged. We were the hardy ones, who had proven our worthiness to be in the frog club. There were gazillions of frogs in that lake. The way that I thought about it was that it wasn't just our lake, it was their lake too.

There were beavers in that lake too. Most people don't remember this, some do, but when we all first moved out to the Ranch, there was a beaver dam on the back side of the lake. I rarely saw the beavers working and only did if it was very early in the morning before people were up for the day. It interested me to watch them swim across to and from their dam, carrying wood. I don't know what happened to them, but I think it was during the year sometime after we all started moving into the circle of tents when they left. There were people who would go swimming early in the morning. The beavers didn't like the people rowing around in the canoes or all the splashing around near the dock either.

The red-winged blackbirds didn't seem to mind us. I heard their shrill calls in the early mornings, *conk-la-ree*, a classic birdcall known by environmentalists as the classic sound of wetlands.

One spring, some of the kids went out in the rowboats on the lake where we had bull frog egg fights. There were two teams, each team would have their own boat. Before the fight, we all swim around in the water and filled our boats with the slimy grapefruit-sized, clumps of eggs that would be plentiful and found floating around in the lily-pads. Each clump of solid slime was filled with tiny black dots, which were the eggs. It was sort of like a snowball fight, except it was summer, and we were in boats and the snowballs were slime balls. The object of the game was to get the other team as slimed as possible. The only way I could avoid getting slimed was to jump in the water and swim off, which I did as quick as I could.

One of our first summers at the Ranch, I and some of the older kids made pea shooters with salmon berry stalks. We would dig out the foamy center of the stalk to create a hollow shooter. Then we sneaked into the bulk food bins and took handfuls of split peas for ammunition. I think it was the boys who initiated this one, but in general, the boys and the girls, we all mostly just played together. We didn't divide off by gender for the most part until much later. We were all close as a group and just ran around together like little Love Family hoodlums.

The lake would freeze during the winter, but it wasn't always thick enough for ice skating. There were at least two winters or more though when it froze so thick that large numbers of people were able to ice skate.

One of my absolute favorite memories on the Ranch: Everyone, the whole ranch practically, went ice skating on the lake. It was dusk and there had been probably 100 people or more out on the ice that day. The lake would creak and moan with the weight of so many people. There were these long cracks in the ice, but it was so thick that the ice was able to handle it, for the most part. After the skating, everyone helped build a humongous bon fire and it was arranged for everyone to have hot cocoa. Maybe it was Presence that brought out this huge supply of metal camping cups to use. I set my cup down on a piece of frozen mud which I thought made a good table. My feet and ankles were sore, but I didn't care. There was singing and laughing…it was so fun to be out there with everyone. It was like 'family day' in the Love Family. My brother Forest was out there too that day. He didn't have skates on. He and a little boy about his age named Brotherhood trudged by, dragging a tree branch. His shoulder length, blond, wavy hair snuck out by his ears from a wool cap tied tightly around his chin. He smiled at me as he passed. His bright blue eyes peered back at mine for a moment, our rosy cheeks in the cool, crisp air, He and Brotherhood both looked quite determined as they purposefully marched off towards the far edge of the lake towards some trees with their branch. I missed my brother and wished that we were closer. I didn't see him very often, and so when I saw him, I felt the tears of his absence in my heart.

There was one year when the ice was thick enough to skate, but it was too thin in some places. That was the year Forest fell through. Love just happened to be standing there when it happened and pulled him out. I didn't see it, but I heard about it because it seemed that everyone was talking about it.

"Oh really?! Wow!" I heard people say.

"Love pulled him out?" Everyone seemed so impressed by the idea of

Love as this hero. I guess if it had been anybody else who had pulled him out, it might not have been that interesting. I was just glad that Forest was OK.

It must've been the following year or maybe the year after that when Love himself fell through the ice. I watched peoples' reactions to the news as it spread like fire around the Ranch.

"Oh God!" people gasped.

Others tried not to laugh. It was like the high and mighty ruler, Love, his holiness fell through the ice.

The Lake, when it was frozen, was perfect for playing Indians and cowboys on our dirt bikes. It was tricky though, because if I wasn't careful, my bike's wheels would slide dangerously out from underneath me. The bike had to take its own pace while I worked to prevent the bike from any tilt. I tried to stay back in the cattails as much as possible where the ice was less slick. Cattale stalks were growing up through the ice and would function as slip guards.

Ethan walked by one day and saw us playing Indians and Cowboys on the ice, and that same week, he sat us all down and read to us out loud the story of Crazy Horse. After he finished the book, we refused to play Indians and cowboys again. The boys said they wished they weren't white. They wished they were Indian, because the Indians were so much more righteous and holy than the white Americans. It was a sad story but one that once we knew, it was impossible to continue playing a game in which the Indians were bad guys.

I didn't have what other kids in the World had, but in some ways, what I had was better. How lucky I was to be able to grow up so close to nature, to be able to have that appreciation for the environment, that so many kids today have lost touch with and don't realize what they missed. The diversity of animal and plant life and the interconnectedness of the relationships between it all astounded me.

Once it began to warm up, there was so much open space at the Ranch. It was the ideal place for softball, soccer, and other field games like capture the flag.

One of my favorite games was to play horses. The grass was never mowed, so we would crawl around in it and make little pathways and nests. Ravah was the stallion and would stomp his hoof and throw his head back with a high pitched, "Nehehehe," and call to his flock, and we would all go galloping off. He blew air through his lips to sputter and snort, which sounded just like a real horse.

Although, if you actually study horses, you will find that the mare is always the leader of the pack, but we were living in a patriarchal society and our group dynamics just played themselves out. One of the older girls would be the mare and would snuggle us babies. We called her mommy and she would nuzzle our heads just like a real mare might.

There were a lot of options in terms of what to do. If we didn't want to play horsy, instead we could take off on a hike to King Lake. One day, instead of going to King Lake, we decided to go to the Look Out. There was maybe four or five of us hiking along. We came to a split in the path in a very lush, woodsy area. I heisted myself over this dead log that was covered with moss. It was always there at this one spot in the path. I guess it was too far out in the woods for anyone to bring a saw and try to remove it. I stopped for a moment or two to enjoy the ferns and moss-covered vine maple just off to the right. I could imagine that it was where the fairies must have lived. As I did so, I suddenly got a pungent whiff of mashish, which I thought was very strange since we were so far out in the woods and far from where everyone lived. But it was a very distinct smell. I knew exactly what it was. I told the other girls who looked at me like I was crazy. I stepped off the path and began sniffing. "There it is again!" I told them feeling sure of myself. The other girls started sniffing too. I smelled it all the time back home as mashish was a regular cultural practice. I stopped to smell in silence. I saw two of the girls wander off behind the trees on the other side of the dead log. One of them said, "I smell it too!" We all had our noses up in the air. I smelled it, but only for a moment because of the light breeze. I could also smell trillium, sword ferns, rotting wood, and tree fungus. One of the girls who was behind me, Gentle said, "Let's see who can find the plant. I'll find it first!" She held her nose upward to catch the scent better and disappeared again, on the other side of the path. I sniffed and kept going and then stopped and sniffed again. There were too many directions, so I got back on the path. She stepped out from behind a tree and grinned at me. We both giggled at our failed attempt to locate the plant. "Who cares anyway," one of the girls finally decided after getting bored with our search, then began walking back towards the path. It was frustrating because I was sure it was there. It seemed odd to smell such a smell way out in the woods. I had no interest in smoking it or picking it or anything like that. I didn't have any idea that in the outside culture it was illegal or that there was anything about it that would need hiding.

Later on that year, something happened that made me wonder. I was playing with Courage's little girl, Peace. She was a year or two younger than I was, and had long, light brown hair and bright blue eyes. I often stayed in Courage's household when I went to town. He lived with his household for a time in a house across the street from Love's Area. Courage, Peace's dad ran his household, but he was also the captain of the Family's ship called the Abundance.

"Can you keep a secret?" Peace asked me.

"Sure," I answered her.

She took me up in the attic and there was this room that was like a little forest, tons of potted mashish plants in rows filling the entire attic. There were special, very bright lights in the room to make sure the plants were getting enough light. When we got in the room, her manner changed, and she began to look scared. "Let's leave," she said. "I could get in big trouble for being in here." We headed out of the attic.

I didn't understand why she would get in trouble just for seeing the plants. The sharing of sacrament/mashish was a normal aspect of our culture. It bothered me, that anyone would think it was something that had to be hidden, and I wondered what it meant.

As a child, I did not know that the Love Family grew fields of mashish in Eastern Washington where the plants would be hidden in the cornfields. I found out years later, that it would look like a cornfield, but each mashish plant was snuggled up close to a corn plant so as not to be noticed by people who might pass by or by airplanes or helicopters flying over.

On the other side of the Ranch, way back in the woods, I knew there were plants on the way to Jordan Store. Since we had to hike across the neighbor's property to get to the road that led to the Store, it wasn't uncommon to smell plants as we crossed his property. Unfortunately for the neighbor, as I was told later, the plants were being put on his property, not our own, because if there was a raid, then the Love Family would not get in trouble for having the plants.

Mashish had to be hidden from people in the World, I figured, because they were lost and living lives that weren't real. We, in the Love Family, were the righteous ones.

We were Jesus Christ. It didn't matter what people in the World thought.

Since I was living in a whole community of hundreds of people who were culturally of one mind regarding mashish, I didn't think much about it. I much preferred to go with my friends on a sleep out. We would just bring our sleeping bags, find a place in the woods and spend the night under the trees. We did not go 'camping,' though, instead we called it, 'a sleep-out.' It didn't seem right to call it camping, since living in tents was a permanent life style back at home.

One day, I and several other girls my age decided to be gone for two nights instead of one night. We didn't plan it well though and ended up realizing that we didn't have enough food. Luckily, one of us brought this large, half-gallon can of peanut butter. I'm not sure where she got it, but that's all we had to eat for two days. Unfortunately, there was no can opener, so we were unable to get into it. Since we were all very hungry, we all worked on the can with sharp rocks. We did manage to puncture a hole in the top with a small rock, but the time it took to get any out of the small sharp hole made it impossible to satisfy anyone's hunger. It was a fun trip though, but due to our hunger, we couldn't stay the second night as we had planned. We ended up calling it a "fast," just to make it sound Love Family sophisticated. In my journal, I had written dramatically that "We almost starved to death!"

Here are some diary entries from the time period when I lived on the Ranch. None of the entries had dates, of course, but from the sounds of the entries, they were probably between 1979 and 1982, so I was most likely between 11 and 13.

Dear Diary,

I went on a hike with Heaven, Shushan, Shisha, and [Gentle]. Vision was our guardian. We went to the Lookout to spend the night. It was already dark when we started out. Eliab knew we were going and left ahead of us, so he could jump out and scare us on our way. That's when I lost my flipflop on the path and had to wear only one for the rest of the trip. Eliab scared us so bad that we all screamed. Sacred jumped 2 feet in the air.

Rachel Israel

Dear Diary,

It is the Year of Prosperity [1979/1980]. All the big girls had a slumber party at Serious's old tent while the big people had a party at the Barn. We had a trading party and told scary stories…

Rachel Israel

Dear Diary,

I invited Esther, [Gentle], Heart, and Keli for a sleep out in the woods near Nobility's household site. [Gentle] and Keli got attacked by mosquitoes and went into the tent. Heber came out and woke us up, warned us a storm was coming. It started pouring. We dragged our wet sleeping bags into the tent just as the thunder and lightning struck. Heart didn't wake up and got left in the storm, so I went back out and carried her in.

Rachel Israel

One of the most memorable camp outs was one that we had just after we all moved into the yurts, probably 1981 due to my memories of which kids were there. It took place in the three-sided cabin, which was on the backside of the lake. Through the woods, past the last household campsite, there was this dilapidated 3-sided cabin. There were younger kids there as well such as

Quan, Zarah, Genuine, Zack, my brother Forest, and at least a couple others, It was enough of us that the three-sided cabin was full of kids. Ethan was our guardian. We had just set up our sleeping bags, when we heard the rustling in the bushes. Since I was one of the older ones there, I was inclined to check it out as a protective measure.

I took the lantern and was stepping through the bushes, looking around. Just to make sure I was on good terms with whatever it was making the noise, I said, "Hello, we're friendly." Suddenly this huge thing jumps out at me. It had white fur and was unrecognizable—I was too scared to do anything but scream. Everyone jumped up, and I heard several screams as we all backed up into a corner of the cabin. Even Ethan was backed up into the corner as well. Two figures came bounding out of the woods, like gorillas. One of them was donned in a brown sheepskin and mud on its face and the other one in a white sheep skin and a papier Mache witches mask. I recognized the witches mask and knew it was Understanding. Someone must have told her we were going to be out there that night. She was a major jokester and loved playing practical jokes on the kids.

Ethan pretended to regain his composure:

"It is Understanding, and I am not sure who the other one—is that [Nobility]?! Ethan asked.

I look over and Understanding had pulled herself out from underneath this sheep skin, and both she and Nobility were laughing so hard that they were doubled over. It took a while for us all to calm down. That was one sleep-out I will never forget.

The Ranch was acres and acres of free space, living close to nature with a gigantic family in tents. In fact, to me, living in a yurt or an Army tent seemed more normal than living in a house. Even before I came to the Love Family, I had lived in a car and then the House of Doors, both at Makena beach. I had lived in a pup-tent when Karen and I had hitchhiked up and down the Al-Can. Then I had lived in pioneer-style log cabins and a tepee in Alaska. Ranch living, Love Family style in Army tents and yurts, was gonna be nothing to me.

In the Love Family, starting in 1979, I lived in a yurt for three years. I was between 11 and 14, which for a kid is a long time, considering the length of a typical childhood. I wasn't a little kid anymore, so it would've been my middle school years or junior high.

When the elders first started moving out of the circle of mostly Army tents into their own yurt sites, it happened slowly over time. The elders didn't all get their yurts at the same time. It was a gradual migration. By the way, Love's household never moved into a yurt site around the lake; he moved into yurts, but he stayed with his household in the main field where the circle of tents had been. The rest of the households were in the wooded portions around the lake, whereas Love was situated in the open field, right next to the lake. His tent scene was at the head, so to speak. It was more centrally located. Maybe he thought it would be more appropriate in terms of his leadership role. From this spot, he would've had more visibility in terms of seeing people coming and going to and from their households to and from the lake and barn areas. It also would've been more convenient for him to come and go from the Ranch since the site was closer to the Barn and the road that led out of there.

Once the elders moved to the yurt sites, Love gradually began to spend more time in the city in his big house on Queen Anne. Even though he was gone, many members of his household continued to live at his yurt site all year round. I didn't keep track of when he was there and when he wasn't, but it seemed he came out periodically for stretches of time. He was usually there though during the summers and for events such as Passover or other traditional gatherings.

Living in the yurts wasn't any better than the Army tents in my experience, but there were a few differences: For one, there was a little more space in the yurt sites for the number of people per household. Also, because the yurts were placed on platforms many of which were high off the ground, there was an additional living space developed underneath many of them. Yurt sites often had more than one yurt and other smaller tents too. Some elders kept their Army tent and brought it to the new site to use for extra living space. The yurt sites were also more private from the other households. Before, when all the households lived in a circle in a field, it was a lot more communal in some ways. Everyone had shared the laundry scene, sauna and out-houses. In the circle of tents, we all shared a common front yard too. The kids would all play together more often as all our houses (tents) were so close together, but after we moved into the yurt sites, it was quite a hike and more trouble to get to the other households. Now it seemed more convenient for kids in the same household, who were of various ages, to play together.

By the time I was living in the yurts, I was getting more mature and expected to share more responsibility. The ladies taught me how to darn my own socks and how to sew. I could fix a hem or mend a tare quite well, if needed. Most of the clothes that we wore in the Love Family were handmade. None of the women had sewing machines, so everything had to be sewn by hand. Living without modern conveniences was good for me though; it taught me how to be resourceful.

I learned what it was like living in a tent in the middle of winter. I slept in a sleeping bag just like most people did. On cold mornings, I learned how to get fully dressed in the bottom of my sleeping bag. That way I could stay cozy warm, until I absolutely had to get out of bed. I slept with my clothes in my sleeping bag. That way, the next morning, they'd be warm when I put them on. The mornings were always the worst as I waited for the fire to be built, and then for the stove to heat up the space. One of the household men was responsible for this chore, so they would do it every morning before everyone was getting up. There was not a lot of space inside my sleeping bag to get dressed when I was half asleep, but anything is possible when it is freezing, and I can see my breath billowing out every time I breath.

After getting dressed, I would roll up my sleeping bag and put it away. During the day, my sleeping bag and a handmade duffle bag that kept my clothes, that was called a 'bolster' bag, would be made into the arms of a couch-like scene on my foam pad. I would braid my own hair, which I was taught to do early on. Once I was finished getting dressed, it was time to sit down for breakfast. Before I could eat, there was chanting and then a prayer, which was custom in all households, as I explained early on.

Every morning, I didn't have to ask what was for breakfast. It was usually a bowl of oatmeal. Since I was the oldest, I would help with breakfast dishes before going to school. I wore my rubber boots, because the Ranch was, for most months out of the year, wet and muddy. It seemed that many people wore the same boots, black with orange trim, but I saw that some of the men had big, Army green or brown boots with beige trim.

Each day, I would hike up for classes, which by then were being held in the Barn in the school rooms that were built for the school. Presence taught me to put cayenne in my boots, which would heat up my feet rather well on my walk to school each morning. He said that's what he did when he went mountain climbing.

When I got home from school that afternoon, I was responsible for doing my chores and helping as needed with the younger children. My help was really needed, because now that I was more capable, it made sense to me that everyone had to pull more weight and help out, including the kids. I already mentioned that daily living responsibilities were divided by gender to a great degree, probably because it was more practical on some levels. It simplified things, and it probably fit neatly in with Love's notions of ancient Israeli biblical culture.

There were times when I was responsible for carrying certain items up to a recycling site in the woods on the opposite side of the Ranch from where I lived. I didn't mind going on the journey and would bring another kid along to keep me company. There was a trail that I had to follow to get there as it was hidden in the woods out of site. Once I got there, there were bins that separated different colored glass, scrap metal, wire, or tin cans. Nowadays, recycling is pretty common, but back when we were doing it at the Ranch, it wasn't; The Love Family had it together, in a certain environmental sense. I usually did not have to bring paper, which would be reused in various ways or just burned in the household stoves. I don't remember ever having to bring plastic as that wasn't something that we had in the Love Family. While I was there, I taught myself how to scrape the rubber coating off copper wire, which I made into friendship bracelets for my friends. Everyone thought they were really great until they started turning our wrists green.

Thankfully I did not have to carry the household compost up to the Barn where there was a worm pit near the garden. Usually it was a younger guy, one of the men in the household who would carry the 5-gallon buckets up each time they needed to go.

Washing dishes was never my favorite responsibility, but in the Love Family, especially early on, dishes were never put on certain individuals. It was a group responsibility after meals.

There were three stations: the wash, the rinse, and the dry. Anyone would start washing, then someone would do the 'bump.' Whoever was washing would now be rinsing. The person who bumped, would now wash. Someone would play guitar, so everyone could sing along while we washed dishes. People would continue to take their turn by joining the line, doing the bump, so that no one had to do one task for very long, and they would each have the opportunity to work at the different stations. I always thought the Love Family way of doing the dishes was novel, egalitarian and downright fun.

The household next to ours had set up a creative way to wash dishes when it was dark. Since we didn't have electricity, at night, an oil lamp or candles were needed to do dishes. If one can imagine a bunch of people in the dark with candlelight or a lantern, washing dishes, singing songs, but we got used to it and didn't even notice it. At the next household over from us, though, they had set up a bicycle near the dish scene, and someone would peddle really fast, so a light would come on. Everyone thought it was so funny to see someone, usually a kid, peddling away as people washed the dishes. The faster it was peddled, the brighter it got. It was also a sort of science experiment where I learned the basic concept behind a battery-free bicycle light which uses the motion of the bicycle wheel to generate electricity.

Even though, there was no electricity, a yurt is white, and during the day, the space inside was bright from natural daylight, especially because each yurt had a dome skylight, just like the nomadic peoples of Central Asia.

A yurt or (ger) is a high-tech Mongolian tepee. Ger means dwelling. It was known to have been used in the 13th century by your average wandering Mongolian. Jenghis Khan's encampment were ger.

The wall framework is composed of lattice-work, much like an oversized 'babygate' in appearance. Atop this framework rests many roof rafters. These rafters rest on a cable atop the baby-gate and come together at the peak of the roof. At the peak they are inserted into a center crown which eliminates the need for a center pole. The center crown or apex of the roof is covered with a clear plexi-glass dome (skylight). The yurt is then covered by weather resistant, heavy canvas tent fabric. Inside the living space, there are three windows consisting of an innermost screen, a middle removable clear plastic sheet and an outer shield made of the canvas wall material. With a wooden floor, and a wood burning stove, the yurt can be very cozy.

Living in tents was not a private experience, so there were times when I heard a sanctioned couple making love. Most people were celibate anyway, but if a younger couple were sanctioned, I saw them put up a tapestry around their bed scene in the yurt to give them a sense of privacy. Sadly, canvass is not a real soundproof barrier. Since the elder and elder lady had a private yurt or tent, they were the ones who had the most privacy of anyone.

Living in tents at the Ranch was not like traditional style camping where there are marshmallows and a campfire and bike riding the next day, etc. No, living in tents was a permanent way of life and hard work. We were totally dependent on wood for heat and to cook since there was no electricity.

There was electricity at the Barn and at the Ranch house, but it wasn't generally used. There was a wood stove in the Ranch house just like everybody else in the tents had, and candles and lanterns were used as well for light.

At some point, the Ranch house burned down though. There was a nice older couple who were visiting at the time who barely escaped with their lives. They were parents of members of the Family. The fire got started because of a candle. The older woman who was visiting was overweight and had a hard time escaping out the small window of the bedroom where she was staying. She got third degree burns and ended up spending weeks in the hospital.

Despite the risks, a wood burning stove was essential to our way of life. Candles and lanterns were our only source of light.

In our yurt, there was a wood burning cook stove with an oven in the kitchen underneath the yurt. It was an old fashioned, antique stove that had to be kept stoked to cook anything.

Whenever I smell olive oil now, it takes me back instantly to the flavors that were so much part of my life then. Maybe Love might've had butter, but other than occasionally, we didn't use butter or other oils, we used mostly just olive oil. I remember the smells that wafted up the wood step ladder into the yurt in the evenings when the household women prepared the meal down below. Olive oil was used to fry bread in the pan, it was used for popping corn for snacks, it was used on any salad that was prepared, and it was used like butter on oatmeal or rice. It was also used to grease the pan for baked bread. It was used to fry leftover oatmeal or rice.

Cooking with wood stoves and using wood for heat came with its own obvious risks. When people were burned, it became legendary in that the story would be told repeatedly to remind people of the dangers. There were times when I got small burns, but some of the kids got more serious burns, like Benjamin when he burned his butt. One day, Benjamin, who was six or seven years old, came in naked after his jump in the lake and walked right up to the stove and backed up to it and stuck his butt right on it. He started screaming. He couldn't sit down for weeks and had to lay on his stomach all the time.

Another time, Heaven was reading with a candle when her sleeping bag caught on fire; she burned her chest, arms and back. Especially in the winter, life centered around the stove. People gathered like magnets around the fire-breathing monster, whose continuous bellow was a constant reminder of its ability to maim. A butt burn was more common as someone tried to get closer to the stove to warm themselves on their backside where the stove is out of sight. Since it was often so cold in the winter, I had to keep turning myself like a marshmallow to warm all sides of me.

The wood burning stove was central to our life and served many purposes in addition to keeping us warm. Wet clothing would hang to dry near it. Musty smelling wool socks and blankets hung strategically to dry around them.

Pots of water would heat for sponge baths, dishwashing or tea. Pots of rice, beans, or oatmeal would cook for meals, and it needed constant maintenance. Somebody had to light it in the morning. Then somebody had to stoke and stir it throughout the day. It was allowed to go out at night, so that's why it was always freezing in the morning. Somebody, mostly the men had to keep wood chopped and stacked nearby, then carry it in to stoke the stove throughout the day. Even some of the houses in town used wood heat.

There was a period during my last couple of years in the Family when I lived in the same household as my mother. I would watch her making bread. She would place the unbaked dough near the wood stove to rise. It made me miss our life in Alaska when we lived in the tepee and she would bake bread or custard pie, using our wood cook stove that had an oven.

At the Ranch, not all of the households had an antique, wood burning stove with an oven, like we did. I knew of one household that just used a camping style cook stove that used propane or white gas.

In terms of water; when we lived in the circle of tents, water had to be hauled in five-gallon buckets from a tap up near the knoll to each of the campsites. It was a daily chore as it was essential to have water for drinking, cooking, bathing and laundry. Once the households began spreading out around the lake, I saw what they called a 'ditch witch' tractor come and dig trenches for water pipes that stretched to our household site. It took time for all the households to get a tap. It happened gradually, over time, so we still had to hall water from a tap until it got there. There was never any running hot water though. That had to be heated on the stove for bathing, dishes, cooking, etc.

There were no toilets. There were only outhouses. When we all lived in the circle of tents, there were shared outhouses by the knoll. Since they were so close to the lake though, the water table was too high to dig permanent pits for them. Instead, there were metal half-barrels that had to be emptied periodically. They were not commercial, plastic Honey Buckets, they were constructed of hand-milled lumber. There was a small mill on the property that was used for such purposes. The barrels would have to be periodically emptied to an area far away from the lake.

After we all moved into the yurts around the lake, each campsite had its own outhouses. They did not have to be emptied, they were more permanent with a huge pit underneath them, so that when it was full it could be moved. The holes would be so deep though that I don't remember our outhouse ever having to be moved, because it never filled all the way up, at least during the years I lived there. In fact, they were so deep that once, one of the young children in our household accidentally dropped a kitten down there, and it was unable to be retrieved, which devastated our household for weeks.

One of the outhouses was a three-sided structure that sat in the woods but that faced the trail, so I could peer through the trees and see who was coming and going from the household as I sat there.

Outhouses were not these shit-dump-sites in the Love Family as they often were at a typical rainbow gathering; they were clean, holy and orderly, with a Bible for reading next to the hole.

For bathing, there was always an outdoor shower, which was usually a bucket with holes in the bottom of it that was hung by a rope from a tree.

In one household, it was hung from the rafters of the sauna structure. Water was heated on the wood stove before being dumped into the bucket. During times when the sauna was not heated, we kept clean by taking a sponge bath in the yurts. It seemed there was always a pot of water on the stove for such purposes. Other times, I would just go jump in the lake which we did often anyway when it was warm enough outside for a swim.

Sometimes, I would hike up to the Barn where there was a communal shower. I say communal, because there were two shower heads there, so that if there were others needing a shower at the same time, then people would just line up and take turns.

Dear Diary,

This evening during setup for dinner, there was a storm. The yurt started falling off the platform. It is 12 feet off the ground, so we ran down the stairs and out. We have to take everything out, so we can move the yurt back. Zarah and I set up a little pup tent temporarily for tonight. The other kids will stay in either Heritage's tent or will sleep in the men's yurt.

Rachel Israel

Dear Diary,

There was a mashish plant sitting in the yurt this afternoon in a five-gallon bucket. The plant is taller than me. Heritage gave me a lesson and explained all about male and female plants and how they germinate each other, so interesting!

Rachel Israel

As I mentioned earlier, in general, responsibilities and chores were divided by gender. The men would be in charge of chopping wood, hauling water and keeping the fire going as well as other more industrial and construction tasks. Pretty much everyone would help with the dishes and laundry, and the adult women oversaw cooking, meal preparation, childcare, and cleaning. Children, such as myself were given chores too, especially as we matured and had demonstrated responsibility.

One summer, it was my chore to milk the goat each day. I had to have been around 12. The goat was stubborn and fought me the entire time. The biggest challenge was tying the goat up. She fought me tooth and hoof. I would bring a Mason jar with me to squirt the milk in. Milking the goat was very important because that was the year, I was living with Helpful and Dedication who had their baby, Glad, who needed milk.

I had to learn how to milk the goat on my own. The first couple of times, I had to wrestle with her, and she won and got away. Then I learned how to get her tied up to the fence in just such a way that she would not be able to struggle so much. She was still combative though, and I had to listen to her constant bleating scream. Eventually, she grudgingly let me do it. If I had had a little bit of grain, it might have helped motivate her, but we did not have grain, we just let them graze.

Milking the goat was just the beginning. I increasingly had more chores as time went on, an I began to be old enough to take on more responsibilities.

One chore that I had was to clean up the candleholders. We used oil lamps and candles for light, as I said, so it became my chore each afternoon to clean them. Before it got dark, I had to dig out the wax that had built up from the previous night, then put new candles in for the evening. I also would put new oil in the lamps and clean them. Sometimes the lamps would need new wicks. Kerosene is a stinky thing to work with, but it was an important job. The entire household depended on this for light. I liked to drip the wax into a puddle and then let it dry just enough to mold it into little shapes. I enjoyed this chore because it took concentration, and it became like a meditation for me as I worked to prepare the candles to light up our household for the evening.

Occasionally, I would go and collect candles for our household from the candle shop that was in the pottery shed up at the Barn. While I was there, I would chat with the Family potter, Solomon. He created beautiful pottery for our community, and he would give me pottery lessons if he had time. On the shelves, in the studio, were beautifully glazed bowls, bongs, cups, vases and other items he had made.

My other chores were to clean the condiment tray. I would clean and refill the soy sauce and olive oil bottles and clean the tray they were carried upon. Then, if needed, I would bring up chopped wood to place by the stove. Other chores on my list were to clean the pottys of the household babies who were potty training and to clean up the sauna platform where laundry was done.

One day, a cat just showed up. This was not the kitty that was accidentally thrown down the outhouse hole. No one seemed to know where this kitty came from, and we lived way out in the woods, so he would've had to wander quite far to even get onto our property, let alone our household. He was a wonderful kitty who everyone called 'Fluffy.' Sometimes I helped carry the leftover beans, oatmeal or rice outside to feed him. In the Love Family, we didn't generally have pets, but somehow by the grace of God, here was Fluffy, this long-haired, orange, cat who just showed up out of the blue. He had gold eyes, like the color of his fur, and he was very, very fluffy.

Anything that usually came in to the Family had to be turned in to Love, but Love was absent a lot in those days, and I had never even heard about animals being turned in. Nobody seemed to have a problem with Fluffy though, much to the delight of most of us in that household.

In general, pets were out. My guess is that pets didn't work very well because if everyone couldn't share it, then it was a 'separate' thing rather than a 'oneness' thing. A relationship with a pet meant that there would be an attachment, and in the Love Family, everyone was trying to avoid personal attachments and instead work on building communal ties. It would have to be a pet that everyone could share and that was impossible due to the size of the Family.

Despite that, pets sometimes showed up. Imagination had a fish tank in his household in town and later got a dog he named Logo. The dog was a gift that was given in exchange for some work that he did for a local pet shop. I did not see much of Logo. My guess is that Logo went out and stayed at this place we called Ekone, which was a horse ranch in Goldendale, Washington.

I felt that Fluffy was a gift from God. We didn't have cat food, but he seemed to like rice and oatmeal well enough. Everyone in the household claimed him and said he belonged to them. He was like his own man though and didn't seem to care about all the rules.

I loved it that Fluffy didn't seem to care one iota about anyone or anything, just a little rebel himself who had slipped through the cracks somehow of the Love Family's rigid idealism. I made sure he got enough attention, even though he mostly just lived in the woods and was not allowed to hang out in the yurt, although he got away with it anyway. Sometimes he would follow us out when we went to go play in the woods. I really enjoyed having him nearby.

We were all devastated though one day when he didn't come home. I heard that maybe the coyotes got him. It was very sad. I had lost a good friend. I still think about Fluffy every so often, and despite trying, I have never found a cat that looked just like him.

Living at the Ranch was an evolution, from when I was sent there with the pox on a quarantine to living in the Army tents to living in the yurts. Once people moved to the Ranch from the houses on Queen Anne, it was my home for years, and even though there were members who stayed in town to maintain the houses, it was most of the community who lived at the Ranch.

My parents, 1968, before I was born

Me @ the Last Exit in Seattle, WA, 1968

Me in Maui circa 1971

Me, Suzanne's dog, Anchor Point, AK, 1973, Courtesy Marty Cummings

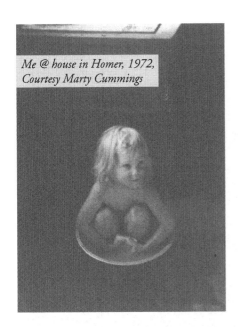

Me @ house in Homer, 1972, Courtesy Marty Cummings

Me, Kindergarten, Homer, AK, 1973, Courtesy Marty Cummings

Marty and Karen @ cabin in Homer, AK, 1973, My metal bathtub hanging on the front of the cabin, Courtesy Marty Cummings

Marty, Mark, Me, Mom, Forest's birth @ Bill's cabin, 1974, Courtesy Marty Cummings

Forest in Cradleboard, 1974, Courtesy Marty Cummings

Me, Forest, Karen, Anchor Point, AK
1974, Courtesy Marty Cummings

Me and Brenda, Anchor Point, AK
1974, Courtesy Marty Cummings

Me, Mom, and Forest, Anchor Point, AK 1974, Courtesy Marty Cummings

Parsons Garden on Flower Day, Queen Anne Hill, Seattle, WA, 1975, Courtesy Marco Ricca

Me and Heaven, Queen Anne Hill, Seattle WA, circa 1978

Love, Activity, Strength, Arlington Ranch, 1979. Courtesy Rich Frishman

Circle of tents, Arlington, WA, L to R: Laughter behind the horse, wearing hat, Meshach, Solidity, Cheerful, Me, Courtesy of Museum of History and Industry, 1977

Circle of tents, Arlington Ranch, 1978, Courtesy Marco Ricca

Lake @ Arlington Ranch,
Courtesy Marco Ricca

Love's Sanctuary, Arlington Ranch,
Courtesy Museum of History and Industry

Me, Arlington Ranch, 1979,
Courtesy Rich Frishman

Me and baby, Arlington Ranch, circa 1979, Courtesy Tobiah

The Barn, Arlington Ranch, Courtesy Museum of History and Industry

Easter. Kids at Arlington Ranch, Courtesy Marco Ricca

The Barn @ Arlington Ranch, Courtesy Marco Ricca

Me, Arlington Ranch, 1981, Courtesy Tom McKnight

Yurt, Arlington Ranch, circa 1983

Arlington Ranch,
Courtesy Marco Ricca

Passover. Men are arranged on the outside circle, women
are arranged on the inner circle, and children are in the
middle, Arlington Ranch, Courtesy of Marco Ricca

Passover. The outer circle are men; the inner circle are women; I am in the center with the children, Arlington Ranch, Courtesy Marco Ricca

Notice there's a woman dancing in the middle, Arlington Ranch, 1979, Courtesy Rich Frishman

Dedication and baby Glad, Arlington Ranch, Courtesy Rich Frishman

Dedication and baby Glad, Arlington Ranch, Courtesy Tom McKnight

Ethan and kids, Arlington Ranch, 1979, Courtesy of Rich Frishman

Ethan and kids, me in the skirt, digging, Arlington Ranch, Courtesy Felicity Erdmann

*School in the garden,
Arlington Ranch, Courtesy
Felicity Erdmann,*

*Silome teaching school in yurt,
Arlington Ranch, circa 1980,
Courtesy Felicity Erdmann*

Eve, Definition, and Baby
Deliberate @ Front Door Inn,
Courtesy Eve

Kids at Cherry Hill

L to R, Sun of Righteousness, Cheerful,
Understanding, Ezra, and Ravah, circa 1975,
Courtesy Understanding Israel

Washington Rainbow Gathering, 1981 Courtesy Gray Eagle

Washington Rainbow Gathering, 1981, Courtesy Gray Eagle

Washington Rainbow Gathering, 1981, Kid's Parade, front, lL to R, me in black shorts, [Mary], Shushan, and Heaven, Courtesy Gray Eagle

Washington Rainbow Gathering, 1981, Understanding's puppet theater, Courtesy Gray Eagle

Me and Fluffy in the yurt, Arlington Ranch

Me and Zarah, Arlington Ranch, around 1981, Courtesy Felicity Erdmann

*Me @ Summit
Alternative high school,
Seattle, WA 1983*

*Me and Gramma Phyllis,
Seattle, WA, 1988*

CHAPTER 9

Ritualistic Sacrifice and the Great Egg Hunt

This chapter goes back in time to the spring of 1976. I had been in the Love Family for almost a year when I celebrated my first Passover. This was during the time before people started migrating out to live permanently on the Ranch. Everyone was still mostly living in town. It was basically our first Passover at the Ranch. Since the property had recently been acquired, it was decided that everyone would meet there and celebrate the holiday in the country. Once it was over, people would return to Seattle, back to their "normal" lives.

Before we came to the Love Family, Passover was usually held in Love's Area. I heard that the previous year, there had been a little Passover lamb running around in Love's yard to the delight of all the children. But there had been numerous complaints from the neighbors about the noise from the lamb's bleating and all the commotion. I once saw a newspaper article with a picture of Reuel driving the sheep down Sixth Avenue towards Serious's Area, but I have been unable to locate the article since then.

It wasn't just that the Ranch was a new property, the neighbors' complaints the previous year was a big reason it was decided to go to the Ranch for Passover this year. In the Love Family, Passover was the biggest and most important holiday of the year. We celebrated it like the ancient Israelites, not like modern Jews, and it did not correlate with the modern day Jewish holiday calendar.

Passover, in the Love Family, was a major event that included Easter and what we called, the 'Fish and Honey Feast.' It was a two-week event, including set up and clean up. The holiday was like a two-week (Love) Family vacation. It was one of the only times when I saw people just relaxing and having fun, so for me, it was great because there seemed to be a lot of free time to just run around with other kids and play without supervision.

Each year, when it was Passover time, the membership from all the different outposts, such as Seattle, Alaska, Hawaii and other properties that were in Eastern Washington and elsewhere, all converged on the Ranch for the events.

As people began set up, there was excitement in the air as the tents were set up and arranged in a huge field by the lake, the same field where the permanent circle of tents was set up the following year.

Love parked his busses in the field where he would stay during the events. The tents were not placed haphazardly; they were neatly set up in a circle, along the perimeter of the field, so there would be a huge gathering space in the middle where there was a firepit. I stayed in a dome-shaped tent with Shivaya and Parvati and their parents who came, just for the events. The dome had clear vinyl walls, so I could see right out into the pasture and into the sky from every panel. I watched the people bustling about carrying rugs, tents, and food. Nearby, there were men building outhouses near the knoll. I watched some people putting up a tepee and thought of Marty in Alaska. *Was he still living in the tepee with Yusef?* I wondered.

My attention shifted purposely away from the sadness of that thought as I noticed all the activity in the field. I saw people setting up pup-tents where they had found a space behind the larger Army tents. There was a car and a van that drove down the path from the barn; Each vehicle found an open spot to park to join the encampment.

First there was set up. A temporary kitchen scene was erected. This was before the Barn had a huge kitchen obviously. Big trucks came through and dropped off boxes of fruit and other food items for the occasion. A lamb was taken from the sheep pasture and set up in a special pen next to the Barn. The lamb was to give its life for the feast as part of the Passover ritual. I would visit the lamb daily and pray for him. I felt sorry for him because I knew he would not survive. Every time I walked by the pen, my heart grew heavy.

I had already had a chance to go and visit the sheep pasture with some of the other kids. I had stood by with the girls and we watched as the boys as they tried to ride the sheep; they competed like it was a rodeo, but it was impossible for them to stay on. The sheep did not like them, and the boys slid off their backs soon after they had a good hold. The boys didn't seem to mind the hard landings and would get right back up on the sheep and try again.

The Passover set up continued for a few days. First, all the tents were set up and people made sure the kitchen was functional and ready. The Barn was cleaned and prepared for the parties, meetings, meditations and gatherings that were held during Passover.

Once the main set up was complete, the whole Family would work on a project together. One year, everyone, including the kids, helped clear the backside of the lake to make a bridge across this swampy area. The bridge was named "Bridge over the River Doubt." It was where we all stood for our Family photo that year at Passover.

This year, everyone cleared brush and landscaped the wooded side of the dirt road that went from the Gatehouse up to the Barn area. It was very hard work but somewhat fun, since we were all out there working together as a family. Neriah was still there that year. She hadn't yet left with her parents who ended up getting in the car accident that killed them. While everyone was working, I, Neriah and some other kids snuck off to play in the woods on the wooded slope above where everyone was working. Neriah said she saw a fairy, so we all stopped and tried to see it too. I think I saw it, but it also looked like it may have been a mosquito.

It wasn't just a work trip; At Passover, there was a lot of parties, but they weren't parties for kids; they were the boring kind where the adults would listen to live, Love Family music and dance for hours. I rarely saw the big people drink wine, but at Passover, during the parties up in the Barn, someone was carrying huge trays of glasses of wine, passing them out to whoever wanted one.

I celebrated eight Passovers in the Love Family. Each Passover was similar to the others in all the big important ways, but there were also things that happened on some years and not others.

There was always dancing in the barn though, and the Love Family band would play. I liked to dance with the adults, but when I got bored, I hid out with my friends under the stairway that led to the upper loft, the same loft that eventually became the school rooms. There was a coat closet at the base of the stairs that was a great hiding place. While we were playing in our fort, no one even knew or probably even cared that we were there, looking out at them as they bustled about to and from the dance floor.

I played this game with the other kids that was like hide and go seek, except that it was on the dance floor, so the challenge was to pretend that I was dancing so that the big people didn't realize that we were really chasing each other around.

The skill was to be quick and prepared to change directions at any given moment. I ran through the dancing people with smiles plastered on their faces, completely unaware of our game. If someone noticed me darting around, I would stop, smile and start dancing again until their suspicion had subsided.

If I wasn't careful, I would accidentally bump into someone who was dancing, which could be very serious, depending on who it was and how fast I was going. I was pretty good at it, and I could pretend to boogie pretty well as I looked around, fearfully, hoping not to be noticed by the adult dancers or by the child who was trying to tag me. To blend, I had to coordinate my game moves to the music in a realistic way, otherwise it would be too obvious. It was sometimes like Russian Roulette, because one time I accidentally bumped into one of the big people. I could tell it made her mad, and she stopped dancing for a moment and glared at me.

"What are you doing?" she asked angrily.

I didn't say anything but must've looked scared.

Her glare shifted to a look of warning, then she returned to dancing.

I got out of there—quick.

The music was extremely loud. There were these huge, black speaker boxes, at least one on each side of the stage that were set up for the events. The music was so loud that I would go downstairs to play with the kids just to avoid it. At least I could hear myself talk downstairs.

Even when I was playing downstairs in the Barn, I could still hear the party going on upstairs. It was like listening to a herd of very coordinated elephants marching around to funky Love Family tunes.

During the days leading up to Passover, the big people would have meetings where everyone read the Bible and the story of Passover, which is in Exodus 12. I knew it by heart since we heard it every year, even the kids. The story is about when the Israelites were saved from slavery by the Egyptian Pharaoh. In order to avoid the plagues, the Israelites were instructed to put the blood of the lamb on their doorposts, so that the angel of death would fly over and not kill their firstborn son. Passover was a celebration and a remembrance of the time God saved our people (the Israelites) from slavery under a severe and demanding Egyptian government. It was a reminder of the absolute power of our Father, God, to redeem us from any situation.

In the Love Family, Passover wasn't just about the Old Testament, Exodus story though; it was also combined with a story from the New Testament about the death of Jesus. Jesus gave up his life, and the lamb too was giving up his life for us.

Passover was holy and ceremonial, but it was also a celebration. That's why in the Love Family, Passover ended with Easter, because Easter celebrated the return of Christ from the dead, the Christ that had returned and was alive in all of us. It was a coming together of the Old and New Testaments.

Everyone wore their finest clothes. All the men wore their robes; the women wore their finest dresses and draped shawls around their shoulders, which was our custom. Part of the preparation for Passover included a baptism for new members. I was baptized at this, first Passover. I already discussed earlier what happened during my baptism.

This year, as they did every year, on the night before Passover, the household women went into the kitchens and got rid of all the leavened bread, including all leavening, baking powder and yeast, which would get removed and burned in the wood stoves. From that moment on, no one could eat leavened bread for eight days. That was what the ancient Israelites did too.

Since I was baptized with the other new members, I was now permitted to be a part of the Passover ritual. Only baptized members could see the lamb sacrificed. I would leave very early in the morning with everyone else to go watch. The only people who would not attend the sacrifice were the younger children, the babies and their caretakers, and of course anyone who wasn't baptized. Usually by then though, since there was a baptism just a few days earlier, most of the adults, unless they were on kid watch, were there to see the lamb give his life.

The ritual was held very early in the morning, so a lot of the younger kids just slept through this part of the ceremony. The older kids were usually expected to go unless they were helping with kid watch, but whether an adult or child, only those who saw the lamb give his life, could eat lamb afterwards at the feast.

Very early in the morning before it was even light, I dressed in my best clothes for the occasion with the other adults from our household. Everyone gathered in the pasture to watch. The group was large, 300 or more, as attendance was expected of most of the membership. Courage, the ship captain, knelt with the lamb in front of everyone who formed a half circle around him and the lamb. There was total silence as everyone stood there and waited for the last arrivals.

After the silence, everyone chanted *"Aaaaah,"* for a period of time, longer than normal it seemed. There was total silence again for a few moments before Love started the prayer. After the prayer, Courage held the lamb tightly and took a huge knife and slowly cut the lambs neck, straight across, from left to right, underneath its head. The blood flowed into a bowl that was underneath it. I couldn't stand watching the lamb die. It wasn't quick. The silence continued as people watched. It was very serious and solemn. There was no whispering or side talk involved. If the lamb struggled, Courage would hold it tighter. There was a rumor that one year, an elder had passed out while cutting the lambs throat, so there were a lot of expectations on Courage to do it right. He had to have had a lot of strength to hold that struggling lamb the way he did and at the same time, cut his throat in just a way to make the blood go into the bowl. No one could leave until the lamb was dead which drew the whole thing out for a long time. He didn't cut the lambs head off, he just cut its throat, so that was why the lamb didn't die right away. The spot where Courage sacrificed the lamb, I would play there often. The grass was dryer and brown there during the summer because it got less rain than the rest of the pasture due to its slight elevation. That was where I used to pick sheep's sorrel. There was a whole patch of it there, that I would go and collect for salads. I loved to munch on its tart leaves and bring it back for the ladies, so they could put it on the dinner salad.

After the lamb was sacrificed there, though, I never played there again. My heart cried for the poor lamb during the whole ritual. Everyone was required to watch though, that was part of the ceremony, so I felt trapped and afraid that someone would see if I looked away.

After the lamb had passed, each household elder would get a portion of the blood to smear on the doorposts as required. That night, the angel of death was to fly over each household. If there was the blood of the lamb on their doorpost, then the angel would fly over without killing the first born. That night in my bed, I imagined a big, black, fierce looking angel flying over our tent during the night.

I was old enough to know that this ritual was a reenactment of events that had taken place in Biblical times. However, I was young, and I had a very active imagination. Plus, growing up in the Love Family as a child, I just accepted that things were the way they were, without questioning whether it was or wasn't. Things that seemed very real there made me wonder, years later, how it could have happened at all. The nature of reality really depends on who you're with and what you mutually believe, that's what I learned.

After the lamb was sacrificed and sometime before the feast, all of the adults would do sacrament, (LSD) so they could, as one former member told me, "get high, meditate, and gain a higher consciousness." Pretty much everyone did it; there were hundreds of people high all at once. Children, like myself, did not generally do sacrament, so instead, we got to go hiking with our guardians, so I never knew what happened when they all got high. My first Passover was years before the King Lake trip where I did sacrament.

The adults who did not want to do sacrament would volunteer to do kid watch or take the kids off the Ranch. One year, Hope volunteered to go on a hike with us in the woods around the property. He pretended to be a zombie and chased us down the hiking trail the whole way. He hung his mouth open and stared at us like he was dead, holding his arms out in front of him as if to clasp them around our little necks. He was very frightening as he yelled out with a drunken slur, over and over, "Get the little people!!!"

The other thing that happened after the lamb was sacrificed was Love would name the previous year. A Love Family year did not start in January. It started in the spring, at Passover. It went from Passover to Passover. Love would announce it when people were feasting and walking around in white. He did not talk about his reasons or thinking on the matter, but they tended to be spiritually significant in terms of events or issues in the previous year leading up to the Passover at hand.

For example, we joined the Family in the Year of Consideration, just after Passover when Love had named the year after Consideration, who had, just a few months before we joined, been kidnapped out of the Family. People had been angry and grieving after he was taken. There was a major effort to have him returned, although unsuccessful. Love named the year after the man, to honor him. It was more of an unspoken acknowledgment, because once Consideration was gone, no one talked about it.

This year, 1976, Love named it the Year of Encouragement. Understanding recalled that, that year, Probity had had a dream about how 'Satan had been bragging that his biggest tool was a wedge called discouragement.' Another thing that may have influenced Love's decision, Understanding speculated, was political strife. In the previous year, there had been divided loyalties amongst the membership that involved two elders.

"Love had recognized Encouragement's authority over Loyalty's," she says, "Loyalty had just been this little upstart who people were listening to over Encouragement. None of that was openly discussed though."

That late afternoon, the feast was amazing. A lot of the food came from Eastern Washington such as Buckets of peach and tomato sauce, wine, and fruit leather, as well as other foods that had been put away from the harvests of the previous summer and fall. Lamb was roasted on the firepit just like it said to do in the Bible.

While the feast ensued, I ran around unsupervised with the other children. It was nice to see the adults eat, relax, and hang out. It seemed everyone took everything so seriously all the time. It was rare to see people just sitting around, laughing and having fun.

Sometime after Passover, in the week before Easter, the kids got wagon rides. We got rides every year; it was just part of the celebration and tradition. The Belgians were brought out to pull the wagon, gigantic, golden Clydesdale horses named Bud and Blondie, that would pull us around to keep us occupied.

I had missed Easter the previous year because my mom, my brother and I had come after it had already happened. I heard it had been in Love's Area and the egg hunt had been in the Kids' House. Understanding told me that the Kids' House stunk like rotten egg for weeks after that because nobody could find one of the remaining eggs from the hunt. It ended up finally being found under the carpet in a place where the boards were loose, and the egg had fallen under the boards.

I was actually very glad when Passover was over. After I saw the lamb give his life, I decided to try and avoid the ceremony in the future. There were years when I got out of it by volunteering to help with kid watch. If I didn't get to eat lamb at the feast, so be it. It made me sick to think how he had lost his life. To me, Passover was just a kill-the-animal and watch-it-suffer thing. I looked forward to Easter though.

Easter came on the heals' of Passover because once the lamb of God had given his life, it was now time to celebrate his resurrection through all of us. Love told everyone that we were the 'children of Israel,' and that we all lived in the 'Kingdom of God.' Every year, I and the other community children were gathered together to hear the story of Passover and then the story of Christ's resurrection. The stories were from the Children's Bible or as told by Understanding, who always added an element of live theater to it, just to make it more entertaining for children.

When we lived at the Ranch, the egg hunt was always held on the knoll. The lineups were next to the barn. There was no Easter bunny and no plastic, candy filled eggs. They were always real chicken eggs. A crew would go and buy them from a local farm, then Family artists would meet to paint eggs. Imagination would organize a point-system where each egg would be assigned a certain number of points. A lot of the eggs were just one point, but then a certain number of them were worth more; it was those higher point eggs that would be intricately painted with delicate scenes. They might have symbols from the Family's lexicon painted in gold lettering on them with a little number to indicate how many points it was. One year I found an egg worth 10 points. It had a little scene with little long-haired people dancing around in a circle. They wore little Love Family outfits.

This was early on and we still had geese, so this year, the golden egg was a goose egg painted gold, but at some point, there were no more geese, and the Golden Egg, in subsequent years, was just a large rock painted gold.

Once the artists were done, the remaining eggs were left for the kids to paint. The day before Easter, the long tables that were low to the ground, were set up in the Barn for egg painting.

It was the morning of the hunt. I got up early and dressed in my best handmade dress. I slipped into my rubber boots, grabbed a bag, container, or whatever I could find and left with the other children from my household. It was early spring, still wet and cool, as we trudged through the fog up the trail, towards the Barn to the line ups. I held up my dress to avoid the mud. In later years, when everyone moved around the lake, it took longer to get to the Barn. I could make out the figures of small groups of children making their way in the same direction, from various household sites, which added to the excitement.

Once I got up to the Barn, all the kids were lined up by size. Each year, as the membership grew, and more babies were born, the number of kids lining up got bigger, which meant that each year, since I was one of the 'big' kids, I had to wait longer as a new row of younger kids, who would go first, was added.

The lines were made up of rows of kids from biggest to smallest. The smaller a child was, the sooner they would get to race towards the knoll and start looking. The adults stood around and watched as each line of kids left the starting point. I liked to watch the younger kids race. They were all different sizes and abilities, and they often raced with their guardian or a parent. When the next row raced, there were fewer guardians and parents and the kids were closer in abilities. When it was my turn, I raced like mad with the other big kids around my age who were all close in our size and abilities, so it was a fierce race as we all charged ahead aggressively.

The knoll was covered with kids pretty much all morning, and then by the early afternoon, it would still be cool, but often the sun would come out and warm things up. Periodically, I hiked down off the knoll and took my eggs to be counted and deposited so I could go back and start again. The knoll was quite wooded, so I was looking for eggs in old, rotted out moss-covered logs and stumps, bushes, under huge ferns and in the trunks of trees. There were areas too that were rocky and steep.

Some of the big people would dress up like clowns and wander around on the knoll for entertainment. Ethan would dress up like a clown with a giant balloon, asking goofy questions. There were others who also dressed up like clowns, Ezra, Dedication, Laughter, and Understanding among others.

Easter was the only time that I knew where I was allowed to talk on the knoll. Otherwise it was designated as a place of total silence for meditation.

The big people stood around, watching us, amused. Later that morning, if the golden egg still hadn't been found, Love would come and give out a clue. By this time, only the hardiest of us would still be looking. Finding the Golden Egg was a big deal. Whoever found it, got to plan a huge party for the kids that would take place later that summer.

After the golden egg was found, everyone would wander down to the prize tables to have their remaining eggs counted. Whoever had the most points got to pick first from the prize table until the last child picked. If there were still unpicked prizes after everyone picked, then it would start over until every prize had been taken. We would all stand around gawking at the tables, our eyes wandering from item to item until it was our turn, hoping and praying that someone else would not pick the prize that was wanted.

By this time, our carefully chosen outfits, a collage of rich colors and ethnic styles and patterns, were soiled from our rough adventures in the brambles, sticker bushes, tree climbing, and digging of our earlier conquests.

The prize tables were covered mostly with handmade toys, but sometimes there were a few carefully chosen store bought toys in large quantities such as one year there were a bunch of cardboard, put-it-together yourself airplanes. When it was my turn, I picked a handmade wooden music box with a picture of a princess playing a harp on it. I loved it so much, that I kept it in my sleeping bag with me each night that year.

We ate hard boiled eggs for weeks after that. It was pretty much the only time there were plenty of eggs. For a month or two, there were still unfound eggs on the knoll that would start to stink. When I was up there, I got this strong whiff of rotten egg that came floating through the breeze. It was just a potent reminder of all the fun we had had on the knoll recently.

Disappointingly, I never found the Golden Egg, but it didn't matter too much because all the kids got to go to the Golden Egg Party anyway later that summer.

That late afternoon/early evening, after the egg hunt, was the Fish and Honey Feast. This was the day that ended the eight days of eating only unleavened bread. The Fish and Honey Feast was a celebration of the Resurrection;

it was considered part of Easter. It was based on the Bible story of what happened just after Jesus was resurrected.

Jesus's disciples were down at the beach, and they saw Jesus for the first time since he had been crucified and entombed. The disciples thought they had seen a ghost, until Jesus proved to them that he was made of flesh and blood by eating fish and honeycomb with them. (*KJV* Luke Chapter 24; 36-43) This story was read out loud from the Bible before anyone could start eating.

That year, all the households gathered in the pasture for the feast. It was like a gigantic, corporate picnic. Each household sat together like a family on their individual blankets in the grass. The fish for the meal would come from Love Family fishing expeditions with the Abundance or sometimes someone would just go buy it.

I did not like fish. The Love Family diet was vegetarian throughout the year, so eating lamb at Passover and then a week later eating fish was a bit much for my pallet. It was just this Biblical thing, but I did enjoy eating the unleavened bread and rolls with honey-butter spread.

After the two weeks of celebrating, everyone helped with cleanup and the tents were taken down. Then most people went back to live in the City or the other outposts, because, remember, as I explained in the last chapter, the first Passover at the Ranch was before everyone moved out there to live permanently. In subsequent years, after the Fish and Honey Feast, instead of taking the tents down, most people would stay at the Ranch, but would go back to "normal" routines.

Later that summer, it was time for the Golden Egg Party. The child who found the Golden Egg at the egg hunt would be considered the king or queen and would help plan the Party for all the Love Family children. There were a lot of adults and caretakers who helped out in one way or another, because it was such a large party, and there were so many kids.

Even though we did not celebrate ages, and we were considered eternal, Love thought of the Golden Egg Party as a shared yearly birthday party for all the kids, although the birthday aspect of it was not emphasized.

The Golden Egg Party was held in different places, depending on where the child wanted the Party. Since it had been at least a couple months since Passover, kids from the houses on Queen Anne Hill and other outposts, would all converge on the Ranch—or wherever it was being held—to celebrate. Often after Passover, I was sent to Eastern Washington with other children to help harvest in the orchards, so when it was time for the Golden Egg Party, we were sent from the orchards directly to wherever the Party was being held.

One year, the Golden Egg Party was in Eastern Washington at the cannery. The Cannery wasn't just a cannery; there was also a large house with a well-landscaped yard, as well as a huge field and a creek on the back of the property. The huge field in the back was where busloads of members would, at certain times of the year, set up large tents. There wasn't enough room in the house for all the people who would pass through from time to time on our way to the orchards to harvest.

The field was empty for the Party, so that is where an obstacle course was set up. I think it was Cheerful's Golden Egg Party that year, and Appreciation had a huge hand in organizing and coordinating the event. I had to float down a small creek on an inner tube and jump over a pit of fire, then climb a horizontal rope ladder across the creek. Each feat that I was able to maneuver, I earned this fake money, that I later spent at a prize table. Unfortunately, I had difficulty with the obstacle course, so I didn't earn much money for the prize tables. I enjoyed the feast afterward, though, that was set up at tables in the Cannery building. We ate baklava and other treats, then afterward went in the hot tub. It was not actually a hot tub, it was a large, round vat that was used to cook the fruit before it went into the cans. The water was so hot, that it took a long time before I could put my big toe in it.

It seemed like there was an obstacle course every year for the Golden Egg Party, even though it was a different kid each year that found the Golden Egg and planned the Party. It was so fun each year that no one wanted to plan anything else.

The previous year, the obstacle course was just in the field next to the lake where all the tents used to be when we lived in the circle of tents. There were different stations in the field, and each station had a challenge involved. I used darts to hit balloons that were pinned up in the shape of a star of David inside of a circle. Nobility manned a station where children would compete against one another using a bowsaw to saw a slice off a log the fastest. Ethan manned what he called, the 'Riddle Booth,' where he told riddles to any kid who showed an interest in hearing them. He had so many stored up in his head that it seemed he never ran out. On another side of the field, there was a horizontal ladder that crossed a stream/mud pit that I had to try and climb across. I ended up being covered in dark, silty mud from my knees down after that one because I didn't get far on the ladder before I had to drop down.

One of the last years I was there, there was a huge treasure hunt at the Ranch. I ran around the lake with the other kids. We went past the different household sites through the woods, looking for clues. Imagination dressed like an ogre and was in the row boat on the lake to scare us away from our task. I and the kids on the hunt stuck together closely and refused to let the ogre stop us.

Each clue pointed to another place somewhere on the Ranch, which meant we had acres and acres to search. One clue ended up being all the way up at the rock gardens on the way to King Lake. Eventually the clues led back to the treasure being discovered on what everyone called "Love's Island." It wasn't actually an island, so I don't know why they called it that. It was just this area on the farthest, back side of the lake that one Passover, everyone had cleared to build a household site for Love; but it never happened, because Love kept his household site in the open field where the circle of tents had been, as I discussed earlier. The lake was shaped like a butterfly, so Love's household was located between the wings, where the lower body of the butterfly would've been. Anyway, Love's Island was where the treasure was buried, underground; We had to dig for it right in that cleared area. It was an all-day deal, running like a pack of wolves around the Ranch and through the woods until we found the treasure. Then the Party was over after we all divvied it up.

Before the Golden Egg Party commenced, it was traditional for there to be a kids' parade. Family musicians would paint their faces and dress up in silly clothes and play instruments as they marched with the kids in the parade. Even Love would march too and wear a silly hat and face paint. There were a lot of clowns. It was just an excuse for everyone to act silly and have a good time. For me, as a child, it was good for me to see people having fun and just letting loose, being that so much of our life was the exact opposite.

After the festivities, everyone shared cake in the Barn, which the 'big people' liked to say was our shared birthday party, but was anything but, since birthday had nothing to do with it. There was a huge cake—and I mean huge—it had to be, since there were so many kids. Can anyone imagine what it must have been like to make a cake for 150 or more children?

One year the cake was so big that it barely fit on the table that it sat on. It was probably at least five feet in one direction. It was a Mt Rainier cake. It had little people on it too. The people looked like they were from the Love Family, because all the figurines of men had long hair and beards, some wore robes and stood with a staff as they would if they were there during biblical times.

One other event, that was part of the Golden Egg Party, which I didn't mention was the piñata. It was a humongous piñata, and they hung it in the Barn by the top of the rafters in the main sanctuary. All the kids gathered around and took turns trying to hit it. One year, someone made it out of chicken wire fencing. The outer portion was papier Mache, but it ended up being a huge problem, because then nobody could break it open for a long time. Eventually, someone had to help it out a little with metal wire cutters. Inside, it wasn't just stuffed with candy, although there was some. It was mostly popcorn balls and other healthful treats, typical of the hippie idealism of the times for raising kids. One year, I ran into the center of the floor and loaded up my skirt with goods. When I came back with my full skirt, there was a toothbrush in there too.

As far as I was concerned, each year, Easter and the Golden Egg Party were, by far, the most fun times I ever had in the Love Family, and even though I didn't appreciate the killing of the lamb at Passover time, there was a lot of free time to just have fun, which helped to balance things out with all the seriousness of everyday life.

BIBLIOGRAPHY (CHAPTER 9)

The Holy Bible (*KJV*, Exodus, Chapter 12; Luke Chapter 24; 36–43)

CHAPTER 10

Hippie Cult School

nce the Golden Egg Party was over, it wouldn't be long before it was Fall and time to go back to school.

I tried to get the most out of school, even though, underneath it, I was sad not to be close to my biological family, and I always missed Marty. The Family had subsumed my mother, Elkanah and my brother Forest too. Subsume, according to Merriam-Webster means, "include or absorb (something) into something else; to include or place within something larger or more comprehensive: to encompass as a subordinate or component element." We were subsumed. It was as if we all got swallowed by this big whale called the Love Family, and my mom was in a different place somewhere in the belly. I knew she was there, living and breathing as part of this being, this fish, but our functions and role within the whale's organs were different. That was how it felt—Like a big fish had swallowed my family.

Elkanah was not assigned to help out in the Family school, so I did not see her there much at all, although there was a period of time when she was helping out with Forest's class. I never saw Forest when I was at school, since he was quite a bit younger. Most of the time, I never even knew where he was or where he was living.

Despite the loss of my mom and my brother, I looked forward to the Family school. When I got involved, I wasn't just like a little duck, following the leader around from place to place. I felt like I had a place where children were the focus. I also felt that way with Understanding when I lived at the Kids' House, but as I got older, I was less involved with her and more involved with school.

My relationships to the other kids and especially to the teachers ended up being my salvation in a way, because school was all about us, the kids. It wasn't about 'We are one.' It wasn't about Love and the strict, dogmatic, spiritual whatever you want to call it. It was a way for me to do what normal kids do—learn, and get my social needs met.

The Love Family school was nothing like the school I had gone to in Alaska, which had been more the standard, conventional, public American elementary school, albeit out in the sticks. The Love Family school, in contrast, was more like a small, private, religious school run within the setting of a hippie commune/cult.

My mom told me that one of the reasons she was drawn to the Family, was because it had a school, but when we got there, there weren't even any books. The children were learning to read simple, three and four-letter words that were written on slate or paper. Love's vision for the school was that we learn through 'living the life.' Eve told me that Love told them over and over, that all we needed was "pencils and reality."

In Alaska, I had been reading chapter books, like Stewart Little and others, but when I got there, in 1975, many of the children were not yet reading. Plus, there weren't that many children early on, maybe only six or eight who were around my age.

Because the group was small, it didn't seem to matter that each of the children were at different places in their knowledge and abilities. We were all considered eternal anyway, so no one was keeping track of how old anybody was.

Once I started going to school, most of how I spent my time there was meditating and learning Bible stories, singing Love Family songs, and going to the park. Pictures of animals that had been cut from National Geographic were shown. They had been pasted on construction paper and used as flash cards. A lot of the animals on the cards were animals I had seen in Alaska near our cabin, moose, bear, and other wild creatures that were common and apart of the environment where we had lived.

At that time, it wasn't legal to home school, so the Love Family took steps to make the school official. It was considered an independent, certified school. All the teachers were college educated, but Eve was the only certified teacher. As the school evolved, there were parent helpers who got involved and helped make the school functional. Some of the parents helped teach individual children who were falling behind, and others helped out in other ways such as to keep the fire going or to help make snacks or meals. Love would designate individuals to help out as needed. For example, if we needed a bus driver for a field trip or we needed extra guardianship for a hike in the woods or a trip to the park, there were members, sometimes parents themselves, who would be assigned if there were no volunteers.

It was a cooperative effort, even though not everyone got involved. In fact, most people weren't, which was a source of frustration to the teachers because things would have been easier with more volunteers. A lot of the members who got involved in the school only did so for a short period of time. Others just lost interest or just decided they didn't want to anymore. It might have been a threatening idea to be with a group of kids who just weren't going to listen. Many of the parents just didn't have time to get involved because Love would not give them the time to be with their kids.

Being with the kids wasn't everyone's gift. Remember too that helping out with kids usually meant helping out with large numbers of kids, not usually just one or two at a time, although it could mean that. When Atarah joined, she was pregnant with her first son, Elisha. At the time that she came, there were five or six other women who were pregnant.

"You always had babies in herds, she says. "When I was a teenager and would baby-sit kids, I thought I'm never having babies. And then when you have like six or eight babies, and you're on baby watch frequently, especially if your one of the underlings…"

There were only a few who taught for the entire eight-year period that I was there, and for the most part, they loved what they did and were good at it.

Eve, who was a certified teacher, developed and distributed the curriculum to each of the teachers, then coordinated and managed the process as it evolved over time. She and the other teachers worked closely with Love, through Serious, to bring down Love's vision for the school.

Family kids had a multi-layered relationship with the teachers, who were more than teachers, they were also family. In public school, kids spend time with teachers only a certain number of hours a day, then they go home. Love Family teachers were at home, too. I lived in the same households with some of the teachers. I lived with Ethan and Dedication on and off over the years in different households. I also lived with two other main teachers, Eve and Definition, at different times and in different households. Not all the kids lived in the same households as the teachers like I did; for those kids though, the teachers were still considered family and apart of the child's close-knit community.

My classmates at school were essentially the same kids that I lived with and played with each day, so it was like being in class with my siblings in some ways. There was a closeness and a level of comfort there that was unique and relaxed. In the Love Family, every single one of my classmates at school knew exactly where I was from and what I was dealing with because they were dealing with it too.

During my first year in the Love Family (1975), Eve and Dedication were running the school, although, I didn't see Eve much because she was taking classes at the University to renew her teacher's credentials. Serious functioned as second in command to Love and was like the principal as well as a liaison between the teachers and Love. Sometimes Serious or Understanding would sit with us and do Bible study or meditation. Understanding told us the stories from the Bible in an animated, theatrical way, acting out the parts of people in the Bible, giving them dialogue as if each story was a play with scenes. Before she joined the Love Family, when she was an airline stewardess, she had taken acting classes in New York. She also had taken improvisation drama classes, and then taught improvisation comedy to kids. As a result, she had a natural gift with theater production and made good use of it with us.

Outside of Bible and meditation, Understanding did not teach academics in the school. She had a lot of activities, that I discuss later, such as field trips, theater arts and multicultural activities that, at times, took precedence over academics. So, because of that, she was in regular correspondence with Eve and the other teachers to coordinate those activities with our school schedule.

Every day during that first year, I would walk with the other children who were in my class and our guardian from the Kids' House to Serious's Area where the schoolhouse was. It was the middle, yellow house where I initially had lived in Encouragement's household, before they were sent to Hawaii, but now Helpful was the elder there. Yes, even the house that was designated for the school had an elder. He was a very relaxed elder and not rule-bound but more just focused on making sure that the school ran smoothly and that everyone was having fun. I loved to listen to him laugh. He had this wonderful laugh, different than any laugh I had ever heard. It was high pitched, rapid fire, like a hyena. When I heard him laugh, I would always laugh with him, even if I didn't know what he was laughing at; that's how contagious his laugh was. He had an accent and was from Memphis. I knew that before he came to the Family, he had been on a spiritual quest and had traveled all over; He had walked barefoot across India and had been on a 39-day vow of silence. Now he was a Love Family elder, overseeing the school.

Helpful's elder lady was a woman named, Dedication, who was my very first Love Family teacher. She was working under the guidance of Eve. When I say "working," I don't mean paid. Remember, this was a commune and anything anybody did was volunteer.

Dedication was a wonderful teacher. She was firm, but patient and loving. She was classically pretty with long, thick, dark brown hair. There was a mole on her face near her mouth. It was dark and distinct, and her full lips would quiver slightly when she sounded out vowels and consonants. In the beginning, she was very involved with the school. She wasn't dramatic or a super-entertainer like Understanding; she was serene and methodical. I found her to be solid and calming to be around. She dealt with us firmly but never harshly.

I sat with the other children on the floor around this table for meals with Dedication. One day, we were brought bowls of split pea soup. Some of the children made faces at it, and one of the kids said, "Icky!" They were refusing to eat it. It was green and thick and lumpy, but I had learned not to be picky at that point from my earlier life of living on the road with my mom. Dedication didn't say anything; she just looked at each one of us slowly as if thinking what to do. Then she had us all stop and pray before the meal. We all closed our eyes and held hands and chanted. After the chant, she did the prayer.

"Thank you, Abba, for things that look icky, but taste great," she says.

The kids usually used the word "Abba" for God, especially the young children. Dedication's prayer before we ate was like this perfect prayer, because we all got through that meal just fine. Each kid took a bite, then another and then another. I saw some of the children's faces look at their soup in amazement, like they might have been thinking how true it was that this gross looking soup actually tasted great! And it did really taste good.

As we ate, Dedication got this small, half smile on her face as if secretly glad that what she said had worked to get us to eat lunch that day.

Dedication had an interesting story in how she had received her virtue name. It was widely known within the Family that she had escaped from the claws of a 'cult deprogrammer.' This happened two years before my mom, Forest and I had joined, so early 1970s. In fact, that is why her name was Dedication, because her escape from the deprogrammers and return to the Love Family was considered a great symbol of her commitment to Love. She was honored for it and received her name for it—Dedication.

In the anti-cult movement that developed in the 1970s, the Love Family had been compared to the Manson Family and the People's Temple. Dedication's parents had hired Ted Patrick, a former community relations aide to Governor Ronald Reagan of California (*Seattle Times*, Jan 31, 1976 A1). Ted Patrick also was a self-proclaimed "cult deprogrammer," and called himself "Black Lightening." He was one of the Family's most outspoken critics and called the Love Family a "collection of drugged-up, spaced out, wired-up, mental zombies." (Patrick and Dulack, 1976: pg. 152)

When Dedication was kidnapped, there was a film crew that captured the abduction and subsequent "deprogramming." It was used as an example of nationwide attempts by parents to get children out of Jesus communes. It aired on the CBS Evening News with Walter Cronkite for three nights in August of 1973, with Roger Mudd introducing the story, and Stephen Young covering it live.

Mr. and Mrs. Crampton ended up being big names in the anti-cult movement. Mrs. Crampton, Dedication's earth mother, allowed the case to be seen on TV, because she wanted to warn people about the dangers of cults. She saw her daughter as an innocent child who didn't know enough to protect herself.

But Dedication was not a kid. She was nineteen years old, a legal adult in Washington State, and sanctioned to a grown man, Helpful. Once you turn eighteen, you are an adult. Corinth had left the nest.

The *Seattle Times* reported that Kathy Crampton [Dedication] was abducted by four people, including her mother, Henrietta Crampton in an effort to separate her from the commune. Efforts to deprogram her took place in San Diego from where she escaped. A reporter notified the Federal Bureau of Investigation and Seattle Police in advance of the plan, but neither the police nor the FBI did anything about it. The Seattle office of the American Civil Liberties Union complained that failure of the police to act in the case was "tantamount to complicity" (*Seattle Times* Sunday Aug. 26, 1973 A16; *Post Intelligencer*, Aug 15, 1973 A3).

I agree with the District attorney for the trial, who argued that there would be chaos if parents who disagreed about the religious doctrine of their children were allowed to kidnap them (*Seattle Times*, Jan 31, 1976 A1). Dedication was one of the grownups, my teacher, and I was just a kid myself, so to think that there were those who saw her as a kid, didn't make sense to me.

On the Fourth of July, 11 days after Ted Patrick's efforts to deprogram her, Kathy/Corinth escaped and hitchhiked back to Seattle. Love renamed her Dedication. Despite the uproar, Dedication did not press charges. The Love Family did not believe in living in the past. Dedication had said, 'every person is free and should be permitted to select a life style.' (*Seattle Times*, Jan 31st, 1976 A1).

Dedication was assisted by a man named Ethan, who would take us on nature walks and taught us about plants and animals. Ethan nicknamed the schoolhouse, "The Yellow Submarine," after we all watched the reel-to-reel Beatles film. I sang the song repeatedly with the teachers and other children. *"We all live in a yellow submarine…"*

Ethan became one of the main teachers there. Many kids, who attend public schools only have a teacher for one year before they switch when they go into the next grade. The teachers in the Family school, I had most of them every year—and in Ethan's case—eight years in a row! It really gave me a chance to get to know these individuals like people and develop relationships with them.

Ethan was tall and slender and had big bushy blond hair and a goatee. Before Ethan came to the Love Family, he was an anti-war demonstrator and a self-described "classic dropout." He felt "alienated from society."

"Somewhere there is a picture of me leading a thousand protesters past 300 policemen," he says. In college, he had studied ecology and nutrition, then he had lived in a commune in California called 'The Land.' It had 60–80 members who lived on about 800 acres. They lived non-hierarchical, like anarchists, in a squatter's village of yurts, tents, and shacks. Members at the Land did carpentry and organic gardening too. Ethan had a degree in community development, so he had helped members of the Land develop a school. When he came to the Family, he was inspired to help with our school too. He was very passionate about learning and seemed genuinely interested in working with the kids.

Ethan was always trying to find a better way of doing things. When he first started, he would read out loud from the Bible and would meditate with us. He played games like tic-tac-toe and counting and took us on nature walks where we would identify birds. He eventually began teaching math, but in unconventional ways, using tangrams, finger math, soma cubes, and Cuisenaire rods.

"There was kind of a hippy trippyness to the Love Family," says Ethan as he looked back on the years he spent in the Love Family as a teacher. "The lifestyle differences, only having one bag, so to have a school with only a piece of slate was kind of cool."

He read this book called *The Barefoot Doctor's Manual*, which taught him that if he was a doctor and got stranded out on a desert island, that he could still be a doctor, because he could use herbs and plants and different things.

"I started looking at teaching that way," Ethan says. "How could I teach without anything?"

The Love Family school didn't have much, but what we did have were people, who were enthusiastic about teaching. To me, it wasn't as much about what I learned. It was more about the people, the teachers and caretakers who seemed to really care about the kids.

By 1976, which was after I had been in the Family for about a year, Eve's role expanded in the school and she began teaching fulltime. She had finished taking classes at the University and got her fifth-year teacher's certification. In addition to developing curriculum for the teachers, which she had already been doing while taking classes, she also began to teach the school age kids, including myself. Dedication took on a lesser role and was more of an assistant to Eve. She still taught, but she began teaching the younger kids.

I missed Dedication as a teacher, but I still lived with her at times, and of course she was still a member of my family, so she didn't disappear; her role just changed. Eventually, years later, when we all moved out to the ranch, she had this cute little baby named Glad. Everyone was so shocked that he was such a big baby when he was born. I kept hearing people say in amazement that he weighed "ten pounds!" The baby's midwife, who had been from New York, kept telling people the baby was "Yuge!"

When Dedication went into labor at the Ranch, I could hear her yelling from across the lake. This was a couple years or so later after we had all moved out to the Ranch and lived in the yurts. Her yelling echoed across the open pasture where we had all once lived. Hearing her yell so loudly scared me a little. She had been such a beloved teacher to me earlier on. I heard that people all over the Ranch could hear her from quite some distance away, since she labored in a yurt that sat right next to the lake where sounds echoed across the lake and open pastures.

Even though I missed Dedication, Eve was a wonderful teacher to me, and I grew to love her tremendously. I don't know about her background before she joined, except that she had been a teacher and had been very independent and had traveled in Europe and other places.

Eve was very loving and dedicated to the school. She devoted her whole life in the Love Family to it. She taught the basics of reading, writing and the English language, but each year, she would change the curriculum as the kids grew and became ready for different material. As I got older, I loved learning about the history of English words, such as Greek and Latin derivatives. I also loved learning poetry, such as Haiku and others.

For a school assignment, Eve assigned me to read the book, *Blubber*, by Judy Blume. *Blubber* is the story of a girl who was overweight who was bullied by her peers. I thought of Sarai as I read the book, and Eve had been one of the women sent to fat camp, which I talked about in an earlier chapter. She was not fat though, as I said, she was just healthy and not anorexic. When she was sent to fat camp, she was bullied, like the girl in *Blubber*, because she was sent as an adult, by the leader of her community, and her adult communal brothers and sisters all went along with it. After reading *Blubber*, I realized what it might be like to be considered "fat," and it concerned me. Especially living in a community where weight was such a big deal for women.

Eve was a good teacher. I wrote her this poem about popcorn since we ate popcorn every day for a snack.

"Popped popcorn pops probably and probably packs a pot."

It seemed we ate so much popcorn in the Love Family that it should've been considered a major food group. It was so good and was our custom to season it with soy sauce and nutritional yeast.

When I lived with Eve, I tried to be helpful and good, and she seemed to appreciate that. I washed the dishes and helped sweep. I helped with the younger children in the household and always tried to find the best ways to serve her. She had a contest once, and I won a prize.

"Whoever can find me a word that I can't spell wins a prize," she said.

I looked everywhere for that one word. I finally found it. She had taught me that 'i' goes before 'e' except after c, so I knew that the word 'conceived" might trip her up. And it did. I won the prize!

She smiled really big, then looked perturbed and said facetiously, "You know, gosh, I can't believe I missed that one."

"I get a prize, right?" I asked.

"That's right!" Eve answered with an approving smile. I won a Bible, which was a little disappointing at the time, but it was still a fun exercise.

Eve spent a lot of time learning different arts and crafts. She would teach herself, mostly, but sometimes she would take classes. I wanted to learn too and occasionally would go with her to the classes. She was doing basketry, so I learned how to make baskets. She would card wool, spin it on a wheel, and make yarn, so I got to learn how to make yarn. She dried flowers and made sachet, so I got to learn how to make sachet. I still have the book she made me that has dried flowers and pressed leaves. Each flower was labeled with information about what sort of flower it was, and sometimes there was a poem or verse on the same page. There were also recipes in it for sachet and potpourri. The title of the book says, *"God's Garden."* The book came with a handmade, wooden briefcase, and in the briefcase, were little bottles of natural oils and scents, like lavender and eucalyptus oil. I received the case and its contents from Eve when I lived in Serious's house in Serious's Area. It was one of the most wonderful gifts I had ever received as a child. No one had ever given me anything that had so much time and love that went into it.

When I was living with Eve at Serious's, I slept upstairs in this bunk that was built right at the top of the stairs. She slept in a single bed over by the window. One night, I was awakened by the sound of a woman crying, so I made my way over to where the sound was coming from. There was Eve, with her hand stuck in the window. I guess she had tried to close the window during the night and it shut on her hand, so I helped her lift up the window and off her hand. Even to this day, she tells me that she remembers when that happened.

Eve had trouble seeing, so I would help thread her needle. When she couldn't thread it herself, she would always use this old timey swear word and say, "Drats!" Family members didn't wear glasses. That made it hard for Eve when she had to take classes at the University, to get through the high volume of college reading assignments.

"How did you do it?" I asked her.

"I would have to close my eyes, open and focus to read a couple of lines, close my eyes and repeat. The only time it was really incredibly difficult for me, was when I had to read anything in the library because of all of the fluorescent lights."

It amazes me what she had to go through to keep the Love Family school legal.

When she was taking classes to get her license renewed between classes, Eve hung out at The Last Exit, the same coffee house in the University District that my mom and I went to before we moved to Alaska. The Love Family traded potatoes with Irv, the owner, so that Eve could have coffee and lunch on the days she took classes. On weekends, she studied in a neighbor's attic.

Eve was sanctioned to Caleb, who was now known as Definition. He was tall and slender and wore his brown hair in a long braid down his back. Both he and Eve were core teachers in the Love Family school. Before he came, Definition had studied mathematics and had been a Vietnam vet. When he first came, it was his job to keep us quiet in the attic during the evening meetings when Serious had to entertain downstairs.

Definition did more than just keep us quiet and distracted. He became our math and history teacher. I still remember chanting the times tables with the other children in Serious's attic. He tried to make it fun.

I am not sure why, but I nicknamed Definition "Deefo." I nicknamed Eve, "Evabirdy." Then years later when Eve had a little baby boy named Deliberate, I nicknamed him Libby Lobby." Who knows where I came up with these nicknames. But it seemed names were always changing anyway there, so why not just change them myself, instead of waiting for Love to do it.

Definition encouraged the kids to ask questions. One day someone asked him, "Why do you have such a big nose?" He laughed, then explained that his nose was broken in a fight when he was young. A fight!? We looked at each other wide-eyed, and he started laughing again.

Definition never took anything too seriously. He could make me laugh by looking at me in a certain goofy way. He would raise and wiggle one eyebrow and grin from ear to ear.

Definition loved to laugh. Sometimes he looked as if he was about to burst with laughter. He threw his head back, grabbed his belly, and positively cackled. His whole body shook when he laughed. Even his arms would flail around as he grabbed his belly. Years later, his earth mother came and lived with us, and it was then, when I heard her laugh, that I knew where his laugh had come from. We always laughed with him even though sometimes it was hard to tell why he thought we were funny. If we got too carried away, he'd say kindly but firmly, "OK now. Let's continue."

Definition told us about his experiences in Vietnam and about his life growing up on Staten Island, in New York. Even though in the Love Family, the past wasn't talked about, he never seemed to pay attention to that when it was just him and the kids, which was great, because I loved hearing about where people came from.

I have so many memories of good times with Definition. I might remember more about him than some of the other kids because, remember, I lived with him and other teachers for substantial periods of time.

Definition mostly spent time with the big kids who were around my age. He played basketball with us. He played card games with us like pinnacle and canasta. At times, he could be quiet and focused. During the card game, he chewed on his mustache, looking intently at his cards, arranging and rearranging them every so often. I noticed that when he was very focused, he would quiver one eyelid.

Definition was our teacher, but he was also a friend. He encouraged reading and had all the bigger girls reading Frank Herbert's *Dune* series, which was great because then we would all sit around and talk about it. He encouraged us to think about what we were reading.

Definition made efforts outside of school to spend time with us, like the time he read *Sacajawea* aloud to us. It wasn't just straight reading; it was also discussion like I said. He wanted to know what we thought about things, and he listened, without making judgments based on Love Family ideology.

One winter, Definition read out loud J.R.R. Tolkien's *The Hobbit*. I was around 10 years old by now and had been living at the Ranch for two years, so fast forward. It was during the second year of living in the circle of tents. To me, listening to him each week, with the other kids there, was sort of like the Love Family version of watching TV.

Just outside the circle of tents in the field next to the lake was the sauna, which was a round, six-sided, wooden cedar structure. At the time, this was the only available place to meet with Definition. It was convenient. It was out of the way from the busyness of life in the household tents. It was quiet and warm since the sauna stove was often kept stoked. Occasionally, people would come and use the sauna, but that wasn't usually a problem.

We were not in the sauna; we were in an enclosed porch area that surrounded the sauna itself, so heat would seep through the walls into the space where we were sitting.

Between the sauna and the dock area of the lake, which was about 30 feet, there was a stream that was crossed by a small wooden foot bridge. There were Alder trees that grew along the stream. It was very close in proximity, so that from the sauna, I could easily hear the people at the dock, depending on how loud they were.

Of course, there were no lights or chairs, so we clustered around Definition near the window frames, which had no glass, but where more light poured in where we sat. Some kids sprawled out on their bellies, some slouched in the customary cross-legged position. From my memory, there had to have been at least ten to fifteen kids.

As he read, I focused on watching the dust particles suspended in the light of the windows, or I stared at the worm holes in the boards where we sat. The holes were smooth, some of them blackened as if burned by fire.

I stood by the window with a view of the circle of tents in the pasture. Each tent was remodeled and looked different one from the next. Some of the tents were built on sturdy platforms with porches built into canvas doorways and had chimneys protruding from the top. It must have been fall, because I saw the trails of smoke, billowing out of the chimneys. When the wind changed, I sometimes would smell a whiff of smoke as it changed directions.

People walked to and fro. Nobody was in much of a hurry. On one side of the pasture, I could hear a baby fussing in one of the tents, and on the other side, men and women sang a Family song:

"God is Love. We are one.
Jesus Christ Is Real.
Eternally I am…
Now's the time. Love's the answer. Jesus is just us.
One with God and Christ my brother…"

I knew the song by heart. I'd sung it hundreds of times, although, I was only half paying attention to the goings on in the pasture as I focused on the story.

When I grew tired of standing, I sat back down with the others. They stared off into the middle distance, our minds far away in Hobbit land. Definition moved to lean against the wall, his mile-long legs stretched out in front of him.

One afternoon when we met at the sauna, there were folks that came and started using the sauna while Definition was reading. Whenever someone poured water on the stove inside, it hissed and sizzled until it burned off. It wasn't super loud, because there was a wall between us and the inner sauna space, but it was loud enough to hear it.

Periodically, naked bodies hurried out the sauna door past us, clomped down the steps and slapped through the mud. Every time the sauna door opened, billows of steam poured out. It was very irritating, as I was having a hard time concentrating on the story with all the distraction.

As they splashed in the lake, we could hear them whooping away in the distance, then I would hear them clomp back across the little bridge back towards the sauna. The loose boards of the bridge knocked against each other as they crossed. They stomped up the stairs, the heavy sauna door opened again, more steam billowed out. Definition kept reading as they came and went, only pausing for a moment and then held the paperback closer to his face.

Other than occasional sauna users, few people interrupted us. Once in a while, someone would wander over and discover us. They might sit down conspicuously and say," Hiii!" with a big smile, curious what all these kids were doing sitting in the sauna porch. Annoyed, we'd exchange glances, then focus more intently on Definition, who continued reading. Eventually, the interloper, who was being ignored, would walk quietly away.

As usual, Definition welcomed discussion.

"Why didn't Bilbo just pull out his sword and fight him?" one of the boys asked.

"Well because," he said, "Bilbo was smarter than that. He knew they were outnumbered and..."

"I think he just thought that..." somebody else speculated.

Definition looked up and studied two different spots in the ceiling boards:

"Well, that is probably true, too," he replied.

It was engaging to have these mini discussions as the story went along. It was just one of those memories that I never forgot.

Each of my teachers, one from the next, were so different, that it is hard to believe they were all in the same Love Family. Appreciation, for example, was my teacher for only about a year. It was towards the end, because, it wasn't too long after that, when the Family started falling apart. When she was my teacher, I was probably around 12 or 13.

Appreciation was tall and had long, full, thick hair. When she started teaching, the other teachers have told me they were so happy she came to help. She didn't have kids of her own and seemed very inspired to make a go of it. I heard that she even got permission and went out and took college courses, just so she was prepared.

The first thing that struck me about her was that on occasion, she came to class clad only in a towel. It wasn't a sexual thing as nudity was quite normal in the Family. As an elder lady, she had plenty of outfits. She just had her own way of doing things. She ran a huge household and was busy. Perhaps she was just too busy to dress.

When Appreciation started teaching, the first thing she did was make sure that everyone knew how to spell her name, so over and over again I chanted with the other children, "A.P.P.R.E.C.I.A.T.I.O.N!"

Every morning, before we started academics, she would do yoga and exercise with us. It had to be rigorous and difficult for her to think we were doing it correctly. If it seemed that we were having too much fun, she would make it harder.

Appreciation taught many subjects, math, writing, geography. She had us chanting the capital cities of all the countries in South America; It seemed sort of ridiculous since we had never had geography before, and generally it wasn't something Love wanted us to learn, unless it was the locations of places in the Bible. But somehow, she did it anyway and no one said anything. It seemed that all over the Barn area, people could hear us chanting loudly.

"The capital of Peru is Lima, Lima!" we all chanted.

One day, we were all late for Appreciation's class. We had all stopped in the pasture to pick mushrooms on our way to class that morning. When we made it to class, we had small jars of mushrooms with us, that we gave to her to see. In the Family, mushrooms were called 'sacrament,' but I also heard them called 'magic mushrooms.' The magic mushrooms were hallucinogenic. While we had been picking the mushrooms, some of the kids ate the mushrooms and then came to class high. I was not one of them, because I wasn't sure if they were edible. I had learned very young about the risks of eating unidentified mushrooms, because I had lived in the wilderness of Alaska, and my mom had warned me not to eat them and told me about a situation she knew about where a bunch of people had eaten the wrong ones and died.

I knew better, but the kids who ate them seemed so sure they were the magic ones. When we got to class, the kids were being rowdy. Here we had just handed Appreciation these jars of mushrooms. I don't think we even thought we were doing anything wrong, but she was so mad. She yelled at us and sent us all down Mattson road for a long run. We were told to run to the sheep pasture and back. I hadn't eaten them, but I had to run too, which I didn't think was fair at all. It was just sacrament. What was the big deal? Plus, we had brought them to her and showed them to her, so we obviously weren't trying to hide anything. Thinking back now, I bet she was just trying to make the rowdy kids tired, so everyone would pay attention, and not knowing who was high and who wasn't, she probably figured just make them all go and sweat it out of their systems.

Appreciation was strict compared to anything I had ever experienced from teachers in the Love Family. She was a good teacher, but to me, she seemed hard to please, and because I was a little bit afraid of her, it made it hard for me to concentrate on her lessons. Plus, some of the kids were getting old enough to start rebelling. Maybe she thought we needed a little discipline. It might've been just who I was too. I, so far, had been very close to the teachers, so when Appreciation came along, I had never lived with her in a household and hardly knew her. I felt like suddenly, I was in a strict, parochial, boarding school.

I guess in the Love Family, just like any school in the world, there are teachers with all sorts of personalities and ways of teaching, and the reality was, that there were people who sometimes had roles that maybe they shouldn't have had. Living outside of the mainstream meant certain things that most people take for granted, such as rules and laws about who should or should not be a teacher, were not a factor. And without oversite, there are consequences, some of them good and some not good.

Ethan's style of teaching was so very different than Appreciation's style. Ethan would just talk to us, not like kids but like real people. There were times when he would get into little arguments with some of the kids he had trouble with, just to prove a point. He had to prove himself, because he wasn't an elder; he didn't even have a virtue name. It was a source of frustration to him.

"You're nobody important, you're just Ethan," I heard one of the kids say to him.

"Fine, you're not going to listen to me? Don't listen to me then, but I don't have to listen to you either," I heard him answer.

I liked Ethan. I thought he was very lenient and tried to give us as much freedom as possible. It seemed that he didn't care about the authoritarian thing and went out of his way to make school fun.

I asked Ethan once what he remembered about me.

"Oh, you were a smarty pants, a goodie two shoes," he says. "When you got in trouble, it was pretty rare. You were the one that always went along with the program. You had some self-discipline."

Sometimes when Ethan saw me, he would start to sing this Worldly song that had my name in it:

Rachel, Rachel, I've been thinking, what a strange world it would be,
if all the men were transported far beyond the northern sea.

I was trying hard to do well in school. I won every spelling bee and tried to get the most out of it. I was reading books far beyond what some of the kids in my class were reading, so eventually they placed me with the teenagers in the upper class. They were a rag tag group of mixed age kids, all of whom were at least two years older, some several years older. I had been doing fractions with Appreciation, which I found I didn't like that well to now doing geometry with Definition, which I enjoyed a lot better. I was obviously the youngest one in the upper class. Love Family school was not organized by grades or ages. It was more organized by ability.

When I was moved up with the teenagers, I had school with them in the upper school rooms. This was during a time when schoolrooms were built in the Barn where the upper loft had been, above the main sanctuary. It seemed around the same time when people first started moving out of the circle of Army tents and into the yurts that spread out around the lake, which would've been 1979. I enjoyed going to school in actual rooms that were especially built for the school, instead of in a tent, out in the pasture or in some elder's sanctuary in town.

Once the school rooms in the Barn were built, from then on, when we were at the Ranch, we had school in those rooms—but we weren't always at the Ranch, so that never became what the teachers were hoping, which was a permanent location for the school.

How it worked was that the school was split by location for the youngest kids—the babies, toddlers, preschoolers and kindergartners, although those terms were not used to categorize them. It was at the Ranch for those whose parents lived at the Ranch, and in town, for those whose parents lived in town (Queen Ann). The kids who lived at other properties that were owned by the Family such as the cannery, winery and others, did school wherever they were living. The moms or others designated would collect the children into groups for age appropriate activities.

In addition to the school that was split by location for the kids at the different outposts and properties, there was a more formal 'School,' for the 'Big Kids,' that was run by designated teachers, including the teachers who I have just described, Dedication, earlier on, then later, Eve, Definition, and Appreciation. There were others who came in later as more and more children entered school age such as Tobiah, Lydia, Ono, Listening, and others who came along or who got involved.

This 'School' was a mobile entity run by Family teachers. I say mobile, because school moved around quite a bit. It wasn't stationed anywhere in particular; It would adapt to the community's needs or to Love's whims, so it would shift locations, depending on where we were sent.

There was no yearly calendar or rigid schedule either. Love wanted us to learn naturally, through our daily life as much as possible.

Daily life in the Love Family changed all the time, so the school would move right along with those changes. For example, even after we all moved out to the Ranch, there were periods of time when we were moved back into the City, and we would have school in one of our houses on Queen Anne. Then each summer, we were often sent to harvest in Eastern Washington. When we were there, which was usually spring and early summer, we had school in the orchards where we were harvesting and camping. There is a picture on a Love Family flyer of one of the teachers, Eve, sitting with several children under the fruit trees for school that day. I am one of the children in that picture, with my hand raised, waiting anxiously to answer a question.

In some ways, it might have been more as gypsies lived, our lives changing with the seasons. Each time we moved, it did not feel unstable or disorganized. I was in school with my brothers and sisters from the community. For the most part, I didn't have to deal with getting a new teacher or having new peers each year. It was just this change of scenery. The Love Family school was simple, and there weren't boxes of supplies or shelving or desks or anything that might have to be moved for a typical school.

One summer, I was in the orchard where we lived in tents, and I walked by one of the kids' tents, and there inside was my brother Forest doing school. He was sitting with other kids his age like Cyrus, Tekoah, Liberty and other little preschool-age kids. He might've been three or four. He was sitting in one of the tents, and they were singing one of the first songs I ever learned in the Love Family. It was perfect for young kids to sing. It was our most basic song.

L. O. V. E., L. O. V. E.
That spells love, that spells love.
Love is what we give, all-the-day long,
L. O. V. E., L. O. V. E.

My memories of learning in a classroom full of fruit trees under the open sky will never be forgotten. There were nights, when all the kids and the teachers would sleep out on a tarp and watch the stars until we fell asleep. At times, in the early mornings, I would go with the other children and help pick fruit with the adults before we did school. The fruit had to picked early before it got too hot, and once it did, everyone stopped picking fruit, and the kids would go do school, and then, there would be lots of free time after that to run around with my friends in the orchards. I had this favorite cherry tree that I would go to, because the cherries off that tree tasted so good. It was a long walk through the orchard and into another orchard but very worth it. It was amazing to me that the cherries on each tree would taste different one tree from the next, as if each tree had its own personality and flavors. I climbed the trees with the other children and collected the hardened amber sap off the trunks to pretend they were magic gems.

When the kids were at Cherry Hill harvesting, we would all live together with the teachers and caretakers in a tent in the orchard or just out on tarps under the starts as I said. But once we were sent back to the Ranch after the harvest, each of the children would go live with their respective households, but still meet for school at a designated place.

For a time, school was held in the Ranch house before it burned down, and later it was held in one of the Army tents when there was a circle of tents in the pasture. Then it was held in the sauna porch area for a while where Definition had read us *The Hobbit*.

The shifting in terms of location often happened because of the larger goals of the Family. For example, there were times, when the kids were needed to help with weeding or hoeing in the garden, so I marched out there with the school to work in the garden instead of classes. We would have school only on rainy days, and on sunny days, we would all be out in the garden with the adult membership getting the beds ready for the spring planting.

Generally, I did not like working in the garden. It was real life, just how Love wanted it, but I did not like the worms and the bugs and the digging. It was hard work too. I enjoyed it somewhat though because we were all out there together. There were musicians like Henry the Fiddler or other young guys who would play guitar as everyone worked. I would sneak over to the hose for a "drink of water" and instead have a spray party with my friends until we would be asked back to work.

Eventually, the Love Family school evolved when Definition and Ethan built the school rooms up in the Barn. We had a more stable location, at least when we were at the Ranch, but even then, we still did rotations in the City and in the orchards.

I liked having school in the Barn where there were classrooms. I had my own desk. Ethan made desks for the kids out of 2x4 end cuts and oak plywood. There was a little shelf underneath where I put my books and lunch, and there was a little bench to sit on. Up till now, we all just sat on the floor or ground wherever we were.

Because of the mobile, even migratory nature of our lifestyle, I was used to just picking up and going at a moments' notice to wherever it was decided we would go. It was often that I had school in the City in the fall and winter. It was held in the sanctuaries of different people's households. There was a time when we used a house near Love's Area on Pleasant Place, in the back alley. I was probably Fourth or Fifth grade then. The teachers used these big slate pieces that leaned up against the wall. I think they were given to us by Coe school.

Then in the spring, we went to the Ranch for Passover, so school would be at the Ranch after the holiday. Then in the summer, we would go to the orchards in Eastern Washington. In the fall, back to the City. It didn't happen every year like that, but it often did happen, just like that.

One might wonder how, with all the moving throughout the year, that we managed to move so many people from place to place. Remember there were hundreds of members and their kids in this community, but not everyone was sent to the orchards, just enough for the harvest work that needed to be done. I was sent with the other children around my age and our guardians to help. It wasn't difficult to load the buses; everyone only had one bag as was always the custom. I had my one bag like everyone else and my sleeping bag. It was easy to grab it and go. People didn't have boxes of stuff that had to be transported. One of the ideals in the Love Family was to get back to living more simply, without all the unnecessary stuff. The whole idea was to get away from the materialism that was so rampant in the larger society, and to focus more on God and living with just the essentials.

I never had to pack. When it was time to load, I just threw my bag on the top of the bus and off we went. There was a huge rack on the top of each bus where all the bags were stored. There was also a lower compartment that could be accessed from the side panels on the outside of the bus, where stuff was kept during the trip.

Having one bag was a big thing in the Love Family. Love stressed the importance of everyone being "ready" just in case. Over time, people would acquire things, but every so often, I was told that it was time to purge everything except the essentials. I learned not to get attached to things. It was just how our life was.

Definition thought that one of the reasons why the Family embraced mobility, was because of the kidnappings.

"Everyone had to be ready to go at a moment's notice," he says. "The entire Family had to be mobile, and the Family school reflected that."

I was ready; I could carry everything I owned, everyone could. And I had been trained about what to do if an intruder from the outside society ever came to try and take someone or to try and hurt people. I was told I would

hear someone yell "Clear out!" Then it would be time for everyone to all quietly hike up to King Lake and hide out until they left.

'Clear Out' was an exercise to teach all the kids what to do, how to
respond in case of 'Armageddon.' I was living in a community that didn't ac-
knowledge outside legal or government systems.

The training was only for the kids. I guess it was assumed that the
adults would be experts already. I knew what to do. One morning, there was
a drill. I heard, "Clear out!" I left right away with the other children from my
household. I knew it didn't matter that the breakfast dishes hadn't been done.
We went towards the hiking trail that would lead to King Lake to join up at
the trail head with the main group of kids and our guardians.

There could be no talking or noise making on the way. Just to make
the training was more realistic, some of the adults hid in the woods as we came
along on the path and pretended to be the "bad guys." If we made any noise,
they would jump out and scare us, but we were not told they were there, at
least I wasn't, so I just hiked along calmly and in silence with the group towards the lake. The plan was that once we got to the Lake, we were supposed
to stay there until we got word that it was safe to go back.

The exercise did not work out at all: First, we never received word that
it was time to return; Second, no one brought any food, so a lot of the kids
were hungry and tired. The hike was way too long for some of the younger
kids, and it took them twice as long to get to the lake where we were supposed
to all meet. A lot of them were fussing, and others were down right miserable. I
hiked to King Lake all the time, but a lot of these younger kids had never been.

Ethan was one of the guardians on the day of the training. He had a
group of younger children with him, including my brother, Forest. He said
that as the kids were hiking along in silence, one of the bad guys jumped out
and tried to grab Forest.

"It scared him half to death, and me too," he says. Ethan got so startled, that he fell backwards into the creek. He struggled to lift himself out of
the water and was so mad, that he went after the attackers. There then ensued an angry wrestling match, which ended with one of the bad guys getting
thrown in the creek.

"It all happened very fast," Ethan says.

After the exercise, no one talked about it, and we never did the training again. People remembered it as a "fiasco." I asked Understanding what she remembered about it. She had been one of the planners for the event.

"Clear-Out was not seen as successful," Understanding says with a scowl on her face, but a moment later, with a hint of pride, concluded, "but we were able to get a large number of kids off the Ranch really fast." That was all she would say.

In the weeks leading up to Clear Out, Understanding told us the Native American story of Chief Leshi. When the early pioneers settled on sacred lands, Chief Leshi was hiding from the White men behind this hillside with his tribe. His son, who was just a baby, was crying, so much so, that the Chief was worried the crying would give them away and everyone in the tribe would die. Faced with this dilemma, Chief Leshi, who had his hand over his son's mouth to muffle the sounds, suffocated his son to death to save the lives of his tribe.

Every story Understanding told had a lesson. The message about why we were doing Clear-Out scared me. I got that it was a real possibility, that there might be people from the outside culture who did not like the Love Family. Perhaps they would try to take people or try to hurt us in some way. It kind of took the fun out of going to King Lake that day, and it was no fun being silent the whole way either. When I usually hiked to King Lake, we would often run the whole way, just to get there sooner, but with all the young children, it took nearly two hours as opposed to what it usually took, which was :45 minutes. After this exercise, I guess I was prepared for the end times, 'Armageddon' if it happened.

Since everyone moved so often, I was good at it. Sometimes the school moved for reasons that had nothing to do with the seasons or harvest schedule; it was based on the needs of the community. Before the migration to the Ranch. Love needed an elder to go to the property in Hawaii, so he sent Encouragement and his whole household to Hawaii. So that house suddenly was empty and became the school house. Serious had his sanctuary back, which was where we had been meeting for school, so now Serious could have meetings and meditations in his own home again. Who knows exactly the reasoning behind certain things; we often never knew but just went along with the decisions that were being made. The way the hierarchy worked was that most people did not often know what was going on, and it wasn't custom to provide everyone with detailed explanations. There were no meetings where everyone was informed of what was happening. The whole idea was just to free everyone up to focus on God. It was to simplify our life, so everyone could rise above the mundane, superficial drama that could bog people down.

Even in the classroom, there was a certain spontaneity, a fluidity, with one thing flowing into another without tension. There were no class periods that would start or stop at a specific time. There were no clocks to separate class periods. There was no loud bell that would warn us that class or recess was over. We didn't have hall passes. When we were done learning this, we would go and do something else, depending on our needs and our attention spans. We were not graded, but we were evaluated. Eve wrote the curriculum and had standards set up that were discussed among teachers. She kept track of each child's progress and evaluated each child individually.

"It a non-grading, very organic system," says Eve.

When Eve had a baby, she would have to nurse him while she was teaching. Nobody cared; it was just very relaxed. It was sort of like home school would be, because the Love Family was home, but it was cooperatively run by teachers and members, so it was an independent entity that existed outside of regular household life.

As the Family grew, the student body grew, and academics became more standardized. I learned basics—but it was limited, because Love wanted us sheltered from Worldly outside influences.

There were no textbooks for the most part. The teachers and others who were helping developed a lot of the school materials that we used. They had to be consistent with Love Family spiritual idealism. Family teachers taught us what they thought we should know and what Love would allow, but they always taught within the Family lens.

The teachers had the help of Family artists who would help illustrate the reading materials for us to color. The drawings were of real Love Family people that I recognized and would wear similar styles of dress. There were illustrations that included the Barn, the sheep pasture, and other imagery from our life such as oil lamps and things one might see in our homes. The themes that were used in our reading, writing, and coloring materials were biblical or taken from Family thinking and philosophies. I have copies of some of the materials that were used during that time. They were given to me years later by former teachers who had been involved in the Family school. Now the materials are part of my personal museum of artifacts from my childhood. One time, I told someone I had them. They had been raised in the Love Family like I had.

"Why would you keep things like that?" they asked with an incredulous expression.

I didn't keep them, I went out and *obtained* them as part of my research for the book.

The school materials that I have collected are not something I spend time pouring over or even talking about. I only have them because I needed them to tell my story, to illustrate what it was like for me to go to school in the Love Family.

There was a coloring book that was made for the school, that came right out of Genesis. It read, "In the beginning God created the heaven and the earth…" Other worksheets were less biblical and more just typical scenes from Love Family life. There were drawings of people enjoying themselves in nature, dressed in typical Love Family style garments. One sheet reads,

"It is fun to love.
I love God.
He loves me.
I am in love.

The other sheet says,

"I am into it.
I can lift us up.
I am so glad to be me."

One illustration showed a boy in the grass raising his arms up as if in prayer. Above him was a Love symbol, which was a circle with a dot in the middle, and there were two doves on each side. The symbolism personalized the worksheets to our culture, so they became original, more interesting.

Other coloring sheets used the names of children who I went to school with. For example, there is a series with children talking about fish.

> "A fish," said Sun.
> "A little fish" said Zoar.
> "A big, big fish! said Cheerful.
> "A big fish and a little fish," said Tirzah.
> "A big fish and three little fish at the dam," said Neriah.
> "Fruit is good," said Activity.
> "I would like some fruit," said Life.
> "Here is some fruit," said Understanding.
> "A plum," said Heaven.
> "An apricot" said Lois, "an orange one."
> "Apples" said Bright...

My name was used in the reading/coloring materials as well, (Lois), so that would tell me about what time period this was created (during the first year I was there and before I was baptized), because my name was still "Lois."

A similar early reading/coloring worksheet series was called, "Our Lamb" It was a short story, that was also about us. It went like this:

> This is a lamb.
> This lamb is Easter.
> "I am a lamb too." Compassion said.
> "I am a lamb too." Cheerful said.
> "I am a lamb too." Aaron said
> "I am a lamb too." Lois said.
> "Look Love," said Jasmine, "See Easter."
> "Easter you are a cute lamb," Love said.
> "Can we feed Easter?" said Tirzah.
> "Yes," said Love, "You can feed Easter some grass."
> "Can I feed her some grass too?" said Bright.
> "Yes, you can all feed Easter. That will help her grow."

"We are all lambs like Easter," Neriah said.

The illustrations of the children and Love are recognizable; I can tell the children apart by their features in the drawings, including a sketch of Love sitting in the grass with the children and the lamb.

Love was against straight academics, but over time, the teachers talked him into some basics—reading, writing, and arithmetic. Eve was teaching primarily language arts, reading, and writing.

Once Eve asked all the kids in her class to write a paper answering the question, 'What is virtue?' This was when we were in the Barn schoolrooms before Appreciation came on board. Another paper I wrote for Eve was called, 'What is culture?' For this paper, I had a choice. I could write a paper discussing culture and what it meant, or I could pick a subculture and write about it. I picked the Moonies.

The 'Moonies' was actually a pejorative term for the worldwide, religious movement called, the Unification Church, founded by Sun Myung Moon. It had thousands of members in the United States in 1973, but it expanded though out the 1970s and 1980s. There were large numbers of Moonies in Korea, Japan, the Philippines, and other countries in East Asia. The church's textbook, the "Divine Principle," taught that God is the Creator and Heavenly Parent, whose dual nature combines both masculinity and femininity and whose center was true love. They had alternative or non-traditional interpretations of the Bible, just like we did, and were open to interfaith ideas as well. In the United States, the group won law suits against deprogrammers from the anti-cult movement. (Wikipedia) It was an interesting assignment for me to learn about another group besides my own.

Love was mostly against history, especially if it was the history of modern outside society, but he was fine with us learning biblical history as well as the histories of other subcultures and of Native and African American histories. It seemed that I was encouraged to learn about the histories of sub-groups, because that would be consistent with living in a cultural, sub-group myself.

Even the math I was learning was innovative, different. Ethan taught what was called, 'finger math.' I still use finger math today and have found it very helpful. Finger math is also called the Korean Abacus or Chisanbop. It is a way to use your finders as an abacus to add, subtract, and multiply where each finger represents a number. On the right hand, each finger represents the ones, and on the left hand, each finder represents the tens.

Ethan also taught math using Cuisenaire rods, which are used for teaching number concepts and the basic operations of arithmetic. We got the Cuisenaire rods because Steve Allen, Logic's dad, donated several large boxes of them. They were little rods in decimal form. Each different sized rod was a different color. I used the rods in school to build trains and to build other designs, but also to do simple equations with them, like red plus red equals purple, which was 2+2=4. It was a concrete example of mathematics, algebra, and fractions.

Ethan set up a sort of math lab where he used Cuisenaire rods and tangrams. He had this chart of all these pictures of what we could do with the tangram. We would do ten minutes every day. Each kid had their own little cardboard set. The idea was that when we would work with the shapes, we would learn how visualize within a space; it is called spatial geometry. With the tangram, I was able to take a space and divide it with shapes, and once I had the seven shapes, I could see how they fit.

In terms of science, classes were less consistent, but when we did have science, it was always taught in the most organic of ways, which was in line with Love's idea of learning through real life. I went, with the other students, on nature walks, collecting pond water in jars to look at under the microscope. During one of the classes, I found this tiny little bundle of sticks. It was the size of the end of my pinkie finger. All the sticks were stuck together in what looked like this miniature beaver dam in the shape of a ball. When I pulled all the little sticks apart, there was this tiny little worm inside. I don't remember what it was, but I just remember being fascinated by it, and it being one of the many wonders of living right on a small lake during those years.

There were times when I had a hard time enjoying biology. The kids were going to dissect a frog that week in class, so I let it be known that I wanted no part of that. Luckily, I was allowed to stay home the day it happened. No one made me do it, and people seemed fine that I was uncomfortable and just didn't want to. I was grateful for that and later, when the kids talked about the frog dissections, I would quickly walk away and did not want to hear about it. It made me sick! Poor innocent little frogs who wanted nothing more than to live in peace in our lake.

Other than the nature walks, science was hit and miss. One year, all the kids were bussed off to the cannery, in Eastern Washington so we could view an eclipse. Each of us got to make our own telescope with a toilet paper roll. That was a fun trip.

Then there was Abishai who had an off and on relationship with the Family school teaching science. He never taught a class, but he would bring the kids to his lab sometimes for experiments. Really early on, like before we moved to the Ranch, he had us collect different types of cheese, which he had us put in a little Petri dish so we could observe mold. His lab was in this area back towards the Kids' House in Love's Area on Queen Anne. Then later he had a lab in the pottery shed out at the Ranch. Every so often, we would go to his lab and check on the cheeses. He seemed a little more excited about it than I was, but it was somewhat interesting. He taught us this word called 'theo-observation.' Theo means God, so God-observation. He felt that everything we observe is God, because God is everywhere.

Another time, Abishai asked the teachers for two children to help him with a science project. Shushan and I got chosen to go with him. He taught us how to make mannitol, which was this imitation, powder-like sugar substance.

"Don't eat it," he warned us, but just take "a little taste" of it. Afterward, he let us each keep a little, miniature bottle of it. I couldn't help but eat it all, and afterward, I had a stomach ache that lasted all afternoon.

What I most remember about Abishai is his creation of these small volcanic eruptions for kids. It was mostly just to entertain, because he would often do it at the Golden Egg Party or other festive events. He would set up this mound. It was probably a foot high, and it looked like a miniature volcano. Once everyone was ready, he would drop a little water onto the mound, and it would explode like a volcano. I am not sure how he did it. I know that there are certain by-products of Alkali metals such as calcium, potassium, or sodium that when mixed with water can become unstable. He also could have used certain peroxides that can also become unstable in the presence of water.

Abishai looked like your typical mad professor. He was a short, wiry, balding man who had wisps of white hair. If he was there in the crowd, I tended to notice him as he always seemed to be walking determined to get somewhere with an air of self-importance. I don't know why, but it also seemed like he was always wearing his robe, at least when he did the demonstrations.

Abishai didn't just look like a mad professor; he really was one in some ways, because before he came to the Family, his name had been Robert Kohn and he had been a tenured biology professor at the University of Washington. He was a leading researcher on primates and a specialist on genetics and DNA. At the University, he had gotten a grant to work with small amounts of marijuana. When he ran out of his supply, he had taken students with him when he was caught at the Canadian border with Kilos of marijuana. After he got out of jail, the University fired him. He went "crazy" from what I've heard. He felt that they had used his arrest as an excuse to fire him and take his research. He basically ended up in a mental hospital before he met the Love Family and joined. Abishai was a part of the Love Family when I got there, so all that must have happened sometime in the late 1960s or early 1970s before we flew in from Alaska to Seattle in 1975.

Love wanted Abishai to make psychedelics and provided him with medical textbooks for his work. Abishai may have done some work on that, but he never became the supplier of such substances for the Family. Instead what he became famous for in the community was creating a miraculous cure for diaper rash. It was called, 'Baby Bottom Balm.' Women were amazed at how well it worked. There were times when I and other children helped him gather cottonwood buds and elder flowers to make it with. He also made the oil that Love used to anoint people. It was made out of apricot kernel, which was used in ancient times in traditional Chinese medicine for treating ulcers and tumors. When we were harvesting in the orchards, he had some of us help him collect apricot pits, then he had this special technique where he would smash them in just such a way that the kernel would pop out unharmed.

That was the extent of the science that I had growing up in the Love Family. I had far more math and English than science.

Definition taught me math the entire time I was there. Then he began to teach history as well as math towards the end. He ended up convincing Love that we needed to learn some ancient history. I learned the history of Sumaria and about the ancient civilizations in Europe in the Middle Ages. At this point, we had already learned a ton of biblical history. We did not learn much current history because Love considered our history as a family to be based on more ancient Israel, and he seemed to be trying to disassociate us as much as possible from histories that he did not consider part of our cultural heritage.

In terms of foreign language, when Mikha'el showed up and became a member, Love right away asked him if he would teach the kids Hebrew classes. He was from Israel. I learned how to pronounce his name, which had a throaty sound that I had never heard before. Mikha'el had shoulder length frizzy, brown hair and a large, classic Jewish nose. He was a very easy going, fun guy with a great sense of humor. He reminded me a little of Presence. He taught me and the other kids in his class the Hebrew alphabet and sentences such as 'hi' and 'how are you? I learned how to pronounce my name, Rachel, in Hebrew and how to write it too. My name, since it had a 'ch' had that same throaty sound. I learned a song in Hebrew, and I sang it with the other children for Love, just to impress him. He did in fact seemed very impressed by our singing. He smiled and became animated as he jumped in and started singing it with us, proudly. We were singing the language of the ancient Israelites and their ancestors, a heritage he had claimed as our own.

"David, Melech Yisrael; Chai, Chai, Vekayam…" (repeat, repeat)

The Lyrics can be translated into English as saying "David, king of Israel, lives and endures."

King David, an early king of Israel was from the tribe of Judah, and in the Love Family, we were seen as descendants from the Tribe of Judah. Love lived and was treated like a king in the tradition of King David. Before I came to the Love Family, I heard that Love was anointed king, just like King David had been anointed in ancient times.

For some reason, Mikha'el didn't stay involved in the school. I think he left the Family, but I am not sure. I heard he came back at some point. While he was there and before he left, I enjoyed learning another language. That class ended up being the extent of the foreign language component in the Love Family school.

My former teacher, who was known as Definition, felt that we need more than just biblical history; he thought we needed to learn about current events and other things that had an impact on the world. He tried to stay in line with what Love wanted as much as possible, but there were times when he would get into discussions with some of the older kids, privately. One day, we were all up in the school room in the Barn where he taught, but it was after class, so we were just sort of hanging out, talking with him. He told us about the threat of nuclear war, about Russia and the cold war. It upset me, because I had no idea that such threats existed. I felt safe in the Love Family. Our life was so cut off from anything that was happening on the outside, that I had little concept of the concerns and threats of modern American life outside of the community.

Dear Diary,

You might get blown up in the war because Reagan is deciding whether or not to blow up the world. I'm scared. I hope there is no war. I will trust in God to save us.

Rachel Israel

Then, shortly after that, I wrote this letter to the president for a school assignment and copied it into my diary:

Dear President Reagan,

You are making too many bombs. You could blow up the world many times. I don't see the benefit. I want a chance to grow up.

Please develop a treaty with the Soviet Union. There would be peace forever.

Love,

Rachel Israel

I was very excited when I got a response, but after I read it, I was a bit disappointed that the letter was signed by a White House secretary. I had assumed that the President would write back to me himself. The response letter basically said, 'We are doing everything we can.'

That experience though was eye opening in terms of my understanding of the outside world, because clearly, Love was the king in this small kingdom, but there was a system of government out there with countries who had bombs!

My mind was further expanded when Understanding took us on a field trip to Olympia to the State capital. We weren't sent there to learn about where laws were made for people who lived in the world, we were sent there by Love to bring the new law of love to them. I was to sing with the other children on the trip for the crowds in the rotunda. The rotunda was like a palace, a round building with a gigantic dome ceiling, measuring 175 feet high from the floor, from the outside, 287 feet high. It's the tallest masonry dome in North America. I had never seen such intricately decorated architecture in my life. In the center of the dome above us hung the largest chandelier ever made by Tiffany's. It was six-foot-wide and weighed five tons, carrying hundreds of lights and thousands of crystal beads. In each corner of the rotunda, sat four Tiffany's statuesque fire posts, replicas of the signal lights used in Ancient Rome to call the first senate into session 2,000 years ago.

Just being there, I was getting a small glimpse of the foundation of the authority structure for outsiders. I saw the vastness of the outside world in comparison to the small community where I was from where Love was in charge. The only way I could process it was just to play. I joined the other kids who were there who were running up and down the marble staircases and sliding down the marble banisters. They were awesome slides! I didn't care that I was wearing my best ethnic, biblical outfit and was about ready to perform. Understanding didn't seem to notice as she was talking to a woman I didn't recognize. Then, a man dressed in a suit and shiny black shoes approached Understanding and asked her to tell us not to slide anymore. Disappointing! Love thought we were going to the capital to propagate his vision to the world. When we sang, a crowd of people quickly gathered around us; I watched the people watching us, smiling, impressed, curious. I smiled on cue back at them then looked around in wonder at the largeness of it all. My eyes had been opened to something much bigger than the small, tribal frame of mind, a place where rules could be made that had nothing whatsoever to do with Love. Woh!

So that was the Love Family school's version of current events.

There was one summer when I was living with Helpful and Dedication in Helpful's household when the whole household would sit together in the evenings and read about the Oneida Community. This would've been 1979, because Helpful had just gotten set up in his yurt site.

I was fascinated by this community. Even as a young child, I was always drawn to history. Being raised in the Love Family, where everyone was so focused on leaving the past behind, in some ways, I was rebelling by even being interested in history at all. All the value was placed on the present moment, and the past was being censored. Without thinking about it, I intuitively understood that history was important. It had valuable things to say about culture, about society, about the world we lived in today and the future. I learned this very young because when history was kept from me, it made me want to understand what I was missing.

So, when Helpful's household read about Oneida, I wanted to know too. Oneida had existed almost 100 years earlier and seemed like the Love Family in many ways.

The Oneidans believed similarly to what we believed, that Jesus had returned, and they were trying to build Jesus's Millennial Kingdom themselves. They tried to be free of sin and perfect in this world, which they called, 'Perfectionism.' Oneida were well off though. They didn't live in tents.

One of the ways they made money was they manufactured silverware, a business that continued, long after the community broke up. In fact, Oneida Limited is one of the world's largest suppliers of silverware, dinner and tableware, and is part of the legacy of that community that still exists today.

Learning to read was a much bigger deal than history or science in the Love Family. One year, after Eve gave out reading tests, there was some concern that some of the kids weren't learning to read. Suddenly there was this push to work on reading outside of school. Back at my household in the evenings, we were told to read the Bible each night, as if we didn't get enough

Bible as it was! That was pretty much the only time I did homework in the Family, so I would read the Bible each evening before bed to improve my reading skills.

I helped in my household to make sure the babies too were doing their homework. I would show them these huge flashcards that had words on them. The cards were large, like a foot long and several inches tall and had giant words like B.O.O.K. in large, black lettering on them. I would read the card to the babies and show them the letters.

They did not seem interested at all. One of the babies grabbed the card and began chewing on it.

I would also help the babies with their math. It was called the baby math system. It was a certain number of dots on large flash cards, that would also say their numerical value. The card would have a number seven on it and seven dots. I frankly could not even get the babies to sit down, let alone read the cards.

It was one of Ethan's brilliant ideas. He had talked Love into baby math.

"It was just a fad that we got into for a while," Eve says.

When Hope was tested, it was found that he was unable to read. This was when he would've been in sixth grade. He didn't go to school; He just decided not to go. Instead, since no one had figured out how to control him, he came and went from the Family on his own; Half the time, no one knew where he went. We knew him as Hope whenever he was in the Family, but when he left, he called himself Eric. Soon after his reading level had been tested, he went and stayed with a relative; it was Truthfulness's sister-in-law, and she put him in Public school. But Hope hated it, because the kids made fun of him that he couldn't read. So, when Hope came back from staying with her, he taught himself to read.

In the orchards, I saw him constantly with his nose in a book, reading the *Hardy Boy* books. He also read books about Alexander the Great too. Later that year, he was tested again, but this time, he tested into a 9th grade reading level. He had jumped three grade levels!

When I first came to the Family, there were no children's books of any kind. There was only the Children's Bible to read. But over time, as the school evolved, we needed books. Eve and the teachers found and collected books that were approved by Love for a little library that we had in the Barn above the school rooms. Now that we had an actual place at the Ranch for the school, the teachers began to create a library. I could not just read any book though; it had to be a book that met certain criteria and had to be consistent with what we believed as a Family.

There were certain books that were considered acceptable reading materials. These were: science fiction, fantasy, or similar genres. At least these books talked about a world that was make believe, often with spiritual underpinnings. I got to read *The Chronicles of Narnia*, *Lord of the Rings*, and other great books, because these books didn't contradict our way of life in the Love Family. I read the *Narnia* series twice. I enjoyed it so much that I would take a flashlight into my sleeping bag at night and read, so no one would know that I was up late.

The *Narnia* series, during that time in history became a sort of hippie phenom and had a large Christian following as well. Aslan, the lion, was seen as symbolic of Jesus Christ in certain ways, and the story of how Jesus was crucified was similar to the story of what happened to Aslan. It was written by the great C.S. Lewis, who while he was popular for his fiction books, he was also a well-known, Christian apologist who wrote nonfiction books on Christianity.

Love allowed the *Narnia* series to be read on a wide scale as a community. The elders would read out loud to groups of members who became very enthusiastic about it. That all got started when it was decided that reading material was needed for the older children to supplement the Bible. Then, it grew from that point, with the teachers encouraging Love that way and putting in efforts to acquire reading materials that were entertaining but that also fit in with the values and beliefs of the community.

Love approved of Frank Herbert's *Dune* series too, so Definition passed out copies for us to read. Love saw the Family like the Fremen tribe in *Dune*. The Fremen were motivated by a religious understanding, like we were. Paul Maudib, their king, was a messiah, which is how Love saw himself. The Freeman had visions and dreams that came from eating mélange, 'the spice' which Love saw as similar to sacrament. As we finished each book, Definition would hand us the next. I saw the similarities, but the Fremen lived on another planet in a desert and had to wear still suits that recycled their sweat.

Definition also got Love to approve James A. Michener's, historical fiction, *The Source*, that was based on biblical history. I was freaked out by that one because it had a lot of violence in it and people getting tortured in medieval ways. I didn't like that, but I was proud of myself that I read it because it was the longest book I had ever read at that point, being 1,888 pages!

The teachers did their best to find books that fit into Family thinking. There was a point when I and some other girls were reading Laura Ingalls Wilder's *Little House on the Prairie* series. We were taking turns with the books as there were not an infinite number of copies to go around. Suddenly, right in the middle of us reading the series, we were told we could not read them anymore. Apparently, the characters in the books had ages, which wasn't consistent with Love Family thinking at all. Love would wax and wane in terms of how rigid he was about books, but he was consistent that none of the books we read could reference age. It was during this time, that some of the books that the teachers had collected for the school were burned.

"Love was pulling us back," Eve explained, "and he felt that the school had 'gone too far,' that "it had evolved away from his original vision of school just being part of life."

I was very upset about not being able to read more about *Little House on the Prairie*. I was somewhat vocal about my feelings. Even after asking questions and complaining, I still did not understand what the big deal was. It was a very disappointing moment, but one I had to accept.

We weren't allowed to have very many books. The Bible and Bible stories were back to being number one. When the teachers would find books for the school, they would take them to Serious, who would take them to Love to make sure they weren't harmful. Ethan shared his thoughts.

"Sometimes Love would approve them, and sometimes instead, he would come back with an entirely new direction for the school," Ethan says. "Love did not care about education. He was not a great supporter of what we did."

The teachers fought for the school, they fought for the rights of the children to learn, but it was challenging for them since Love often did not agree on things. Every so often Love would come through and purge the library of "unsuitable" material. I heard that he sold half of the books for butter once. Despite this, or maybe because of it, I loved to read.

I learned how to carry on whole conversations with people while I read, so I could keep reading.

"Uh huh, ok sure," I would answer if I was asked to do something.

Then later, I would get in trouble because I didn't do it. And they would say, "You were sitting right there, and you said you would," they would complain.

I would have no recollection, so in the end, it didn't work, but it did temporarily, until I at least could finish the chapter.

I read with the other girls who were around my age. It wasn't for school, it was just to keep ourselves entertained since we didn't have television. I and some of the girls in my class would lay around on the floor in one of the empty school rooms and read our books. Even reading a book was this communal activity. I used one of the girls for a pillow. She would lie on her stomach and I would use the small of her back which fit my head perfectly.

When it came to basically anything beyond the basics, the teachers were dealing with a censor. It wasn't easy for them, since there was no money for books. They were resourceful though and found ways to acquire them.

"Then occasionally, Love would come through and throw 90% of them out," Definition recalled. "In the end, it meant that the teachers had little to work with and basically came down to the fact that the kids didn't need to know anything more than what [Love] was willing to tell them." There were a lot of reasons why the books were thrown out. "A lot of it had to do with the idea that we were eternal, so anything that referred to anything but that idea, which they all do, unless they are totally fantasy books, [Love] wouldn't relate to that."

Eve bitterly recalled the time when Love made them burn half the books.

"His stance was 'How can we have our kids' reading about lifestyles that we are trying to not live like,'" she says. "Books had to be very limited, no pictures, only certain story lines, etc. Love had decided it had gone too far and we should go back to only reading the Bible."

Teachers had to work within Love's parameters. As educators, they passed on the cultural heritage. It was not completely a one-way street though. Love and Serious did decide lots of things for the school, but Family teachers influenced Love as well. Definition talked him into ancient history. Eve talked him into books. Ethan talked him into finger math and tangrams. Understanding talked him into milk money for the little ones.

If it wasn't contrary to our beliefs or way of life, and if it didn't cost anything, then the chances were high that a teacher's idea would be approved. But they had to go through the right channels, i.e., Serious and Love. Essentially, the ideas had to be practical, realistic, and contribute in some way to Love's vision for the school.

When I interviewed former Love Family teachers for this chapter, I got a sense of the frustration that they must have felt. Definition explained what it was like dealing with Love.

"He put all this value on what we did, but what could we do without tools!" Definition harped.

Over time though, Love came to trust more in their judgment. For example, Love believed that the kids didn't need to know any history outside of the Bible, but Definition argued with him that we did need to know some things, especially from a contextual point of view, because we didn't know anything.

"Once I got him to agree with my logic, it loosened up a bit," Definition says. "It was still tight though. Love wasn't against geography all together—but no straight teaching of geography. If it came up in the other things we would talk about, then that was fine—where were these civilizations located?"

The question Love may have been asking himself was: How can I teach these children in a way that perpetuates our culture? Why should we teach our children how to survive in a culture we don't approve of?

Maybe he thought that if we learned about the outside society, that we would one day leave him; and it is true that the less exposure to outside influences, the more likely a group will survive. That is true throughout history. Intentional communities and utopian experiments tend to dissolve as they mix with outside influences. This is true even of large-scale cultures and societies, so it really was a dilemma that a spiritual community such as ours would've had to deal with one way or another.

In the last year or so that I was there, there was less oversight by Love on what books we were reading, as he seemed constantly absent. That is when we would go in packs to the library and check out boxes of books to read. Every two weeks, I got to go and fill up a huge cardboard box. I checked out and read a lot of the classics.

I was gleaning information about the outside world. The World was a place I could learn about in books. I didn't need to be told about the World, because I could find out for myself. I had begun reading books that I knew would never have been approved for us to read. I was checking out any book that struck my fancy. No one was screening, and no one seemed to notice at all what I was doing. Looking back of course I realize that this last year was the Families most disorganized year. Books were giving me a window into the world that I had never quite had, a world of romance and people could do things without Love's approval.

I was a fast reader and went through a lot of the classics this way. The teachers arranged to have occasional visits from the book mobile, but we still went to the library because of our voracious appetites for books that the mobile could not keep up with.

Increasingly, there was more rule breaking and things became more disorganized. It was entering into the later days (1982–83). There were large scale conflicts going on and the teachers were becoming frustrated with Love about money.

"There were now 120 school age kids, and more materials were needed, as well as high school level text books," says Eve.

Ethan explained that originally, it was "cool" that all we had was a slate and a pencil each, but toward the end "it became a problem." There were rumors that Love was spending money on cocaine, and it "pissed" the teachers off because the school needed books, tools, and supplies.

"We wanted to cover more than just the basics," Ethan says. "People started taking over the schoolrooms with band equipment." The way Ethan saw it was this:

"We were camped out in army tents, in yurts, and in the Barn, and were biding our time until we got to a better place, until more people came with more money, so we could build a real school. But it never happened, says Ethan. "Years would go by and we would still be doing the same thing—camping out together. The visions were small. Wouldn't it be nice to have a blackboard? Wouldn't it be nice to have an overhead projector?"

"As the family got bigger, the school did too, and more things were needed," Eve explained. "Serious was bowing down to everything Love would say. We'd try getting Serious to ask for things for the school but after a year of trying to get Serious to do this and no results, I started going to Love myself and said that 'things needed to change…' I just thought he was being a jerk about the school needs. It was very frustrating."

I wasn't aware of how the teachers were struggling. I felt like I generally got some basics in terms of math and English, but I didn't have much to compare it to either; it certainly did not seem like it was the intention at the time to give us anything comparable to what kids were getting in the world. Instead, there seemed to be the opposite with just as much emphasis and value placed on non-academic learning.

Love's ideas about what he thought we should be learning included the arts. He encouraged Family artists to teach the kids what they knew, but Love was somewhat frustrated though, from what I understand, that more artists and craftsmen did not get more involved in teaching the kids, but there were those who did help out from time to time.

I was sent to go be an apprentice to Eden where I learned to string a large loom to weave textiles with different yarns and threads. Other times, I was sent to go learn from Family artists, like Imagination, Dignity, and Grace.

There was one year when I had belly dancing lessons. This was during the first year that we lived in the circle of tents (1977). Piety was there who was the lady who had taken care of me in the Ranch house when I had chicken pox earlier on. There were two or three other girls my age who were there too, but mostly it was a group of adult women. It was glorious, the feeling of shimmying around with chiffon hip scarves wrapped around my waist. I danced using the gold finger symbols or 'zills' as they are called, rolling my belly as I was instructed. I layered myself with the coin jewelry that would jingle with every move, and of course, the costumes were a bit oversized, but so much fun.

We had horses at the Ranch, so there were members who taught horse-back riding lessons at times and general animal care.

I learned a lot about horses and animals from Vision. Vision often did not fit into typical gender norms. I would see her out working, riding on the tractors, and for special events, she would ride naked on the horse, like a circus lady. She would stand on its back as it galloped across the pasture as everyone cheered. She was like a one-woman circus show and for just a few moments, as I watched her ride across the pasture, my spirit would ride with her, proud and free.

Vision also taught me and three or four other girls a dance class, and afterward we performed for everyone at a party up in the Barn. The performance was set to Steve Miller's "Fly Like an Eagle." The dance began with me pretending to be a seed in the ground; As the song got going, I would sprout into a flower that would dance around to the rest of the song. I wore this beautiful tapestry around me that hugged me like protective soil. As the seed (me) began to sprout, I carried the scarf with me as a streamer as I skipped across the Barn floor to the music.

Another time, I got to go with Logic and Simplicity on a trip to San Francisco. Love asked them to take a couple of kids, so we could learn about Simplicity's role as head seamstress for the Family. Heaven got to go too. I don't know when this was, but from the pictures of the trip that I have, I was probably around ten or eleven, which would've made it around 1978-79. It was early on because the fabric that was bought was the same fabric that was used to make the 12 tribes of Israel banners that were hung in the Barn.

Logic drove in a Volkswagen bus to a well-known fabric district where Simplicity bought large bolts of 100% cotton fabric for the Family. While on the trip, we were taken to see the San Francisco Zoo. After that, they took us to go see China Town where Simplicity bought Heaven and I each a folding silk hand-held fan.

What I actually remember the most from the trip was not the part where we went to buy fabric or the zoo, but it was a side trip we took to visit the Foundation of Revelation located in San Francisco not far from the fabric district.

The Foundation of Revelation was a spiritual community headed by a man named "Father," who was from India. The community lived in two houses that were attached. We also visited their farm in the country where there were about 100 people living. Heaven and I stayed there for a couple of days or more. I am not sure where Logic and Simplicity went, but we spent the time with a girl around our age named Sherry who was being raised in that community. During our stay there, I got to watch the movie cartoon, *Charlotte's Web* and eat Hostess Twinkies for the first time in my life. We ran around with Sherry without supervision which was so much fun in contrast to the restrictive life we had in the Love Family back home.

I met Father, their leader in one of the upper rooms. He was East Indian and had long dark hair and a long graying beard. He was surrounded by women who waited on him. When we came into the room where he sat cross legged on the floor, he did not say hi. He was totally silent the whole time. It seemed a little weird but compared to what? By this time, I had seen some pretty different stuff. At the time, I knew from meditation and fasting in the Love Family that Father was most likely engaged in some sort of spiritual exercise in self-restraint.

In fact, he was and had been on a vow of silence for nearly two years. Father, the spiritual guru of the Foundation of Revelation who sat before me, like Buddha, believed that silence was the inevitable path that leads to truth.

A vow of silence is a spiritual practice taken in a monkhood like context where one renounces Worldly pursuits and devotes him or herself fully to spiritual pursuits. A vow of silence, also known in Hinduism as Mauna translates in English to "silence." Mauna comes from the noun muni, meaning sage or hermit and is a common word in most Indian languages which means blissful calmness, tranquil quietude, perfect stillness. What he was attempting to achieve through 'mauna' was 'satya,' translated as 'truth' and meaning an existence that is pure, holy and perfect, and can only be experienced through the medium of silence.

There was something else that happened there which stuck out in my mind well after we left. Heaven and I stayed in a room that was the children's room, so it had blocks and other toys in there. We slept on the floor in our sleeping bags with Sherry.

Just as we were setting up our beds, I heard a loud clomping noise as somebody stomped up the front porch. Sherry ran to the door and locked it, just as whoever it was came to the door. I could hear the door handle jingle as the person tried violently to open the door from the outside. Sherry seemed calm and nonchalant, while I was scared and wondered what was going on. Apparently, the man was trying to get away after he had stolen a woman's purse less than a block away. Soon after, there were police outside who were apprehending the man.

The way Sherry responded, like it was just another day in an ordinary life in San Francisco, seemed odd. For me, the whole thing was shocking and scary. It really opened my eyes to the realities of life outside of my small, safe community. We didn't have to lock our doors at the Ranch. What doors, they were tent flaps! Robbery? The whole idea was new to me, and why would anyone want to be so mean as to take someone's belongings by force. It seemed horrible!

The entire trip was really something else and made a strong impression on me. It was fun though cruising around in a Volkswagen with Logic and Simplicity, going across the Golden Gate Bridge into another city. What an adventure it was to visit this interesting community and see and experience things I had never seen. It was supposed to be a learning experience. Well, I did learn, just not about fabric. That's how things were in the Love Family. It was called the school of life.

I learned a lot of things like that. I learned about birth that way. In the Love Family birth was natural and just part of life. Women had their babies at home, in our own community. There were midwives that assisted at the births. I got to watch several births that way. It wasn't traumatic. I thought it was interesting to watch their little heads come out.

Years later when I went to a public high school, I took this class called family psychology where the teacher showed the class a video of a live human birth. The video was a very small black and white screen; frankly I could hardly see what was going on even very close up where I was sitting in the front of the class. It almost seemed purposely blurry. Maybe these high school students couldn't handle it? It was strange to me and almost seemed as if they were trying to hide the truth of birth, this beautiful and amazing experience that is so natural and just part of life.

When I was growing up on the Ranch, I saw baby animals born too, not infrequently, especially early on when we had so many animals. It seemed that whoever was around would just run and help. I was so amazed to see a little horse born. I could hardly tell that it was a horse, except that the baby had these very long legs that slid out. This was learning about real life!

Once, when Ethan was teaching his class to some of the younger kids, one of the goats went into labor during the class; he had to go right away and help. In addition to teaching, Ethan also helped with the animals. He was the most knowledgeable about the goats. During this time, each household had a goat that was tied somewhere nearby that they would take care of. When the goat went into labor, somebody went and got Ethan to help.

"All my students were with me," he says. The mother goat was screaming, trying to push the baby out. "I had to reach inside her and pull it out because it was stuck. My class watched the whole thing. It just took a few minutes."

There was a whole realm of learning that took place outside of the classroom and seeing and being a part of birth was just a small part. There was an abundance of learning opportunity in day-to-day life, which was more in line with Love's thinking about what he wanted school to be for us, instead of just straight academics.

Whenever there were activities going on that had any sort of important learning implications, any of the kids who were around or who could participate were encouraged to do so. One day, I was up at the Barn. I was just walking through on my way somewhere when suddenly, I was rounded up and invited to help learn how to prepare and tan a sheep's skin. First, I helped pour salt on the skin. Then it had to soak in this disgusting water. I was told the sheep's brains were in the water, which didn't sit well with me at all. After it soaked, I helped stroke the skin with a wire brush. When my learning experience was over, I was so glad to be on my way afterward to different things.

In the early spring, it was time to sheer the sheep, and there would be tons of wool to clean. In my household, I was taught how to card wool, how to make felt, and how to spin the wool on a spinning wheel to make yarn. The Love Family always had a pasture full of sheep as long as I was there.

Not all the kids were chosen for every learning experience though, so there may be people who were also raised in the Love Family who don't remember the same things I do. A lot of it was just random and spontaneous things that happened, and I just happened to be there at the right time and place or wrong, depending on what it was.

I may not have had as much academics as kids on the outside, but I certainly had the opportunity to learn crafts, like sewing and embroidery. There was one season when all the girls would get together and sew a quilt for Love. We would have been probably 8 or 9 then, very early on, when I was living in the Kids' House. A girl who already knew how to sew, Asahel was just a few years older than us headed the project. Each of us embroidered a different patch with a different letter. I think I had the "L," someone had "O," someone else had "V," and someone had "E." We would meet once a week until it was finished. When we were each complete, we were taught how to sew all the patches together into the quilt, which was then presented to Love.

One day I heard that all the kids were supposed to go up to the Barn and help Appreciation sacrifice the chickens. It was not ceremonial; there was no prayer. She had some of the people from her household assist. I helped catch the chickens with the other kids. I ran after them, and in teams we would corner them and bring them to the garden where there was a fire pit. I watched as some of the boys helped hold the chickens down while their heads were chopped off. Then the chicken would be put in a huge stainless-steel pot of boiling water to loosen feathers. To my horror, one of the chickens whose head had been chopped off got away and ran off to the woods. We ran after it to try and catch it. By this time, I was in a state of trauma. I loved the chickens and thought they were the most wonderful creatures. Plus, I had been living in a mostly vegetarian community, except at Passover and Fish and Honey Feast, so I could not understand why we were killing the chickens. There was no explanation provided. I was just doing what I was told, and it was to learn. The chicken was running off into the woods. Someone got out a bow and shot at it as it ran off into the woods. They got it. I couldn't believe it was happening. I worked with the other children up in the Barn kitchens to pluck them and prepare them to cook. As we took their organs apart, one of the little girls, Purity got all excited because she had found a button inside the gizzard, someone else found a pin. To me, it was all very disgusting, and I felt sick to my stomach the whole time. The next day, there was a chicken feast up in the Barn. All the kids were there. I don't remember much of the feast other than

I thought it was weird. I took a nibble but I was not interested. Where was Understanding? Where was Love? Why?

For years, I never understood how I could have such a horrible memory without an explanation. Then years later, I talked to Phaedra who told me that the reason why we sacrificed those chickens that day was because she had called Child Protective Services (CPS) and complained that she wasn't getting enough meat. Phaedra was in the Love Family without her parents. She was a foster child and was under the care of one of the members, so Love received money each month for her care. I am not sure how the check was written or how they arranged the details, but that was her situation. Once she called CPS, there were social workers who planned to come out the next day to investigate how children were being cared for and fed. There wasn't time to come up with a better plan. It finally made sense. The kids were helping to prepare the chickens for the social workers, who were served the next day during their visit, to show that, yes indeed, children were getting meat. I didn't appreciate that learning experience.

Some learning opportunities were segregated by gender because I heard that the boys got to learn knife throwing and archery, and they would be assigned to apprentice some of the men and do wood working and construction. I did not get to do that. I was doing more of the sewing and weaving type crafts. I was taught how to make bread. It wasn't totally segregated that way though, because I also got to do archery at times, and I heard the boys got to learn how to weave.

Then there was a special hike planned for the kids; it was planned as a learning experience where we would learn survival education with Presence. Presence taught us how to use a compass and what to do if we ever got lost.

On that hike, Heaven and I were goofing off and lost track of time. We finally realized that we had gotten separated from the group. We stayed put just as we had been trained to do. We called to Presence and the group and heard them call back, very faintly. As they got closer and closer, their voices got louder and louder, until finally we became officially found.

Once everyone was together again, we all kept going and made it to a place in the woods above the waterfall where there was a stream. We camped out for three days, learning how to survive in the wild. We had to haul all our bedding and food up there. We took turns lugging water back to the camp from a stream in a canvas bucket. We had to boil the water before we used it. It was not fun per se, as it was supposed to be this training. To me, it was ridiculous to be doing it when our life on the Ranch was like survival in so many ways. I did not need this training. Daily life in the Love Family taught me enough about that. My friend Heaven called it the "Stupid Girl's hike, because she forgot her sleeping bag and no one realized it till we were up there.

On the way, Seth hurt his finger. I went immediately to Presence and got the first aid kit and attended to his finger with much care. It was fun as I pretended to be his nurse and put salve and gauze on it to stop the bleeding.

"You would make a good nurse," Seth told me afterwards.

It was a great compliment. I liked the idea that maybe I was like Bliss, who I admired greatly, and who had taken care of me early on when I had been sick.

......

I may not have learned the exact same things that kids learned in schools on the outside. Instead, I was living in a spiritual community that was trying to preserve its heritage and culture by limiting outside influences. For better or for worse, there may have been this ongoing assumption that this 'heaven on earth' was forever. I was not being prepared for life on the outside, I was being prepared for life on the inside, and to that end, it was probably an ok education.

I felt like I had a place, a role in the Love Family. I was a student, and even though the academics were hit and miss in some ways, I was there to learn whatever they were going to give me. I appreciated that there were those who were fighting for the kids, trying to give us what we needed against the odds. I tried to be a good girl. I was one of the first ones to raise my hand with the answer when a teacher asked a question. I tried to set a good example for the younger children. As one of the older ones, I was always ultra-aware of how children imitate one another and how group dynamics can play out and have such a great impact on the spirit of a group. I could see that on a larger scale with the adults in the community, but I could also see that on a smaller scale with the children.

I am going to end this chapter with a quote from Steve Allen's book called, *Beloved Son; A story of the Jesus Cults*, (1982). Steve Allen was a famous American television personality, musician, composer, actor, comedian, and writer as many people know. He was the first host of the *Tonight Show* and hosted numerous game and variety shows. His book, *Beloved Son*, was just one of many books that he wrote. He wrote over 50 books.

In *Beloved Son*, Steve Allen tries to understand why his son Brian, (aka Logic) joined the Love Family. Steve Allen does not disown him or try to have him kidnapped and deprogrammed. Instead he was supportive of his right to believe as he chose.

Steve Allen visited the Love Family often. He had two grandchildren there, Purity and Liberty. He made comments about the Love Family children in his book. He wrote that our communal upbringing made us "different," but that it provided us with "other values." He observed that the children dressed in "simple, communal attire, strangely reminiscent of both pioneer and early Christian dress." He wrote, "They have not been raised in traditional American schools, not brought up on the mean streets of our large cities, not subjected to television, commercial bombardments, polluted air, loud mindless music."

Steve Allen had made efforts for the school such as buying the Cuisenaire rods and the other ways that he helped the Family. He concluded his observation of the children: "They are sweet, free spirits, though in no way wild or uncontrolled. They laugh readily, have a remarkably well-developed sense of humor for children so young, and are well behaved."

BIBLIOGRAPHY (CHAPTER 10)

Allen, Steve. (1982). *Beloved Son; A Story of the Jesus Cults*. The Bobbs-Merrill Company, Inc.

Bradley, Liesje. (2014). *Placenta Traditions*. Birth to Earth website of New Zealand.

[Bright]. Personal Interview. January 11 and 17, 2002.

Brown, Larry. *Seattle Times*. No Charges Planned in Abduction. August 26, 1973 pg. A16.

Bryant, Hilda. *Seattle Post-Intelligencer*. Love Family is Gaining Ground. Sunday May 14, 1978 A13–14 BM.

Clever, Dick. *Seattle Post-Intelligencer*. Strange Tale of Filmed Kidnap. August 15, 1973 A3

[Definition and Eve]. Joint Personal Interviews. June 27 and September 30, 2001.

[Ethan]. Personal Interview, January 3, 2002.

[Ethan] Personal Interview with Chuck LeWarne. February 18, 1998.

Hinterberger, John. *Seattle Times*. A Minesweeper for the Love Family: Owners for Kathy Jo. January 31, 1976 A1.

Israel, Understanding. Personal Interview, February 14, 2004.

Merriam-Webster, Incorporated, (On-line Dictionary).

Ruppert, Ray. Seattle Times. Sure Israel Travels Halfway Around World to Rejoin Commune. October 20, 1976 B11.

Ruppert, Ray. *Seattle Times*. The Stress of Faith. April 17, 1975 C2.

Ruppert, Ray. *Seattle Times*. Sure Israel Taken From Sect—by Court. May 12, 1976. A9.

Shrief, Lynnea. (2016). *Placenta history*. Independent Placenta Encapsulation Network (IPEN). 2016.

[Zarah]. Personal Interview. December 12, 2001.

CHAPTER 11

Shared Parenting: Moms and Dads Galore

Before I came to the Love Family, I was living in a traditional, nuclear family. It was the most "normal" family I had had at that point. I had a mom, Karen, a step dad, Marty, and a little brother, Forest. I think warmly of those times when Marty would hunt for small animals with our wolf-dog Yusef, and my mom would grind flour to make bread. I sometimes helped gather kindling in the woods or helped take care of Forest.

But the moment that we stepped foot inside the Front Door Inn on Queen Anne Hill, our lives were transformed. I was no longer, Lois, Karen's daughter; I was known on my own merits as Rachel, Family member, kid.

I had a new family now, hundreds. I was now a part of a huge group of kids, who were like my brothers and sisters, and who I lived with and played with each day.

My biological mother, who was now going by the name Elkanah, was also a member of my new family, but her role in my life was nothing more than my "earth" mother. Earth mother means the woman who gave birth to me—not considered in the realm of the spiritual plane. My new spiritual family was all that mattered now. There wasn't any special significance placed on my relationship with her. In other words, she did not have primary parental authority over me and was not taking care of my basic needs. I was being raised communally now, living in a society that idealized the ideas of cooperative or shared parenting.

In the following chapter, I'm going to be discussing the Love Family's version of shared parenting. Who took care of the children? How did they do it? What was it like for me, living in a community that espoused these ideals?

How shared parenting worked out in practice was that certain members were designated to take care of the children. If Elkanah had been inspired that way, she could have volunteered herself to be a part of the kids' scene with other designated caretakers, but that would not have given her a special relationship with me. She would be taking care of me and everybody else's kids, and it was a huge group of kids. While it was 15 or so when we first got there in 1975, it was many more than that over time. Like I said earlier, there were 269 children in the Love Family (while I was there), 134 of whom were born there. Many more children were born after I left in 1983.

So, during the time when I was there, even if Elkanah had taken more of a role with the kids' scene, she still would not have been making the primary decisions.

She would have been under the authority of Understanding and other primary caretakers, who in turn would have been under Love's authority. If she had chosen to oppose anything that was happening to me or to the other kids, she did not have any authority to challenge it. Everyone, including the moms, were focused on the dominant theme, Love's vision for the children. If there were moms who were involved, they were helpers, delegated to certain tasks such as helping to make snacks or helping the kids get cleaned up or gathered onto a bus.

Elkanah was helping with Forest's class. It was more common for the moms to be involved if their kids were younger. Part of it was her personality; if she had been a super entertainer, a teacher, or talented with large numbers of children, she could've been more involved as a caretaker, like Understanding or Ethan, but she wasn't. Even then, Ethan and Understanding were still under the dominion of Love and their attention had to be distributed to many.

Usually the moms were more involved with the kids' scene when their kids were young. But even if a mom was helping with the kids, it wouldn't have been accepted for her to give her own child special attention. That's not how it worked. It was communal.

I wasn't the only one who was there whose biological parents were no longer directly involved. When I first got there and became a part of the kid scene, it didn't take long for me to get to know everyone. Many of the kids were parentless. The group now acted as a surrogate family. This was true for those kids whose parents had dropped them off there and for those kids whose parents were there but not involved. Although, as I said, for the babies and young kids, their mothers were more involved in the households, but as the child got older, that was less and less true.

I was close with my peers. There was a year when I got a diary as a gift, but I didn't see it as mine, I just assumed that even though I got it, that I would share it. Every other aspect of our lives was shared. It was our diary. At slumber parties, we all would take turns writing in it. Although, my best friend Heaven and I took more turns than the others, until she got her own diary later on. Close enough to share a diary—that's how close we were.

One reason why we were all so close was because communal ties had replaced family ties. Love was trying to limit outside influences, the outside influences of close bonds of attachment between parents and their kids. How could he create a society where everyone shared one mind in Christ, if each member had their own separate families who would be a constant distraction? How could the parent serve him if the parent's total focus was their own child?

In general, members were discouraged from keeping up with their families or friends outside of the community too, although, if they were friendly, they could visit us—and I mean all of us. If my gramma Phyllis wanted to visit, she would not just go walking up to the house where my mom lived; she would have to go through the "center." She would go to the Front Door Inn, then Love would be notified through a messenger. I heard there had been complaints that relatives had come to visit but hadn't even seen their offspring while they were there. A lot of parents of adult members were heart broken. I can't imagine raising a child to then have them change their name and identity and choose a lifestyle that excluded me from their lives.

I heard there was one point, and this was early on, when Love asked members to write their families and tell them off, that they had new families now. From what I heard, a lot of members did it.

Visitors did not usually get one-on-one time with their relative. They would be expected to participate in group life during their stay. When my gramma Phyllis came, she would not always be hosted by my mom, she would be hosted by multiple members, sometimes by Love himself. Love often as-signed Wisdom to host her, who was one of the "oldest" members; Wisdom was graying and was likely old enough to be a grandmother herself. Other times, especially towards the end, my gramma would just be hosted by the household where my mom was living. At the very end, when Love was absent a lot and when things became disorganized, my gramma would take Elkanah off the Ranch, take her into Arlington to shop or out to eat. I sometimes got to go too. But that wasn't the norm.

Communication with outsiders was done either my mail or person to person. Letters to outsiders were personally delivered and not usually mailed, especially early on. Remember I talked earlier about how Consideration hand delivered a Love Family Charter to Billy Graham. It wasn't sent. They had to hitchhike across the country to deliver it. A member would also sometimes have to hitchhike across the country to deliver a message to a relative.

Even within the Family, Love would send messages out via personal messengers. That was how people knew what was going on from day to day. That would mean that the messenger would have to go to every household with the message. The messages came from top down too, not the other way around.

When we still had the property in Alaska, there were letters sent back and forth with updates about life. The letters were sent from everyone at one outpost to, or from, everyone at the other outpost. I once saw on the letters that were sent from the Hawaii outpost to the Front Door Inn. It was passed around, so everyone could see it. It was a warm update about things happening such as a baby that was born and some of the activities that were happening. Letters were essential, because it was not custom to use phones in the Love Family.

Incoming mail also went through the center. Even though the Family owned many houses, various properties and outposts, all mail went to one address where it would be read or opened under Love's guidance for review as to how it would be handled.

The Love Family was structured in a way that discouraged interaction with outsiders, even family, which led to everyone being even more dependent on one another to meet their needs for a sense of belonging and connection.

Essentially, I had been cut off from the opportunity to build relationships with biological relatives outside of the community. I had a dad out there; I had an aunt, uncles, cousins, grandparents, not including good friends that my parents had known who I never saw again. The only way that I could've had a relationship with them was if they had come to the Love Family and participated in the life. A lot of relatives said, 'No way!' My uncles, for example, thought it was "too weird" and never returned after their first visit.

The only relative that came to visit was my gramma Phyllis. Her visits, though, said something about who she was. For someone in her generation, she was very progressive in her thinking. As I discussed, she had been involved in the early Natural Birth Movement,' which, at that time, was basically Lamaze exercises and a midwife instead of a doctor, but that was considered radical. Nowadays, that's not uncommon. She had also been involved in political efforts for voting rights of Blacks in New Hampshire, Virginia.

My grandmother was the 1st Vice President in the Women's League of Voters at the State level. She remembered that they had to hire security at the voting booths. At one rally, she and a group of women she was working with had a rock thrown at them through a window. Attached to the rock was a note.

"It basically said, 'Get lost,' Phyllis remembered. "I was from the North; I was a damn Yankee!" The unsafe conditions of her activities were the main reason my grandpa insisted that they move out of state to Washington. She also was progressive in her spiritual thinking and was into a lot of New Age and alternative spiritual ideas that would've made her more open-minded to the Love Family's way of thinking.

Phyllis really looked forward to coming for her visits where she was hosted by friendly people.

"I loved going out and getting all those hugs," was one of the things she would say she missed the most after we left in the mid-eighties.

They wanted her to join. No, she wasn't going to do that, but she was once talked into staying overnight. She was set up in her own bed in one the Army tents. She never did it again and said it was the most uncomfortable night she ever had.

My gramma Phyllis was introverted and kept most of her thoughts and feelings to herself, but occasionally she would say things: "There were some really good ideas," she commented one time about the Love Family. I knew, for her, that meant a lot, because she was really "into ideas."

Other than my grandmother who would visit on occasion, like many members, my communal ties were all I had.

There wasn't a lot of mixing with outsiders; the Love Family was its own secret society, mostly cut off from the outside world. The adult members took extra precautions to make sure I was protected from exposure to Worldly influences. That was the main reason for a lot of things. It was the reason I didn't get a lot of TV growing up. For the most part, there were no televisions in the Love Family. On occasion though, I could see a film. The films were carefully screened for the children to make sure they did not contradict the Love Family belief structure. And this would be true of any child raised in a strict, religious family, I suppose, but for me, my religious family was just very unusual.

I was told that Logic was able, with the help of his dad, Steve Allen, to acquire a 16mm motion picture projector, which gave us the ability to check out films on occasion from the local library. I saw a clay animation film called "Closed Mondays," a seven-minute film about a man who visits a museum who sees works of art come to life. We also, as I have mentioned, saw the Beatles Yellow Submarine. We saw Fantasia. These were all films that we saw early on, when we had school with Dedication in the yellow, middle house in Serious's Area.

Sometime after that, it might've been a couple years later, there ended up being a television in Love's big house. They kept it locked up in Cube City. Then eventually, years after that, towards the end and just before I left, there was another one that was kept at the Ranch, up in the Barn for group showings.

That's how we got to see the musical drama, *Oliver*, the 1968 version. It was rented through the King County library system. They thought it would be beneficial because we would learn about homeless children in an orphanage. Plus, since it was a musical, it was thought that it would be beneficial to some of the older kids who were now singing and performing as part of the Love Family's drama group.

It was the next evening after we had seen *Oliver*. There was a group of us running around together playing. We wandered into the storeroom into the lower portion of the Barn where the animal feed and bulk foods were kept. We were playing in the storeroom and saw that there were huge bins full of nuts. We stuffed our pockets full of them. We weren't doing it to steal, like some of the adults thought, we were doing it because we were pretending to be squirrels. But they had heard us singing earlier that day "You've got to pick a pocket or two."

We all got in trouble once it was discovered we had taken the nuts. Understanding remembered it clearly.

"It was a scandal!" Understanding says. "There was an emergency elders' meeting where it was determined that you kids had stolen the nuts. You had seen *Oliver*, and it was all the media's fault."

We all got in big trouble and got swats! It was the big kids, mostly, about eight to 10 of us. It was really fun playing squirrel till we got in trouble. I was terrified as we all lined up for the swat. One by one, we filed into the back bedroom of the Ranch house. Strength did the deed with the polished rod that he kept there just for that purpose. Strength was a burley looking guy, tall, heavyset man with a ruddy complexion. He had shoulder length, thin, wispy strawberry blond hair and a beard and mustache. He was a big guy and always had this expression on his face that was like a scowl. He wasn't mean though. Strength was a very loving guy, a very high-status elder—he was the head of the Ranch. I heard years later that he did not appreciate being designated to give the swat. It hurt, of course, but the fear was worse, as I waited in line for my turn. I had to wait for like eight or more kids to go before me, and I saw each one as they left his room. Terrifying! I guess we should never have taken the nuts, but I don't think any of us thought it was the gravely serious situation that it was made out to be. After that, there was more censorship which meant even less television than we already had which was hardly any.

That was a good example of how decisions about our behavior and the discipline that might result, were often made—by the community, not our parents. We no longer belonged to our parents; we belonged to the community.

"The Love Family gave people a chance to take on the spirit of adoption," says Ethan. "It was an opportunity. I was able to do that, freely. Whoever I lived with, I adopted them as if they were my own."

Consideration wrote about the nature of the relationship between children and their parents:

"Children did not have one person that they called "mommy" or "daddy," he wrote. "We saw them as our children for we were all their parents in the Lord. They were God's children. When a child came with someone they were usually separated from the mother unless the mother was nursing. It was not good for the child to be dependent on one person (263)."

I already discussed earlier that when a couple came to the Family, they gave up their former relationships to become a new person that was a part of a larger community. They also gave up their former relationships with their parents and other relatives and friends. Well, when people joined, they also gave up their parental bonds and any idea of ownership over their children that they might have had.

The past was really the past now. Larry/Consideration wrote about the loss of his parents when he wrote:

"I called them Betty and Abe, for my new mother was New Jerusalem and my Father was God, and they had simply been my earthly parents that had given birth to the temple I was in, meaning my body. They did not understand this." (144–45).

I learned this too. It was explained to me that Elkanah was my "earth mother." I came to learn that she was no longer the most important person in my life. Love was.

Consideration's parents tried to accept it, but they had a hard time, and it may have led to their decision to hire Ted Patrick to kidnap him out of the Love Family. They were convinced that he was in enough danger that it was necessary to remove him by force.

One of the reasons my mom had explained that she had left Alaska was because she had followed our friend Suzanne to the Love Family. Even though we had been close to Suzanne before, once we joined, it was like that relationship was over. The nature of relationships was different in the Love Family. It was less about personal one-on-one relationships and more about each person's relationship to everyone as a group. I did not see that people had personal friendships, at least not openly.

Suzanne became Radiance early on and was in Love's household, serving Truthfulness. Because of that, she was way higher up in the food chain than Elkanah, my mom who was at the bottom. Radiance was friendly after that, but she never acknowledged that we had anything special with her before we joined. Even though that was just the way things were in the Love Family, it was a bit hurtful, and I never could fully understand it. When I saw her, I thought back to the times that she had taken me skiing behind the cabin and how she had visited at my school in Anchor Point, but now, when she saw me, she smiled genuinely, but it was empty and without recognition of our previous connection. That was then, this was now.

Exclusive relationships and attachments were problematic because they were seen as a threat to communal ties within the group, as were the emotional attachments between parents and their children. Most communal utopian groups throughout time, have had some form of shared parenting.

There have been great philosophers and thinkers who have proposed radical ideas in how to restructure family life.

The famous Ralph Waldo Emerson was an American essayist, lecturer and poet who led the Transcendentalist movement in the mid-19th century and wrote the popular book Walden. Emerson was a close friend of Henry David Thoreau and believed that close ties between parents and children were incompatible with true communal life (Muncy, 1974).

Another influential thinker was French philosopher Francois Marie Charles Fourier who wrote about utopian socialism. He thought that the ties between parent and child must be broken in the interest of human happiness (Owen & Fourier, 1969, pp. 209–10, 214).

Even Plato—In "The Republic," which is one of the most influential works of all time, both intellectually and historically, lists rules for the 'guardians' and proposed that for the ideal state, children should be reared by the state and never even told who their parents were.

I have tended to be more drawn to more recent philosophies regarding attachments in human relationships. Attachments are not something to discard; they are important to human survival. They are protective bonds between family members that contribute greatly to our sense of self and compel us to help another survive. An attachment between a mother and child or even between adults in a loving relationship—when there is an attachment, the mother, by instinct, is bound to protect the child. The child, who is properly attached, looks to the mother to fulfill its needs. The husband bound to protect the wife from abuse, predators, whatever. Without exclusive relationships of attachment, people are left vulnerable. But are exclusive emotional attachments between people a threat to communal life?

Burrhus Frederick Skinner thought so. He was considered a pioneer of modern behaviorism. In his influential book, *Walden II*, he discusses an experimental utopian community that is run by scientists. The scientists attempt, through behavioral engineering, to create a utopian community. They dissolve the nuclear family by placing the responsibility of child-rearing in the hands of the larger community.

In *Walden II*, B.F. Skinner wrote: "We have to attenuate [make thinner] the child-parent relation for several reasons. Group care is better than parental care. In the old pre-scientific days, the early education of the child could be left to the parents…But with the rise of a science of behavior all is changed…"

The goal, according to Skinner, was to have every adult member of *Walden II* regard all the children as his own, and to have every child think of every adult as his parent. A parent was never to single out his own child for special favors; to do so exclusively was "taboo." The idea was that a child would never receive any services or special favors that it didn't also frequently receive from others. "We have untied the apron strings," Skinner wrote, "Love and affection are psychological and cultural, and blood relationships can be happily forgotten." (Skinner, 1948. p.131–133) Really?

Walden II wasn't just a book, there were actual intentional communities that existed such as Twin Oaks (1967) and others, that were based on the behaviorist principles of this book. Plus, the ideas put forth in *Walden II* and many other books since, regarding restructuring the nuclear family and society in general, were idealized and very influential, especially during the resurgence of countercultural groups of the 1960s, 1970s and the 1980s.

Walden II has been typically referred to as "a communal utopian group," and even though there are stark differences between *Walden II* and the Love Family, surprisingly, there are similarities. Was the Love Family a communal utopian group?

The Love Family could be described loosely as communal, because it was a group of people who lived together, worked together and shared everything in common. But it doesn't make it into the 'commune' boat because most definitions of commune specify that a commune is non-hierarchical, that people are equal, including men and women. As my chapter on the hierarchy described, the Love Family was very hierarchical. It had a leader, and that leader had absolute, unchecked power.

Then was it a cult? According to most definitions, a cult is a religious or social group with socially deviant, novel, extreme or dangerous beliefs or practices. One could argue that the Love Family fit that definition.

Of course, the problem with the term cult is that it's a subjective term that lacks a consistent definition. It has been controversial and is often used pejoratively as an attack against groups with whom one disagrees.

But just because the Love Family easily meets most definitions of the term cult, doesn't mean that the Love Family also couldn't be classified in other ways. Other definitions can be used more neutrally and in a wider context, such as intentional community.

According to Wikipedia, an intentional community is a planned residential community designed from the start to have a high degree of social cohesion and teamwork. The members of an intentional community typically hold a common social, political, religious, or spiritual vision and often follow an alternative lifestyle. According to this definition, the Love Family was an intentional community.

Another term that seems to fit is a 'new religious movement,' or NRM. An NRM is a religious community or spiritual group of modern origins, which has a peripheral place within its society's dominant religious culture. Yep.

It could also be classified as a 'utopian community,' which has been more often applied to communities in America in the 18th and 19th centuries such as the Oneida community (1848–1880) and many others. Utopian communities, led by charismatic leaders, who had high religious or secular moral ideals, often experimented wildly with different models of government, marriage, labor and wealth.

The Love Family was not easy to define or package up neatly. There was an African American man who had visited the Love Family for a few days one year. He was a prominent community leader based out of Harlem. Years later, I had the opportunity to ask him what he had thought of the Love Family during his visit. There was a long silent pause as he struggled for the right words, then he answered with a hint of sarcasm and a chuckle:

"It was totally "Out-of-the-box," he says, "Here they had come from a background of wealth and privilege, and given all that up…"

Here's another one: How about a 'revitalization movement?' A revitalization movement is defined as: "a deliberate, organized, conscious effort by members of a society to construct a more satisfying culture" (Wallace, 1956: 265). Bingo! One could say that was exactly what the Love Family was trying to do.

Partridge explains that "Revitalization movements are religious movements which arise out of situations of extreme individual and societal stress." These movements arise at times "when it becomes increasingly difficult for individual members of a society to follow culturally patterned ideals, behaviors, and beliefs." (Partridge, 1973, pg. 77)

As a child raised in the Love Family, I have learned that I have to just accept that where I came from isn't going to be easily defined. I don't think it has to be. It's OK with me that it doesn't fit neatly into any one classification. To me, that's just how life is.

No matter how a community is defined, many of the more well-known groups, were more explicit than the Love Family about attenuating (making thinner) exclusive relationships between members.

In the Oneida community, the children were raised and schooled communally. They practiced what was called 'complex marriage,' which was that they discouraged exclusive, possessive relationships between the sexes. "Instead there would be a complex marriage in which all loved each other and placed the concerns of the community above their private selfish interests" (as cited in Foster, 1997, pg. 88, 262). That possessive love also applied to relationships between parents and their children.

Oneida children did not belong to their parents, they belonged to God and the community. "From the time they were fifteen months old, they all lived together and were taught the principles of Christian conduct and Bible communism by the foster fathers and mothers assigned to duty at the Children's House." (Klaw, 1993, pg. 142).

Parental love in the Oneida community was seen as "possessive love," even "idolatrous." Adults in the Oneida community were encouraged to befriend and even make protégés of other people's children. This was seen as healthier because they were untainted by possessive parental love.

"Letting parents raise their own children would divide the community into little clusters of adults and children whose loyalty to one another must inevitably conflict with the greater loyalty they owed, if they wished to be true Christians, to God and to his appointed deputy at Oneida," (147).

"A mother's natural love for [her] own child was called 'philoprogenitiveness' and was seen as a sign of a bad spirit and was subjected to punishment." (142)

Playing with dolls was not allowed as it was seen as a sign of philoprogenitiveness. "The 'doll spirit' was the same spirit that seduces women to be so taken up with their children that they have no time to attend to Christ." (147–48) There were doll burnings.

At least in the Love Family, there may have been some books burned, but there weren't doll burnings! I would have been very upset to have my one and only hand-made doll that I got one Christmas, burned.

The punishment at Oneida was extended separation. Peirrepont Noyes, the son of the leader who founded Oneida, was raised in the Oneida community and wrote, "I remember my mother's terror lest my crying be heard. She knew that Father Noyes frowned on any excess of parental affection as he did on all forms of 'special love,' and she feared that such demonstrations might deprive her of some of my regular visits." (Noyes, pg. 66)

The children in Oneida were taught a song by Oneida's first schoolmistress who the children called, "Mother."

> *"I-spirit*
> *With me never shall stay,*
> *We-spirit*
> *Makes us happy and gay."* (Klaw, 147)

That song sounds like something I might have been taught, if the Love Family had been around a 100 years earlier.

Another 19th century socialistic community called, New Harmony or the Owenites, followed the utopian vision of one man, Robert Owen. Owen believed that a new utopian, social order could be brought about by controlling individual character. Children as young as one-year old were placed in the new infant school with the purpose of "replacing initial negative family influence with a positive environment for instilling desired values and fashioning superior character." (Brewer, 1997, p.94)

The Shakers had similar ideas of reconstructing family relationships. They were another religious sect of the 19th century that had branched off from the Quakers in England. They called them the 'Shakers' because they danced ecstatically and spoke in tongues. The Shakers regarded marriage and possession of property as symptoms of a lower order (Holloway, 1966). When families joined, husbands and wives became brothers and sisters, and children were cared for and educated communally (Brewer, 1997). If parents brought children, they were separated from them, and children could only see their parents once a year, privately in the presence of an elder. (Holloway, 1966). This was seen as "shielding the children from the unwanted negative influence of their parents and families." (Brewer, 1997, p.114)

In the Love Family, I often felt like a free floater. In other words, because we all lived so closely, I was free to live in whatever household I wanted. I was known to be well behaved and helpful, and it seemed that I was welcomed no matter where I went. When we lived in the circle of tents, which was the second year (1978) when all the Army tents were being expanded into shacktents, I was invited to live in Love's household for a while. I stayed in the tent behind the sanctuary tent where some of Love's kids were staying with their guardians. I just chose to go live there, I think because Vision lived there, and I wanted to live with her for a while.

That same year, I ended up living with Certain and Goodness who by this time were no longer the elders at the Front Door Inn where I had first met them. Now they had a large, green Army tent that was set up on a wooden platform that was 3 or 4 feet off the ground. It was one of the higher platforms than the other household tents because we used to play under it. I had decided that I now wanted to live with my mom, who I learned was staying there as well. While I was there, Elkanah and I began to have this sort of contentious relationship. She and I were getting into these little arguments. The other householders started complaining about it. I guess it was irritating to listen to, so it was decided that I should go live elsewhere.

That's when I was sent to go live in Frankness's household who had a totally different scene, which was just past the sauna and 2 households over, in the same field. I was fine with that as the attachment with my mother was not strong anymore. Since her parental authority over me was not recognized by the community, I looked to other members of my family for support now like the teachers and caretakers. I loved Elkanah, but her practically non-existent role in my life was a source of internal conflict. When I was sent to live elsewhere after our conflict, I find it interesting that the first response to conflict between a parent and child was separation. There was no one who took note of it as a sign of a problem. No one asked, What is going on here? Maybe we should look at this. Ethan explained:

"Love made it clear that children would not be living with their parents," he says. "The Family was about overcoming jealousy, overcoming ownership. You were married to everyone. It was all about the value of the tribe. We all take care of everybody."

Understanding agreed and told me that Love talked "frequently" about it:

"'Love talked frequently about it," says Understanding. "He would say, 'the children belong to all of us,' or he would say, 'We have to all take responsibility for the children in the houses.'"

A lot of people helped out with childcare, but mostly, it was designated caretakers, guardians or teachers who took care of me. Shared parenting in the Love Family meant that some people got more of their fair share of taking care of kids, it seemed, and others were not sharing enough.

Ethan got plenty of his fair share. He was not just a teacher in the Love Family school, he also took care of kids when they were not in school, as a caretaker and guardian. That's what he did the entire time he was there.

There was this game we played with Ethan. He called it, "Hike and go seek." We would all be hiking down the path through the woods. There might have been anywhere from 15 to 20 or more kids there. I would run ahead with half the kids and hide no more than ten feet from the path. If Ethan couldn't find us before he passed us, then we got to go hide again. We played that game all the way home from King Lake one time.

Before Ethan came along, it was just Understanding and her helpers. I had gone to Cherry Hill with a group of kids and Understanding to help pick fruit. I was around eight or so. It was one of my first harvest seasons, so probably spring 1976. Ethan remembered that one night there was a Mexican who came into the kids' tent and was bothering us, so he was assigned to move into the tent with us. He guarded the entrance just in case the Mexican came back. There were Mexicans that were picking fruit in nearby orchards.

"Understanding was like a mother hen," Ethan says. "No one else wanted to be around the children because it wasn't an important part of the Family," he explained. "It was a necessary thing; they had kids and they loved the children, but they didn't want to spend time with them. I saw a niche for myself that I could easily get into."

From then on, Ethan was a regular part of the kids' scene. "They were shuffled around a lot," Ethan remembered. "In other words, they weren't with their parents. Love would say, 'Okay, take all the kids over to the Roza for the summer...' I was with them; I was the person doing it," Ethan explained.

"We had a bus load of kids...It was like providing a service," Ethan says. "We are taking your kids to summer camp—so you can do what you need to do."

"No one wanted to watch the kids," Understanding explained, "so I began showing up every day to help out. I saw that I had to have a clean enough scene around me so that they could be children and have a childhood," she says.

Understanding told me that at one-time, there were 100 children in her care. She was the legal guardian for a few of them.

"Some of the moms snuck out in the middle of the night so I wasn't able to get papers, Understanding explained, "but many of the moms would sign a paper that gave me the complete authority to seek medical care and to make all decisions in their absence."

In other words, there were moms who came, dropped their kids off, and then left the Family for good, leaving them in Understanding's care. Maybe these moms felt that the Love Family had more to offer their children than they could offer them, or maybe they just saw an opportunity, a place where somebody would take care of their kids for free.

When Understanding came to the Love Family, she saw a role for herself right away, taking care of children. She just started showing up every day for what the Family called, "kid watch." When Love saw her gift with children, he set her up in one of the houses that became known as the Kids' House. From then on, Understanding was like Love's chief nanny and head caretaker for children. In the Love Family, the term "caretaker" was used a couple of ways: It was used for the chief yards keepers who lived in the 'caretaker's house.' But it was more often used for anyone who was in a role taking care of children.

Understanding made sure the kids in her care were fed. When I lived at the Kids' House with her, I ate the food that the community ate, like rice and oatmeal and other community staples, but in addition to that, I ate things that only Understanding was provided like eggs, granola, cheese, peanut butter, applesauce, milk and other things I needed because I was a growing child.

Who provided Understanding with these foods for the kids? People did not have paying jobs in the Love Family, at least for most of the years that I was there, so if no one was working, then how were we eating? Again, it was a shared parenting philosophy in terms of how the children were being cared for and fed. There were not enough donations from in-coming members to feed the Family.

A man named Sure was a big part of the reason that anyone had food in the Love Family. He was a man of medium height, with long, bushy, dark brown hair. It was because of Sure that I ate in the Love Family. Sure helped make sure that Understanding had food at the Kids' House, but he also made sure that the entire Love Family had food.

Sure was an elder and a householder, but it seemed his most important role was making sure that the Love Family was supplied with staples, bulk foods such as rice, oatmeal, beans, soy sauce, olive oil, and other foods that were a regular part of our diet. He very cleverly developed relationships with large grocers and warehouses, where he would buy food wholesale from them and resell it to small grocers. Within the network that he built, there were also relationships where he would trade for goods, some of which were for profit as well. It was through Sure that the Family got to know Chuck the Cheese Man, a Jewish wholesaler.

On Holy Day, I ate delicious cheeses that we got from Chuck the

Cheese Man. It was Gjetost and Jarlsberg cheeses. Jarlsberg cheese was like Swiss cheese with holes but it was a mild, slightly sweet, buttery flavored cheese. Gjetost was my favorite. It was a dark brown Norwegian goat cheese with a fudge-like consistency and a slightly sweet, almost caramel like flavor. Just one little piece could last a couple minutes in my mouth since it would melt slowly.

Apparently, Sure and other Family men like Happiness, Zest and others would put in a certain number of hours of labor in exchange for certain items like cheese, flour and other items that the Family needed. We also had a relationship with certain dairies like 'Country Charm,' where I heard that Steadfast and Menahem would go and work on their farm in exchange for milk for the Family. These relationships that were forged and that helped feed the Family were ongoing relationships that were maintained for all the years that I lived in the Family.

Eventually, Sure developed a little health food grocery store that brought in profit for Love and for the Family. He turned the basement of a house that the Family rented on the corner, which was less than one block from the Front Door Inn, into a little grocery store, called, 'The Village Store.' There were fresh produce and other fine foods, and there were other items on the shelves too like natural soaps, creams and lip balms etc.

My friend Sarai lived with Sure's household for a while and I would visit her there. He was an elder, and his household stayed in the upper portion of the house, above the store. Most everyone in Sure's household helped in the Village Store. Sarai and I were put to work at once. I had to weigh out certain foods like nuts and dates on a scale and place the sticker labels with the prices on the bags after they were weighed. Then I would help put them on the shelves. I enjoyed helping. While I was there, she and I got to eat the most delicious toast I'd ever had. The bread that we used for the toast was one of the loaves that Ishmael made. Ishmael made bread for the Family and it was also sold at the Village Store. He was said to have made 100 loaves a day, some of which were sent to the Kids' House for kids like me. Ishmael was a short, balding man with shoulder length, wispy blond hair and a strawberry blond beard that never grew much. He wore a long, green apron while he baked and because he was such a short man, the apron reached down to the floor like a very long, oversized dress.

Sarai and I ate the toast with green mint jelly, something I'd never seen before. Sure had the most delicious foods in his household cupboards too. There were little jars of things I didn't even recognize. Sure was the food guy, so him having fine foods that no one else had, seemed to make sense. Although, I wondered how it could be, since in the Family, everyone ate the same foods, usually. Love ate better, more fanciful foods with more variety, but he was sort of a special case, being that he was the king and all. I didn't think about it much, I was just there to enjoy my time with Sarai. While I was there, I got to know Sebrahim, who was sanctioned to Sure. She was very beautiful and was from Holland; She looked like one of those porcelain dolls, I had thought. She had very light, golden blond hair and bright, blue eyes with pale, ivory skin; she had a strong accent too and taught me how to say, 'I love you' and other simple phrases in Dutch.

Sure had the name Sure for a reason. He was sure he wanted to be in the Love Family. Sure, like Dedication and like Consideration, was one of those few people who were unlucky enough to have parents that could afford to hire Ted Patrick, the famous cult deprogrammer, to kidnap them out of the Love Family. In Sure's case, there were several unsuccessful attempts to abduct him.

The third attempt was unsuccessful, like the previous two, but it was at least more successful than the others due to the time it took for him to escape the deprogrammers and return to the Love Family—a full year and a half! It happened right after we left Alaska and flew to Seattle to visit at the Front Door Inn, so late summer, early fall of 1975. That's when Sure was kidnapped from the Love Family homestead in Homer.

Definition, my former teacher told me what happened. He knew because before he joined, he had gone up to Alaska to work on the pipeline and somehow had made it up to Homer where he met the Family, so he was living there too when the attempt happened.

Definition and the other Love Family members who were living at the homestead, had all just gotten out of the sauna and were all going towards the tent to get dressed when they got an unexpected visit from six or seven Anchorage Policemen with shotguns in full riot gear. There was a plane circling overhead that was in communication with the men on the ground. Sure snuck out the back and hid, and it then became like a "Mexican Stand-off," because the police refused to leave until they had Sure with them.

Sure's father had paid off an Anchorage Superior Court Judge $100,000 to get a Writ of Habeas Corpus to force Sure to leave with them. Sure was the son of a very wealthy Jewish man who lived in Boston, and who owned a lot of real estate right around Harvard. As Sure was hiding out, the sergeant convinced Frankness, who was the elder there during this time, that all Sure had to do was appear in court and say that he was not being held against his will, that he was not being coerced. Then he would be released, and he could come back to the Love Family if he chose.

Frankness convinced Sure to come out of hiding and go with them. Once they had him in court, Sure was not allowed to speak, and he was sent under armed guard back to Boston to his father. He was held captive there in his father's mansion for a month. Just like they did with Consideration, they screwed down all the windows and made the house like a jail while the deprogrammers tried to convince him out of his beliefs about the Love Family. Sure was argumentative and told them the Love Family were the people of Israel. Sure's father said, 'You don't know anything about Israel. You want to go to Israel?' Sure agreed, and his father flew him to Israel where he was stripped of his passport and all money. They put him in a yeshiva for wayward Jews, where they would reeducate him on what it meant to be a Jew. Sure's father was able to keep a close eye on him because Sure's brother had already emigrated to Israel and was a member of the Mossad, which was the Israeli Intelligence Agency, similar to the CIA in the U.S. This fact made it even harder for Sure to sneak around in Israel.

Sure was there in the yeshiva for a month or two until he found a way to escape. He was illegal without his passport, so he went to the American Embassy and got his passport updated. He found a house with ex-patriots and was able to get a job in a pizza parlor for a while, trying to save enough money for airfare. Unfortunately, once he had enough money, he was unable to fly out of there because the Israeli police had him under surveillance. So instead, he went to Haifah, a shipping port, and snuck aboard a ship and went down and hid in the hold. The ship went to somewhere near Athens in Greece. Once he was in Greece, he hitchhiked across Europe to Southern France where he worked in a vineyard and saved enough money for a plane ticket. He then flew to Boston and went and saw his grandfather who empathized with his situation and bought him a ticket to Seattle. It took a full year and half before he was able to return to the Love Family.

I already knew about what happened to Sure, because I had heard about it while I was in the Family, most people knew, but Definition had a lot of the finer details since he had been there when Sure was taken and had talked to Sure at length when he had finally returned.

The newspapers were also following the story. The *Seattle Times* wrote several articles about Sure's ordeal. All of the information in the articles confirms the details that Definition gave me about what happened. One article was titled, "Sure Israel travels half way around the world to rejoin commune." In the article, Sure talked about what drove him to the lengths he went through to return to the Love Family. He was quoted as saying, "[The Love Family] is where I can live my ideals. I love everyone here. This is definitely my home." (*Seattle Times* Oct 20, 1976 B11) See also, *Seattle Times*, Thursday April 17, 1975 pg. C2 and *Seattle Times* Wednesday May 12, 1976 pg. A9.

Sure's pilgrimage to Israel didn't exactly work out the way his father wanted it to. These kidnappings just irritate me, because here they were these grownups with all the rights and privileges that come along with being a legal adult, when their parents were still holding on, unable to let go of the power, and here I was a real, authentic, genuine, bona fide kid, and no one was trying to kidnap me. I am glad Sure made it back though. Here was a man who went to great lengths to be in the Love Family, then he had such an important role as someone who worked to make sure the Family was fed, including the children.

I am sure without him, it might not have worked as well as it did, but it didn't matter, because I was living in a community that believed the best way to live was to get away from money and just 'live on faith.' When people would join, they would turn in money or properties, and it was seen in spiritual terms, that God was looking out for us.

The whole idea was to break away, at least as much as possible, from the economic cycle. I heard many times people talking about getting away from the "rat race." I wasn't sure what they meant back then, other than it being just another pejorative term applied to life outside the community.

I understand now that what they were talking about was a society, with people racing to get ahead financially, like rats in a maze, competing to get the most cheese. It could be seen as an endless, self-defeating, or pointless pursuit that leaves little time for relaxation or enjoyment.

In the Love Family, there was no hamster cage treadmill. I was learning very young that "stuff" wasn't important, it was just considered superficial and had no spiritual redeeming value. If we just had faith, everything that we needed would be provided; but we still had to eat, although people went on fasts just to prove that we didn't even need food either. I needed to eat!

On a most basic level, I think everyone knew we needed food. The Family found creative ways to make sure there was enough for everyone. Sure's food trade was a big part of that, but there were also other tremendous efforts to barter and trade for certain things that were needed.

Part of what we did to help feed the Family was our efforts in the orchards of Eastern Washington.

We had relationships with people who owned orchards and large farms. These relationships were set up long before I came to the Family and remained in place every year that I was there. We would ask if we could glean in exchange for picking in their orchards for them. A large group of members would be sent each season to help with the harvest. Gleaning is the ancient practice of collecting the leftover fruits and vegetables from a harvest and providing them to the needy.

The custom has its roots in the Book of Leviticus with God's command to Moses:

> "And when ye reap the harvest of your land, thou shalt not make clean riddance of the corners of thy field when thou reapest, neither shalt thou gather any gleaning of thy harvest: thou shalt leave them unto the poor, and to the stranger: I am the LORD your God." Le 23:22

References to gleaning are littered throughout the Bible: De 24:21; Mic 7:1; Ob 1:5; Jer 49:9, 6:9; Isa 17:6, 24:13; Jud 8:2; Le 19:9, 19:10; Ru 2:2, 2:3, 2:7, 2:8, 2:15, 2:16, 2:17, 2:18, 2:19, 2:23.

Dr Winterscheid, Goodwin, and Bob Lincoln were some of the names of the men who owned the orchards where we worked, but there were many others. They let us camp in their orchards and pick fruit. We were also friends with a guy named Gonzalez who had a tomato farm.

Understanding usually took the kids to help out during the summers. The kids and I would help pick cherries, apricots, peaches, tomatoes, grapes, asparagus, and other fruits and vegetables. A lot of what we gleaned was sent back to the Family in Seattle and the Ranch in Arlington. Sometimes we would help them harvest for money, and Love would send a portion of it to Strength at the Ranch to buy feed for the horses or for milk when we did not have relationships with the dairy farmers.

We were also gleaners for a couple named Fred and Sharie Prior. The land was on the Columbia River. We would trade labor for their potatoes. The Love Family called that place, "Potato Heaven." We got a little bit of money but mostly it was a labor trade that helped feed the family.

Once, I got to go with Helpful and Dedication to Potato Heaven to stay for a couple of weeks. Dinah was there too, who was a girl around my age. They let Dinah and I help separate the dirt clods from the potatoes as they went by on the conveyor belt. We even got a ride on a huge tractor. I had to wear these ugly goggles for the ride. Dedication would have school with us in the house where they had turtles. Dinah and I helped to clean their tank out every couple of days.

On the potato farm, there was an experimental government sprinkler system and bird sanctuary, so throughout the day, I would see these huge flocks of birds go by as the potato diggers went up one way and down the other.

Another way that the Love Family got food was through the cannery. A man known to us as Joab joined, but it was before I got there. The Love Family, just a reminder, was formed in 1968, which meant that it was going on for seven years before I even got there. Anyway, when Joab joined, he brought the cannery.

The cannery did not produce much food to be sold. It mostly was to prepare food into cans and buckets for the Family. At the Kids' House, Understanding would open the five-gallon buckets and put peaches on our oatmeal.

There were times I was sent with the kids to help out at the cannery.

After the peaches came out of the boilers, I was supposed to peel the skin off. Even though the skin slid right off, like a sock, the slippery peaches were so hot that it burned my hands to do it. It was very hard work.

The Love Family also owned vineyards in Eastern Washington, in Granger. The vineyards were next to the Yakima river and were called, Israel Brothers. Israel Brothers made wine and other products for the Family, and also for sale. I never got to go there, even though I saw from the pictures that a lot of kids went there and helped with harvesting the grapes.

It seemed to me that 'having faith' really did work. A lot of free food was given to the Love Family. For example, the warehouses, including Chuck the Cheese Man, would give us foods that were past date. Foods like bananas, tomatoes, fruits, lettuce, and banana's. And when we had bananas boy, we had bananas! It was a smorgasbord! I ate one right after the other, just like I did in Maui at Makena Beach when I was little.

Also, the Love Family received certain quantities of USDA food. We were considered qualified since we provided free food to the public at the Front Door Inn. At the Kids' House, there were cans of applesauce and peanut butter and other food items. My understanding was that the government food was not supposed to be given to the kids at the Kids' House; it was only supposed to be for the public that was served at the Front Door Inn, but I got to eat I t anyway, and I can't help but be glad of it as it meant I got a lot more variety in my diet as a result.

The Abundance, the ship that the Family owned, was never a big moneymaking operation, but the fish was sold to wholesale buyers who in turn would sell it to groceries and restaurants. The money would go to Love. Operation costs just to keep it going, such as equipment, fuel and repairs were so high though, that it ended up being more just for fun. There was a ton of fish that were caught for the Fish and Honey Feast, but that was just once a year. A lot of the fish was just given to our Queen Anne neighbors as gifts.

Another way that the Family survived was through donors. There were a lot of people who were not members and who did not live with us, but who supported us and gave us money or things that were needed. John Bradford was one of our biggest donors; he was our good friend and almost like a celebrity to us in some ways because he gave to us so generously. Then we also had members like Richness and others who brought in a lot of money for our differing needs.

In the *Seattle Post-Intelligencer*, Sunday May 14th, 1978, business owners shared their views of the Love Family, some of which were not flattering. One businessman is quoted as saying, "They have nothing to offer this business community. Our society wouldn't survive if we all did what they do. We'd have no tax base. They are trying to get tax exemptions because they say they belong to the church. And they get their water from the city for free. They dug up some city ordinance that says charitable organizations don't have to pay for their water."

Despite what some of the area business owners thought, the Love Family, thanks to Sure and others, had plenty of positive relationships with business owners across the city that were mutually beneficial and were not cause for complaint.

Coincidentally, both Forest and I are photographed in this article I just quoted. I am standing with two boys, Ravah and Meshak and a man known as Solidity. In the photo, Solidity is holding the reigns of a horse pulling a homemade horse drawn cart used for small jobs on the Ranch. We are all just standing there in the encampment of tents in the main field. On the backside of that page, in the article, there is a picture of Forest who was probably around four years old. He is sitting on the front steps of the Ranch Gatehouse with Submission. Forest would play often with her son, Brotherhood. Forest was said to be nibbling hot nuts, and when asked how old he was, said, "I'm just a little bit." I guess he hadn't yet learned to say the word, 'eternal.'

Finally, even with all those different ways we got food, we liked the idea of trying to be self-sufficient, so there was a lot of produce that we grew at the Ranch. Years later, I heard someone complain that we weren't as self-sufficient as we could've been, maybe as we should've been. It's a good point. Maybe there was a lot of potential there that was lost, but as a child, I spent a lot of time in the garden at our ranch in Arlington, helping to do what was needed. I was sent to the Barn to pick lettuce or Swiss chard or other vegetables from the garden for dinner many evenings. There were some years where we depended more on the garden than other years. I would stuff a gunnysack full when it was Swiss chard because it had to be enough for the whole household to eat—probably about 15 people or more, including kids, so I would stuff it down as tight as I could, because I knew it would cook down to almost nothing once it was boiled in the pot, just like it does with spinich. Except the leaves were larger, thicker, stronger flavored. The leaves were shiny, almost a rubbery feel when I ran my finger along them. The stems were tasty too, with the consistency of celery, but sweet, tender, with a spinach flavor.

Once Sure got the food to the Love Family, it was a team effort after that to make sure it was distributed to the households. There were key people who worked together to make sure the kids had food.

Understanding would ask Helpful for things that she needed for the kids, and he would go and talk to Love, or she would ask Strength or different elders, and they would go talk to Love for her. Sometimes she would go talk directly to Love herself about her needs for the kids. Once, she said that she went in to talk to Love. On her way, she saw a man named Fun who was on his way out, after having talked to Love. Fun stopped and complained to Understanding that Love would not give him money to buy a Martin guitar.

"He was really mad at Love," she says. So then Understanding went in to talk to Love:

'If you could have anything you wanted, what would it be?' he asked her.

Understanding told him that if she could have anything, she would want milk for the kids. She also told Love she wanted Bibles for the kids and to be able to do things for the kids that were culturally enriching. "Love wrote me a check right then: $1000 for milk, $1000 for Bibles, and $1000 for cultural arts programs," she says. "Remember that cartoon Bible?" she asked me.

I did remember it. Every household got one. They were great but not nearly as great as her just telling us the stories herself in the animated and fun way that she told them.

With the money Love gave her for culturally enriching programs, Understanding bought theater tickets for us kids at Poncho theater and put money aside as well for gas for the buses so we could all go. I went to several plays at Poncho Theater. I saw the ballet Swan Lake as well as the musical Annie, about the little orphan girl. It was so much fun to get away from the Ranch, and afterward, I sang the songs with the other kids such as "Tomorrow! Tomorrow! I love ya, tomorrow, you're only a day away." Then the other song we sang from the movie was, "It's a hard knock life, for us, in the Love Family!" We substituted Love Family for "orphanage." We sang that one back at home, as we worked in the garden. It was a hard knock life, in certain ways, growing up in the Love Family.

Luckily, Understanding got what was called the 'cut-rate' on tickets because we were a school. I really enjoyed going to see live theater, the musicals and ballet, especially since I had begun to be involved in Understanding's Drama Group, which I devote a whole chapter to later on.

I'm glad Love gave her the money for the shows. They were culturally enriching. When Fun went in, he had said he wanted a Martin guitar, and I guess Love had ruled that that was selfish. Often Understanding's requests to Love were needs-related, so she was often accommodated. She would tell him the kids needed boots and he would send Wisdom out to go get them. She also often went to Love for materials for the school, like books.

"Love would not give me the money directly," Understanding explained. "He would appoint someone to get it for me."

I looked forward to hot cocoa at the Kid's House. There were times when it was served after the morning meditation.

"Love appointed Sure to go find cocoa for me," Understanding says, "then he even appointed someone to come over and make the cocoa for me." If she needed help such as extra guardianship for the kids, she would ask Love, and he would request the help from different households for her.

Over time when the number of kids grew, there was a change. The younger kids and Love's kids stayed under Understanding's direct care, but the older or more mature kids, like me, went and lived in the households. Understanding still took care of me, just less so. She was doing a far majority of it prior to that change, but gradually more and more people were joining and bringing kids with them, and more and more babies were being born to current members. There were just too many kids for Understanding to take care of by herself, even with the helpers that she had. That change began taking place once the households started to spread out around the lake, (1979). After that, if I needed flip flops or rubber boots, the elder lady of my household would put my need on a list. The elder lady was responsible for keeping track of the needs of everyone in her household. There was also a group of women who were designated as shoppers, and they would end up with the needs lists. Key people like Wisdom, Clarity, Devotion, Reaiah, or Duel would go in teams to thrift stores or factory outlets. The lists would be turned in at the ladies' meetings. We did not know sizes, we did it by measuring inches. Wisdom would take the lists to Chubby and Tubby.

"Wisdom was really good with that tape measure," Understanding remembered. "She would whip it out at the thrift store and she knew by heart the kids' waist and leg lengths. She knew what would fit every kid."

Zarah remembered a lot about Understanding.

"She had a positive influence on me and was someone I always respected, says Zarah. "She had a kids' circus, and I was a performer on stage. This taught me to be creative, and how to orchestrate and be productive with a lot of people. I got to be involved with the arts and creating... What I learned from her became a large part of who I became later."

There was one year when we watched Mary Poppins. It was after that movie that I decided that Understanding was like her. Understanding even carried that black, suitcase-like purse around with her just like Mary Poppins did. In the suitcase, she had puppets and other story props like a large, oversized toothbrush among other items.

There were children who for one reason or another were not a part of Understanding's kid scene. They missed out. As the number of kids grew over the years, there really needed to be more of her, more Understandings. One for each household—really!

Understanding taught me how to brush my teeth. It was her, not our parents who had a direct line to the tooth fairy. Her role as the head kid lady never ended, even after the kids' scene evolved to where the households were picking up more of the slack.

One year, I lost a tooth, and Understanding told me to put it under my pillow for the tooth fairy. In the morning, I got a handmade draw-string bag. It was reversible; it was purple velvet on the outside and pink satin on the inside.

Years and years later, long after I had left the community and was all grown up, Understanding showed me this little bag. It was a draw-string, ethnic, hand-woven bag about two by three inches big. She had it hidden away and just brought it out to show me. She laid out the contents on a table between us. All these little teeth fell out on the table. Each little tooth was wrapped individually in a piece of paper that read the child's name on it. Other teeth had fallen out of their papers and were just loose in the bag. It made me want to cry to see the teeth. Here she had loved us so much that she had saved our teeth!

One early memory I have took place in the first year, so 1975. I'm at the Kids House, under Understanding's care. I go into the bedroom that I shared with the kids who lived at the Kids' House. I walk in the door and look up to the left. My bed is on a shelf built above a closet. To get to the bed, I had to climb onto a queen bunkbed, then across another bunk behind it that was higher up. Then, there was a short ladder from the end of that bunk that climbed to my bed above the closet.

I climb up on top of the lumpy blankets to hoist myself up. Suddenly, a huge something jumps out of my bedding and comes at me! I fly backwards, screaming but landed safely on the bunk just below.

It's Understanding, with a wicked expression on her face. We crack up.

"You should've seen your face!" she laughs. She thought it was funnier than I did at the time.

It was so unexpected. She did stuff like that a lot just to break things up.

Understanding would fall asleep, right in the middle of telling a story. Literally, she would start snoring as she was sitting there, so each time, just as she was nodding off, we had to wake her up just to continue the story. I thought it was so funny that when she woke up and continued telling the story, she still sounded half asleep and would not know where she had left off, so I would remind her, and gradually, she would start sounding more coherent.

Understanding was overworked. So much so that she started complaining because she was always taking care of the kids and never got to go to the parties.

"I never even got a glass of wine," she says, so Israel and Happiness, because their kids were always at the Kids House, got her some wine. They called it "troop wine." She hid it under her bed in bottles, and on special occasions, she and the women would have a glass. But one day, Love found out about it, and when she came back from a ladies' meeting, she noticed that the wine was gone.

"When I came back," she says, "my bed had been pulled out in the army tent and they had gone through everything under my bed and confiscated the wine. Israel got in trouble."

Understanding contributed greatly to my moral development. By reading to us from the picture Bible, by developing characters in her stories who dramatized good and evil spirits, by all the examples in her stories and plays, she encouraged us to do the right thing. She showed us that our behavior had consequences. Bright told me what he thought of Understanding:

"I learned a strong sense of who I wanted to aspire to and who I approved of and who I didn't. The Bible stories had a lot to do with that," he says. "She instilled in us a deep-seated value system of morals and ethics."

Bright might have been a year younger than I. He had long brown hair that he parted down the middle, which turned almost blond in the summers. Usually he wore it in a braid, that hung down his back, almost to his waist, but when he wore it out it was wavy and golden, cascading down his back. He had a baby face cuteness about him, and was serious, not goofy—mature, not chatty. He chewed his tongue when he was concentrating real hard on something.

Bright says that he only had good memories of Understanding.

"She was one of the few people that went out of their way to be with the kids," he says. "She genuinely seemed to really love what she did." The first time that Bright went to buy shoes, it was with Understanding. "Before then I had stubbed my toes constantly, constantly had bloody toes, from walking around on the cement of Seattle on Queen Anne, barefoot." Bright remembered that she gave him a belt that an Indian chief had given her.

Understanding took care of me the most, but there were a lot of other people who were involved with the kids' scene over the years. When I first came to the Love Family with my mom, there was a nice man named Ezra who would sit with us and play circle time games. This was the same Ezra who years later became the candlestick maker. I sat with the other kids on the floor around him. Everyone in the Love Family sat in the lotus on the floor, so I was taught to sit that way from the get-go.

The lotus position or asana originated from the ancient meditative practices of India. The feet are placed on the thighs in a cross-legged position, which encourages proper breathing for meditative practice and fosters physical stability. They called it the lotus because the position resembles a lotus flower.

We all sat in a half circle around Ezra.

"We're goin' on a lion hunt," says Ezra.

"Going on a lion hunt," we repeat, and paddle our thighs with our hands for walking sounds.

"I don't see a lion," says Ezra.

"I don't see a lion," we chorus.

We get stuck in the mud and our footsteps slow down: pad-dle, pad-dle, pad-dle. We stop, hold our hands to our brows to shield us from the African sun.

"Wait, I see one!" says Ezra

Slap-slap-slap-slap-slap, we run like mad.

Ezra played the recorder and often wore a red rubber clown nose. When I squeezed his nose, it squeaked, but it was really his mouth making that loud funny noise. He could mime, and he made silly faces at us, blew up balloons and painted our faces.

"Tell us a story! Tell us a story!" we begged.

Reason told Rocky and Bullwinkle stories, Definition told us about Nanook of the North. Ethan told the story of Jump the Giant and another about donkeys. Understanding told us stories about Ignorant and the Grabbits and Snatchems. Stories were our version of TV. The children belonged to everybody, but certain individuals were more involved than others.

I saw the adult members like my parents, all of them to one degree or another. That was how Love wanted it. I found a newspaper article where Love was quoted describing the relationship between one of the adult members and the kids. It was a report about something that happened. Imagination was Canadian and had somehow been detained at the Canadian border. I don't know why he was there and the article didn't say. He was refusing to recognize his former name. He was being deported and was said to have overstayed his six-month visitor status. In the article, the *Seattle Times* described him as a teacher and quoted Love as saying that he was an "uncle and daddy to 25 children there." (*Seattle times* May 12, 1976 A9). I was one of those 25 children. Imagination didn't even have any children of his own at that point. Later on, he had a little boy named Deliverance.

I was once chosen to go on this ski trip.

Presence and Able had come to Understanding and asked her which children they could take.

Understanding chose Heaven and I to go.

"Why did you choose us?" I asked.

She explained several reasons: "You and Heaven were close," she explained. "and because you were reliably well behaved. Love wanted there to be children when we went into the World. He was concerned about how we represented ourselves to outsiders.

If there were children present, our community seemed more attractive in that we looked family oriented. It was an odd time to be pulled out of school right in the middle of a school year, but off we went.

I liked Presence a lot, and I looked forward to the trip. I sometimes went to visit him in what everyone called his "tooth booth" that was sitting out by the knoll.

One day, Shushan and I went there, and no one was there. It was open as it usually was, and so we went inside. We found a cigarette butt on the floor, which was weird because people did not smoke cigarettes in the Love Family. Shushan took the butt and tried to smoke it. We laughed so hard. Presence was very relaxed and an easygoing kind of guy. He kind of looked like a mountain man, burley. Even when it was braided, I could still tell he had frizzy hair.

Able, the other guy who would be on the trip, was this tall, slender guy who had eyes that bulged—bug eyes. On this trip, just for fun, Able would open up his eyes real wide to look scary and chase Heaven and I around growling like a monster. He would laugh so hard when we ran away from him squealing with fear. I didn't know him that well before the trip, but he ended up being great fun.

We all went to stay for a couple weeks in a chalet outside of Boise Idaho. The chalet was owned by Richness's mom. To get to the cabin, we had to cross country ski. I had done that many times when I used to live in Alaska in Suzanne's log cabin. The snow was so deep at the chalet that it completely enveloped the cabin to where I could only see the roof as we approached.

During the days, Presence and Able, who were like a couple of big kids themselves, would take off cross country skiing for the day, and Heaven and I would stay at the cabin and play Heart sound tracks and eat the cocoa mix that we discovered in the cupboards of the cabin. In the evenings, we all sat around the table and ate meals from all the frozen foods that were stocked there.

On our way out of there, we all stopped and stayed with Richness's mom, in Boise. Just as we arrived at her house, a bunch of family members came through in the blue bus on their way back from the West Virginia Gathering. A rainbow gathering is a huge hippie festival and sometimes three-week-long camping trip that is held in a different state each year. The Love Family always went to the Gatherings as a family, so that is how I know it was 1980 when Heaven and I went on this trip with Presence and Able.

Anyway, while we were at Richness's mom's, we got out a couple of huge black garbage bags and climbed up this small hill behind her house and slid down a few times. Presence and Able also took us skiing at Dollar mountain. They took Heaven and I all the way to the top of the highest ski lift and left us there. Maybe they thought that would be the best way to learn how to ski. Heaven and I basically rolled down the slope tangled in each other's skis.

When we got back to the Ranch, it was apparently the middle of the school year, and everyone seemed surprised to see us. We were tan, because Heaven and I had sunbathed at the chalet. Yeah, even though there was very deep snow everywhere, it was actually warm, and we had laid out in the snow on a blanket to sunbathe.

There was no formula in the Love Family. Things just happened out of the blue for seemingly no reason at all. At times, that was what shared parenting looked like. Elkanah, my mom didn't even know I went. It was a memorable trip though, and I was very glad I had been chosen to go.

Presence and Able were very stable, longtime, well established members. There wasn't a question of whether they were qualified to take two girls on a ski trip in the middle of the school year for a week or more. Early on especially, not just anyone could be with the kids. A new member had to be in the Family and prove themselves as a trustworthy person for at least a year before they could be responsible for children. There was a point when that began to change though, as I discussed earlier. Childcare became less centralized and became the responsibility of people in the households. As the Family grew and as the group of children got bigger and bigger, there just weren't enough people who were interested in taking care of the kids.

The early expectations about childcare no longer applied: new members were designated to kid watch without much thought, and others who were willing but less qualified were readily accepted.

I distinctly remember it, because I didn't like it. It seemed that when we all lived in the circle of tents, things were more communal in the classic sense. Before, the kids were together and taken care of by Understanding and other caretakers, but when we were divided up into the households, it was a big change and hard to get used to. Communal bonds had replaced the bonds with our parents for many of the kids, so the change from living with my peers in the same household to living in different households without them was a significant adjustment. Luckily, I was still pretty involved at school and with Understanding, at times, such as when she planned outings or drama group activities for the kids.

No matter how close I was to my peers or to teachers and caretakers, I still missed my mom, and she missed me. Whenever I saw her, she would hug me so tight that I had a hard time prying her loose. I could tell by her questions that she was desperate for information about how I was doing. I asked her, years later, to tell me what she remembered about our then relationship.

"I had some uncomfortable feelings about how I was losing contact with you," she says. "but I also knew that you seemed to be doing really well. People loved you, and you were involved in a bunch of stuff with Understanding."

I was having a lot of fun with different things I was doing, but I was also mixed up. When I did see my mom, I felt angry with her. Where was the strong woman who I had once known who had taken care of me? It seemed now that she was weak and was no longer making the decisions. I missed who she had once been to me, but clearly, she was no longer that person. The loss was painful, but no one in this group seemed to take notice, and because things were so strict, I had to focus on getting along and trying to get my needs met in other ways. What would crying do for me? It might just get me put in some closet somewhere or get everyone on my case for being negative.

That's exactly what happened to Sun. He showed that he was unhappy about being separated from his parents, through his behavior. I was able to keep it to myself—He was not. Sun, little angel face with blond curls dancing around his shoulders. Blue, mischievous eyes. He was nomadic, like I was. He lived in lots of different households, like I did, but the reason he was nomadic was that no one wanted to deal with him because he couldn't be controlled, and because of it, he often wasn't allowed to be with the other kids; he was assigned a personal guardian. He was such a handful though that he was often handed off, and another guardian would take a shot. I found it very sad that it seemed no one wanted him. He would do things that made it very difficult for anyone to want to watch him, such as the time he fed one of the children poisonous berries. Another time he tricked Compassion into drinking lemon soap water, telling her it was lemonade. She drank it, then gagged up bubbles. He ate bird poop and gave it to other kids. He picked gum off the street to chew.

One day, Understanding took the kids to Rogers Park on Queen Anne. Again, this was early on, when I was living at the Kid's House and before I moved to the Ranch in 1977. Every time Sun would see a wrapper on the ground, he would run and pick it up, look at it, then throw it back down on the ground. He was looking for a treat. Eventually he found one. It was an ice cream cone melted on the sidewalk with a stick in it. He picked it up and started eating it.

Sun's mom, Miriam, just happened to be on this walk. Understanding had secretly arranged for her to meet us on our way to the park. When Miriam saw her son pick up the ice cream cone and start eating it, "she was shocked and dismayed," Understanding recalled.

The reason Miriam had to meet her son in secret was because she wasn't welcome in the Love Family. It had been decided that she was a bad influence on Sun. Understanding explained that she felt sorry for her and for Sun, and that's why she arranged the meeting.

"Sun was mistreated," Understanding remembered. "but no one knew how to manage him." His behavior was "such a problem, that he was unable to live at the Kids' House" with the other children. "He needed special, one-on-one guardianship," Understanding explained.

When I first came to the Family, I walked into the bathroom at the

Kid's House one morning and saw him sleeping in the bathtub on a piece of plastic. This was his punishment for wetting the bed.

At times, Sun lived with his dad, Serious, but Serious was busy helping Love run the Family, and Serious's elder lady, Probity, was also busy, running Serious's household. Plus, she and Serious had a couple children of their own, so he had nobody looking out for him, nobody to protect him.

"Maybe all he needed was for someone to wake him up in the middle of the night and take him to the bathroom," Understanding guessed.

"Why was she 'blocked' from seeing him," I asked her.

"I would have to ask Serious about that," Understanding answered. "...She would come for short visits, but she wasn't welcome to stay very long. She would leave sobbing."

"Why? What was wrong with her that she would not be welcome?" I asked.

"She wouldn't submit to the hierarchy. She was known as an honest, powerful, tell-it-how-it-is type of person. She was called, 'Worldly' and was said to be a bad influence on him. The Family took very strong steps to block her from seeing him."

I loved Sun. He was like a brother, and even though he was always getting in trouble, I admired him for being a little rebel. I guess he was like his mom, in this way. He would not give in, even though he was living in a culture where there was absolutely no room for protest.

Sun became known as a "problem child," and a "challenge." I didn't see him that way though. I saw him as a child who didn't easily bow down to authority, head strong, a survivor, always figuring out how to get his needs met, including food, money, and attention, good or bad.

Miriam wasn't willing to fight for her legal rights as his mother. She would've had to take Serious to court. I am not sure why she didn't do that, but it doesn't surprise me that she chose not to. It is hard for anybody to deal with divorce and all the legal challenges of a child custody case, but there were additional complications for Love Family women that made it harder for them.

A Love Family woman was not just fighting the father, she was fighting the community, a community who stood behind *him*. The Love Family was very reluctant to relinquish ownership of children whose parents had left or were kicked out. Children who came to live in the Love Family were now considered to be children of the community. The rules of the outside society did not apply.

One example was a baby boy named Light. His mother's name was Godliness, and she had been one of those who had been kidnapped out of the Love Family by Ted Patrick. This happened before I came to the Love Family.

When they kidnapped Godliness, she didn't have her baby with her. Somebody had been watching him. After she was kidnapped, the Family refused to give her baby back to her. It took a court injunction to get the baby released back to her. Steve Allen discussed it in his book *Beloved Son*. The newspaper articles about it vary slightly from the personal accounts of members who were there, but, from what I gather, Love, Logic and Serious were thrown in jail over it, and they were not released until the baby was given back. Yeah, it took jailing the three highest status elders in the Family for the baby to be released back to its mother.

Another example was Neriah. Her parents had taken her to visit her grandparents, and while they were gone, they were in a car accident. Both parents, who were known as Salem and Nathaniel died, so the grandparents got custody of her and kept her. This happened about a year or so after I had been in the Love Family. It seemed that it was close to the time or during the period when everyone moved out to the Ranch.

When I heard about the accident, I was standing on the front Barn stairway that led into the the Barn's second floor. Eventually that stairway was removed, but this was early on, during the transition when people moved to live more permanently at the Ranch. In the two weeks leading up to her trip out, Neriah and I and some other girls had discovered this pile of dirt and debris under some trees near the Barn where we had taken to making fairy houses each day.

Then she left and we heard about the accident; Her parents were dead, and she had been placed with her grandmother. Everyone was devastated. I was devastated. I had been close to her, like a sister.

The Love Family refused to accept that Neriah wasn't coming back. Love sent several members to go try and retrieve her from her grandparent's house. There was more than one trip that occurred where men hitchhiked across the country trying to get her back, even knowing that the custody had already been granted to the grandparents. I don't think anyone ever gave up, because there were other trips over the years, attempts to try and see her.

But this is just another example of how reticent the Family was to give up its members and especially children who were seen as belonging to the community.

Moms stayed so they could be with their kids, just not wanting to deal with the hassle of fighting Love and a large community of people who would go to great lengths to prevent the children from being taken away. Remember Clear-out?

How could it be that women in our own country, in the United States, had fewer rights over their own children? The reason is partly that the Love Family was very isolated from the mainstream culture and didn't believe in the legal institutions that were taken for granted elsewhere. Not only did they not believe in it, they actively fought against it year after year as can be seen with the many arrests and refusals to provide legal names and birthdates to law enforcement, often resulting in violence and harassment against us. The Love Family was so stubborn that, as I have explained, they ended up having to provide us with identification that was specially made for us. The police made an exception for us to save themselves the headache of trying to figure out what to do with us.

What would a Love Family woman have done in court? The court-room would have been packed with a bunch of ethnically dressed long haired and bearded members of the Love Family. None of the witnesses would have been able to be identified, other than with these cards, that listed their Love Family names, many of whom didn't have one. It most definitely would've been in the papers. The *Seattle Times* and the *Seattle Post-Intelligencer* were on us constantly and regularly published salacious articles about the community.

The Love Family was a society structured very differently in terms of how the children were cared for. It was—these are our kids, not yours, we are one, and we all share the children. If a woman left the Love Family or was kicked out, it was not assumed that she would just take her kids with her. If she tried, she would be physically stopped. Once she left, she would have to go to court and legally fight the community to get her children back. I talked to Understanding about this, and she concurred:

"It was true. Women were told to walk down the road if you want to go but leave the children here. It was harassment. And there was a sort of brow beating that we got and pressure on us—Me, Beauty, Quiet, [Probity], and Yaar are just a few I can think of but there were others…"

I spoke to Bright about how his mom left him and his brother in the Family for periods of time. Bright mostly lived with his dad, Humility.

"There was a big power play around children in the Family," he says. "The idea of her even taking us with her would have been a huge deal. That was a sensitive issue."

For many women in the Love Family, they would never consider fighting the Family. For one, many did not have any money to fight, because they had turned everything in when they joined. Some had relatives in the world who had money, but they were not confident that the courts would even listen to them since they did not have ID, they had no record of themselves as people with work or housing histories. They didn't even have birth certificates for their children or official custody, since they had lived in a community that had disavowed all that.

Very few women who were in the Love Family had relationships with their parents or relatives anymore to even ask for money, because when they joined, Love had asked them to give up former identities. Many had given up relationships with their parents and other supports as well when they joined. This is important because for a woman to decide to fight a legal battle, she must consider her support network. The only support network that many women had were their friends in the Love Family.

It was even more complicated than that because once a woman in the Family had children, the child or children were bonded to their friends who were like brothers and sisters now. The children were attached now to many other individuals who had shared in the parenting for years, so more often than not, the children refused to leave anyway. And if she left with them, they demanded that she bring them back. On top of everything, there was now a battle with her kids about leaving.

There was a time when I was worried that my mom would take me out. I didn't want to leave my friends and school. I enjoyed my activities with

Understanding and other caretakers. The Family was the only family that I knew. My attachment to my own mother was weak after years of being in the Family. The thought of living on the outside, with so many unknowns away from my community was a frightening thought.

In the Love Family, parenting was shared. Raising kids was just another communal activity, like gardening. Share is such a nice word – to share in the responsibility of childcare. I had hundreds of parents and one big papa, Love. The more parents you have, the more you get, right? But what do you get more of? Attention? Food? Hugs? Fun?
For some of us it meant more time with somebody else, but less time with our parents. What is more about that?

In my case, I didn't know my real dad, so Love was the closest thing to a male figure to me that would've been like a dad, other than Marty, who was now way in the past. The elder of my household, whichever household I was in, was closer to me in some ways, but he was not the most influential over my life. In terms of the major decisions that a dad would make for his child, such as, what I ate, what school I went to, what clothes I wore, what activities I would do, who I could and couldn't associate with, pretty much every aspect of my life was decided by Love.

One day, I was at Jordan River with a bunch of kids and our guardians. The Love Family called it the Jordan River, after the Jordan River in the Middle East. The real Jordan was the significant site where the Israelites had crossed into the Promised Land and where Jesus of Nazareth was baptized by John the Baptist. Outside of the Love Family, the "Jordan" was known as the Stillaguamish river, a river in northwest Washington in the United States. It runs 22 miles from near Arlington and flows into the Puget Sound. The river's watershed drains part of the Cascade Range north of Seattle.

That day, I was playing with Seth. I had this small, battery operated radio with me. I wasn't supposed to have it, but no one saw it. I had it hidden in my shirt. Seth and I went off by ourselves to listen to the radio in hopes that no one would notice. We were standing by the river listening to songs. This song came on the radio. It was called, Twilight Zone by Golden Earing. Seth got all excited and told me that his dad, Bob, who lived in the world, was in a band and that his dad's band played that song. Seth told me that Certain wasn't his real dad, and that he had gotten to visit his real dad, Bob.

As he talked, I wondered about my own dad, who I will call, 'Mike.' I knew he was out there in the World too, just like Seth's dad. But I didn't get to visit him, and he didn't visit me. Elkanah never talked about Mike, except one time she told me that he played baseball. I wondered about him from time to time, but I didn't dwell on it, since I didn't know much more than that. It bothered me more about Marty, who was still living up in Alaska and who had been like a dad to me before we came to the Love Family. We continued listening to the song. *When the bullet hits the bone.*

One of my peers, who went by the name Ravah, was in the Family with his mom, Clarity. His dad wasn't there either. He told me exactly what he thought of shared parenting:

"There were certain guardians who should never have been put in charge of kids," says Ravah angrily. "Couples were strongly influenced to separate, and children and families split apart, so no one had special treatment. Love's kids got special treatment—and the children paid!"

Bright also talked to me about shared parenting:

"With kids and parents there was this disconnect there, this distance, and that has some effect on our relationships now."

The Love Family completely restructured family relationships. Instead of a nuclear family with one mom and one dad in one house, I had mothers and fathers galore.

In the Love Family, as I have said, most of the biological parents, unless they were elders, had very little say over what their children did or where they went. Zarah remembered when they "shipped" her to China Bend.

"They thought it would be fun for me," she says. "But no one explained it to me. Years later, I had it out with my mom about things, and she said that a lot of times she wasn't even notified. She was out at the Ranch and there was no phone...So after I would be shipped out, she would hear later that I had been moved."

Family hierarchy was a pyramid, with Love at the top, the elders in the middle, and everyone else on the bottom. There were hierarchies within hierarchies, too – among elders, within households. The hierarchy pyramid affected our relationships with our parents. Is our earth parent an elder or not?

If so, elder of what? a household? the Ranch? Hawaii? Some kids lived a life of privilege, but most of the kids did not live a life of privilege.

The few kids who did have parents near the top of the food chain, didn't necessarily have parents with any more to offer either. It didn't usually mean more access, more affection, or more time with their parents, although in some cases it did. Elders' kids didn't necessarily benefit from their parents' status. Elders and elder ladies usually didn't do childcare or household chores; they delegated, at least in the households I was in, and I was in quite a few over time. If your parents were elders, they were still submitted to Love who made all the decisions.

Zarah came to the Family with her mom after her parents divorced. The first thing that she remembered was being baptized.

"At that time," Zarah says, "I remember thinking to myself, I am in charge of myself here. I was seeing my mom being all passive, giving herself into this everyone else. But everyone else to me was like a bunch of people that I didn't trust."

I felt similarly. It was a lot to get used to. Suddenly, my mom was no longer in charge. I'd like to think that maybe I was a little more tenacious than some because when I joined, we had lived in very rustic conditions in the wilderness of Alaska and had been hitchhiking around. My mom had always expected me to be a little more independent. But it was still hard.

I no longer looked to my mom to fulfill my needs. At Christmas time, the gifts that I received were from Love. They were hand made by members, but I often didn't know who had made them.

About two weeks before Christmas, I heard there was an elf shop where artists and craftsmen would all get together on a regular basis and make toys for the kids. Once they were finished and wrapped, the toys would be turned in to the center for Love, and personal helpers like Understanding and others would then decide, with Love's approval, who was getting what.

Ravah called Family gift giving "wacked." Bright called gift giving in the Family "twisted." One of the problems was that because Love was the only official giver of gifts, people were less motivated to give.

Ever since I could remember, my mom had sewn me clothes. In the Love Family she didn't do it as often, but sometimes I would receive clothes she had made for me. This time, she made a dress for me. Well, she hoped it would go to me after she turned it in. It was a satin, light blue, princess dress with crystal beads attached to the bodice and a gold cord around the waist. It was beautiful and the sort of thing one might see Princess Anna wearing in the movie Frozen. But when she turned it in, which she was required to do, Truthfulness gave it to her daughter, Gentle. Privately, it was very disappointing for my mom, but for me, I don't remember dwelling on it or it being a source of resentment. That was just the way things were, and I was learning not to have expectations or to get too attached.

My mom was "sad" that I didn't get the dress, but she was "also honored" in a way. Truthfulness, who was sanctioned to Love, was like a queen, with the highest status of any woman in the Family, and Truthfulness had thought the dress was good enough to give to her daughter Gentle.

Ravah talked more about gift giving in the Family:

"Love's kids got Worldly toys that were better," says Ravah, "I remember not liking that," he says. Love's kids "got bikes" and "a new sled" and things like that. But all Ravah got that year was an eight-inch by eight-inch wooden block with his name on one side and a letter of the alphabet on the other side. "We weren't getting those kinds of gifts, but they were," says Ravah bitterly. "I tried to be buddy-buddy with Love's kids, so I could get in on it. They got to take trips, like to Hawaii—It was a total monarchy—and we knew it!"

One year, we all received a gift at Christmas. It was a very large train-set on display, unveiled for the kids to all share. The set had miniature, doll sized yurts and tepees, little people and animals, even a little Barn with a star of David window. Afterward though, I heard the boys complaining that the trainset was set up in Love's house. It was a permanent display and set upon a table that filled an entire room in Love's house. How would we even be able to play with it? This was a legitimate concern since most of us would go back to the Ranch after the feast and not even be in the city, plus, even if some of the kids were in the city, it is not like we could just go walking in to Love's house to play with the train. As I explained before, Love's house was a sanctuary and very "invite only" sort of place. People didn't even go into Love's Area without having a good reason for it. Only Love's kids would have access to it.

Ethan told me a story of something that happened to him: He was at one of the rainbow gatherings and he traded some tangrams for a bunch of pocket knives, and when he turned them in, he never saw them again.

"Did it bother you?" I asked him.

"No, it didn't bother me," he answered, casually, then paused. "On second thought, there was always a little bit of selfishness where you wanted to keep one for yourself, but that was the game we played. The whole idea was to give to the center, and then everything would be given to you that you needed."

I remember hearing all the time, 'Don't 'want.' Live simply without all the unnecessary 'stuff.' Stuff always had negative connotations. 'Just have faith and trust God to provide.'

Giving is a wonderful thing because it builds relationships, it forges bonds. It encourages attachments. But in the Love Family, everything came from the Center (Love), and everything went from the Center (Love); Love was the only one who ever received or gave anything, which limited people's inspiration towards giving.

It was Christmastime and I was given a doll. I knew it came from Elishama who had just returned from Mexico, even though officially it was from Love. The doll obviously looked Spanish. It had long, jet black hair, pale skin, and a bright orange satin dress with black lace trim. Another Christmas, I got a handmade doll. I called it my Simplicity doll, because I knew that even though the doll wasn't from Simplicity, I knew that she had made it. I had been told that Dignity painted its face. It had long, brown yarn hair and a beautifully stitched satin maroon dress. It even looked like Simplicity who had very fine facial features and long, brown hair, longer than most women there. The legs of the doll were attached by buttons, so they were able to rotate. Her arms and legs were made of cloth that was hand sewn. I still have that doll. It's been so many years now that it looks like an old, washed out hippie doll. It's been ruined as it accidentally was washed in the washing machine, but it is a treasure to me because the doll is still so beautiful to me and is a reminder of my life in the Love Family.

Gentle, Love's daughter had boxes of handmade dolls. There were times when I went to sleepover with her at Love's house. Every time I went, all she wanted to do was to play with her dolls. I didn't mind. I only had one doll, so it was really fun to play with her and her dolls. She had these elaborate games involving all the dolls interacting. There was a boy doll but most of her dolls looked like Love Family women, a cloth body with long, yarn hair, a hand painted face, and a long, handmade dress.

Most of the gifts I ever received in the Love Family were handmade. Twice a year, everybody helped make toys in what was called, 'Elf Shop.' There were toys that were needed at Christmastime, and there were also toys needed for the Easter Egg hunt prize table at Passover. Wood craftsmen would make toys like wooden airplanes, trains and trucks. The women would get together and make dolls. Imagination, a family artist would often head up the elf shop. One year, they made us Inca looms; another year, they made wooden tangrams. There was a year a lot of the big kids got used bikes but that had been remodeled and fixed up like new.

Each year, that Christmas was celebrated, I got one nice present. One year I got a six-pointed star-of-David Chinese checkers. It was hand-carved wood and painted with Israel symbology with six sets of different colored marbles for each point of the star. There were other images painted on it too, such as a peace symbol and a bright yellow sunshine that had a smiling face. I loved it.

There was a decorated Christmas tree in Love's house for everyone to share. None of the households had their own tree. At the Ranch, the shared tree would be up in the Barn.

Christmas was not a big holiday in the Family and wasn't celebrated every year.

Toys were generally not store bought for us, but there were times when certain items would be bartered for or bought in a large quantity, especially as the birthrate had skyrocketed and there were so many children needing gifts.

You would think that with such a large family there would be plenty of attention to go around, but it wasn't so. When I did get it, I almost exploded with happiness. Like when Vision made me a skirt.

She made me a red dancing skirt, with an elastic waist band. It had so much material that it spun out almost parallel to the ground like a tutu would. I won a dance contest on Cookie Day because of it.

Years later, I asked her if she remembered making me that skirt.

No, she didn't even remember it.

I thought, how could something that meant so much to me be so inconsequential to her? No other child got a skirt like I did; How could I not be special?

Whenever Vision saw me wearing it, she would smile, and I could feel her sending me love. It made me feel special and important. I wore it almost every day for a while.

That sort of attention wasn't there, and if it ever was, it was rare. I needed to be singled out and given something special, just for me, which would prove my worthiness. So I imagined it, even if it wasn't really there. Most people might think that was pitiful, and it was, but it was also a fantasy that helped me feel like my needs for attention were being met.

A lot of my memories involve times when gifts were exchanged. Maybe because it was so rare and special to get a gift.

One Christmas, Elkanah snuck me and Forest out, and she took us to Gramma Phyllis's house. She could easily do that, because Christmas wasn't usually celebrated in the Love Family on the same calendar day as Christmas in the World. So, I celebrated Christmas with my Love Family peers, then I went to Grammas on the actual day of Christmas.

My gramma Phyllis had an apartment in Bellevue. Yeah, suddenly, Elkanah was my mom again, and I was being whisked off to gramma's house for the day. My uncles were there, Jim and Johnny. I didn't even know I had uncles. Gramma served a ham which was against Love Family thinking totally, but I guess I knew I wasn't Dorothy and we certainly weren't in Kansas anymore.

Gramma's apartment was decorated to the hilt with her own tree with ornaments and lights. I was probably around twelve. There was a picture of me there that day, sitting in Gramma's rocking chair holding her cat. I wore an ethnic, ankle length red skirt. I rocked back and forth. It was soothing. My uncles watched me brushing my hair.

"She's gonna be a knock out someday," one said to the other. The other one nodded in agreement.

Whatever that meant, I had thought. There was a lot of awkward silence as my uncles opened their presents from Elkanah, their sister. Elkanah's gift to her brothers: ethnically decorated candlesticks. I had helped decorate them with crayon. To us, the handmade candlesticks were probably the most normal gift that we would've had to give.

While I watched Elkanah hand her brothers the presents, my thoughts flashed back a couple weeks earlier. I had gone with a large group of children from the Ranch to sell candlesticks in Arlington, door-to-door. Appreciation coordinated the event. We had boxes of candles stacked in the vehicles we came in. Every single one of those candlestick sets were gone by the end of the night. We were all divided off into small teams, hitting different neighborhoods, block-by-block in Arlington. Once they opened their door, I held up the candlesticks for them to see.

I heard many people say that there were a lot "Rednecks" in Arlington who hated us. There was some ambivalence for sure, but that night, every door we came to, the people were friendly and curious, wanted to ask us a lot of questions. Some bought just one pair, others bought several. We did not have even close to enough candles, because almost everyone whose door we knocked on, bought some. In the end, we had plenty of money for that movie that we all got to go see in the theater. It was a movie called, *Time Bandits* (1981).

My mind had drifted. It was Christmas at my gramma's, and my uncles opened the Christmas paper and saw the candlesticks. Then they looked at one another with odd expressions, snickered and said, "Thanks!" They seemed disappointed.

My mother watched their reactions and looked down, ashamed. I could tell she felt sad and disappointed that her brothers weren't happy. She smiled superficially at them, and they said, "Great!" but I could tell, they weren't very thrilled to have them. I just sat there and observed this interaction, not quite understanding what it meant.

We depended each night on the candles for light. I guess they did not need them as they surely had electricity in their homes and didn't live in a tent. My uncles gave me an ant farm as their gift to me. They didn't like our candlesticks, but I did not like their ant farm either. I lived on the Ranch and I saw ant farms everywhere every day. It bothered me that the ants weren't free; they were stuck in this compartment. How could they be happy? I thought. On the Ranch, I liked to watch the ants. They marched around, just like the song says. I brought the ant farm to the Ranch, and instead of turning it in to

Love, I just opened it and let the ants go free. That made me happy.

My uncles never did appreciate or understand my mother's lifestyle and maybe the gift reminded them of that. The Christmas at Gramma's wasn't fun at all, but rather awkward and boring, sitting there with relatives I didn't know.

Then that evening, it was over, and away we went back to the commune, to my life as I knew it. I did not see my uncles again after that for several years or more.

In the Love Family, the incentive to give was lost as everyone scampered around trying to impress Love. I didn't receive gifts that often anyway, but when I did, they were from him. One of the things that people forgot in the Love Family is that when a child receives a gift, it is their opportunity to get personalized attention. The meaning behind a gift is priceless in terms of what a child receives. A gift is not just a commercial object, a symbol of how American culture has gone astray. A gift can be a symbol of love passed from one to another.

I got very little personal attention in the Family. Most of the attention that I got was from the other children. If there was a gift to be had, it was often to all of us from everyone (Love). One year, I opened a card at Christmas, and it said that I and some of the other girls around my age had been gifted with 12 ballet lessons which we were to take in Arlington with a woman named Martha LeValley. I ended up really appreciating those lessons. Apparently, Appreciation had talked to Love and had arranged the lessons. I wrote about them in my then diary:

Dear Diary,

Passover is gone and Easter too and I'm in the town of Snohomish for ballet with some other kids. My ballet teacher says, "you are not riding a bus, you are driving it!" This means don't be lazy, keep your muscles tight. We are just starting to learn leaps and twirls. I have had eight lessons so far. Good night.

Rachel Israel

I appreciated the lessons that Appreciation arranged for the girls. She did things like that, that no one else did. One time, she arranged for all the kids at the Ranch to have swimming lessons in Arlington. She was also the one that arranged for the pie making party up in the Barn that ended up being so fun.

But like I was saying, most of the attention that I received, was not given to me as an individual. It was given to me, as a group. It was fun being in the group and having fun in the community setting, but it also kind of left me emotionally starved for attention, because I never had a chance to feel like I was special, that I got something that no one else got. When I got a bike for Christmas that year, all the kids also got bikes. It was very communal in that way. They were trying *not* to give us individualized attention. That was the whole idea.

Bright felt similarly to how I felt about the lack of attention.

"Even though I knew that people cared," says Bright, "it was very rare when children actually received that personalized, one-on-one attention…the kids sort of don't belong to anybody, we are just this big community. If the kids were getting attention, it was as a big group. And there needed to be a balance…We were just sort of clumped together."

Ravah also shared some thoughts with me about what it was like for him being cared for in the community:

"I was one of the luckier ones to have a parent in the Family," he says. "but there were many, many times when I missed my mother very much. I had a lot of role models who I admired and respected and learned from, but the one who I most wanted to be with, wasn't there — my mom. And that was because of policies, but it was also because of her, who she was."

For Zarah, the personal affection from her mother was absent.

"Something that I held in for a long time was that my mom didn't show me personalized affection," she says. "Mercy would get secret notes from her mom, notes that said, I love you. I never got anything like that," Zarah complained.

For me, personally, I didn't need "secret notes." Secret notes wouldn't have been enough. I would have needed her to spend regular one-on-one time with me and to be the one making the decisions. From time to time she would ask me how I was doing. How's school? I didn't want to tell her; I was mad at her.

"Why don't you hug me back?" she asked. She looked hurt.

It felt wrong to me that I had to tell her what I was doing in my life. Shouldn't she already know, since she was my mother? When adults see each other, grownups have to "catch up." I was still a young girl, not ready to just keep her updated once in a while like a teenager whose gone off to college.

I felt totally abandoned by her, permanently. At least when I was a little kid and she left me, she always came back, even if it took her a couple weeks or a month. This time, it wasn't like that. We had joined the Love Family, and I had lost her for good.

Before we joined the Family, I saw my mom as a role model, a tough do-it-yourselfer. Once we joined the Love Family, my mom seemed to have lost all the power that she had, when we were on the road, or in Maui, or in Alaska when we teamed up with Marty. She had staked out property and was a take-charge sort of person. When she was hitchhiking around, she carried a knife in her boot. When we joined the Family, she lost all that, and I lost her, the only person who had consistently taken care of me until that point. Out of survival, I endeared myself to the teachers and caretakers who genuinely seemed to care about the children.

......

It makes sense to me, after having been raised the way I was, why people will continue to be drawn to communal life, a life where people live together, work together, and raise children together, especially living in the World we live in today where people live in huge overpopulated cities, without a sense of meaning or purpose.

I grew up in community. I know what it's like to have a sense of belonging and to live as a member of a tribe. It had a small town feel where everybody knows everybody and works together toward common goals.

I felt safe and protected, and there were members of my community, such as Understanding and other teachers and caretakers who were involved and trying to build a kid-centered world where I could get what I needed.

On the other hand, it sucked that I lived in a society where my relationship with my mother or with other relatives outside of the community were not valued, and that her authority as my mother and protector were absent. Love made all the decisions about my care and his primary interest was not me, it was the community, or some would argue himself. I say that because Love was not consulting with the parents. In addition to all the meetings he was having with elders, he should've also had meetings with parents, to get their feedback about how their children were being cared for.

I didn't get much personal, individualized attention. I needed that and not just group care by a bunch of people, most of whom were not that involved. I needed to feel like an individual, like I was special and unique and not just separated off to get group attention by designated caretakers. This has had a real negative impact on my life, contributing to years of suffering with depression and anxiety, which have been very difficult to overcome.

Shared parenting is a great idea, it takes a village to raise a child, but communal bonds, even caring, loving attachments from significant others will never replace a child's relationship to his or her parents, parents who are born with the instinct to protect, kill if needed anyone who intends to harm their child. Why mess with this relationship unless there are no alternatives? The primacy of that bond has remained stable throughout human history for good reason: It works the best.

When you take parents away from their children, it leaves children vulnerable, and parents aren't able to fulfill their protective roles. Then you have a bunch of unrelated individuals living together and taking care of children—Not a good combination.

There is a saying, "Don't throw the baby out with the bathwater." If there is any lesson to ever be learned and passed on to future generations, let that quote be used as a guide to those seeking change. Some things need changing, yes, but not everything!

Early utopian communities such as the Oneida and Shaker communities and many others since then, have been revered and idealized since their time by popular theorists and writers, as well as by people today who are interested in intentional communities, urban co-ops, cohousing groups, eco-villages and rural communities.

Each group that comes along seems to make the same mistakes as the last one. People crave community. People want change. But do people have to keep learning the same lessons? It is my feeling that the movement towards building alternative communities of all sorts will never take foot hold until there is a full-on self-examination of how people have experimented with building community in the past. And that lessons learned are being processed and applied as new communities are formed. Otherwise, it's just going to be this fringe thing where people end up hurt.

The Love Family was a social experiment, just as many others that went before it and plenty of others that have and will come after it. But it was not an isolated experiment that Love invented from scratch. Many of the ideas behind it, like shared parenting, had been tried before by other communities throughout time in America and elsewhere. There are always people who are going to be drawn to what communes try and offer, which is a life where everyone lives and works together, shares everything in common, and raises children together.

Since people are going to just keep doing it, the question must be asked: How can this be done better? How can we get beyond these primitive applications of the shared parenting model? What we need are people, who are willing to share their stories about what worked and what didn't work and give examples from their own lives. What did they learn? Sometimes, there's nothing more convincing than someone's personal story. It's my opinion, that the way forward from here, is just to pass on the knowledge so that hopefully people involved in the movement will make better choices.

BIBLIOGRAPHY (CHAPTER 11)

Allen, Steve. (1982). *Beloved Son; A Story of the Jesus Cults.* Pgs. 79, 89–90. Bobbs-Merill Company, Inc. Indianapolis/New York.

[Atarah]. Personal Interview. August 7, 2002. Seattle, WA.

Brewer, Priscilla. (1997). Ed. Donald E. Pitzer. *America's Communal Utopias.* The University of N. Carolina Press: Chapel Hill and London.

[Bright]. Personal Interview. January 11 & 17, 2002. Des Moines, WA.

Bryant, Hilda. *Seattle Post-Intelligencer.* Sunday May 14, 1978. A13 and BM.

[Definition]. Personal Interview. June 27 & Sept. 30, 2001. Seattle, WA (Magnolia Hill).

[Definition]. Personal Interview. March 13, 2003. Lake Forest Park, WA.

[Karen]. Personal Interview. November 10 & 19, 2001. Maple Valley, WA to Vashon Is.

[Ethan]. Interview conducted by Chuck LeWarne. February 18, 1998.

[Ethan]. Personal Interview. January 3, 2002. Seattle, WA (Magnolia Hill).

[Forest]. Personal Interview, February 23, 2002. Portland, OR.

Foster, Lawrence. (1991). *Women, Family, and Utopia: Communal Experiments of the Shakers, the Oneida Community, and the Mormons.* Syracuse University Press, Syracuse New York.

Holloway, Mark. (1966). *Communities in America*, 1680–1880. 2nd Ed. Dover Publications, Inc., New York.

Israel, Larry (Consideration). 1978. Unpublished Manuscript.

Israel, Understanding. Personal Interview. May 5, June 10, Jul 15, December 9, 14, & 29, all 2001, and May 9, 2002. Arlington, WA.

Israel, Understanding. Personal Interview. February 14, 2004. Lake Forest Park, WA.

Klaw, Spencer. (1993). *The Life and Death of the Oneida Community.* pgs. 142, 147–8 Allan Lane; The Penguin Press, New York.

[Lydia]. Personal Interview. February 20, 2002. Seattle, WA.

Muncy, Raymond Lee. (1973). *Sex and Marriage in Utopian Communities.* Penguin Books.

Noyes, Pierrepont. (1937). *My Father's House: An Oneida Boyhood.* Farrar & Rinehart, Inc. New York, Toronto.

Owen, R. & Fourier, C. (1969). Al Morton. *The Life and Ideas of Robert Owen.* International Publishers; New York.

Partrige, William L. (1973). *The Hippie Ghetto; A Natural History of a Subculture.* Georgia State University. Waveland Press Inc. Prospect Heights, Illinois.

[Ravah]. Personal Interview. March 19 & April 8, 2002, 8:30pm.

Ruppert, Ray. *Seattle Times*. Sure Israel Travels Halfway Around the World to Rejoin Commune. October 20, 1976 B11.

Ruppert, Ray. *Seattle Times*. Sure Israel Taken from Sect—by Court This Time. May 12, 1976 B11.

Ruppert, Ray. *Seattle Times*. The Stress of Faith April 17, 1975 C2.

Skinner, B.F. (1948). *Walden II*. Hackett Publishing Company.

Wallace, Anthony F.C. (1956). Revitalization Movements. *American Anthropologist*, 58: 264–281. Pg. 265.

Zablocki, Benjamin. (1980). *The Joyful Community: An Account of the Bruderhof: A Communal Movement Now in Its Third Generation*. University of Chicago Press (1971, reissued 1980) ISBN 0226977498.

Zablocki, Benjamin, (1980). *Alienation and Charisma: A Study of Contemporary American Communes*. The Free Press.

[Zarah]. Personal Interview. December 13, 2001 and February 2, 2002. Maple Valley, WA.

CHAPTER 12

The Juicy Details—
Living without Modern Medicine

I was raised in a community that didn't believe in conventional medicine, which meant that people generally did not go to the doctor when they were sick.

Back during the first few months after I came to the Love Family, when I was living at Encouragement's, one day, I walked into the sanctuary, and there, lying on the floor was a man. All around him were gathered household members, including the elder and elder lady. There were probably seven or eight people all kneeling around him on the floor. Each person had their hands on him and they were chanting. I stood there a bit dumb founded. The chanting went on for another minute or two, then the elder, Encouragement prayed as everyone else silently listened with their hands still on the man. Someone saw me watching, and I was beckoned to join the prayer. A couple people moved to the side to make room for me. I squeezed in and put my hands on him. His body was covered in hands. My hands were one of the smallest hands among the many. I closed my eyes like everyone else, and like I was told, imagined a healing, white light flowing through me, through my hands and into his body.

I came to learn that this was called 'laying hands,' and it was a spiritual form of treating illness. I can see his face, but I don't remember who that guy was, what his name was, but within a short period of time, he was up and walking around, bright and smiling, as if he'd never been sick.

Since I was just a child, it did not amaze me to see this healing, as it might have someone else who might have been more familiar with mainstream medicine. My mom was pretty unconventional in her thinking regarding Western medicine as it was. We had only rarely seen a doctor, and when we were living in Alaska, she had delivered her own baby.

Instead, the healing was just something to take in and accept as just the way things were. It startled me more than anything, especially walking in on all these people kneeling on the floor, chanting, around this man who was lying there.

It was a faith healing. Even today, laying hands is not uncommon in certain religions, especially Christian. The Bible is littered with references about the laying on of hands:

> Wherefore I put thee in remembrance that thou stir up the gift of God, which is in thee by the putting on of my hands. (2 Timothy, 1:6, *KJV*).

> Now when the sun was setting, all they that had any sick with [diverse] diseases brought them unto him; and he laid his hands on every one of them and healed them. (Luke 4:40, *KJV*)

I saw people laying hands on Benjamin once. Benjamin also lived at Encouragement's household early on. He might've been maybe five and lived there without his parents. That day, Benjamin was crying and getting more and more upset and agitated. They had tried separation—a swat—nothing was working, and when Benjamin cried, boy he cried! He would become angrier and angrier as people tried various ways to get him to calm down. Discipline did not work. He would end up in a rage, and his crying would begin to sound like growling as snot ran down his nose and chin, his face, wet and swollen from all the tears. I was told that he had a "spirit."

They had decided to lay hands on him in prayer, to "cast the spirit out." After everyone laid hands on him, chanted and prayed, Benjamin was still and quiet for a few moments as he looked curiously at everyone chanting. His crying stopped and he became calm. Everyone waited in suspense to see if it was going to last. It did. There was a sigh of relief in the room. Then one of the household women ushered him off into another room, and that was that.

That was my initial impression of the power of prayer. No one sat me down and explained it to me; I just went about my business of being a kid in the Love Family, making a mental note of everything I saw happening around me. I was seeing a lot of things for the first time and was, at that time, in the process of adjusting to a whole new culture.

Then there was a situation where I got hurt, and I ended up getting caught in the crossfire between Family ideology and the need for medical care. It happened at Cherry Hill. It was my first harvest season, so must've been Spring of 1976 when Love sent Understanding to help harvest fruit in Eastern Washington. I went along with the crew of kids who went with her. Cherry Hill was the name of an orchard on a big hill, which overlooked the Yakima River. It was a place in Eastern Washington where we gleaned and camped.

Several converted school buses filled with Love Family members made the trip over the mountain passes towards Cherry Hill. Elkanah and Forest came too, though I had little to do with them, because by this time, we did not live together anymore.

On our way to Cherry Hill, we all stopped at the Cannery, which we usually did on our way to the orchards. The Family also owned a vineyard near Cherry Hill in Granger, next to the Yakima River. But I never went there.

I very much enjoyed stopping at the cannery and have many fond memories of playing there with the other children. There was a big beautiful back yard area with a large willow tree and eucalyptus bushes.

We went out to play. Each of the kids who were there broke off the branches of the willow and made whips that would whistle through the air as we chased each other around with them. The whips actually had a pretty good sting, so I ran like mad to avoid getting hit. I would go hide behind the bushes and pick and smell the eucalyptus berries near the willow while I waited to be found.

Then I would run off with the other kids into the nearby fields near the cannery where we would play in the empty cement water channels we called, 'aquaducts' that would irrigate the nearby orchards and farms.

Eastern Washington was so different than being in the houses on Queen Anne Hill or out at the farm in Arlington where we lived in the forest in tents and where it rained most months of the year. In Eastern Washington, it was hot and dry. There were few trees other than the fruit trees in the nearby orchards and a few shrubs. I watched the boys try and catch the crickets in the long, golden grasses. I liked to enjoy the little pink morning glories everywhere that would close at night and open in the morning, which to me, seemed to work like magic.

When we got to Cherry Hill, I was taught how to pick the fruit correctly but only helped pick for short periods. A lot of the kids were too young to climb the tall ladders that were used. Plus, the caretakers intuitively understood that our attention spans required that we could only do so much to help before we just became a distraction to the adults. The adults would get up early while it was still cool enough to work, and they would, as my mom remembered, "pick their butts off" until it was too hot to continue. I sometimes could not see the pickers who were hiding in the trees, up on tall ladders with buckets strapped to their waists. I could hear the cherries go kerplunk into the buckets, then as the bucket filled up, the sound of the cherry went thud as it hit the other cherries. As they picked, there was always a young Family guy who would be playing guitar, and there was singing to help pass the time.

In the evenings, we got to know these Mexican families that were migrant workers. They would be sitting around their campfires singing. We would all join in together, singing La Bamba and other classics. They felt comfortable hanging out with us. It was a really warm and positive relationship between our two cultures. They might be picking in a nearby orchard.

I had a hard time at first getting used to the heat. Some of the only relief I got was by taking a cold shower. A bucket with holes in the bottom of it hung from a tree by a rope. After you fill the bucket up with water, someone would pull the rope until the bucket was high enough to stand under and take a shower.

At first a lot of people didn't have shoes. The heat was so scorching that one day I carried this pitcher of cold water and would pour it on the ground in front of me and then take a step, pour, take a step, until I realized that it took way too long to get anywhere. This was before we got the flip-flops. Then one day, there was a huge shipment. They were all identical but just different sizes, black, rubber soles, canvas toe piece. There were so many flip-flops that at nights they were always piled up at the entrances to the tents, and when I got up in the morning it was impossible to detect which pair were mine. There were times when one of my flip-flops was slightly longer than another, but it didn't matter. Thongs solved the problem of the hot ground.

As the season progressed, the Family moved from orchard to orchard, picking the different fruits that became ready to harvest. We would pitch our tents and set up camp each time we moved. A full kitchen was set up in the orchard where we would share meals, communally. There was a cooking crew, and sometimes Elkanah was assigned to it. We ate salads, rice, noodles, grains, and lots and lots of fruit. I especially enjoyed eating the dried cherries, which still had the pits in them. They took longer to eat than a typical dried cherry, because I had to gnaw on them a while to get the fruit off the pit. There was also a crew that would make fruit leather out of the seasonal cherries or apricots.

Much time was spent in the communal outhouses on the outskirts of the orchards, especially necessary, because we were eating so many cherries, which everyone knows what happens when one eats too many cherries. The outhouses became a real bonding experience. Each outhouse had two or three or four holes cut into the plywood side by side. Then there were openings cut high in the sides, near the roof, which allowed breezes to drift in so there was fresh air. Instead of being disgusted or embarrassed by having to pee right next to someone else, we had huge silly giggling fits. Out of sight in the outhouse, we could relax and talk and laugh, and mostly no one even knew we were there.

When we weren't goofing off in the outhouses, we played in empty fruit crates or climbed trees in neighboring orchards looking for the juiciest fruit to eat. Sometimes I sat with another girl in the tepee and crocheted.

Every day, the caretakers would take us to what we called 'the warebox' to swim. The warebox was square, about half the size of a small swimming pool and was connected to the irrigation system of water, which was distributed into the orchards. If we weren't swimming there, we would play in the orchards nearby that were not being picked.

Water from the warebox would flow into the orchard where we were camped. I played with the other kids in the water daily, making dams and tunnels. Without being aware of it, one time, we accidentally redirected the water right out of the orchard into the peach orchard. When it was discovered, it made the owner so mad, that he asked the Love Family to leave the orchard that year.

The day I got hurt was the day that Understanding had a contest for all the kids to see who could pick up the most apricots. There was an apricot orchard right in the middle of the cherry orchard. I carried my egg carton and collected apricots that had fallen to the ground they were so ripe. I filled up my egg carton and emptied it onto the drying rack nearby. The drying racks were huge pieces of corrugated metal sheeting that were up about a foot off the ground on top of logs.

Once I deposited my apricots onto the racks, we would split each apricot open, take the pit out and place both halves face up on the rack. There was supposed to be a prize for the winner who collected the most, but because I got hurt that day, the contest was called off.

Holding my egg carton to my chest, I dashed past one of the metal drying racks, and something happened to my leg. I heard a ripping/tearing sound. When I looked down, blood streamed down my leg. My calf was sliced open. Everyone came running. There was a sort of panic. No one gathered around me to pray and lay hands.

The Love Family believed that God healed everything. If one became ill, they "had a spirit," and an Elder would lay hands on you and pray. Occasionally we used herbs or plants like Aloe Vera and comfrey leaf for burns. But I knew I was in trouble when Understanding rushed over and gasped, "Oh my Goll!" Her expression scared me even more than all the attention. I needed help.

Evidently there was a hastily-called elders meeting to discuss what to do. Since the cut was so deep and serious, Understanding recommended that I be taken to the hospital without asking Love's permission. It would take too long to send someone to a neighbor's house to call him, since we didn't have a phone in the orchard. The elders agreed. Helpful and Dedication decided to take me to the hospital. Helpful asked my mom to come too, so she could give the doctors permission to treat me.

When we got to the hospital, right away there was a problem. Helpful and Dedication argued against the tetanus shot the doctors were insisting on. Helpful refused it on the basis that it "wasn't part of our belief structure," and my mom and Dedication backed him up. Despite the controversy, the doctors were very patient and kind to me and asked if I wanted to see the wound before they stitched me up.

"It looks like the inside of a grapefruit," I observed, and the doctors laughed. My mom remembered it well:

"It was a big cut and scary," she says.

The doctors were frustrated, but Helpful, Dedication and my mom stood firm and refused to let them give me a shot.

"I stuck to the guns," says my mom. "We were not into shots. I didn't believe in the medical trip even before I joined the family."

Even before I came to the Love Family, I had been born into a family with a lineage of thinking that was not mainstream. Both my biological parents were raised in Christian Science. Christian Scientists try to avoid conventional medical treatment. Instead they focus on prayer and believe that God heals.

"We knew it was beyond us," Understanding remembered. "Dedication boiled water to clean the wound because we knew that the camp scene might not be clean. We could clean you, but we couldn't sew you up—That was a real shock," Understanding says.

Afterward, a lady from the Public Health Department came to see what sort of living conditions we were living in. She was very nice, and while she was there, she taught some of the ladies how to sew up wounds.

Bright and Ravah were both there that day as well and told me what they remembered:

"I remember Cherry Hill and you cutting your leg on the thing that they would dry the fruit on," Bright says. "It still makes me cringe because I remember seeing your leg."

"I was running with you," Ravah says. "I remember how deep it was and the great panic. Understanding held the wound closed until they arranged to take you for help. When she took her hand off, it wasn't gushing anymore."

On the way home from the hospital, I recounted the argument between the doctors and Helpful. For a couple moments, it had been heated. The more persistent the doctors were, the more resistant Helpful was to the shot. Helpful did most the talking. Dedication and my mom backed him up and provided input as needed to show the doctors a united front.

"Do you want to stop for some ice cream?" Helpful said on the way back to our home in the orchard.

"No," I said. I had no appetite and was still trying to digest all that had happened.

"You don't want ice cream?!" He moaned, sounding disappointed, like he really wanted that ice cream himself.

"When we got back from the hospital, Love was mad at us," Helpful says. "I'm glad we took you when we did; He wouldn't have let us go if we had asked him."

I too am glad they took me. No one would've known how to take care of my injury. Afterward, when my leg was all bandaged up, I wasn't allowed to play in the warebox anymore. That was really the worst part. I wasn't allowed to get it wet. I still went to the warebox though, so I could just be with the other kids and watch. Hope was there with us and saw me sitting there. He came over and picked me up and pretended to throw me in. I screamed, thinking he might really toss me in the water. He laughed as he sat me down safely, much to my relief.

Once we returned to Seattle and back at the Kids' House, Dedication offered me some vitamin E oil to put on my scar. She said it would help it go away. I refused the oil. I didn't want it to go away. I wanted to keep it just like the scar from the shot in Maui, I wanted it to stay there as a reminder to me of what happened, as if I would ever forget. I never saw it as ugly or as something to hide, even though the scar was so pronounced that even today, it still sits there in all its glory, reminding me of my childhood, being raised in a community that did not believe in Westernized, conventional medicine.

There was an evolution, though, in Love Family thinking regarding treating illness over the years. In the early days, it was strict in terms of using the spiritual realm to heal; later, things loosened up a bit, and there was more openness to natural remedies. It was never either/or though; the emphasis was always spiritual at its foundation, but as I will explain, there were always exceptions that were made in different situations that arose.

The one thing that always stayed the same was that there were absolutely no drugs—not even aspirin. When my teacher Ethan came to the Love Family, he was into herbology, and for the first few years, they didn't let him talk about it.

"It's all spiritual," they told him.

"Nobody wanted to attribute healing powers to anything other than prayer, laying on of hands and meditation," Ethan says, "but later, it became more accepted. We had nurses that would give healing ointments. Jael had band-aids."

Even with the gradual changes, the spiritual thinking about illness and death remained the same. I was taught that people got sick or died because they were being negative. People talked about spirits all the time.

"You have a "bad spirit," I heard people say. "You need to drop that spirit," or "You are not in your right spirit." When we had lice, it was seen as a spiritual battle where we needed to, "clean up our act." When things happened, it was the spirit world with a message.

"Spirit was a big one," Understanding says. "It had Native American roots, where everything was seen to have a spirit, and they all worked together," she explained. "Spirit could cause jealousy, lust, hate, but the main ones were referred to as either negative or positive spirits. The body was seen as a sacred temple and you could choose what spirits lived in your body."

As a child, I was learning to solve life's problems through personal change and transformation. That was evident as can be seen in my then diary from that time period:

Dear Diary,

I have a pesty spirit and a helpful spirit and a lazy spirit in me; I know that I will get the pesty and lazy spirit out of me sometime. I think I am selfish and need to change myself. Because nobody likes me and it's not them I should blame.

Rachel Israel

Consideration talked in his manuscript (1978) about his then perspectives about the causes of illness: "The next day," he wrote, "I took out my contact lenses, since they had told me that to have glasses was not to have faith that God would heal my eyes, and I broke them into pieces…(159). The only reason anyone in the world got sick was because people didn't fight off the bad spirits (275)."

I already talked earlier about how Eve struggled to get her reading done without glasses. This was when she went back to college to renew her teacher's certificate.

Fortunately, there were at least four to five registered nurses who joined, and they helped deal with cuts and minor burns and other common ailments. But they had to work within the context of a community that did not believe in conventional medicine, which was the foundation of their training.

I talked to Bliss about how it felt to be a nurse in the Love Family. She had joined in 1971 after graduating from nursing school. When Bliss came, she became involved in the Family school and taught some of the younger kid's physiology and anatomy.

"When I came, I was the only one with any medical experience," she says. "Medical information was not respected though, and Courage, following Love's orders, burned all my medical books."

Before joining the Family, Bliss described herself as "partially disgruntled with mainstream medicine." She recalled that she had "seen electric shock treatment be given to people for having smoked weed and knew that chemotherapy was making people very ill and immuno-resistant. "I had classmates from my previous high school go to Vietnam and die," Bliss says soberly. "It made the world a more depressing place."

"It was difficult," Bliss explained, "because [the Love Family] belief system constantly challenged my background." It was "really scary," Bliss says. "I was responsible for this huge community of people, then to have to try and help people based on a model of thinking that excluded modern medicine was a challenge."

"I just did a lot of mothering," she explained, "and a lot of common sense remedies." If someone got a wound, she would use comfrey, or if someone got sick, she might try wrapping the chest in wool, fluids, ice—"We would try anything," she says.

Then, when a bunch of the kids got worms, Bliss gathered the kids together, and one by one, she examined us, then told our households to feed us garlic every day. It was awful, but it took care of the problem. Bliss says that when she first came, Gentle had burned her leg and foot on a pot of hot soup. "I saw people putting butter on it," she says. "I couldn't believe it."

When Gentle burned herself and when Benjamin burned his butt on the wood stove, Bliss instructed people to put Aloe Vera on the burns to aid with the healing. It seemed that every household had its own Aloe Vera plant, at least the households that I lived at. There were a couple times when I got small burns after accidentally touching the wood stove; I would automatically just go and break off a leaf and smear it on myself.

When I got my ears pierced, they got infected. Bliss gave me a hot washcloth to soak my lobes, then afterward, she applied a salve of lanolin and golden seal. I was amazed when the next day, the infection was mostly gone.

Bliss had a unique role, because not only was she a nurse, she was also sanctioned to Love, which gave her more of a direct line to Love than the other nurses.

"If I thought someone needed to go to the hospital," Bliss explained, "I would, on rare occasions, recommend that to Love, but I tried not to," she says, "because I was trying to have faith myself." Love "usually listened" to her, but "there were times when he didn't."

Love didn't listen to Bliss, though, when she asked to go to the doctor for a medical problem of her own. She could've died because she didn't go until it was almost too late. She had terrible headaches for three years. At first, they thought Bliss was pregnant. She was sick and weak, then she started getting blurry vision. She lost so much weight that she began to look skinny as a toothpick. She was told it was 'jealousy, negativity, in her head.'

"Finally, I just went without his approval," Bliss told me. It saved her life. The doctors found a tumor the size of an "orange" growing in her head.

I didn't know what going on with Bliss at the time. I saw her though and thought she did not look well, but it wasn't generally discussed and was dealt with privately in Love's household.

I always loved Bliss and had remembered the times when she took care of me from time to time. When she was around, I always watched her. She always made people feel loved and cared for. I wanted to be like her.

The Love Family's beliefs about sickness and natural ways to heal fascinated me. I was always curious to learn about the healing qualities of plants. In Alaska, my mom had been into it, and now here in the Family, Bliss and others were into it too. It just seemed natural and part of life.

Someone told me that the sticky milk inside the stem of a dandelion could be used to treat warts. Cheerful had warts, so each day, when we went out to play, he would come to me for his treatment. I would pick a dandelion and pop the stem in half, and when the sticky, white resin would seep out, I would dab it on his warts. I was a nurse, like Bliss.

I also learned that sickness could be controlled with my mind. When I was living in the yurt, there was a time when I got sick. I was coughing. I felt terrible and stopped going outside to play. One of the household women confronted me about being sick.

"Don't feed it! It's not real," she told me.

I looked at her confused.

"Thoughts create," she continued. "Tell yourself, I am well, I feel great," she instructed.

I didn't have anything to lose and was extremely bored, so I decided to try and apply what she said. I convinced myself that I wasn't sick, and that I felt great. It was the middle of winter, but I went and opened the huge wooden, yurt door, that opened to the outside. I looked out at the trees in the woods. The sun was shining even though it was freezing. If a sick thought came into my mind, I would say to myself, Nope! Then, I accepted and embraced the thoughts that came into my mind that told myself, I am well. I feel great now. It seemed that the longer I did it, the better I felt, so I kept doing it. Within a very short time, I decided that my sickness was gone. Resolutely, I got dressed and went out to play. I was done being sick. It seemed to work.

I never forgot that. I got up out of my bed and that was it. I had convinced myself out of being ill. That was when I began to understand how powerful my thoughts could be. I could heal myself by refusing to accept sick thoughts. Be gone negative spirit!

There was one thing though that didn't seem to respond to prayer or any of the ways of the spiritual thinking that might have helped, and that was when I got asthma.

One day, out at the Ranch, I came home from berry picking and found myself having a difficult time breathing. I tried to erase the symptoms with my thinking, but it didn't work.

No one took me to the doctor of course, but thankfully, no one lectured me about having a negative spirit. The household women speculated that maybe I was allergic to mold or to the trees. It did seem to start giving me trouble right about the time we moved from the Army tents, which were in the open pasture to the yurts, which were set up in the woods where it was a lot wetter.

Whatever it was, it was no fun. I don't know if Bliss had recommended it or if someone else just figured it out, but every time I had an attack, I was given a shot of black coffee. It helped sometimes, but other times, I would just have to suffer, often for hours until it went away. This was the downside to living in a community that did not believe in going to doctors.

Prayer and laying hands were always tried first to get rid of any negative spirits that could be causing it. If that didn't work, they tried other natural means. It didn't always make sense to me. If I cut my leg at Cherry Hill, well then, they rushed me off to the hospital. If I had asthma, well then just give her coffee. At other times, use my mind, prayer. Rather than try to make sense of it, I just got the message that going to the doctor was bad and especially taking medicines. There was always something better than that.

Going to the doctor was avoided at all costs, but there seemed to be a different attitude about going to the dentist, which may've been influenced somewhat by the fact that an actual dentist had joined, Presence. Presence only worked on adult's teeth though, because it was such a huge community, and he only fixed teeth sometimes. I heard there was quite a waiting list.

The kids didn't see Presence for dental work. I went on the busses with loads of kids every six months or so. Understanding would take us to the free clinic in Georgetown. I loved going and always heard how beautiful my teeth were.

Even though Presence did not work on the kids' teeth, he worked with Understanding to make sure all the kids knew how to floss and brush correctly. When we had all stopped at the cannery on our way to Cherry Hill, they had passed out floss—so we could all practice.

That is when Understanding started a storytelling program on teeth brushing. She would do full-scale puppet shows about the importance of brushing our teeth. She used her huge toothbrush as a prop for the show.

How was it that the kids were allowed to go to the dentist but not the doctor? I asked her.

"Love very much endorsed having the children's teeth taken care of," Understanding answered. "Love did not talk much about it, but he never fought us a bit."

I never understood the mixed message that said, we don't believe in doctors but it's fine to go to the dentist. I enjoyed it though, as it was a chance to pick from the prize basket they kept at the clinic.

In time, there was a change that began to appear. As more and more babies were born, people began to sneak to the doctor. I didn't know about this at the time. I found out later. It was a large enough community to where people could get away with it without Love finding out, especially towards the end.

On the surface, going to the doctor was still not accepted practice, but there were those who took the liberty to just go anyway. Women began to sneak out to get birth control. Understanding told me that Wisdom and Truthfulness were the ones who "made the decision" to let women get birth control "in secret." In a world where women have so many choices, as they do today, here were women living in a community where they had to sneak to do their own family planning.

Understanding herself broke the rules and snuck Azar down to get medical care for his ear infections. Azar was a little boy that she adopted from South America. She didn't ask, she just snuck out of there without being detected. When she got back, she "told everyone at the ladies' meetings" what she learned. So, then "Wisdom snuck Clean and Guidance" to a doctor for ear care. Then "Imagination took his daughter Birth," and "Eliab took his daughter, Flowing." I even remember my own mother, Elkanah snuck me out once to have a doctor look at my feet. The doctor said I had "pes planus" or fallen arches, basically flat feet and "nothing to worry about."

On our way to the foot doctor, we took a Metro bus across town to the clinic. I felt uncomfortable on the way. I knew it was not the accepted thing to go to the doctor, and my feet seemed just fine to me. It seemed odd to be snuck out in this way, but I didn't ask questions. There were people on the bus who were staring at us. I thought it was the way we were dressed, decked out in our Love Family, ethnic/hippie/Old Testament garb. I don't think I had even been on a city bus before either, since most of the travel we did before the Love Family was hitchhiking around, and in the Love Family we had our own vehicles.

There were a lot of exceptions when it came to the kids, especially more in the last years I was there. I would say that for the adults, making an exception was rare. It had to be really bad for them to go.

One major exception that happened was when Bright was hit by a car. He was badly hurt. He was riding his bike with Ravah in the neighborhood where we had houses on Queen Anne Hill. After he was hit, a neighbor called Harborview, and he was taken directly to the hospital. He would've died if he hadn't gone.

"I bit my tongue in half and it was so swollen that he couldn't breathe," Bright remembered. "I had to have a tracheotomy." Bright's "jaw was broken." His "face was torn up" and he was "bleeding profusely."

I was one of the kids who was chosen to visit him in the hospital that day. Understanding took me and Gentle, because she and I were to be his co-stars in an upcoming play for the Drama group. I was frightened to see him lying there with tubes in his mouth, watching television. It was a very uncomfortable visit, as I loved Bright very much and hoped that he would be ok. Even though they were rare, the exceptions stood out the most.

In general, people were told to "Just have faith." That's what Atarah was told when her six-month-old baby wasn't breathing properly. She told me what happened.

Her baby was having "petty mal seizures." Just to keep him breathing, Atarah would "splash water or blow" on his face. It helped somewhat, but then her baby began to get worse. "He had stopped breathing for ten minutes." After consulting with Wisdom and Appreciation, who then consulted with Bliss, who then consulted with Love, Atarah took her baby to the hospital. When she went to the hospital, she had to hold him in her arms during "two spinal taps." He "would've died" if she hadn't taken him. When she got back to the community with her baby, even though she had gotten permission to take him through the right channels, she got "a lot of judgment" from the membership for taking him and "for not buying into the prescribed way of thinking."

"I was judged as having no faith," Atarah says, "and to me, the whole thing was full of God." Atarah remembered sitting in the waiting room with Imagination and Wisdom: "We were meditating and all of us felt an overwhelming sense of the God force saying he was going to be OK."

I don't know how Atarah's visit to the hospital was paid for. That wasn't something I thought to ask her, but no one had health insurance; None of the kids had medical coupons. Getting any form of welfare was not part of the Love Family belief system. It was just assumed that if we had enough faith, we wouldn't need that sort of assistance. And while there were those willing to break the rules to get medical care for a child, there were those who would do anything to avoid it.

The hepatitis epidemic was a good example of that. The hepatitis outbreak was the one that most people who were there remember the most. But it wasn't the first epidemic to come along. Apparently, before I came to the Family, there was a scabies outbreak. Understanding told me all about that one.

"A lot of people suffered for a long time before they got help," Understanding remembered. There were "open sores, so people got staph infection in the wounds. Dedication had scabies all over her face."

"People were trying to hide the sores," Understanding says. They "were oozing" and "spreading" among "vast numbers of people" in the community. Then, someone snuck out to the doctor to get help. Once the medical staff heard that there were others who were suffering, they sent healthcare workers to the Family to check it out. There were sensitivities regarding medical care, so there was "a private meeting" set up for those afflicted. "Love finally relented and allowed everyone to get treated," says Understanding. "Love said, 'Let them give our bodies a physical cure, so we can go on with our spiritual.'"

I wasn't in the Love Family when they got the scabies, but I got them when I lived in Alaska, so I know what it was like.

There were other health problems that came along from time to time, such as lice. The problems were often introduced into the Family after members would return from rainbow gatherings. Other things were brought in by new people or visitors such as when I caught chicken pox from Shivaya and Parvati.

Lice was a big deal that took up a lot of time. Much time was spent checking heads and boiling laundry. A lot of the epidemics that took place were sometimes referred to as 'plagues,' that gave them biblical significance. I was told many times the story, in Exodus, of how Egypt was afflicted with the ten plagues before Pharoah let the Israelites go. The plagues included lice, boils, frogs, the water being turned to blood and the locus, among others.

There was no plague in the Bible, though, about people turning yellow, but that is what happened in the Love Family. It was the biggest and most well-known epidemic there was. Large numbers of people caught hepatitis A, resulting in a huge effort to control the spread of it and led to major changes in the way we lived as a family.

In the Love Family, everyone called it 'Yellow Fever.' In the next few paragraphs, I will talk about what happened. Yellow Fever was such a major event in the history of the Love Family, that pretty much everyone remembers some aspect of it. I was old enough that I remember a lot about what happened too.

I was at the Roza with the caretakers when it started. The Roza is not the name of a town, it is the name of an irrigation district in the Yakima River Basin where we picked fruit. 'The Roza' was one of the places where we camped and stayed during the harvesting season. Even though we all camped at the Roza, we had the use of a house there. The house and our camping scene next to it was located close to a town called Zillah, in Eastern, Washington.

It was the spring of 1977. What happened was that people had left the Roza and had gone to the Rainbow Gathering. Then after the Gathering, everyone came back to the Roza to pick fruit. When they returned, there were a man and a woman who came back from the Gathering with us to help pick fruit. People hoped that they would join. Their names were, 'Carlos and Rainsong.'

After Carlos and Rainsong had been with us for a few days, they started turning yellow and were throwing up. People were concerned that maybe what they had was contagious, so they were asked to leave. They left, but it was too late.

A week and a half later, Loyalty's whole household became so sick that they refused to come out of their tent. They never said, 'I am not feeling well,' instead they said, 'I am laying down, I have the spirit.'

There were a lot of people living together and sharing everything, such as meals and outhouses, so there was a great potential for anything that came in to be spread very quickly to large numbers of people.

Then, Understanding and the kids, including myself and several of our guardians that were there, all left to go back to the Ranch for the Golden Egg Party. At the Ranch, we lived as we normally did, going to outhouses and participating in the dish lines and sharing meals, etc. No one, at that point, knew how contagious the sickness was.

After the Golden Egg Party at the Ranch, the kids were sent back to the Roza. When we got there, there were more people sick than when we had left. There were 20 or 30 people who were sick. No one could explain tome why the kids were sent back after knowing that so many were sick there, but maybe it was just that there were no phones and the disease spread so quickly that people didn't know what was going on.

Once we arrived, a man named Waterfall came for visit. Waterfall came with his wife Goddess and their son Galahad. They were former Source members. Waterfall saw how many people were sick, and he talked to Understanding about taking some measures to prevent any further spread of whatever it was. One of the things he recommended was to close off the warebox, drain it, and bleach it out. He thought that might help. So, we were no longer allowed to swim in the warebox. Since that was the only relief from the heat, a lot of the kids were miserable and crying. By now, the tent of 'big people' who were sick had grown. Most of them couldn't get out of bed and were throwing up all over the place.

One of the things that amazes me about all this was that the Love Family was so unprepared. And I guess that is typical of any communicable disease that hits any population, so the Love Family was no exception. I was living in a large community of people with very poor hand washing facilitations. There were no bacterial soaps of any kind. There were no phones, and there were different members traveling from one outpost to another without knowing how serious it was.

By the end of summer, still none of the kids were sick, so we were sent back to the Ranch for school. After we left, Jael, one of the Family nurses, came out to the Roza, and she knew exactly what it was—Hepatitis A. That's when everyone started calling it "Yellow Fever," because people were turning yellow. When Jael saw what was going on, she quarantined the Roza.

Back in Seattle, people on Queen Anne were getting sick and being quarantined in Love's Area in the big house as it was being remodeled.

At the Ranch, people were starting to get sick; their eyes were turning yellow, they had severe nausea and other symptoms. The Ranch house went under quarantine as well. There was a tent near the lake.

The rule was, 'you had to stay there until your eyes were clear.' For some people it took 3 days, for others it took 3 weeks or 3 months. Just at the Ranch, 50–60 people all had it at the same time. Jael was the one who made the decision about whether someone was clear or not. There was no involvement with public health; These were self-quarantines.

I was sent into quarantine too, even though I never got sick. I was eating over at Love's household. Fresh, Salome and some other women were frying up tofu in a pan. Wisdom was nearby taking care of Perfection. I loved tofu, and I could hear it sizzling in the pan as I sat waiting for more. We were dipping it in soy sauce and calling it 'toe food.' Fresh and the ladies laughed at us when they heard us say 'toe food.'

"No, it's tofu," the ladies corrected us. They were still laughing when a messenger came in the tent and told us not to eat anymore of the tofu. I was very disappointed since it was my turn for more. Some of the younger kids started crying and throwing a tantrum. The messenger said that there were some people who thought it might have been the tofu that was making people sick. So just to be sure, tofu was out.

Later that afternoon, I complained of a stomach ache and was immediately sent to the Army tent of quarantined people. When I moved in, there were a lot of people who were in bed. No one was having meetings or carrying about normal business.

My stomachache was gone by that evening. I never got sick, and I didn't turn yellow—but because I went into that tent that was under quarantine—I wasn't allowed to leave. While I was there though, I just helped with dishes and clean up and did whatever I could do to make people comfortable. I was happy to be helping, which I liked to do, however, it was depressing for me because I couldn't play with the other children. I just had to live in this dark tent with all these yellow looking, sick people.

Then, Henry the Fiddler showed up, who was a good friend to the Love Family. He knew how to help, since he had dealt with a hepatitis outbreak at Steve Gaskin's Farm. Henry the Fiddler's advice led to big changes in the way that we lived.

Instead of composting human waste, there began to be huge pits dug for outhouses. Before, when the outhouses were full, there were men that would just carry the waste to special compost piles in fields. I sometimes saw them carrying the buckets across the pasture. It took four men to carry them. They were barrels sawed in half, or 30-gallon honey buckets.

Another change was that now there were separate outhouse holes for men and women, and the field where the waste had been dumped and stored was quarantined off. Then, we started using Betadine soap and everyone began washing hands. We also started using toilet paper in the outhouses instead of newspaper and phone books.

The Yellow Fever outbreak was the main reason why people moved out of the circle and started spreading out around the lake. We had been living in our own cesspool. The area where we were camping next to the lake was a kind of a marsh. They said we were all living too close together and just making 'a soup of pollution,' so the next year, instead of putting up a tent in the circle, each household was given a home site around the lake.

The next year at Passover, Love named the year, the 'Year of Cleanliness,' after the major effort that was made to deal with the health problem the previous year.

Yellow Fever was the worst health problem the Love Family had ever dealt with, at that point, but luckily, no one there ever died from it. Hepatitis A is rarely fatal, although it can sometimes lead to liver failure and other more serious forms of hepatitis. Even though there were no deaths related to the hepatitis epidemic, there were deaths related to other things.

Three years before we came, in 1972, two men named Solidity and Reverence had died. They had inhaled glue by themselves 'without supervision.' Yes, apparently there was this short-lived phase early on when the membership would inhale glue together. Consideration discussed the matter in his manuscript (1978) since he was a member during that time. Understanding also had been a member during that time and shared with me what she remembered. Plus, there were articles about it in the papers.

"Once the bodies were found unconscious," Consideration wrote, "Love attempted artificial respiration on them and shouted for them to 'Come back!' Everyone silently prayed as they waited. Police cars and a fire engine showed up, and there was a confrontation. The Family would not let the police take the bodies. The police agreed. "They prayed all night, hoping the bodies would be resurrected. By the third day, they had not come back. Love claimed the reason was because Reverence had been disobedient and had not breathed under supervision. (pp. 226-228)

The Love Family had not called it glue though, they called it, "Tell-U-All," and saw it as a religious rite. It was actually an industrial solvent called toluene. In a usually well-controlled setting, members would inhale the substance and have psychedelic experiences together.

A Seattle based bi-weekly newspaper serving the Pacific Northwest, whose chief purpose was to document local music reported that, "Love and other Family elders would administer the drug to the faithful by pouring small amounts into plastic bags. The flock would then inhale the fumes and undergo a quasi-psychedelic experience." (*The Rocket*, August 1984 pg. 23.) "Reverence (William Eddy, 26) and Solidity Israel (Gregory Lemaster, 22) died of toluene poisoning." This was not the same "Solidity" that I came to know later on.

"The men were found dead with plastic bags over their heads in the living room of a Family home at 817 W. Armour St." the Times had reported (*Seattle Times* January 25, Tues. 1972 A20). There was a "3-day vigil before burial, because "the sect refused to surrender the bodies until a "resurrection" period had elapsed" (*Seattle Times* Oct. 21, 1978 A11).

After the deaths, the Family quit breathing glue ever again. I never even heard about it until years after I left the community and ran across some newspaper articles about it when I was doing some research for the book.

But Solidity and Reverence's deaths weren't related to the Love Family's beliefs about doctors. Serenity's death was though. I always felt sad about her death, even though I was not close to her, and she wasn't a regular part of the kid scene.

Serenity was one of the adults, but she had only been 16 when she joined. She was such a petite woman though, that I thought she looked like Snow White in the Disney story. She was sick for years before she finally died, because she refused to have a surgery that she needed. And here she had total faith in God and served Love with her soul as her body slowly shut down. She lived as long as she did though, because towards the end of her life, her mom came and forced her to go to the hospital. But it was too late. The last time I saw her was when we lived in the circle of tents. I saw her walking off towards the knoll, towards the tooth booth.

Serenity wasn't the only one whose death could've been prevented. There were babies born that might have lived if they would've gotten the appropriate medical care. There were 13 babies total who died, and that number does not include the number of miscarriages that may have been associated with the lack of medical attention. Some of the babies were dead when they were born, and others were dead at birth. Why did they die?

"We had no sensitivity to diet, no sensitivity about milk or protein, and no sensitivity about pregnant women and what they needed," Understanding says. "It was just this ignorant trip."

Thirteen may sound like a small number compared to the 134 babies who were born there and lived, but that any baby died at all is a tragedy. A majority of them who died were either born stillborn or died within the first few moments after birth; a minority of them died in their sleep after they had been born.

I have a list detailing every baby who died, when they died, who their parents were, and some details about the circumstances around their death. It is part of a larger list of every kid who was born into or who lived in the Love Family. When I created the list, it seemed to only make sense to include the babies who died. It seemed unfair to exclude them. I compiled the list from my own memory with the help of former teachers and caretakers and others who had also grown up in the Love Family.

I am not going to share all the details of that list, however, because of some understandable sensitivities. But I am going to discuss the deaths more generally, since they had a big impact on me. That babies died or that women might not have had proper maternity care is important to my story, because I came from a place, a world, a society that was based on a foundation of beliefs about health care that placed people and children at risk—of death!

Understanding had a lot to say about the babies who died. She was "deeply affected" by the deaths, since she was close to the children and would have expected that the children who died, if they hadn't died, would have become part of the kid scene under her care. When a baby died, she "visited each mom" and "talked to them about what happened and prayed with them."

"They would have been part of my world—the children's world," Understanding says. "These were the newest members of our community, and so I felt a sense of grief."

I felt sad too. It kind of confused me as to how I was supposed to understand death, considering I was being taught that we were eternal and would live forever.

When Preservation died, it upset me to learn that she had suffocated in the blankets between her parents in the night. I ate over there at their tent all the time. I would frequently go peek at her dead body during her wake. In the Love Family, it was our custom that when someone died, they would be kept for three days before they were buried to see if God wanted to bring them back. Preservation was kept in a small four-man tent in the main pasture where all the Army tents were. I would go and just watch her through the little bug mesh screen window of the tent and wait, hoping she would open her eyes and be resurrected.

It must have been 1978 because I believe the Army tents in the circle of tents had been remodeled with kitchens and entranceways by then. Preservation looked very peaceful, like she was sleeping, but very still and unmoving. Would she come back? Was Preservation eternal? I tried to avoid thinking about the relevant biblical passage, but it was impossible not to think of it:

> "…for dust thou art, and unto dust shalt thou return." (Genesis 3:19, KJV)."

Another baby that died, a boy, was placed in wake in a small trailer and hauled into the woods, which was on a hiking trail that led to King Lake. The babies did not all die at once, of course. They took place over time. I am guessing it was the following year after Preservation's death because she was already gone by then. Every time I hiked to King Lake, I would see the little trailer nestled in the trees where the baby lie in wake. It made me uncomfortable when I saw it: I wondered what would happen if the baby resurrected and no one was there to know about it. How would he survive?

After the wake, they buried it right there in the area where the trailer was.

"Love felt it would be more peaceful up away from the pasture," Understanding explained. "They took the trailer away after the wake. Love didn't want the wake down there with all of us by the tents like it had been for Preservation."

Then a year or two later, Energy died. After her wake, the kids were asked to go and help bury her.

"Come on you kids, we need you to help us out!" we were asked.
I and the other kids who were there all jumped in the back of the truck with the shovels, a box, and a group of adult men, members from Strength and Appreciation's household.

The truck drove to a woodsy location in Arlington. I don't know where it was exactly. When we got there, the kids were instructed to go into the woods and collect pieces of wood and rocks that were to be placed on top of the grave. I was too young to use a big shovel. It was mostly the men that helped dig the grave, although in my memory, they let some of the boys help too. Maybe this was learning through our daily life, which was learning the natural way. I saw babies born, and now I saw them when they were dead and needed to be buried.

It was a huge pit. It took a while for them to dig it. Then, after the baby was buried, we all stood together in a circle around the grave and prayed. We were eternal, right? But death seemed pretty real when I am helping bury the baby.

It is hard to even explain to myself how I could be raised in a place where I had been a witness to prayer healings; I had been taught from an early age about the mind-body connection and the power of my thoughts to heal myself. And at the same time, I was being raised in a place where babies died because of our faith, because people just refused to go to doctors or get needed medical care.

It is impossible to know exactly how many miscarriages took place without talking to everyone who was in the Love Family, but I imagine the number was quite high. My guess is that our infant mortality rate was probably closer to the rates in some third world countries, and even to some areas of the United States where women's economic status, diet, and access to medical care is compromised. Was this infant mortality rate just to be expected because of our life situation? We were an isolated religious, community with certain beliefs. It shouldn't be surprising.

"I think what disturbs me," Understanding says, "is that we built a society where children could be nameless. And if you don't have a birth certificate, then you don't have a death certificate. When [Congenial's] kids died, they couldn't get death certificates because they didn't have birth certificates," she explained. Those children, "in some ways," were "non-persons. The babies and the children were vulnerable and easy to victimize," continued Understanding, "because their graves weren't marked; there were no investigations; there were no birth records to even show they existed. There were not enough people looking after their interests," Understanding concluded. "They had a right to live. They had a right to go to the doctor and be in a hospital where they could have cleared their wind-pipes, so they could have lived."

I felt sad about the babies who died as they would've been like brothers or sisters to me. Understanding pressed the point to me:

"If nobody knows about you then who is there to protect you, who even knows if you died and they buried you in the back pasture. And if our society were absolutely perfect and full of enlightened angels then fine, but we were not. There was evil and corruption in the Family, just like there was in society."

Years before any of these babies died, there was a mother of a Love Family adult member who was interviewed by a *Seattle Times* reporter. This mother was worried about her daughter who had joined the Love Family and had been sanctioned to a man. The mother expressed her concern to the reporter, and again, this was way before any of those babies had died. She had said to the reporter, 'They do not believe in medication. They have assigned a husband for my daughter though there is no record of any marriage. If she had a baby and it needed medical attention and died, we'd never know about it.' (*Seattle Times* March 13, 1974 A15). Predictive!

There were at least 134 children that were born in the Love Family when I was there, children who lived. I wasn't born there. I had a birth certificate because I came when I was almost seven years old. I had been born in a hospital some years before we even joined. But my dad never came to visit me. If something had happened to me, no one would've known. Something bad could've happened to any of the almost 270 kids, whether they were born there or whether they came like I did, and no one in the outside society would've known about it. I guess that's true no matter what society one lives in. There are missing children reported every day. But our community was isolated and disconnected from the typical supports that people take for granted every day in conventional society, such as birth certificates and schools that keep records of attendance etc.

It's kind of spooky, especially considering how consolidated the power base. In other words, as I discussed earlier how the hierarchy worked, there were no checks and balances on the leadership. People believed so strongly in Love's authority, that people put him over their own needs and the needs of their children and families. Is that why they call it, 'blind faith?'

"Why did we have to live like we were in a third world country?" Understanding cried. "This is America, and it was a violation of a child's rights as a human being. Women were not getting the medical care that they needed, medical care that was available in their own country!"

There was a child that died. His name was Worth. He was probably four or five when he died. When I first came to the Love Family, this little boy lived with his parents in Meekness's household. They lived in Serious's Area in the house next to the yellow, schoolhouse. I went over there from time to time, and when I saw Worth, he was very blue looking. His skin was blue. His lips were blue. No one told me why he was blue, but I knew something wasn't quite right, because he wasn't growing, and he was not being taken care of by the caretakers, which was unusual. All the kids in the Love Family, especially early on were being taken care of by Understanding and other caretakers and teachers. I would see his parents taking him for his walks. It took an hour for him to walk one block.

I learned later that he apparently had a bad heart and needed surgery. They had faith that God would heal him, so they didn't take him to have the surgery. Then one day, they took him to the dentist and got caught; The receptionist saw Worth and that he obviously needed medical care, and she called CPS. To avoid CPS, they ran off to Hawaii and lived in the house that the Family owned there. It might've been there where he died, but if he had had that surgery, maybe he would be alive today.

The deaths scared me, and I had no way to process them other than to write about them, since there was no public discourse about them in my community.

Dear diary,

What I Think About Death:

I think I'll live forever, my spirit will at least, but I also think my body will pass away. I don't know it, but I think it. Sometimes I think it won't be fair if the world blows up now, because I didn't get a chance to grow up, like Big People did. That's why I wrote the president a letter, but it didn't help because he doesn't even get the letter. His secretary wrote me back. I will pray.

Rachel Israel

Dear Diary,

Today I had a conversation with Danny about reincarnation. He is visiting with his dad. I really don't know what to think about reincarnation. I can't remember any of my past lives, but I want to believe him. I wonder what personality or form I was? I want to guess I was a famous queen with many servants and nice things. Or maybe I was a princess in a green pasture sitting in the shade of an apple tree. I'd like to think I was a lady in Bible times wearing a veil over my face all the time, though that would be a nuisance. I thought we were eternal and that we would live forever but now I'm not sure. Definition told me about nuclear bombs.

Rachel Israel

Dear Diary,

Just in case I die,

...all of my pretty clothes go to Zarah, Heaven, Mercy and [Gentle], in that order.

My skirts, jeans, and socks go to whoever needs them. My costumes go to Understanding and the Drama Group. My looms and beading projects go to Eve. My deck of cards goes to Forest. My Marco Polo roller-skates go to Ravah, and my Pinochle deck goes to Bright."

Rachel Israel

Dear Diary,

I dreamed that Compassion and I were going to be put to death. Both of our heads were cut off. We looked down at our bodies and said, "Death is not so bad after all."

Rachel Israel

After all these years, I still don't know what I think about death, but there is nothing so sure as the evidence of a scar on my leg that reminds me of when I was cut at Cherry Hill. Looking at it is like looking at a photograph because of the memories it conjures up. I see doctors arguing with Helpful and Dedication in the hallway outside my hospital room. I see Hope picking me up and pretending to toss me in the warebox. I see the hot, dry climate of Cherry Hill and our tents, camping in the apricot and cherry orchards. I see myself, a young child in a community with an alternative belief system that seemed to clash with the predominant beliefs of the world outside.

The scar on my leg reminds me of what happened and where I come from, but for me, it was also something more. There was a reason why I didn't want the vitamin E. I didn't want my scar to go away, because it was concrete evidence that it even happened in the first place. There were no medical records that were kept. I have no photographs of me and kids running around in the orchards.

I spent years as a child in a community that focused on the now, on the present moment. The past was the past. The future didn't matter either. All that mattered was right now, but even back then, I wanted to believe that my past was valuable. After all, it was part of my story that made me who I am. It must be important.

When now is the time, all the time, I ended up feeling that I didn't have a right to my own history. Like Marty, like my life in Alaska before we got there, like anything that ever happened to me in the Love Family such as when I cut my leg in the orchard. I knew that once it was over, it would be done, and no one would ever talk about again—as if it never happened. What happened the week before or last year, who knows? There was no record of it, because the Family was so focused on staying present. There was no record keeping of things that happened there, no evaluation of events with talk of lessons learned.

My attachment to the scar was my way of keeping a part of the past with me. It was my own secret way of rebelling against those ideals, something that I can keep when it's all over, a reminder of the progression of time, my own strength and of healing, and of my ability to move on and to survive.

I was raised in a community where I saw firsthand the power of faith; I learned very young, the power of prayer. I also learned about the mind body connection and how important it is to understand how thoughts create reality, but I also saw a darker side where I lived in a community where babies died because of people's faith, and where people had to sneak out to get birth control or get their child evaluated for an ear infection.

There has to be a better way, a way where people can have faith and where people can use the power of their minds to heal themselves and others but can still go to the doctor when needed without shame, without secrecy. That is what I have tried to do in my life. I am very guarded about the medical profession. I tend to research everything and don't just accept a doctor's evaluation right off. At the same time, I try to find a balance because obviously, there is a role for doctors when the time presents itself. I always have tried to make myself well and do what is possible to prevent illness through diet and exercise but have still kept a certain respect for mainstream medicine, that could step in where I could not, if needed.

BIBLIOGRAPHY (CHAPTER 12)

Atarah. Personal Interview. August 7, 2002. Seattle, WA.

[Bright]. Personal Interview. January 11, 2002. Des Moines, WA.

[Bliss]. Personal Interview, March 5, 2002. 5:30pm.

[Ethan]. Personal Interview, January 3, 2002. Magnolia Hill, Seattle, WA.

[Definition]. Personal Interview. September 30, 2001. Magnolia Hill, Seattle, WA.

Hannula, Don. *Seattle Times*. Love Family Reports Father's Kidnapping. March 13, 1974. A15.

Hannula, Don. *Seattle Times*. Last Time, Says Father. March 13, 1974. A15.

Hinterberger, John. *Seattle Times*. It's Right for One but Wrong for Another. October 21, 1978 A11.

Hinterberger, John. *Seattle Times*. Sect Wants to Rule Magnolia and Queen Anne. January 25, 1972 Tues. A20.

Israel, Larry. (Consideration) 1978. Unpublished Manuscript. Pg. 159 and 275.

Israel, Understanding. Personal Interviews. May 5, 2001, January 20, 2002, and February 14, 2004. Arlington, WA.

[Ravah]. Personal Communication. March 19, 2002 (7:55pm).

CHAPTER 13

Big Foot, Patch Adams, and the Far Corners of Your Mind

One of the lucky things that I got to do in the Love Family as a child was be involved in the Drama Group. It was a theater group put together by Understanding and others for the kids. We did some performing for the membership as well as some performing outside of the community at different local venues. Besides giving me theater skills, it also opened my eyes a bit to the outside world, because we were performing outside of the Family.

Up till this point, my perspectives were limited about the world because I wasn't exposed to it much. The exposure to the world that I got as being part of the Drama Group was limited though. A lot of our performing was done for people in the counterculture at large, so even though we were performing outside the community, we were still kept from exposure to mainstream culture. All the same, it was still good experience and taught me something about life on the outside. Plus, it got me away from the Love Family, doing something interesting and different.

To provide some perspective, let me explain in more detail my views as a child about the world outside of the community. Growing up in the Love Family—there was a sense of safety that I have never felt since. It was a tight knit community. We didn't have to lock our doors at night; we didn't have to worry about burglars; If we needed food, we would go to the 'store' that was in a room up at the Barn where staples were kept. I collected vegetables from our garden for our household when needed. There were not the modern conveniences such as phones or television that might have widened my perspectives about the World. What I knew was pretty much what I was being told and a few early memories of my life on the road with my mom before the Family, including our life in Alaska.

There wasn't a lot of mixing with folks on the outside. We were an isolated group, by design. Nobody knew what was going on in the Love Family. The papers didn't know what was going on. Our Queen Anne neighbors didn't know what was going on. Parents and relatives of Family members also mostly did not know what was going on. Even members within the Family did not know what was going on. The information channels were pretty top down. People were so focused on staying present and being positive that we ended up living as a culture, in a sort of insulated bubble.

I lived in a "kingdom," in "heaven on earth," in "God's family." I was told that the world outside was from Satan, and that 'our people' were wandering out there, confused, lost, lonely and searching for the truth. What gave us hope was that we knew they would all eventually come home, to us, even Marty. God just woke us up first. We were Christ reborn, risen from the dead, and had become "the first fruits of them that slept" (1 Cor. 15:20).

I hadn't chosen this. I was only there because my mom had brought me. I had a lot of questions and was curious and yearned for information about the outside World that would help me to understand what they were talking about. I had lived out there but only when I was very young. I had good memories of living out there with Marty in Alaska, and in our travels on the road. I had met and stayed with a lot of nice people, so I wasn't sure what I thought.

Years later, I had the chance to talk to Ravah about what it was like for him growing up in the Family and what he knew then about 'the World.' He didn't have much awareness of the world outside, he says, but he remembered that he and some other boys were in the back of the bus, going to the rainbow gathering one year. They were maybe around 10 or 11 at the time. They were looking out the window, and they saw "this kid" looking at them. He was making fun of them.

"And we made fun of him right back," Ravah says. "That was the first time when I realized we were different," he says. "Before that, I thought that we were what normal was." From that point on, Ravah began to feel self-conscious, "embarrassed" about his family. "We were sheltered from the world," Ravah explained. "I began stepping out. There were encounters. I wasn't going to wear those tunics and robes! I wanted to wear blue jeans."

Zarah says she "knew we were different." She could tell because, "It was obvious" that the children from Coe school would take the bus or walk a few blocks up the street to their school, but she and her peers from the Love Family would just walk and go enter into nearby private residences for school.

"The neighbors encouraged their dog to come and take our shoes off the porch," Zarah says. "Things like that, that were just pointless, being mean, just because we were Love Family." She remembered doing this walkathon and was going around and asking for donations. Someone was just about to donate:

"Are you from that love group?" they asked her.

"Yeah!" she answered proudly and happily.

Immediately they closed the door in her face.

"That's when I realized that people didn't like us. That was my first experience with hatred," Zarah says.

I did not have any negative or unfriendly interactions with outside children like Ravah or Zarah did. From what I could tell, from the few interactions I had had with outsiders, I knew that they were curious about us. I never picked up that there was judgment or disapproval in the interactions I had, but I hadn't had many interactions in the first place.

I wasn't sure I believed that the world was where Satan lived, that out there, people were "lost." I wanted to believe that the World was not a bad place at all but just a different place. I was withholding my judgment. I had an unquenched thirst for information about the outside, but it would be years before I would ever figure out just how isolated and unconventional my family really was.

My prior experience was limited, so there was no way I could understand. I could not make an informed comparison, as most adult members had the opportunity to do when they joined.

The boundary though between the World and the Love Family, between us and them was clearly defined. Since I didn't know much about the World; it was mostly this vague concept from which everything was measured against. It never made a whole lot of sense to me how the World could be a bad place when that was where I was from, and I was good, right? Our life with Marty had been a good life. I never had felt lost or scared out there. The tepee was warm and cozy. Yusef would greet me every day when I got off the school bus, so I figured that there were many different ways of living the hippie good life.

There was such determination within the Family to keep separate. It was to such a degree that it sometimes seemed as if the World didn't exist. It was invisible. Even when we lived on Queen Anne hill so close to people who were living in the World, it was as if they weren't there. Our map included the Love Family and that was the only reality that anyone ever accepted. Everything else either wasn't acknowledged or was ignored. In a sense, it was like walking down the street with tunnel vision, but everybody had this tunnel vision, so it was like everyone was colluding to create a certain worldview. I was only allowed to see the world through that tunnel vision.

There were times when I walked to or from the Front Door Inn to Love's Area, and on the way, we walked by Coe School. I watched the kids play on the playground behind the fence. It seemed so chaotic, their play so unstructured compared to ours. Little girls playing jump-rope here, other girls and boys running there. Others were over playing on the monkey bars—it seemed so crazy. In my community, people did things together. Everything was so orchestrated, so organized and structured. It seemed that on the Coe playground, there were so many children and just a few teachers roaming about with them. There was no centralized point from which everything else made sense; It made me dizzy just to watch it. No one on that playground was family. Most of them didn't even know one another outside of school. At the end of the day, all the kids left to go to their own private homes. After living in the Love Family for as long as I had, it became hard to imagine.

I was walking by Coe School once again, and a couple of girls came up to the fence:

"Hi," they said to us and smiled. "What's your name? How old are you?" they asked, one question after the next.

Peace gave them a fake, 'Worldly' sounding name and made up how old she was.

I didn't really see a need to do that, so I just chuckled to myself and stood there quietly.

The Coe School girls went back to play, and we went on our merry way back to Love's Area. There was no rule about talking to outsiders, but it was something we didn't generally do, unless there was some sanctioned reason for it.

In other utopian, religious communities, the division between us and them was more officially defined. For example, at Oneida, their religious and moral training powerfully reinforced their sense of being different from–and spiritually superior to–children in the world outside…"Oneida children were forbidden even to speak to outside children," (Klaw, 1993, 149). Children from the Shaker community were taught to "never even look at the world's folks" (Holloway, 1966).

What the Amish children are taught: "It is the duty of a Christian to keep himself "unspotted from the world" and "separate from the desires, intent, and goals of the Worldly person." Another Amish rule: "One should not dress and behave like the world." Furthermore, no Amish shall marry a non-Amish person, nor shall they enter into a business partnership with an outsider. "For those who wished to have automobiles, radios, or the usual comforts of modern living, they faced the threat of being excommunicated and shunned." (Hostettler & Huntington, 1971 pg. 5–7)

Mennonite children are taught to believe that the Christian as a citizen in Christ's kingdom is called to leave the Worldly Kingdom and "live a life of separation without being unequally yoked with the institutions of 'the world.' The dual Kingdoms were historically conceptualized and contrasted as good versus evil and righteousness against sin." (Kraybill, 1977, pg.7) In the Love Family, I often heard biblical verse that emphasized the division:

> They are not of the world, even as I am not of the world. We are in the world, but we are not of it." (I John 17:16)

> Do not love the world or the things in the world. If anyone loves the world the love of the father is not in him. (I John 2:15, *KJV*)

Why do these groups have to do this? Why do they create this 'us and them' mentality with so much judgement against outsiders? I found one educator and author who has written books on communitarian societies, including books on the Amish and the Hutterites. John A. Hostettler came up with a reason: "In order to survive in an industrialized nation like the United

States," he wrote, "most sects have had to retreat to a spatial and psychic togetherness...interpersonal relations and cohesion within the community become more and more essential for the successful functioning of the community." (Hostettler & Huntington, 1971, pg. 9)

This makes sense to me. In order for the Love Family to survive and function as it did, it had to define itself by what it was not. 'This is who we are,' and 'that is who they are,' and by doing that, it built cohesion. And that's really true of everybody, in a way, we define ourselves by who we are not, and in this way, it forms a stable identity and gives us membership into a definable group, otherwise, if we define ourselves as like or similar to, everybody else, then there is no distinction that defines and separates, and that can make people feel uncomfortable or lost.

Arbitrary divisions between groups, with one being pitted against the other, function to build in-group cohesion and also protect the group from outside threats whether perceived or real.

For me, the more I understand, the easier it is for me to accept that growing up in the Love Family was not this freak accident with all these crazy people, and I just happened to be there. It was a complex set of social and psychological dynamics set within a unique period in history.

There are so many different ways of looking at things, its mind boggling! But I don't mind that. It's OK that I don't understand everything. I try, though, to make sense of it, as much as I can.

As a child, I certainly was taught that the World, which was the customs and norms of the outside society, that that was NOT how it was done in the 'Kingdom of Heaven.' People out there had 'lost their vision.' 'Eventually they would come home.' Plus, the overt message that I received, by the fact that Worldly influences were totally kept from me, was that I was being protected from those influences. And if I had to be protected, then the influences must be bad.

One of the things that got me out of that isolation was the Drama Group. I consider that my experience and involvement in the Drama Group was one of the coolest things I ever did in the Love Family.

The Drama Group went through an evolution. At first, it was just the kids singing Love Family songs and doing little theatrical skits for members of our Family. But, when Love saw us perform, he became inspired and encouraged Understanding, and the other caretakers, to build theater into our lives as part of school. Understanding acquired a large puppet theater, and we began to sing as the opening act for her puppet shows. Glory and Solomon were talented Family musicians, who would play the guitar while we sang for the crowds. We sang for Love and for different guests; even Steve Allen when he would visit. We sang at Love Family events. It wasn't just strictly singing; it was also learning to perform, to smile to animate the songs through nonverbals with our body, hands and facial expressions.

As the show improved, we began to perform outside the Family. We performed at peace concerts at Volunteer and Gasworks park; We were the opening act for one of the Love Family bands called, 'The National Band.' Gideon helped arrange for us to perform at Seattle area churches and halls. Understanding arranged with Native elders for us to perform at the Indian Pow Wow and the Reservation. Each time we performed in a public place, I would go through the motions on cue. I had sung the songs so many hundreds of times by now. What I really enjoyed was people watching. It was an opportunity to observe the Worldly people in the audience who were just there, watching our show.

Usually, we performed for a live audience, but one time, we got on the radio waves at KRAB. KRAB was an FM radio station that was on the air between 1962 and 1984. It mostly provided educational content without commercials and was one of the forerunners of what would become community radio.

I rehearsed the songs that we would sing. There was this song that Understanding and Solomon wrote called, "We Are One." It was simple, but each verse said, 'We are one' in a different language.

When we started singing in the studio, one of the kids accused another kid of "hogging" the mic and it went live on the air. Understanding remembered it well:

"Purity wanted the mic and somebody else said, 'You already had it. I have not. Yes, you did, Give it to me!' And the whole thing went out over the radio and we were never invited back. One kid actually punched another kid. It was horrible!" Understanding remembered.

I remember the fight, but I didn't understand that it was being aired live and that lots of people were listening. To me, it was just us, a bunch of kids in this small, overcrowded room with no windows, with one microphone that we all had to share. Most of our performances up till then were without fancy equipment. We were used to performing to a live audience. We had no experience performing for people who weren't there right in front of us. Plus, we didn't even listen to the radio in the Family, so I didn't really have a concept about what we were even doing.

Apparently, Love never found out about that KRAB radio fiasco. He had wanted us to do it to show the world that the Love Family were peacemakers.

"What it really showed," says Understanding, "was that we had no control over our children. Afterward, people were coming up to me, scratching their heads. 'I thought you were the Love Family,' they would say."

The KRAB radio embarrassment was just one small blip. There were a lot of performances that we did over time. I don't remember every show.

One of the things that I appreciated the most about those times were our trips into the outside world, to see live theater. After Love gave Understanding that money so that the children could do 'culturally enriching activities,' she went about making the arrangements for us to take trips to see the performing arts and shows that were in the Seattle area. She thought it would be helpful to be exposed to that since we were learning how to perform on stage.

We went to see plays at Poncho Theater, which were located at Woodland Park Zoo. This was before it became what most people know as the Seattle Children's Theater, which is currently located at the Seattle Center.

When it was time to load, we all piled into the buses like a school would for a typical fieldtrip. Then, when we got there, we would all file in and fill up two or three rows of seats.

We saw a lot of different plays but the ones I remember the most were Helen Keller, which a lot of people know is a true story about a little girl who was deaf and blind; I also remember Heidi, a show about a little girl who goes up in the mountains and lives with her grandfather who tends goats. But the one that really sticks out in my mind the most was a play called, "Outside."

It was about four teenagers who lived in outer space. Their mother was a computer that was built into the orb that they all lived in. It was a sheltered existence until one of the boys accidentally found the 'outside.' He figured out that there was a much larger universe outside of the orb. At first, when he found out, his siblings didn't believe him. The computer (their mother) tried to stop him. Eventually they all figured it out and were able to leave the orb. They were free. I could relate to this story. I felt like those teenagers on that orb who found their loyalties divided. They wanted to learn the truth, but they also desired to remain safe under the care of a computer mother (the Love Family) who took care of their every need. In some ways, I felt like I lived in an orb in space, and maybe someday, I would want to be free too, just like these teenagers.

It was wonderful to see theater, and I was able to relate it to what we were doing in the Drama Group. Plus, it was so great to see stories about people who didn't live in the Love Family. It helped me to understand the outside world.

Love wanted the kids doing quality theater. He made sure Understanding had the money to do it, and that she had people helping her. He had really high standards that influenced the amount of effort and energy that went into our productions. There were lots of people who helped to make it all work such as Fresh, Jezreal, Radiance, and others who helped with everything from food, to extra guardianship, to costume and set design. Family musicians, such as Solomon, Integrity and others helped create the music for our productions. There were elders like Logic and others who helped with coordination to make sure we had vehicles, food and places to stay if we were going into town or somewhere else. There were Family seamstresses who helped to sew costumes. My mom was involved with that.

I think the Drama Group was one of those coordinated efforts in the Love Family that worked out well for the kids. Unlucky for any kid that didn't get to be apart of that. There were a ton of kids who were just too young, others who just didn't have it together enough, and some who were just not in the right place at the right time.

How did the drama group get started," I asked Understanding.

"It started with a performance that we did for Love," she says. "It happened very early on when Hope was probably around nine or ten." Courage had written a song called, "The Soldier of the Lord." When Hope heard it, he asked if he could act it out:

'Can we make swords and shields?' he asked.

Reliah was in town (Understanding's twin sister), and she bought some black light paint to paint the arrows with. During the show, the arrows could be seen in the dark, flying through the air. Courage sang the song; Hope was the soldier of the Lord; and Elimelech was the evil guy throwing the arrows like spears. On the arrows were written words like lust, want, greed, etc. Hope wore the 'shield of faith' and the 'helmet of salvation.'

When the show was ready, Love and all the elders were brought in to see it, but when Love saw it he was "very disappointed." He told everyone that it had to be 'better quality.' He said, 'there needed to be real swords and shields.' He did not like the cardboard that was used. He thought 'the costumes should've been real leather.'

"We were totally deflated," Understanding says. "We had worked so hard. We thought we had this great thing, and Love thought it wasn't real enough. He thought the costumes needed to have more time into them. After that I did not want to try drama in front of Love again. But as you know," she says to me, "we continued doing drama."

Over time, the Drama Group evolved to where we were doing higher quality performances and getting opportunities to travel. One of the reasons that happened was that a man joined who later became known, as Laughter.

Laughter had been a member of the Source Family, and after Yahowah died, he came with others from that group to the Love Family. When he came, I was living at Love's Annex, which was the house right next to Love's house that eventually was remodeled and became a part of Love's big house. Encouragement was the elder; he had just come back from Hawaii. Benjamin was there. I hadn't yet caught chicken pox from Parvati and Shivaya. It was either late1975 or early spring of 1976.

Laughter showed up and was staying in a small room on the main floor of the Annex with the woman who came with him who became known as Modesty. I used to go visit him. Laughter was a short guy, with shoulder length wavy brown hair and a beard. There was a big, bold, and bright energy inside of him. He had these dynamic, engaging eyes and had an amazing ability to make people laugh. Laughter was, by far, the funniest man I had ever met, and each moment I was in his presence, I found my mood was lifted. He was a gifted mime and would, in an empty room, convincingly go up and down a staircase or elevator right there in front of us. In that same room, he could convince me that he was in a glass box; and moments later, he would be mounting a motorcycle, preparing to ride right out of the room. In the empty room, which was the sanctuary of Encouragements then household, He would convincingly jump on an invisible trampoline. He used no props whatsoever. His props were invisible. It was a totally magic experience being around him and going to his room to talk to him was what I did every day until I got chicken pox and was sent to the Ranch on the quarantine.

Sometime before Laughter came to the Love Family, it might've been before he joined the Source, he had a close, almost father-son relationship with Marcel Marceau, who was the most famous mime of our time.

Marceau's last name was actually Mangel but he adopted the name Marceau during the German occupation of France during WWII. His father was sent to a concentration camp; his mother survived. When France entered the war, Marceau joined the French resistance and helped numerous children escape concentration camps. He did many things in his life: He was an actor in movies and most famous for his creation of the character 'Bip the Clown;' Marceau saw mime as the 'art of silence,' and opened the first school for pantomime, in Paris, then brought mime to the U.S. through the Marceau Foundation. He was known all over the world and had a longtime friendship with Michael Jackson who used what he learned from Marceau in his dance steps.

When Laughter came to the Love Family, he had already been very involved in theater and had studied with the most well-known. It only made sense that right away he got involved with the Drama Group. Laughter brought a very formalized, professional training to the Drama group, and I got to learn mime and drama from him with the other children who were involved.

"I could act and I could write, but I was only doing it for fun," Understanding explained. "But Laughter had exceptional organizational and directing skills. He and Understanding "were complimentary" and "worked well together" to mobilize the theater troupe.

Laughter brought discipline. He would play 'freeze' games with us.

We would have free play until he said "Freeze!" Then each of us would hold real still, and he would walk around our frozen figures and try to make us laugh. No matter how funny he was, we had to be completely still and silent. He also taught us how to control our breathing, so that we did not move as we breathed. Laughter called it, 'Point of Focus.' It was extremely hard to not giggle when he walked right up to me and made a goofy face or did a little comedy skit right in front of me.

Laughter taught us to mime. I would move my hands in such a way to make it appear as if I were trapped inside a glass box, just like he could do. My hands moved along each of the four walls in such a way to make it appear as if there were four corners to the box.

I mean kids taking a drama class—it was one of more "normal" things I did as a kid. I enjoyed that it was something to focus on that took me away from all the spirituality and meditation that was so much a part of the culture. Here I could just be with the other kids and with awesome people like Understanding and Laughter. I got to learn theater skills to which I could apply to performances that people seemed to really enjoy. The Drama Group would perform for Love Family events and at least for a time, everybody would be smiling and focused on us, instead of focused on Love. It was just the sort of attention that I needed and gave me a role and a purpose.

Steve Allen's son David, Logic's brother, came to visit the Love Family and told his dad about the visit. Steve Allen put David's comments in his book, "Beloved Son." David described his visit to the Love Family:

'We stopped at a house in which one of the teachers, a woman named Understanding was working with another teacher, [Laughter,] and a group of children. They were putting on improvisational plays. The theme of the play we walked in on was, "Be sure to floss your teeth or you will not have any teeth to floss later in life." (Allen, 1982, pg.172)

Even though Laughter seemed so focused on what we were doing in the Drama Group, he never lost his total commitment to his belief in Love and the ideals of our life style. There was an incident that took place in which he was arrested. This took place during the second year we lived in the circle of tents. I found news articles about it, but I am not listing the reference so as to protect the identities of Laughter and others who were involved.

The news articles report that Laughter was arrested on his way to get ice to make ice cream with for the Golden Egg Party when he was arrested and thrown in jail for driving without a driver's license and refusing to give the officer his real name or his birthdate. Another article reports that [Laughter] wouldn't agree to show up for trial…because they lived only in the present, and there was no way of their knowing where the Lord wanted them to be on that date.

Laughter served 13 days in jail until the hearing. More than 50 people from the Love Family packed the courtroom." Laughter was found guilty, but all the charges were dismissed. The obstruction of justice charge was dismissed because of his constitutional guarantee of religious freedom. The driving without a license charge was also dismissed because the police could not prove that Laughter Israel was a resident.

It is hard for me to believe, knowing Laughter as I did that something of this nature would even happen to him, considering how well liked he was. He probably had everyone in that jail cell, so entertained and laughing that they didn't want him to leave, although, I'm sure it was a lot worse than that.

Laughter had been arrested, and I already talked earlier about Understanding's arrest for the same charges. So here I was I was being taught and schooled in the dramatic and theater arts by some very creative and talented people but also by some staunchly idealistic people.

None of the arrests were talked about openly, so of course, I didn't know about them. What I do remember is that at some point, Laughter began teaching circus arts. Of course, I was interested and excited about doing it.

One of my favorite things was going to the Circus with Understanding. She had maintained friendships with several people from the Barnum and Bailey Circus such as Gunther Gebel-Williams, the legendary animal trainer. He helped get us tickets several years in a row. She was given special passes one year, and I got to go down to the main floor during the show and ride one of the carriages that went around the outside of the rings as part of a festive procession at the beginning of the show.

Understanding also developed friendships with the trapeze artists, a family from South America who traveled with the Circus. There were times when they would come and visit the Family. On one of their visits, Understanding took their two sons with us to the Space Needle on an outing. They were about our age and were trapeze artists themselves, who performed with their parents in the show. Tito was the name of one of the boys; I can't remember the name of the other one. I was nervous about being up so high in the Needle, but Tito and his brother weren't nervous at all. I watched amazed as they climbed the metal ropes that surrounded the observation deck, which are no longer there today, probably for this reason: kids can climb. When Tito climbed the metal ropes, Understanding turned white as a ghost and looked shocked. Staff came right away and asked Tito to get down.

When we went to the circus, it was fun to watch Tito fly from one swing to another, way above, up near the roof of the tents with his family. He was used to heights. I had been to the circus several times, I had met some of the people that performed in it, and I was interested right away in learning circus arts when the opportunity came along. And it did. Laughter started teaching the kids in the drama group circus arts.

Back at the Ranch, there were kids who gathered up in the Barn sanctuary. Laughter passed out juggling scarves and told us we were going to learn how to juggle. There were three scarves, one was neon pink, another was neon green and the third was a neon yellow. They were lightweight, nylon scarves that floated gently, making tossing, tracking, and catching them easy. There was at least 10–15 kids that were involved in the Drama Group, but some of the kids were switched out with other kids for various reasons. Maybe they were having difficulty with the high level of discipline that was required, or maybe they were switched to give other kids a chance.

Once we learned how to juggle scarves, Laughter taught us how to juggle balls. It got progressively more challenging, two balls, then three. I could never do four. Eventually I could juggle three clubs though. It was great fun and a wonderful mental as well as physical challenge.

Then I got a unicycle for Christmas that year. Sun and Tamlyn got one too so the three of us would all practice together up in the Barn. The unicycles were from Love, but I think Laughter must've had a say in who got them, since it was the three of us who he had seen practicing on his unicycle.

It wasn't nearly as hard to learn as I thought it would be. Laughter showed me how to place all my weight on the seat and easily maneuver myself across the floor. Once I could do that, he wanted me to learn to juggle clubs while riding the unicycle. I practiced every chance I got, but it was challenging, because I had to do two very challenging things at once. I ended up being able to do it, but only for a few seconds. A few seconds is actually pretty good for what I was trying to do.

Laughter taught a lot of trampoline work as well as floor gymnastics. I enjoyed it so much that I really wished that I could jump on that trampoline for the entire day and that would be my life except for eating. I learned how to do flips and other fancy tricks. Laughter was very patient with me and worked through the challenges that came up such as my tendency to throw my right shoulder forward which caused me to lose balance and veer off kilter as I flipped.

I think it was the first time in my childhood thus far when I felt a true sense of what I was meant to do. I was motivated and passionate about learning everything that Laughter had to teach. It seemed that once we learned one thing, he was adding another, such as the tight wire. I got to the point where I could get across it but never could get to where I was juggling or sitting on a chair on the wire, like Laughter did.

I came to appreciate Laughter so much that I made him a handwoven headband that he wore for several years. It was a rainbow strip that I wove on my inkle loom. As I said, men in the Love Family typically wore a headband to hold back their hair out of their face. He's wearing it in a lot of the pictures I have seen of that time period.

Dear Diary,

I am learning to ride my unicycle and juggle at the same time for the Drama Group.

Rachel Israel

"The Drama Group was one of the most positive things there was," Ravah agreed as he discussed what he remembered about the Drama Group. "I learned a lot from Understanding because she had us doing some very interesting things, that were real learning experiences and that were joyful, like the gymnastics," he says. There was only one play that he didn't especially like and that was that one on tooth decay that ended up on KOMO 4 News: "That was just one of those things that the adults thought was absolutely adorable and that I thought was absolutely stupid," Ravah says.

In addition to all the regular performing that we were doing such as the singing and skits, the Drama Group evolved to where we were doing a few larger scale performances. One of the shows we did was a full-scale musical about the story of the birth of Christ. I had a main part where I would come out on stage and sing, "For unto to you is born this day in the city of David, a Savior which Christ the Lord…" The lyrics were mostly taken out of the Bible, Luke II, but Eli put it to music. We practiced that one for hours, days, weeks…

There was this phase of rehearsals where both Laughter and Understanding became irritated with me, because I was having difficulty singing as loudly as they wanted me to. They really wanted me to belt it out without reserve. My voice was cracking after a while as I had to sing it over and over for them, and I don't think I ever got as loud as they wanted me to, but I must've been good enough, because I got to keep my lead role.

A lot of the lyrics for the songs we sang in the shows came right out of the Bible. Other songs were written by Solomon, who was one of the few musicians who wanted to work with the kids. He was on the stage with us, playing the guitar and leading us into our different vocal parts. He was a very kind hearted, easy going guy who had a lot of energy and patience, and as I explained earlier, became the Love Family potter. He rarely got frustrated, but when he did, he would just grin and chuckle until it got worked out.

I will never forget that music. It is forever etched in my mind as we sang the songs so many times during rehearsals, then many more times during the shows. I had a part of helping to create one of the songs that was a part of the Christmas show.

Understanding sent me to go visit Integrity who was a Family musician and elder who now had a yurted household around the lake. It was my task to go and visit Integrity and help him write a song, so I hiked along the path that led to his site. When I got there, I handed him the paper with the lyrics on it and sat near him on a tree stump while he began to write the music.

I guess it helped him to have a child nearby for him to look at as he wrote it. He looked at me intently as he began strumming cords on the guitar. I just sat there quietly, waiting for him to give me instruction. He just strummed away, then began to sing along to the cords. After about ten minutes or so, he told me I could go. I left. It seemed a little weird to me that I was supposed to help him write a song, but all I did was sit there while he did it himself.

Doll song

Christmas is a melody that lives within your heart
Feeling joy in giving, makes the music start
It can last the whole year through and never should run out
As we keep on giving love and share our gift about.

Repeat

It was a pivotal moment in the show when Purity, Logic's daughter was carried across the stage, dressed like an angel, looking as if she was flying. Nobility, who was very tall and strong, lifted her up and carried her, horizontally, to make it look realistic.

I had a solo part as well as Gentle and Bright, but Bright got in that car accident on his bike, and no one believed he could do it. He was supposed to sing, "Fear not, behold, I bring to you good tidings of great joy…" We had been in the middle of rehearsals when he got hit by that car and cut his tongue. I talked earlier about how Understanding had taken Gentle and I to go visit him in the hospital. Gentle and I would've been his solo companions on stage. Understanding remembered the situation well and discussed it with me:

"We meditated and prayed for him because they said he might not speak again," she says. "We asked him to sing the solo part even though he could hardly talk. He said no and sat in the audience, but when the time came he got up there and he sang. Clarity cried. There were tears coming down her face. It was such a brave thing for him to do, as he was somewhat on the shy side and was still healing up. It was such a wonderful feeling to see him sing."

The Christmas Wish was big, but not nearly as big as a play we performed called the *Far Corners of Your Mind*, written by Understanding. It was the largest of our productions. Laughter tirelessly helped us rehearse our lines:

"Quiet! OK now you do it this way; get your mind into this," Laughter would say. He brought discipline in learning our lines and made sure we were on time to rehearsals.

The Far Corner's play was a futuristic story about a family's trip to a museum located at a place called, 'The Far Corners of Your Mind.' This museum held all the earth's evil spirits, spirits which had been frozen into statutes and placed in remote seclusion. Heaven and I played the lead roles as sisters who go visit the museum with our parents, Mary and Laughter.

As a family, we toured the museum and looked at the exhibits (statues). We were told not to touch the statues, or they would unfreeze and go back and haunt earth's people. Each frozen statue was a different negative spirit. A lady was getting robbed at gun point. She had a plastered scream on her face as she clung to her purse. The robber had a stocking over his head and held a gun to her side. Each held very still, trying to look like a statute.

"Oh. I remember when earth had problems like this," our father, Laughter would say as he looked at the statutes.

My sister and I point at the statutes:

"Look!" we exclaim. We stare at the statues with innocent curiosity and apprehension.

Another frozen statute was of two kids in a fight. They were dressed in pajamas and were frozen in a struggle over a stuffed animal.

After seeing this, my sister and I look at each other in shock and tried to imagine fighting.

"Thank God I never had to deal with this!" our mom says relieved. She then looked lovingly at us as if we were the best little children and she was so lucky to have us.

Another set of statutes was a lady wearing a bathrobe and wearing pink hair curlers. She held a newspaper that had been rolled up and was frozen as she had been beating her child with it. She appeared to be dragging her child off by the ear.

We go from statute to statute in the museum. All of the exhibits had names such as Greed, Want, Disobedience, War and Jealousy.

We finally came upon a statute of a witch. I look fearfully at the witch.

My sister moved closer to it in curiosity, while I moved away, visibly disturbed.

Understanding who played the witch, stood frozen in a long black gown. Her papier Mache mask looked diseased with a large nose and warts. She was frozen in time and didn't move a millimeter. I notice the museum guide begin to walk over to us in quick strides:

"Remember, don't touch—," he warned.

It was too late. My sister (Heaven) reached out and touched the witch as the guide approached.

"Nooooo!" the museum guide yelled as he broke into a run towards us and called for security.

I and my family are terror stricken, as we watched the witch slowly stretch and come alive.

"Come alive! Come alive!" the witch began screaming.

My sister and I clung to each other in fear.

"Come alive, my children! And I will RULE THE WORLD!" The witch begins to lose control in a heckle which almost knocks her over.

The statues slowly came to life: The robber grabbed the victim and yelled,

"Gimme your money!" The robber comes to life. His victim begins screaming.

The mom wearing a bathrobe and hair curlers unfreezes, then drags her child across the floor, yelling:

"Come here you little brat!"

Her child starts throwing a tantrum, kicking and hitting.

"It's mine!" and "Gimme!" The two children in a fight over a toy slowly come to life and begin fighting.

The witch notices security guards coming through the main entrance and begins to hackle:

"Yes! Yes, my children." The witch says and can't contain her glee.

With the stage a chaotic mess, my sister and I get down on our hands and knees and pray:

"Dear God. Please save us from the witch!" we pray.

When the witch hears our prayer, she screams in agony:

"No! No! Don't do that!" she begs.

Our prayers are answered. The statutes begin to freeze up again into their poses, and the earth and my family are saved.

"Why were Heaven and I chosen for the lead role?" I asked Understanding.

"You were the most talented," she answered. "and I knew you would work well together." Understanding continued: "You were close and got along well; You were buddies and did things together. You were even closer to her than [Gentle] was. You shared a bedroom together at the Kids' House. You liked the same kinds of things. When Love and Truthfulness took her on towards the end and in the last year, her relationships with the other kids changed; She and Gentle became closer as she became part of the privileged palace crew."

The Far Corners was a hit. Sometimes, we would do the show when the National Band would play at local venues. John the Wine Man would bring grape juice, and seltzer water was added for carbonation. Dignity, one of the Family artists, played the synthesizer during the show, and set it up so that when the witch came alive, her evil voice would echo when she talked into the microphone.

Gideon arranged for us to do a formal presentation in the basement of a Catholic Church where there was a performance hall. The audience was packed after several buses of Love Family members showed up. I saw Elkanah take a seat in one of the rows; she had sewed my costume for the play. She came up to me after the show with tears on her cheeks.

"I am so proud of you," she said. Ethan came up to me as well and said,

"That was great, Rachel, congratulations." He was dressed up too.

There were so many people in the hall afterward that I became overwhelmed and felt like leaving. I saw Laughter carrying a tray of paper cups of carbonated grape juice. He had quickly put white face paint on after the show and a red clown nose and was trying to be very entertaining to people as he passed out juice. It was hot in the room, and his white face paint was dripping down the side of his face, which he didn't seem to notice. I took a cup and snuck out the back door which went behind the stage. Heaven was there by herself, fixing her hair up in the mirror. I sat down to rest and keep her company.

We did the show again and again at different venues. I enjoyed the experience every time and especially getting out into the theater world with Laughter and Understanding, away from every day Love Family life.

One of our shows was for Steve Allen. Love invited him to a show at Love's big house. I heard afterward that Steve Allen loved the show. He wrote a synopsis and review of it in his book, "Beloved Son."

Steve Allen wrote: "One sketch was particularly clever. A group of visitors alive in a future century were being conducted through a museum described as "*The Far Corners of Your Mind*…Little Purity was very effective— and hilarious—as she acted out Disobedience. The moral lesson of the play was such that the production could have been presented in any church, synagogue or ethical society in the world." (Allen, 1982, p. 237).

I asked my mom what she remembered from that day:

"The lights dimmed, and the show (Christmas Show) was put on, and you were like this star," she says. "I remember seeing you up there soloing into the microphone with this really pretty voice and all confident. You sang quite professionally," she says. That show in the Catholic church basement was a double performance. It must've been Christmastime, because we did the Christmas play before *Far Corners*. It seemed we had moved beyond the point of being just a bunch of commune kids singing religious songs to our Family.

After Steve Allen saw our show, Love asked Understanding to create something for the 1981 Washington Rainbow Gathering, which was going to be held near Usk, in the Kanisku National Forest. He wanted the Drama Group to perform at an important event at the Gathering called the Peace Pole Pageant. He commissioned Raeiah to make us matching costumes, but there were other people who helped out with the costumes too, including my mom. The outfits were ethnic, but in a showy way, matching cotton dresses for the girls and pants and shirts for the boys, all made with bright, primary colors such as blues, reds, and yellows.

Instead of just wearing our Love Family outfits which were ethnic and different as it was, now we would be performing in our new costumes, which were like Love Family outfits on steroids. In addition, Understanding worked to perfect her show on the importance of brushing teeth.

Rainbow gatherings were held every year, in a different state. Love usually sent a delegation each year to represent the Love Family. Before Love decided to send the Drama Group to the Gathering, I had already been to a couple gatherings by then, New Mexico, (1977) and Oregon, (1978).

Love wanted Understanding to take a group of children each time, because it was important to him, as I have mentioned, that the Family represent itself as a family-oriented community. We were representing the Love Family to the world. Everyone was looking at us there. In fact, a lot of people joined the Love Family by meeting us at the gatherings. Plus, we knew a lot of people there who were a part of the Rainbow Family, the group that organized the gatherings each year. We also knew others who were prominent figures in the counterculture, such as Wavy Gravy the well-known hippie clown and Patch Adams among many others.

In Eastern Washington, cherry harvest was just finishing up, so we left for the Washington Rainbow Gathering directly from Cherry Hill. The Gathering was held during the first week of July every year. Everyone piled into the fleet of repainted school buses and other Love Family vehicles, and we caravanned across the State towards the location. For the Family, it would be at least a two to three-week adventure, sometimes longer including setup and cleanup of our tents and scene plus helping the organizers do general cleanup after the gathering was over. On the way, everyone sang Love Family songs to pass the time, and Understanding told the kids stories.

The buses had been remodeled to meet our needs. There was typically a kitchen and cushioned bunks along each side of the main isle inside the bus. Love's bus had a hot tub and an upper compartment with beds, From the outside, it looked like a mini wood cabin sitting on top of a bus.

Below this upper cabin was a lower compartment where there was a wood stove and seating areas, then the rest of the remaining space was divided up into room-like compartments with curtains that divided each section. The buses were not covered in hippie peace symbols and flowers etc., like I often saw a lot of the busses at the gatherings. Instead they were nicely painted a light or dark blue with a yellow strip going down the side. The 'blue bus,' which I usually rode in with Understanding and the kids, had an eagle's face leading each yellow striped, side panel. Love's bus was similar, but it was light blue with a yellow stripe, a little fancier with Family symbols on it such as the star of David with the cross in the middle and a circle around the points. There was also a lion painted on the front of Love's bus, a biblical symbol of the tribe of Judah.

I really enjoyed going on these adventures with my family. When the bus stopped for gas, the kids on the trip were allowed to switch onto another bus or vehicle. Switching was fun because then I could play with the other kids who were in other vehicles. I played with the CB, so I could talk with my friends as we traveled. I imitated Trust, one of the drivers by talking trucker talk saying, "10–4" or "over and out." Plus, I already knew some trucker talk from my days of hitchhiking on the road with my mom.

One of our stops was at a small lake that was not too far off the road, just a short hike. Everyone seemed so happy to get out, stretch their legs and go skinny dipping. While the big people swam, Understanding served bowls of Grape Nuts or Shredded Wheat to the kids, boxes that had been given to her by Sure before she left. I had never eaten boxed cereals before.

On the next leg of the trip, I hung out with Peace in the back curtained compartment of the bus and listened to Courage's Bob Marley tapes. We popped the tape in the cassette player. In a deep voice, Bob Marley sang, Sip your cup now, in his Jamaican-English accent. It just so happened that as we were listening to that song, we were each really sipping on a cup of tea. Each time he would sing, Sip your cup now, Peace and I would sip our cup and then fall over in laughter. For some reason, it just got funnier and funnier as we went along, so we pressed rewind several times and got more cups of tea. It got pretty silly actually to where we were howling with laughter on the floor of the bus. It was amazing how much fun it could be on a long ride to the Rainbow Gathering.

I could not wait to get there. And this time, we had a purpose, to perform our show at the Peace Pole Pageant. The Rainbow Gathering was a place that gave me a glimpse of life on the outside where there were people who didn't live in the Love Family. And traveling with the Drama Group meant that I was there with all my friends too, all of whom were part of my close-knit tribe.

For anyone who doesn't know what a rainbow gathering is, it is a week-long camp out where up to 20–30,000 people from all over the States, North America and Europe come. It lasts two months long, including set up and clean up but officially commences between July 1st and July 7th. Rainbow Gatherings have been taking place since the early 1970s. They include a kids' parade organized by Wavy Gravy on July Fourth after a silent meditation for world peace. It was inspired originally by Woodstock, but it is different than Woodstock in that it is not a music festival, although there are plenty of musicians there, but it is more of a non-commercial, countercultural communal campout. Aside from trade and barter, everything is free. It is non-hierarchical, so there is no official leadership; Decisions are made by group consensus.

There are all sorts of people from the counterculture who go to the rainbow gatherings. People of all ages and walks of life are welcome. Many different spiritual groups unite at this gathering, groups that have nothing to do with each other outside of the setting of the gathering. A lot of people come from communes or other groups. There are plenty who go to volunteer and help the organizers, who live communally all year round, to set up outhouses, kitchens, walkways, and spaces for people to gather and camp.

Each gathering is set up similarly, even though they are held in a different state each year. They have what is called 'Kid City,' which was a place specially set up for kids to gather. They have a MASH tent, where there are volunteer doctors.

One of my favorite places to go is to the trading circle, a place where people trade their crafts and trinkets since the Gatherings are non-commercial and money is useless. Other important places typical of the Gatherings are the food kitchens and other designated places for people to gather. Between these main areas are well-defined pathways, mapped out with signs for people to follow so they know where they're going.

Gatherings are not just a thing of the past, they still take place every year. The purpose of the Gathering is "both to further the cause of world peace by prayer and to create a peaceful and cohesive nonhierarchical society that can serve as a model for reforming 'Babylon,' the industrialized world" (Niman, 1997, 31–32). The Gatherings are built on a "foundation of ecological living" and "disconnecting from technology."

The locations of the Gatherings are usually primitive with no running water that often has to be hauled from somewhere back to the kitchens, tents and campsites. Since there are often thousands of people all camping out together, there were times when everyone was asked to boil the water before using it, to disinfect it, so as to prevent the spread of diseases that might be going around.

Even though the organizers were very together, and a lot of work was put into the planning, it often seemed dirty, though mostly because it was primitive camping but also because gathering goers were typically hippies who could care less about superficial efforts to make themselves neat looking; it was all about being natural and 'real' and not playing social games with appearance. It was once explained to me that wearing deodorant was not needed, because sweating and the smell of sweat was natural. There was no need to hide it, just get used to it, then I won't smell it anymore.

The Love Family had a very clean set up that people at the Gathering noticed and remembered, because it was different. We were a very distinct presence at the Gathering. We stood out for how organized and clean we were. A lot of people said that the Love Family vision and scenery was "incredibly beautiful."

That's really the message that I was being taught in the Love Family, that it was important for my environment to be clean and orderly, a vision of beauty, and in that way, the Love Family was setting itself apart from a lot of hippies in general, because the hippies were rebelling against a lot of that and trying to get back to being more natural, more genuine.

If one were to walk into a Love Family group at a rainbow gathering, they would see order; the tents were placed in orderly fashion, everything was clean. The Family made beautiful rock paths around the tents where we slept. There was a well-made kitchen. If people from the gathering came to visit, they were served meals on a clean porcelain plate.

There were stark differences. Rainbow gathering camps were very unsanitary, and in the early years of the gathering, many people got sick, passing around disease, and not just the flu. At the Love Family camp, however, if someone got invited into Love's tent they'd see he sat like a king and people waited on him hand and foot. He'd bring the musicians in and they'd play for him.

At the Gathering, I was fascinated by the people I saw. It was so unstructured, anarchistic. At our campsite, our neat little yurts sat there, like a private clan. We acted alike, we dressed alike, we were structured as a family, we would sit the same. Our tents at the Gathering were swept up neatly and there were carpets inside. Our dress was totally different than most as we dressed ethnically and kept ourselves squeaky clean. Women served the meals, Love was the head, people bowed to each other, etc. It was the Love Family, but it was as if we had been picked up and put in another land, like Dorothy's house was picked up out of Kansas and placed in munchkin land. We were no longer in our safe, secluded, isolated, everything in control Ranch, where I knew where every outhouse was. No, there were maps just to find the "Shitters," which was what they called outhouses. There were certain designated trees with cardboard signs that had arrows pointing the way down the path.

I loved to see the diversity at the gatherings. I would see people from different cultural and spiritual groups. Love would hold gatherings in his sanctuary tent and meet with the visitors and potential new members, of which it seemed that there was a constant stream.

Our reputation among the organizers and gathering goers was mixed, somewhat controversial, because we had a leader and that was against the philosophies of many in the counterculture, which was to be more anarchistic and anti-establishment.

"One member of the Rainbow Family, who worked closely with the Love Family when plans were being made for the 1981 Gathering in Washington State, complained that Family members could not make even trivial decisions without first getting approval from one of their elders." (Balch, 1998, pg. 67).

When I was there, I felt a part of a bigger whole. It was exhilarating. I wasn't just this kid from the Love Family; I was from a community that was connected to a larger network of people. Thousands of people from all walks of the counterculture all comingling. It was an amazing thing to witness. Being there made me feel as if I were a part of a large piece of colorful fabric, instead of just a patch on someone's pocket.

By the time I arrived at the Washington Rainbow Gathering, I had already been to two gatherings, although I went to four total while in the Love Family. I went to New Mexico 1977 and Oregon 1978, then after Washington 1981, I went to Idaho 1982.

The first gathering I went to was New Mexico in 1977. That would've been no more than a year and a half after I had come to the Love Family. Even though I was only around eight and a half, I actually remember quite a bit about my first gathering.

The New Mexico Gathering was located by Burnt Corral Canyon in the Gila National Forest. The Love Family took the Belgians, so I got to ride on the wagon into the Gathering site. The wagon stopped to rest on the way in, right in the middle of an orange grove. I didn't know that oranges grew on trees, so it was amazing to see. I got out and found a couple oranges on the ground and took them with me before going on our way.

It was a scorching, New Mexico, dry heat, but there was a beautiful, slow-moving river that lazily crawled right through the middle of the Gathering site; people took advantage of it and used it like a massive conveyor for fruit, which would be collected at the kitchens when it arrived. I saw people floating down the river too, going from one place to another. It looked like a pleasant way to travel. I was too young and hadn't yet learned to swim, so we just played in the water right where the river came closest to our campsite.

Our tents were set up near huge rock formations. I would go and collect the rocks because they were so interesting to hold and look at; they were these black pumice rocks that had tiny crystals growing on them that looked like little fairy castles imbedded in them.

I was amazed by the environment, but my memories of things that took place at the New Mexico Gathering were bad. The first thing that happened was I lost the ruby ring that Love had given me after I was baptized at the Ranch a year earlier. The ring slipped off my finger and zig zagged to the bottom of the river. The water was clear, so I saw it land in the sand below. When I tried to retrieve it, it seemed to disappear. Ravah, one of the boys swimming with me, tried to help me find it and dove for it over and over, but then finally gave up. It was disappointing as I enjoyed showing off my ring and hearing people compliment me on it. Maybe I was no longer Love's princess of God. I wondered. Either way, for now, the ring would forever rest in the New

Mexico river bed.

Another bad thing was several mishaps with the critters. First, I got bit by a gigantic black wasp. In my memory, it was at least two inches long. I was in the tent with Seth and Peace when I suddenly felt a searing pain on my wrist. I saw the wasp fly off, which scared me more than the actual bite. A grown up named Solidity came running when he heard me scream. Solidity was a Family musician and helped drive the horses on this trip. Solidity began sucking on my wrist where I was bit, then each time he sucked, he spit. I watched, startled, confused. He explained to me that he was sucking the venom out.

Then he walked me down to the river and dug up a handful of mud and placed it on my wrist, right on the spot where I had been bitten. He explained that when the mud dried, it would continue to suck the poison out. I carefully carried the mud around for the next couple hours or so, waiting for it to dry.

Another critter that I got to meet was a scorpion. I had been playing when one of the kids lifted up a rock, and there it was. I had never seen one of those before either. Again, no one was hurt; we all just stood there looking at it until our guardian put the rock back over it so it could go about its business and we could go about ours.

The third creature I got to meet was a tarantula, which was sitting near a place in the rocks where we were playing. He didn't hurt anyone; He was just minding his own business, but it was at that point that I decided not to play in the rocks anymore and from then on, I played at the river.

The last bad thing that happened was when we got in trouble. We had been playing behind one of the tents with toy cars. One of the boys had been given a good-sized bag of toy cars by someone at the Gathering, not someone from the Love Family.

Finally, we had something interesting to do. We started going out every day and dug tunnels and obstacle courses for the cars. I had my favorite car, which was a Volkswagen Beatle, which no one else seemed to want. We were really getting into this game and started going out every chance we got. But then one of the big people saw us and went and told their elder. It wasn't long before we were told we couldn't play with cars anymore. "The cars were

Worldly," it was explained to us, and they were confiscated. I was disappoint-ed, but the boys were angry and Cheerful and Ravah made their disappoint-ment widely known.

On the last day, everyone worked together to clean-up the scene be-fore we left. I helped by spreading grass seeds on the areas where the tents had been. That was the first rainbow gathering I ever went to—scary critters, getting in trouble, losing my ring, and just seeing the setting that was so amazing. That was New Mexico.

Oregon, the following year, was very different, and since I was a year older, nine and a half now, my memories were a bit clearer. The setting was more familiar too in terms of climate and critters since it was held in the Northwest, by White Horse Meadows in the Umpqua National Forest of Or-egon, just one state away from Washington.

The hike in was torture. I was hiking along with Ethan and just to keep myself from falling over with exhaustion, I was asking him questions about things I saw along the way.

"Why is that man just lying there like that? I asked. There was a naked man lying in the trees, staring up at the sky.

"He's probably on drugs" he said matter-of-factly," which didn't sound at all like the standard Love Family answer.

What kind of tree is that?" I asked. Ethan was unique in that he would actually give me a thoughtful answer. He was very knowledgeable about a lot of different subjects and was willing to share it, as opposed to so many in the Love Family that just kept to the party line. I kept asking Ethan questions, and he kept on answering them, until finally he had grown exasperated:

"Has anyone ever told you that you ask too many questions? He asked me. He was carrying way more than I was, and his face was dripping with sweat.

I took the hint.

When we finally got there, and people were setting up camp, it was discovered that there weren't enough tents for the kids to have our own tent, so Understanding distributed us individually into the different tents that were available. I ended up sleeping in a tent with Elkanah, and Forest was there too, who must've been around four by then. There wasn't enough bedding either, so I had to share a sleeping bag with him. One morning I woke up, soaking wet and was so upset about it that bedding was quickly donated to me from various people for the next nights. I hadn't slept in the same tent with my mom since before we joined, which had been almost three years by then, so I wasn't that thrilled to be under the same "roof" with her, especially after she was determined to make me sleep with Forest.

During the day, I would go with the other kids to be with Understanding, while Elkanah worked hard at the communal kitchen with other members. When she wasn't working in the kitchen, she was helping take care of Kim, an Asian woman with no legs who had met the Love Family while at the Gathering and had decided to stay at our campsite. Elkanah kept quite busy getting her around and fed.

I would say that the Oregon Rainbow Gathering was my least favorite of all Gatherings, but at least, there were no tarantulas, scorpions, or giant wasps. But there was no tent for the kids, and I was used to us being all together at night, especially in a strange place such as the Rainbow Gathering. Plus, Love kept pulling me, Heaven, Gentle, and other kids around our age into his sanctuary tent for gatherings. He was trying to impress the visitors and potential new members who were being hosted and groomed to join.

I spent a lot of time trying to avoid Love. Heaven and I would try to sneak off, so he wouldn't see us. I did enough meditating and sitting in meetings back at home; that was the last thing I wanted to do at a rainbow gathering.

Unfortunately, it was sometimes unavoidable. Heaven and I got caught and had to sit for a long period right next to Love. He put Heaven on one side of him, and me on the other side, right at the head of the circle. I hated it, because then Love was in the middle, between us; I couldn't even whisper in her ear during the meeting to cope with the boredom.

Other times, we were successful. She and I would casually wander off, hoping no one would notice. One of those times we wandered off, we stopped and watched the belly dancers. There were two women and a man who were belly dancing in the middle of a huge circle of people, maybe a hundred or so. Back at the Ranch, I had taken belly-dancing classes with Piety and knew some of the moves, so I wanted to see what was happening.

Another time, we went to the trading post. I heard that Cheerful had traded a large Hershey's chocolate bar for a ¼ stick of dynamite and a hit of acid. It "shocked" Understanding, and she took Cheerful back and asked him to tell her who it was, so they could trade it back, plus, then she could find out who would do such a trade with a child. The culprit had left, and they were unable to figure out where he had gone, so Richness took the 1/4 stick of dynamite, and he and Cheerful went and blew it off in a faraway pasture.

The trading post was a grassy area where people traded goods, trinkets, food, and things they didn't want anymore. Each trader had a small blanket or tapestry laid out on the ground with everything they were trading. Heaven and I wandered about looking at all the goods for trade. I came across these earrings. They were sterling silver, little naked fairies. I could have them, but in return, I agreed to give the lady the necklace around my neck. I had made it; it was a small bag that I had crocheted out of rainbow colored yarn. In the bag, I kept this crystal rock that I had taken from the New Mexico Rainbow Gathering that I had found near our tent. The lady seemed eager to have it. Those were the first earrings I ever had, and I had to save them for a year until my ears were pierced so I could finally wear them.

Going to see the belly dancers and going to the trading post was about the most fun I had at the Oregon Gathering that year. When we slipped back into our campsite, I was relieved that no one had even noticed we were gone.

When we reentered the campsite where our tents were, there were people carrying a stretcher out of the camp. There appeared to be somebody under the blanket. Something was going on as people were looking very serious and scurrying about. Somebody told me that it was a woman, and that she was dead. They were carrying her through the Gathering asking people to look at her as they were trying to figure out who she was. She had, apparently been high on acid, which I didn't know what that was because in the Family LSD (acid) was called 'sacrament.' But I heard she had taken it and had jumped off a cliff to her death. It sounded terrible and upset me for a while just thinking about it and not clearly understanding why somebody would do that. This was a few years before the King Lake sacrament trip.

Fast forward. I was on my way to the Washington Rainbow Gathering of 1981. I was with the Drama Group, and we were to perform that year at the

Peace Pole Pageant at Love's request. I would've been 12 ½ by then.

When we pulled into the parking lot, it was so big, and there were so many vehicles that it took a long time to park; miles of vehicles, it seemed. Many of them were old beaters, dusty from the long dirt road that we came in on. I was mesmerized by the parking lot. So many Volkswagen buses and bugs and a lot of old school buses and vans that had been repainted with trippy designs, peace symbols and poetry, anti-war slogans, and butterflies.

The hike in was even worse than Oregon had been. This time I was old enough to help carry more things, and I got stuck carrying some heavy items, plus, my own duffle and sleeping bag.

I wondered if I would make it, since I was thirsty, and the heat was unbearable. Every so often there were volunteers by the road side offering travelers water, but at the last water site, they had run out. I saw that there were those who just didn't make it. They just decided to set up camp along the trail in. Some people had tents, others were just make shift campsites out of pieces of tarp or sticks they found in the woods. There were tons of unfamiliar faces and people everywhere. I could handle it well as I had already been to two Gatherings—New Mexico and Oregon, which I discussed earlier; I was curious about everything, and I had memories of being in countercultural hot spots before we met the Family when my mom and I were hitchhiking around. It was fun to be off the Ranch and doing something interesting, something different than the same old Love Family routine.

As soon as I got there, people were starting to set up camp, so to get the kids out of the way, Understanding took us to Kid City. It felt like a long walk, especially since I had just hiked in, and I had carried a lot. The location was beautiful with big, huge, open areas of grass surrounded by forest, way out, it seemed, in the middle of nowhere. We hiked on a narrow, dirt path that wound up and down little hills as we made the trek. I was fascinated by all I saw. It was like walking through a page of 'Where's Waldo,' except Waldo was traveling through an almost Woodstock-like hippie camping land. I saw people hugging, laughing, eating, rubbing each other's backs, dancing, drumming, setting up their tents and camp scenes, milling about. Not everyone was naked but there were quite a few people who were. We went by what was called, 'Teepee Village,' which was an area where a ton of teepees were erected, maybe 30-50 from the aerial pictures I saw later on.

When we finally got to Kid City, Wavy Gravy was there. He wore a clown outfit that looked like a tie dyed, homemade patchwork quilt, and a rather large, red, rubber clown nose. He had a rainbow colored frizzy wig that stuck out from his cowboy hat. At the time, I had no idea that he was famous. To me, he was just this clown at the rainbow gathering.

Apparently, there was a lot about Wavy Gravy that I didn't know. He had a background in theater. He had been a member of a secret society of clowns and comics dedicated to ending Vietnam using political theater. He got started wearing his clown outfit because it decreased his chances of being arrested at antiwar protests and demonstrations. Wavy Gravy wore a lot of hats though, so to speak: He was the official clown of the Grateful Dead; He had two radio shows; He'd been on television; He was a part of the Hog Farm, a communal experiment that evolved into an entertainment organization; He wrote many books; He taught theater; He was a part of a security team for all three Woodstock festivals; He did a lot of other different things over the years, too many to list here. There was a documentary that came out in 2010 about him called, "Saint Misbehavin: The Wavy Gravy Movie."

At Kid City, I was too hot, tired and hungry to care much about Wavy Gravy, and it seemed like forever before Understanding was done talking to him, before she took us to the food kitchens to get us fed.

The food kitchens were free standing structures, many made from plywood and tapestries or whatever people could find. There was no running water. The kitchens were dirty. None of the food looked very appetizing. Big vats of soup or something were slopped onto people's plates. There were long lines. I saw that people used Frisbees, empty tin cans or any object that would hold food for their plates. For camping way out in the middle of nowhere, it seemed people were just grateful for a hot meal. The only kitchen I wanted to go to was called Cookie Castle. It didn't look like a castle though, it looked like all the other primitive kitchens. When I took a bite of the cookie, I didn't want to finish it, since it had a weird texture and flavor. I much preferred to eat at the Love Family kitchen where it was clean, and the food was familiar.

The next day, Understanding took the kids to go find water. There was a tap, but it was a long walk to get there. It was very hot, and we were thirsty and tired. We walked by a small pond that was full of people soaping up and washing themselves. Some of them were washing their laundry. It was disappointing to see them there as we had wanted desperately to swim to cool off, but there were so many people washing up that there was no room in the water. Understanding told us not to drink the water because it might not be clean. She said just put a little on our heads to help cool us off. It did seem to help until we were able to find drinking water.

On our way back to the Love Family campsite, Understanding made us wait while she went over and was talking to Patch. At the time of this Gathering, Patch Adams and Love were friends;

"They were both big leaders with big visions," Understanding says.

I watched Understanding and Patch talking. Patch had a big grin on his face and was very engaged in telling Understanding something. She stood there, her arms crossed, seemingly very interested in what he was saying. I overheard some of the conversation. Understanding was telling Patch that we would be performing at the Peace Pole Pageant. She looked over at us and pointed and was animatedly telling him all about it. Then they walked off a little to talk to the rangers. I could not hear what they were saying. There were two rangers who were there; They had gotten off their horses and were chatting with Patch and Understanding. I was trying to figure out what they were talking about by watching them talk, but it was hard to tell. Courage and Laughter were also there, talking with the rangers. I wondered what they were talking about, since they all looked so serious. Finally, Understanding looked as if she were done talking and waved them good bye and approached us.

"OK kids, we need to have a serious talk," Understanding says. She had a very serious expression on her face, which for her, was not normal.

We all gathered around her to listen.

"Big Foot had been spotted near the outhouse," she told us. She still called it an outhouse. Apparently, the rangers had taken a cement imprint of the huge footprint that had been found there and were there to warn people. "Make sure, if you go to the outhouse, that you don't go alone, and make sure you take a friend with you," she warned.

Just great! Big Foot had been spotted at the shitter. 'Shitters' were just holes in the ground with a piece of plywood over the top that had a hole cut into it to squat over. Sometimes there were more than one hole cut so multiple people could go at the same time. I hated it. I much preferred the clean, holy outhouses at the Ranch. One shitter was a pit dug back in the forest with just a fallen log over it, so I had to sit on the log with hang my butt over it. It was hard to hang far enough over it to make my leto go in the hole since I was only a kid and had a small frame. I was worried I would fall in if I hung over the log too far, and there was never any privacy. People would just come walking up and if there was room, they would just sit down over the hole next to me. It's like a lot of things in the counterculture where convention is just thrown out the window. Who needs privacy anymore? That was just a convention of Babylon.

I was very concerned about Big Foot. I was just a kid and believed every word of it. From time to time, Understanding told us practical jokes, but this was convincing. The rangers were involved and Patch Adams too. I hated going to the shitters in the first place, but now to learn that Big Foot was there. It had apparently been spotted at the shitter right by the Love Family campsite too, which made it worse, because now I had to hike to another one, which was further away and not as private. I got a map and found one and had to follow the arrows, which were nailed to trees along the way to indicate which way to go. I found myself worrying about who might be there when I showed up. After going a couple times, I found that it was just easier to hold it.

The joke didn't last for more than a couple days, because there were kids besides me who were refusing to go to the bathroom. Understanding saw that we were taking it too seriously and had to tell us it was just a joke. She said it was Patch Adam's idea and that he wanted people to laugh. He was doing talks at the Gathering, talking about how laughter is the best medicine. He thought the joke would be therapeutic in some way. At the time, I did not find it funny at all, although I do now, looking back. Right before she told us that it was a joke, we had all been sitting around the fire that evening, and she had someone jump out wearing a gorilla suit that belonged to Patch. One little girl was so frightened by the gorilla/Bigfoot, that it was arranged for her to leave the Gathering early and go back to the City.

I never knew what was going to happen at the rainbow gatherings. On another occasion, Heaven and I noticed that there were people crowding into one of the yurts for what might be a meeting or a gathering of some sort.

We had gotten pretty good at disappearing as we had learned to do at the Oregon Gathering three years earlier. It wasn't that hard to do since there were thousands of people at the Gathering besides the Love Family, and Gathering goers were constantly passing by our tents. I could easily slip out of the camp without being noticed and blend with the passers. No one saw us.

As soon as we hit the trail, it wasn't long before we came upon a group of people engaged in an intense drumming circle. I would guess there were easily 100 people there. Half of them were going one way, and half of them were going the other, past each other. There were no kids there, but Heaven and I were adventurous in our spirits and jumped into the circle. I literally had to jump in because the people were body to body moving their limbs in unison in certain rhythmic motions. To join the group, one had to follow suit, as it was a fast-paced, closed-space event. We got in there and were doing the movements. She was going one direction, and I was in the other group going the other direction, so every time we passed each other, we would grin and giggle at each other. Everyone was stomping their feet and their arms were in the air waving around in certain coordinated movements. It reminded me of some of the photos I had seen in National Geographic of an African tribe.

I was exhausted after a while. Heaven and I gave each other the look and quickly stepped out of the circle that just kept going with just as much intensity as when we entered. It was amazing to step out and to feel the light breeze and freedom. Even though it was a hot day, the drumming circle was so tightly knit with bodies that it was almost like a sauna. Walking away from that drumming circle and back to the Love Family yurts—I'll never forget that feeling. It was like a paradigm of our life in the Family, where everyone is doing the same thing in a dream like state, and then to suddenly be released into the free and crazy outside world of a Rainbow Gathering—Wow!

Despite a two-day ordeal of being afraid to go to the bathroom because of Big Foot, we still did some performing at the Gathering like Love had asked.

I stood with the other Family children in front of a castle prop, which Understanding used for her toothbrush show. Imagination, a Family artist hand painted the castle intricately, and its hinges opened and shut little windows and doorways for puppets to maneuver.

Before Understanding went on stage, we would all file out in front of the puppet stage and sing our songs. We wore our new costumes that had been recently made for us. Our first number was a song called "Little Fish Swimming in the Ocean." There were about 10 to 15 of us from the Drama Group who were there performing. We had learned to be animated as we sang and to smile the whole time. I noticed the crowd get bigger as we sang:

"Little fish swimming in the ocean." I wiggled my hand with the other kids as if our hands were fishes swimming.

"Big bird flying high in the sky." We held our hand up to our eyes and looked up as if searching for a bird.

"I wanna tell you everything that I know and more." We all pointed to our chests with a smug look on our faces, as if we knew everything.

"There's a time when the rain is falling and a time when the sun is shining high." We all moved our fingers horizontally to indicate rain, then made a circle with our arms to indicate a sun.

Our next number was more Bible based. It was a song called "Little barefooted boy." We animated this one too just like the other songs we sang. It was from Matthew 14:13-21 about the miracle that Jesus performed when he multiplied loaves of bread and fishes for 5,000 people.

"Little barefooted boy, running in the sand
What you got in that basket in your hand?
There's five thousand people waiting to be fed.
What you gonna do with that fish and bread?

"To sum it all up, you simply divide
Watch that bread just multiply
Add a little faith, subtract all your doubt
And watch it all work out

"You've got to give it away, pass it around,
Twelve full baskets sitting on the ground
I can tell by the smile and the twinkle in your eye,
The master has taught you how to multiply."

There was another show that we did at the Washington Gathering that was not planned ahead of time. The idea was hatched out, again, by Patch Adams who was trying hard to bring laughter to the Gathering. He had seen us perform and liked our show, especially Understanding's toothbrush segment. So, Patch asked Love if we would perform a skit for people at the Gathering about prehistoric peoples and how they used to take care of one another. There was this pond-sized mud puddle off yonder, and it was Patch's idea for us to put mud on our bodies and act it out. We would be naked, but we would be covered in mud. Some of us didn't want to do it, but we did it anyway, because Patch asked us to do it, and Love agreed.

Once we were all covered with mud, the show began. It wasn't just us kids; it was also Understanding, Laughter, and a couple of Patch's volunteer doctor friends.

When the show began, the boys made a "fire." They got two rocks and banged them together to build it. Understanding had to wear the gorilla suit that she got from Patch. She says that wearing the gorilla suit was awful:

"It was awful," she says. "I felt like I was suffocating the whole time. I was actually hyperventilating because it was so hot inside the suit."

One of Patch's doctor friends wore a giraffe suit. I screeched with the other children as if I were an ape. We picked imaginary bugs off each other and ate them. Laughter came out wearing a huge sheep skin, and the boys threw spears (sticks) at him. There was no specific plot, only an intimate glimpse of prehistoric life. People from the Gathering gathered around us and watched, smiling and laughing. There was even someone there filming from the *Spokane News*.

I guess it was a hit. I did not like this show though. I was uncomfortable being naked in what seemed like such a public place, even if we were covered in mud and no one could tell what we looked like. When I heard other girls complaining, I went and told Understanding:

"We don't like this!" I told her.

"I am really sorry," Understanding said apologetically. "From now on, you girls can wear underwear or even a halter top, and I'll ask the boys if they want to wear loin cloths."

It didn't help much. I still hated it.

It was the Fourth of July, almost time for us to perform at the Peace Pole Pageant. The Peace Pole Pageant was a yearly event where people would present things. There were talking circles where people would pass the stick around. It was traditional, in a Native American way, in that only the person holding the stick could talk. I saw the sticks were decorated with crystals and Native beads and feathers. When I saw them talking, it seemed to me that the conversations were more serious. Some were about problems happening at the Gathering and what to do about it; other conversations were about different societal ills. Others were spiritually oriented meditation or focus groups. I saw the Peace Pole Pageant when I was at the Oregon Rainbow Gathering, so I knew what it was. I had watched it from the sidelines and was just curious as it seemed so very different from the hierarchical way that decisions were made in the Love Family.

Each year, before the Pageant though, there was a kids' parade. I and the other girls around my age wore sequined costumes that belonged to the Drama Group. Someone handed me a baton to twirl. It was traditional. Each year at the Gathering, on the Fourth of July, the kids' parade would commence. Hippie kids from all over the Gathering would gather for the event. It was led by Wavy Gravy. There were thousands of people at the Gathering, so one can imagine just how many children there might have been marching in this parade. As we marched, we sang, John Lennon, All we are saying, is give peace a chance... We sang it over and over and over as we marched towards the silent meditation for world peace.

On the day of the parade, it was also traditional that the adults are silent that day. There was fasting and then a long silent meditation. While we were marching in the parade, they would be meditating in silence. The kids' parade was far enough away at its start that no one heard us. It was planned just right, so that when we do finally arrive at the meditation, we are supposed to break the silence at noon when everyone is chanting. Then the adults are supposed to stream off the mountain to greet us as we get there.

Ideally, it's supposed to be perfectly coordinated, and usually it was. At past gatherings' the kids could be seen from a distance as the people silently meditated, so Wavy Gravy and those coordinators and elders knew when we would parade in, but at Washington, no one could see or hear where they were meditating, and we came noisily marching up singing. A lady came running up to the front of the parade:

"The silence hasn't been broken yet!" the lady panted.

Suddenly the parade came to a stop. For the longest time, we stood there not knowing what was going on. Wavy Gravy was discussing something with the messenger at the front of the parade. I was hot and thirsty as I waited. The lady wanted us to march back to Kid City and start again because they were still in silence. It hadn't taken us as long as they thought it would for us to arrive. I was thirsty and did not want to go back to Kid City and start again but the lady insisted. We weren't that far from the front of the parade, so we could see the the lady and Wavy Gravy. The meditators were not happy to hear us arrive. Wavy Gravy was arguing loudly with the lady until he finally agreed. Not the best year for that parade, but it was still fun marching along in those sequined outfits and twirling those batons.

Now that the parade was over, the Peace Pole Pageant would be held. It was either the day after the Fourth of July or the day after that, I can't remember exactly. But it was the whole reason why Love even wanted us to go to the Washington Rainbow Gathering in the first place, which was to perform at the Pageant.

I don't remember if it was raining on the way over there or if it started when we got there. I just remember being there and it was pouring rain. Here we were dressed up in our ethnic costumes, ready to present ourselves as some of the best that the Love Family had to offer, and we weren't even able to do it because of the rain. It wasn't just a light rain; it was pouring. No one knew exactly what to do about it, but it was decided that everyone there would form a huge impromptu circle, probably to keep everyone from leaving. There were a lot of people, probably two or three hundred, maybe more, just standing there in the pouring rain. A few people found tarps, pieces of cardboard, plastic or whatever they could find, trying to take cover as best as possible, but most of the people had nothing, not even raincoats or umbrellas.

As everyone stood there in a circle in the rain, they began to sing what I heard was called the rain song. I guess it was supposed to make the rain stop, but it didn't make the rain stop. It just seemed to rain harder the louder people sang. They sang, *"I was lost! Now I'm found! Got my head in the stars and my feet on the ground!"* The crowd sang the same verse over and over, asking for some sort of divine intervention. As time went on, the rain continued, and they sang more and more passionately. I saw people getting drenched with their faces turned upward towards the sky wearing huge grins of joy. The rain became heavier and thunder struck; this seemed to excite people even more. It was a total deluge. Amazingly, there was no hint of disappointment at the Pageant that people had prepared for weeks if not months, presentations and performances that were now not going to happen. The rain never did stop, but we did end up singing the rain song with everybody. We stood there singing away with all the spirit we could muster. Glory was there. Love stood there with us with his entourage. Understanding, Laughter, the entire kid scene and all our helpers and caretakers. We were all out there for a long time in this downpour. I looked over and Bright's skin was all blue. He wasn't blue from being cold, because it wasn't cold out there that day. He was blue because the wet material from his costume had stained his skin.

We didn't perform at the Peace Pole Pageant that year, and we weren't able to perform in our costumes after that, because the costumes had gotten so wet, that they were ruined and needed special attention that wasn't available at the Gathering. But we had performed it already quite a bit for gathering goers before the pageant.

Patch Adams had already seen our show and was impressed. He asked Love if we could travel with him. He was at the Gathering helping in the MASH tent with other volunteer doctors. After the Gathering, he planned to go on tour from small town to small town giving talks as part of his attempt to revive the touring Chautauqua. Traditionally, a touring or circuit Chautauqua brought entertainment and culture to small towns and communities with speakers, teachers, musicians, entertainers, preachers, and specialists. It was popular in the late 19th and early 20th centuries and was like Vaudeville, except that Chautauqua was more geared towards intellectuals as its lectures dominated the circuits.

Patch's talk was called "Laughter is the Best Medicine," and he believed that humor and play are essential to physical and emotional health. His talk was full of improvisational humor. He wore a rubber clown nose during the talk. He said your attitude and what you put in your body makes a difference. He was trying to raise money for the Gesundheit! Institute that he founded, which was a free community hospital and healthcare eco-community.

Patch had teamed up with the Flying Karamazov Brothers who were also at the Washington Rainbow Gathering where they had performed. They were a juggling and comedy troupe that consisted at that time of three hippie guys—Ivan, Dmitri, and Alyosha. They weren't really brothers, they had taken their name from a Fyodor Dostoevsky novel, *The Brothers Karamazov* and had identified with characters from that novel. I found them very funny and entertaining, especially since Laughter had been training us to juggle, and we were into the circus arts.

After the Washington Rainbow Gathering, we went on tour with Patch Adams for two weeks. Love was proud that Patch had been so impressed with us, so he arranged for Understanding and the Drama Group kids to have the use of the blue bus for the trip, which meant that some of the members who came to the Gathering in it would now have to hitchhike back home instead of going in the caravan back with everyone else. Appreciation helped pack the bus up with stuff we needed, including homemade bread and granola for breakfasts.

We would sing our songs, Understanding would do her toothbrush show, and then we would also be performing the prehistoric people's mud show that Patch loved so well.

At the small towns where we performed, sometimes there were only a few people there in the audience, and at other times, there were huge crowds. When Patch wasn't performing on stage, he would go and do his talks at different places in the small towns. He was running the business and PR side of things, so the Chautauqua went smoothly. The Flying Karamazov Brothers, with the help of their girlfriends, gave us sandwiches and juice each day for lunch and rice for dinners, which was very kind of them, since we didn't have much food with us.

Patch and his wife Linda rode with us in our bus. The Flying Karamazov Brothers had their own bus, and other performers on the trip brought their own vehicles. One of my strongest memories of Patch was a situation that took place between shows.

Everyone was standing around after lunch. There were people milling about the stage area where equipment was being moved to the buses. There were people just sitting around after having seen the show. I was just finishing up my sandwich as were the other children, when suddenly, a lady fell over. I didn't know who she was, but it looked like she was dead. No one knew what happened to her.

"Go get my medical bag!" Patch yelled at Understanding.

Understanding ran to go get his medical bag. While she was gone, Patch checked the lady's vitals. As he was checking them, Understanding came running toward Patch with his medical bag, but before she got there, she tripped and fell. The contents of the bag fell out all over the steps of the stage. I saw a rubber nose and a bunch of different party style noise makers fall out, the type that one might suspect would belong to a clown or to kids at a party. There was no stethoscope, tongue depressor, specimen bottles, medicines or other items one might suspect a doctor to carry.

"Oh no! I heard Understanding wail. "I must have gotten the wrong one!"

"That is the right one, please bring it to me!" Patch responded firmly as a doctor would.

Understanding brought the bag to him and he proceeded to use his "tools" of humor. Patch was leaning over the woman who was lying on the ground. I will never forget that stunned expression on her face when she came to awareness and saw Patch smiling down at her with the biggest grin on his face, wearing his clown nose and holding this obnoxious looking joker puppet.

That was the first time when I began to understand how serious Patch was about the importance of humor to human health. To me, since I thought she was dead, it seemed like he had performed a miracle and brought her back to life with his clown act. She had just fainted, and Patch must've known all along that she wasn't dead.

In the Love Family, people saw illness and disease as stemming from negative spirits, but here Patch had a whole new way of looking it. He had demonstrated in one spontaneous moment how to apply some of what he believed to a real-life situation.

During the show and between acts, Patch would narrate and introduce the lineup of performances as well as doing his own lecture on laughter and health. We went on stage right after the Karamazov Brothers. Every time they went out there, I watched them intently and enjoyed it each time. I knew how to juggle clubs, but they did it with fire and had flaming clubs that they would toss around magically as if it were easy. Then they told jokes at the same time. Amazing!

One bad thing happened. Understanding had to make a major adjustment to her part of the show. She was not able to perform the part of her show that had a tooth witch, because there were real witches and warlocks that were traveling with Patch, and they were very offended when they saw the tooth witch. The show was changed immediately to avoid further upset. Understanding wrote more storylines to replace the tooth witch, and a couple of the kids got new parts in the show.

Then, in Strawberry Patch, Oregon, Heaven refused to go on stage. She was upset because everyone was eating strawberry shortcake, and we didn't get any because there was no money for that. Her being upset, upset me, and she and I got into an argument. Meanwhile, the crowd was all there waiting for us to come out on stage. Understanding was begging Heaven to go on. Dr. Patch had already announced us. Luckily for us, there was a magician guy with a goat that had a horn like a unicorn. He saved us by performing with his "unicorn" during the time we were supposed to be on stage.

It was fun to travel with Patch, but we were not used to the pace. We were not used to performing at that level for the Public. There were a lot of shows, sometimes one right after the other, so it was exhausting, and there was a lot of pressure on us to perform on cue.

Towards the end of the tour, we performed at the Oregon Country Fair, which was a sort of hippie fair that was in the woods in Southern Oregon. The Brothers went on stage and juggled naked for that show. It didn't seem like that big of a deal to me since there seemed to be people everywhere at the Oregon Country Fair who were naked as it was a real countercultural affair. There were lots of people there who were expressing themselves in different ways. After our Oregon Country Fair show, there were some nice people who provided us with a meal, and some kind lady gave all the girls in the Drama

Group flower crowns. They were made with real dried flowers, some carnations, satin ribbons and a hanging beaded streamer. I skipped around with the other girls, wearing my crown and feeling like a little hippie princess.

I loved being at the fair. I felt right at home with all the people from different alternative walks of life. I enjoyed looking at all the crafts and going to the performances. I also enjoyed seeing the costumes that were part of the parade, giant papier Mache creations and walkers on stilts. The food booths offered natural foods like hempseed burgers or alfalfa sprout sandwiches. It kind of reminded me of my life before I came to the Family—Living and traveling to and from different hippie hot spots, which was the only other life that I had known. It was the 'World,' a place where there was a rich diversity in what people were allowed to express—so different from the Love Family. I missed that world, and because I was in the Drama Group, I got to go out and still be a part of it when I went to Gatherings and other countercultural affairs such the Oregon Country Fair.

Theater was good for me, because it brought out my character a bit, which was helpful since I had a tendency towards shyness. It was good for me to see that the Love Family was not the center of the universe; It was a non-Love Family world that I got to be a part of—theater, travel, adventure. Love wanted to show us off, so the Love Family had a face out in the World through the music and performances of the Drama group. All the theater and musical work that I did was very in line with Love Family thinking and culture.

Being a part of the Drama Group was one of the best things that I got out of growing up in the Love Family: Training with Laughter and learning mime, drama, and circus arts; Going on adventures to rainbow gatherings; Performing in plays and musicals; Traveling with Patch Adams—thank you to all the people who made that happen, for their inspiration and dedication and to all the others who helped out so that it was even possible.

BIBLIOGRAPHY (CHAPTER 13)

Balch, Rob. (1998). *The Love Family: Its Formative Years. Sects, Cults, and Spiritual Communities,* Ed. William Zellner and Marc Petrowsky. Pg. 67.

Hostettler & Huntington, (1971). *Children in Amish Society: Socialization and Community Education.* Published by Holt McDougal.

Israel Understanding. Personal Communication. July 15, 2001. Arlington, WA.

Israel, Understanding. Personal Communication. February 10, 2002. 5pm.

Niman, Michael I. (1997). *People of the Rainbow: A Nomadic Utopia.* Univ Tennessee Press.

[Ravah]. Personal Communication. Tuesday March 19, 2002. 7:45–8:55PM.

CHAPTER 14

Polygamy:
The Experiment

wish that every chapter of this memoir was like the Drama Group chapter, full of adventures and learning new things. It hasn't worked out that way, and especially this chapter in which I discuss one of the more difficult experiences I had there, living as a child in a community in which adult members experimented with polygamous relationships.

I would say that my whole adult life I have been wiser beyond my years because of what I'm going to talk about in this chapter. One example in point: In my 20s, I was taking a college math class that was way beyond my level of knowledge, so I got a tutor. He helped me pass that class. His name was James. He was the perfect tutor, because he would get all animated and excited when he talked about math, and it was contagious. Once I began to get a handle on it, James began to show an interest in dating me. He was good looking, very attentive and sweet, but after talking to him on the phone a few times, I just found that I wasn't that interested.

James would talk on and on about his ideas of men's and women's relationships. He felt that men should have multiple wives, and that monogamy wasn't natural. He would list out all these arguments, trying to convince me that monogamous relationships were humanity gone astray. I argued with him. I said, if that is true then why do those sorts of relationships make people so unhappy. I told him that his ideas about this seemed a bit self-serving, male centered. I told him that he wasn't taking any account of how women felt about it, or what it was like for children to be raised in polygamous families. And what about how men felt about it? He hadn't talked to any real men who had actually experienced it. He was dismissive and thought he knew everything. He was young, hadn't done anything with his life yet. These sorts of relationships don't work, I insisted. He scoffed and argued right back. He seemed so passionate about it, as if he had all the answers, and didn't seem a bit concerned for my arguments against it, which in my mind was exactly my point.

I stopped returning his calls. He had irritated me that much to where I said, "You know what—Good bye, James." I was probably the wrong person for James to talk to about this issue.

I knew it didn't work, because I was raised in the Love Family, which was one big social experiment conducted by non-scientists. And part of the experiment had to do with polygamous relationships, but in the Love Family, it wasn't called polygamy, it was called, "multiple relationships."

What multiple relationships looked like were that certain elders were sanctioned to more than one woman at a time. In the following chapter, I share my memories of living with my mom when she was sanctioned into a multiple relationship.

Let me start from the beginning. As I explained earlier, after Yellow Fever, the households moved out of the circle of tents and starting in 1979, gradually began spreading out around the lake into the yurts. Right around that same time, as I have mentioned, there was a big change in the structure of the kids' scene. There were now so many kids, too many for Understanding, so she was sent into town to take care of Love's kids, who were a rather large group by now, probably 10 or more. In addition to Love's kids, she would also take care of some of the kids whose parents lived in town.

The kids whose parents lived at the Ranch, like myself, were sent to live in the households with our parents. Those who did not have a biological parent in the Family were sent into an available household where they would have appropriate guardianship.

It was at this point when I was sent to go live in the household where my mom lived, Nobility's household. Nobility was a new elder and had not been an elder for long when I was sent there. I mostly had known him by his Bible name, Matthew and had never been in the same household with him. I first noticed him at Cherry Hill; He was tall and had long red hair. I didn't often take note of every young guy that came along; there were so many that were joining. The new faces often just blended with all the rest as they all took on new mannerisms typical of Love Family behaviors. Young men came in, and in order to be accepted, they became a quiet, humble servant, disassociating themselves from their former, individual selves to become part of the oneness. But not Matthew; My impression of him was that he was charismatic, popular with the ladies, and had an uncanny ability to make people laugh. His household was situated across the back pasture, nestled up against the trees, not too far from where the Passover lamb was sacrificed each year. He had a large Army tent and several smaller tents. Since he had just recently become an elder, it is my guess that there had been no room for his tents in the circle of tents, so that's why he may have been set up across that pasture.

A woman whose Bible name was Moriah was there too, who was in position to be Nobility's elder lady. She was super fun and would have contests with the kids in the household to see who had the cleanest teeth, and whoever won got a prize; I looked forward to opening my mouth as wide as possible for her to look at my teeth for a possible win.

Moriah had been a nurse before she came to the Family and offered to pierce my ears. I was so happy that I would finally get a chance to wear the sterling fairy earrings that I had traded for at the Oregon Rainbow Gathering. When the time came, she put clothes pins on my earlobes to numb them since we didn't have ice. Once my lobes were numb, she stuck a needle through and planted the tip into a potato on the back side of my ear, so it would not stab me when the needle came through. She didn't let me wear earrings right away until the holes in my ears healed. I had to wear dental floss for earrings. It made me happy though to finally have pierced ears, and I was grateful to her.

I liked living there but was only there for a short while, because then I went and lived for a few months with Eve and Definition. They were now living up at Frankness's old site, which was an Army tent site that was up a trail near the Barn. After that, I also lived for another few months with Helpful and Dedication at their new site, which was the first yurt site on the backside of the lake. No one seemed to make a big deal out of me moving about, and I now preferred to live with the teachers anyway.

While I was living with Helpful and Dedication, something happened. I heard that Dedication had left the Family. I wasn't sure why she had left, but I felt sad that she wasn't there anymore. I suspect that her leaving was the reason I was sent back to Nobility's, where my mom was living.

It was now 1980 and I'd been in the Love Family for five years by now. I would've had to have been almost 12. I hadn't even been to the Washington Rainbow Gathering with the Drama Group yet, which didn't happen for another year.

When I went back into Nobility's household, everyone was in the middle of transition to the new site. One of the things that I did to help was to paint a rust colored, clear varnish on the floorboards of the platform that the yurt would soon sit on. Zarah was living in that household too, and she helped me paint. It took us several hours to complete the job, and it was hard work, especially since we were still young and I had never done that before, but I was excited to be moving into a yurt, as I had never lived in one before. There was a tall ladder we had to climb just to get up onto the platform. This is where I would sleep from now on with the other household women and children, and other than excursions out from time to time with the Drama Group or school fieldtrips, I pretty much stayed in Nobility's household for the remaining three years I lived in the Love Family.

When I returned to the household, there was something else going on. Elkanah was now sanctioned to Nobility as his second lady. No longer was it just Love and his two women, Truthfulness and Bliss, or Integrity with his two women, Together and Submission, as it had been for so long. Now Love was allowing other elders to give it a shot. Thus far, Elkanah had not been sanctioned and had been celibate for years, so the idea of her even being in a relationship that wasn't with Marty, was a new idea. I felt sad, especially when Marty came for a visit once, and when he was there, I could tell he was sad about it too.

Another thing that was different was that Moriah was no longer the newest member of the household. She had been made Nobility's elder lady and was now going by the name Honorable. I noticed that even though Nobility was the spiritual leader and symbolic head of the household, he left most of the household decisions up to his elder lady, Honorable, and it seemed to me that she ultimately was the main source of power behind him; he deferred to her and mostly did not undermine or challenge her authority.

Honorable had a lot of power in the household as the elder lady, but she had additional status because of her decision to allow Elkanah to be Nobility's second lady. Honorable was now seen as the ideal of what Love wanted women to be—open, accepting, virtuous. She had overcome jealousy and possessiveness, the tools of Satan who tried to divide and separate. Theoretically, for my mom, being a second lady to an elder should have raised her status as well, but it didn't. It back-fired on her. Even though Honorable had "blessed" the relationship, in reality, she wasn't dealing at all very well, was incredibly jealous. No one was happy.

Things were very different now. Honorable still had tooth brushing contests, but she had changed towards me. I caught her looking at me several times with what I could only describe as hatred. It startled me at first, then I grew concerned since she had such power over me and everyone in the household. It hurt my feelings too, since she had initially been so nice to me the year before when she was a new member and her name had been Moriah. I was used to very talented, loving people taking care of me such as different caretakers, teachers and guardians, so her antipathy towards me was confusing. I had always been a pretty good kid; I had always been pretty well liked.

It didn't take me long to figure out what was going on. She was extremely jealous of my mom. Honorable had welcomed Elkanah into her relationship with all the perks that went along with that choice such as increased status and admiration, but when it came down to it, unsurprisingly, she couldn't handle it.

Honorable was an elder lady and had status and connections, something my mom didn't have, so she used it. At elder ladies' meetings, Honorable passed false rumors and told lies about my mom such as that Elkanah was a "big problem." She also talked to elders and whoever she could, trying to build her case, and that caused Elkanah to be confronted by others in the community who didn't understand what was going on. It was all designed to have a negative impact on Elkanah's social standing in the community. It was a campaign to undermine my mom's reputation, so she would leave the Family. I guess another option would've been to just leave herself, but she had recently joined, and that was probably the last thing on her mind. Of course, once she had accepted Elkanah into the relationship, she probably didn't feel that she could back out of it without seriously undermining Nobilities new eldership.

My guess is that it probably seemed easier to her to just try to make

Elkanah leave. If Elkanah didn't leave the Family, Honorable could at least kick her out of the household. But in order to do that, she had to have a case built against her and have Nobility, the elder, and the other householders convinced that Elkanah was the problem. Honorable set about making things unlivable for my mom.

My mom didn't leave the Family, at least not right away, and it took a while for Nobility to be convinced of Honorable's lies. He loved Elkanah and had his reputation as an elder to uphold.

Understanding attended the elder ladies' meetings and clearly remembered the situation being discussed:

"I remember [Honorable] talking about it at the meetings. She had us all thinking that Elkanah was argumentative and creating all these problems," Understanding says. "At one of the meetings, Wisdom spoke up and defended [Elkanah], and told everyone at the meeting how well she thought Elkanah was doing and that she was being picked on."

Despite the rumors and attacks on her reputation, my mom was not going to just easily leave. She had been in the Love Family for many years before Honorable came along and had been celibate the entire time. An elder had taken an interest in her, and their love had been honored by Love. Honorable herself had allowed it to happen. Plus, within a relatively short period of time, Nobility became the father of two of Elkanah's children, two sons. Her two other children, Forest and I, she thought, "seemed to be doing really well."

When Honorable became pregnant, it wasn't too long after that when Elkanah became pregnant too. When Honorable's baby was born, she was named Brilliant; When my mom's baby was born, he was named Boldness. It seemed that once Boldness was born, Honorable's hostilities intensified. She "forbid" Nobility from "getting together" (sex) with Elkanah, but he did it anyway, and within time, my mom was pregnant again. Coincidentally, Honorable became pregnant again too.

I am not sure if the gender of the babies had much to do with the timing of the births; My mom, coming into the relationship, and soon after, birthing two boys, while Honorable raced to save her place in the relationship, having two girls. I know in biblical times it sure would've been a big deal, and the Love Family was culturally modeled after the Old Testament in certain important ways.

Girl or boy—It would be hard enough to deal with another woman in the relationship, but it would be very threatening indeed that the second lady would be having his children.

"She was cruel to me," my mom says. "I didn't have baby clothes and she wouldn't give me time to make some. She worked me to death, trying to make me lose the baby."

Maybe in Bible times, multiple relationships went a lot better; not likely though, but it is hard to say since the Bible does not go into much detail about women's lives from women's perspectives.

What the Bible does say was that Elkanah was the name of a man who had two wives, Hannah and Peninnah. Peninnah had many children and Hannah had none. There happened to be a lot of conflict between the two wives as the story goes. I include an excerpt here from the *New Living Translation* because the *King James Version* is not as clear. What it says was that Peninnah would taunt Hannah and make fun of her because the Lord had kept her from having children. Each time, Hannah would be reduced to tears and would not even eat. (Samuel 1:1, verse 1–24, NLT) It would make sense to me that the more children a woman might've had, especially sons, the more power she might've had in her relationship, and I suspect, it was power these women from the Bible were fighting over, not whether they were barren.

Even my own Love Family name—Rachel. Rachel was a woman in the Bible who was in a multiple relationship. She was the second wife of Jacob whose first wife was called Leah. Rachel and Leah were sisters. Rachel was the pretty one, who was jealous of Leah because Leah had many sons, while Rachel was unable to conceive. Rachel ended up having one son, Joseph, and then, when her second son came along, Benjamin, she died during childbirth. The Bible talks about the conflict between these two sisters, and how the conflict between them had a negative impact on their children, causing lifelong family feuds that were a direct result of the relational politics between the parents. (Genesis, Chapter 29 and 32)

Meanwhile, fast forward to the Love Family where people were trying out polygamous relationships, and from what I could tell, they didn't seem to work out well at all. Then things began to get worse.

"Nobility became physically abusive," my mom explained. "I tried to tell people, but no one would believe me."

What a horrible idea, multiple relationships! It seems so obvious that it would be a recipe for disaster.

Elkanah told me that she "talked to people to try and get help," but Nobility would immediately find out and that's when the violence started. He might've been trying to stop Elkanah was talking about it. Those she told were unwilling or afraid to get involved and help her, even those who were considered closer to her and people she thought were her friends. This was not the sort of thing that people talked about. In the Family, everyone was holding each other accountable to be positive and light. Maybe people were concerned that getting involved would put themselves in the crossfire and possibly threaten their own standing in the community. Maybe their friendship with Honorable, an elder lady, took precedence, politically over their friendship with my mom. Maybe it had nothing to do with the women. Maybe it was the elder Nobility himself. He was an elder, but he was a lower rung, younger elder. Fortunately for him, it didn't matter though, that he was a younger elder, because he was close to Love, which added to his overall status. Plus, he had a reputation for being what I heard people say was a "loose cannon." Maybe they were afraid of him or how he would react if they tried to get involved on Elkanah's behalf. For whatever reason, no one felt comfortable getting involved.

Maybe Nobility was trying to teach Elkanah a lesson to stop her from talking about what he thought was their private problems. I imagine he, as an elder, was worried about his reputation. Or maybe, he was escalating the situation between Honorable and Elkanah in order to assist his elder lady with her "problem," to where my mom would have no other option but to leave. My guess is that, my mom not leaving would've been quite frustrating. Was Honorable encouraging the abuse? She never said anything against it, that I was aware of. It seemed to me that householders were jumping into the mess, on Honorable's side, as a way of endearing themselves to the elder lady, the most powerful woman in the household. There was back-stabbing, side takings, and switching sides. There was a lot more going on in that household than it would've appeared on the outside. It's possible that the situation, for Nobility, triggered some underlying violent tendencies toward women. I don't know.

I saw bruises on my mom's body. It seemed that Honorable tried to keep my mom and I separate, but one day, Elkanah snuck me off in the woods to go berry picking. We found a huckleberry bush that seemed bursting with berries where we stopped to pick. We were by the three-sided cabin. While we picked, she showed me bruises where her rib was broken. It hurt her so bad that she was not able to touch it. I didn't know what to say or do, I just felt really bad for her.

Back at the household, I heard Nobility make fun of her at the household meetings. He called her 'Bush Woman,' then everyone laughed. He made fun of how she lived in Alaska and tanned hides like the Eskimos. It made me angry. I was happy in Alaska and had so many good memories of our life there with Marty. I was proud of Alaska, and I knew she was too. How could he be so mean?

Dear Diary

[Nobility] calls Elkanah a 'jerk' and a 'big fat pig' all the time and I can't stand it. In my mind [he] is low class."

Rachel Israel

For those of you who think that maybe I don't really remember seeing bruises on my mom and hearing these things, I was between the ages of 12 and 14 when this was going on, well past the age of a young child who gets confused or makes thing up to get attention. When this happened, she snuck out to see a doctor in Arlington to get it checked out. It was probably 1982 when this happened.

The situation between Honorable and Elkanah took on new proportions that year when the Love Family began to lose some of its cohesion; Love was absent a lot and suspicions were building that he may've had a drug problem (cocaine). This was a period when the leadership was in trouble, so, in some ways, things were not as strict or as tightly controlled as they had been, which might've had some impact on the situation in Nobility's household that unfolded.

I could see that my mom was unhappy and in a bad situation, but I felt helpless to do anything. When she saw one of my Drama Group shows, I saw her crying in the audience afterward, and she practically fell on me when I came out. She was so happy for me and proud; but back at the household, she was sad, fearful for herself and her situation, with a baby on the way.

I wondered if Honorable began using me to hurt my mom. At times, it felt that way. Honorable began to assign me to be her personal helper. I was like her personal servant. I heard people refer to me more than once as Honorable's "handmaiden," which was a term used in the Old Testament. It was used to refer to a mistress's servant who would also often be assigned as a concubine or inferior wife to a mistress's husband whose role was to bear him "seed." The term was used for me almost as complimentary and had biblical connotations of religious humility.

Honorable needed a lot of help because she had a household to run and within a relatively short period of time, two young daughters. I was referred to as her 'handmaiden,' because I was only allowed to help her—not my mom. Honorable would arrange the household schedule so that Elkanah had no help from the other grown household women either. This was terrible because in a commune, everyone worked together, and everyone helped one another, one of the benefits of communal life. There was a sisterhood that the women shared, in the tasks of daily life. Without that network, Elkanah was on her own in the household, which was a very isolating and frightening position. In the Love Family, communal ties replaced the family ties and supports that people might've had before they joined, leaving people even more prone to dependency. Honorable made sure that my mom was isolated from the supports that were taken for granted in the community. For example, she would assign her to kid watch repeatedly, so she would miss the parties up at the Barn or other Family festive events. I would sometimes offer to stay and do kid watch so Elkanah could go, but Honorable would say no.

Honorable was my direct elder, so I had to do what she asked me to do. I dared not challenge her for fear of the consequences on myself as well as Elkanah. Honorable was an elder lady in a bad situation. No matter what her intention was when this all began, here was another woman (Elkanah) in a sexual relationship with her man (Nobility) who now has children with him. All Honorable had to fight back against this situation was the fact that she was an elder lady. She had a substantial amount of power within the household, and she had behind the scenes power on a larger scale as an elder lady in the Love Family with connections to all the elders in the community, especially the other elder ladies. My mom didn't have anything. Usually, if a woman was sanctioned to an elder, her status would increase, but Honorable made sure that didn't happen when Elkanah was sanctioned into the relationship.

The whole thing was ridiculous considering that Love was trying to create relationships that were not characterized by ideas of ownership and exclusivity. But obviously, that is a fantasy, that doesn't work.

As Honorable's personal handmaiden, it was my job to wash the rugs and linens in her yurt. Since Honorable was the elder lady, she had her own yurt that she shared with her daughter, Brilliant, then later her youngest daughter too. As an elder lady, it was not Honorable's role to wash laundry or do the menial labor that was essential to the day; Just like most of the elder ladies in the Family, it was their role to delegate what needed to be done to the lower household women. Just a year or two earlier, when she was Moriah, we had done the laundry together, and she was fun to work with, but now, things had changed. I didn't want to be doing laundry and working like a servant for Honorable, I wanted to be playing with my friends, being a kid, having fun.

Another thing that would happen is that Honorable would make me and Elkanah 'purge' our stuff. A lot of people had to purge from time to time. We all had to share such close quarters. People naturally acquire things over time, so I learned that occasionally, it was time to sort one's belongings and get rid of anything that might not be needed. All anyone was ever allowed in the Love Family was just one bag, so I learned to get rid of anything that wasn't totally essential. It was something that people did to keep things uncluttered and simplified, but it was also seen in spiritual terms, because living without getting attached to stuff and learning to let go was part of the spiritual thinking in the community. 'Let go and let God' I heard that enough times.

There were times though when Honorable expected me and Elkanah to purge things that meant something special, and no one else would be expected to purge. I talked about it in my then Diary:

Dear Diary

"[Honorable] is mean to Elkanah and me all the time now. She used to be so nice. God help me! She purged things of mine and Elkanah's that we didn't want to get rid of. She got rid of things that were special to me, like my music box with the fairy on the lid that I got from the Easter prize table.

Rachel Israel

I used to sleep with that music box, in my sleeping bag. That's how much I loved it.

I wasn't just washing the laundry from Honorable's yurt. It became my job to also wash the laundry and diapers of all the babies in the household, including my own laundry. At one point, there were five in diapers, two of whom were actual infants, three of whom were just beginning to potty train. The diapers were not disposable—they were cloth.

I spent a lot of time at the laundry scene. There was no washing machine, there was no dryer, there was no hot water. There was just a cold water tap at the sauna platform, powdered soap, a plunger, and a washboard. To dry the laundry, I rung everything out by hand and hauled it to the knoll in five-gallon buckets where there were clotheslines. It was rustic, like it might have been 100 years earlier.

I filled the buckets up again and again for the rinses. The motto was 'rinse, rinse, rinse, until the water is clear.' It took a lot of cold rinses when it was soiled diapers. Luckily, I had Zarah to help me. She would wash her laundry and her little brother Reconcile's diapers, which made the job easier. His name was Reconciliation, but we just called him Reconcile because it was easier to say. Zarah was younger than I, around eight but a big help. She was big for her age, so everybody thought she was closer to my age. Zarah helped me haul the laundry in buckets to the clothes lines, then we had to return about two days later to collect the dry laundry and bring it home.

It became obvious that I was overwhelmed by all the work I was expected to do, so Nobility and Honorable made it clear that Zarah was to be under my direction. It was too much responsibility, so I was happy to have the help; I was in a position with her as a sort of child elder, and in older to meet the responsibilities, I had to tell her what to do, so that everything got done. At times, she did not like me telling her what to do, and at times we argued, which irritated the other household members who would complain to Nobility. It was so bad, that one day, Zarah and I had been arguing, and there had been complaints, so he took us out in the woods and we had to pick out a stick by which we then both got a swat. "Spare the rod and spoil the child," I guess. It was hard not to argue considering what we were both having to put up with. Despite our arguments, we were close. Zarah was a great help and strong, and I could count on her to help me carry the five-gallon buckets of wet laundry to the clothes lines. I had written:

Dear Diary,

"Zarah has long, brown hair, brown eyes and a little button nose. She is 3'8" and her skin is slightly darker than mine and she's very cute all together."

Rachel Israel

Despite our arguments, there was an alliance between Zarah and I that made the job seem easier. She told me that one of her favorite memories of me was when we used to walk arm in arm together everywhere:

"It was pretty amazing that you and I did that," she says. "because there was a real big difference between the big kids and the little kids, kind of click-like. You were always really cool with me and would include me in things. You didn't mind me paling around as a younger sister." Zarah also remembered that, when we had the chance, we would play in the woods or jump on the trampoline. "We would sing a lot together. You used to write in your journal all the time," she says.

I wish that was all I had done back then was write in my diary and jump on the trampoline. But unfortunately, there was little time for play. There were buckets and buckets of children's and babies' laundry every day.

Since there was no hot water, I had to wring the clothes with my hands, even in the coldest part of the winter, which meant that the water I stuck my hands in was icy cold. My hands were stiff, turning slightly blue because the water was so cold when I wrung out the laundry, especially during the winter months.

As Zarah and I washed the laundry, we would sing or talk about our lives. She was more than just a help washing the laundry. Even though she was a few years younger, she also was a good friend and sister who I could talk to. She shared with me a memory of me during that time.

One night, she was out scrubbing Reconciliation's leto diapers. It was the middle of winter and freezing. I wasn't helping her, because we had worked it out that she would do her own and her brother's laundry.

"There were those wooden walkways between the yurts," Zarah says. "and my tears were the warmest things dropping onto my hands. You danced around in the moonlight, and you sang and kept me company in that way. It was kind of a cute memory of you but bitter-sweet." I thought it was unfair but I knew that it wasn't your job."

Zarah and I used to compete to see who had the biggest arm muscles. Having a buddy in hell to goof off with, if it wasn't for her, it would've been a lot worse. One year, there was no plunger, so we had to get in and stomp the poopy diapers with our feet. This was before we had the tap water, so I would have to take the buckets down to the lake and fill them up. I figured at the time that if I stomped them with my feet instead of swishing them with my hands that it would feel as if I didn't have to touch the leto. But it ended up being just as gross.

Our laundry scene was connected to the sauna, which was built on a platform where people cleaned themselves. If one needed warm water to wash, one had to heat it on the stove in the sauna and use the camping shower or take a sponge bath.

The Barn was maybe a ten or fifteen-minute walk, depending on where one was coming from. It had hot water, and there were a washer and dryer there, but there were too many people living at the Ranch for it to be practical to share them, so they were reserved for people who lived in Strength and Appreciation's household. The washer and dryer were overused though and ended up not working half the time anyway.

One day, I saw Shushan in the Barn laundry room; she was in there washing clothes. I just happened by and had some extra time. The washer wasn't working, so I helped her wash them. That was when there was this antique wringer in the laundry room. Once the laundry was washed, there were two rollers that if you crank the handle, the laundry gets wrung out between the rollers. It was an arduous task but better than wringing them out by hand, especially when we were doing it together.

Shushan had this wonderful sense of humor, so we just got through it by laughing the whole time. We made up this little nonsense song that went *"Mahini Mahim, Mahini Mahim."* We chanted it over and over as we washed the diapers. It didn't mean anything, it just sounded funny. As we washed the clothes, we just kept getting sillier with the song and really getting into it and then started a little dance that went with it too, which made it even funnier, and finally the laundry was done. Laundry was hard work, but whenever I could, I just made the best of it.

I had a lot to make the best of, because not only was I responsible for washing the babies' laundry, Honorable had me taking care of the babies themselves. The adult women in our household, who were moms, nursed their babies, bathed them and put them to bed, but during the day or when I wasn't in school, I was doing childcare. When I was taking care of the kids, the moms were freed up to go to household or Family meetings, or they might be cooking or cleaning or doing whatever the elder lady had them doing.

I was like a little mom in Nobility's household. I was put in charge of the kids' scene just like Understanding was put in charge of kids in the Love Family. Nobility had once made a comment about what he remembered about me:

"You were like a little Understanding," he told me.

I helped to serve the bowls that had been prepared for the young children before I sat down to eat with them. After one of the younger household women prepared the meal for the children, she did the prayer, then, I would look after everyone as we ate. The children in the household, who were around elementary age, were Zarah, Forest, Quan, and Genuine. For a time, a little boy named Zack was there too. Then there were the five babies, three of whom were preschool age, two of whom were infants. There were older kids there as well, teens such as Boaz and Naaman. Sun and Shama were there for a time, who were around my age. After the meal, I would do clean-up and dishes with whoever was old enough to help, usually Forest and Zarah.

In order to wash dishes, someone had to haul water from the sauna tap to the yurt, then the water could be placed on the wood stove in pots to heat. Eventually trenches were dug and finally the main yurt had a cold water tap in the kitchen, which was also piped up into the upper portion of the yurt where there was a sink.

Twice a day, I would also help feed the babies. There were three at first. Brilliant was Honorable's baby girl. Reconcile was Zarah's baby brother, and Boldness was my brother, Elkanah's new baby. This memory was before Honorable and Elkanah had their second baby with Nobility. All three would be lined up in the little walker seats that we had for them on the drop cloth. Each baby had their own wooden bowl of oatmeal or mashed peas or potatoes. I sometimes had Zarah's help but not always. I was feeding three babies at the same time, so there were mix-ups. I had to keep track of which spoon went into which baby's mouth, and because, like baby birds, they all had their mouths open at the same time, I had to go fast to keep up with them. If I didn't go fast enough, one or more of the babies would start fussing and kicking their legs out from their walker in expectation. I did my best to keep up with them.

Feeding three babies sounds like an ordinary, expected experience of a mom who maybe had triplets or what it's like to work at a day care center, but I wasn't a mom or old enough to work, I was a girl and still several years from adulthood. It helped though, that I was used to seeing all the children in the Love Family like siblings and members of my family. I naturally took on the role of big sis/guardian to the younger children in the household and tried to mother them as best I could.

I learned how to change a diaper really fast. I knew all the tricks, like running a pin through my hair to neutralize the static, so it slid right into the cloth. With three babies in the household, anyone that has ever taken care of a baby knows—that is a lot of diapers! An average infant goes through easily 12 diapers a day. It was a minimum of 36 diapers a day to start—cloth diapers!

The three babies became toddlers eventually, but then Honorable and El-kanah each had another baby, so then really there were actually five in diapers, until the older three were potty trained. Kids aren't potty trained overnight either. It was a gradual process, I learned.

With so many diapers, there was a huge push in the household to potty train. Many times a day, I took potties out to the outhouse to empty them, then took them over to the sauna/laundry scene to wash them out.

Even though I tried not to favor one child over another, I couldn't help but want to feel closer to my own biological sibling, Boldness, and when he met certain mile markers, I felt extra happy for him and kept track of them in my diary.

Dear Diary,

Woopee! Boldness just did his first leto in the potty. I am so glad. I wish he could get a present for that.

Happy go leto day!

Rachel Israel

Then there was naptime. Zarah and I weren't allowed to go play until the babies were down for their naps. They would all nap at the same time in Honorable's yurt, where it was quiet, so Zarah and I patted them until they drifted off. The problem was that there were three, so I had to pat two at the same time while Zarah patted just Reconcile. It was so frustrating to pat them for endless periods of time. Just when it seemed they were asleep, we would attempt to sneak off, and they would lift their heads and start crying again. I was learning early what it was like to be a mom.

Taking care of the babies was hard work, but I also learned to try and make it fun. I took what I learned from Understanding to entertain them. When they got old enough, I would put on little puppet shows for them in the yurt, and Zarah and I would take them on walks every day to the trampoline or the swing set up at the Barn, just like mini fieldtrips.

It was fun to go to the trampoline, but I had to be so careful with the babies, because they were so light that they could easily go flying off if I didn't hold them tight as I jumped. The swing set at the Barn near the garden was better, because there were three swings, one for each baby, and then it was just a matter of pushing them, one at a time. They were old enough to hang onto the swings at that point.

If we didn't go to the trampoline or the swingset, we instead would take them on a little hike to pick berries. There were lots of hiking trails from our campsite that went to the back meadow.

It was quite an operation, being as young as I was, walking with three toddlers and the other young children from the household to the Barn or trampoline. It took so long that Zarah and I would just carry them on our hips until we got too tired.

Years later, when I had some back problems, my chiropractor asked me:

"Did you carry a baby on your hip when you were young?" he says.

"Yes, I did," I answered.

He then speculated that maybe that is why one of my hips stuck out further than the other one. I was still growing, and the babies just got plumper and plumper.

Yes, those plump, heavy little babies, carrying them around made me strong. When they were little, I could actually throw them above my head and make them giggle. Then I would lie down and put them on my feet, so they could play airplane.

I knew even then that I was being over-depended on in terms of the household labor, but at the same time, I knew of other girls my age who had a lot of responsibility too. When I spent the night with Heaven, we had to help take care of babies and young children when I was there too. This was in Love's household, though. They had a lot more kids than even we had in Nobility's household, but they also had a crew of adult women who were primarily responsible for the children there, people like Fresh, Radiance, Jezreal, Silome, and many others. But in Nobility's household, Zarah and I were the crew.

In some ways, I didn't mind helping. I felt motherless, and it was the only way I knew how to gather praise and approval in a society where I didn't get much attention in the first place, but I also felt used in a vicious battle between the elder lady and my mom.

I was on my way out of Honorable's yurt after having just collected her rugs, when I accidentally ran into her. As I was apologizing, she was giving me the evil eye with a glazed over expression, as if her mind was somewhere else. It was that same look! I had seen her look at my mom that way. I wanted to shake her. I wished that I could just say, "Hello?! I am not Elkanah! I am me, Rachel. Instead, I just smiled as sweetly as possible. The smartest thing that I could do in that situation was just to try to endear myself to her as a reminder of my value to her as her helper. It sometimes worked, and her expression would shift to where I saw recognition register in her eyes. She would see me smiling up at her, and she would suddenly awaken as if from a reverie. She would then smile back at me with a puzzled expression on her face. It seemed that she was superficially nice to me on the surface, maybe to keep me from an all-out rebellion. After all, I was doing a substantial amount of the household labor, such as laundry and childcare in addition to my chores.

She wasn't just doing it for the help though. She could've assigned the adult women to be more involved in laundry and childcare; she also did it to try and punish my mom. She was trying to force Elkanah to leave the household, the Family, whatever.

There were times when she would hold me back from activities that took me away from the household, and that is when I began to do some back-talking. I needed to be with Understanding and my peers. They were going on fieldtrips and other fun outings.

Dear Diary,

[Honorable] won't let me go to ballet class this Saturday in town. She wants me to help with the babies.

Rachel Israel

When I had responsibility in Nobility's household, I didn't come into it with no prior experience. I helped out with the younger children in the different households where I lived, but I wasn't asked to do it, I usually just did it on my own. I could see that I was needed. It was just fun then. I enjoyed helping out. When I lived with Eve and Definition, I would sometimes help watch Deliberate who was Eve's little baby.

I was watching Deliberate one day in the kitchen. This was about a year before I moved back to Nobility's household after living with Eve and Definition at Frankness's old site, up near the Barn. The kitchen was attached to the main Army tent by a little wooden walkway. The kitchen itself sat on a platform; its walls were built with planks and clear plastic sheeting, so it was very bright inside. There was an old fashioned, wood burning cook stove in the corner, a hand-built table in the center.

Deliberate was crawling around on the floor, near the sink and dish area. I had turned my back for just a moment, and I go to pick him up, and his fingers were in his mouth. He was chewing on something. I knew I had to be careful about that, so I did my hook swipe and pulled out a slug. I felt sick and freaked out. Heart was there, a little girl who had come with her mother, Hannah from the Source. I was so grossed out, that I became agitated and began announcing the incident to the whole household. Definition came into the kitchen to see what all the commotion was about and started laughing. He was quite humored by it:

"Slugs are good, I'll eat some slugs," he bragged as he left the kitchen.

Twenty minutes later, he came back in the kitchen with a handful of slugs. He put them in a frying pan with some oil and began to sauté them.

By this time, I was so disgusted that I had to leave, but later when I came back into the kitchen, he had already eaten them and was rubbing his belly:

"They were good," he bellowed, then he just laughed and laughed like it was so funny.

At the time, I did not find it that funny, although I am sure the household did. Now, looking back, I find it hilarious. Definition was a character! I loved him very much. Of course, the Ranch was covered in slugs; they were so great in number that they could be seen just about anywhere I went, except not usually in the tents or kitchen. Their slime was very difficult to remove and gross. I was learning: never turn my back on a baby, even for a minute.

A few months later, for some reason, Eve and Definition moved and were staying in the tepee in Nobility's household before he got the yurts. Whenever I got the chance, I would help with Deliberate who was now walking. People were impressed when they saw me take care of him. I heard someone say I had "natural ability." Then Eve was assigned to go to the Rainbow Gathering that year. Deliberate's gramma, who was staying in the household at the time, was to take care of him with my help, since he was too young to go. I was 11 years old. I knew what the date was, because I had asked my teacher Ethan what year it was. He told me without even thinking about it, and I had written in down in my diary.

Eve was now gone. Deliberate was now a toddler but barely. He was walking, but not very well, because I still carried him quite a bit in his backpack.

Deliberate's gramma, for some reason, ended up not being able to take care of him. I'm not sure where she went. Suddenly, I was Deliberate's primary caregiver. No one else helped me with him; I was on my own. I had to carry him on my back, twice a day up to the Barn for meals, since at that time, everyone would gather there for shared meals. It was quite a little trek as he was a heavy baby. During the day, I would play with him, and while he napped, I would wash his laundry, including all his diapers. That is when Moriah, who later became Honorable, was friendly, and we would wash laundry together. I put Deliberate to bed each night, patting him to sleep and singing him lullabies. It was more responsibility than I had ever had at that point, but I did it like a champ and enjoyed it for the most part. Deliberate was a cute baby and I grew to love him as if he were my own.

After three weeks, Eve returned from the rainbow gathering. I clearly remember the day. I was in the pasture with Deliberate. It was a warm evening in early August and Deliberate and I wandered through the meadow together, picking daisies. In the distance, I saw Eve come running across the pasture toward us with open arms.

Deliberate looked at her with a blank expression on his face. He then looked back at me confused, then he looked back at her. Because he was so young, three weeks probably felt like a lot longer to him.

She picked him up and hugged him with a huge smile on her face. He started whimpering. Eve got a guilty expression on her face:

"Oh, I think he might be a little mad at me," Eve says to me. She picked him up and started walking back towards the tents. I saw him peering back at me as she went. He looked back at me standing there, watching them walk away. He looked confused, sad. Suddenly, it was over. I was no longer a mom. I was back to being a child, at least for the time being. Little did I know at that point that it would not be long before I was taking care of more babies than just one. But in those three weeks, I learned a lot about life. I learned how much responsibility it is taking care of a baby. I learned a little bit of what that relationship is like between a mother and her child, how close, how bonded it can be.

I had been more of a sibling to Deliberate, then suddenly, a maternal figure to him, then, back to more of a sibling, because then Eve went back to being a maternal figure to me as well as my teacher who was his mother. It kind of ripped my heart out actually. He had loved me with all his heart and looked to me to fill his every need. Then, as she took him away, I felt the same thing a mother would feel as he cried, as if I were abandoning him.

Fast forward a year, and now I was living at Nobility's yurt site. I was now around 12 and the one in charge of the household babies and young children. I needed help with one of the younger children, so I went and interrupted a household meeting and was shooed out of the meeting and told to "just give em a swat." Basically, the message I was getting was to just figure it out myself, which I did. I was determined to protect and love the children in that household, the most important of which was to protect them from these idiots.

Meanwhile, Elkanah's situation worsened. After Honorable had bad mouthed Elkanah at the elder ladies' meetings and to everyone she knew, Honorable had peoples' sympathy. Once she had peoples' sympathy, she felt secure kicking my mom, who was nine months pregnant, out of the household. Of course, Honorable had to have Nobility's permission, since he was the elder of the household. He finally gave in to his elder lady.

Nobility had "always promised" Elkanah that he would not kick her out of the household, even though he knew that was what Honorable wanted. He stood firm, but I guess the pressure was too great from his elder lady who would constantly run to him with lies about my mom, trying to convince him that Elkanah was too big of a problem to keep in the household.

Dear Diary

"[Honorable] sent Elkanah out of the household. [Nobility] just went along with it. I know she said for just two weeks, but I know [Honorable] hates her and doesn't want her to come back at all. She wants [Nobility] all to herself. I wish I could change things and for someone to understand me. I just have Zarah to talk to."

Rachel Israel

Well of course she wanted him all to herself. Before they had come to the Love Family, Nobility and Honorable had been married, although they had broken up and had joined separately. They were one of those couples that were an exception to the rule. Love had allowed them to get back together after they joined. It's interesting to think about that point, because Love was trying to create a community where prior attachments were absent, in the spirit of true communal life. That was why he usually didn't allow a couple to be together if they had been together before. And now, they were trying a polygamous relationship, when there had been a prior attachment. How much did that contribute to the overall situation that unfolded?

When Elkanah was kicked out, no other household invited her to stay with them. The false rumors that had been spread, stuck, and people didn't want to get involved. She ended up staying at Frankness's old Army tent campsite, which was where Eve and Definition were living after Nobility moved his household to his yurt site. Most households by now had moved to a yurt site.

My mom was really "scared." Her second baby was due any day now, and there had been no arrangement by Honorable, who was a nurse, for the delivery. Elkanah was at this strange campsite without the father of her baby on hand and without her other children, me, Forest, or Boldness. I was told that I would have to stay back, while she was gone and help take care of Boldness, Forest, and the other children in the household, which I was already doing a lot of anyway, so it would only be a bit heavier without her.

I have tried to understand why Elkanah would've been kicked out when her baby was due any day. I can only assume that maybe Honorable thought the cruelty would push Elkanah over the edge enough to leave the Family. Maybe, she just couldn't handle the stress of a multiple relationship any longer, especially since Elkanah had not left on her own as maybe she had hoped. Maybe she never let it go that this baby had been conceived in the first place, especially after she had told Nobility he was not allowed to get together with my mom. In reality, this was another woman giving birth to another child by the father of her children.

Even though I don't think Honorable's behavior was very kind, I can understand her reaction. This is almost typical of the sorts of things that can happen in multiple (polygamous) relationships. She was acting like any other woman would've acted in a similar situation.

Now Elkanah was by herself. It was very humiliating for her, especially because having a baby in the Family was usually a celebration. It was also humiliating for me as her daughter who had to sit by while all this was happening and watch Elkanah's situation get worse and worse. I began to see it as a threat to my own status and membership in the community. If she left the Family, what would happen to me? I didn't like the idea of being there without her, but I also knew she didn't have anywhere to go. When she first brought me to the Love Family, it was just me and Forest, but now she had a toddler and very soon, a newborn as well. Nobility and Honorable had made it very clear in the household that Elkanah would not be able to take Boldness if she left the Family. Boldness was not even two years old yet, but this was just one more reason to not leave. This meant, in order to leave, she would "have to sneak" out, since she was "afraid" of Nobility, and "what he might do to try and stop" her if she tried to take her children with her.

While Elkanah was kicked out of the household, there was a meeting upstairs one night. Everyone in the household, maybe eight, nine adults were sitting on the floor in a circle in the main living area of the yurt floor. It was a casual meeting where Nobility was entertaining everyone, and people were laughing and joking around. I was not at the meeting, but I was in the same room; I was taking care of the kids. Boldness started fussing and I could not console him. Here he was a young toddler and his mother (Elkanah) had disappeared. Boldness toddled into the center of the circle where everyone was sitting and looked around at everybody. He was fussing. For some reason the top of the yurt, a six-sided plexi-glass dome was sitting nearby. Sometimes, on a nice day, the yurt top was removed, so there was sunlight and fresh air that would brighten the yurt. It must've been the spring or summer of 1982. Boldness's fussing became more urgent and the meeting was interrupted by the commotion. In a spontaneous moment, the yurt dome was put on top of Boldness. The dome was maybe three or four feet wide and the same distance in height. Nobility's character was that he was funny, and the household was constantly full of laughter because of him. He was cracking jokes about how funny it looked to see Boldness under the dome, fussing. Everyone at the meeting started laughing and pointing at the baby under the dome. Boldness looked out at all these people laughing at him and started crying even harder, which caused everyone to laugh even harder. Maybe I just didn't have much of a sense of humor at that point. I was watching this whole thing wondering why people thought it was so funny. It was making me angry. With Elkanah gone, I began to feel even more protective of Boldness than before when she was around. Finally, the laughter subsided, but it was a long few minutes before anyone empathized with his plight and turned him loose.

I just can never shake that memory of his little face, screaming angrily as everyone watched and laughed. His face grew red with rage, while tears of laughter fell down their cheeks. He was a little cutie pie too. His hair was a light blond, very fine, so he almost looked bald. He was a chubby baby, with big round full cheeks and playful, laughing blue eyes. He had been teething and had two bunny teeth that had just come through his gums.

With Elkanah gone, I tried to love Boldness up as much as possible to make it easier for him, just like I did with Deliberate when Eve was gone. I made up little nicknames for him like Bobo and Boldy. I wrote in my diary for him:

Dear Diary,

A poem for my brother Boldness;

Boldness he's a boy
Boldness he's my joy
Boldy boy, goldy joy
He's my boy; he's not coy
good Boldness boy

Rachel Israel

I began to feel like a protective mother hen with the children in the household. I tried to keep them under my wing as much as possible. I was on my own with Boldness, but I still had all the responsibilities of laundry and watching the other babies and young children in the household too. Plus, I also had a lot of daily tasks like dishes, sweeping and cleaning up, cleaning and refilling the condiment tray, cleaning and preparing lanterns and candles, and other chores, which I discussed in more detail in a previous chapter.

Dear Diary,

After doing my chores and helping with dishes and clean-up, I don't have enough time to do my homework. No one understands."

Rachel Israel

I liked to help, but it became stressful, because it seemed everyone was depending on me. Especially after the dome episode and after it became clear that I would also be expected to be the disciplinarian.

I was upstairs in the yurt once, and one of the household women overheard me complaining to Zarah about wishing I could go play or go swimming instead of taking care of the kids that day. That's when I got a long lecture about the power of positivity and how negativity gets you nowhere, etc. The woman giving me the lecture was one of the younger women in the household. She had the brightest red hair that anyone had ever seen and seemed to like to walk around naked everywhere. I turned her off in my head and just watched her mouth move. It was the same old line, over and over. Feelings didn't matter, be positive crap, and no one was listening or paying attention to what the kids needed.

On top of everything, I began to notice that there were men in the household that were creepy. My protective instincts were kicking in. Before I even came to the Love Family, my mother had taught me to trust my instincts. When we had lived on the road and had been hitchhiking around, she had to use them to protect me.

I trusted my feelings when I felt a distinct creepiness about certain individuals in the household. Boaz, a tall, slender teenager who had red hair had put his hand on my leg a couple times trying to entice me to "like" him. There were others—a man who I will call Asteroid, who was new and another man who was a regular householder named Nethinim.

I won't say who, but I heard comments directed towards the children that had a subtle sexual vibe to them. Then I sometimes heard the children say things that led me to believe that something might have happened that was inappropriate. One little girl in the household told me that one of the adult men in the household had "licked" her "mena." Mena was the Family word for Vagina. I overheard the younger women in the household talking about how Asteroid thought that kids had sexual needs that needed to be satisfied. I heard something else as well from one of the younger household women, that something had happened to Shama. Shama was around my age and lived in our household for a time. I didn't know exactly what had taken place, but it sounded like she may have been raped.

I began to be more vigilant around the men in the household. I knew we were not safe. The tone of voice I used with the men would be mean. I would say things to them, speaking for all the kids, like, "We don't like you anyway, so just leave us alone!" I was mean to any man because I began to not trust anybody. Years later, there was a man who confronted me about how "mean" I was to him. It was Benaiah; I had hurt his feelings. I apologized to him but at the time, I was trying to protect myself and the children from abuse. No one from the household, like Honorable or Nobility discussed my behavior towards the men, and I never got in trouble for being disrespectful, so I just kept doing it. Maybe they weren't paying attention that much or maybe they just overlooked it because of how much responsibility I had with the children and laundry. I was in charge and if any child misbehaved, they had been warned to do what I asked, or they would get a swat from Nobility. The kids began to see me like a mom and I knew that I had back-up if needed.

The creepy feelings I felt were not imagined, because in the end, after they left the Family, I heard that Boaz, Nethinim, and Asteroid, all ended up charged and prosecuted for sexually abusing little children. I could tell that there was something about them that wasn't quite right, but it seemed no one was paying attention except for me.

I had no one I could talk to about it except for Zarah. If I told my mom Elkanah, she would have been powerless to do anything, and if she tried to defend the children, she would have put herself as risk for more abuse, as had already been shown.

I told Zarah to stay away from certain individuals who I felt weren't safe. Years later, she remembered:

"When you were around, I stayed away from them," Zarah says. "Your influence helped me later when he was going to try and be a pervert to me in the yurt. But if you weren't around, I would play with them. They were fun with kids. I got piggy back rides and stuff."

At the time, it scared me to think that I had to protect the children because I was just a child myself. Before I went to live in Nobility's household, I already tended to be somewhat quiet and thoughtful. But living there made me more serious as I had to become like a little adult out of necessity.

Sexual abuse was not a topic in the Love Family. No one talked to me about what it was or what to do if it ever happened to me. I just had to figure it out.

Then, Big Lois asked me and Zarah to come talk to her. She was in Love's household at the time and was no longer sanctioned to Encouragement.

"What happened?" she asked. She wanted specifics.

I felt like I was under an inquisition. Someone had obviously told her that I had been complaining about the creepy men in our household. I told her some of the things I had observed and heard, but she kept reaching for something more that I couldn't give her. "You aren't being specific enough," she insisted.

I clammed up. I saw what happened to Elkanah when she complained. I saw what happened to any member who complained. Usually they were booted if they couldn't get it together, brow beaten or raked over the coals. I had learned by now not to be open about my feelings.

When Big Lois brought me in to talk about sexual abuse, she addressed it in such a frank, sincere way, showing genuine concern, that I didn't know how to deal with it. I had no context for it, so I wasn't sure how to respond. I don't know why Love didn't address it in the community. Maybe he was concerned about how bad publicity could impact the community and was trying to minimize any threat that could arise that might disrupt our life as a family. Maybe there were more sinister reasons.

Whatever the case, it wasn't part of Love's vision. Here you had this community that was totally cut off from society and that didn't go by the laws and rules that were developed to protect people. There was this assumption that we didn't need all that, that we were Jesus Christ and beyond all that, which, of course, made the Love Family a perfect haven for predators, because sexual abuse wasn't even a topic of conversation. Someone who had those tendencies could easily slip through the cracks and go join the Love Family where they would take on a new identity and life, including a new name. One could essentially disappear! They would join and have access to children in a shared parenting community, especially towards the end.

As the community began to disintegrate, it became more disorganized. As it lost its cohesion, there was less oversight of people coming into the Family and going into the households, leaving the kids vulnerable to predators.

If Love had laid down guidelines for the community to follow, it would've set a precedence. He should have said, 'this will not be tolerated.' But he didn't. People would've listened to him. They worshiped the ground he walked on.

One of the things that made the children especially vulnerable was the fact that no one was keeping track of how old anybody was. Whether a girl was eleven or seventeen, who knew? Age is one way that people make those determinations. There was no official turning point where a child would become an adult. I always felt that I had a choice, that if I wanted to, I could just start going to morning meetings and doing what the big people were doing. I could just decide that I didn't want to be in the kids' scene anymore. Abigail wasn't that much older than me, and she was sanctioned and had a baby. I wasn't exactly sure how that had gone down, but the idea of that frightened me. There were other kids that made that choice. Asahel was one example of that. Even at a very young age, she took on a lot of responsibility. When I first came, I was around seven, so she must've been around 11 or 12, and she was teaching a group of younger kids a class in quilting. She would help Understanding take care of kids, and she would do what the adults were doing, gardening, going to meetings, etc. My understanding was that she had joined the Love family on her own, without parents. She had had a vision from God that brought her home. Her vision, which I don't remember the exact details of, was very similar to some of the dreams and visions that I heard other members say they had, that had guided them to Love, to the Kingdom of Heaven, to Israel. Many had revelations of oneness and love, many of the same tenants in the Love Family. I was pretty mature for my age, but not like Asahel. I was not interested at all in leaving the kid scene. I knew I wasn't ready for that.

I was too young to have to worry about sexual abusers in my household. My fears of something happening to one of the children made me feel frightened, and I took on a sort of hyper vigilance that seemed required for the task of protecting them. Gone were the innocent days of my early childhood when I lived with Understanding in the Kids' House and ate granola and yogurt and watched puppet shows.

If I did end up going somewhere with Understanding on some field trip, I now worried about who would take care of the babies and young children without me, or what could happen to them while I was gone.

It was hard worrying about the children, taking care of babies, and washing diapers, but the hardest part of having so much responsibility was that it felt proscribed by Honorable who seemed to be using me to hurt Elkanah. I became bitter and resentful. I overheard the ladies of the household complaining that I wasn't "humble" enough and that I would "talk back."

A lot of my resentment was over being kept back from Drama Group activities and field trips with Understanding and other caretakers. What I really wanted was to just be with the other kids my age and do kid stuff.

Dear Diary,

[Honorable] won't let me go to town with the other big kids. She wants my help with laundry and babies. Its two weeks from Passover and we are on a break from school. I'm mad. Today was boring because all I did was watch babies and help.

Rachel Israel

Years later, after I no longer lived in the Love Family, I went out, one year, for Passover at the Ranch. I was somewhere in my mid-twenties. When I was out there, I ran into an ex member who had been known as Tobiah. Tobiah taught biology in the Family school for a time. I asked him what he remembered about me. With a knowing expression on his face, he made a comment to another ex-member standing next to him:

"She was like 12 going on age 40," he says, which at the time, was exactly how I felt. Tobiah had a closer chance to observe me too because he lived in the household next door during that time. I would visit him over there when I went to see Eve and Definition who ended up living at that site. There were others there too who lived there that I was close to such as my friend Sarai.

Suddenly, I heard my mom was going into labor, and I was sent to go see her. As I said earlier, she had been kicked out of the household and was staying up at Eve and Definition's, which most people knew as Frankness's old site.

From Nobility's, I hiked across the pasture, past the lake, another pasture, past the knoll to the Barn, then headed from the Barn, up the trail through the trees to where the campsite was located. It might've been a fifteen-minute walk or more for a kid. It was a very picturesque setting with the giant Army tent, which sat on a wooden platform, nestled in the trees. I had fond memories there when I had lived with Eve and Definition two years earlier. I had slept in my own bunk bed that was built way up near the top of the roof of the tent, where there was a small plastic sheeted window, overlooking the main trail, where I could watch folks going past on their way to other households, to or from the Barn.

There was no one there when I got there, except a couple householders. I had been to several births by then. Usually when someone had a baby, at least the births I went to, the room was full of people and festive. There might be music, singing, and chanting.

The Army tent was quiet and dark. Elkanah was set up in a bed near the window near one side of the tent. I don't know if people just didn't know about it, or if her reputation was so wrecked and beyond repair that people just didn't come, because she was seen as such a pariah. Even though we had not had much of a relationship for many years, I still loved her, and it made me feel terrible to see her without the community's support. I felt a mixture of feelings—sadness, anger, shame and frustration.

It was sad to see her in this situation. Before we met the Love Family, when we lived in Alaska, we had had lots of good friends and it seemed like every day, we had different visitors that would come to our cabin or tepee. People came and offered to help when Forest was born. She and Marty both had been well liked people. Once she had been in the Family for a while, she seemed to have changed. Now she was ultra-shy, bitter, unhappy. I can't quite describe how painful it was to see my own mother rejected in this way, and by this time, she had dedicated at least eight years to the Love Family.

I knew what was going on, but I just didn't know what to do about it. There had been a conscious campaign to drive my mom out. Spreading false rumors as a way to turn people against someone is a form of bullying. When people see that, they may be less friendly to that person who is being talked about because they're afraid of the consequences of getting involved or of being the next target.

I did what I could to help as my mom waited for the next contraction. My mom seemed so happy to see me and I could tell she was happy that I was there as she waited for the midwife to show up.

There were a few women who were trained, registered nurses or midwives when they came to the Love Family—Honorable, Virtue, Jael, Bliss, Magdiel and Mispah that I know of. Having babies at home naturally fit in with Love Family thinking about health, which was against conventional, modern medicine. Home birth was natural.

Mispah ended up my mom's midwife. Before she came to the Family, Mispah had been a midwife for the Farm at their huge birthing center, which was out in the Midwest somewhere. The Farm was a commune headed by Steve Gaskin. There were thousands of people who were a part of the Farm. People from the world paid to have their babies there. Mispah had gone to do her laundry at the Barn and someone came running—"She is having the baby right now!"

My mom wasn't worried. She had been her own midwife when Forest was born in Alaska, so even though Mispah wasn't there when the baby started coming out, Elkanah, didn't panic. She could've delivered her own baby if she had to.

Ten minutes later, Mispah showed up. It became my job to bring a constant stream of clean, warm washcloths from the kitchen. Eve ended up being there as well since she and Definition were householders at that site during that time, which meant they were in line to become elders. Eve handed me the washcloths as fast as I could take them.

My brother came out just fine. Nobility showed up for the birth just moments after the baby came out. Apparently, Honorable had told him he wasn't allowed to come, but he was able to sneak out of there anyway at the last minute.

Even though hardly anyone was there, I was there. It felt like a magical moment when the baby arrived. People don't realize how beautiful birth is anymore when most babies are born in the hospital with doctors everywhere and bright lights.

I grew up in a society where birth was just a natural part of life. It took place as it has for peoples and cultures throughout time, in the peace and serenity of the forest or somewhere close to nature. It might have been how it was when people lived in tribes, small communities, or villages, way before birth became the giant industry that it is today where a large percentage of women are on an IV, have C-sections and are dosed with large quantities of medications in small hospital rooms by doctors and medical staff who they don't know.

When Elkanah's baby was born, he wasn't circumcised, just like all male Love Family babies. Children ran around naked all the time, so it was obvious that no one was getting circumcised. In a religious sense, this would've made us gentiles or non-Jews, according to the Bible, but that is not why we did it. We did it that way because it just seemed more natural. It also was more in line with the hippie idealism of the times, an idealism that underlay a lot of the Family's culture.

By the time I had seen this birth, I had seen a lot of babies born. When I lived with Eve and Definition, and we were staying in the Army tent in the circle of tents, before the households spread out around the lake. Eve went into labor, and I watched it from the top bunk just a few feet away.

No one had a camera there, but I was so amazed that I got out a piece of paper and a pencil and began to sketch what I was seeing.

Afterward, I gave Eve one of the sketches of the labor.

"That's really good!" she exclaimed and she kept it. The sketch she kept was of Deliberate's head coming out of her vagina. The head looked pointed; it wasn't round and hadn't taken shape yet.

A year later, when I was living in the Army tent across the back pasture that was Nobility's first household site, I listened all night long to the sounds of Shemuel having her baby. I drifted in and out of sleep, listening to the heavy breathing sounds of pained grunting and distressed moaning with the midwife giving instructions. Then, by early morning, everyone cheering, "It's a girl!"

That little baby was named Joy. Shortly after the baby was born, Honorable kicked the baby's mother, Shemuel out of the Family. Apparently, Shemuel had 'gotten together' with Nobility, and they were not sanctioned, so Shemuel with a newborn and a five-year-old little girl named Amanda were kicked to the curb. It was a big no-no to get together with someone who wasn't sanctioned, so Honorable had a strong case in kicking Shemuel out.

Before the Ranch house burned down, I saw Piety have her baby there in the back bedroom. The room had been so packed with people that I had a hard time getting in the door and through the bodies to where I could see what was happening. Since I was a kid, I was shuffled through the crowd, and I ended up with a front row place where I could see the drama unfold right in front of me. I had to have been around nine, maybe 10 then.

If word went out that someone was having a baby, people would come running from the different households. People would just show up to join the party. It was a new person, a new virtue coming in. Everyone wanted to know—Who is this?!

Birth wasn't this private event that takes place removed from the home in the sterility of a hospital under the care of doctors and nurses who are mostly unknown to the birthing mother. It was usually a joyous, social event, under the care of midwives who were family. At least it was that way for most of the years.

When I saw my little brother born though, it was not that way. It was totally depressing with no one there, and I could tell she felt humiliated.

Once my mom had the baby, she decided to leave the Family and go try and find a place for us to live. She was determined to come back and get me, Forest and Boldness and take us all out of there as soon as she had something lined up. Before she left, she was allowed to come back to Nobility's household, but only because she told Honorable she had decided to leave the Family.

Finally, Honorable would get what she wanted. No one in the household dared to try and talk Elkanah out of it. Before she left, Strength and Appreciation volunteered to help take care of Forest. They promised that once she returned, they would give him back to her.

Mom had an old friend named Don come and get her and take her to stay with Shemuel, who now lived in Southern Oregon. Her baby, Joy, was now walking. While there, my mom tried to find work and a place for us to live.

"There I was, I didn't have a name," she says. "I didn't have ID and I didn't have any money; I didn't know what to do." Plus, she had an infant with her, my new brother, that was just a few weeks old. She thought she had something lined up, but it fell through. She knew she had to get back to us, so she decided to come back to the Family and come up with a better plan.

When she got back, my new baby brother was given a Bible name, Jacob. He was not honored with a virtue name as all babies usually were who were born in the Family, because she had left the Family, a symbol for all who knew her of her failure.

When Elkanah went to Strength and Appreciation to get Forest back, they refused to let her have him. Honorable had told them that my mom was too "unstable" to have him back, that it was best he stay with them. When I went to the barn during that period, I would sometimes see Forest. I didn't know what was going on and why he wasn't living with my mom. Younger kids usually lived with their parents. One day, I was up in the Barn, and there was Forest being picked on by Cheerful. I told Cheerful to back off. "You leave my brother alone!" I told him. Even Forest, who was six years younger than I remembered that.

The decision for Forest to live with Strength and Appreciation had been coordinated by Honorable. My mom did not have much recourse to challenge them other than to just go talk to her elder, Nobility, and Nobility wasn't willing to challenge his elder lady or challenge Strength and Appreciation, very high status elders who were in charge of the Ranch.

The way that things got resolved in the Family was you went through a certain order. You went through the elder of your household; that was Elkanah's connection to Love. In those days, Love was absent a lot, and no one was being allowed to see him. Love and Nobility were close during that time period, and I doubt Love would've challenged his friend on what he may have thought was a personal matter.

When my mom went to Nobility for help on how to get Forest back from Strength and Appreciation, I overheard the whole thing. I was changing Boldness's diaper during the household meeting when the discussion took place.

"You don't need your fuckin kid!" Nobility laughed in front of everybody.

My mom left the meeting crying.

He followed her outside, and I heard some noises go "thud thud" and heard my mom cry out.

The next day, I saw two huge bruises on her side, and she told me he had "kicked" her "twice." My gramma Phyllis came to visit that week and saw the bruises. From that day on, Phyllis refused to ever visit us again at the Ranch.

I can't ever explain how terrible it was to think my mom was being hurt, and I knew she wanted to leave the Family. One day, I was at the sauna with Hope. He was goading me with comments about my mom's martyrdom.

He had obviously been hearing the rumors.

"Why is Elkanah such a martyr?" he asked. He made a face when he said it, so even though I didn't know what martyr meant, I knew it was not good. He had heard the rumors that were being spread about her, but he had no idea what was going on in our household. If Elkanah was so unhappy, Honorable rhetorically must've asked her elder associates, then why doesn't she just leave?

I was scared. It was because of my mom that Honorable seemed to hate me. Would I be hurt like Elkanah was being hurt? I wanted to help my mom, but it seemed there was nothing I could do.

It was a whole year before my mom got Forest back. During that year, she "wrote letters" to people, trying to arrange to get help so she could leave the Love Family.

"It was really horrible," my mom says. "I was just trying to get out of the Family."

I talked to Forest about his experience, during that year when he was living with Strength and Appreciation. I was surprised he had remembered so much since he had only been seven.

"I missed my mom," he says. "I wasn't quite sure why I was there. Mom used to sneak me out on these walks. Suddenly I was cut off from everyone in the household I had been close to. I didn't have clothes to wear and no mom to tuck me in."

Forest says he was "spoiled" while he was there. He says there was "no structure," that he "watched a lot of TV" and "played with Legos."

"I would say, 'Hey! You know what's on TV tonight?' Forest remembered. "Strength had to take me aside and say, 'Hey, cool it!' because no one else had television." Back at [Nobility]'s household, Forest says, "there were no luxuries there, but at least you had the structure."

While Forest was living with Strength and Appreciation, he got to go to Disneyland and stay with Steve Allen for a couple of weeks. The reason they all went was that there was that earthquake in California, the Coalinga earthquake, of 1983, and 40–50 Family people went down to help out in the recovery effort.

While the adults were helping with reconstructing earthquake damage, he and Cheerful mostly stayed back and got to swim in Steve Allen's piano shaped swimming pool, then Steve Allen taught the boys how to play pool:

"Cheerful and I were playing in the yard, and we got in trouble," he says. "Apparently there were rattlesnakes down there."

Soon after that trip, Forest was suddenly placed back in the household at Nobility's:

"I was confused by it," he says. "Did I do something wrong or what?"

The reason that Forest was returned so suddenly to my mom was not because Honorable had a change of heart, it was because Strength and Appreciation had decided to leave the Family, and the members of their household were left struggling with relocating. My mom explained what she remembered:

"When I got him back, most of the clothes I had made him were missing and his head was full of lice," she says.

......

Multiple relationships didn't work. Look what happened to Forest. It is interesting to me that a lot of the problems that resulted seemed to be related to the fact the when an elder had more than one woman, one of the women had the power of elder lady, and the other woman did not. They were not equal. There was no checks and balances, so of course one should have figured how that would end up, especially when children were being born into this dynamic.

There were other elders, besides Nobility, who were trying out multiple relationships, and people said it was "working out." I don't know what all went on in those relationships, but I have heard rumors that they were not the ideal that people were led to believe. Even in Love's relationship, I was told by unnamed sources that Love would lecture Truthfulness about her jealousy during meetings in front of everyone, and that he favored Bliss's kids over Truthfulness's. I can only imagine what those women went through.

I asked Understanding to talk about what some of the discussions were at the ladies' meetings around the subject of multiple relationships:

"We sat around as women and talked all the time about our dissatisfaction with the polygamy thing," Understanding says. "Oh, we hated it! We talked about it a lot because people would break down emotionally." In the meetings, there were women who would ask Love why it had to be, and "they would tell him that they couldn't handle it, and that they didn't like it." Understanding remembered that Love would come in to the ladies' meeting and talk about it. She deepened her voice when she quoted Love from her memory: 'We all know that the old woman of the world wants to own her man,' Love would say. 'There is a tendency in women to just be a witch. They want to scare everybody else out.' Love would continue, 'I promised when God helped me build this family that we weren't going to have that, we were going to end jealousy on this planet.' If a woman spoke up or challenged Love, Understanding says, "We felt we were forced to shut up. Love would talk, and he wouldn't give us a chance to talk."

When women protested, their words fell on deaf ears. Love's ignorance reminds me of James, my tone-deaf tutor in college who was so convinced in the rightness of his views that monogamy was this oppressive model for relationships.

I wish the women who had been there would've stood up together in opposition to this awful oppression, but that didn't happen. Instead women tried to landmine and backstab each other. That was the only power they thought they had. Understanding explained:

"What we would do is make alliances and friendships to try and make the other woman look really bad," she explained. "Like if a beautiful woman came in, we wouldn't help her. People would make her look really bad and clumsy and pass rumors about her."

One situation that Understanding remembered happening was when all the women who lived in Cube City "shut out" [Glory] and Empathy.

"We couldn't stand them," Understanding says. "We wouldn't do anything for them. Love had to come down that time and read us the riot act because we wouldn't watch their kids."

"When the women ganged up on someone, it wasn't pleasant, she continued, "We turned the cold shoulder at you and if you had kids, we would make up excuses or whatever." Some of the women were even staking out territories, thinking well if I have two kids, maybe I'll own him more than her, she doesn't even have any kids."

Why would women accept multiple relationships? Did the community have that much to offer that women would overlook this? Was their desire to avoid the messiness and pain of leaving, stronger than their desire to protect themselves and their children from this crap? Understanding's answer: "Accepting the polygamy thing was one of the calling cards for upward mobility," she says. "The more giving and sharing you were in your relationship, the more glorified you were; you would get your virtue name—and that is why I bowed out and didn't even have guys," Understanding explained, "because I knew I couldn't win in that thing—I knew I couldn't handle that."

My old teacher, Definition had some thoughts to share on the issue. I include his perspective here, as I think it is important to hear from a man's perspective too, and he is a good one to ask, since he ended up in a multiple relationship himself.

> Everyone was trying to emulate Love and of course, he had two wives. Having another woman fit into the vision. The problem with men and women in the Family had to do with men. The women did not like it that the elder of the house had more than one woman, it always caused trouble. That is the way Love wanted it though. It's a male fantasy but it turns into a disaster. You don't see it until it happens to you and you realize what a mess it is. When you can't ever really satisfy anybody, somebody is always going to be mad. Some of the Family's core ideas about men and women didn't work.

Even if one were to take the polygamy out of it, there would still be the problem of Love deciding who was going to be with who that would eventually become an issue as it did in the Oneida community.

At Oneida, couples would frequently fall in love with each other. There were reports of frequent criticisms of men and women who failed to suppress one of these exclusive or special attachments. If it was suspected that a person refused attentions due to greater love for another, they would be severely criticized for lack of appropriate public spirit, and public ostracism of exclusive couples was severe (Zablocki, 1971).

Adult Oneida members wanted sexual freedom or to be able to choose sexual partners without Noyes consent. Others complained that some women were doing it too much and others were being neglected. (Klaw, 1993).

The whole idea in the Oneida community was to have a 'complex marriage' where there were no exclusive attachments. That was the idea in the Love Family too, that there was no such thing as ownership, that we were all married to each other, and that Love was the one who decided who would be with whom.

What is interesting to me about what happened in Oneida was that here there was this community where they decided there were not going to be any exclusive, special ties between men and women, and the people couldn't handle it; they were drawn, instinctively towards exclusive pairings. In secret, couples were pairing off and having secret, monogamous-like attachments. What this tells me is that people like James, my math tutor and other evolutionary theorists are missing something very important when they say that exclusive, monogamous ties are unnatural—Take it away and people can't get enough of this monogamy thing.

Sometimes, there's a reason why things are done the way they are. Not everything needs changing. I appreciate idealistic, passionate people, however, there needs to be discrimination, deep thought about what is being targeted for change. There needs to be discussion by more than just one person. One would think, after as long as humans have been around on this planet, that over time, they would've learned by trial and error what works and what doesn't when it comes to the most basic of human relationships where procreation is involved.

Even today, there are still pockets of people who are trying to make polygamy work. It seems to exist in societies and cultures that are male dominated, where men are making the decisions, and where women do not have a voice, where women's concerns and feelings are not highly valued.

This is exactly what happened in the Love Family. It was a patriarchal community where there were few checks and balances. At the top, was a man, Love, making all the decisions through his elders, who were also men. After what I saw, women's lack of voice or real power within the community was why multiple relationships happened. And every woman that joined the Love Family allowed that to happen by naively agreeing to go along with it or overlooking it and not being willing to stand together as a group and say no.

It was a world where women had such little power that they were willing to put up with bullshit like multiple relationships, relationships in which everyone was unhappy, including the children. The shame that I had to carry, because my mother was humiliated in front of everyone, and no one did anything to help her had a hugely negative impact on me. And it had a lasting effect for years after that on my biological family once we left the community, as I will discuss in the next chapter.

There was no domestic violence hotline in the Love Family. There was no Child Protective Services. There was no court of appeals.

I had been taken care of communally, having essentially no personal relationship with my mother for years, and then towards the end, I finally had a chance to live with her, and this is what was happening.

I have wondered: Whose fault was it that that happened, really? Elkanah and Nobility wanted to be together. Honorable accepted it, then dealt with it in the only way she knew, with the only power she had. But who decided that polygamy was acceptable in the first place? Love. And who designed the hierarchy that made status and power, among women, such as commodity in demand, where women had to prove themselves by squelching their natural impulses and need for monogamy? In other words, I am speculating that women's lack of power in general led to a sort of desperation that led women to seek one of the only ways they were given to raise themselves up in that society. They were seeking recognition and admiration. Do we have to push each other down to raise ourselves up? What is a sisterhood really, if it's not raising each other up and joining forces to fight back against our shared oppression?

I have tried to love Honorable and Nobility no matter what I went through. I have tried, just as I was taught in the Love Family, to just forgive. I try to understand what it must have been like to be them and to be in their situation, but it has been hard because they hurt me and my family so much. It was hard enough being raised in the Love Family to begin with, but my experience in that household during the last two or three years that I was there, were by far, the most difficult years growing up in that environment.

In the next chapter, I will discuss my last year in the Love Family and some of the changes that began happening on a wide scale throughout the community.

BIBLIOGRAPHY (CHAPTER 14)

[Karen]. Personal Interviews. July 11 & November 10, 2001) West Seattle.

Israel, Understanding. Personal Interview. September 15, 2002. Lake Forest Park, WA.

Klaw, Spencer. (1993). *Without Sin: The Life and Death of the Oneida Community*. New York: Allen Lane, Penguin Press.

Kephart, William M. (1963). *Experimental Family Organization: An Historico-Cultural Report on the Oneida Community, Marriage and Family Living* 25 (3), pp. 261–271.

LeWarne, Chuck P. (2009). *The Love Israel Family: Urban Commune, Rural Commune* University of Washington Press, Seattle, WA.

[Zarah]. Personal Interview. December 13, 2001 Maple Valley, WA.

CHAPTER 15

Mounting Disorganization

My third year in Nobility's household ended up being my last year in the Love Family. It was the period between the time I got back from the 1982 Idaho Rainbow Gathering to mid-August of 1983.

I have several memories that stand out. One took place in the fall. There had been a Cookie Day party up in the Barn for the kids. "Cookie Day" was the Love Family's version of Halloween. The kids in town would walk the neighborhood and visit each of the Family houses, asking for cookies. The kids at the Ranch would walk from homesite to homesite. Later that night, there was a party up in the barn for the kids.

Elkanah had sewed me a costume in her free time when she went to go take a turn at Potato Heaven that year. It was a Scotchman outfit. I learned how to do a little Scottish jig that I practiced every chance I got to show off my costume. She made Forest into a Pakistani with a turban, sash, and ethnic balloon pants, which to me, didn't seem all that different from how I saw some of the men dress every day, minus the turban.

Eve and Definition dressed up like pirates. Nobility dressed up like 'Darkness' with black war paint on his face and hid out under the bridge. As kids would pass by, he would jump out and try to scare them.

The sanctuary in the barn was decorated to the hilt with bales of hay, pumpkins and scarecrows. It was dimly lit with candles which seemed to cast shadows everywhere throughout the space. I decorated a heart shaped cookie, and even though I was supposed to give it to someone I love, I decided to eat it instead. There was a couples' dance contest and Zarah and I won. We got a gingerbread house to share as our prize. There is a picture that I saw somewhere of her and I taking a bite. I was amazed that we won since we didn't practice or anything, but Zarah and I were close, and as we danced, we coordinated our movements together, so it turned out to look as if we had.

During this last year, I noticed that things began to happen; there were subtle changes in the culture. It affected me personally because I could do things that I would never have been allowed to do before.

For example, just a week after that Cookie Day party in the Barn, there had been another party for the adults. Some of the big kids, including myself, formed a band and planned to perform as the opening act for the Love Family band that would play that night. There was electricity in the Barn, and no one seemed to notice us borrowing the band equipment for our weekly practices.

At that time, every Saturday night, there would be a huge party up in the Barn, and the band would play. It was loud, and the dance floor would be packed. The big people would drink wine that came from the Love Family winery. It was a very tame party, social drinking only. I did not see anyone get sloshed or act inappropriate in any way. There were servers who would bring out trays with wine glasses and pass them out to people, almost like a catered event.

I looked forward to putting on the show. I had done quite a bit of performing with the Drama Group in the last few years, so we put a lot into it. Before the show, us girls helped braid and fix one another's hair. We used the school supplies in the school rooms to decorate our outfits. I found an old skirt down in the storeroom that I cut up and made into a miniskirt. With a big black marker, I wrote PUNK on my shirt and found an old pair of cowboy boots in a box under the stairway to wear. We used paint from the art box to make it look as if we wore makeup. Ravah would play base. Bright was on drums, and Boaz played guitar. Dinah was on keyboards since Cheerful didn't want to do it. Mary, Heaven, Gentle and I would sing. The boys put something in their hair to make it spike out, so we all would look like little greasers, the opposite of ethnic, Love Family hippie kids.

The fact that we all did this, that no one stopped us, was truly amazing and unbeknownst to me, clearly was a sign of the lack of continuity that was present during that last year.

That night, in front of easily over 100 or more people, we all got up there to play our song. We had many practices, so we didn't sound all that bad. We all rocked out in our rebel gear as the party on-lookers watched in shock and near horror. Everyone was stunned. When I looked out into the audience, I could visibly see peoples' mouths drop open and their jaws just hang there as they stared at us.

Part of the shock was our outfits, which were so outrageous, but the other part of peoples' shock was the song that we performed—the lyrics!

"On our Halloween night, everybody is a fright,
We just wanna be a scare, chase the boys and pull their hair.

I just wanna be a punk, always eating dirty junk,
Smoking, toking every night, nothing seems to work out right.

I am always out with Paul, 'cause he gives me alcohol.
I am always getting drunk, that's why people call me punk..."

I don't know what people were thinking that night after our performance, but we clearly made an impression. If the Family had been more cohesive at that point, we would have been stopped before I even put that miniskirt on. There was an aspect of what we did that was devious; it was putting up the finger to everyone for what we had been through and taking advantage of the loose rules and environment where people began to challenge the status quo.

A few months later, spring of 1983, it was Passover time again. Everyone was partying, and the kids were running around in the fields. Hope set up the music equipment by the knoll. They were able to get electricity all the way down there from the Barn. He set up an electric guitar and other equipment. It was near the outhouses that were there by the trees near the knoll. I walked by and stopped short in my tracks to see what was going on. Hope was singing and playing the guitar for the Cars song, "Shake it Up." It was very loud, and certainly shook things up because I saw people walking by, just staring at him as if not sure whether to stop and enjoy it or whether to keep walking. I saw people chuckle in amusement. In the Love Family, we didn't play music from the World, and if we did, they were songs that were not about shaking things up. It was Hope, doing his own thing. Once again, he was trying to shake things up so to speak. He was a total rebel till the end. He wasn't going along with the program, and no one was able to stop him. They had tried earlier on by beating it out of him, but he was now too big to spank now; He was probably 17 or so by then and had taken to lifting weights. Every time I hear that song now, I think of Hope. I wonder if he played that song on purpose, knowing that the Love Family was on the verge of blowing apart.

That summer, after the Golden Egg Party, Love invited the big kids into town for a feast at his house. It was supposed to be an honor. We were all bussed into town. Love's house was a gigantic house with multiple floors. In the main sanctuary, Love served us scallops, which I thought were gross. It didn't make any sense to me that he would be serving them, since as a culture we were mostly vegetarian and followed Old Testament rules regarding pork and shellfish. The rules were different when it was the king who decided, apparently.

After the feast, Love invited some of the kids to smoke mashish with him. Most of us had never smoked mashish before, but maybe he thought we were old enough now. I was probably almost 14 by then, but I'm sure Love knew that there were some of us who had taken an interest, and maybe he was just trying to make us think he was cool. Love passed around the tau, and then we all went off to play hide and seek.

There was an upper floor in Love's house that was under construction in certain places. I went and hid in these rafters. I was hidden so well that no one found me for a long time. I began to feel physically very strange. I sat there for at least a half hour waiting for it to go away but it never did. I began to feel scared, hiding there for what seemed like an eternity. I thought, *I don't like this mashish.*

Another thing that happened that was indicative of major change going on was one day, I was up at the Barn and this huge truck shows up. It was full of blue jeans. They all said, 'Fresh Squeeze' on them. I sorted through piles and piles of them to find a pair that fit me. I was looking forward to wearing them, as I was sick and tired of always wearing a long dress or a long skirt all the time. It was difficult to find a pair that fit me though and that didn't need to be repaired. Each pair of jeans had something wrong with them, like the zipper needed repair, or one leg was longer than the other and other miner factory mistakes. A bunch of people began wearing these Fresh Squeeze jeans. I thought it was weird since most people never wore blue jeans in the Love Family. There were a couple guys who wore them when they worked in the gardens, but definitely not the women or the girls. There also were several women that I had seen wearing makeup, which puzzled me since Family women never did that. I took note of it in my diary:

Dear Diary,

The ladies and girls can wear pants now instead of just long dresses and long skirts and blouses. Make-up is not a total disgrace. Is our culture falling apart?

Rachel Israel

I liked some of the changes, but they were odd enough that I wondered if something was wrong. Nobody seemed to care when I ran off with the other kids to Jordan Store by ourselves, without a guardian, to swim in the river or to visit Claudia, the store owner. I brought my jewelry to Claudia, so she could pick something out that she liked, and in exchange, she let me pick out a handful of penny candies. She let some of the other girls I was with do that too. Something was different, and especially considering how rigid our culture had been up to this point.

I was playing without guardianship with groups of children my age, and I noticed that the oversight was missing in terms of screening adults that were coming in. As I discussed earlier, usually if a visitor came to the Family, they were taken in by a household or by Love and hosted and fed and talked to. They might go to meetings and be observed to see if they were a fit for the Family, but there were individuals during this time who were coming and going, and no one seemed to care. I saw people were joining who didn't seem to fit and didn't seem to be getting with the program. For example, this young man came in, who I will call 'Nathan.' He was a slender guy with short, blond hair and a goatee. I am not sure whose household he was in. He couldn't have been more than 19 or 20. Most people were young like Nathan when they joined, but it had been a few years by now, and most of the adults were somewhere over 30. Nathan was taking the kids on boat rides on the lake, and he came and went from the Ranch as he pleased. He didn't take on a Bible name and wasn't attending meetings. It did not seem to me as if anyone even noticed him. He gave me the creeps, so I just avoided him. Coincidentally, I heard rumors years later after I left the community, that he really was a creep.

Anyway, there was another guy who used to visit the Ranch that I thought was strange. I noticed him because I used to go up to the Barn with jugs that I would fill with milk for the household, but lately, every time I went to the Barn, there was this guy who was just hanging out in the parking area. His name was Eddy, and he wasn't in any household; he was just visiting in his van.

Eddy, my guess, was maybe 60. He was balding and had graying, short curly hair. He was unkempt, had a pot belly and beard stubble all over his chin and cheeks, as if he had recently stopped shaving. I had seen him several times up at the Barn, talking to some kids who were crowding around his van. Usually I just got my milk and left but one day, I went over there just to see what was going on. When I got to the van, he had this box of candy bars that he was passing out to the kids who were there. A chocolate bar was a rare gift in those days, so I got one and walked off chewing on it.

Then I went over and was standing near the Barn washroom where I had set my milk jugs. I was talking to Naaman and some other younger kids who just happened to be there. Zarah was there, because she had come with me to get milk. We were just chatting, and Eddy walked over from his van:

"Is that candy bar good?" he asked me with a grin.

"Yes! Thank you!" I answered him.

"How about a thank you kiss?" he asked. This was right in front of Naaman and the other kids.

"Thanks, but no thanks!" I told him politely and took another bite of the chocolate bar.

"I insist," he stepped closer to me and put his cheek up about an inch away from my mouth.

The others looked on watching the interaction, not sure how to react.

Eddy wasn't going to accept no. He pointed to his cheek, as if I needed instructions.

I felt pressured to give him a quick peck on the cheek and be done with it since everyone was still just standing there, watching. But instead, to my shock and horror, when I went to plant him a kiss on his cheek, he turned so his mouth would be the recipient of the kiss, and he put his tongue in my mouth right as I went to kiss his cheek. I cringed backwards in dismay and disgust. Everyone was silent, then Naaman broke the silence with uncontrollable laughter, as if it were funny. I ran from the group into the washroom and began washing my mouth out with soap. Zarah followed me and provided support. I hardly knew this unshaven, creepy guy and here he had done this to me in front of my friends. And Naaman had laughed. I was mortified and totally disgusted.

Once I was done washing my mouth out in the Barn washroom, which I did repeatedly, Zarah and I grabbed our jugs of milk and began the trek from the Barn towards our household.Even after washing it repeatedly, my mouth still felt dirty.

Eddy wasn't even a member; he was a visitor who had unsupervised access to children. People weren't paying attention, and there were creeps like this who were coming and going without notice. *What was going on?* I thought.

This was during a time when some of the kids my age had played spin the bottle out in the pasture. I wasn't there but I heard a lot about it from Heaven. I was sort of glad that I hadn't been there, actually, as I was not interested in kissing boys. Us kids had always been like siblings, like brothers and sisters, and to think they had been kissing was beyond what I felt like trying to understand.

Then, Appreciation had a slumber party up in the Barn for the kids, and Seth and I had parked our sleeping bags up in the Barn library with some other kids. We had each settled into our sleeping bags. Seth asked to French kiss me.

"Yuck, no way!" I told him.

"Please! Please!" he kept begging me.

"No! That's gross!" I kept insisting.

This was not long after Eddy had groomed me with that candy bar and then tried to kiss me, so the idea of kissing with tongues was too much to stomach.

Plus remember that I already was dealing with perverts who had been allowed to come in to Nobility's household. Every day, I worried about their access to the children I was caring for. I wasn't too worried about myself. I told them off or gave them the look, and they seemed to intuitively keep their distance from me. It was a constant concern though, especially since there were changes in the culture that were unsettling.

Dear Diary,

We do not eat pork, but Nobility bought a ham for our household. Something is really wrong lately. Heaven invited me to breakfast tomorrow.

Rachel Israel

The next morning, I walked over to Love's household for breakfast. I couldn't think of another time when I had been invited for breakfast anywhere. Usually I just went over there for dinner or a sleepover. Some of the women were making mushroom omelets. Eggs were not common in my household, but it was a staple in Love's household. I looked forward to having eggs, and I had never eaten omelets before. I ate breakfast with all of Love's children and other children who were in the household. There were at least 15 kids there, probably more. The kids ages ranged anywhere from around three or four to around 13. I was one of the oldest ones there. Most of the children were under eight or nine though.

After breakfast, suddenly some men in suits came to visit Love, and the kids and myself were scurried out on a walk—real quick.

The next thing I remember, we were all walking down Mattson Road. I saw Life turn into a cartoon character as he ran off towards the front of the group. He got smaller and smaller as he ran. I looked at Heaven to see if she had seen it. We looked at each other and busted up laughing. It was then that she told me that the mushrooms in the omelet had been magic (hallucinogenic). Every kid on that walk ate those omelets because I helped serve that morning. That was the strangest walk I had ever been on, but it seemed there were a lot of strange things that were happening lately.

Another strange thing happened. There was a party up in the Barn where the kids were being given wine. There were trays coming out of the Barn kitchen with glasses of wine and grape juice, and the kids were crowding around and asking for juice. There were huge speakers in the Barn, so it was very loud. The dance floor was packed with adults. I don't remember who it was that gave it to us, but several kids were given glasses of wine. It was just another example of something odd, something different happening that I wasn't used to seeing. It was different enough that I took note of it in my then diary:

Dear Diary,

I drank four glasses of red wine in a contest to see who could drink the fastest. I felt really weird afterward, and during the party in the Barn, I sat by myself under the stairway where there is a secret hide-out. I don't like wine.

Rachel Israel

Then there was this very memorable, but strange hike that I went on with some of the other girls around my age. We took off by ourselves one day on a hike to the Lookout. There were at least five of us.

On the way up, there was a conversation. They were angry at Love. It was a very serious conversation, and the girls were particularly upset. I didn't know exactly what they were talking about, but I heard them say something about Love and a man named Israel. Another girl said that Love had made her do things to him that were inappropriate. I was quiet and just listened, not quite sure what was going on. I began to feel sick to my stomach.

"When I turn 18, I am gonna get the hell out of here!" one girl cried out.

It frightened me how angry and hurt they sounded. As we hiked along the trail, a couple of the girls started picking mushrooms and eating them. Every time they saw a mushroom, they would run off the path and eat it. One of the girls took a maternal tone with us, as she often did:

"You better not eat just any old mushroom; you have to make sure it's not poisonous!" she scolded. "You could die!"

"Who cares!" one of the other girls exclaimed.

I picked a puffball and chewed on it, but I knew it was edible. It seemed that they must have wanted to die because they were eating mushrooms that looked poisonous to me. I kept hiking but I was worried about them. We made it to the top of the Lookout. It was always quite a hike to the top.

"OK fine, if we are going to die, then we are going to die, there is no point in eating anymore," one of the girls announced.

I couldn't believe what I was hearing. I had spent a good majority of my childhood with these girls; they were like sisters to me. The view at the top of the Look-Out was usually fantastic but this time, it was dismal. A feeling of doom enveloped me. I looked way down and saw the little miniature tents and yurts in the pasture by the lake. It looked the same as it always did, but this time, I hung way back from the edge in the trees because when I stood near the edge, it felt like I would fall off to my death. We were all there together, but it seemed we were each far, far away with our thoughts and not close like we usually were. I always remembered that hike as being called the 'suicide hike.' Maybe the girls had called it that, or maybe I just thought of it that way.

I never forgot that hike though, because it really confirmed to me that something bad was happening in our community. What was going on? I could feel it; things that had always been the same were crumbling. That sense of safety that I had always taken for granted, was no longer there.

Even though Dedication had already been gone for a year, rumors began to circulate about why she left. I could tell that people were really concerned about this as they told it. There was fear in people's eyes, and shock. They said she had gone to Love to complain that she didn't have milk for her kids, and that Love did not address her concern at all but instead, offered her some lines of cocaine. It seemed that now that things were beginning to unravel, it was now safe to openly discuss why Dedication had left. I usually didn't hear about stuff like this, and it bothered me. What did it mean?

I didn't know what cocaine was, but I had heard a rumor that Love was doing it. I was just sad to hear it. Dedication had been my first teacher in the Love Family. Helpful was devastated, of course, as they had a son together named Glad and Helpful loved his elder lady very much. When she left, he lost his elder status, although not officially.

A lot of people had come and gone over the years but not people like Dedication. When she left, it sent ripples through the community. No one could believe it since she had been one of the few who had been kidnapped out of the Family early on by Ted Patrick. The whole thing had been seen live on TV, and she had escaped the viper's claws to return to the Love Family, where Love honored her dedication to him by giving her a virtue name—Dedication. It was almost legendary.

Love had offered Dedication lines; she had left the meeting angry. No one knew exactly what happened there, but with all the changes, I now had a serious question, was the Family was falling apart?

I didn't know what was going on behind the scenes, and only found out years later by talking to people. Understanding told me:

"Cocaine had been going on for at least a couple of years," she says, "but it was just like bad weather." Then in the last year, it grew into a real problem. "Love and [Truthfulness] began to look like ghosts. They were skinny and gaunt."

Ethan grew "concerned" as well after he saw Love walking down Sixth Avenue "looking like a drug addict:"

"He looked terrible, Ethan says. "He had big black rings under his eyes which looked all sunken in. No one was being allowed to see him," Ethan continued. "People were getting upset because there was no money for the other stuff that was needed."

Rumors began to circulate that Love was doing cocaine with the main elders in the city and Strength, who was the main elder at the Ranch.

"Some of these elders came to the realization that cocaine was becoming a problem, and they stopped including themselves," says Understanding. "The circle of elders doing cocaine became smaller. People turned on each other and began ratting on each other."

In 1982, a huge elders meeting was held. "Love left the meeting pissed off because he couldn't make people do things; he had lost his power and respect. After that, he always had a guard at the door and was totally unavailable to people."

I didn't know what to make of the rumors. Unbeknownst to me, there were secret meetings being held to discuss financial things going on.

"The elders were discussing dividing up the Ranch," says Understanding.

I began to complain too, at least to Zarah. I was sick of the same old food. It was getting bad. The diet was always simple, but it got worse to where there were times when there was no milk or rice. In my diary, I wrote:

Dear Diary,

I am sick of leftover beans.

Rachel Israel

At the time, I didn't know that the reason why there was not enough food was because there was no money. Rents weren't getting paid.

"Love permitted certain people to work if they gave him a percentage of the profits," says Ethan. "It wasn't the majority. Most people continued the Family lifestyle. Very few people went out and got a job," he says. "Nobody had birth certificates, driver's licenses, social security numbers, housing or work history, so the work that people got was limited to private, self-employment businesses, mostly." Small "organized teams" of men or women would go after "different moneymaking ventures."

Businesses were started such as yard work, landscaping, and construction. There were carpenters, plumbers, remodelers, landscapers, and house painters. There were catering, plumbing and electrical services. The Wood Shop made custom cabinets, doors, wooden toys and crafts. The cannery and winery made some money. There was a logging business. The men were going into forested areas and cutting up dead trees that had fallen; Then they would split it into firewood and sell it.

It wasn't just groups of men. Lydia told me that she worked in the honey business where they imported, repackaged and sold honey foam. It was kept in a warehouse shared by John the Wineman.

"Honey foam is cool stuff," says Lydia. "We would get these big barrels of honey and there was honey foam on top that would be put into jars," she says. The jars of honey foam were also distributed into the households, and we had honey foam that we could put on our bread or on our oatmeal. It was delicious!

It wasn't just Lydia. There were other talented women artists and craftswomen who started businesses too, such as Simplicity and others.

There was a rumor that the Family was drug dealing as a way to support the Family, but that wasn't true. Multiple sources have told me that the drug dealing was only for Love's benefit, to support his drug use, never for any benefit to the community in general.

For those who worked, they were allowed to keep 10% of their income for their personal households. Unfortunately, there was no fair way in place to share in that available resource. For example, the school, which everyone benefited from, did not generate income, so it did not receive any of the funds from the 10%.

How it worked was that Meekness was the business manager, and [Truthfulness] was the bookkeeper. Once the money, that the businesses made, went to Love, he would divide it up to pay the different bills such as rent, utilities and operational expenses, and food and supplies. Whatever was leftover, Love would decide what to do with. He could take a bunch of people to Hawaii or to a rainbow gathering. He could plan a big party or event, or he could buy the brick factory, an airplane, or whatever he wanted, such as cocaine. There was no board. There were no committees. There was no voting mechanism or opinion/satisfaction surveys.

Before the membership started working, the community had been more isolated and "safe" from outside monied influence. It had been mostly money free and spiritually based, with little bits of money and lots of bartering. The whole mentality had been to avoid working at all costs. Now Love was asking people to work.

"It was ridiculous!" I heard one ex-member say, as they looked back on that time.

Why did the Love Family begin to fall apart? I asked my former teacher, Ethan:

"It came down to Love couldn't take care of our kids," says Ethan. "It is related to money in that you couldn't buy applesauce for your little baby.

You couldn't go get bananas because you didn't have any money. There wasn't any milk for the kids."

"There began to be 'the haves and the have nots,' says Ethan. "I remember seeing Heritage walking back to his household with a six pack of beer, and I thought, I don't even have apple sauce for my baby."

How the breakup started was that certain people just got up and left.

"Out of the blue," Ethan says, "Joppa, Diligence and their kids just vanished—gone, and no one knew why." Dedication had left that way too. It was shocking when people who had lived together for years just left without saying good bye.

During this same period, there began to be certain individuals who were later described as the 'rule breakers.' It was only a few people, but as things became more disorganized—Love wasn't around much—and the amount of rule breaking grew.

It just so happened that Nobility, was one of the most notorious rule breakers. I was so happy, though, when he would bring home snickers bars and cookies for the household.

"It wasn't unwelcome," says my mom, "but it was scandalous! One day, he shocked the household by bringing home a large bottle of cheap, red wine."

Usually when people broke the rules, Love would do something about it, but he became unavailable, which left the community without the normal controls. All the rule breaking added to the overall chaos during that period.

I wasn't a rule breaker. The babies and young children in my household needed me, and I was going to do my best to take care of them, despite all the change and conflict in our household.

I was still being targeted by Honorable for no other reason than because I was my mother's daughter, which led to a build up inside me of anger and resentment towards her. I argued with her, as if I were a teenager and she was my overbearing mother, which made things worse, of course.

On top of everything, Nobility was adding household women to the multiple relationship. So even though it wasn't working out at all between Honorable and Elkanah, two other women in the household were brought into the already chaotic multiple relationship. This made things even worse than they already were.

The two women that were added came into the relationship siding with the elder lady, Honorable. If they had sided with Elkanah, I seriously doubt they would've been invited. So, in order to establish themselves in the relationship, they must've felt they had to appease the elder lady to except them. Honorable didn't have to except two new women into the relationship with Nobility. Why did she do it after what she went through with Elkanah? All I can assume based on what was happening was that it was a tactical move to gain support against my mom and make the already unlivable situation worse, so my mom would leave sooner. My mom would've been happy to leave sooner. She was trying to build a plan to where she could get out with all her children as Nobility had threatened her if she took Boldness.

Meanwhile, on July 12, 1983, a petition was signed by most of the elders and a few other people. Most people didn't know about it. It was kept confidential except for those who were involved. It was a typed letter to Love that listed out three main complaints. It accused Love of making himself "an exception to his own directives, agreements and advice." It accused him of "alienating" himself, socially, and showing "little or no involvement in the daily life of people, over which he held absolute authority." It also accused Love of separating himself from the people, economically, by "exercising a privilege," denied by him to others, "to gain and use large sums of money for personal pleasure." The petition stated that these areas where Love had alienated himself were "creating a mounting disorganization," and that at the root of all these problems was a "gap between absolute authority and unfulfilled responsibility."

In the final page of the petition, Love was asked to "relinquish authority to those who are responsible," and to "apologize for his gross self-indulgence and his oppression of people, especially women."

"The elders were basically asking Love to step down as business manager and let them run their own businesses and keep the money," says Ethan. "They were basically trying to keep the money out of his control," he says, "because he was using it for dope."

There must be somebody out there who knows and heard exactly what Love said in response. Somebody who was standing right there when he said it. But what I heard was that he essentially said, 'no way,' and that's when people started leaving. It became "a free for all" where people were taking things off the Ranch and taking things out of the houses on Queen Ann and leaving with it.

"I was with the kids in this yurt," Understanding remembered, "when someone came in and proceeded to detach the sink, then they left with it."

"All the money was in [Love's] control," Ethan says. "All the property was in his name, and so the only power you had was to leave. Because staying there just meant that you would continue to contribute to what he was doing that was unfair to everybody else."

"From the petition on, the Family fell apart pretty fast," my mom explained. "It did not slowly disintegrate over a long period of time—It took about a year max."

That first year after the petition, about 100–150 people left. "Then all hell broke loose, my mom continued." Then really the rules didn't apply anymore. "Love was selling off the assets. No one knew where the money was going. He lost it in a fairly short period of time. It doesn't take long for cocaine to start turning you into a weirdo."

"After everyone was starting to leave the family," Understanding says, "Things were so bad that Love was sleeping during the day and wasn't even aware that I was going down to the food bank. The person at the door would keep me from even talking to him."

From when the petition was signed, in July, things were deteriorating—fast. The teachers were leaving and there would be no one to teach in the fall.

"Appreciation, who had been teaching the previous year, went to Love to discuss the possibility of putting the kids in public school. Understanding remembered her visit.

"I picked up undercurrents in Love's house that he was not pleased with her ideas," she says.

Sometime after the meeting, Love sent Understanding to talk to Appreciation, to tell her he was adamant that the children were not to be put in public school.

"They were already having meetings, discussing the issues that were at stake," Understanding says. "They wanted to divide the Ranch up. They had lost faith in Love. Appreciation was the head lady at the Ranch with Strength and together they made the decision to put you kids in school. She knew she could do it because things were falling apart anyway."

I heard the rumor about public school, although from reading the entry in my diary, I obviously didn't know what was going on:

Dear Diary,

Love and Definition are thinking about putting us in World school. Does that mean we would start having ages and not be eternal anymore? Is our family going to fall apart if that happens?

Rachel Israel

The next thing that happened was that I was being told to pack my bolster and sleeping bag, I was going to the City to go to school. I was fine with that. I always liked going to the City, and at that point, with all the stress I had been under, it sounded like a welcome relief from watching babies and doing laundry. I wasn't told many details, and I didn't ask.

I was used to decisions just coming down with no explanation whatsoever. I didn't know about the petition. I didn't know that people had started leaving the Family in large numbers. I didn't know that the teachers wouldn't be teaching in the fall or that they were even leaving. I didn't even know what school I would be going to. I just assumed, that the kids were going to town to do school on Queen Anne in one of the Family homes as we often did during certain times of the year.

I got a ride into town with Gentle. Wisdom was in the front seat of the Volkswagen bug. I don't remember who was driving. That morning, they had made brownies in our household, and when Gentle came to get me, I was handed two of them, one for each of us. I gave one of them to Gentle and of course, since we were hungry, we ate them right away.

On the way to town, I began to feel different and everything began to be funny. I was laughing at everything. I was giggling at things and poking Gentle in the arm and saying, "Isn't that funny?"

"Shhh!" Gentle glared at me. She was trying to tell me to tone it down.

I didn't understand what she meant, so I kept laughing.

"If Wisdom knew that the brownies were mashish, she would be mad," Gentle whispered in my ear. *The brownies were mashish?* I wondered to myself.

That didn't make sense at all, since Wisdom was also a member of the Love Family, and mashish was considered a sacrament, but I quieted down all the same. Then I wondered why they had given them to me in the first place. I knew that it wasn't custom for the children to have sacrament, even though exceptions had been made. Generally, the kids were not offered mashish, but weird things had been happening lately.

I was excited. In the Family, I loved going to town and staying in the houses in the City. Life seemed easier there than life on the Ranch, and like I said, I was used to just picking up, at a moment's notice, getting in the bus and going wherever I was assigned to go, wherever Love wanted the kids that day or that week. It would be so very different this time, but I didn't know exactly how. I wasn't used to questioning. When something "came down," people didn't question, that was what was happening.

BIBLIOGRAPHY (CHAPTER 15)

[Karen]. Personal Interview. October 21, 2001. West Seattle.

[Ethan], Interview with Chuck LeWarne. February 18, 1998.

Israel, Understanding. Personal Communication. June 10, July 15, July 20, November 4, all 2001) Arlington, WA.

[Lydia]. Personal Communication. February 20, 2001 Magnolia Hill, Seattle.

CHAPTER 16

Culture Shock

t was August 1983, a month after the petition had been signed, when I began living with Asaph and Hanifah, long time Love Family members. They had two daughters, one of whom was right around my age, the other was just a year or so younger.

Asaph and Hanifah lived in a house, right around the corner from Love's Area on Smith Street. When I got there, there were other Family people living there too, such as Humility and some people who had been in his household, including Bright, who I was told would be going to school with me.

As soon as I was settled in, it immediately was evident that even though these were people from the Love Family living there, that it was not the Love Family as I had known it anymore. We were not chanting or praying before meals, there was no sanctuary or Bible centerpiece. There were foods in the refrigerator that we didn't usually eat such as tortillas. Hanifah and Asaph took us kids out to the Spaghetti Factory for dinner. I had never eaten in a restaurant in the Love Family! Asaph had a job working at the radio station, although I don't remember the name of it or what exactly he did there. Hanifah had a little baby named Lively.

It was comforting to me that Bright was there too and that he would be going to school with me, but he had changed. I had always teased him, it was a playful teasing. Usually he had teased me right back, but now when I teased him, he became angry and made terrible faces at me.

"Leave me alone!" he would snarl. He wouldn't even let me call him Bright anymore.

"It's Mark!" he would say angrily. He had cut his hair very short, and he wore blue jeans and a black jacket, so he didn't even look like Bright anymore.

I soon learned that I would not be going to school in one of the Family houses as I had thought we might; No, instead we were going to be put in a public alternative school called Summit. I had no idea what to expect since my memories of going to kindergarten in Alaska were now vague after years of going to school in the Love Family.

My biggest concern though during this time was about my best friend Heaven. Even though there were several kids from the Love Family who were also going to be going to Summit, Heaven was not, and since we were close in the Family, I was sad feeling that she wouldn't be there with me. Even though she was not at Summit, I often went over to her house for sleepovers or just to hang out.

Heaven was still living in Love's household; even as large numbers of members were transitioning out. They were streaming out of the Family like oil out of an underground pipe when a leak has just been sprung. I didn't know about that though, instead I was just focused on dealing with a lot of changes and trying to maintain my connections with the kids whom I had been raised with.

Love was living in his big house just right around the corner from Asaph and Hanifah's house. Heaven was staying in Cube City, which, as I described earlier on, was a room full of little cupboards and compartments where people, mostly kids, slept on the lower floor of Love's house.

Usually Truthfulness would say yes when Heaven and I asked her for spend-the-nights, but one day I went over there, and I asked her if Heaven could spend the night at my house, at Asaph and Hanifah's house.

"No, Heaven has been bad," Truthfulness answered as if she were mad.

"I miss Heaven, I haven't seen her in a long time," I naively whined.

"I don't care whether you see Heaven ever again!" she said angrily. She had never said no before, and I was shocked that she would say that to me in that tone. I went down to Cube City to ask Heaven about it.

"No, I haven't been bad, she is just trying to control my life," Heaven explained. She filled me in on the situation in Love's house. Love and Truthfulness were moving to California. Heaven was being made to go with them.

"No, you're not going! You're gonna run away!" I told her.

"Where am I gonna go?!" she asked with a frightened expression.

When I went home that night, I talked to Hanifah about Heaven's situation. Hanifah told me that Richness, who was now going by the name Daniel Greuner, was suing Love for all the property and money that he had given Love over the years. Other people were accusing Love of things and writing threatening letters, so Love was leaving the state to avoid prosecution.

I wasn't paying attention to the slew of news coverage in the papers about how the Love Family was breaking up and about the legal battle between Love and Richness. All I cared about was Heaven. What was she going to do?

Hanifah told me to call two former members who had been known as Holiness and Bathsheba. Maybe they would let Heaven stay with them.

I knew them quite well and that they had a little baby girl named Moderation. But now they had changed their names and had their own home.

I called them up—Yeah, there was actually a phone at Asaph and Hanifah's which I learned to use. I asked them if Heaven could stay with them, so she didn't have to go to California with Love:

"Sure!" they agreed.

I was thankful they didn't even have to think about it.

They gave me directions to their house.

We had to sneak Heaven out of Love's house. The plan was we would leave after dark when everyone thought she had gone to bed.

I felt an urgency to get her out of there. I had heard a rumor that Love had planned to sexually initiate the big girls into womanhood. The 'big girls' were all now between 11 and 15). It would have been me, and I was now 14 and several others around my age. Love had talked about this initiation at meetings. It was one of the things that upset people, who were now starting to leave the Family in droves. I was disgusted with the idea, and knew I had to get Heaven out of there—quick—especially if Love was planning on taking her to California.

When I got to her cubical, Elimelech was there, and he hung out with us until it was dark. I hadn't seen him in the last three or four years and didn't know what happened to him. His name was now Dean.

He told us how he left to finish high school, then joined the Navy where he had been assigned to a fast attack nuclear submarine that snuck around in Russian waters during the cold war. He said if there was a nuclear war, that to survive, I would have to go live in the air-tight, walk-in cooler up at the corner grocery store, to avoid the fallout. I had lived in a lot of places, but never in an airtight, walk-in cooler! It upset me so bad that I had a nightmare that night.

Dear Diary,

I had a nightmare last night. I dreamed that there was a nuclear war, and I could not find my friends. I finally found them, and we began hugging, but then my friends shriveled away and all that was left was their clothes. I asked people where my friends were, but they didn't know and urged me towards the building where there were food lines and guards.

Rachel Israel

I was already scared that if we were caught, I might never see Heaven again, and that Love would take off with her to California, forever, as far as I knew; but with the threat of nuclear war, maybe none of it mattered anyway.

As soon as it was dark, Heaven quickly packed her bag, and we snuck out of there. We had to walk in the dark to Holiness and Bathsheba's house, before they moved to Government Way. It wasn't too far, but it was a long way for us. I had never walked by myself much and certainly never after dark. In town, I occasionally, I would walk with other kids to the Front Door Inn from Love's Area, but that was always usually during the day and only a couple of blocks up the street.

We got safely to Holiness and Bathsheba's house, and that was where Heaven would stay. I was so relieved that she had a safe place to live now, but I was scared that Love and Truthfulness would find out where she was and would snatch her back up. All that mattered now was that she was safe and that she got to go to school with us.

Back at Asaph and Hanifah's, Understanding showed up at the door, and asked to talk to me in private. She hadn't left the Family and was still living with Love. She told me that Heaven would not be able to go to school with me at Summit, because she had been reported as a runaway and could be picked up by the police if she didn't come home. I didn't know if I should tell Understanding where Heaven was. If I told her where Heaven was, then Heaven would have to go back and live with Love and be taken away to California. If I didn't tell her where she was, then Heaven could be picked up by the police and taken back to Love anyway. I didn't really know how it worked, but either way, it did not sound good. I ended up telling Understanding where she was, and Understanding said she would warn Heaven and talk to her about what her options were. My hopes of going to school with my best friend from the Love Family were over.

Fortunately, and I am not sure how it was worked out, but somehow, Heaven remained living with Holiness and Bathsheba at their house, and she ended up going to Summit just as I had wanted. Maybe they got a hold of Heaven's mom to get permission. I am not sure, but we stayed close for the first year that we were at Summit together. I often spent the night at her house, at Holiness and Bathsheba's. We would go jogging at Discovery Park or down to the Ballard Locks to kill time. After school, we would stop in at Woolworths and have our picture taken in the photo booth or visit Bathsheba's sister who ran a flower stand on 1st Avenue.

I started school at Summit Alternative in September of 1983, just a few weeks after I had left the Ranch. Summit was a public alternative school, K–12. There were around seven of us from the Love Family, although that number dwindled because not everyone ended up sticking it out.

I didn't have any clothes for school, so my gramma Phyllis took me to the store and bought me a backpack and my school supplies. She planned to help me until my mom left the Family and got settled. Elkanah was still living out at the Ranch, trying to figure out a place to live and how to leave safely with Forest, Boldness and Jacob. Nobility's household was one of the last remaining households at the Ranch.

To get to school, I had to take two city buses across town. I had to transfer in downtown Seattle. The school was a large brick building in South Seattle, off of 23rd up the street from Rainier, not the best part of town in those days.

I had only taken a city bus one-time. It was when Elkanah had snuck me out to go see a foot doctor. For years now, I had just walked to school, through the woods, past the lake, past the knoll and up to the Barn. That was now the past. This was the World, and I was now living in the big city, a place that I had only wondered about.

Taking a bus across town was a shock to see the World in all its glory. I had always been curious about the World, but now that I was actually there, it was like a nightmare that I couldn't wake up from.

I was on the bus on my way to school. I looked out the window and saw this man on Third Avenue in downtown Seattle. The man walked aimlessly, as if he had no direction. I had been taught that 'everyone in the World was lost, but that eventually they would all come home to the Kingdom of God. This man truly looked lost. He had long hair and a long beard. He had disheveled, dirty clothes on. There were all sorts of people everywhere, but he caught my eye, because he was eating a bus schedule. I stared at him, as if mesmerized. He was chewing on it, then he would struggle as he tried to swallow the bite. I couldn't understand it. No one had told me that in the World, there were such thing as people who were so hungry that they had no food and had to eat paper. He seemed to be swallowing the pieces, then he would rip off another bite and put it in his mouth. It was shocking and upsetting. When my mom and I were on the road, before we met the Love Family, we were homeless in a sense, but my mom had her 'act together' and was resourceful and creative when it was time to find a meal. This man did not have his act together. I felt sorry for him.

On one of my first trips across town, I was at the bus stop and this black man approached me:

"What's your name?" he says sleazily. I didn't know him and felt uncomfortable:

"I don't know," I answered him, uncomfortable with his personal question.

"I bet you would know if I pushed you into the street!" the man insisted. He looked serious and as if he was about to literally throw me into the street:

"It's Rachel," I fearfully told him my name.

"Do you want to earn some quick money, Rachel? The Black man asked sincerely. "There's no taxes, it's easy."

I had no idea what he was even talking about, and surely, I must have looked confused.

There were other, yucky things that happened to me on the bus, drunk men who would sit right next to me, almost on top of me and talk to me. There were men that followed me off the bus who wouldn't leave me alone. I wasn't exceptionally beautiful or anything. I was just young, almost 15, and a freshman in high school, and this was a rude awakening in terms of what I was learning about the World.

One of the brighter things for me during this time was music. It seemed like every student at Summit could listen to whatever band they wanted to listen to. In the Love Family, we sang the same old songs, over and over again; it was the only music there was. It brought me great joy to listen to as many bands as I could, to figure out who I liked best. There were a wide range of experiences and feelings that were being expressed in the music. It was thrilling, and a feeling of freedom overcame me sometimes at the vastness and size of the outside World. Love Family music—while it was beautiful and dear to my heart—was spiritual and about oneness, God, and love.

The lyrics of some of the music of the World was more the opposite of spiritual. There were songs with lyrics that were violent and that talked about women in demeaning, sexual terms, glorifying male dominance. When I listened to it, it made me feel like a piece of meat for every wild animal that just happened to see me. I tried to avoid listening to that music.

It didn't help that in the news constantly were reports of the latest victims of the Green River Killer and other news of women being sexually assaulted. The news and the harassment I got just waiting for the bus to take me to or from school was creating this impression that the World was not a safe place for me.

I was sickened that large percentages of women in the outside culture were victims of sexual and physical violence with no societal outrage or obvious dissent. Especially after seeing what my mom went through in the Love Family. It was discouraging and frustrating to see such passivity in a world where there was so much oppression.

This was the world? What a horrible place! I thought. I was heart-broken and disappointed. I wanted to believe that the world was this great place that had just gotten this bad rap for all those years. I couldn't go anywhere, it seemed, without getting honked at. I got lewd comments thrown at me. I felt vulnerable, scared, lost. I wondered if girls raised in the World were used to it, but I could tell they didn't like it either and were struggling to make sense of it too. It was a shock to witness and experience since I wasn't used to seeing that, and the injustice of it made me angry.

I had come from a place where it seemed everyone was the same. I had been taught to love, but now, I was in a world where it seemed people would take advantage of any weakness they saw in me. Sometimes I heard different kids tell me they thought I was "naïve," or "gullible."

For example, it was picture day, and I had $20 in a little pouch that I planned to give to the school for my picture order. My gramma had given it to me. I was downstairs in the girls' bathroom, brushing my hair and getting ready for the picture. Two African American girls walked in and were also getting ready for their pictures. It was Cecile and Sunshine, and this Native American girl I had befriended named Tracy. I put my little purse on the counter and walked into the bathroom stall. When I came out, the purse was gone. Cecile, Sunshine, and my friend Tracy were quickly walking out of the bathroom. I ran after them and asked them, "Did you see what happened to my little pouch?"

"No, sorry," they answered without looking back. They had been the only ones in the bathroom, and so I figured they had taken it. I was devastated. Later Tracy told me that Sunshine had taken it.

I was so hurt that anyone could be so cruel and so uncaring as to steal from me. Even though the school let me have my picture taken anyway, I cried so hard that day that my eyes and cheeks were swollen and red, and I had a very serious expression on my face.

I think for any child to get something stolen from them would be upsetting, but for me, having come from the Love Family, from such a sheltered society where I never was taught to watch out for thieves, it was shocking that someone would have such little regard for my feelings.

The academic piece, for me, compared to the social piece, was a cinch. In some subjects, I was ahead of things, but in other areas, I was behind. To make up for certain areas where I was lacking, I had to spend extra time doing homework. I also took time to use the teacher's office hours to get extra help whenever I could. I didn't mind making the extra effort. The teachers were supportive and seemed pleased with my efforts. It was something I had more control over.

The social deficit though was substantial, and it was impossible for me to do any quick catching up. Most of my challenges at Summit stemmed from my lack of a cultural consciousness for what most of the kids just knew already.

I stood there with this group of girls who I had made friends with, and they were all talking about the *Little Rascals*. I had no idea what they were talking about. I should've just kept my mouth shut, but I didn't do that:

"What are you talking about?" I asked naively.

"*The Little Rascals*," someone answered.

"Who are they?" I asked.

They all stopped for a couple of moments and stared at me, looking befuddled.

"It's a TV show, where have you been?" somebody finally answered.

I wasn't going to say, "In the Love Family." There were so many of these types of interactions that I began to feel stupid.

It was a lot of change to take in and process. There was this day I just happened upon this old book that was in a 'free' box at the school. It was called *Future Shock* by Alvin Toffler, (1970). It caught my attention and so I took a look. Toffler defined the term "future shock" as a certain psychological state of individuals and entire societies. His shortest definition for the term was "a personal perception of too much change in too short a period of time."

He was talking about what was happening to me! I read that book so fast, then began to find other things that spoke to me about my experience. I learned about another term, 'culture shock.'

The term culture shock, first used in an article by anthropologist Kalervo Oberg (1960), described a state of anxiety that arises from not knowing how to behave in a new culture. According to Wanda Lee, Studies of life stress have found that the cumulative change involved in moving from one culture to another is often so great that it puts a person at risk for serious illness or depression (1999).

I was lucky that I knew English, I thought. I couldn't imagine how stressful it might be for people who didn't even speak the language to come to another country and deal with the stress of culture shock as well. Although, there was a sort of language that was used in the Love Family, with a lot of words that were only used there.

I read Oberg's article. He discussed the issue of recovery from culture shock, He wrote that, one of the things that you can do to get over culture shock as quickly as possible is to "get to know the people of the host country."

And that's what I began to do. My biggest asset though, in dealing with my deficits, were that I knew how to be quiet and just observe what was going on around me: that came naturally. I learned a lot that way. I had a tendency, even as a young child to be very quiet, observant and thoughtful. I had always been terribly curious about most things. But I also had the disadvantage of being a highly sensitive person which made me get overwhelmed with the intensity of my feelings as I dealt with the challenges that emphasized my discomfort.

I watched people. There was a lot of staring into eyes in the Love Family. Suddenly I was living in a culture where people didn't do that, but I had had years of staring. In the World, people didn't do that unless there was a reason for it. In the Family, it was a way to connect and be close to people. Guys in the world would think it was a come on, so I had to be careful where I looked. People seemed visibly uncomfortable when I would look at them. I guess to them, my intense little eyes looking into their soul just freaked 'em out.

I used to watch this girl, who I will call Julie. I would make a point to always say hi to her each time I saw her. She seemed to appreciate that I was a friendly face to her, someone she could talk to. I wondered why the other students were not friendly to her. *Why did they call Julie names? Why did they make fun of her?* It was like she was this pariah. After what happened to my mom, I wasn't going to do that to anyone.

Julie had very light, long blond hair, pretty blue eyes, but her face was covered in terrible acne. I would see her stride down the hall confident, proud, wearing very tight fitting short skirts and revealing blouses, always high-heals, tons of make-up. She had this throaty laugh that carried itself quite far and sounded as if she needed to clear her throat when she did it. No one talked to her, except a couple girls, Elaina and Mica. They would bring teeny-bopper magazines to school that had Scott Baiou and other heart throbs on the covers. They just kept to themselves mostly, until they were all together, then they would break loose the magazines and the whole table would be guffawing away, right in the middle of science class. The teacher didn't even seem to notice.

I talked to Julie whenever I got the chance as she made me curious about how such a creature could even exist. The kids, (and this was a high school,) would call her names I had never heard before like "slut" and other demeaning epithets. I felt sorry for her. One day in class, she gave me a Christmas card. I opened it and there was this card that she had decorated with holly berries and hand calligraphic lettering.

Times are tuff, life is hard, here's your fuckin Christmas card.

I guess she passed one out to everyone in the classroom. Julie baffled me but there was something more about her. It was the fact that she could care less what anyone thought about her. She would stride by, looking so proud of who she was without a care in the world for what anybody thought of her. She was, it seemed, totally detached from anybody's idea of what was cool. She was hardened though. She had this invisible armor that gave her a pass to be happy anyway, despite all. She was everything that I was not. I didn't have any armor. I didn't have an attitude. I wasn't belligerent and sassy; but when I realized how strong she was in her mind, how brave she was to face such judgment and consternation for how she presented herself, I began to understand what I was up against socially.

I was talking to Julie one day, and she told me that she was a prostitute. I didn't know what that meant but I sort of figured it out. On the bus ride back home from school, I saw her standing on the street a few times on First Avenue, conspicuously standing there, as if waiting for a ride. I felt sad for her that she spent her time like that and wondered if something really bad might have happened to her.

It seemed to me that I could learn more about the World by watching those who were rejected than watching those who were the accepted, popular, cool kids. Why? Because it seemed there was this friction there where there were opposing forces and perspectives that each deserved attention, forces that were clashing up against one another to where I could see more clearly. It seemed on some levels, that everyone was pushing up against the cultural norms and expectations, and each person I met was trying to find a way to express themselves within these confines, trying to find a way towards integration without losing themselves in the process. *What was going on in this culture that would lead to people like Julie?* I wondered.

I made friends with this girl named Tracy. She a was heavy set girl, Native American with dark, almost black, short hair and dark brown eyes. Her skin was badly scared from acne. She also had that throaty laugh like Julie. Maybe it had to do with the fact that they both smoked cigarettes. Tracy was another one that just didn't seem to care what anyone thought. *Maybe I could learn how to do that? To not care.* It seemed the only way, because if I cared too much, it was a painful realization that I would never figure out how to be cool, because there was too much that I didn't know.

Tracy and I left the school at lunchtime and went and sat on a log on a side street while she smoked her cigarette. She told me about her Native heritage and her criminal record. She had been busted for drugs and alcohol many times and told me her war stories of her dealings with the police. She said she had been busted for "weed." I didn't have any war stories, but I told her that I had been in the Love Family where people smoked marijuana, which was called mashish, and it was just part of the culture. She didn't believe me, at first.

"Woh!" She exclaimed when I had her convinced. "That is how it should be."

In a sense, we were both minorities. She was Native American and I was from the Love Family.

One day, I brought her back to my house to see where I lived. She wanted to see this place where people thought smoking pot was normal. At the time, I was living with Dinah's dad where I stayed for a few weeks. Her dad and step mom were artists. When Tracy saw my house, she gasped and looked horrified.

"It is scary here!" she said as she looked around at the house. "How come you don't have any furniture? The house is so cold. Why do you sleep on the floor in your sleeping bag?" I could tell by her facial expressions that she didn't like my house. There were 3D art objects about the house that were very modern. Dinah's dad and stepmom were countercultural hippie types, but they had never lived in the Love Family. While Tracy was there, we got stoned together, which Dinah's dad thought was funny. He was very tall and had long red hair that was in a braid.

After that, Tracy and I stopped hanging out, and she became closer to her other friends who happened to be Cecile and Sunshine, the African American girls who had taken my $20 that day. I wondered if bringing her home had been a good idea. I decided at that point to never bring any more friends home. Tracy told me later that when she saw my house, it "freaked" her out. I didn't want to freak people out.

Not everyone had that reaction though. I finally found someone I could relate to and who didn't judge me. Her name was Kate. We would make up Haiku poems to pass the time and pass them to each other during class as if they were secret messages. I told her about things that confused me, and she seemed to understand. She was confused about some of the things I was confused by, and she hadn't even been raised in the Love Family. She talked about her life, her family. She was in foster care and her parents had moved to Baltimore. She missed her mom. I was sad and felt like I had lost my family too. *Get to know people of the host country.*

One day, Kate and I went out to get stoned at Rocket Park, which was a park that was right behind the school. We made our way into the bushes. Another friend of ours named Caroline was there too. She was this skinny, African American girl with an afro. She told me she had gotten pregnant and had a baby, and that it was lost in a terrible fire. She was really nice, but I could only imagine what a horrible thing she had been through.

We got stoned that day—it seemed that at Summit a lot of kids and even teachers did that; it was a relaxed school and had an open attitude towards marijuana. From where I had come from, that didn't seem unusual to me at all. But at Summit, there also were administration who obviously were very against it; one teacher ended up getting fired because of it. I figured that marijuana was fine—but make sure you try and hide it from certain people.

The double message was a bit confusing.

After we got stoned and when it was time to go back to class, Caroline brought out this bottle of perfume, and we all took turns spraying ourselves with it. I had spent my whole childhood around adult folks who thought of marijuana/mashish as sacred, holy, a spiritual, tribal ritual, that was shared and culturally revered in many ways. It had been a culturally based norm. Now I was in a world that seemed itself very confused, conflicted about it. I wasn't sure if I had to worry about getting busted, expelled, arrested? It made no sense. All these conflicting messages, stay away from drugs like marijuana which is the gateway drug to hell, just say no, but there was this whole segment of student life that seemed to evolve around marijuana and that included some of the teachers.

It irritated me, and I decided to do some research and find out for myself what the deal was. I was driven to understand it. My report for school included an oral component. I wanted to present a balanced perspective, but I could not find one piece of information that showed me that there was a legitimate concern. I only found stuff that proved it was good for you and had a lot of healing properties. It made no sense to me. It never did. I thought it was ridiculous. Plus, from what I saw, moneyed interests had played a large role in the decisions that were made about it.

Then trying to understand why alcohol was tolerated when it caused so many human health problems and deaths was, to me, flat-out outrageous and totally nonsensical.

This was the early 1980s, so it was a very different society than it is today where states are beginning to legalize. Back then, there was this huge push in the schools to 'Just say no to drugs.' It was the Reagan era.

I got a lot of mixed messages about marijuana, half of which seemed based on misinformation if not outright lies and corruption. It had the effect of making me more skeptical and less trusting of authority in the outside culture. It made me less inclined to want to conform to social pressures and expectations.

When I went out to Rocket Park to smoke a bowl, it was less coming from a place of rebellion and especially after my report, it was more out of a decision that I made that marijuana was harmless, if not beneficial. Like a lot of things in my life at that point, I just had to figure it out for myself.

Summit was a good match for me in a lot of ways, because there were a lot of people there like me, independent, creative thinkers. A lot of the kids there had parents who were liberal, countercultural types or who were alternative in some way or another.

Academically, there was a different philosophy at Summit than the public schools. They encouraged me to think for myself and to take on self-initiative. It was more focused on the arts and building creativity. Just like in the Love Family, I did not get a letter grade at Summit.

Summit was a small, K–12, public alternative school. Al Jones was the original principal, and his goal had been for Summit to be for the creatively gifted. It had about 350 students and was located between Martin Luther King Way and 23rd on the corner of 23rd and Massachusetts in the Coleman building. It is the same building, by the way, that eventually came to house the African American history museum.

At Summit, it may not have been the most rigorous in terms of its academic standards, but that is not what they were trying to do. It was more about letting kids learn to take initiative, almost in some ways like the Montessori model. I took a lot of art classes and participated in art activities such as the Imagination Celebration. I took science class with a short, balding, wiry looking instructor named Duane. In his class, I got to make a rocket, and I got to go set it off in Rocket Park next to the school. I don't know if there is any coincidence in the name of the park and that class activity. There was a whole martial arts component as well where I learned tai chi, including the sword form.

Tai Chi is an internal Chinese martial art. It is a series of movements performed in a slow focused manner accompanied by deep breathing. It is practiced for its self-defense training and health benefits. It was probably just what I needed to help me learn to relax and take the edge off all the change. In music class, we sang Beatles songs and other classic 1960s tunes. Connie, the teacher was fun and would take us on field trips to her house or to Pike Place Market and different places, excursions about town that taught us about different kinds of music.

It was a very relaxed school. Some of the teachers smoked pot themselves and would let us smoke it in class if we had class outside that day. I sat in the grass in Rocket Park. It was a writing class and the teacher did not seem to care that the students were passing a pipe around during class. In the Love Family, I had sat many times in a circle of people and the tau had been passed around me, but now it was passed to me as it went around.

I came into art class late, stoned. My eyes were probably glowing. I sat down and the art teacher, Sandra, looked at me with this knowing expression on her face. She looked troubled and deeply sad, as if she felt sorry for me. What sort of school was this? I thought. Make up your minds! I was so used to being in a community where everyone thought the exact same thing. It was disconcerting to have an administration and teachers who were clearly not all on the same page.

I had a lot to learn. One day I was down at the park with a girl named Sharla, and she saw me drink out of the men's urinal. We had gone into the men's restroom, just goofing off. For some reason, there was water in the urinal. She gave me a strange look that day. I found out later that she always remembered that about me, that she had thought it was weird. She was confused as to why I would do it. She had thought maybe I was "just too stoned." But that wasn't it. The truth was that I didn't know that it was a urinal. I thought it was a drinking fountain. I had only rarely been in a public restroom, and I had never been in a men's restroom. I was used to outhouses. Sounds crazy but men did not stand up to pee in the Love Family either, so I didn't assume that the urinal was for that purpose.

I dared not tell people that I was from the Love Family. Whenever I had told someone, their reaction was not positive. They would say, "Weird." They would look confused and would scowl. Although, there was a couple of Jewish kids who when they saw me, they always found an opening to ask more questions about the Love Family. They seemed genuinely curious. They didn't scowl; they thought the Love Family sounded "cool." I answered a couple questions, but that just seemed to make them even more curious. I didn't think it was that "cool." I figured the less I said, the better.

I didn't want others to think of me as weird, but I also knew that I was different. It was hard to find the commonalities with other kids. Some of them already knew about my past, and that was bad enough. Sun was there for a time, and he had been telling the kids where we had come from, just to be mean; He knew we didn't want them to know. The school administration and all the teachers knew. At least I wasn't picked on like some of the other Family kids who went into public schools near the Ranch.

Back at the Ranch, there were still families there in transition, trying to figure out what to do, as more and more people left. Zarah was still out there. All the teachers had gone, so there was no one to teach the remaining kids. So some of the parents placed their kids in public school in Arlington. Zarah was placed into Sixth grade. She told me about how she was treated by the other kids, who would approach her aggressively and try to intimidate her.

"I hated it," she says. "I didn't admit to anyone that I had been part of the Love Family. They would ask in a mean way, like 'Are you from that Love bunch?' I would say no, because it was called the Love Family, not the Love Bunch."

Zarah was in school in Arlington, which was not that far from the Ranch, and there were rumors being passed about the Love Family. Whereas I was at Summit, in Seattle, and quite further than where she was, and no one, that I knew of had heard about the Love Family at Summit until we got there.

My own brother Forest, who was also still out there at the Ranch during this time, was put in public school too. There was some debate about whether he should be put in Third or Fourth grade. He was grateful that they ended up putting him in Third:

"It was so hard," he told me. "The kids made fun of me, that I was an Israel. They all knew, because the school was K–12 and the seniors told the younger kids."

When the Oneida broke up, the kids, who were being raised there, had to adjust to life outside the Community, just like we did. Pierrepont Noyes, was raised in Oneida. His father was the founder of the community, John Humphrey Noyes. That would be like one of Love's sons. Pierrepont went through a great adjustment when the community, he was raised in, split up. Eventually he became a successful business man and writer.

One of the books he wrote was called, *My Father's House: An Oneida Boyhood* (1937) about his life in Oneida and what happened to him during their breakup.

When Oneida broke up, the children of that community had to transition into schools on the outside. He wrote about how he was bullied and taunted, called names.

> "We had not gone far when a loud yelling attracted our attention; looking back, we saw a mob of Turkey Street boys running down the road toward us, their actions suggesting hostile intent. When they came nearer, they jeered; called us 'Christ boys, bastards,' and 'God-damn goody Community boys.'" (Noyes, 1937, 116)

Kids from the Love Family went through similar abuse from their Worldly counterparts. When Forest took the bus to and from school, all the kids, no matter what grade they were in, would ride together.

"Those bus rides were the worst part--they would yell at me, and I got beat up once," he says. "I remember not wanting to tell people my name. Brotherhood started going by John, and I told mom I wanted that name, but she wouldn't let me."

I think it was rough for a lot of us, but for the kids who were left at the Ranch while everyone was leaving, it had to have been bad.

"There were rumors going around that they were selling the Ranch," Forest says. "I was still living at the Ranch and we ate nothing but kale that last year; there was no food because the Family was breaking up."

It was rough for me, but at least at Asaph and Hanifah's I had plenty to eat. I talked to Bright and asked him what it was like going to public school after years of growing up in the Love Family:

"I found it hellacious!" he says. "I was completely miserable." On his first day of school, Bright looked at the list of names and noticed that his name was listed as 'Bright Israel.' He thought *Oh no!* The teacher began reading the roll call out loud to the class. Bright was "terrified of being there in the first place," but he quickly got up and quietly told the teacher to call him by his new, Worldly name before the teacher got to his name on the list. The teacher caught it just in time. "My ass was saved," he says.

"The kids were running around hitting each other and saying, 'Psych!'" explained Bright, which was a sort of fad word that kids were saying which meant, 'tricked you.' "The biggest shock," he says, "was going from an environment where I knew everybody to an environment where I didn't know anybody. I mean some of the people I grew up with were there, but we were so dispersed; we were in different classes. Some of us were in different grades and homerooms."

The day before school started, Bright changed his name. "I just picked it out of the air," he says. "I was not going to go there with the name Bright, or Sunhawk, which was my birth name. It wasn't gonna happen."

Bright, whom I didn't remember as being shy at all, was now "extremely self-conscious. Being 13 is a challenge in the first place. I didn't want to stand out; I was just there to go to school, having grown up in this alternative thing that nobody would understand."

Ravah also discussed with me what his experience was like:

"I didn't really want to tell people that I had been in a religious cult," he says. "Suddenly, I understood how large the outside world was. I was used to relating to people as brother to brother or sister to sister, and so now it was like relating from stranger to stranger."

When Oneida broke up, Pierrepont Noyes suffered culture shock, like I did, but that term wasn't around back then. He wrote: "The shock of the breakup still colored my emotions; there still haunted my consciousness a feeling best described as a plant pulled up by the roots…" (216–17).

Yep, that's how I felt. He wrote, "My knowledge of good and evil progressed still further, and the world outside became more and more a reality; a disturbing reality, but I suspect, increasingly interesting by contrast with the simplicity of our utopian isolation." (118)

Oneida was a long time ago, almost 100 years earlier than the Love Family, and yet it's comparable. How can that be, considering how different things were in America in 1881? In my opinion it's even more comparable than some of the other groups that sprung from the hippie counterculture. I was raised in a very different society than most people I have ever met—or will ever meet.

The teachers at Summit knew who we were, and that we had an unusual background. Connie, my music teacher remembered me as "quiet, calm." She said that I often shared information with the class that was unique.

She remembered that one day, she had asked the class what an aura was. I was the only one who raised my hand, then explained to the class that it was an energy light field that surrounds the body and that can sometimes be seen around one's head.

I talked to the principal, whose name was Barb. I wanted to know what her impressions of us were. Before we even got there, she remembered the man who came to sign us up. She said he was tall, and had long, dark brown hair and a beard.

"He had an "otherworldly" presence about him," Barb says.

'It will be difficult for them,' the man told her.

She didn't remember what his name was but thought it might've been Serious.

Barb says she pulled all the teachers together for a meeting to discuss what to do. She wasn't sure how to place us, because none of us had records or identification. She didn't even know who our parents were.

"You seemed withdrawn, apprehensive, scared, not really trusting," she says. "I suspected abuse, but I didn't know. Some of you didn't work out and left, but there were others who stayed on."

Barb was not concerned about whether we would be fit academically, even though she knew we "had low skill levels." She was more concerned about how to make us comfortable. So she set up a special meeting for us.

"How can we make you comfortable?" she asked us kindly.

No one said anything.

"You were all on the border between survival and freaking out," says Barb.

Jody, another teacher there used these terms to describe us: "guarded, quiet, withdrawn." He watched the way we interacted with the other students:

"When kids referred back to assumed knowledge, there was a lot that didn't register," Jody says.

Rachel, my home teacher remembered me. She said that I was "shy and quiet." Her impression of us as a group:

"You were distinct in your own way and lacked the attitude of I'm cool," she remembered. "You hadn't learned to hide or cover up," she guessed. "I wasn't sure what was going on," she admitted.

What was going on for me was that I was miserable but doing the best I could under the circumstances. I may have looked "calm," but on the inside, I was anything but. I would say it was one of the most difficult times of my life. I had a place to live with Asaph and Hanifah and their daughters who were my friends, but I was only there temporarily until Elkanah left the Family and could back on her feet.

I didn't have a dad that I knew of, and my mother, Elkanah was still living at the Ranch. People were leaving the Family in droves. Understanding was gone. She had gone with Love and a few other remaining loyalists and their kids to California, including Gentle, whom I was closer to than Love's other children. The teachers were all gone. I had no idea what happened to them; It was as if they dropped off the face of the earth. I found out later, though, that Eve and Definition had gone with their kids to Arizona to build a new life for themselves there. Ethan was running a school for ex members' kids out of one of the houses that used to be a Family home. All the kids there in his school were young; preschool and early elementary age kids. He had a little child now to take care of–Discretion. Hanifah and Asaph were kind to me and tried to help. Hanifah put me on a girls' basketball team through the Queen Anne Community Center, and Asaph helped me with my presentation for school. He helped me build an abacus to present to my classmates, which was a tool that early peoples used for math.

It was nice that Asaph and Hanifah's daughters lived there. I had lived with Dinah when I lived in Helpful and Dedication's household, and she and I had gone on that trip to Potato Heaven. But they didn't go to Summit. Except for the kids who went to Summit, I never saw most of the kids, that I had been raised with, again, and didn't know what happened to them.

For a short time, and before Love left for California, I used to go over to Love's Area and hang out with some of the kids who were still around. Like I said, Asaph and Hanifah's were less than two blocks from Love's Area.

Even though she didn't go to Summit, Hadassah was still around for a time. She was tagging along with her older sister who was friends with Hope's girlfriend. That's how it was that I was invited to hang out one day over at Imagination's old house. Love's Area was mostly empty. There were a few stragglers who were in transition, trying to figure out where to go. Love was not paying attention, because he was absorbed in dealing with litigation and legal threats, getting ready to leave the State. I went over with Hadassah, and all these teenagers are crammed up into this secret attic in Imagination's old house. It had an Alice in Wonderland type feel because I never even knew the attic existed. Somebody had to give me a hand up. One by one, each of us heisted ourselves up into this ceiling, this trap door that went up into this overcrowded, stuffy, dark and unfinished space. It was Hope, Elimelech, Hadassah, Jael's daughter, Hope's girlfriend, Abigail and me. Most of them were probably two to five years older than me. Hadassah and I were the youngest. When I got up there, everyone was making strawberry daiquiris. Somebody handed me a glass and a bottle of liquor. There was laughter, and everyone was joking around and having fun. It reminded me of the mad hatter's tea party, except instead, it was daiquiris and Love Family teenagers. I didn't know how to make a daiquiri, so Hope made one for me. It was strange drinking alcohol with Hope and Elimelech after all those years in the Love Family when they had been nothing more than community big brothers.

It was a strange time. There was another night when Elimelech had a couple bottles of liquor, and we all went on this walk in the middle of the night. We went up and down the streets in the neighborhood behind the Front Door Inn. We were totally drunk, stumbling down the street. Then we went through this old lady's yard. She came out and was yelling at us. Elimelech was trying to ditch Life and Deaf David.

Later that night, we all went into Ken's Market and bought candy. That's when I felt sick and vomited all the way down the candy isle, as I ran out of the store and down the street. Ken's market was no more than a couple blocks up the street from Asaph and Hanifah's, going the other way from Love's Area. It was almost kiddie corner from the Front Door Inn.

When I got home, I was still sick and continued to throw up as I ran up the stairs to the bathroom. Hanifah stood there looking concerned.

"Are you OK? What's going on? She asked frantically.

I was honest with her and just told her that I had been drinking alcohol.

Her look of concern turned quickly to disbelief, and shock.

It scared me to see her look at me like that. What was happening to me? Heaven came busting in the door right at that moment and apologized to Hanifah, then she helped clean me up in the bathroom and helped clean the stairs.

Hanifah went and talked to the lady at Ken's Market. She apologized for me and told the lady I was alright.

What must Hanifah have thought, this innocent commune girl—drunk?! And her girls were so well behaved.

Other than Hanifah that night, no one had asked me if I was OK. No one even told me there was such thing as divorce.

A divorce between two parents is a difficult thing for any child to endure, but this was no typical divorce. Hundreds of people were involved. I call it a mass exodus, because literally, hundreds of people left the Family and started new lives in the World.

It wasn't a divorce though, because the Love Family did not end; people stayed and stuck it out. Once Love returned from California and went back to the Ranch, there were people who remained and regrouped, a few loyalists and their kids. Understanding told me that after everyone left, there actually were still almost 50 kids, including all of Love's kids; the number of adults who remained was less than half that. The mass exodus was happening, but I wasn't aware of its magnitude, because I was so busy with school and trying to adjust.

At first, before I developed my own social group at Summit, I would spend time with the other kids from the Love Family who were there at Summit with me. We frequently would all get together on weekends. Hanging out with my Love Family brothers and sisters on weekends was the only thing that felt familiar. We all ended up over at Solidity and Listening's house. They were ex members who lived in a house near Parsons Gardens. They had taken in one of the boys who went to Summit, and because he lived there, that's where we would all meet. Listening and Solidity were now going by their former Worldly names.

Everyone I knew from the Love Family were now changing their names and going by their Worldly or birth names, but I have and will refer to them by their Family names to keep their privacy, unless they have given me permission. I kept my name, Rachel Israel. I felt grateful that I didn't have a virtue name, and my Bible name was a common name, so I did not have to deal with peoples' reactions to an unusual name.

I looked forward to the weekend where I would meet with kids I had known my whole life up till that point. At Solidity and Listening's house, we would get stoned and play Dungeons and Dragons. Or we would all listen to rock music, like the Scorpions or Pink Floyd and get drunk and stumble around together at night in their neighborhood.

We all would get together on the weekends, but at school, it seemed that we were not as close. It almost reminded me of that movie, "The Breakfast Club" where the kids were close friends when they were hanging out in detention, but when they were at school, they would pass one another in the hall and not even say hi.

It seemed we were all trying to pass off as normal kids, and our association with each other was too much of a reminder of where we came from. When I said hi to one of the Love Family boys, he would pass me in the hall and pretend he didn't see me. Ravah would sit as far as possible from me on the bus. Mary sat with her new friends at lunch. Bright was always off by himself and didn't want to be bothered by anyone. Heaven and I stayed close though, and we had mutual friends, so fortunately, our paths naturally crossed at school.

None of us were in the same grade level or homerooms. Mary had been placed in either 10th or 11th grade and was trying to get help with her transcripts. She wasn't going to be able to graduate, because she didn't have any credits after years of going to school in the Love Family.

I was sad. I had lost my way of life, my family, my community, almost everyone I had known, and my relationships with kids at Summit I had known my whole life were changing.

We distanced ourselves from each other, just trying to understand where we had come to be, and we were grappling with all the different social dynamics. Here we were thrown into this environment where all of our roles were being reformulated with each other and with the world around us. We were all living in different places at that point and in different situations.

I focused on school and on my new friends like Kate and others who I associated with, but underneath it, I felt the pain of the separation of all of us. I missed the closeness that we all had. What had held us together—for so many years—was no longer there, so it seemed we drifted apart. I was the only one who went into Ninth Grade. A few of us went into Eighth Grade, and a couple of us went into 10 and 11th grades.

There was this party over at Solidity and Listening's house. It was a going away party for the boy who lived with them. He would no longer be going to Summit. He was moving to another country. I don't remember the exact details on why. I think he had relatives there.

It was one of the most memorable parties for me. There was a sadness there that was amplified. Towards the end of the party, there was a group hug that I will never forget. I cried my eyes out. I heard others crying too and saw tears running down their faces. When the boy, who was leaving, said good bye, it was like we were all saying good bye to each other. It would never be the same, and we knew it. Who we had been to each other was over.

From that party onward, it seemed we began to focus even more on our own social groups. After he left, we did not go to any more parties at Solidity's and Listening's house, which was too bad because their house had been a central meeting place for our group since we had left the Love Family.

Luckily for most of us, our respective social groups overlapped somewhat so we still saw each other at different gatherings, just not as often. When I saw them, there was never any acknowledgment of our shared past. It certainly was never a topic of conversation. Sometimes I would say, 'Remember this?' or 'Remember that?' which only seemed to irritate them, so I just dropped it.

In the next chapter, I discuss what happened when my mom finally left the Love Family. I also intend to go into detail about what ended up happening in the triangle between my mom, Nobility, and Honorable and how it affected me once they were all no longer living in the Love Family and were now living in the World.

BIBLIOGRAPHY (CHAPTER 16)

[Bright]. Personal Interview. Des Moines, WA. January 11, 2002.

Cemeno, Barb. Personal Communication. October 24, 2001.

Coffman, Connie. Personal Communicatio. October 24, 2001.

Forest. Personal Communication, Portland, OR February 23, 2002.

Gray, Rachel. Personal Communication. October 25, 2001.

Granitor, Jody. Personal Communication. October 18, 2001.

[Ravah]. Personal Interview. March 19, 2002.

[Zarah] Personal Interview. December 13, 2001. Maple Valley, WA.

CHAPTER 17

Dravus Street and Ingraham High School

Over a year later, in 1984, Elkanah had finally left the Family. I was looking forward to leaving Asaph and Hanifah's. They took good care of me, but I wanted to be with my mom again. I had lost her for so many years in the Love Family when other people were taking care of me, so I wanted to believe that going to live with her would be the answer to all my problems. *Maybe I just needed a mom*, I had thought. I stayed with Gramma for a while, at her apartment in Bellevue, then stayed with my mom in a hotel for a time before I ended up living with her in an apartment on lower Queen Anne on Dravus Street.

It was July when I moved in because I asked her if she planned to take us to the fireworks show. Her response:

"Oh God no, I am not into that stupid American shit."

Oh okay, so her old hippie self that I had lost when she joined the Love Family was still in there somewhere.

At first, it seemed to be working out. I got to have my own room, which was nice, because back at Asaph and Hanifah's house, I had just shared a room with their two daughters. Our life was beginning to normalize; Elkanah changed her name back to her birth name, Karen.

I was happy that she discarded her Love Family name, because then I could introduce her to my friends with a normal sounding name, and there would be no questions.

I wanted a normal relationship with my mom, but it seemed that the instant I moved in, there was a clash. It shouldn't have surprised me since in the Love Family, we never lived together for long and didn't have a typical mother daughter bond. I had fantasized that our relationship would become more than it had ever been, because that is what I now needed desperately in my life, since everyone who had ever been like a parent to me was now gone.

I had a boyfriend that I brought over one day. When I went to close the door of my room, she freaked out and there was a yelling match that ended in my boyfriend leaving in a hurry. It embarrassed me terribly. I had wanted to impress him and show him that I had a real bed and a room of my own, that I didn't sleep in a sleeping bag anymore or live in a tent in a commune. After he left, I got a big lecture about using birth control—I wasn't even sexually active.

There was conflict between us over food. She would not let me eat whatever I wanted out of the kitchen. I was hungry, and she wouldn't let me snack on peanuts. I thought it was ridiculous. *Was this her attempt to parent me?* I asked myself. I thought of it more as a joke. Here other people had raised me my whole childhood, and now that I was a teenager, 15-year old, she wanted to tell me what to do. Our relationship was estranged at best. Here I had struggled for the last year with no one to guide me, no one to understand how stressful it had been, how alone, how abandoned I felt.

I was mad at her. She seemed totally unavailable, uninterested in me and what I was going through. I didn't understand how hard it was for her either. I didn't understand what a struggle it was to be a single mom and trying to survive in a world that she had not been a part of for almost ten years.

I tried to help her. I would babysit for my brothers, Boldness and Jacob, who were two and four years old now. Forest was now around nine.

One night, I was watching the boys for her, so she could go out on a date with this guy, who was the brother of a former Love Family member.

While they were gone, and while my brothers slept, I noticed there was a man's head that was peeking in the bathroom window at me. Instinctually, I ran and locked all the doors. I called Definition for help. This was way before cell phones, so I couldn't just call my mom. Eve and Definition hadn't yet moved to Arizona. Definition left his house immediately and came and sat with me for a couple hours. I wouldn't let him leave. I was already sensitized to the powerlessness of the women in the Love Family, so it was frightening to me that there was this risk of being attacked for my gender. I had seen some statistics about the incidence of domestic violence and sexual assault, and it had scared me.

What was wrong with this culture that this sort of thing would be tolerated? It seemed to me that the attitudes about it were dismissive, without resistance or real protest. Pop culture seemed to encourage it! It just seemed so wrong, such blatant discrimination.

In the Love Family, the sexism was institutionalized which means that it was part of the doctrine—the man is the head, the woman is the heart; but in the culture outside, sexism was not institutionalized, and yet, it was everywhere. The law mandated equality, but in reality, that was not the way it worked out. It was an interesting contrast to me and one that I noticed and thought about. Especially since I had come out of a community where things like sexual assault and domestic violence were not talked about. There were no TVs or newspapers in the Family, like there were in the World, to blare it out so everyone knew. It seemed that everything I was learning about the World upset me.

My mom wasn't who I needed her to be. She was struggling. Maybe my problems to her paled in comparison to what she thought she was dealing with. I think anybody coming out of the Love family would've been dealing with culture shock, but as a child raised there with no real prior experience in the world, the Love Family was all I had known. I was now considered a dependent.

Elkanah was dealing with a major cultural transition for sure. She had survived an intensely abusive situation in the Love Family. She had no license, no identification, no record of housing or employment, and besides me, she had three little kids to take care of. Nobility, the father of two of her children, had refused to help her out. We had no family either who were in a position to help us, although, initially, we did stay with Gramma for a while in her apartment in Bellevue. Elkanah was a single mom, basically, with two young children and two older, school age children, Forest who was nine and me, 15.

When the Family broke up, Nobility, had to make a choice between Honorable and Elkanah, both of whom had two of his children. He couldn't keep both, especially after everything that had happened in his household at the Ranch. Even if it had worked out in the Love Family between his two women, it wouldn't have been acceptable to keep both in the modern society where ex members were trying to fit in, blend, live normal lives.

He chose his elder lady, Honorable, of course. Honorable's mom had the resources to help them get into a nice home. Plus, Honorable had a nurs-

ing degree and was able to make a decent wage right away. Nobility was working as well, under the counter, doing construction projects for ex-members.
They had two incomes and help from relatives.

Elkanah had nothing and couldn't even get welfare. Back in her hippie
days, she had been against welfare and the government and anything it had to
offer. But now, things had changed to where she felt she had no choice. She
had to get back on her feet somehow, so she could feed us. But she couldn't
even get welfare until she could produce birth certificates for her children, and
in order to get birth certificates, she had to establish paternity. She established
paternity, and she finally got welfare, but DSHS went right after Nobility
who had no official income, because he was working under the counter, so of
course, the next thing DSHS did was to begin garnishing Honorable's wages.

Honorable hated my mom, and now welfare was garnishing her wages because of her. Must've been rough. Maybe if Nobility had just helped
Elkanah out, helped buy his kids some food or loaned her some money to
buy them clothes, maybe she wouldn't have had to go to welfare! Maybe he
could've helped pay for childcare, so she could have found a job while Forest
and I were in school.

Honorable was so angry, that she spread false rumors amongst ex
members. She told everyone that my mom was trying to take the kids away
from Nobility, and that my mom was prosecuting him, neither of which was
true. Nobility must've believed that lie, because he started coming around
angry and had threatened to kill my mom if she took the kids away. As I said,
my mom was only trying to get welfare, so she could get back on her feet, since
Nobility had refused to help her out.

Nobility made up a story that the reason he had taken Elkanah as his
second lady was because Love had personally asked him to, as if she were a
charity case. The story went that if Nobility didn't take her, maybe she would
leave the Family, and Love was worried that he would lose Forest and I—total hogwash. During the time that Love supposedly asked Nobility to "take"
my mom, Love was, by all accounts, beginning to become increasingly isolated from Family life. Many were already suspicious that he was strung out
on cocaine. Besides, Love never tried to stop members from leaving; He was
constantly kicking people out who were problematic. If Elkanah had been

a problem before she was sanctioned to Nobility, she would've been kicked out. Elkanah wasn't popular or well spoken, but she hadn't been considered a problem or argumentative before she was sanctioned to Nobility. In fact, she was doing well enough that two other elders, at different times, had considered inviting her into their household, so she could be sanctioned into their relationship. She had done quite well in the households where she had lived too, mostly Encouragement's and Helpful's. Love wasn't worried she would leave with Forest and I. She had already left us there twice when she went into the World for periods of time for different reasons. Love had no reason to fear she'd leave with us.

Also, all of the rumors that were passed started shortly after Elkanah was sanctioned to Nobility, not before. I was in that household when they first became sanctioned. They certainly didn't act like it was an arrangement, and they seemed happy together at first, before reality set in about the multiple relationship. And finally, if Elkanah had been a problem before she was sanctioned to Nobility, I would have been aware of it. The community was tight knit, everybody knew everybody's business, and even though, we didn't live together, I always knew how she was doing, because how she was doing, her status and reputation, impacted me. For example, as soon as Honorable began passing rumors, I began to get wind of them. My mom, at times, would confide in me, or I would hear comments from people.

These lies were not trivial. These lies had a serious impact on my experience coming out of the Love Family and made the culture shock way worse. The lies bolstered Nobility and Honorable's story that had been made up to make them look as if they had a plausible story, just so that no one would believe my mom about what had been done to her. Once the Family broke up, she wanted people to know the truth, since people were still keeping their distance from her. They were keeping their distance when everyone needed each other the most. It seemed that Honorable purposely wanted people to keep their distance from my mom, so she wouldn't get help and be able to tell them her story.

Karen described this time period as one where she was "living out of churches." She had absolutely no intentions of taking the children from Nobility. That was a lie. Nobility had threatened to kill her, and all she was doing was following the advice of her attorney, which was to get custody of her own children, which she had to do anyway in order to get welfare. She only did what she had to do to survive.

She didn't have enough to feed her children. One of the things that we fought about when I first moved in with her was over food. I was hungry, and when I went to get food out of the kitchen, she would get mad at me.

Honorable spread the false rumors far and wide amongst ex members. The difference this time was that now most people had left the Family and were all forming alliances and helping one another get back on their feet. The continued strife going on between Elkanah, Nobility and Honorable and the way it was portrayed came down to, no one would help my mom, and subsequently me and my brothers. When she saw ex members, they would come up to her and ask, "How could you do that to him?" Remember, they were already convinced my mom was a problem just the year before when Honorable would complain about her at elder ladies' meetings and after Honorable spread false rumors around the community about her.

Honorable had people convinced. Somebody called welfare and tried to report Karen for fraud, saying she had some guy living there, but that wasn't true at all. She did have somebody that she was dating, but he was not living there. Whoever this was that called, was just trying to make it difficult for her after what Nobility and Honorable were telling people.

Honorable was poisoning the waters for Elkanah during a time when ex members needed each other the most to help one another get back on their feet after years in the Love Family. The politics of the polygamous relationship followed us all right out of the Love Family and into the World.

Why would Honorable do this? I don't know, but my guess is they still wanted my mom to shut up about what happened in that household. And they were continuing to protect their own alliances. Plus, Honorable still had to have been mad after what she herself went through, having to share her man, the father of her children, and then she had such trouble getting rid of my mom, which she never was able to do. It only happened because the Family broke up. Then, after all that, Nobility had chosen her, but he had these two sons from my mom. So my mom was never fully out of the picture, at least not while my brothers were growing up.

A lot of the ex-members relied on each other for help. They needed each other. When people left the Family, they had nothing to show for all those years of devotion. Dan Greuner, who had been Richness, was suing Love for all the money he had donated, a legal battle that stretched out for years. He had lost millions in property value alone of his Dupont inheritance. Richness was no more of a sucker though, than anyone else, just because the sum that he gave was larger. People gave houses, cars, and entire lifetime savings, which was more asset to them than Gruener's money was to him. Most people didn't have the money to sue Love, so they literally lost everything. Even people who just had a few hundred dollars in their pocket didn't get to leave with it. When people left, they were struggling to survive after putting in years of dedication to the community and the causes they believed in. That's why they were turning to each other for help.

Elkanah was not able to tap into that network at all. There was a point when she wanted to give up and was considering moving back to Alaska to be with Marty. I had always missed Marty, but I didn't want to leave again and have to adjust to more change. When she approached me with the idea, I screamed in her face, "I am not going to be dragged off to Alaska like some sack of potatoes!"

I was 15 and had just started my second year at Summit and had a group of friends that I felt close to, and after all the loss from the breakup of my community and the only family I had known for the last eight years, I was not about to just pick up and leave, again. There was no way I would move off back to Alaska. I would run away if I had to! From my mom's perspective, she was considering all options and had to figure out what to do.

It didn't have to be this way. The Love Family could've been smart. They could have planned ahead for just in case there was a break-up or in case people left. Other communities did just that.

In the Shaker community, when members joined, they relinquished their property, but at any time they returned to the World, they would resume ownership. (Holloway, 1966)

When the Oneida community broke up, loyalists and dissidents worked together to divide community property and money equally in a fair-minded way.

It wasn't chaos when Oneida broke up. Everyone was taken care of, including the children, the elderly and disabled members. Every member had the right to housing and food, owned by the company. No one was abandoned and left to themselves. All former members were given rent at cost at the mansion. Every child's education was paid for until the age of 16. Everyone got $30 worth of furniture, which must've been a lot back 100 years ago. Ex-Oneida members also received one-half of the value of the property or funds they brought into the community in shares of stock. Widowers were given two-thirds and widows one third of the amounts brought in by themselves and their deceased partners.

All the rights and terms were drawn up into a contract. It was called the 'Agreement to Divide and Reorganize' and was signed by nine-tenths of Oneida's adult members. According to one author, Oneida consisted of 213 adults, 77 children under 21, 64 of whom were under 10. When they signed the Agreement, they had to agree that all bygones would be bygones, and they had to relinquish their right to sue in order to get their stipends and stock (Klaw, 1993).

No, in the Love Family, there was no contract. All the property and money were in Love's name, and he wasn't t sharing it; no, instead he was fighting anyone who wanted a piece of it, starting with Dan Greuner.

I wasn't worried about money; I was totally overwhelmed by all the change and just dealing with culture shock and the new social landscape that was before me. I finally had my mom back, but I felt alone and scared. She was in survival mode and wasn't sure how she was going to feed us. She had changed. She was angry and resentful. I wanted her to love me and to finally be my mom after so many years of surviving in the Love Family without her, but I couldn't seem to reach her.

One day I was in the kitchen, and I called her "Mom." I had always called her by her first name, my whole life, no matter what her name was, but I thought that maybe if I called her mom, that she would wake up and remember that I was her daughter. To her, it must have seemed out of the blue when I said it, because she stopped, froze for a second or two before continuing to chop the lettuce, like she was wondering if she heard that right and not quite sure how she felt about it. I needed her to love me. I needed a parent.

Unfortunately, I couldn't make a connection with her. It seemed she only saw me as a burden to make her life harder. One day, we were arguing, and she slapped me in the face. I guess I had become a typical teenager, and she couldn't handle it. I had tried to shut the door to my room when my boyfriend came over. I had eaten food without her permission, and I also wanted to talk on the phone with my friends from school. I didn't understand what the problem was.

I don't think I was all that bad, considering other kids my age and what they put their parents through, but for whatever reason, she was not in a place in her life where she was prepared to deal with me. She had a lot on her plate, I got that, but it seemed that she did not have normal feelings for me as a mother would. How could she? I hadn't been under her care since I had been almost seven years old.

I came home from school one day and all my belongings had been thrown on the front lawn.

"Your dad will be here in 20 minutes to pick you up," she barked.

"What dad? I don't even know my dad!" I screamed at her.

It frightened me to think of some guy coming to take me away. I was angry. I was hurt. How could she have done this? It seemed so cruel after what I had been through in the last year or so, and she hadn't even discussed it with me to see how I felt about it. Was I going to wake up from this terrible nightmare? No, it was real, all my stuff was still sitting out in the yard. Some of it was on the sidewalk outside the gate ready for pick up.

Twenty minutes later, Mike was there. I didn't remember anything about my dad. He was a total stranger. He had short, dark, curly hair, hazel eyes, medium height and build. He wore khaki pants and a dressy sweater. This was my dad? I thought. He smiled at me, but it didn't put me at ease, and I wasn't able to manage a smile back.

When I was a young child and before we met the Love Family, there were times my mom would leave me with people I didn't know. I had followed her on all her adventures, hitchhiking around, living in hippie communes, living on a hippie beach in Maui, living as a survivalist in Alaska, and living in the Love Family. I had survived major culture shock and public school. It felt like I had gone to the ends of the earth for her, without much resistance at all;

I only tried to please her and be a good girl. I almost never got in trouble. Now that I was no longer being taken care of by other people, it seemed that now I was considered a burden. I overheard her talking about me over the phone earlier that day.

"I just can't handle her!" my mom had whined to my gramma Phyllis.

A lot of why I became argumentative was because she was not being very nice to me. She told me I couldn't talk on the phone, and she didn't provide me with a reason. For anyone that has ever had to raise a 15-year-old, can you imagine telling them they can't talk on the phone? She made me go to bed early in the evening, so she could watch television by herself. It was hard for me to understand how my presence was such a stressor. Teenagers don't go to bed at 7pm—of course I argued with her. I just wanted to be a normal teenager like my friends, to have a mom that cared. Plus, we didn't really have an established relationship where she had been an authority, and she was trying to parent me in this inappropriate way. She had never been like that before we joined the Love Family. We had been close, but I was a lot younger then. Now, I was almost grown up, and she had three other kids, who were still quite young.

I had been kicked to the curb, abandoned once again. My dad got my things and loaded up his car. As he drove off with me, I was silent, but inside my head, I screamed over and over, wishing I were dead.

Ingraham High School

I was 15 1/2 years old and had just completed the first half of my second year at Summit. I arrived at my dad's house on the brink of total shut down mode. I began to feel a darkness inside me; it was a toxic sludge of rage and self-hate that began to take hold. No matter what was going on, it was there, eating at my insides. It was hard to feel good about myself when I had been nothing more than a throwaway.

So far, since the Love Family had crashed, it was still recent and raw. I was trying to get used to a new world, a new society without anyone I had known. I had hoped my mom would rescue me, not send me off to live with someone I didn't know.

When we arrived at my dad's house, I met his wife, who I will call 'April.' April helped me carry my things to a small back bedroom. She watched me as I put my things into order. She was smiling and acting very welcoming, but I could also tell by her smile and her eyes that she was a little afraid. For me too, it was awkward and frightening. I looked around at the furniture, the beige carpet, and the art on the walls. It looked clean and homey. I could tell that Mike and April wanted me to be happy about meeting them and seeing my new home, but I felt empty, numb, and nothing was making sense.

I called my dad by his first name and my new stepmother by her first name too. I had always called parental figures by their first names my whole life, so it just seemed to make sense to me to do that. I didn't know them, and it seemed too weird to call them mom and dad. They didn't seem to mind.

At first, Mike and April seemed like a conventional, mainstream couple. They both worked at United Airlines in white-collar positions. They had no other children except me, and there was finally enough food. I ate things that I had never seen before—avocado, all sorts of different crackers, cheeses, cereals, and potato chips. I now found myself with a tendency to overeat.

Soon after I arrived at Mike and April's house, they helped me plan my 16th birthday party. I had never had a birthday party before. I invited Ravah and Heaven from my old Love Family days, and we ate pizza and watched scary movies. I thought to myself that living with my dad might not be so bad after all.

Then, I celebrated Christmas. It seemed so different from how it was growing up in the Love Family. It did not seem like a celebration of the birth of Christ, it seemed more like a celebration of Santa Clause. I was speechless when I opened my presents and there was a television and a stereo for my room.

I was moving closer to what I thought would be a "normal" life. April had my hair trimmed at a fancy salon and bought me trendy clothes for school. They wanted me to throw my hippie skirts and blouses in the trash.

They did not understand what had happened to me or where I had been all those years, and I didn't understand where my dad had been either. When I asked him, he told me that he had driven out to the Ranch to visit me one-time, but when he got to the Gatehouse, he just sat in his car.

"I just didn't have the nerve to go in," he says.

I asked myself questions, wondering why he had been absent from my life. He didn't provide me with much explanation. If he didn't have the "nerve" to come visit me, what was he afraid of? If I had been a boy, would he have tried harder? I wondered if it was because of my step mom, April.

She did seem jealous of me, as I was a constant reminder to her of his former relationship with my mom, which was entirely understandable. She knew that my mom and dad had been high school sweethearts, and that my dad had loved my mom very much. It seemed that every time my dad would talk to me, April would interrupt and storm into the room looking angry, then she'd give us the silent treatment until he left me to my own devices.

April was 20 years older than Mike, but there didn't seem to be anything significant about that, other than it seemed she put herself under a lot of pressure to look younger. Plus, when I was growing up in the Love Family, no one had kept track of how old they were, so I wasn't aware that their age difference was unusual.

Mike's mother, my grandmother, had died when Mike was young, just a few years before my mom had left him. For whatever reason, my dad, seemed to avoid giving me any personalized attention whenever April was around, and she was always around. *Maybe it was because of the drinking*, I wondered. Mike always had a Coors beer in his hand, and April held a perpetual cocktail glass in her hand. They were always drunk, so I never felt as if I could get close to them and get to know them. April would get so sloshed that it was hard to track a conversation with her. Mike would just drink one Coors right after the other and stay glued to the television watching baseball or football.

Years later, my dad remembered when I grabbed the glass of Vodka out of April's hand and slammed it on the coffee table. "Why do you do this!?" I angrily cried. I needed a mom. She wasn't it.

Karen had taken my brothers and left the State, and they were now living in Portland. My best friend Kate, from Summit, left too: she went to be with her family who lived in Baltimore. My best friend from the Love Family, Heaven, had moved to California to live with her relatives. Even my boyfriend from Summit had moved to New York with his family. I was trying to find a new normal, but the pieces just kept falling away.

I was finally living, at age 16, what I thought was a pretty normal life, that might have been similar to what most kids in America had. I lived with a mom and dad in a house and went to a normal school, at least that is how it must have seemed from the outside. But on the inside, I had lost everyone and was now living in a foreign country.

As soon as I moved in with my dad, I was taken out of Summit and began school at a large public school three blocks from our house, Ingraham. I was glad that I didn't have to take the city bus to school each day anymore, but it was another rough adjustment during a time when there was already a lot of changes and loss.

At Ingraham, they had frequent assemblies in the gym. All the students—there were around 1500—would chant the Pledge of Allegiance each time. I didn't know the Pledge; I had never learned it. Summit hadn't done that, so I just mouthed the words, so it would look like I knew it. It made me feel stupid when the whole school, except me knew it. When they were learning the Pledge in elementary school, I was learning how to sing 'We are one,' in seven different languages.

Ingraham was a large public school. All the kids had divided themselves into stereotyped groups—preps, jocks, wavers, rockers, punks. I did not fit into any of the groups that were available. I found it curious how they grouped themselves off into stereotyped boxes.

The trendy clothes didn't help at all either. In fact, they seemed more of a liability. I felt so crisp and brand new in my neon pink and green shirt and elastic stretch pants that April had bought me. These African American girls passed me in the hall and stopped to question me about my clothes:

"Where'd you get those pants?" They said it snidely. "Where'd you get that shirt? Jay Jacobs?! Ha ha ha" It wasn't just those girls, there were other times I was called "weird." Someone told me they thought I "must be on another plane of existence." I wondered that myself.

When I got to Ingraham high school, it was clear that it was more academically challenging compared to Summit.

I didn't mind the challenge; it just gave me something to focus on that at least I could overcome with hard work. I actually enjoyed the challenge of school because it was concrete and something I could master with enough effort. I was motivated and confident. I knew I could do this part.

The social piece was way harder. Summit had been almost like a small private school compared to Ingraham, which was a big public school. The difference was drastic. I didn't realize what I was getting into. If I did, I would have pushed harder to stay at Summit. Who cares about the long bus rides.

At Ingraham, there were a lot of drugs, and there was way more unwanted sexual attention. I couldn't go anywhere, it seemed without getting weird cat calls or inappropriate advances from teenage boys and men. It happened so frequently now, that it became just part of the background noise, part of what seemed to be seen as a normal aspect of American culture. It might have been more obvious to me as an outsider, who had been raised in a different society, than someone else who was socialized from a young age in the World. Why was it like this in the World? I wondered.

Not even a junior in high school, and I began to read. I read a lot of books about feminism and sexuality. If no one was going to explain it to me, I was going to find out for myself. I read famous feminist icon, Bell Hooks, Audre Lorde, Shere Hite, Gloria Steinem, Andrea Dworkin, Adrienne Rich and others. I read the Dance of Anger by Harriet Learner. It wasn't today's world where I could just look it up on the internet. I went to the library and bought books with the money I earned from a paper route. I was afraid of succumbing to the waves of social control as I knew what a mistake that was in the Love Family. I wanted to make up my own mind.

I didn't fall into the neatly defined groups that seemed to provide a basis for organizing student social life. Eventually, I fell in with a group of misfits and rebels where I felt I could at least be myself. I had a resistance mentality already that I think came from my background of being raised in counterculture.

I saw fistfights just outside the school. Punches were thrown, this kids' head was shoved into the cement right in front of me. This was on the west side of the school, half a block from the grocery store. It was scary.

My cousin Robert went to Ingraham too. He lived two houses down from my dad's house. He tried to help. Maybe he knew that I was in over my head. He was popular, well-adjusted, and had a lot of friends. He introduced me to them and encouraged me to join the clubs and student associations. I tried to get involved, but it didn't work. I was too frightened, awkward, and self-conscious. It seemed that there were so many rigid rules, unspoken standards, and expectations for behavior for which I had no familiarity. There was a lot that just seemed foreign. It was easier to just say, forget it. I felt like somebody put too many frozen bananas in the blender and it just shorted out and shut down.

I stopped trying to fit in. Instead, I kept up my Summit friendships and ended up going to a lot of parties at my friend Rebecca's house. When her parents were gone, everyone there would get drunk and stoned and listen to Led Zeppelin. Ravah and Heaven and some of the other Love Family kids from Summit would show up. It felt more like family when I was at Rebecca's, than it did when I was at my dad's.

I'll never forget when Kate came from Baltimore for a visit.

"God, Rachel," Kate exclaimed, "You have really changed. You seem really angry!" We had been down at Green Lake, and we had gone into a public restroom when I had attempted to take the sink off the wall.

"Why?!" she asked me.

"Because its fuuuun!" I answered with a devious expression on my face.

She looked at me shocked.

We left the restroom. On our way out, I threw some litter on the ground. That's when she gave me this long lecture on the importance of keeping the environment clean. Kate was pretty progressive in her thinking and beyond her years maturity wise. I had been like that too before I went to Ingraham.

Yada yada yada, I had thought.

Later that day, she looked me over for the longest time:

"Rachel, you've really gained weight!?" she stated with concern in her voice.

It was good to see her but I had changed. She was right. I was no longer that innocent, sweet girl, fresh from the commune who passed Haiku poetry back and forth with her in class at Summit.

I became closer friends with Rebecca's brother Daniel, who was a couple of years younger than I was. He and I used to go sneak into the basement window of this church near their house and make long distance calls to Heaven in California. I am not sure what possessed me to do this, other than

I had shut myself off from my feelings and just quit caring about what other people thought. No one seemed to give a rat's ass about me.

We were there at the church one day, and we had wandered back behind the sanctuary where there were a couple of small offices. One of the offices had art supplies. Daniel took a can of white spray paint and sprayed peace symbols all over the podium and pew where there was seating for the congregation. I did not find this as funny as Daniel found it, and in fact, I pressured him to leave before we got caught.

"Come on Daniel, let's go," I whined.

He thought my whining was funny.

We actually did get caught, because the next time we were there making calls, some lady from the church came by and found us. Daniel, who was around 14, instantly pretended to be a homeless waif who was only there because he was starving. He grabbed a piece of bread and began stuffing it in his mouth, hungrily. I ran out of there so fast and got on a Metro bus and went home. I later heard that there was a police description of me as a young girl, with long, blond hair, wearing a long, white dress with rainbow embroidery around the neckline. I was still wearing my hippie dresses from my Summit days.

When Rebecca found out, she was not happy about it and it created some distance between us for a time.

My gramma Phyllis tried to help me. When I quit ballet class, she started taking me to church each Sunday. She bought me a pretty dress to wear to church and shoes to go with it. I wore it every Sunday. Afterward, she would take me out for pie. Even though it seemed all the pieces of my life had fallen away, my gramma was there trying to help me piece myself back together every Sunday. She thought I needed church. I found it very boring, but I enjoyed being with her each week and being able to complain about Mike and April.

I had gone from listening to regular rock to harder core stuff like speed metal and punk. One day in church the Pastor gave this long lecture about AC/DC and how full of the devil they were. The Pastor was looking out into the audience with an expression of incredulity like how could this be happening to our youth? Just that past weekend, I had gone to an AC/DC concert at the Tacoma Dome, and it had been the most fun I had had in a long time. I thought to myself, this world, this place where I now live, is the place where death occurs, the place where people are mortal. I am no longer in the Love Family where everyone was trying to create heaven on earth. The kingdom of heaven (The Love Family) was no more everlasting than Satan's palace in hell! I wasn't into it.

The Pastor used the example of the song, "Highway to Hell," to say that "Kids today are so misguided that they are walking themselves right into the pit of fire." It made no sense to me. I liked the song and had listened to it many times. How would I know that the highway to hell didn't actually lead to a bigger and better world? Or maybe this was hell and I had already taken the road to hell when the Family broke up, and I was now stuck in this nether world, going to church. Or maybe the Love Family was hell. Who knew? I was going to church during a time in my life when religion was probably not the best thing for me, despite my grandmother's good intentions.

Music was my only refuge in those days. I listened to a lot of different music. I went through a Bob Dylan phase. I listened to new age music. My Led Zeppelin phase never ended, since I believed, and still do, that they were one of the greatest rock and roll band there ever was.

I went through a major Metallica phase. All the intense feelings that I was going through, hopelessness, the anger, the rage, the disappointment, the sadness, the loss, the confusion—all of it could be channeled out of me.

I went to a lot of rock concerts in those days, but I went to Metallica four times. This was before they became a mainstream rock band when they were putting out albums like "Ride the Lightning, Garage Days," and "And Justice for All." They were more thrash metal, before "Master of Puppets" came out. Their music seemed to express what I was feeling, which was the pain of loss, the shock of change without support, and anger towards the cruelty of being dropped into this abyss of a nightmare. It was complete nihilism and rejection of anything associated with the World, this new culture that I was thrust into. There was nothing about the World that I could relate to. I was done. Metallica's "Fade to Black" spoke to me, which was a song about suicide. I didn't want to die but I could relate to the pain that was expressed in the lyrics.

There is nothing more for me
Need the end to set me free.

Without thinking about it, dropping out was the same choice my mom had made, and it was the same choice that members of the Love Family had made, so it wasn't hard for me to make that choice. I wasn't alone now. I was a member of a sort of underworld, an alternative society of others who also wanted nothing to do with it. It was community. We had each other's back. I was finally free.

I quit following the arbitrary rules that Mike and April made for me. A curfew never made any sense, and it was never explained to me why there would be one. Why would there be separate rules for them than for me? I grew up in the Love Family where there were not separate rules for adults and kids. Plus, I was unmotivated to follow Mike and April's rules since there was no relationship; they never spent any time with me or talked to me about things. April had told me one time, "I love you, but I don't like you." I guess it was possible to love someone but not like them? I had never heard about that.

In class one day, a freshman girl came up to me. She was a skinny, petite, Hispanic girl.

"Are you hard core?" she asked me admiringly.

I was baffled by the question and silent as I tried to figure out what to say. I was Sun. I was Hope. I was Julie. I was done. I didn't care what anybody thought. No one was going to hurt me anymore. I could tell that she wanted me to say, 'Yes, I am hard core.'

"I am done with labels," I said to her, disinterested, bored.

She got a knowing expression on her face and went and sat down for class, like she had finally figured me out.

The next Monday, she was wearing a leather jacket and boots and way too much black eyeliner on. She strode into the classroom with a new confident gait. I chuckled. I had given up being cool, and I could see that she had a long way to go.

"You have walls around you," a guy I dated had once commented.

I did have walls, walls of protection. I had given up trying to fit in, socially. Finally, I didn't care what anybody thought. In the Love Family, I had been forced to adjust to that culture, but now I was in the World, and I didn't have to fit in, I could just be myself. I wasn't going to be controlled by society as I had been controlled by the society I was raised in. I could think and feel how I wanted to think and feel.

Each day, at lunch, I went out to what was called the "Elephant Farm." It was just a wooded area near the school where kids could hang out without the school administration sneaking up on them. Every so often, small bands of admin would sneak up on us and bust those who were caught smoking pot.

My boyfriend was suspended, then the administration treated him terribly, just generally harassment to where he would be pulled into the office for the slightest little thing; it got so bad that he ended up dropping out just to get away from it. When I saw what happened to him, it scared me to think that people in authority would spend their time just trying to police and control as opposed to trying to help and understand. They had singled him out, labeled him as a trouble maker, and then treated him accordingly. When he left the school, he was always angry after that towards the school. He blamed the school that he didn't graduate. After what I saw, I wondered if he was right.

Little by little, I was learning what was real and what was bull and kept trying to make sense of things. One day, I took a friend of mine named Patricia to the Elephant Farm. I had seen her in church from time to time.

I had just left the campus. Patricia caught up with me on my way off the grounds, going to the Elephant Farm. This was during my lunch period. She followed me on this little pathway through the woods into a clearing where a thick crowd of students were smoking pot. When she saw them, she started reciting biblical verse:

"Yea though I walk through the shadow of death, I will fear no evil…" she recited as we walked. It was the lyrics of a popular Love Family song. I thought she was trying to be funny, at first, but she had this very serious expression on her face. I was standing there next to some other friends of mine; Patricia was next to me. One of my friends offered me a hit off his pipe. I went to take the pipe, and suddenly Patricia started in on me with a lecture about how God doesn't want me smoking marijuana. This was in front of probably five or six people who were standing off from the main group.

"Rachel, you're not planning on smoking that are you?" she asked condescendingly.

"What is your problem?!" I asked her casually as I took a hit.

She gasped, then stomped off angrily.

Frankly, I thought she was being ridiculous. Smoking pot seemed to connect me with my higher self, to my spiritual core. It grounded me.

After that, Patricia left me alone. She must have thought of herself as a failure. I realized that she had tried to help me. She did help me but not in the way that she thought she would. I never forgot that experience because it helped me realize more fully that traditional, mainstream Christianity was the wrong path for me, at least in my life then.

Christianity, it seemed, after going to church with Gramma Phyllis and associating with Patricia, just seemed like this judgmental, rigid faith that had all these nonsensical rules and limitations. I was told that this was satanic and that was demonic, and there was no understanding about what it might mean in a bigger sense about our society or about how people were feeling. The lyrics of a song aren't just lyrics; they are expressions, like art, of what people are feeling and the stories of people's lives that aren't being told. When I went to church, I never felt that the Pastor said anything that helped me in my life. There was never any advice that seemed to apply to me. Music taught me that I wasn't alone, that there were others who were feeling what I was feeling, and that it could be okay, and it was something healing to share and to grow from.

So, in a religious sense I felt lost, but on deeper level, I strongly believed in God. I always prayed about things and felt, on an intuitive level, connected to something much larger than what it seemed on the surface. I think no matter how dark things were, as I was going along, I was looking for the deeper meaning, and what was happening on the spiritual plane drew me forward.

Part of my evolution was going through culture shock and learning how to adjust to the outside culture. In order to do that, I had to go through the darkness, so I could find the light to draw me out. High school was a very intense experience. But it wasn't all bad. The journey through darkness led to finding freedom and realizing that I had a choice. I didn't have to conform and be accepted. I could just be myself and make my own decisions.

As a child, Experience Change was the name I was given in my dream. The dream had been a nightmare, because I knew what it meant, and it's been true, really. Experiencing change is a nightmare, at times, but it's also been a part of my evolution, which has helped me to self-actualize and find my potential.

The Love Family needed to evolve, it could have, but it didn't. In any relationship whether it's between two people or whether it's between 300, 600 or even a million, people are constant changing and evolving forward, and there's a need, if the relationships are going to work, for there to be adaptation to those changes. Otherwise, it's going to be just like an earthquake fault, making the shifts that change the landscape of the earth, releasing the built-up pressure and scattering everybody. I went through that traumatic shift, so I know a lot about experiencing change and how essential it is to survival.

CHAPTER 18

Politics—The Loyalists and the Secessionists

In high school, no one knew where I had come from. I had hidden it from everyone, including myself. I completely shut off my past that included growing up in the Love Family. I didn't talk about it. I didn't tell people. It was like this black box that was there, but that I didn't access. Occasionally, I would tell someone, but it wasn't a part of who I was anymore. They wouldn't understand anyway. It was more likely that someone understood if they were way older than me, because then they might have been more familiar with the counterculture and some of the events that took place during those times. But most of my friends were around my age or younger which meant that all they knew were the stereotypes they saw on television, of hippies or some vague notion of what a commune was without any context. God forbid, I ever use the word cult to say where I came from because the idea of it to anyone was just this big, scary word that conjures up images of animal or child sacrifice and other bizarre things. The subject was hexed.

There was no reason to talk about it, really. But clearly, my perspectives were greatly influenced by what had happened to me, so in some ways, it was put away, but on other levels, it was always present, no matter how far I traversed.

I wanted to never open that black box again. On the other hand, I felt like a huge piece of who I was, was missing. I was a transplant, but my roots had been grown in Love Family soil. It was a strange, unfamiliar world that I was in now, and I desperately missed that sense of community that I had been so used to.

I had stayed away because I was angry. I was angry at my mom for dumping me off at my dad's, but my anger was much greater than just her. I was mad at everyone who had been a part of the Love Family, not at any one person. I felt betrayed and abandoned to the World, this place that I had been taught was this terrible, big bad hell out there, and in some ways, what I had been taught about the World seemed about right.

After high school, I lost touch with mostly everyone who I had known from the Love Family. I kept my distance as I tried to assimilate and adjust to life on the outside. It had been ten years since I left the Love Family. I began to wonder what happened to everyone. I had lost so many people that I had loved. After being away for so long, I wanted to come back and reconnect, so I could find people who would understand what I had been through. I also wanted to understand what had happened and why. How could Love let this happen? How could they just leave without a fight? Where was everybody?

I began to reach out. Every so often, I would show up at some ex-member's birthday party, wedding, or some other get together. Some of the former members who had been musicians had formed bands that performed around town at different venues, and I occasionally would end up there and see people I used to know.

Honestly, it took a lot of courage on my part to show up at one of these events, because then I had to deal, face-to-face with all the thoughts that usually stayed in my black box. The result of which, not always, but could be downright upsetting. When I was there, I was always disappointed that there seemed to be very few people who would show up who I had been close to, like the kids. None of the kids who were around my age ever showed up. If they did, it was rare. Mostly, it was the adult ex-members who were trying to stay in touch. It was nice to see them anyway, and especially those who had been more involved with the kid scene.

They didn't just happen to be there, there were a large group of people and their extended friends, family and associates that stayed in contact with one another as a group, especially early on after the exodus. When I went, I sort of felt like an outlier. They had all joined the Love Family as adults. I had never joined, although I had been a baptized member. I had only been there in the first place though, because my parent was there.

That difference affected my whole outlook. When I was there, I was quiet mostly and just observed what was going on around me. I was friendly, but I was in my head, trying to take it all in and process it.

I got something to eat, chatted, but mostly, I just observed. The Love Family had divorced so to speak, although the divorce was never complete, because not everyone left. So now everyone had been clumped and rebranded into certain groups. There was Group A, Group B, and Group C. Group A were the Love Family staunch loyalists. They were those who had stayed loyal to Love and had stayed in the Love Family, although there were a few people in Group A who did not live in the Love Family anymore, but still mostly just associated with current Love Family members. Then there was Group B folks.

Group B were people who had left the Love Family, most of whom were bitter, mad at Love. This was the largest group because most people had left, only a few stayed. Group B were like the secessionists as opposed to the Group A loyalists.

Then, finally, there was Group C people. Group C were anyone that did not fit neatly into either Group A or Group B. They were friendly with both groups though. They would go visit their friends at the Ranch, then I might see them show up at some group B get together later on. They had friends on both sides of the isle.

When I went to a gathering, it was for the most part a Group B gathering, because I had left when they did. At one such event, where Understanding had been present, I heard that she had been confronted and judged because she had kept her name. This judgment affected her standing in the Group B crowd. There were those who just couldn't accept her decision. They felt she should have renounced her name in opposition to Love himself as a symbolic gesture of protest. There were certain ex-members who had been elders in the Love Family who kept their status amongst Group B members. They were kind of like leaders of the pack in a way, and from what I observed, they had a lot of influence in the group dynamics that played out.

Since I kept in touch with Understanding over the years, she told me exactly what happened to her after the mass exodus. Understanding didn't keep her name out of some blind loyalty to Love, she kept her name because Love tried to take her name from her when she was kicked out, and she refused to let him do it. It was despite Love that she kept her name, and so what? She did what she felt was right for her. She stayed but she became a sort of outspoken rebel to where Love kicked her out of the Family at least twice.

There was also judgment and gossip against Understanding, because after she had been kicked out, she had returned to the Love Family. I guess they could not understand why she would have wanted to return to what they thought was such a horrible place, a place a lot of them had lived for many years themselves.

Understanding stayed, but it seemed to me that it wasn't out of some blind fanaticism. It was more out of a moral obligation towards the children that remained out there, children who had been in her care their whole lives. She had two young children of her own now too. Their dad was a Group A, loyalist. She had planned to leave, but her kids had begged her to go back, so they could be with their friends, their dad, and their community. I occasionally went out to visit her at the Ranch.

She didn't give up on Love, but she became a rebel as a result of her attempts to change things for the better. She was kicked out the first time because she put her kids in public school, and remember, this was all after the mass exodus of 1983 and 1984. She had left with Love to California, and then they all returned to the Ranch to regroup and start over fresh with those who now saw themselves as the 'true believers.'

Against Love's wishes, she had her kids tested and found out they were academically below standard, so she put them in a special program in public school to help them. I guess Love had decided that the children would be homeschooled until at least seventh grade. Despite that, she returned and began a campaign to try and protect the kids that remained at the Ranch from drugs and alcohol. Understanding found it "a losing battle" though, because "the children were living in a community where drugs were sanctioned and a part of the culture."

She challenged Love, over and over, to the point where the loyalist community turned on her. While Group B sent her to the curb because she kept her name and went back to Love after so many had left, Group A rejected her as well because she wasn't loyal to Love enough.

When she was kicked out, predictably, Love refused to let her take her own children out of the Family, so she ended up taking Love to court in order to establish paternity, so she could get custody of her children. There was a front-page article about the situation in the Seattle Times, May 11, 1997, pg. 1.

Then, Understanding underwent another full on battle with Love over the issue of sexual abuse. Several children had told her they were being sexually abused, and she had taken their reports to Love, who did nothing, and instead accused her of being on a 'witch hunt.' That's why she was kicked out the second time. What angered Love the most though was that she had gone to the police with the kids reports. She felt she had no other choice, since Love had refused to put protections in place or to confront the offenders. Once again, Love's concern for the survival of the community was more important than the safety and wellbeing of the children.

"The Family will almost always cover itself to protect itself from bad publicity," Understanding says. "There is this feeling of it's us and them. We can't tell anything about 'us,' or 'them' will come in and take our land away, take our houses away, take our children away or try to break up their family."

"Why did you stick it out?" I asked her. This was years later after she finally left for good.

"My survival was at stake, as far as my own kids," Understanding answered directly, "and I felt responsible for all of the kids that remained. We had no books, we had no teachers—we didn't even have food when we came back from California," she continued. "The kids' teeth were abscessing; they needed medical attention. And that's what put me at odds with Love because I decided that my first job was kids, not him."

Years later, Understanding finally left. Once she had the main boxes situated at her apartment in Arlington, I was sitting with her, helping her organize her stuff into plastic storage bins. I came across this small, hand-sized velvet draw-strong bag.

"What is it?" I asked.

"Oh—that's your teeth!" she answered evenly.

"What?!" I asked surprised. I looked inside the bag. There were all these little pieces of paper folded up. One by one, I unfolded the papers. Each one had the name of a child scrawled on it and inside a small tooth. There were loose teeth at the bottom of the sack that had fallen out of their papers. It had been many years since I was old enough to be losing teeth, so she must've saved the bag for a long time. As I unfolded each paper and read the note, I came across one that said 'Rachel,' and there lo and behold was one of my baby teeth. I looked at Understanding in disbelief. It apparently was unmistakable proof that somehow the tooth fairy of my childhood had been in fact Understanding herself.

"I just didn't know what to do with them, and I couldn't just get rid of them," she says, apologetically. "Do you think they would want them back?"

"I don't know," I answered. It was incredible to me that here she had saved our teeth for all these years, just like a parent would.

Understanding continued to love us, even though so many of us had left, and she stayed because there were still children there who needed her, just like we had needed her.

I asked Understanding what it was like for the kids that stayed when so many people left. She shared with me a story about something that happened during the break up period. She was walking up near Ken's Market on Queen Anne with some of the kids whose parents had stayed. Activity saw Strength getting in his car after having left the store. She was so happy to see him. It had been a month since he had left the Love Family. Activity ran up to his car and began pounding on the window.

"Strength! Strength!" she cried.

Strength refused to roll down the window and say hi to her. After a minute, he slowly rolled down the window:

"My name is not Strength," he says with a growl.

"Why do you hate my dad?" Activity asked, innocently.

"Your dad made some decisions that I can't agree with," he answered gruffly. Slowly the window rolled back up again, then he backed up his car out of the parking lot and left.

"She was devastated and started crying," says Understanding," then continued, "The kids whose parents' stayed felt abandoned by their caretakers," she explained. "Many of them also lost their closest childhood friends, who were no longer a part of their lives when their friend's parent's left. There were no explanations, no good-byes. There was a long period of adjustment," Understanding says. "They were rebelling, hurt, angry, and couldn't be controlled. Before I had a team of people helping me, but now there was nobody left."

"How did the adults do?" I asked. They also had lost many of their closest friends.

"No one talked about it," Understanding answered.

"Did they ask about people or kids who had left?" I asked.

"If I brought up how one of you kids was doing," Understanding explained, "the response was a blank expression—emotional Alzheimer's. It was like you didn't even exist anymore. A group silence ensued."

The Love Family breakup was hard on everybody, no matter which side of the fence they were on. I suppose it must've been similar to the division and warring that takes place in a typical divorce where children are involved, with one parent pitted against another. Except, this was a community with hundreds of people splintered off into rivaling factions and uncompromising loyalties.

It was very similar to what happened to the kids who were raised in Oneida. When the Community disbanded, the membership, including the children were split down political lines. Pierrepont Noyes wrote about what that was like for him as a child, and remember, he was the son of the founder.

"If the storm which swept away my past left no permanent scars, it certainly made new creases in my brain and some of them very deep," Noyes wrote.

"My belief in the impeccable lives and spiritual authority of all Community men and women had been shattered, first by their own charges and countercharges against each other, then by jibes of outsiders with whom we now associated freely…" explained Noyes who went on to write, "The results of the dissension as a sort of poison of a secondary partisanship which now began to separate children who had all their lives regarded each other as brothers and sisters…" There were "group whisperings" that eventually led to "a definite sorting up into youthful loyalists and seceders." (Noyes, 1937, 156)

I didn't feel like I belonged in any group, but it seemed that amongst the kids, I was being pigeon holed no matter what group I went towards. When I saw some of the kids whose parents were group B ex-members, if I said anything positive about my childhood experience, I was considered too pro Love, which didn't really resonate at all with how I felt. On the other hand, if I went to a gathering where there were kids whose parents were Group A, loyalists, then if I said anything negative about Love or the Love Family, I was seen as too anti-Love, "too negative," I was told. I was censored no matter who I talked to or what I said. I didn't feel like I fit into any of the categories. Yet everything I said was screened for red flags in terms of who my loyalties belonged to.

I went out to the Ranch a few times, a couple of those times were to go to the Garlic Festival, which was an event that the remaining members started doing to raise funds to help pay bills. When I talked to the people who stayed and who lived there, I felt that all they wanted was to get me to "come home." I didn't really feel supported by anyone who stayed loyal to Love, except for Understanding and a couple others. I felt like I was struggling and trying to make a life for myself, but who I was or what I was doing in the world outside of the community was meaningless to them. All that mattered was the Love Family. It seemed that they were not interested in me and my struggles in Babylon;

"Of course, it is like that out there," they told me, "that's why you need to come home here and just be present and part of the oneness."

I didn't know what I wanted, but I knew that my time in the Love Family had expired. Despite how hard it seemed in the World, going back, with so many people missing, just didn't seem like an option. They were loving though and didn't play the social games.

I was bound and determined to find my way on the outside; I knew that was my mission. My visits to the Ranch were to just say hi to people I loved and missed and to see the place where I spent my childhood, so I could process and understand what had happened.

It was very strange feeling to see the remaining members who had stayed loyal to Love. It was like going back in time, but when I got there, everybody was missing. It would be like going back in time to your childhood home, and your mom's there and your sister's there, but your dad and your brother and the family dog is missing. *This isn't how I remember it!* To me, it was like going to a ghost town. And the remaining members acted like nothing had happened. And none of their personalities had changed or their circumstances, which may sound obvious, but for those of us who left, it was a major contrast.

The people who left were not the same people they had been. They had gone back to their former personalities. They weren't recognizable. Their life circumstances were totally different, and nothing resembled their former selves except their faces. It was like an evil trick and totally weird.

I saw the Group B, Secessionists more often, because I had left, but I really didn't fit into either of those groups. Technically, I must have been Group C, because I was friendly with certain individuals who were in each of the groups.

I have a memory from during that time. It was shortly after high school. I must've been early 20s, because I went to a bar with a couple ex-members. There was a band playing. I recognized some of the band members as also being ex-members of the Love Family. I talked to a man who had been named Diligence. He had been one of the first members to leave, and when he left with his elder lady Joppa and his kids in the middle of the night, everyone had been shocked.

Diligence had a Worldly name now and had his own business. He was an indoor plumbing guy, selling toilets. Solidity, who was of course, also going by his Worldly name, was a member of the band playing. I saw that Listening was there dancing. She stopped dancing and came over and gave me a big hug. I had known her since my Alaska days. The ex-members who were there told me what their Worldly names were, but I forgot them. I am not sure if I actually forgot them or if it was more comfortable for me to just "forget" them. It felt very strange calling them by these new names. I guess it shouldn't have since I should've been used to people changing their names all the time throughout my entire childhood. And maybe it might not have been so weird if they had a Bible name, another Virtue name or even a hippie name, but they were names like 'Bob,' 'Joe,' or 'Pat.' I had never called anyone from my childhood by such a "normal" sounding name before. It wasn't just the names, it was also that they had conventional lives, most not even in the counterculture at all but regular guys with normal jobs in their own houses. It seemed very strange to me after knowing them the way I did.

That night at the bar, I was reintroduced to people I hadn't seen since my childhood. One of the ex-members at that bar, chose not to recognize me. It was very offensive. Like here we lived together, day in and day out. You helped take care of me? Really? You don't remember me? I guess it's been a long time. It was just a few years later. Were they that out-of-it? I wondered.

Or maybe they just decided that politically, I wasn't cool enough, I wasn't in the right groupings. Maybe it was my mom, Elkanah who had had such low status and all those troubles in Nobility's household. How could they not recognize me? I wondered. I didn't look very different at all. I never grew another inch and I kept my long blond hair. I lived with them for 8 years. Maybe they hadn't been paying attention to the kids, and I had been just another community urchin, running about with the groups of children.

When I went to a get together, where ex-members were present, I saw people with their new names, new haircuts, new clothing and attitude—it was surreal. I was trying to process it all, who people were when I knew them, who they were now, who I was then, who I was now, everything that was lost, everything that had changed. I would start drowning in my thoughts. I had only known these people as their Love Family selves, I hadn't known them before, so their new identities, to me, just seemed fake, ridiculous.

They had short hair now. They wore Worldly clothes. I went out to Whidbey Island for a reunion get together. It was on someone's private property. It was wooded and there was a nice house. I think it belonged to Solidity and Listening, but I couldn't be sure. A huge number of ex members were there partying for the weekend, maybe 100 or more.

I saw people setting up their tents. I talked to different people I had known, listened in on people's conversations. It was very boring. No one even mentioned the Love Family at all. It was mums the word. I heard superficial conversations about the weather and peoples' jobs. Everyone was standing around, mingling. There was a band, it was ex-members who were musicians. There was a food table. It was like a corporate champagne party. I noticed a sort of cliquish behavior. When I said something, it seemed to pass by everyone's sniff test to make sure I wasn't on the wrong side. Remember, this was a 'Group B' function.

Later on, at this event, I was sitting next to two women. The women were talking and I was just listening. They began to talk about the Love Family, and so my ears perked up. They went back and forth for a couple minutes. I couldn't hear exactly what was being said. I was standing nearby, eavesdropping on them. The women were sitting on the ground between two tents. Then suddenly, one of the women got all uptight and asked to change the subject. I heard their voices raise and I heard the word, "Love." The other woman got up and went to go "get food."

I went over to the food table and there was a BBQ pit where Bathsheba was passing out ribs. I put my plate out there and it was passed over more than once. Puzzled, I stepped back to watch what was going on, and I realized that there were all these former elders standing there. She was making sure they got ribs first before anyone else got them. Maybe there weren't enough.

I saw Nobility there. He was totally drunk and wrestling with Quan and my brother Jacob who were a lot taller than I had remembered them earlier on. It was very entertaining to watch, because Nobility was this huge, tall guy, his face was red from too much wine. He could barely handle Quan and Jacob. I had a flashback of him in the yurt wrestling with the kids. He would often take on up to eight of the young kids for gigantic wrestling scenes. All the little toddlers and young kids like Genuine and Quan and others would pile on top of him, and back then, even with so many of them, they were no match for him. All the household would gather around and cheer the kids on. But now, Nobility was stumbling about, and Quan and Jacob were kicking his butt.

I saw Certain and Goodness there sitting by their tent. They had new, Worldly names now as well, just like most of the ex-members. Goodness asked about me and seemed genuinely caring. I am standing there talking to them and Strength walks up. He has short hair. I hadn't yet heard about the story of how he had treated Activity in the parking lot at Ken's Market, so when I saw him, I said, "Hi Strength." And I actually called him 'Strength' because I didn't know what his new name was. I threw my arms around him to hug him. It was just a spontaneous gesture. I didn't even think about it; it just seemed the natural thing to do. He had been like a poppa in a way, head of the Ranch but always nice to the kids, never uptight or lecturing.

Strength didn't hug me back. He stood there stiff as a board while I hugged him.

I stepped back, surprised, confused. Did I do something wrong? I wasn't sure at the time, but now I have come to realize it probably had to do with calling him 'Strength.'

Another similar thing happened at an entirely different event. I was over at Bliss's house, and she was having a birthday party. This was about five years out of high school. I was in her back yard talking to a couple of ex-members, two women. One of them was Perseverance, and the other one was, I think, Uprightness. I was chatting with them. I began to tell them how I had gone out to the Ranch to visit for the Garlic Festival.

Both women suddenly became quiet. They looked at me, then looked at each other.

"Excuse me, I have to go see about something," one of the women said. She got up and walked away.

The other one quickly found an excuse to talk to someone else nearby.

There I was standing by myself, feeling stupid. *Did I say something wrong again?* It was very hurtful. Here I had just been this kid; I had never even made the choice to join the Love Family, but somehow, I had failed their little cool test because—oops—I had gone to the Ranch to visit.

Perseverance and Uprightness didn't know me anymore, and I guess the birthday party was group B folks where it was not acceptable to even go to the Ranch, my childhood home for so many years. They wanted to know whose camp I was in, and me going to the Ranch put me in the category of group A people. I didn't really feel like I was in any camp, but no matter who I met from the Love Family, those dynamics were present.

I went to enjoy the festival. I went to see my childhood home. I went to see people I loved and to know what was going on out there. It didn't mean I was on Love's side. Most definitely not. When I had gone out to the Garlic Festival, it was a little weird, because Truthfulness was not going to allow me to park in the special VIP parking that was for friends and family. Like I was raised out here, remember? I'm not considered friends or family? Really?

Every time I reached out, it was just one weird situation after the next. Everyone was pointing fingers and mad. There was little to no effort to work things out. They left after giving Love one little petition to which he responded negatively. There were meetings and talks, but once Love said, 'No way!' that was it. Maybe they thought that Love would never be moved to reason, but there was hardly any effort to fight back and demand the changes that were needed. Everyone could have teamed it and refused to back down. Leaving was kind of chicken shit in my opinion. On the other hand, even if they had worked it out, I would've left on my own. I wanted the freedom to make my own decisions, to build my own life. I never would have been one to return, despite what I was suffering. In my mind, my suffering became the motivational source from which I fought to make a life for myself. Going back would've been like giving up.

Some of the ex-member women asked me to babysit, which I was happy to do since I was in high school and needed money to buy music. I babysat Purity and Liberty for Simplicity and Logic. I babysat Miracle for Salome. I babysat Elisha for Atarah. I babysat Discernment for Pleasant and Reason. I even at times babysat for Honorable and Eve's little kids while they went out. I only charged a couple dollars an hour. I wanted to help them out as I still saw them as family. It was a nice arrangement, but once I stopped babysitting for them, I never heard from them again. I guess in the World, there was no context for our relationship anymore.

Every so often, I would go out to the Ranch and visit Understanding. Not too long before the Love Family mass exodus, she had been sanctioned and had two sons, so after I had left the community, I went out to see her family. They lived in the old yurt site that was situated next to where I used to live in Nobility's household. This was before she was kicked out. It was very strange to drive down the gravel road, park, walk past the Barn, past the knoll, across the pasture, past the lake, across another pasture and through the woods to her home site. To see her living there in those same rustic conditions, living communally under Love's total authority, was hard for me to even fathom after what I had been through since I left. There were no longer hundreds of people living out there. There were just a couple dozen.

I would also visit Understanding after she was kicked out for standing up to Love. And as I mentioned, I went to visit her when she had an apartment in Arlington.

She told me what had happened to her, why she was kicked out and how she was trying to protect the kids who still lived out there. I respected her for that since I had been a kid out there at one time, and I had needed her too.

I told her what was going on in my life. She listened.

"Love always made me uncomfortable," I admitted. "I was afraid of him."

"Most people were afraid of him, but not Love's kids," Understanding countered. She used to watch closely when Love's kids would go in and ask him for something. "They were so unaffected by his power and just treated him like a human being," she continued, "and that's all he really was, just a human being, and yet we all treated him like this God."

"We were afraid of him," Understanding explained, "and I think he was aware that he caused others to feel scared around him. That's how he maintained his power, but we gave him that power too."

What she said reminded me of what I heard Ethan once say:

"It was a control trip, but it was one that we gave him," he had said.

Then I went to a party at Eve and Definition's house, which was Honorable's birthday party. I kept in touch with her for years, even after everything I had gone through under her authority. I never held any grudges against her because I knew that she wasn't evil. She had just been caught up in the dynamics of the Love Family hierarchy. I knew that if it had been me, dealing with another woman sharing in my personal relationship—was there anything I wouldn't have done to save my family, save my children from losing their dad? I also understood that power corrupts no matter who's got it, that no matter how nice someone is, that with unchecked power, even the most likeable, honest person can succumb to the pressures that lead to corruption.

Honorable was nice to me during that party and acted like nothing bad had ever happened. She had come to visit me once and gave me a nice coat. I would visit her from time to time when she lived in Darrington, which was not too far from Arlington. She was kind of like family, in a way, through my brothers' relationship with their dad, Nobility. I forgave her, because I was trying to let it go, just like everyone who left was trying to put the past behind them. I just purposely didn't think about what she had done to my mom and how she had targeted me too. I never forgot it though.

At this same birthday party, which was Honorable's birthday party, I was eves-dropping on a conversation in the kitchen. It was a woman I had known as Fairness. She was talking to another woman. I don't remember who the second woman was. They were talking about another ex-member, a woman—I didn't know who they were talking about. One of the women was saying, "It was obvious by what she said that she wasn't invited, and if she shows up, I won't be afraid to tell her she's not welcome."

The exclusive mentality was irritating, but it wasn't the only thing that I observed about Group B politics. There was also this victim mentality. They had all decided, that Love was the bad guy, a corrupt overlord who had betrayed them. As a group, they tended to conform to the idea that Love was the reason why they were angry. No one was taking any responsibility for the choices they had made, not even the elders, who had, by the arm of Love, helped run the Love Family. Some of them were refusing to call him Love and insisted that his name was Paul Erdman.

Then, about ten years after the breakup, 1994, some of the kids who had been raised in the Love Family had a reunion of sorts. I helped to plan it. We all stayed at a resort in La Push Washington for the weekend. One of the girls brought matching t-shirts for everyone, and on the t-shirt, in big, bold, red lettering, it said, "NO ELDERS." In the group photo that was taken, everyone was wearing one. Apparently, it was realized after the fact that no one would want to wear them outside of the context of this reunion and piss off real elders (old folks). I found it humorous. Here it seemed we had all decided who was to blame. It didn't say "No Love" Here we were, all grown up now, young adults. What the t-shirt said would only make sense to us. I wondered what it would be like for an ex-member, who had been a real 'elder' in the Love Family, how they would feel when they saw me wearing my 'NO ELDERS' t-shirt to a group B event. When I got home from the reunion, I put the shirt away in a trunk in my attic.

After the reunion, I was at a group B event, and I overheard a discussion. Several ex-members were debating whether they had been brainwashed or not. I guess one could make that argument, but it made more sense to me that in fact, they could not have been brainwashed because they weren't in prison or behind locked doors. They had all made the choice to be there in the first place and had willingly relinquished their autonomy. If they could brainwash themselves, then they could un-brainwash themselves as well, and many did when they ended up leaving on their own. As I said earlier, their personalities and identities were transformed overnight once they left the Family. I could just as well make the argument that they were more like victims of domestic mental abuse. If they became weak and dependent, then it was by choice. Everyone knew where the door was. At any time, they could've left.

Usually, a victim of domestic violence is not said to have stayed in an abusive relationship because she was brainwashed; usually, it is said that she stayed for various reasons: the kids, financial dependency, learned helplessness, etc.

I heard someone argue, "Well, yes, I did make the choice to be there, but once I joined, it was hard to leave."

Sure, but just because it was hard to leave doesn't mean you were brainwashed.

Almost every ex-member I have talked to said they felt "betrayed" by Love. I felt betrayed by everyone. If they hadn't given Love God-like power, he wouldn't have been able to "betray" them in such a devastating way. Never give that much power to anybody—ever!

When Hitler killed all those Jews, there was an army that did it for him, and those people were held accountable! Some of them rotted in prisons for the rest of their lives. Love could not be held solely responsible for what happened. I don't think Love was more responsible than anyone else.

No one, that I know of, wrote Love a letter saying, *Dear Love, I am sorry, that I expected you to be somebody that it was impossible for you to be, and then vilified you when you failed to live up to my unrealistic expectations.*

For years as a child, it was drilled into me that Love was the answer. I was inculcated with the teachings, and now everyone was saying that Love was this big bad man who had taken it all for himself and had lived like a king, while they had been living in squalor. Well of course Love lived like a king, because he was treated like a king. Everyone fell in line with the thinking that this man should have absolute power, and for years, he did. His absolute power was the basis for the whole thing. Every single person in the Love Family made it possible for Love to be who he was. People would've done anything in the world to make sure that this guy had more cheese. Love didn't force himself on anyone. People handed him the bottle and he drank. Then he wanted more, and so they gave him more. It seemed that after people realized what they had done, they tried to blame Love. In my view, Love was guilty of being a human being when people tried to make him a God.

"Love's drunk" they were saying.

"Yes of course, Love was drunk, you were handing him the bottle." To me, after what I have seen, the old adage sounds right—power corrupts—and it wouldn't have mattered much if it had been someone else in Love's shoes. If you give anyone absolute power over you, with no checks and balances, that'll be the end of you.

I heard a man who had gone by the name of Heritage once say, "Love went from someone who was loved, admired, and feared, to someone who was mocked and pitied."
Love fell out of good graces because he couldn't handle the absolute power that he'd been given. Predictable.

Everyone knew that it was an experiment. In college, I studied in-depth, research methods and statistics, as part of degree requirements, and I hated those classes, mostly because they were taught by a Japanese woman with a very strong accent. But one thing I came away with is that in conduct-ing an experiment, one must control for all the variables. That was impossible in the Love Family. It was impossible for Love to conceptualize the magnitude of what he was asking of the members, and I don't think the members were able to fully conceptualize what Love was asking of them either, because they were blinded by the love that was shared and by the tiny glimpse of hope for a better world that was promised.

Those who were adults in the Love Family each must wrangle with their own thoughts and feelings about what happened to them and why. As a child growing up there, I also have had to wrangle with what happened to me and why. Other kids raised in the Love Family, whether they were the kids of members who stayed or of those who left, it seems there are various per-spectives and opinions on who is more responsible than who. It's been a very hot-button subject, but since I am writing my story, my view is that I spread the responsibility around pretty evenly. The world I was raised in may have been conceptualized and envisioned by Love, but it was the adult membership who put it into action and who taught me the way of the Love Family. They passed on the knowledge to me that Love gave them. The adult membership enforced the unspoken rules and 'agreements' that Love handed them, to each other and to me. Thus, it has been impossible for me to take on the victim mentality that a lot of the ex-members took on, which was that Love was seen as the bad guy who screwed everybody over. Love became an addict, but who was supplying him with all those drugs? Love was on a power trip, but that was the whole idea, from the very beginning.

The whole reason for this discussion is that my perspective as a child diverged pretty dramatically from the perspectives of ex-members in general, especially early on after the breakup. And I felt just as much betrayed by them as they felt betrayed by Love.

So, it seemed to me, after the breakup that what I was hearing was that everything I had been told growing up was now considered bullshit, but to me, it was no more bullshit that what I was hearing now. I didn't trust them anymore.

The Love Family as I knew it disintegrated, I was not shielded; it was like a war. I was not informed about what was going on and why. This was a major, major change in my life. I had been told not to go out in the World, and now I was in it because my parent chose not to stay.

I started college and was immediately drawn to the fields of sociology and psychology. I was taking a social psychology class at a community college, and I befriended this man who had schizophrenia who was also taking the class. His name was Frank, and he believed that the government was after him.

He would tell me how they were monitoring him and where they put cameras to watch him. He said that when people coughed in class that it was a message to him from the government.

I tried not to cough when he was in the classroom. It didn't help.

He thought that I was from the government too.

I tried to convince him otherwise.

He seemed to appreciate my kindness, and we would meet for coffee sometimes in the school cafeteria. I would see him, hurrying down the hall to class, looking frightened, harried. He didn't have any friends. I took pity on him and wanted to understand how someone would end up like that.

"I can prove to you that I am not from the government," I told him; "Here, let me show you how ridiculous that is," and I proceeded to try and take apart the light fixture, so he could see that there was no camera in there.

"No. It's no use," he replied. "If I were to ever stop believing that the government was after me, I would have to accept that I just wasted 10 years of my life believing something that is not true. I don't think I could do that."

"Man, you're only 29!" I insisted, pleadingly.

It was people like Frank that fascinated me. *Get to know people from the host country.* It was me, trying to understand why people believe and do the things they do.

Why did people stay, after so many left? Were they like Frank? When I went out to visit at the Garlic Festival and talked to people, they wanted me to come back, to rejoin. I guess I was old enough now to make that decision. Even though I never would have gone back, there were those who were raised there who eventually did go back, even though their parents had left.

I talked to my dear friend and Family sister, who had been known as Zarah, who left a year or so after I left. She shared her perspective with me about the Love Family.

"The Family is warped," she declared.

"What do you mean by that?" I asked.

"There is just so much resentment from the breakup, and it is still the king and his serfdom," Zarah says. "The Ranch is not paid off, but guess what? Love has a huge TV," Zarah contined, "The Barn is remodeled any time he wants. He has a six chicken BBQ pit, with his own house and servants to run it. He has a hot tub, and then there are people like Noah, who is a wood worker who "doesn't even have his own staircase that is made out of wood—It is just shit like that," she says.

When Zarah went out to the Garlic Festival one year, her brother parked in the wrong spot; he parked up near Love's Barn, (house) and she was going up there to help him move his truck, when Truthfulness and Love stopped them.

"Their only concern was whether we had paid or not," Zarah says angrily. "They didn't even recognize that, 'hey this is Reconciliation who was born out here.' They were just so focused on 'Did you pay?!'"

Love and Truthfulness had security come and take Zarah and her brother off the premises.

"I just don't like the whole hypocrisy," Zarah says. "The universal family that I believe in cares about the whole world, not just their own little Love Family."

Bright discussed his feelings about the breakup.

"I think that the things said in that letter [petition] says it pretty clear," Bright says, "that whoever is making the decisions should not be strung out on drugs and spending the common funds." Bright's perspective was that the Family needed to evolve into "something more egalitarian." He expressed frustration that "people didn't try harder to confront Love and to just band together as one—this one individual cannot keep us down." Bright expressed his views to me calmly but firmly with angry undertones. "[Love] is a very self-serving individual," Bright says, "and [Truthfulness] is a very dishonest self-serving individual too," he continued. "[Love's] name should have been Lust, and [Truthfulness's] name should have been [Falsity], and Serious should have been Goofy."

I laughed when he said it, but he didn't; he looked very serious. He went on to express the "frustration" and "sadness" that such a huge amount of effort resulted in something that failed, collapsed. "It had so much potential," he says sadly.

My own perspective is that it needed to evolve as well. For me personally, it could not have evolved enough for me to want to spend my life there though; I was destined to make my way out in the World, one way or the other. Maybe it would have been unreasonable to think that Love could've been reasoned with, but with a lot of pressure and intervention from a majority of people, it might not have had to end that way with people so mad, bitter, grouping off and taking sides.

I would have left no doubt. In the Love Family, women were not allowed to be anything more than the domestic role. I wanted to go to college, I wanted to make something of myself. I heard that [Probity] had asked Love to take classes and wanted to become a midwife, but Love said no. I was too much of a rebel in my spirit to ever be told I couldn't follow my dreams. In fact, I once broke up with a guy because a domestic role was all he wanted for me, and I wanted to go to college, which he could not understand. If I had gone back to the Love Family after it had reorganized itself, I would have been the one who challenged the status quo, probably would've been kicked out, like Understanding. There was nothing there for me to aspire to other than elder lady, and my experience was that no way would I have wanted to do that.

I came across this book about the Bruderhof community, and it discussed the hidden costs of tribalization, and in many ways, the Love Family was a tribe. It said: "To the cynical, the fate of contemporary communes is always the same old story – young idealists starting out in a burst of enthusiasm to create a better world, and ending, sadder but wiser, with their dreams in ruins." The story that one hears from communes that have disintegrated is always the same, "Emotional garbage which had been thought buried safely, deep beneath the ground, comes seeping into the communal drinking water with poisonous results." The two lessons that might be drawn from this, Zablocki explained, are one, that men are basically evil and incapable of living together harmoniously, or two, that the costs of commune formation are greater than has generally been anticipated." (Zablocki, 1971, 321)

I told Bright that I was writing a memoir of what it was like growing up in the Love Family.

"Why?" Bright asked incredulously. He looked confused. "I have put all that behind me."

I put it behind me too. My past hasn't held me back from anything. I've done all sorts of things in my life since growing up and being a part of that. But in order to share my story, I have to go back and remember what happened. And I feel that writing my story is part of my evolution forward. It had been in my black box for a long time. Most people I have known throughout my adult life have no clue that I grew up that way. But I always knew that someday I would write my story. I wanted to share what had happened to me and what I had learned from it about life. As a child, I had had that dream about the *Book of Life* and had read the *Diary of Anne Frank*. It was my destiny, if there's such thing.

Time passes. I was engaged to be married, and my fiancé and I decided that we each would bring photos of our childhoods to put together in a sort of slideshow for the wedding guests, but I had no photos of my childhood. I didn't have any evidence that my childhood had happened at all. Some people have boxes full of mementos from their childhood—trophies from sports leagues, team shots, yearbooks from their elementary school—Framed family photos lined along their parents' walls. I had nothing, except my memories of Love Family life, my memories of people I had known and things that had happened along the way. The only thing I could find were newspaper articles, most of which were sensationalized garbage and half-truths.

I had one item; it was a doll that I had gotten for Christmas one year. Simplicity had made it; Dignity had painted her face—that's all I had—and my Love Family diary. This was way before Chuck LeWarne had written his historical account of the Love Family and it was before sociologist Rob Balch had researched the Love Family and had written his article, both of which were the first intelligent things to be written about the Love Family, other than newspaper articles. Maybe if I had a couple photos, it would give me a sense of my history, and even if no one ever saw them, I would have something that made me feel like I came from somewhere. I wasn't just plopped into high school out of the middle of nowhere, a transplant from another planet, even though that's sometimes how it felt. Plus, I still planned to write my memoirs someday and would need a few photos to include in my photo section.

I asked everyone I knew if I could make copies of their photos for a book I would write. But I couldn't get anyone to respond. The excuses were often, 'I don't have time' or 'I don't know where they are.'

I understood, so I offered to help find them, to help organize them and put them into nice albums. This was about our history. It seemed important to me. But it seemed no one wanted to help. I thought it was weird. I explained all my reasons: I told them I was writing a memoir, that I was getting married and needed photos for the wedding, and that I didn't have any photos of my childhood. My calls weren't returned. I wondered if I was being discouraged from writing.

Four or five years went by, and I wasn't making any progress. Any rational person would've just given up, but to me, photos of my childhood represented my history, something that it seemed no one wanted to even talk about. The more resistance I got, the more persistent I became. I didn't understand why I was having so much difficulty. The more time passed, the more irritating it was. I didn't see why I couldn't have them. Maybe they wanted me to give up. I began to wonder if the story of the Love Family was purposely being repressed. My childhood was being squelched into non-existence. There were other things that happened that led me to wonder this.

I was going to go down another avenue. I had decided to try and understand why the Family had broken up. I heard that a certain elder had a copy of the petition. He was one of the ones who signed it. It was the same petition that the elders had signed that they had presented to Love. Understanding had told me who had a copy of it, so I asked this certain elder for it when I saw him at an ex-members birthday party. It was a group B party.

"Why do you want to see it?" he asked, in a matter of fact, indignant tone, "You were not involved."

"I want to know my history;" I answered firmly. "I want to know what happened."

He didn't seem swayed by that at all, so rather than argue with him, I just let it go.

"Did you get a copy?" Understanding asked me later.

"No," I answered. I told her what the former elder had said and how he had responded.

"Oh! Oh! Of the little dirty secrets!" she exclaimed loudly. We were in the back bedroom talking since the party was so loud. Understanding continued: "Your life was torn apart by that paper—my life was torn apart by that paper. Hello? You don't think that we aren't going to want to see what the heck the paper says! Otherwise, it is just washed down the drain," she says with passionate anger. "These issues had a great impact on your life and on other people in your family!"

She was right. Eventually, I did get a copy of it, when it became more widely available. But at the time I had asked for it, hardly anyone had seen it; it wasn't being shared or copied around at all. It was still very hush-hush.

After this incident, and my other troubles getting photos, it all seemed to start making sense. This was a cover up! They were worried. Maybe they would lose their job. Maybe they would lose friends or contacts if people found out that they had been a part of the Love Family. And remember, this was early on after the breakup, after the battle lines had been drawn and everyone was reeling and defensive, still scrambling to build new lives.

One of the ex-members, who refused to let me have copies of her photos, began to pass rumors that I had been "rude" to her.

I had been the opposite of rude. I had been patient and purposely sweet and had offered to help, because I knew that if I wasn't, I would never see those photos. I was persistent though, and that probably was irritating to her, but I was always very well-mannered about it. I wrote her a letter, explaining how much it would mean to me to have photos of my childhood. I wasn't giving up. She didn't like that. The false rumors that she passed telling people I was rude to her, seemed to be her way of saying 'back off.' It pushed my buttons, especially after the false rumors had been passed about my mom.

I read a story once about someone who was raised in the Farm commune. He had a lot of problems getting photos after the Farm broke up and discussed it in his Blog posts. One article I read was titled, "Growing Up on a Hippie Commune." (https://hippycommune.wordpress.com/2015/05/06/a-picture-worth-a-1000-wonders/).

No one wanted the author to have proof that maybe this really happened to him. Maybe they thought that if he didn't have pictures, it would be easier to say maybe he's making it all up. Maybe they were afraid they might be exposed. I understand. Must be rough, but I don't want to feel censored. I need to be able to tell my truth.

It was painful to challenge people I loved to let me see the truth of my history, but I wasn't going to just give up. It wasn't just their story to hide, as hard as it had been, it was also my story, my truth, that I would have to bear for the rest of my life.

The idea that I was writing made certain ex-members uncomfortable. I heard comments like, "It would offend too many people," and "How can you write about it when everyone had a different experience." If I had been an elder or someone who would carry on the party line, would I have gotten more support? If I had been Logic or Frankness or Humility, or Imagination, would it have helped? I was just little lowly Rachel. Nobody important, just a kid, back-of-the-lake scum.

I kept pursuing photos. One woman agreed to let me copy some of her photos, but first, they had to read my manuscript and make sure it wasn't "negative." I was like, *Oh boy, here we go again.* It was the same old Love Family thinking.

That was the last straw. I still have a copy of her response letter. I was being censored basically. I must make the Family look good, or else I was out of luck.

I thought, no one is going to stop me from telling my story. I became even more determined. I would write my story without photos. I don't need photos! I can just tell my story, no need to show. It is standard to include a photo section, but I decided it wouldn't matter. I started taking writing classes.

Luckily for me, over time, people became less defensive about their involvement in the Love Family. It seems, since then, that there has been more of an openness about the past. The photos are now being coordinated, and there are plans to put them on a website so that people have better access.

I began writing my story in earnest and trying to piece it together. People started coming through for me. They wanted to help. I was able to finally see the petition and other documents as well as photos. I was so happy to finally see the them. There we all were in our ethnic regalia playing, dancing, chanting, gardening and there was the Barn and the lake. I was really from someplace that actually existed.

It seems now like so long ago, although, it has had a deep and lasting impact on me. It wasn't just this phase in my life; it was my childhood. It's a world that I come from that I can never visit; I can't just buy a plane ticket and go, as if it were some other country. To me, looking at a photo is in some ways like flying back home for a moment, but without it being an interactive experience. The people are frozen in time, smiles plastered on their faces, a two-dimensional plane devoid of the movement, smells, and sounds that I can only imagine now. There I am again, perpetually carrying my sleeping bag across the pasture. There's that same family meeting. They are images of a single instant in time. It's almost like the 'Far Corners of Your Mind' where the spirits were frozen to—for better or for worse—never be awoken again.

......

"How did growing up in the Love Family affect you?" Understanding once asked me. She was gathering information for an article she was writing for the Communal Studies Association.

"I'll have to get back to you on that," I answered. The question was so broad, that I had no idea how to answer her.

I thought about it, took some notes, but it seemed impossible to summarize something of that magnitude. I did finally get back to give her a few main points.

I then used those main points and expanded upon them to create a five-page summary that will end this final chapter of my personal narrative.

To be honest, it has not been easy having the history that I have, but I consider myself very blessed to have done as well as I have. Amongst my Love Family peers, there have been high rates of alcoholism, drug addiction and depression. There have been drug related deaths. Many are survivors of childhood sexual and physical abuse. Others have had problems with severe mental illness. There have been three suicides at the time I am writing this—Hope, Activity, and Purity. Hope shot himself; Purity poisoned herself with carbon monoxide; Activity hung herself. The suicides were all hard, but Hope's was the worst; I had nightmares about it for years, still do occasionally. The deaths and other problems are constant reminders of what a struggle it has been. I try to pretend that it's been easy, and that I'm alright, but when one of us dies or I hear of the terrible problems one of us faces, it hurts. I understand, more than I want to admit, how easy it could be to want to just slip off into oblivion, to just want to throw in the towel.

The impact of growing up in the Love Family has hit me hard. First, I know what it is like to suffer great loss. My relationship with my mom never recovered after all the years of separation. My mom didn't take care of me; Other people did, and that's been very hard for both of us to overcome. I think it would've been hard, no matter what, to heal, after so many years of living in that environment, but it was especially hard for her after what she went through with Nobility and Honorable. Plus, even though we both had lived in the same community, our experiences were so very different in critical ways.

I was taken care of by some of the same people that turned on her, who looked the other way or who were caught up in the same political system that drove her down.

I'm sad that my mom was hurt, but I'm also grateful that there were a few people in the Love Family who made a difference in my life. It is because of them that I had just the right amount of resiliency and tenacity to make a good go of it in the World. There were angels looking out for me, but there is nothing that can ever fill the black hole of pain that is left in my heart where my mom and dad and other family belonged, except for God, and that is an ongoing project.

I also lost the opportunity to have a normal sibling relationship with my brothers. For the most part, I didn't live in the same households with Forest. Furthermore, he was quite a bit younger and wasn't as involved in the kids' scene like I was. As a result of that separation and lack of shared experience, Forest and I were left with this invisible space between us that had a permanent impact on how our relationship evolved. Boldness and Jacob were so young when we left the community, that they had no idea what I went through growing up. And because they were so much younger than me, I was out on my own while they were still in elementary school; While I was mostly raised in the Love Family, my brothers were so young when we left the community that they were mostly raised in the World. Karen was very involved and present while they were growing up, so between us, again, that absence of shared experience—it was devastating!

My relationship with my dad never had much of a chance. It seemed to me that he was never interested in building a real relationship with me. My mom once told me that 'He was weak.' I didn't know what she meant by that. I just knew I needed a dad, but it seemed that he didn't know how to relate to me. Whenever I called him to talk or would visit him, he would say he didn't feel well. He didn't respond to invitations and would make up excuses. When I saw him, he would laugh nervously or seem irritable or grumpy. I'm not sure if he held it against me that I wouldn't follow his curfew during my last two years of high school. My impression was that the role of dad didn't come naturally to him. No matter what, I never assumed he wanted me to get lost, so I didn't give up on him for a long time. I thought I would eventually win his heart, but it never seemed to happen. Each time I reached out, the message I got was that he wasn't interested. I got my hopes up a couple times when he helped me out with my bills when I was in community college, then later helped pay for my wedding. I thought if he gave me money, it meant he cared, but it didn't change things.

I never knew my dad for most of the years of my childhood. I was his only child, but he hadn't raised me. He never even visited me, so he had no idea what I had been through. I didn't hold it against him. I had to forgive him for not knowing how to build a relationship with his long-lost daughter. It wasn't the Hollywood ending I was hoping for. I was not even two years old, when my mom left him, and we ended up in Maui and beyond. I've survived a lot of stuff, including being raised with no dad.

On top of the loss of my biological family, I suffered the loss of my spiritual family, my community, and the only real family I had known. I quit going to ex-member events, since I rarely ever saw any of the kids I was raised with there. Being a kid in the Love Family was not the same as being one of the 'big people.' Then just trying to relate to them coming to terms with their past was really hard. If adult ex-members talked about the Love Family, it was always talked about as if it were some big mistake. When they refer to it this way, I feel as if I were part of the wreckage of some terrible accident. I understand why they feel that way, but it hurts to think of my childhood as someone's 'mistake' and something they don't even want to admit happened. It may be easier for me to say, since I never had to reckon with myself about why I joined the Love Family or why I stayed, but the way I feel about growing up the way I did, is that it's not going to be my shameful secret. Secrecy breeds shame. This was my childhood, for better and for worse. There's power in owning one's story. There's a reason why I had that dream that my name was 'Experience.' I never told anyone, because I didn't want that name. I knew, even then, that experiences could be beautiful and joyful, but I also knew they could be painful and terrible. In the dream, I was afraid, but now I realize, that every experience teaches us something new about ourselves and helps us evolve to something better. There is a lot of wisdom that can be learned as a culture and as a society from those who are willing to share what they learned from their experiences, especially experiences where people have moved against the grain to try to change society.

As a child of the Love Israel Family, I went through culture shock, that was extremely stressful. It took me years to adjust to life on the outside. No one taught me how to survive in the World, because no one thought that is what I would need. As a result, I was unprepared. After a few bruises and skinned knees so to speak, I ended up learning quite a bit by trial and error. Sounds cliché, but it was basically the school of hard knocks. By the time I was 24, I had major surgery to remove a brain tumor the size of a walnut. It wasn't as big as Bliss's tumor had been, but it was big enough to warrant immediate surgery. My doctor thought maybe it was caused by stress. It can take years for a tumor to grow to that size; "It might've been growing for ten years," the doctor had told me. I found it odd when he said that, because it had, in fact, been just about ten years since the mid-eighties breakup when I was diagnosed with that tumor.

Over time, the culture shock faded as I adjusted to life on the outside, but I don't think I'm ever going to feel like a native in this land. I am from America, but I am from somewhere else, a stranger in a strange land, in some ways, and it seems that no matter how many years have passed, I will continue to feel like an outsider, always looking in with wonder and amazement—and sometimes horror—at my discoveries about how people get along and how the world works.

The culture shock took a toll on me. Back when members were leaving the community in mass numbers, I was put into high school at Summit. It had only been a few months since I had left the Ranch. I was sitting in class and the kids were exchanging pictures that were to be in the yearbook. One of the girls in the class looked at my picture closely and commented to me that she thought I looked "old" in my picture. I think it was the serious expression on my face, plus, I had been crying on picture day after my money had been stolen. I didn't respond after she commented. I just sat there pondering the idea. I did feel old inside. I hadn't even been a teenager for that long, and already, I felt like I had been on a long journey. It seemed that high school students were like little kids in big bodies; They knew things that I didn't know about what was cool and what wasn't. But I knew things that they didn't know too. When she said that I looked old, I wondered and thought about it, because that's how I felt, in some ways, but I didn't think it showed. I had been raised to believe I had eternal life, that getting sick and dying were all in my mind. But now I was in the World and someone told me that I looked old.

Even though I had a lot to learn about how the outside world worked, I knew so much more about things other kids knew nothing about. I knew what it might be like to live in a 3rd world country, without modern conveniences or the privileges of democracy; I knew how to live without hospitals or modern medicine, phones, clocks or electricity. I knew what it might be like to live in a dictatorship where there's no separation between church and state, where the rules of the greater outside society no longer existed.

By the time, I was in high school, I had lived in a culture where polygamy wasn't just this thing that people say exists in some parts of the world. It was accepted practice. I understood what certain words meant, words like cult deprogrammer, censorship, and Armageddon.

How did knowing all this affect me? For one, I have had difficulties trusting authority. When I got my first job, I was working in fast food. When the manager would come around and check on us, I would begin to feel terrified. My hands would shake. I thought I would pass out, and all the manager did was stand there and look at me as I worked for a few seconds. I had lived in a world where one man had been in total control, where there was no checks and balances, so anytime I see a situation where someone is in a position of power, I am always very skeptical and suspicious. Absolute power corrupts absolutely—I learned that the hard way.

It isn't just fear of authority. I'm careful about conformity too. Conformity is dangerous. I saw what can happen to people who were hurt when no one stood up to protect themselves or others. Conformity so terrifies me that I avoid groups. Groups are what make up our society! I have a master's degree in psychology, which is the study of individual behavior, but I have a bachelor's degree in sociology, which is the study of group behavior. But I studied group behavior as an outsider looking in. This was an advantage academically, but it was my way of trying to get mastery over the social forces that control human behavior. My fear has never gone away, that I will be swallowed alive by vicious politics and group think. Group think, according to Wikipedia is, "the practice of thinking or making decisions as a group in a way that discourages creativity or individual responsibility." I have been more comfortable in the role of rebel, in one form or another, and being drawn to independent minded, creative types. I don't follow crowds unless I have thought it through—carefully.

The thing that had the worst effect on me, though, was the mind control. Just living in a community where everyone had to think the same positive thoughts. Thoughts were predetermined as everyone shared one clean, holy mind. I wasn't allowed to have negative thoughts, to complain, to voice dissent, to cry, to be angry, to be scared, so it seemed I was being told I didn't have a right to my own feelings. It was just normal to watch everyone squelching their natural human responses. I have learned since then that my thoughts and feelings are important. I pay attention to them. Anger, fear, doubt—those are good—because they help me take care of myself and help me figure out what to do next. Feelings are like sense organs.

Thought control wasn't all bad though, because it taught me the creative power that thoughts have, which has been invaluable to me in facing life's problems. A lot of the mental training too such as the meditation and other exercises in focus and self-restraint that were a part of my life growing up, have made me stronger and better able to deal with life's problems.

It took time for me to understand how the Love Family made me into the person that I am today. All the loss has made me into someone who can empathize with others who have suffered great loss themselves and has given me the motivation to help others overcome adversity.

Living in a patriarchal community and seeing how women were affected made me into the strong feminist that I am today. Living in a society governed by a man who had such great power made me into someone who places great value on human rights, multiculturalism, diversity and equality.

Being cared for by people who were so radical and idealistic in their lives gave me the courage to walk my own path and strive to live out my own ideals and goals. To live in a culture that was so creative and unconventional taught me that anything was possible, if I just put my mind to it.

Nothing about my childhood was totally negative, because it made me into the person I am today. I made the best of it, basically. Otherwise, I would have felt like a victim. No one else, but me, was going to be my champion. I had always taken care of myself, trying to figure out what to do with the circumstances that were before me, so I knew what I had to do, just like a little hitchhiker, but just not waiting for the ride. I was bound and determined to get there, one way or the other. Once I get there, I sometimes wonder if where I ended up was really where I wanted to be, but it's not about that, it's about the journey.

I have to see it like it was an adventure to write about; otherwise, I might cave in to self-pity, shame, anger, and sadness. It was my attitude and instinct that led me forward. I was not alone though. God was guiding me each step of the way, looking out for me. Some of my peers from the Love Family went the other way and became cynical, almost nihilistic about religion. That didn't happen to me. Well, it did at first, but eventually, even though I didn't end up very religious, I came to realize my connection to God had always been there. I consider that was one of the good things that I took away from my Love Family experience. I was deeply impacted by the spirituality in the community, and my connection to the spiritual realm has been a big resource to me in facing my challenges.

Another thing that affected me positively was the teachings. 'Love is the answer,' and it really is; it's what Jesus taught for one, and it's really true, because a lot of world's problems could do with a little love. I believe also that 'we are one.' That all the world's peoples' share a God consciousness, and that if we all were more aware of that, there wouldn't be so much fighting and unhappiness. Finally, 'Now is the time,' for people to wake up and work together and make the planet healthy and able to sustain life for generations to come. Now is the time to say no to tyranny and abuse and to embrace the power we all have within us to stand up for what's right and work together to make this society a more healthful place.

I try to 'stay present,' be mindful and dwell on positive thoughts, but because of how I saw that ideal taken to the extreme, I tend to place a high value on thinking about it holistically. I have an awareness of the future and how it guides me forward and gives me hope; I also have done my best to honor the past, especially in the lessons to be learned from it.

The outside world has been lonely and painful, with so many challenges that I have had to make the best of. Failure was never an option though. I worked very hard to overcome the challenges of being raised in the Love Family, including therapy when needed. I refused to let the circumstances of my childhood stop me from succeeding at following my dreams and goals. I have done well in life, despite my crazy childhood, despite all the loss, despite the culture shock. I am college educated; I have had a successful career. I am happily married; I have two beautiful children; We have friends. It turned out OK. I had to work really hard to do it though. I could write another whole book about what it took, what I had to go through to get where I am today, although I'm not planning on it. There will be no sequel.

It wasn't all bad. I have a lot of good memories of my life growing up in the Love Family. Memories of people I was close to, such as the children and the teachers and caretakers who were involved with the kids. I got to experience a lot of amazing things in my life that not many people ever do: I know what it's like to live on a primitive hippie beach on a tropical island. I have memories of life on the road and living in log cabins, tepees, Army tents and yurts. I got to learn theater and travel with the drama group, performing. I got to go to rainbow gatherings and visit different communes. I got firsthand experience living in an intentional community and learned what it's like to live with a large group of people who chose a very different path for themselves. Even though it is not the path I would've chosen, it gave me a worldview where I learned that anything is possible when people put their minds together. What I learned throughout my childhood was that there are many ways people can choose to live their lives.

What that means to me, in looking at some of the current problems our society faces, is that we don't have to live like this. We all have a lot of power to change things, that we don't realize we have. I don't like groups because they are hotbeds for the destructive forces of conformity, but I'm also fascinated and curious about the complexities and power that humans have when they group together. Norms must be established for any group to properly function. In groups, we have the power to change the world, and I know, that in the Love Family, no matter how off base they were in different ways, most people had good intentions, and many worked very hard to create a better world.

One of the interesting things about the Love Family is that, it never ended. Love died in 2016, but it's like the never-ending story. The community continues to thrive, despite the loss of members over the years and despite the many hardships, starting when they lost the Ranch. The remaining loyalists, their children and their grandchildren still get together for Passover, Easter, and other events and celebrations. Many still consider themselves family and live somewhat communally on shared property in various locations in Washington.

In the end, what it all comes down to, is the same thing that it came down to in 1968 when the Love Family began, and that is: More and more people in this world are ready for change. The Love Family was proof that anything is possible when people put their minds together—literally and figuratively. The real question is, can we learn from the past mistakes of those who've courageously tried to change the World?

A lot of folks are afraid of what it could mean to step out of this matrix, this web that we're all caught up in. It's risky, there are so many unknowns. But where is this all heading if we continue down this road? In my opinion, my childhood was tough, in certain ways, but things like that have to happen, in order to teach us not to give up, but to teach us how to proceed, how to move forward. And that's not going to happen unless more people get over their shame, guilt, pride, hurt, anger, whatever it is, and realize they have a valuable story to share and to pass on to future generations, who are trying to figure out what to do, what not to do. Being raised the way I was, crossing over from one culture into another, gave me a countercultural perspective: I was in multiple environments where people were setting their own ground rules and rebelling against the conventions that keep people trapped and leave them hopeless. I am a product of the waves of cultural resistance that overtook mainstream culture in the late 1960s. My message is—Don't let fear, shame, guilt, anger, sadness, disappointment stop us from knowing the truth of our power as a people. Experience Change!

BIBLIOGRAPHY (CHAPTER 18)

[Bright]. Personal Interview. Des Moines, WA. January 11, 2002.

[Ethan]. Interview with Chuck LeWarne. February 18, 1998.

Israel, Understanding. Personal Communication. June 10, July 15, July 20, November 4, all 2001) Arlington, WA.

[Zarah]. Personal Interview. December 13, 2001. Maple Valley, WA.

Made in the USA
San Bernardino, CA
11 February 2019